MCAD
MCSE
MCDBA
Self-Paced Training Kit

Second Edition

Microsoft
SQL SERVER™ 2000
DATABASE DESIGN
AND IMPLEMENTATION

Exam 70-229

PUBLISHED BY
Microsoft Press
A Division of Microsoft Corporation
One Microsoft Way
Redmond, Washington 98052-6399

Library of Congress Cataloging-in-Publication Data
MCAD/MCSE/MCDBA Self-Paced Training Kit. Microsoft SQL Server 2000 database
   design and implementation, exam 70-229 / Microsoft Corporation.
      p. cm.
   Includes index.
   ISBN 0-7356-1960-3
    1. Electronic data processing personnel--Certification.   2. Microsoft
software--Examinations--Study guides.   3. Databases--Design--Examinations.   4. SQL
server.   I. Title: Microsoft SQL Server 2000 database design and implementation, exam
70-229.   II. Microsoft Corporation.

   QA76.3.M325566   2003
   005.75'85--dc21   2003046485

Printed and bound in the United States of America.

2 3 4 5 6 7 8 9   QWT   8 7 6 5 4 3

Distributed in Canada by H.B. Fenn and Company Ltd.

A CIP catalogue record for this book is available from the British Library.

Microsoft Press books are available through booksellers and distributors worldwide. For further information about international editions, contact your local Microsoft Corporation office or contact Microsoft
Press International directly at fax (425) 936-7329. Visit our Web site at www.microsoft.com/mspress. Send
comments to *tkinput@microsoft.com*.

Acquisitions Editor: Kathy Harding
Project Editor: Valerie Woolley

Body Part No. X09-59427

Contents

About This Book

Welcome to *MCAD/MCSE/MCDBA Self-Paced Training Kit: Microsoft SQL Server 2000 Database Design and Implementation, Exam 70-229, Second Edition.* This training kit introduces you to SQL Server 2000 and provides detailed information about how to design and implement a SQL Server database. The training kit takes you through the steps of how to plan and implement a database, create and maintain database objects, and implement data integrity. You will also be introduced to Transact-SQL, and you will learn how to use Transact-SQL to query a SQL Server database and manage and manipulate data stored in that database. Finally, the training kit describes how to manage SQL Server security and how to maintain and optimize a SQL Server database.

Note For more information on becoming a Microsoft Certified Systems Engineer, see the section titled "The Microsoft Certified Professional Program" later in this chapter.

Before You Begin Part 1

Each chapter in Part 1 is divided into lessons. Most lessons include hands-on procedures that allow you to practice or demonstrate a particular concept or skill. Each lesson ends with a short summary of the information presented in that lesson, and each chapter ends with a set of review questions to test your knowledge of the chapter material.

The "Getting Started" section of this chapter provides important setup instructions that describe the hardware and software requirements to complete the procedures in this course. Read through this section thoroughly before you start the lessons.

Intended Audience

This book was developed for information technology (IT) professionals who need to design, plan, implement, and support Microsoft SQL Server 2000 or who plan to take the related Microsoft Certified Professional exam 70-229: Designing and Implementing Databases with Microsoft SQL Server 2000 Enterprise Edition.

Prerequisites

This course requires that students meet the following prerequisites:

- Working knowledge of the Windows interface is required.
- Understanding of basic Microsoft network functions and terminology is required.
- One year of experience with relational databases is recommended. You should have supported or designed a relational database and you should understand the fundamental concepts of relational database design.
- Three to six months of SQL Server experience is recommended. You should have installed SQL Server and worked with SQL Server client tools.

Reference Materials

You might find the following reference materials useful:

- *Designing Relational Database Systems*, Rebecca M. Riordan, Microsoft Press, 1999
- *Inside SQL Server 2000*, Kalen Delaney (based on the first edition by Ron Soukup), Microsoft Press, 2000
- Microsoft TechNet, available online at *http://www.microsoft.com/technet/*
- MSDN Online, available at *http://msdn.microsoft.com/sqlserver/*
- SQL Server Books Online, available on the product CD-ROM
- *SQL Server Magazine* (Information about the magazine is available at *http://www.sqlmag.com/.*)
- Technical and product information available online at *http://www.microsoft.com /sql/*

About the CD-ROM

This book contains both a Supplemental Course Materials CD-ROM and a 120-day Evaluation Edition of Microsoft SQL Server 2000.

The Supplemental Course Materials CD-ROM contains files required to perform the hands-on procedures, as well as information designed to supplement the lesson material. These files can be used directly from the CD-ROM or copied onto your hard disk by using the setup program. For more information regarding the contents of this CD-ROM, see the section titled "Getting Started" later in this introduction.

A complete version of this book is also available online with a variety of viewing options available. For information about using the online book, see the section, "About the eBook," later in this introduction.

Features of This Book

Each chapter opens with a "Before You Begin" section, which prepares you for completing the chapter.

▶ The chapters are then broken into lessons. Whenever possible, lessons contain practices that give you an opportunity to use the skills being presented or to explore the part of the application being described. All practices offer step-by-step procedures that are identified with a bullet symbol *like the one to the left of this paragraph.*

The "Review" section at the end of the chapter allows you to test what you have learned in the chapter's lessons.

The Appendix, "Questions and Answers," contains all of the book's questions and corresponding answers.

Notes

Several types of Notes appear throughout the lessons.

- Notes marked *Tip* contain explanations of possible results or alternative methods.
- Notes marked *Important* contain information that is essential to completing a task.
- Notes marked *Note* contain supplemental information.
- Notes marked *Caution* contain warnings about possible loss of data.

Conventions

The following conventions are used throughout this book.

Notational Conventions

- Characters or commands that you type appear in **bold lowercase** type.
- *Italic* in syntax statements indicates placeholders for variable information. *Italic* is also used for book titles.
- Names of files and folders appear in Title Caps, except when you are to type them directly. Unless otherwise indicated, you can use all lowercase letters when you type a filename in a dialog box or at a command prompt.
- Filename extensions appear in all lowercase.
- Acronyms appear in all uppercase.
- Monospace type represents code samples, examples of screen text, or entries that you might type at a command prompt or in initialization files.

- Square brackets ([ ]) are used in syntax statements to enclose optional items. For example, [*filename*] in command syntax indicates that you can choose to type a filename with the command. Type only the information within the brackets, not the brackets themselves.

- Braces ({ }) are used in syntax statements to enclose required items. Type only the information within the braces, not the braces themselves.

- Icons represent specific sections in the book, as follows:

Icon	Represents
	A hands-on exercise. You should perform the exercise to give yourself an opportunity to use the skills being presented in the lesson.
?	Chapter review questions. These questions at the end of each chapter allow you to test what you have learned in the lessons. You will find the answers to the review questions in the Appendix, "Questions and Answers," at the end of the book.

Keyboard Conventions

- A plus sign (+) between two key names means that you must press those keys at the same time. For example, "Press ALT+TAB" means that you hold down ALT while you press TAB.

- A comma (,) between two or more key names means that you must press each of the keys consecutively, not together. For example, "Press ALT, F, X" means that you press and release each key in sequence. "Press ALT+W, L" means that you first press ALT and W together, and then release them and press L.

- You can choose menu commands with the keyboard. Press the ALT key to activate the menu bar, and then sequentially press the keys that correspond to the highlighted or underlined letter of the menu name and the command name. For some commands, you can also press a key combination listed in the menu.

- You can select or clear check boxes or option buttons in dialog boxes with the keyboard. Press the ALT key, and then press the key that corresponds to the underlined letter of the option name. Or you can press TAB until the option is highlighted, and then press the spacebar to select or clear the check box or option button.

- You can cancel the display of a dialog box by pressing the ESC key.

Chapter and Appendix Overview

This self-paced training course combines notes, hands-on procedures, and review questions to teach you how to design and implement databases with SQL Server 2000. It is designed to be completed from beginning to end, but in some cases you can choose a customized track and complete only the sections that interest you. (See the next section, "Finding the Best Starting Point for You," for more information.) If you choose the customized track option, see the "Before You Begin" section in each chapter. Any hands-on procedures that require preliminary work from preceding chapters refer to the appropriate chapters.

Part 1 is divided into the following sections and chapters:

- The "About This Book" section contains a self-paced training overview and introduces the components of this training. Read this section thoroughly to get the greatest educational value from this self-paced training and to plan which lessons you will complete.
- Chapter 1, "Introduction to Microsoft SQL Server 2000," introduces you to SQL Server 2000 and explains what SQL Server is. The chapter provides a cohesive overview of SQL Server so that you can understand how all the pieces fit together.
- Chapter 2, "Using Transact-SQL on a SQL Server Database," introduces you to Transact-SQL and provides details about how to create and execute Transact-SQL statements in order to manage a SQL Server database and its data. The chapter also introduces you to the SQL Server programming tools that allow you to use Transact-SQL to interface with the database.
- Chapter 3, "Designing a SQL Server Database," introduces you to the process of creating a SQL Server database. It describes the basic concepts of database design and provides information about planning a database, identifying system requirements, and developing a logical data model.
- Chapter 4, "Implementing SQL Server Databases and Tables," explains how to create and manage a SQL Server database. It then discusses data types and how to identify which ones to use when creating a table. The chapter also describes how to create these tables—using the data type information—and how to modify the tables after they have been created.
- Chapter 5, "Implementing Data Integrity," provides an overview of the various methods that you can use to maintain data integrity and a description of the types of data integrity that you will find in a SQL Server database. The chapter also provides detailed information about the various types of integrity constraints that you can use to enforce data integrity and how to implement them in a database.
- Chapter 6, "Accessing and Modifying Data," provides detailed information about four Transact-SQL statements (SELECT, INSERT, UPDATE, and DELETE) and describes how each statement is used in Query Analyzer to retrieve and modify data. This chapter also introduces you to other methods for adding, modifying, and deleting data.
- Chapter 7, "Managing and Manipulating Data," describes more techniques for managing and manipulating data, including how to import and export data, how to manipulate heterogeneous data, how to use Transact-SQL cursors, and how to extract data in XML format.
- Chapter 8, "Implementing Stored Procedures," introduces you to the types of stored procedures available in SQL Server 2000 and how to create, execute, and alter them. You are also introduced to programming stored procedures.

- Chapter 9, "Implementing Triggers," introduces you to triggers and how to use them to extend data integrity and implement complex business logic. You will learn when it is appropriate to implement triggers and when basic constraints will suffice. You will also learn how to program triggers and how to use system commands and functions commonly used in trigger programming.

- Chapter 10, "Implementing Views," introduces you to views and the various functionality that they support. You will learn how to use views to insert, update, and modify data.

- Chapter 11, "Implementing Indexes," introduces you to the structure and purpose of indexes and the types and characteristics of indexes. You will learn how to determine when an index is appropriate, the type of index to create, and how to create it.

- Chapter 12, "Managing SQL Server Transactions and Locks," introduces you to the fundamentals of transactions and locks and describes how transactions and locks are used to process data modifications.

- Chapter 13, "Designing and Administering SQL Server 2000 Security," introduces you to SQL Server security. You will learn how to design SQL Server security to accommodate user requirements and protect the database from unauthorized access.

- Chapter 14, "SQL Server Monitoring and Tuning," examines how to use SQL Profiler to monitor a database system and explores methods of improving database performance through partitioning and index tuning.

Following Part 2 you will find:

- The Appendix, "Questions and Answers," lists all of the review questions from the book and the suggested answers.

- The Glossary provides definitions for SQL Server terminology.

Finding the Best Starting Point for You

Because this book is self-paced, you can skip some lessons and revisit them later. But note that you must complete the procedures in certain chapters before you can complete the procedures in other chapters:

- The exercises in Chapter 3, "Designing a SQL Server Database," must be completed before you can complete the exercises in Chapter 4, "Implementing SQL Server Databases and Tables." The exercises in Chapter 4 must be completed before you can complete the exercises in Chapter 5, "Implementing Data Integrity."

- The exercises in Chapter 3, "Designing a SQL Server Database;" Chapter 4, "Implementing SQL Server Databases and Tables;" and Chapter 5, "Implementing Data Integrity," must be completed before you can complete the exercises in Chapter 6, "Accessing and Modifying Data," and Chapter 7, "Managing and Manipulating Data."

- The exercises in Chapter 3, "Designing a SQL Server Database;" Chapter 4, "Implementing SQL Server Databases and Tables;" Chapter 5, "Implementing Data Integrity;" and Chapter 7, "Managing and Manipulating Data," must be completed before you can complete all of the exercises in the chapters that follow Chapter 7.

Use the following table to find the best starting point for you.

If you	Follow this learning path
Are preparing to take the Microsoft Certified Professional exam 70-229, *Designing and Implementing Databases with Microsoft SQL Server 2000 Enterprise Edition*	Read the "Getting Started" section. Then work from Chapter 1, "Introduction to Microsoft SQL Server 2000," through Chapter 7, "Managing and Manipulating Data." Work through the remaining chapters in any order.
Want to review information about specific topics from the exam	Use the "Where to Find Specific Skills in This Book" section that follows this table.

Where to Find Specific Skills in This Book

The following tables provide a list of the skills measured on certification exam 70-229, Designing and Implementing Databases with Microsoft SQL Server 2000 Enterprise Edition. The table provides the skill and where in this book you will find the lesson relating to that skill.

Note   Exam skills are subject to change without prior notice and at the sole discretion of Microsoft.

Skill Being Measured	Location in Book
Developing a Logical Data Model	
1.1 Define entities.	Chapter 3, Lessons 1 and 2
1.2 Design entity keys.	Chapter 5, Lessons 1 and 2
1.3 Design attribute domain integrity.	Chapter 4, Lessons 2 and 3 Chapter 5, Lessons 1 and 2
Implementing the Physical Database	
2.1 Create and alter databases.	Chapter 3, Lessons 1, 2, 3, and 4 Chapter 4, Lesson 1
2.2 Create and alter database objects.	Chapter 2, Lesson 4 Chapter 4, Lessons 1 and 3 Chapter 5, Lessons 1 and 2 Chapter 8, Lessons 1, 2, and 3 Chapter 9, Lessons 1, 2, and 3 Chapter 10, Lessons 1, 2, and 3 Chapter 11, Lessons 1 and 2

Skill Being Measured	Location in Book
Implementing the Physical Database (continued)	
2.3 Alter database objects to support replication and partitioned views.	Chapter 14, Lesson 2
2.4 Troubleshoot failed object creation.	Chapter 14, Lesson 1
Retrieving and Modifying Data	
3.1 Import and export data.	Chapter 7, Lesson 1
3.2 Manipulate heterogeneous data.	Chapter 7, Lesson 2
3.3 Retrieve, filter, group, summarize, and modify data by using Transact-SQL.	Chapter 6, Lessons 1, 2, and 3
3.4 Manage result sets by using cursors and Transact-SQL.	Chapter 6, Lessons 1, 2, and 3 Chapter 7, Lesson 3
3.5 Extract data in XML format.	Chapter 7, Lesson 4
Programming Business Logic	
4.1 Manage data manipulation by using stored procedures, transactions, triggers, user-defined functions, and views.	Chapter 2, Lesson 3 Chapter 8, Lessons 1, 2, and 3 Chapter 9, Lessons 1, 2, and 3 Chapter 10, Lessons 1, 2, and 3 Chapter 12, Lessons 1, 2, and 3
4.2 Enforce procedural business logic by using stored procedures, transactions, triggers, user-defined functions, and views.	Chapter 2, Lesson 3 Chapter 8, Lessons 1, 2, and 3 Chapter 9, Lessons 1, 2, and 3 Chapter 10, Lessons 1, 2, and 3 Chapter 12, Lessons 1, 2, and 3
4.3 Troubleshoot and optimize programming objects.	Chapter 14, Lesson 1
Tuning and Optimizing Data Access	
5.1 Analyze the query execution plan.	Chapter 14, Lesson 1
5.2 Capture, analyze, and replay SQL Profiler traces.	Chapter 14, Lesson 1
5.3 Create and implement indexing strategies.	Chapter 11, Lessons 1 and 2
5.4 Analyze index use by using the Index Tuning wizard.	Chapter 11, Lessons 1 and 2
5.5 Monitor and troubleshoot database activity by using SQL Profiler.	Chapter 14, Lesson 1
Designing a Database Security Plan	
6.1 Control data access by using stored procedures, triggers, user-defined functions, and views.	Chapter 2, Lesson 3 Chapter 8, Lessons 1, 2, and 3 Chapter 9, Lessons 1, 2, and 3 Chapter 10, Lessons 1, 2, and 3 Chapter 13, Lessons 1, 2, and 3

Skill Being Measured	Location in Book
Designing a Database Security Plan (continued)	
6.2 Define object-level security, including column-level permissions, by using Grant, Revoke, and Deny.	Chapter 13, Lessons 1, 2, and 3
6.3 Create and manage application roles.	Chapter 13, Lessons 1, 2, and 3

Getting Started

This self-paced training course contains hands-on procedures to help you learn about Microsoft SQL Server 2000 Enterprise Edition.

Hardware Requirements

Your computer must meet the minimum hardware requirements for Windows 2000 Server. In addition, you must meet the following minimum configuration to support SQL Server 2000 Enterprise Edition. All hardware should be on the Microsoft Windows 2000 Server Hardware Compatibility List (HCL). The latest version of the HCL can be downloaded from the Hardware Compatibility List Web page at *http://www.microsoft.com/hwdq/hcl/*.

- 166-MHz or higher Pentium processor
- 64 MB RAM (minimum), 128 MB or more recommended
- SQL Server database components: 95 MB to 270 MB, 250 MB typical
- CD-ROM drive
- Microsoft Mouse or compatible pointing device

Software Requirements

The following software is required to complete the procedures in this course.

- Windows 2000 Server
- SQL Server 2000 Enterprise Edition

Caution   The 120-day Evaluation Edition provided with this training kit is not the full retail product and is provided only for the purposes of training and evaluation. Microsoft Technical Support does not support this evaluation edition. For additional support information regarding this book and the CD-ROM (including answers to commonly asked questions about installation and use), visit the Microsoft Press Technical Support web site at *http://www.microsoft.com/mspress /support/*. You can also e-mail *tkinput@microsoft.com*, or send a letter to Microsoft Press, Attn: Microsoft Press Technical Support, One Microsoft Way, Redmond, WA 98502-6399.

Setup Instructions

Set up your computer according to the manufacturer's instructions. Use default installation options when setting up SQL Server 2000. The Windows 2000 computer should be set up as a stand-alone server.

About the eBook

The Supplemental Course Materials CD-ROM includes an electronic version of the book that you can view on screen by using Adobe Acrobat Reader. For more information, see the README.TXT file included in the root folder of the Supplemental Course Materials CD-ROM.

Before You Begin Part 2

Part 2 lets you identify any areas in which you might need additional training. To help you get the training you need to successfully pass the certification exams, Microsoft Press publishes a complete line of self-paced training kits and other study materials. For comprehensive information about the topics covered in the Designing and Implementing Databases with Microsoft SQL Server 2000 Enterprise Edition exam, see Part 1.

Note   You can find a complete list of MCP exams and their related objectives on the Microsoft Certified Professional Web site at *http://www.microsoft.com /traincert/mcp*.

The Components of Part 2

The electronic assessment is a practice certification test that helps you evaluate your skills. It provides instant scoring feedback, so you can determine areas in which additional study might be helpful before you take the certification exam. Although your score on the electronic assessment does not necessarily indicate what your score will be on the certification exam, it does give you the opportunity to answer questions that are similar to those on the actual certification exam.

Part 2 of the book is organized by the exam's objectives. Each chapter of the book pertains to one of the six primary groups of objectives on the actual exam, called the Objective Domains. Each Objective Domain lists the tested skills you need to master to adequately answer the exam questions. Because the certification exams focus on real-world skills, the Tested Skills and Suggested Practices lists provide practices that emphasize the practical application of the exam objectives. Each Objective Domain also provides suggestions for further reading or additional resources to help you understand the objectives and increase your ability to perform the task or skills specified by the objectives.

Within each Objective Domain, you will find the related objectives that are covered on the exam. Each objective provides you with the following:

- **Key terms** you must know to understand the objective. Knowing these terms can help you answer the objective's questions correctly.
- Several sample exam questions with the correct answers. The answers are accompanied by explanations of each correct and incorrect answer. (These questions match the questions on the electronic assessment.)

You use the electronic assessment to determine the exam objectives that you need to study, and then use Part 2 to learn more about those particular objectives and discover additional study materials to supplement your knowledge. You can also use Part 2 to research the answers to specific sample test questions. Keep in mind that to pass the exam, you should understand not only the answer to the question, but also the concepts on which the correct answer is based.

MCP Exam Prerequisites

No exams or classes are required before you take the Designing and Implementing Databases with Microsoft SQL Server 2000 Enterprise Edition exam. However, in addition to the skills tested by the exam, you should have a working knowledge of the design and implementation of databases using SQL Server 2000. This knowledge should include:

- Logical database design
- Implementing physical databases, including creating and altering databases and database objects
- Retrieving and modifying data
- Programming business logic, including stored procedures, triggers, and transactions
- Tuning and optimizing queries and data access
- Designing a database security plan

Note   After you have determined that you are ready for the exam, use the Get More MCP Information link provided in the home page of the electronic assessment tool for information on scheduling for the exam. You can schedule exams up to six weeks in advance, or as late as one working day before the exam date.

Know the Products

Microsoft's certification program relies on exams that measure your ability to perform a specific job function or set of tasks. Microsoft develops the exams by analyzing the tasks performed by people who are currently working in the field. Therefore, the specific knowledge, skills, and abilities relating to the job are reflected in the certification exam.

Because the certification exams are based on real-world tasks, you need to gain hands-on experience with the applicable technology in order to master the exam. In a sense, you might consider hands-on experience in an organizational environment to be a prerequisite for passing an MCP exam. Many of the questions relate directly to Microsoft products or technology, so use opportunities at your organization or home to practice using the relevant tools.

Using Part 2

Although you can use Part 2 in a number of ways, you might start your studies by taking the electronic assessment as a pretest. After completing the exam, review your results for each Objective Domain and focus your studies first on the Objective Domains for which you received the lowest scores. The electronic assessment allows you to print your results, and a printed report of how you fared can be useful when reviewing the exam material in this book.

After you have taken the electronic assessment, use Part 2 to learn more about the Objective Domains that you find difficult and to find listings of appropriate study materials that might supplement your knowledge. By reviewing why the answers are correct or incorrect, you can determine whether you need to study the objective topics more.

You can also use Part 2 to focus on the exact objectives that you need to master. Each objective in the book contains several questions that help you determine whether you understand the information related to that particular skill. The book is also designed for you to answer each question before reviewing the correct answer and answer choice explanations.

The best method to prepare for the MCP exam is to use Part 2 of the book in conjunction with the electronic assessment and other study materials. Thoroughly studying and practicing the material, combined with substantial real-world experience, can help you fully prepare for the MCP exam.

Understanding the Conventions for Part 2

Before you begin Part 2, it is important that you understand the terms and conventions used in the electronic assessment and book.

Question Numbering System

The electronic assessment and Part 2 contain reference numbers for each question. Understanding the numbering format will help you use Part 2 more effectively. When Microsoft creates the exams, the questions are grouped by job skills called *Objectives*. These Objectives are then organized by sections known as *Objective Domains*. Each question can be identified by the Objective Domain and the Objective it covers. The question numbers follow this format:

Test Number.Objective Domain.Objective.Question Number

For example, question number 70-229.02.01.003 means this is question three (003) for the first Objective (01) in the second Objective Domain (02) of the Designing and Implementing Databases with Microsoft SQL Server 2000 Enterprise Edition exam (70- 229). Refer to the "Exam Objectives Summary" section later in this introduction to locate the numbers associated with particular objectives. Each question is numbered based on its presentation in the printed book. You can use this numbering system to reference questions on the electronic assessment or in Part 2. Even though the questions in the book are organized by objective, questions in the electronic assessment and actual certification exam are presented in random order.

Using the Electronic Assessment

The electronic assessment simulates the actual MCP exam. Each iteration of the electronic assessment consists of 50 questions covering all the objectives for the Installing, Configuring, and Administering Microsoft SQL Server 2000 Enterprise Edition exam. (MCP certification exams consist of approximately 50–70 questions.) Just like a real certification exam, you see questions from the objectives in random order during the practice test. Similar to the certification exam, the electronic assessment allows you to mark questions and review them after you finish the test.

To increase its value as a study aid, you can take the electronic assessment multiple times. Each time you are presented with a different set of questions in a revised order; however, some questions may be repeated.

If you have used one of the certification exam preparation tests available from Microsoft, the electronic assessment should look familiar. The difference is that this electronic assessment gives you the opportunity to learn as you take the exam.

Installing and Running the Electronic Assessment Software

Before you begin using the electronic assessment, you need to install the software. You need a computer with the following minimum configuration:

- Multimedia PC with a 75 MHz Pentium or higher processor
- 16 MB RAM for Microsoft Windows 95 or Windows 98, or
- 32 MB RAM for Windows NT, or

- 64 MB RAM for Windows 2000
- Microsoft Internet Explorer 5.01 or later
- 17 MB of available hard disk space (additional 70 MB minimum of hard disk space to install Internet Explorer 5.5 from this CD-ROM)
- A double-speed CD-ROM drive or better
- Super VGA display with at least 256 colors

▶ **To install the electronic assessment**

1. Insert the Supplemental Course Materials CD-ROM into your CD-ROM drive.

   A starting menu will display automatically, with links to the resources included on the CD-ROM.

   Note   If your system does not have Microsoft Internet Explorer 5.01 or later, you can install Internet Explorer 6.0 now by selecting the appropriate option on the menu.

   ---

2. Click the link to the exam you want to install.

   A dialog box appears, indicating you will install the exam to your computer.

3. Click Next.

   The License Agreement dialog box appears.

4. To continue with the installation of the electronic assessment engine, you must accept the License Agreement by clicking Yes.

5. The Choose Destination Location dialog box appears showing a default installation directory. Either accept the default or change the installation directory if needed. Click Next to copy the files to your hard drive.

6. A Question dialog box appears asking whether you would like Setup to create a desktop shortcut for this program. If you click Yes, an icon will be placed on your desktop.

7. The Setup Complete dialog box appears. Select whether you want to view the Readme.txt file after closing the Setup program, and then click Finish.

   The electronic assessment software is completely installed. If you chose to view the Readme.txt file, it will launch in a new window. For optimal viewing, enable word wrap.

▶ **To start the electronic assessment**

1. From the Start menu, point to Programs, point to MCSE Readiness Review, and then click MCSE RR Exam 70-229.

   The electronic assessment program starts.

2. Click Start Test.

   Information about the electronic assessment program appears.

3. Click OK.

Taking the Electronic Assessment

The electronic assessment consists of 50 multiple-choice questions, and as in the certification exam, you can skip questions or mark them for later review. Each exam question contains a question number that you can use to refer back to Part 2 of the book.

Before you end the electronic assessment, make sure you answer all the questions. When the exam is graded, unanswered questions are counted as incorrect and will lower your score. Similarly, on the actual certification exam you should complete all questions or they will be counted as incorrect. No trick questions appear on the exam. The correct answer will always be among the list of choices. Some questions may have more than one correct answer, and this will be indicated in the question. A good strategy is to eliminate the most obvious incorrect answers first to make it easier for you to select the correct answer.

You have 75 minutes to complete the electronic assessment. During the exam you will see a timer indicating the amount of time you have remaining. This will help you to gauge the amount of time you should use to answer each question and to complete the exam. The amount of time you are given on the actual certification exam varies with each exam. Generally, certification exams take approximately 100 minutes to complete, but they can vary from 60 to 300 minutes.

Ending and Grading the Electronic Assessment

When you click the Score Test button, you have the opportunity to review the questions you marked or left incomplete. (This format is not similar to the one used on the actual certification exam, in which you can verify whether you are satisfied with your answers and then click the Grade Test button.) The electronic assessment is graded when you click the Score Test button, and the software presents your section scores and your total score.

Note   You can always end a test without grading your electronic assessment by clicking the Home button.

After your electronic assessment is graded, you can view the correct and incorrect answers by clicking the Review Questions button.

Interpreting the Electronic Assessment Results

The Score screen shows you the number of questions in each Objective Domain section, the number of questions you answered correctly, and a percentage grade for each section. You can use the Score screen to determine where to spend additional time studying. On the actual certification exam, the number of questions and passing score will depend on the exam you are taking. The electronic assessment records your score each time you grade an exam so that you can track your progress over time.

► **To view your progress and exam records**

1. From the electronic assessment Main menu, click View History. Each test attempt score appears.

2. Click a test attempt date/time to view your score for each objective domain.

   Review these scores to determine which Objective Domains you should study further. You can also use the scores to determine your progress.

Ordering More Questions

Self Test Software offers practice tests to help you prepare for a variety of MCP certification exams. These practice tests contain hundreds of additional questions and are similar to the electronic assessment. For a fee, you can order exam practice tests for this exam and other Microsoft certification exams. Click the Order More Questions link on the electronic assessment tool home page for more information.

Using Part 2 of This Book

You can use Part 2 of this book as a supplement to the electronic assessment, or as a stand-alone study aid. If you decide to use the book as a stand-alone study aid, review the Contents or the list of objectives to find topics of interest or an appropriate starting point for you. To get the greatest benefit from the book, use the electronic assessment as a pretest to determine the Objective Domains for which you should spend the most study time. Or, if you would like to research specific questions while taking the electronic assessment, you can use the question number located on the question screen to reference the question number in Part 2 of the book.

One way to determine areas in which additional study may be helpful is to carefully review your individual section scores from the electronic assessment and note objective areas where your score could be improved. The section scores correlate to the Objective Domains listed in Part 2 of the book.

Reviewing the Objectives

Each Objective Domain in the book contains an introduction and a list of practice skills. Each list of practice skills describes suggested tasks you can perform to help you understand the objectives. Some of the tasks suggest reading additional material, whereas others are hands-on practices with software or hardware. You should pay particular attention to the hands-on practices, as the certification exam reflects real-world knowledge you can gain only by working with the software or technology. Increasing your real-world experience with the relevant products and technologies will improve your performance on the exam.

After you choose the objectives you want to study, turn to the Contents to locate the objectives in Part 2 of the book. You can study each objective separately, but you might need to understand the concepts explained in other objectives.

Make sure you understand the key terms for each objective. You will need a thorough understanding of these terms to answer the objective's questions correctly. Key term definitions are located in the Glossary of this book.

Reviewing the Questions

Each objective includes questions followed by the possible answers. After you review the question and select a probable answer, turn to the Answer section to determine if you answered the question correctly. (For information about the question numbering format, see "Question Numbering System," earlier in this introduction.)

Part 2 briefly discusses each possible answer and explains why each answer is correct or incorrect. After reviewing each explanation, if you feel you need more information about a topic, question, or answer, refer to the Further Readings section for that domain for more information.

The answers to the questions in Part 2 are based on current industry specifications and standards. However, the information provided by the answers is subject to change as technology improves and changes.

Exam Objectives Summary

The Designing and Implementing Databases with Microsoft SQL Server 2000 Enterprise Edition certification exam (70-229) measures your ability to implement, administer, and troubleshoot SQL Server 2000 Enterprise Edition.

Before taking the exam, you should be proficient with the job skills presented in the following sections. The sections provide the exam objectives and the corresponding objective numbers (which you can use to reference the questions in the electronic assessment and book) grouped by Objective Domains.

Objective Domain 1: Developing a Logical Data Model

The objectives in Objective Domain 1 are as follows:

- Objective 1.1 (70-229.01.01)—Define entities.
- Objective 1.2 (70-229.01.02)—Design entity keys.
- Objective 1.3 (70-229.01.03)—Design attribute domain integrity.

Objective Domain 2: Implementing the Physical Database

The objectives in Objective Domain 2 are as follows:

- Objective 2.1 (70-229.02.01)—Create and alter databases.
- Objective 2.2 (70-229.02.02)—Create and alter database objects.
- Objective 2.3 (70-229.02.03)—Alter database objects to support replication and partitioned views.
- Objective 2.4 (70-229.02.04)—Troubleshoot failed object creation.

Objective Domain 3: Retrieving and Modifying Data

The objectives in Objective Domain 3 are as follows:

- Objective 3.1 (70-229.03.01)—Import and export data.
- Objective 3.2 (70-229.03.02)—Manipulate heterogeneous data.
- Objective 3.3 (70-229.03.03)—Retrieve, filter, group, summarize, and modify data by using Transact-SQL.
- Objective 3.4 (70-229.03.04)—Manage result sets by using cursors and Transact-SQL.
- Objective 3.5 (70-229.03.05)—Extract data in XML format.

Objective Domain 4: Programming Business Logic

The objectives in Objective Domain 4 are as follows:

- Objective 4.1 (70-229.04.01)—Manage data manipulation by using stored procedures, transactions, triggers, user-defined functions, and views.
- Objective 4.2 (70-229.04.02)—Enforce procedural business logic by using stored procedures, transactions, triggers, user-defined functions, and views.
- Objective 4.3 (70-229.04.03)—Troubleshoot and optimize programming objects.

Objective Domain 5: Tuning and Optimizing Data Access

The objectives in Objective Domain 5 are as follows:

- Objective 5.1 (70-229.05.01)—Analyze the query execution plan.
- Objective 5.2 (70-229.05.02)—Capture, analyze, and replay SQL Profiler traces.
- Objective 5.3 (70-229.05.03)—Create and implement indexing strategies.
- Objective 5.4 (70-229.05.04)—Improve index use by using the Index Tuning Wizard.
- Objective 5.5 (70-229.05.05)—Monitor and troubleshoot database activity by using SQL Profiler.

Objective Domain 6: Designing a Database Security Plan

The objectives in Objective Domain 6 are as follows:

- Objective 6.1 (70-229.06.01)—Control data access by using stored procedures, triggers, user-defined functions, and views.
- Objective 6.2 (70-229.06.02)—Define object-level security including column-level permissions by using GRANT, REVOKE, and DENY.
- Objective 6.3 (70-229.06.03)—Create and manage application roles.

Getting More Help

A variety of resources are available to help you study for the exam. Your options include instructor-led classes, seminars, self-paced training kits, or other learning materials. The materials described here are created to prepare you for MCP exams. Each training resource fits a different type of learning style and budget.

Microsoft Official Curriculum (MOC)

Microsoft Official Curriculum (MOC) courses are technical training courses developed by Microsoft product groups to educate computer professionals who use Microsoft technology. The courses are developed with the same objectives used for Microsoft certification, and MOC courses are available to support most exams for the MCSE certification. The courses are available in instructor-led, online, or self-paced formats to fit your preferred learning style.

Self-Paced Training

Microsoft Press self-paced training kits cover a variety of Microsoft technical products. The self-paced kits are based on MOC courses, feature lessons, hands-on practices, multimedia presentations, practice files, and demonstration software. They can help you understand the concepts and get the experience you need to take the corresponding MCP exam.

MCP Approved Study Guides

MCP Approved Study Guides, available through several organizations, are learning tools that help you prepare for MCP exams. The study guides are available in a variety of formats to match your learning style, including books, compact discs, online content, and videos. These guides come in a wide range of prices to fit your budget.

Microsoft Seminar Series

Microsoft Solution Providers and other organizations are often a source of information to help you prepare for an MCP exam. For example, many solution providers will present seminars to help industry professionals understand a particular product technology, such as networking. For information on all Microsoft-sponsored events, visit *http://www.microsoft.com/events*.

The Microsoft Certified Professional Program

The Microsoft Certified Professional (MCP) program provides the best method to prove your command of current Microsoft products and technologies. Microsoft, an industry leader in certification, is on the forefront of testing methodology. Our exams and corresponding certifications are developed to validate your mastery of critical competencies as you design and develop, or implement and support, solutions with Microsoft products and technologies. Computer professionals who become Microsoft certified are recognized as experts and are sought after industry-wide.

The Microsoft Certified Professional program offers five certifications, based on specific areas of technical expertise:

- **Microsoft Certified Professional (MCP).**   Demonstrated in-depth knowledge of at least one Microsoft operating system. Candidates may pass additional Microsoft certification exams to further qualify their skills with Microsoft BackOffice products, development tools, or desktop programs.

- **Microsoft Certified Systems Administrator (MCSA) on Microsoft Windows 2000.**   Individuals who implement, manage, and troubleshoot existing network and system environments based on Microsoft Windows 2000 and Windows Server 2003 operating systems.

- **Microsoft Certified Systems Engineer (MCSE).**   Qualified to effectively analyze the business requirements, and design and implement the infrastructure for business solutions based on Microsoft Windows 2000 platform and Microsoft .NET Enterprise Servers.

- **Microsoft Certified Database Administrator (MCDBA).**   Individuals who derive physical database designs, develop logical data models, create physical databases, create data services by using Transact-SQL, manage and maintain databases, configure and manage security, monitor and optimize databases, and install and configure Microsoft SQL Server.

- **Microsoft Certified Solution Developer (MCSD).**   Qualified to design and develop custom business solutions with Microsoft development tools, technologies, and platforms, including Microsoft Office and Microsoft BackOffice.

- **Microsoft Certified Trainer (MCT).**   Instructionally and technically qualified to deliver Microsoft Official Curriculum through a Microsoft Certified Technical Education Center (CTEC).

Microsoft Certification Benefits

Microsoft certification, one of the most comprehensive certification programs available for assessing and maintaining software-related skills, is a valuable measure of an individual's knowledge and expertise. Microsoft certification is awarded to individuals who have successfully demonstrated their ability to perform specific tasks and implement solutions with Microsoft products. Not only does this provide an objective measure for employers to consider; it also provides guidance for what an individual should know to be proficient. And as with any skills-assessment and benchmarking measure, certification brings a variety of benefits: to the individual, and to employers and organizations.

Microsoft Certification Benefits for Individuals

Microsoft Certified Professionals receive the following benefits:

- Industry recognition of your knowledge and proficiency with Microsoft products and technologies.
- Microsoft Developer Network (MSDN) subscription. MCPs receive rebates or discounts on a one-year subscription to the Microsoft Developer Network (*http://msdn.microsoft.com/subscriptions/*) during the first year of certification. (Fulfillment details will vary, depending on your location; please see your Welcome Kit.)
- Access to technical and product information directly from Microsoft through a secured area of the MCP Web site (go to *http://www.microsoft.com/traincert /mcp/mccpsecure.asp/*).
- Access to exclusive discounts on products and services from selected companies. Individuals who are currently certified can learn more about exclusive discounts by visiting the MCP secured Web site (go to *http://www.microsoft.com /traincert/mcp/mccpsecure.asp/* and select the "Other Benefits" link) upon certification.
- MCP logo, certificate, transcript, wallet card, and lapel pin to identify you as a Microsoft Certified Professional (MCP) to colleagues and clients. Electronic files of logos and transcript may be downloaded from the MCP secured Web site upon certification.
- Invitations to Microsoft conferences, technical training sessions, and special events.
- Free access to *Microsoft Certified Professional Magazine Online*, a career and professional development magazine. Secured content on the *Microsoft Certified Professional Magazine Online* Web site includes the current issue (available only to MCPs), additional online-only content and columns, an MCP-only database, and regular chats with Microsoft and other technical experts.

- Discount on membership to PASS (for MCPs only), the Professional Association for SQL Server. In addition to playing a key role in the only worldwide, user-run SQL Server user group endorsed by Microsoft, members enjoy unique access to a world of educational opportunities (go to *http://www.microsoft.com /traincert/mcp/mcpsecure.asp/*).

An additional benefit is received by Microsoft Certified Systems Engineers (MCSEs):

- 50 percent rebate or discount off the estimated retail price of a one-year subscription to *TechNet* or *TechNet Plus* during the first year of certification. (Fulfillment details will vary, depending on your location. Please see your Welcome Kit.) In addition about 95 percent of the CD-ROM content is available free online at the *TechNet* Web site (*http://www.microsoft.com/technet/*).

Additional benefits are received by Microsoft Certified System Database Administrators (MCDBAs):

- 50 percent rebate or discount off the estimated retail price of a one-year subscription to *TechNet* or *TechNet Plus* during the first year of certification. (Fulfillment details will vary, depending on your location. Please see your Welcome Kit.) In addition about 95 percent of the CD-ROM content is available free online at the *TechNet* Web site (*http://mail.microsoft.com/technet/*).
- A one-year subscription to *SQL Server Magazine*. Written by industry experts, the magazine contains technical and how-to tips and advice—a must for anyone working with SQL Server.

Microsoft Certification Benefits for Employers and Organizations

Through certification, computer professionals can maximize the return on investment in Microsoft technology. Research shows that Microsoft certification provides organizations with:

- Excellent return on training and certification investments by providing a standard method of determining training needs and measuring results.
- Increased customer satisfaction and decreased support costs through improved service, increased productivity, and greater technical self-sufficiency.
- Reliable benchmark for hiring, promoting, and career planning.
- Recognition and rewards for productive employees by validating their expertise.
- Retraining options for existing employees so they can work effectively with new technologies.
- Assurance of quality when outsourcing computer services.

Requirements for Becoming a Microsoft Certified Professional

The certification requirements differ for each certification and are specific to the products and job functions addressed by the certification.

To become a Microsoft Certified Professional, you must pass rigorous certification exams that provide a valid and reliable measure of technical proficiency and expertise. These exams are designed to test your expertise and ability to perform a role or task with a product, and are developed with the input of professionals in the industry. Questions in the exams reflect how Microsoft products are used in actual organizations, giving them "real-world" relevance.

- Microsoft Certified Professional candidates are required to pass one operating system exam. Candidates may pass additional Microsoft certification exams to further qualify their skills with other Microsoft products, development tools, or desktop applications.

- Microsoft Certified Systems Engineers are required to pass five core exams and two elective exams. Microsoft Certified Database Administrators are required to pass three core exams and one elective exam that provide a valid and reliable measure of technical proficiency and expertise.

- Microsoft Certified Systems Administrators are required to pass three core exams and one elective exam that provide a valid and reliable measure of technical proficiency and expertise.

- Microsoft Certified Database Administrators are required to pass three core Microsoft Windows operating system technology exams and one elective that provide a valid and reliable measure of technical proficiency and expertise.

- Microsoft Certified Solution Developers are required to pass three core Microsoft Windows operating system technology exams and one elective that provide a valid and reliable measure of technical proficiency and expertise.

- Microsoft Certified Trainers are required to meet instructional and technical requirements specific to each Microsoft Official Curriculum course they are certified to deliver. The MCT program requires on-going training to meet the requirements for the annual renewal of the certification. For more information on becoming a Microsoft Certified Trainer, visit *http://www.microsoft.com /traincert/mcp/mct/*.

Technical Support

Every effort has been made to ensure the accuracy of this book and the contents of the Supplemental Course Materials CD-ROM. If you have any comments, questions, or ideas regarding this book or the Supplemental Course Materials CD-ROM, please send them to Microsoft Press, using either of the following methods:

Microsoft Press provides corrections for books through the World Wide Web at the following address:

http://www.microsoft.com/mspress/support

To query the Technical Support Knowledge Base about a question or issue that you may have, go to:

http://www.microsoft.com/support/search.asp

E-mail:

TKINPUT@MICROSOFT.COM

Postal mail:

Microsoft Press
Attn: Microsoft Training Kit Series Editor
One Microsoft Way Redmond, WA 98052-6399

SQL Server 2000 Evaluation Edition Software Support

The SQL Server 2000 Evaluation Edition included with this book is unsupported by both Microsoft and Microsoft Press, and should not be used on a primary work computer. For online support information related to the full version of SQL Server 2000 (much of which will also apply to the Evaluation Edition), you can connect to *http://www.microsoft.com/support/*.

For information about ordering the full version of any Microsoft software, please call Microsoft Sales at (800) 936-3500 or visit *http://www.microsoft.com*. Information about issues related to the use of the SQL Server 2000 Evaluation Edition with this training kit is posted to the Support section of the Microsoft Press Web site (*http://mspress.microsoft.com/support*).

PART 1

Self-Paced Training for Microsoft SQL Server 2000 Database Design and Implementation

C H A P T E R 1

Introduction to Microsoft SQL Server 2000

About this Chapter

This chapter introduces you to SQL Server 2000 by describing the components of SQL Server and explaining how those components work together to provide a relational database management system (RDBMS). Many of the topics discussed in this chapter will be described in greater detail in later chapters. The purpose of this chapter, however, is to give you a cohesive overview of SQL Server so that you can understand how all the pieces fit together.

Before You Begin

There are no special requirements necessary to complete the lessons in this chapter, although a working knowledge of the previous versions of SQL Server would be helpful.

Lesson 1: Overview of SQL Server 2000

Microsoft SQL Server 2000 is a complete database and analysis solution for rapidly delivering the next generation of scalable Web applications. SQL Server 2000 is a key component in supporting e-commerce, line-of-business, and data warehousing applications, while offering the scalability necessary to support growing, dynamic environments. SQL Server 2000 includes rich support for Extensible Markup Language (XML) and other Internet language formats; performance and availability features to ensure uptime; and advanced management and tuning functionality to automate routine tasks and lower the total cost of ownership. Additionally, SQL Server 2000 takes full advantage of Microsoft Windows 2000 by integrating with Active Directory Services and supporting up to 32 processors and 64 gigabytes (GB) of Random Access Memory (RAM).

After this lesson, you will be able to:
- Describe the SQL Server 2000 RDBMS, including its essential components.
- Describe several of the important features of SQL Server 2000.
- Identify the various editions of SQL Server 2000.

Estimated lesson time: 20 minutes

What Is SQL Server 2000?

SQL Server 2000 is an RDBMS that uses Transact-SQL to send requests between a client computer and a SQL Server 2000 computer. An RDBMS includes databases, the database engine, and the applications that are necessary to manage the data and the components of the RDBMS. The RDBMS organizes data into related rows and columns within the database. The RDBMS is responsible for enforcing the database structure, including the following tasks:

- Maintaining the relationships among data in the database
- Ensuring that data is stored correctly and that the rules defining data relationships are not violated
- Recovering all data to a point of known consistency in case of system failures

The database component of SQL Server 2000 is a Structured Query Language (SQL)-compatible, scalable, relational database with integrated XML support for Internet applications. SQL Server 2000 builds upon the modern, extensible foundation of SQL Server 7.0. The following sections introduce you to the fundamentals of databases, relational databases, SQL, and XML.

Databases

A database is similar to a data file in that it is a storage place for data. Like most types of data files, a database does not present information directly to a user; rather, the user runs an application that accesses data from the database and presents it to the user in an understandable format.

Database systems are more powerful than data files because the data is more highly organized. In a well-designed database, there are no duplicate pieces of data that the user or application has to update at the same time. Related pieces of data are grouped together in a single structure or record, and you can define relationships among these structures and records.

When working with data files, an application must be coded to work with the specific structure of each data file. In contrast, a database contains a catalog that applications use to determine how data is organized. Generic database applications can use the catalog to present users with data from different databases dynamically, without being tied to a specific data format.

Relational Databases

Although there are different ways to organize data in a database, a relational database is one of the most effective systems. A relational database system uses mathematical set theory to effectively organize data. In a relational database, data is collected into tables (called relations in relational database theory).

A table represents some class of objects that are important to an organization. For example, a company might have a database with a table for employees, a table for customers, and another table for stores. Each table is built from columns and rows (attributes and tuples, respectively, in relational database theory). Each column represents an attribute of the object class represented by the table, such that the employees' table might have columns for attributes such as first name, last name, employee ID, department, pay grade, and job title. Each row represents an instance of the object class represented by the table. For example, one row in the employees' table might represent an employee who has employee ID 12345.

You can usually find many different ways to organize data into tables. Relational database theory defines a process called normalization, which ensures that the set of tables you define will organize your data effectively. Normalization is discussed in more detail in Chapter 3, "Designing a SQL Server Database."

SQL

To work with data in a database, you must use a set of commands and statements (a language) supported by the database management system (DBMS) software. You can use several different languages with relational databases; the most common is SQL. The American National Standards Institute (ANSI) and the International Organization for Standardization (ISO) define software standards, including standards for SQL. SQL Server 2000 supports Entry Level SQL-92, the SQL standard published by ANSI and ISO in 1992. The dialect of SQL supported by SQL Server is called Transact-SQL, and Transact-SQL is the primary language used by SQL Server applications. Transact-SQL is discussed in more detail in Chapter 2, "Using Transact-SQL on a SQL Server 2000 Database."

XML

XML is the emerging standard format for data on the Internet. *XML* is a set of tags that can be included in a text document in order to define the structure of the document.

Although most SQL statements return their results in a relational (tabular) result set, the SQL Server 2000 database component supports a FOR XML clause that causes the results to be returned as an XML document. SQL Server 2000 also supports XPath queries from Internet and intranet applications. You can add XML documents to SQL Server databases, and you can use the OPENXML clause to display the data from the document as a relational result set. XML is discussed in more detail in Chapter 7, "Managing and Manipulating Data."

SQL Server 2000 Features

SQL Server 2000 includes a number of features that support ease of installation, deployment, and use; scalability; data warehousing; and system integration with other server software.

Ease of Installation, Deployment, and Use

SQL Server 2000 includes many tools and features that simplify the process of installing, deploying, managing, and using databases. SQL Server 2000 provides database administrators with all of the tools that are required to fine-tune SQL Server 2000 installations that run production online systems. SQL Server 2000 is also capable of operating efficiently on a small, single-user system with minimal administrative overhead.

The installation or upgrade of SQL Server 2000 is driven by a Graphical User Interface (GUI) application that guides users in providing the information that SQL Server 2000 Setup needs. The Setup program itself automatically detects whether an earlier version of SQL Server is present, and after SQL Server 2000 is installed, it asks users whether they want to launch the SQL Server 2000 Upgrade wizard to quickly guide them through the upgrade process. The entire installation or upgrade process is accomplished quickly and with minimal input from the users.

SQL Server 2000 reconfigures itself automatically and dynamically while running. As more users connect to SQL Server 2000, it can dynamically acquire additional resources, such as memory. As the workload falls, SQL Server 2000 frees the resources back to the system. If other applications are started on the server, SQL Server 2000 will detect the additional allocations of virtual memory to those applications and reduce its use of virtual memory in order to reduce paging overhead. SQL Server 2000 can also increase or decrease the size of a database automatically as data is inserted or deleted.

SQL Server 2000 offers database administrators several tools for managing their systems, such as SQL Server Enterprise Manager and SQL Profiler. The administration tools are discussed in more detail in Lesson 2, "Components of SQL Server 2000."

Scalability

The SQL Server 2000 database engine is a robust server that can manage terabyte databases being accessed by thousands of users. At the same time, when running at its default settings, SQL Server 2000 has features such as dynamic self-tuning that enable it to work effectively on laptops and desktops without burdening users with administrative tasks.

SQL Server 2000 includes several features that extend the scalability of the system. For example, SQL Server 2000 dynamically adjusts the granularity of locking to the appropriate level for each table referenced by a query and has high-speed optimizations that support Very Large Database (VLDB) environments. In addition, SQL Server 2000 can build parallel execution plans that split the processing of a SQL statement into several parts. Each part can be run on a different Central Processing Unit (CPU), and the complete result set is built more quickly than if the different parts were executed serially.

Many of the features that support the extended scalability of SQL Server 2000 are discussed in more detail throughout the training kit.

Data Warehousing

A *data warehouse* is a database that is specifically structured to enable flexible queries of the data set and decision-making analysis of the result set. A data warehouse typically contains data representing the business history of an organization. A *data mart* is a subset of the contents of a data warehouse. A data mart tends to contain data that is focused at the department level, or on a specific business area. SQL Server 2000 includes several components that improve the capability to build data warehouses that effectively support decision support processing needs:

- **Data Warehousing Framework.**   A set of components and Application Programming Interfaces (APIs) that implement the data warehousing features of SQL Server 2000.
- **Data Transformation Services (DTS).**   A set of services that aids in building a data warehouse or data mart.
- **Meta Data Services.**   A set of ActiveX interfaces and information models that define the database schema and data transformations implemented by the Data Warehousing Framework. A schema is a method for defining and organizing data, which is also called metadata.

- **Analysis Services.**   A set of services that provide OLAP processing capabilities against heterogeneous OLE DB data sources.
- **English Query.**   An application development product that enables users to ask questions in English, rather than in a computer language such as SQL.

System Integration

SQL Server 2000 works with other products to form a stable and secure data store for Internet and intranet systems:

- SQL Server 2000 works with Windows 2000 Server and Windows NT Server security and encryption facilities to implement secure data storage.
- SQL Server 2000 forms a high-performance data storage service for Web applications running under Microsoft Internet Information Services.
- SQL Server 2000 can be used with Site Server to build and maintain large, sophisticated e-commerce Web sites.
- The SQL Server 2000 TCP/IP Sockets communications support can be integrated with Microsoft Proxy Server to implement secure Internet and intranet communications.

SQL Server 2000 is scalable to levels of performance capable of handling extremely large Internet sites. In addition, the SQL Server 2000 database engine includes native support for XML, and the Web Assistant Wizard helps you to generate Hypertext Markup Language (HTML) pages from SQL Server 2000 data and to post SQL Server 2000 data to Hypertext Transport Protocol (HTTP) and File Transfer Protocol (FTP) locations.

SQL Server supports Windows Authentication, which enables Windows NT and Windows 2000 user and domain accounts to be used as SQL Server 2000 login accounts. Users are validated by Windows 2000 when they connect to the network. When a connection is formed with SQL Server, the SQL Server client software requests a trusted connection, which can be granted only if they have been validated by Windows NT or Windows 2000. SQL Server, then, does not have to validate users separately. Users are not required to have separate logins and passwords for each SQL Server system to which they connect.

SQL Server 2000 can send and receive e-mail and pages from Microsoft Exchange or other Message Application Programming Interface (MAPI)–compliant mail servers. This function enables SQL Server 2000 batches, stored procedures, or triggers to send e-mail. SQL Server 2000 events and alerts can be set to scnd e-mail or pages automatically to the server administrators in case of severe or pending problems.

Editions of SQL Server 2000

SQL Server 2000 is available in different editions to accommodate the unique performance, run-time, and price requirements of different organizations and individuals.

- **SQL Server 2000 Enterprise Edition.**   This edition is the complete SQL Server offering for any organization. The Enterprise Edition offers the advanced scalability and reliability features that are necessary for mission-critical line-of-business and Internet scenarios, including Distributed Partitioned Views, log shipping, and enhanced failover clustering. This edition also takes full advantage of the highest-end hardware, with support for up to 32 CPUs and 64 GB of RAM. In addition, the SQL Server 2000 Enterprise Edition includes advanced analysis features.

- **SQL Server 2000 Standard Edition.**   This edition is the affordable option for small- and medium-sized organizations that do not require advanced scalability and availability features or all of the more advanced analysis features of the SQL Server 2000 Enterprise Edition. You can use the Standard Edition on symmetric multi-processing systems with up to four CPUs and 2 GB of RAM.

- **SQL Server 2000 Personal Edition.**   This edition includes a full set of management tools and most of the functionality of the Standard Edition, but it is optimized for personal use. In addition to running on Microsoft's server operating systems, the Personal Edition runs on non-server operating systems, including Windows 2000 Professional, Windows NT Workstation 4.0, and Windows 98. Dual-processor systems are also supported. While this edition supports databases of any size, its performance is optimized for single users and small workgroups and degrades with workloads generated by more than five concurrent users.

- **SQL Server 2000 Developer Edition.**   This SQL Server offering enables developers to build any type of application on top of SQL Server. This edition includes all of the functionality of the Enterprise Edition but with a special development and test end-user license agreement (EULA) that prohibits production deployment.

- **SQL Server 2000 Desktop Engine (MSDE).**   This edition has the basic database engine features of SQL Server 2000. This edition does not include a user interface, management tools, analysis capabilities, merge replication support, client access licenses, developer libraries, or Books Online. This edition also limits the database size and user workload. Desktop Engine has the smallest footprint of any edition of SQL Server 2000 and is thus an ideal embedded or offline data store.

- **SQL Server 2000 Windows CE Edition.**   This edition is the version of SQL Server 2000 for devices and appliances running Windows CE. This edition is programmatically compatible with the other editions of SQL Server 2000, so developers can leverage their existing skills and applications to extend the power of a relational data store to solutions running on new classes of devices.

Lesson Summary

Microsoft SQL Server 2000 is a complete database and analysis solution for rapidly delivering the next generation of scalable Web applications. SQL Server is an RDBMS that uses Transact-SQL to send requests between a client computer and a SQL Server 2000 computer. A database is similar to a data file in that it is a storage place for data; however, a database system is more powerful than a data file. The data in a database is more highly organized. A relational database is a type of database that uses mathematical set theory to organize data. In a relational database, data is collected into tables. SQL Server 2000 includes a number of features that support ease of installation, deployment, and use; scalability; data warehousing; and system integration with other server software. In addition, SQL Server 2000 is available in different editions to accommodate the unique performance, run-time, and price requirements of different organizations and individuals.

Lesson 2: Components of SQL Server 2000

As described in Lesson 1, SQL Server 2000 is an RDBMS. An RDBMS, by its very nature, is made up of a number of components, including the database engine, various applications and tools, and any databases, whether they are predefined and bundled with the system or added to the RDBMS after it is installed. This lesson provides you with an overview of the main components that make up the SQL Server 2000 RDBMS.

After this lesson, you will be able to:

■   Identify and describe the various components that make up SQL Server 2000.

Estimated lesson time: 25 minutes

Overview of the SQL Server 2000 Components

SQL Server 2000 is made up of many components, such as the relational database engine, Analysis Services, and English Query. All of these components play a role in providing a complete database and analysis solution, working together to create a comprehensive RDBMS (as shown in Figure 1.1)

SQL Server 2000 Relational Database Engine

The SQL Server 2000 relational database engine is a modern, highly scalable engine for storing data. The database engine stores data in tables. Each table represents some object class that is of interest to the organization, such as vehicles, employees, or customers. The table has columns that each represent an attribute of the object modeled by the table (such as weight, name, or cost) and rows that each represent a single occurrence of the type of object modeled by the table (such as the car with license plate number ABC-123 or the employee with ID 123456). An application submits a SQL statement to the database engine, which returns the result to the application in the form of a tabular result set. An Internet application submits either a SQL statement or an XPath query to the database engine, which returns the result as an XML document. The relational database engine provides support for the common Microsoft data access interfaces, such as ActiveX Data Objects (ADO), OLE DB, and Open Database Connectivity (ODBC).

The relational database engine is highly scalable. The SQL Server 2000 Enterprise Edition can support groups of database servers that cooperate to form terabyte databases that are accessed by thousands of users at the same time. The database engine also tunes itself, dynamically acquiring resources as more users connect to the database and then freeing the resources as the users log off. In other words, the smaller editions of SQL Server can be used for individuals or small workgroups that do not have dedicated database administrators. Even large Enterprise Edition database servers running in production are easy to administer by using the GUI administration utilities that are part of the product.

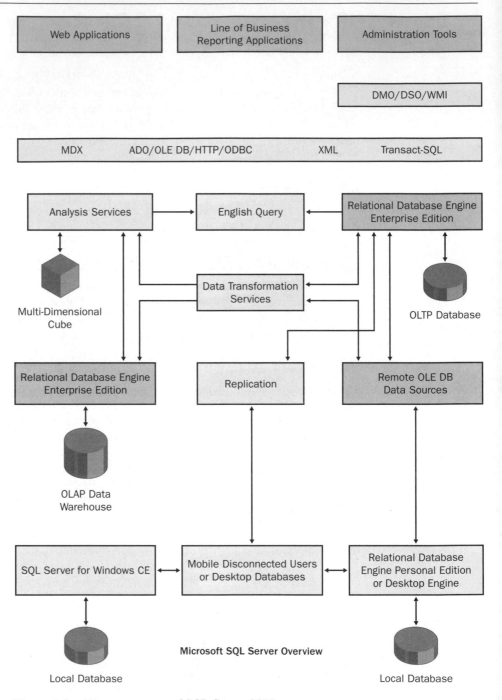

Figure 1.1.   The components of SQL Server 2000.

The relational database engine is also highly secure. Login authentication can be integrated with Windows Authentication so that no passwords are stored in SQL Server or sent across the network (where they could be read by network sniffers). Sites can set up C2 security-level auditing of all users accessing the database and can use Secure Sockets Layer (SSL) encryption to encrypt all data transferred between applications and the database. For details about the database engine's architecture, refer to Lesson 3, "Overview of SQL Server 2000 Architecture."

SQL Server 2000 Replication

SQL Server 2000 replication enables sites to maintain multiple copies of data on different computers, in order to improve overall system performance, while ensuring that all the different copies are kept synchronized. For example, a department could maintain the department sales data on a departmental server but use replication to update the sales data in the corporate computer. Several mobile, disconnected users could disconnect from the network, work throughout the day, and at the end of the day use merge replication to merge their work records back into the main database.

Replication is an important and powerful technology for distributing data and certain types of database objects (stored procedures, views, and user-defined functions) across an enterprise. SQL Server Replication uses a publish-and-subscribe metaphor. The publisher, or owner, of the data to be replicated defines articles (analogous to tables in a database) that will be available to subscribers (or those locations receiving copies of the original publication).

The merge replication model enables many or all subscribers to a publication, as well as the publisher, to make updates to replicated data. In any environment where subscribers are frequently disconnected from their network (a remote sales force, for example), merge replication is an ideal solution. Subscribers can modify or add data while on the road, then return to their office or connect to their Local Area Network (LAN) via modem to merge their modified data with the original copy (the publisher).

SQL Server 2000 DTS

Many organizations need to centralize data in order to improve corporate decision making. This data can be stored in a large variety of formats in a number of different places, however. By using DTS, you can build data warehouses and data marts in SQL Server by importing and transferring data from multiple heterogeneous sources interactively or automatically on a regularly scheduled basis.

SQL Server 2000 DTS greatly improves the process of building Online Analytical Processing (OLAP) data warehouses. In addition, large Online Transaction Processing (OLTP) databases are finely tuned to support a large number of concurrent users who are actively adding and modifying data. OLTP databases are also structured to record the details of every transaction. Trying to perform sophisticated analyses in order to discover trends in sales over a number of months and years would require scanning huge numbers of records, and the heavy processing load would drag down the performance of the OLTP databases.

Data warehouses and data marts are built from the data in an OLTP system that is extracted and transformed into a form more suited for OLAP processing. OLTP detail rows are periodically pulled into a staging database, where they are summarized and the summary data is stored in a data warehouse or data mart. DTS supports extracting data from one source, performing sometimes complex transformations, and then storing the summarized, transformed data in another data source. The component greatly simplifies the process of extracting data from multiple OLTP systems and building it into an OLAP data warehouse or data mart.

SQL Server 2000 Analysis Services

Analysis Services provides tools for analyzing the data stored in data warehouses and data marts. Data warehouses and data marts store their summarized data in fact tables. A fact table is a central table in a data warehouse schema that contains numerical measures and keys relating facts to dimension tables. Typically, base fact tables contain data that describes specific events within a business, such as bank transactions or product sales. Applications work with Analysis Services data by using multi-dimensional extensions to ADO and OLE DB. Processing OLAP queries on multi-dimensional Analysis Services cubes is substantially faster than attempting the same queries on the detail data recorded in OLTP databases.

The Analysis Services system includes a server that manages multi-dimensional cubes of data for analysis and that provides rapid client access to cube information. Analysis Services organizes data from a data warehouse into cubes with precalculated aggregation data in order to provide rapid answers to complex analytical queries. Analysis Services also facilitates the creation of data mining models from both multi-dimensional and relational data sources. You can apply data mining models to both types of data. Microsoft Excel and applications from other vendors use PivotTable Service, the OLE DB–compliant provider, to retrieve data from the server and present it to the user or to create local data cubes for offline analysis.

SQL Server 2000 English Query

SQL Server 2000 English Query helps you to build applications that can customize themselves to ad hoc user questions. An English Query administrator defines for the English Query engine all of the logical relationships among the tables and columns of a database or the cubes in a data warehouse or data mart. An application can then present the user with a box where he or she can enter a character string with a question (written in English) about the data in the database or data warehouse. The application passes the string to the English Query engine, which analyzes the string against the relationships that are defined among the tables or cubes. English Query then returns to the application a SQL statement or a Multi-Dimensional Expression (MDX) query that will return the answer to the user's question.

With English Query, developers can turn their relational databases into English Query applications, which make it possible for end users to pose questions in English instead of forming a query with a SQL statement. The English Query model editor appears within the Microsoft Visual Studio version 6.0 development environment. With Visual Studio, database information is specified in such a way that English Query can process English questions about its particular tables, fields, and data.

English Query features include wizards that will automatically create a project (.eqp) and a model (.eqm) for the application. After the project has been tested, it can be compiled into an English Query application (.eqd) and then deployed. The SQL Project wizard speeds the English Query project creation process by automatically creating the entities and relationships for the database that you choose.

Before you deploy an English Query application, you should thoroughly test it to ensure that all of the necessary entities and relationships exist to return accurate results. The Model Test window provides built-in debugging while enabling you to further modify and refine your EQ project.

SQL Server Meta Data Services

SQL Server Meta Data Services provides a way to store and manage metadata about information systems and applications. This technology serves as a hub for data and component definitions, development and deployment models, reusable software components, and data warehousing descriptions. Product components consist of the repository engine, tools, APIs, standard information models, a browser, and a Software Development Kit (SDK).

SQL Server 2000 Meta Data Services is a set of services that helps you to manage metadata. Using Microsoft Meta Data Services requires understanding metadata characteristics. Metadata describes the structure and meaning of data, as well as the structure and meaning of applications and processes. You must remember that metadata is abstract, that it has a context, and that it can be used for multiple purposes in a development environment.

In software design, the application and database structures that represent or store data can be abstracted into metadata classification schemes that make sense to developers and designers. A table or form is derived from an object, which in turn can be derived from a class.

Metadata contains multiple levels of abstraction. You can describe a data instance, then describe that description, and continue to describe subsequent descriptions until you reach some practical limit. Typically, metadata descriptions used in software development extend to two or three levels of abstraction. In real terms, a data instance of "loan table" can be described as a database table name. A database table can be described as a database table object. Finally, an abstract class that formalizes the fixed set of characteristics to which all derived objects must conform can describe a database table object.

The distinction between data and metadata is often called the type/instance distinction. A model designer articulates a type (such as a class or a relationship), and a software developer articulates an instance (such as a table class or a table-has-columns relationship).

The distinction between instance and type is context-sensitive. What is metadata in one scenario becomes data in another scenario. For example, in a typical RDBMS, the system catalog describes the tables and columns that contain your data. You can think of the data in the system catalog as metadata because it describes data definitions. With the right software tool, however, you can manipulate it as you would manipulate any other data. Examples of manipulating metadata include viewing data lineage or table versioning information, or identifying all tables that express financial data by searching for columns that have a currency-based data type. In this scenario, standard metadata (such as the system catalog) becomes data that you can manipulate.

SQL Server Books Online

SQL Server Books Online is the online documentation provided with SQL Server 2000. You can find information in SQL Server Books Online by taking any of the following actions:

- Navigating through the contents
- Typing a keyword in the index
- Typing a word or phrase and performing a search

SQL Server Books Online also includes Help files, which are the topics found when you click the Help button on a dialog box or when you press F1. These topics are found in the "Using the SQL Server Tools" section.

The complete SQL Server Books Online documentation for SQL Server 2000 cannot be opened from the SQL Server 2000 compact disc. SQL Server Books Online must be installed to your local hard drive before you can open it. The installation documentation in the Microsoft SQL Server 2000 introduction manual does not include some items that arose after the manual was printed. These items are covered in both SQL Server Books Online and the SQL Server Setup Help file.

You can perform a custom setup of SQL Server 2000 and select only the Books Online component to install the SQL Server Books Online documentation on the hard disk of your computer. SQL Server Books Online is a collection of HTML Help documents and requires Microsoft Internet Explorer 5.0 or later. You can download Internet Explorer 5.0 from *http://www.microsoft.com/windows/ie/*.

SQL Server 2000 Tools

SQL Server 2000 includes many graphical and command-prompt utilities that help users, programmers, and administrators to perform a variety of tasks, including the following:

- Administering and configuring SQL Server
- Determining the catalog information in a copy of SQL Server
- Designing and testing queries for retrieving data
- Copying, importing, exporting, and transforming data
- Providing diagnostic information
- Starting and stopping SQL Server

Command Prompt Tools

The command-prompt utilities are installed automatically when you install the SQL Server 2000 utilities on a computer running Windows 2000, Windows NT, Windows 95, or Windows 98. The following table lists many of the SQL Server command-line utilities and the folders where they are installed by default. Note that the MSSQL subfolder is the folder name for the default instance of SQL Server 2000. For each named instance of SQL Server 2000, the corresponding folder name is MSSQL$<i>instance_name</i>.

Utilities	Folder
console	
sqlagent	
sqldiag	
sqlmaint	
sqlservr	
vswitch	x:\Program Files\Microsoft SQL Server\MSSQL\Binn
bcp	
dtsrun	
dtswiz	
isql	
isqlw	
itwiz	
odbccmpt	
osql	
rebuildm	
sqlftwiz	x:\Program Files\Microsoft SQL Server\80\Tools\Binn
distrib	
logread	
replmerg	
snapshot	x:\Program Files\Microsoft SQL Server\80\Com

During installation, the *x*:\Program Files\Microsoft SQL Server\80\Tools\Binn folder is added to the system path. You can run the utilities in this folder at any command prompt. For a utility that is not in this folder, you must either run the utility from a command prompt in the directory in which it is installed, explicitly specify the path, or add the folder path to the operating system search path.

The following utilities are no longer installed by SQL Server 2000 Setup:

- makepipe
- odbcping
- readpipe

If you need to run these utilities, you can run them from the \x86\Binn folder on the SQL Server 2000 installation CD-ROM, or manually copy the utilities to your computer. For a description of each of the command-line utilities available in SQL Server 2000, refer to SQL Server Books Online.

User Interface Tools

SQL Server 2000 provides an extensive set of user interface tools to work with and to administer SQL Server. This section provides an overview of many of these tools. For information about any of the user interface tools available in SQL Server, refer to the SQL Server Books Online.

SQL Server Enterprise Manager

SQL Server Enterprise Manager is the primary administrative tool for SQL Server 2000 and provides a Microsoft Management Console (MMC)–compliant user interface that helps you to perform a variety of administrative tasks:

- Defining groups of servers running SQL Server
- Registering individual servers in a group
- Configuring all SQL Server options for each registered server
- Creating and administering all SQL Server databases, objects, logins, users, and permissions in each registered server
- Defining and executing all SQL Server administrative tasks on each registered server
- Designing and testing SQL statements, batches, and scripts interactively by invoking SQL Query Analyzer
- Invoking the various wizards defined for SQL Server

MMC is a tool that presents a common interface for managing different server applications in a Microsoft Windows network. Server applications include a component called a snap-in that presents MMC users with a user interface for managing the server application. SQL Server Enterprise Manager is the Microsoft SQL Server 2000 MMC snap-in.

SQL Server Agent

SQL Server Agent runs on the server that is running instances of SQL Server 2000 or earlier versions of SQL Server. SQL Server Agent is responsible for the following tasks:

- Running SQL Server tasks that are scheduled to occur at specific times or intervals
- Detecting specific conditions for which administrators have defined an action, such as alerting someone through pages or e-mail, or issuing a task that will address the conditions
- Running replication tasks defined by administrators

SQL Profiler

SQL Profiler is a tool that captures SQL Server 2000 events from a server. The events are saved in a trace file that can later be analyzed or used to replay a specific series of steps when trying to diagnose a problem. SQL Profiler is used for a variety of activities, including the following:

- Stepping through problem queries to find the cause of the problem
- Finding and diagnosing slow running queries
- Capturing the series of SQL statements that lead to a problem
- Monitoring the performance of SQL Server to tune workloads

SQL Profiler also supports auditing the actions performed on instances of SQL Server. Security-related actions are stored for later review by a security administrator.

SQL Server Client Network Utility

The Client Network utility is used to manage the client Net-Libraries and to define server alias names. You can also use this utility to set the default options used by DB-Library applications.

Most users will never need to use the Client Network utility. To connect to SQL Server 2000, users can specify the network name of the server where SQL Server is running, and optionally, the name of the instance of SQL Server.

SQL Server Network Utility

The Server Network utility is used to manage the server Net-Libraries and can be used to specify several types of information:

- The network protocol stacks on which an instance of SQL Server 2000 listens for client requests

- The sequence in which server Net-Libraries are considered when establishing connections from applications
- New network addresses on which an instance of SQL Server 2000 listens

Most administrators will never need to use the Server Network utility. They will specify during setup the server Net-Libraries on which SQL Server will listen.

SQL Server Service Manager

SQL Server Service Manager is used to start, stop, and pause the SQL Server 2000 components on the server. These components run as services on Microsoft Windows NT or Windows 2000 and as separate executable programs on Windows 95 and Windows 98:

- **SQL Server service.** This service implements the SQL Server database engine. There is one SQL Server service for each instance of SQL Server running on the computer.
- **SQL Server Agent service.** This service implements the agent that runs scheduled SQL Server administrative tasks. There is one SQL Server Agent service for each instance of SQL Server running on the computer.
- **Microsoft Search service (Windows NT and Windows 2000 only).** This service implements the full-text search engine. There is only one service, regardless of the number of SQL Server instances on the computer.
- **MSDTC service (Windows NT and Windows 2000 only).** This service manages distributed transactions. There is only one service, regardless of the number of SQL Server instances on the computer.
- **MSSQLServerOLAPService service (Windows NT and Windows 2000 only).** This service implements SQL Server 2000 Analysis Services. There is only one service, regardless of the number of SQL Server instances on the computer.

SQL Server Service Manager is a taskbar application that follows the standard behavior of taskbar applications. When minimized, the SQL Server Service Manager icon appears in the taskbar status area. To get a menu that includes all of the tasks that SQL Server Service Manager supports, right-click the taskbar icon.

SQL Query Analyzer

SQL Server 2000 SQL Query Analyzer is a graphical tool that helps you to perform a variety of tasks:

- Creating queries and other SQL scripts and executing them against SQL Server databases
- Creating commonly used database objects from predefined scripts

- Copying existing database objects
- Executing stored procedures without knowing the parameters
- Debugging stored procedures
- Debugging query performance problems
- Locating objects within databases or viewing and working with objects
- Inserting, updating, or deleting rows in a table
- Creating keyboard shortcuts for frequently used queries
- Adding frequently used commands to the Tools menu

You can run SQL Query Analyzer directly from the Start menu or from inside SQL Server Enterprise Manager. You can also run SQL Query Analyzer by executing the isqlw utility from a command prompt.

SQL Server 2000 Built-In Wizards

SQL Server 2000 contains several wizards to walk administrators and programmers through the steps needed to perform complex administrative tasks and to assist all users to view and modify data with SQL Server databases. SQL Server Books Online describes these wizards in detail.

Lesson Summary

SQL Server 2000 is an RDBMS that is made up of a number of components. The database engine is a modern, highly scalable engine that stores data in tables. SQL Server 2000 replication helps sites to maintain multiple copies of data on different computers in order to improve overall system performance while making sure that the different copies of data are kept synchronized. DTS helps you to build data warehouses and data marts in SQL Server by importing and transferring data from multiple heterogeneous sources interactively or automatically on a regularly scheduled basis. Analysis Services provides tools for analyzing the data stored in data warehouses and data marts. SQL Server 2000 English Query helps you to build applications that can customize themselves to ad hoc user questions. SQL Server 2000 Meta Data Services provides a way to store and manage metadata relating to information systems and applications. SQL Server Books Online is the online documentation provided with SQL Server 2000. SQL Server 2000 includes many graphical and command-prompt utilities that help users, programmers, and administrators perform a variety of tasks.

Lesson 3: Overview of SQL Server 2000 Architecture

The data storage and analysis needs of a modern corporation or government organization are very complex. SQL Server 2000 provides a set of components that work together to meet the needs of the largest data processing systems and commercial Web sites while providing easy-to-use data storage services to an individual or small business. This lesson introduces you to the SQL Server 2000 architecture and describes how the various components work together to manage data effectively.

After this lesson, you will be able to:

■   Identify and describe the various components that make up the SQL Server architecture.

Estimated lesson time: 30 minutes

Database Architecture

SQL Server 2000 data is stored in databases. The data in a database is organized into the logical components that are visible to users, while the database itself is physically implemented as two or more files on disk.

When using a database, you work primarily with the logical components (such as tables, views, procedures, and users). The physical implementation of files is largely transparent. Typically, only the database administrator needs to work with the physical implementation. Figure 1.2 illustrates the difference between the user view and the physical implementation of a database.

Each instance of SQL Server has four system databases (master, tempdb, msdb, and model) and one or more user databases. Some organizations have only one user database that contains all of their data; some organizations have different databases for each group in their organization. They might also have a database used by a single application. For example, an organization could have one database for sales, one for payroll, one for a document management application, and so on. Some applications use only one database; other applications might access several databases. Figure 1.3 shows the SQL Server system databases and several user databases.

You do not need to run multiple copies of the SQL Server database engine in order for multiple users to access the databases on a server. An instance of the SQL Server Standard Edition or Enterprise Edition is capable of handling thousands of users who are working in multiple databases at the same time. Each instance of SQL Server makes all databases in the instance available to all users who connect to the instance (subject to the defined security permissions).

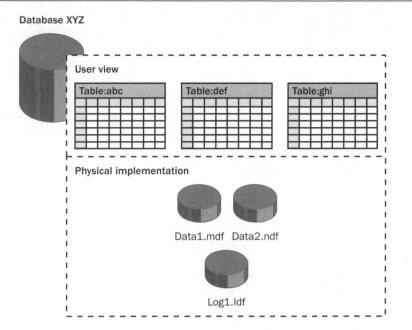

Figure 1.2.   User view and physical implementation of a database.

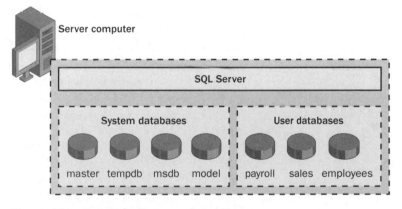

Figure 1.3.   System databases and user databases.

If you connect to an instance of SQL Server, your connection is associated with a particular database on the server. This database is called the current database. You are usually connected to a database defined as your default database by the system administrator, although you can use connection options in the database APIs to specify another database. You can switch from one database to another by using either the Transact-SQL USE *<database_name>* statement or by using an API function that changes your current database context.

SQL Server 2000 enables you to detach a database from an instance of SQL Server, then reattach it to another instance or even attach the database back to the same instance. If you have a SQL Server database file, you can tell SQL Server when you connect to attach that database file using a specific database name.

Logical Database Components

The logical database components include objects, collations, logins, users, roles, and groups.

Database Objects

The data in a SQL Server 2000 database is organized into several different objects, which users see when they connect to the database. The following table provides a brief description of the main objects in a database. These objects are discussed in more detail in subsequent chapters.

Object	Description
Table	A two-dimensional object consisting of rows and columns that is used to store data in a relational database. Each table stores information about one of the types of objects modeled by the database. For example, an education database might have one table for teachers, a second for students, and a third for classes.
Data type	An attribute that specifies what type of information can be stored in a column, parameter, or variable. SQL Server provides system-supplied data types; you can also create user-defined data types.
View	A database object that can be referenced the same way as a table in SQL statements. Views are defined by using a *SELECT* statement and are analogous to an object that contains the result set of this statement.
Stored procedure	A precompiled collection of Transact-SQL statements stored under a name and processed as a unit. SQL Server supplies stored procedures for managing SQL Server and for displaying information about databases and users. SQL Server–supplied stored procedures are called *system stored procedures*.
Function	A piece of code that operates as a single logical unit. A function is called by name, accepts optional input parameters, and returns a status and optional output parameters. Many programming languages support functions, including C, Visual Basic, and Transact-SQL. Transact-SQL supplies built-in functions that cannot be modified and supports user-defined functions that users can create and modify.
Index	In a relational database, a database object that provides fast access to data in the rows of a table, based on key values. Indexes can also enforce uniqueness on the rows in a table. SQL Server supports clustered and non-clustered indexes. The primary key of a table is automatically indexed. In full-text search, a full-text index stores information about significant words and their location within a given column.

Object	Description
Constraint	A property assigned to a table column that prevents certain types of invalid data values from being placed in the column. For example, a UNIQUE or PRIMARY KEY constraint prevents you from inserting a value that is a duplicate of an existing value; a CHECK constraint prevents you from inserting a value that does not match a search condition; and NOT NULL prevents empty values.
Rule	A database object that is bound to columns or user-defined data types and specifies which data values are acceptable in a column. CHECK constraints provide the same functionality and are preferred because they are in the SQL-92 standard.
Default	A data value, option setting, collation, or name assigned automatically by the system if a user does not specify the value, setting, collation, or name; also known as an action that is taken automatically at certain events if a user has not specified the action to take.
Trigger	A stored procedure that is executed when data in a specified table is modified. Triggers are often created to enforce referential integrity or consistency among logically related data in different tables.

Collations

Collations control the physical storage of character strings in SQL Server 2000. A collation specifies the bit patterns that represent each character and the rules by which characters are sorted and compared.

An object in a SQL Server 2000 database can use a collation different from another object within that same database. Separate SQL Server 2000 collations can be specified down to the level of columns. Each column in a table can be assigned different collations. Earlier versions of SQL Server support only one collation for each instance of SQL Server. All databases and database objects that are created in an instance of SQL Server 7.0 or earlier have the same collation.

SQL Server 2000 supports several collations. A collation encodes the rules governing the proper use of characters for either a language, such as Macedonian or Polish, or an alphabet, such as Latin1_General (the Latin alphabet used by western European languages).

Each SQL Server collation specifies three properties:

- The sort order to use for Unicode data types (*nchar*, *nvarchar*, and *ntext*)
- The sort order to use for non-Unicode character data types (*char*, *varchar*, and *text*)
- The code page used to store non-Unicode character data

Note   You cannot specify the equivalent of a code page for the Unicode data types (*nchar*, *nvarchar*, and *ntext*). The double-byte bit patterns used for Unicode characters are defined by the Unicode standard and cannot be changed.

SQL Server 2000 collations can be specified at any level. When you install an instance of SQL Server 2000, you specify the default collation for that instance. When you create a database, you can specify its default collation; if you do not specify a collation, the default collation for the database is the default collation for the instance. Whenever you define a character column, variable, or parameter, you can specify the collation of the object; if you do not specify a collation, the object is created with the default collation of the database.

Logins, Users, Roles, and Groups

Logins, users, roles, and groups are the foundation for the security mechanisms of SQL Server 2000. Users who connect to SQL Server must identify themselves by using a Specific Login Identifier (ID). Users can then see only the tables and views that they are authorized to see and can execute only the stored procedures and administrative functions that they are authorized to execute. This system of security is based on the IDs used to identify users. The following table provides a description of each type of security mechanism:

Security Mechanism	Description
Logins	Login identifiers are associated with users when they connect to SQL Server 2000. Login IDs are the account names that control access to the SQL Server system. A user cannot connect to SQL Server without first specifying a valid login ID. Members of the Sysadmin fixed server role define login IDs.
Users	A user identifier identifies a user within a database. All permissions and ownership of objects in the database are controlled by the user account. User accounts are specific to a database; for example, the xyz user account in the sales database is different from the xyz user account in the inventory database, although both accounts have the same ID. User IDs are defined by members of the Db_owner fixed database role.
Roles	A role is like a user group in a Windows 2000 domain. It allows you to collect users into a single unit so that you can apply permissions against those users. Permissions that are granted to, denied to, or revoked from a role also apply to any members of the role. You can establish a role that represents a job performed by a class of workers in your organization and grant the appropriate permissions to that role. As workers rotate into the job, you simply add them as a member of the role. As they rotate out of the job, you can remove them from the role. You do not have to repeatedly grant, deny, and revoke permissions to or from each person as he or she accepts or leaves the job. The permissions are applied automatically when the users become members of the role. A role is similar to a Windows security group.
Groups	There are no groups in SQL Server 2000 or SQL Server 7.0. You can, however, manage SQL Server security at the level of an entire Windows NT or Windows 2000 group.

Physical Database Architecture

This section describes the way in which SQL Server 2000 files and databases are organized. The organization of SQL Server 2000 and SQL Server 7.0 is different from the organization of data in SQL Server 6.5 or earlier.

Pages and Extents

The fundamental unit of data storage in SQL Server is the page. In SQL Server 2000, the page size is 8 kilobytes (KB). In other words, SQL Server 2000 databases contain 128 pages per megabyte (MB).

The start of each page is a 96-byte header used to store system information, such as the type of page, the amount of free space on the page, and the object ID of the object owning the page.

Data pages contain all of the data in data rows (except *text*, *ntext*, and image data, which are stored in separate pages). Data rows are placed serially on the page (starting immediately after the header). A row offset table starts at the end of the page. The row offset table contains one entry for each row on the page, and each entry records how far the first byte of the row is from the start of the page. The entries in the row offset table are in reverse sequence from the sequence of the rows on the page, as shown in Figure 1.4.

Extents are the basic unit in which space is allocated to tables and indexes. An extent is eight contiguous pages, or 64 KB. In other words, SQL Server 2000 databases have 16 extents per megabyte.

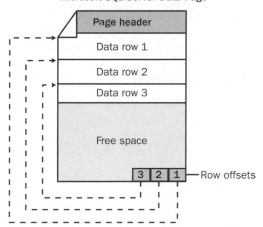

Microsoft SQL Server Data Page

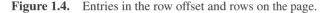

Figure 1.4.   Entries in the row offset and rows on the page.

To make its space allocation efficient, SQL Server 2000 does not allocate entire extents to tables that have small amounts of data. SQL Server 2000 has two types of extents:

- A single object owns uniform extents; only the owning object can use all eight pages in the extent.
- Up to eight objects share mixed extents.

A new table or index is usually allocated pages from mixed extents. When the table or index grows to the point that it has eight pages, it is switched to uniform extents. If you create an index on an existing table that has enough rows to generate eight pages in the index, all allocations to the index are in uniform extents.

Database Files and Filegroups

SQL Server 2000 maps a database over a set of operating-system files. Data and log information are never mixed on the same file, and individual files are used only by one database.

SQL Server 2000 databases have three types of files:

- **Primary data files.**   The primary data file is the starting point of the database and points to the other files in the database. Every database has one primary data file. The recommended filename extension for primary data files is .mdf.
- **Secondary data files.**   Secondary data files comprise all of the data files other than the primary data file. Some databases might not have any secondary data files, while others might have multiple secondary data files. The recommended filename extension for secondary data files is .ndf.
- **Log files.**   Log files hold all of the log information used to recover the database. There must be at least one log file for each database, although there can be more than one. The recommended filename extension for log files is .ldf.

Space Allocation and Reuse

SQL Server 2000 is effective at quickly allocating pages to objects and reusing space freed up by deleted rows. These operations are internal to the system and use data structures not visible to users, yet these processes and structures are occasionally referenced in SQL Server messages.

SQL Server uses two types of allocation maps to record the allocation of extents:

- **Global Allocation Map (GAM).**   GAM pages record which extents have been allocated. Each GAM covers 64,000 extents (or nearly 4 GB of data). The GAM has one bit for each extent in the interval it covers. If the bit is 1, the extent is free; if the bit is 0, the extent is allocated.

- **Shared Global Allocation Map (SGAM).**   SGAM pages record which extents are currently used as mixed extents and have at least one unused page. Each SGAM covers 64,000 extents (or nearly 4 GB of data). The SGAM has one bit for each extent in the interval it covers. If the bit is 1, the extent is being used as a mixed extent and has free pages; if the bit is 0, the extent is either not used as a mixed extent or it is a mixed extent whose pages are all in use.

Table and Index Architecture

SQL Server 2000 supports indexes on views. The first index allowed on a view is a clustered index. At the time a *CREATE INDEX* statement is executed on a view, the result set for the view materializes and is stored in the database with the same structure as a table that has a clustered index.

The data rows for each table or indexed view are stored in a collection of 8 KB data pages. Each data page has a 96-byte header containing system information, such as the identifier of the table that owns the page. The page header also includes pointers to the next and previous pages that are used if the pages are linked in a list. A row offset table is at the end of the page. Data rows fill the rest of the page, as shown in Figure 1.5.

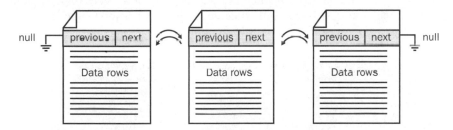

Figure 1.5.   Organization of data pages.

SQL Server 2000 tables use one of two methods to organize their data pages—clustered tables and heaps:

- **Clustered tables.**   Clustered tables are tables that have a clustered index. The data rows are stored in order based on the clustered index key. The index is implemented as a B-tree structure that supports the fast retrieval of the rows based on their clustered index key values. The pages in each level of the index, including the data pages in the leaf level, are linked in a doubly linked list, but navigation from one level to another is done using key values.
- **Heaps.**   Heaps are tables that have no clustered index. The data rows are not stored in any particular order, and there is no particular order to the sequence of the data pages. The data pages are not linked in a linked list.

Indexed views have the same storage structure as clustered tables.

SQL Server also supports up to 249 non-clustered indexes on each table or indexed view. The non-clustered indexes also have a B-tree structure but utilize it differently than clustered indexes. The difference is that non-clustered indexes have no effect on the order of the data rows. Clustered tables and indexed views keep their data rows in order based on the clustered index key. The collection of data pages for a heap is not affected if non-clustered indexes are defined for the table. The data pages remain in a heap unless a clustered index is defined.

Transaction Log Architecture

Every SQL Server 2000 database has a transaction log that records all transactions and the database modifications made by each transaction. This record of transactions and their modifications supports three operations:

- Recovery of individual transactions
- Recovery of all incomplete transactions when SQL Server is started
- Rolling a restored database forward to just before the point of failure

Relational Database Engine Architecture

The server components of SQL Server 2000 receive SQL statements from clients and process those SQL statements. Figure 1.6 shows the major components involved with processing a SQL statement that is received from a SQL Server client.

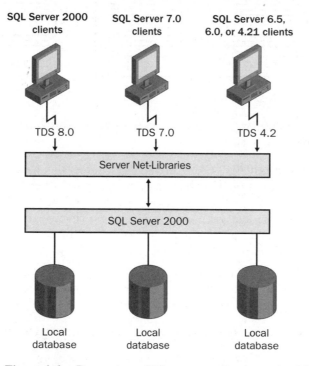

Figure 1.6. Processing a SQL statement that is received from a client.

Tabular Data Stream

SQL statements are sent from clients by using an application-level protocol specific to SQL Server, called Tabular Data Stream (TDS). SQL Server 2000 accepts the following versions of TDS:

- TDS 8.0, sent by clients who are running versions of the SQL Server client components from SQL Server 2000. TDS 8.0 clients support all the features of SQL Server 2000.
- TDS 7.0, sent by clients who are running versions of the SQL Server client components from SQL Server version 7.0. TDS 7.0 clients do not support features introduced in SQL Server 2000, and the server sometimes has to adjust the data that it sends back to those clients.
- TDS 4.2, sent by clients who are running SQL Server client components from SQL Server 6.5, 6.0, and 4.21a. TDS 4.2 clients do not support features introduced in either SQL Server 2000 or SQL Server 7.0, and the server sometimes has to adjust the data that it sends back to those clients.

Server Net-Libraries

TDS packets are built by the Microsoft OLE DB Provider for SQL Server, the SQL Server Open Database Connectivity (ODBC) driver, or the DB-Library dynamic link library (DLL). The TDS packets are then passed to a SQL Server client Net-Library, which encapsulates them into network protocol packets. On the server, the network protocol packets are received by a server Net-Library that extracts the TDS packets and passes them to the relational database engine. This process is reversed when results are returned to the client.

Each server can be listening simultaneously on several network protocols and will be running one server Net-Library for each protocol on which it is listening.

Relational Database Engine

The database server processes all requests passed to it from the server Net-Libraries. The server then compiles all the SQL statements into execution plans and uses the plans to access the requested data and build the result set that is returned to the client.

The relational database engine of SQL Server 2000 has two main parts: the relational engine and the storage engine. One of the most important architectural changes made in SQL Server 7.0 (and carried over to SQL Server 2000) was to strictly separate the relational and storage engine components within the server and to have them use the OLE DB API to communicate with each other, as shown in Figure 1.7.

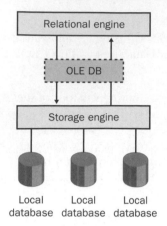

Figure 1.7.   Relational engine components.

Query Processor Architecture

SQL statements are the only commands sent from applications to SQL Server 2000. All of the work done by an instance of SQL Server is the result of accepting, interpreting, and executing SQL statements. SQL Server 2000 executes SQL statements by using one of the following processes:

- Single SQL statement processing
- Batch processing
- Stored procedure and trigger execution
- Execution plan caching and reuse
- Parallel query processing

Memory Architecture

SQL Server 2000 dynamically acquires and frees memory as needed. Typically, it is not necessary for an administrator to specify how much memory should be allocated to SQL Server, although the option still exists and is required in some environments. When running multiple instances of SQL Server on a computer, each instance can dynamically acquire and free memory to adjust for changes in the workload of the instance.

SQL Server 2000 Enterprise Edition introduces support for using Windows 2000 Address Windowing Extensions (AWE) to address approximately 8 GB of memory for instances running on Windows 2000 Advanced Server and approximately 64 GB for instances running on Windows 2000 Data Center. Each instance using this additional memory, however, must statically allocate the memory it needs.

Input/Output (I/O) Architecture

The primary purpose of a database is to store and retrieve data, so performing a lot of disk reads and writes is one of the inherent attributes of a database engine. Disk input/output (I/O) operations consume many resources and take a relatively long time to complete. Much of the logic in relational database software concerns making the pattern of I/O usage highly efficient.

SQL Server 2000 allocates much of its virtual memory to a buffer cache and uses the cache to reduce physical I/O. Each instance of SQL Server 2000 has its own buffer cache. Data is read from the database disk files into the buffer cache. Multiple logical reads of the data can be satisfied without requiring the data to be physically read again. The data remains in the cache until it has not been referenced for some time and the database needs the buffer area to read in more data. Data is written back to the disk only if it is modified. Data can be changed multiple times by logical writes before a physical write transfers the new data back to the disk.

The I/O from an instance of SQL Server is divided into logical and physical I/O. A logical read occurs every time the database engine requests a page from the buffer cache. If the page is not currently in the buffer cache, a physical read is then performed in order to read the page into the buffer cache. If the page is currently in the cache, no physical read is generated. The buffer cache simply uses the page that is already in memory. A logical write occurs when data is modified in a page in memory. A physical write occurs when the page is written to disk. A page can remain in memory long enough to have more than one logical write made before it is physically written to disk.

Full-Text Query Architecture

The SQL Server 2000 full-text query component supports sophisticated searches on character string columns. This capability is implemented by the Microsoft Search service, which has two roles:

- **Indexing support.**   Implements the full-text catalogs and indexes defined for a database. Microsoft Search accepts definitions of full-text catalogs as well as the tables and columns making up the indexes in each catalog. This tool also implements requests to populate the full-text indexes.

- **Querying support.**   Processes full-text search queries and determines which entries in the index meet the full-text selection criteria. For each entry that meets the selection criteria, it returns the identity of the row plus a ranking value to the MSSQLServer service, where this information is used to construct the query result set. The types of queries supported include searching for words or phrases, words in close proximity to each other, and inflectional forms of verbs and nouns.

The full-text catalogs and indexes are not stored in a SQL Server database. They are stored in separate files that are managed by the Microsoft Search service. The full-text catalog files are not recovered during a SQL Server recovery. They also cannot be backed up and restored by using the Transact-*SQL BACKUP* and *RESTORE* statements. The full-text catalogs must be resynchronized separately after a recovery or restore operation. The full-text catalog files are accessible only to the Microsoft Search service and to the Windows NT or Windows 2000 system administrator.

Transactions Architecture

SQL Server 2000 maintains the consistency and integrity of each database, despite errors that occur in the system. Every application that updates data in a SQL Server database does so by using transactions. A transaction is a logical unit of work made up of a series of statements (selects, inserts, updates, or deletes). If no errors are encountered during a transaction, all of the modifications in the transaction become a permanent part of the database. If errors are encountered, none of the modifications are made to the database.

A transaction goes through several phases:

1. Before the transaction starts, the database is in a consistent state.
2. The application signals the start of a transaction. This process can be initiated explicitly with the *BEGIN TRANSACTION* statement. Alternatively, the application can set options to run in implicit transaction mode; the first Transact-SQL statement executed after the completion of a prior transaction starts a new transaction automatically. No record is written to the log when the transaction starts; the first record is written to the log when the application generates the first log record for data modification.
3. The application starts modifying data. These modifications are made one table at a time. As a series of modifications are made, they might leave the database in a temporarily inconsistent intermediate state.
4. When the application reaches a point where all of the modifications have completed successfully and the database is once again consistent, the application commits the transaction. This step makes all of the modifications a permanent part of the database.
5. If the application encounters some error that prevents it from completing the transaction, it undoes (or rolls back) all of the data modifications. This process returns the database to the point of consistency it was at before the transaction started.

SQL Server applications can also run in autocommit mode. In autocommit mode, each individual Transact-SQL statement is committed automatically if it is successful and is rolled back automatically if it generates an error. There is no need for an application running in autocommit mode to issue statements that specifically start or end a transaction.

All Transact-SQL statements run in a transaction: an explicit transaction, an implicit transaction, or an autocommit transaction. All SQL Server transactions that include data modifications either reach a new point of consistency and are committed or are rolled back to the original point of consistency. Transactions are not left in an intermediate state in which the database is not consistent.

Administration Architecture

Each new version of SQL Server seeks to automate or eliminate some of the repetitive work performed by database administrators. Because database administrators are typically among the people most highly trained in database issues at a site, these improvements enable a valuable resource—the administrator—to spend more time working on database design and application data access issues.

Many components contribute to the effectiveness of SQL Server 2000 administration:

- The SQL Server 2000 database server reduces administration work in many environments by dynamically acquiring and freeing resources. The server automatically acquires system resources (such as memory and disk space) when needed and frees the resources when they are no longer required. Although large OLTP systems with critical performance needs are still monitored by trained administrators, SQL Server 2000 can also be used to implement smaller desktop or workgroup databases that do not require constant administrator attention.

- SQL Server 2000 provides a set of graphical tools that help administrators perform administrative tasks easily and efficiently.

- SQL Server 2000 provides a set of services that help administrators schedule the automatic execution of repetitive tasks.

- Administrators of SQL Server 2000 can program the server to handle exception conditions or to at least send e-mail or pages to the on-duty administrator.

- SQL Server 2000 publishes the same administration APIs used by the SQL Server utilities. These APIs support all of the administration tasks of SQL Server. This functionality enables developers of applications that use SQL Server 2000 as their data store to completely shield users from the administration of SQL Server 2000.

Data Definition Language, Data Manipulation Language, and Stored Procedures

Transact-SQL is the language used for all commands sent to SQL Server 2000 from any application. Transact-SQL contains statements that support all administrative work done in SQL Server. These statements fall into two main categories:

- **Data Definition Language/Data Manipulation Language.**   Data definition language (DDL) is used to define and manage all of the objects in a SQL database, and data manipulation language (DML) is used to select, insert, update, and delete data in the objects that are defined using DDL. The Transact-SQL DDL that is used to manage objects such as databases, tables, and views is based on SQL-92 DDL statements (with extensions). For each object class, there are usually *CREATE*, *ALTER*, and *DROP* statements such as *CREATE TABLE*, *ALTER TABLE*, and *DROP TABLE*. Permissions are controlled using the *SQL-92 GRANT* and *REVOKE* statements and the Transact-SQL *DENY* statement.

- **System stored procedures.**   Administrative tasks not covered by the SQL-92 DDL and DML are typically performed using system stored procedures. These stored procedures have names that start with *sp_* or *xp_*, and they are installed when SQL Server is installed.

SQL Distributed Management Framework

The SQL Distributed Management Framework (SQL-DMF) is an integrated framework of objects, services, and components that are used to manage SQL Server 2000. SQL-DMF provides a flexible and scalable management framework that is adaptable to the requirements of an organization. This tool lessens the need for user-attended maintenance tasks (such as database backup and alert notification) by providing services that interact directly with SQL Server 2000.

The key components of SQL-DMF support the proactive management of the instances of SQL Server on your network by enabling you to define the following information:

- All SQL Server objects and their permissions
- Repetitive administrative actions to be taken at specified intervals or times
- Corrective actions to be taken when specific conditions are detected

Figure 1.8 shows the main components of SQL-DMF.

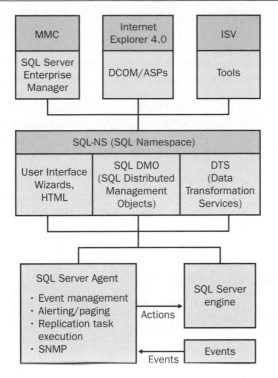

Figure 1.8.   The components that make up SQL-DMF.

Graphical Tools

SQL Server 2000 includes many graphical utilities that help users, programmers, and administrators perform the following tasks:

- Administering and configuring SQL Server
- Determining the catalog information in a copy of SQL Server
- Designing and testing queries for retrieving data

In addition to these tools, SQL Server contains several wizards to walk administrators and programmers through the steps needed to perform more complex administrative tasks.

Automated Administration Architecture

SQL Server 2000 provides a number of features that enable administrators to program the server to administer itself for many repetitive actions or exception conditions. This functionality enables the administrators to spend more time on activities such as designing databases and working with programmers on efficient database access coding techniques. Applications from any vendor can choose SQL Server as their data storage component and minimize the administrative requirements of customers by automating administrative tasks.

These automation features are not limited to database administration tasks such as scheduling backups. They can also be used to help automate the business practices that the database supports. Applications can be scheduled to run at specific times or intervals. Specific conditions detected in the system can be used to trigger these applications if they need to be executed before the next scheduled time.

The features that support the automation of administrative tasks are SQL Server Agent, jobs, events and alerts, operators, and triggers.

Backup/Restore Architecture

The backup and restore components of SQL Server 2000 allow you to create a copy of a database. This copy is stored in a location protected from the potential failures of the server running the instance of SQL Server. If the server running the instance of SQL Server fails or if the database is somehow damaged, the backup copy can be used to recreate or restore the database.

Data Import/Export Architecture

SQL Server 2000 includes several components that support importing and exporting data, including DTS, replication, bulk copying, and distributed queries.

DTS

Data Transformation Services can be used to import and export data between heterogeneous OLE DB and ODBC data sources. A DTS package is defined that specifies the source and target OLE DB data sources; the package can then be executed on an as-required basis or at scheduled times or intervals. A single DTS package can cover multiple tables. DTS packages are not limited to transferring data straight from one table to another, because the package can specify a query as the source of the data. This functionality enables packages to transform data, such as by running a query that returns aggregate summary values instead of the raw data.

Replication

Replication is used to create copies of data in separate databases and keep these copies synchronized by replicating modifications in one copy to all the others. If it is acceptable for each site to have data that might be a minute or so out of date, replication enables the distribution of data without the overhead of requiring distributed transactions to ensure all sites have an exact copy of the current data. Replication can therefore support the distribution of data for a relatively low cost in network and computing resources.

Bulk Copying

The bulk copy feature of SQL Server provides for the efficient transfer of large amounts of data. Bulk copying transfers data into or out of one table at a time.

Distributed Queries

Transact-SQL statements use distributed queries to reference data in an OLE DB data source. The OLE DB data sources can be another instance of SQL Server or a heterogeneous data source, such as a Microsoft Access database or Oracle database.

Data Integrity Validation

Transact-SQL uses a set of DBCC statements to verify the integrity of a database. The DBCC statements in SQL Server 2000 and SQL Server 7.0 contain several improvements to the DBCC statements used in SQL Server 6.5:

- The need to run the statements is reduced significantly. Architectural changes in SQL Server have improved the robustness of the databases to the point that you do not have to verify their integrity as often.

- It is not necessary to run DBCC validation statements as part of your normal backup or maintenance procedures. You should run them as part of a system check before major changes, such as before a hardware or software upgrade or after a hardware failure. You should also run them if you suspect any problems with the system.

- SQL Server 2000 introduces a new PHYSICAL_ONLY option that enables a DBCC statement to run faster by checking only for the types of problems that are likely to be generated by a hardware problem. Run a DBCC check with PHYSICAL_ONLY if you suspect a hardware problem on your database server.

- The DBCC statements themselves also run significantly faster. Checks of complex databases typically run 8 to 10 times faster, and checks of some individual objects have run more than 300 times faster. In SQL Server 6.5, DBCC CHECKDB processed the tables serially. For each table, it first checked the structure of the underlying data and then checked each index individually. This procedure resulted in a very random pattern of reads. In SQL Server 2000, DBCC CHECKDB performs a serial scan of the database while performing parallel checks of multiple objects as it proceeds. SQL Server 2000 also takes advantage of multiple processors when running parallel DBCC statements.

- The level of locks required by SQL Server 2000 DBCC statements is much lower than in SQL Server 7.0. SQL Server 2000 DBCC statements can now be run concurrently with data modification statements, significantly lowering their impact on users who are working in the database.

- The SQL Server 2000 DBCC statements can repair minor problems they might encounter. The statements have the option to repair certain errors in the B-tree structures of indexes or errors in some of the allocation structures.

Replication Architecture

Replication is a set of technologies that allows you to keep copies of the same data on multiple sites, sometimes covering hundreds of sites. Replication uses a publish-subscribe model for distributing data:

- The Publisher is a server that is the source of data to be replicated. The Publisher defines an article for each table or other database object to be used as a replication source. One or more related articles from the same database are organized into a publication. Publications are convenient ways to group together related data and objects that you want to replicate.

- The Subscriber is a server that receives the data replicated by the publisher. The Subscriber defines a subscription to a particular publication. The subscription specifies when the Subscriber receives the publication from the Publisher and maps the articles to tables and other database objects in the Subscriber.

- The Distributor is a server that performs various tasks when moving articles from Publishers to Subscribers. The actual tasks performed depend on the type of replication performed.

SQL Server 2000 also supports replication to and from heterogeneous data sources. OLE DB or ODBC data sources can subscribe to SQL Server publications. SQL Server can also receive data replicated from a number of data sources, including Microsoft Exchange, Microsoft Access, Oracle, and DB2.

Data Warehousing and Online Analytical Processing (OLAP)

SQL Server 2000 provides components that can be used to build data warehouses or data marts. The data warehouses or data marts can be used for sophisticated enterprise intelligence systems that process the types of queries used to discover trends and analyze critical factors. These systems are called OLAP systems. The data in data warehouses and data marts is organized differently than in traditional transaction-processing databases.

Enterprise-level relational database management software, such as SQL Server 2000, was designed originally to centrally store the data generated by the daily transactions of large companies or government organizations. Over the decades, these databases have grown to be highly efficient systems for recording the data required to perform the daily operations of the enterprise. Because the system is based on computers and records the business transactions of the enterprise, these systems are known as Online Transaction-Processing (OLTP) systems.

OLTP Systems

The data in OLTP systems is organized primarily to support transactions such as the following:

- Recording an order entered from a point-of-sale terminal or through a Web site
- Placing an order for more supplies when inventory drops to a defined level
- Tracking components as they are assembled into a final product in a manufacturing facility
- Recording employee data
- Recording the identities of license holders, such as restaurants or drivers

Individual transactions are completed quickly and access relatively small amounts of data. OLTP systems are designed and tuned to process hundreds or thousands of transactions being entered at the same time.

Although OLTP systems excel at recording the data required to support daily operations, OLTP data is not organized in a manner that easily provides the information required by managers to plan the work of their organizations. Managers often need summary information from which they can analyze trends that affect their organization or team.

OLAP Systems

Systems designed to handle the types of queries used to discover trends and critical factors are called OLAP systems. OLAP queries typically require large amounts of data. For example, the head of a government motor vehicle licensing department could ask for a report that shows the number of each make and model of vehicle registered by the department each year for the past 20 years. Running this type of query against the original detail data in an OLTP system has two effects:

- The query takes a long time to aggregate (sum) all of the detail records for the last 20 years, so the report is not ready in a timely manner.
- The query generates a very heavy workload that, at least, slows down the normal users of the system from recording transactions at their normal pace.

Another issue is that many large enterprises do not have only one OLTP system that records all the transaction data. Most large enterprises have multiple OLTP systems, many of which were developed at different times and use different software and hardware. In many cases, the codes and names used to identify items in one system are different from the codes and names used in another. Managers who are running OLAP queries generally need to be able to reference the data from several of these OLTP systems.

Online analytical processing systems operate on OLAP data in data warehouses or data marts. A data warehouse stores enterprise-level OLAP data, while a data mart is smaller and typically covers a single function in an organization.

Application Development Architecture

Applications use two components to access a database: an API or a Uniform Resource Locator (URL) and a database language.

API or URL

- An API defines how to code an application to connect to a database and pass commands to the database. An object model API is usually language-independent and defines a set of objects, properties, and interfaces; a C or Visual Basic API defines a set of functions for applications written in C, C++, or Visual Basic.

- A URL is a string, or stream, that an Internet application can use to access resources on the Internet or an intranet. Microsoft SQL Server 2000 provides an Internet Server Application Programming Interface (ISAPI) DLL that Microsoft Internet Information Services (IIS) applications use to build URLs that reference instances of SQL Server 2000.

APIs Supported by SQL Server

SQL Server supports a number of APIs for building general-purpose database applications. The supported APIs include open APIs with publicly defined specifications supported by several database vendors, such as the following:

- ActiveX Data Objects (ADO)
- OLE DB
- ODBC and the object APIs built over ODBC: Remote Data Objects (RDO) and Data-Access Objects (DAO)
- Embedded SQL for C (ESQL)
- The legacy DB-Library for C API that was developed specifically to be used with earlier versions of SQL Server that predate the SQL-92 standard

Internet applications can also use URLs that specify IIS virtual roots referencing an instance of SQL Server. The URL can contain an XPath query, a Transact-SQL statement, or a template. In addition to using URLs, Internet applications can also use ADO or OLE DB to work with data in the form of XML documents.

Database Language

A database language defines the syntax of the commands sent to the database. The commands sent through the API enable the application to access and modify data. They also enable the application to create and modify objects in the database. All commands are subject to the permissions granted to the user. SQL Server 2000 supports two languages: (1) Transact-SQL and (2) Internet applications running on IIS and using XPath queries with mapping schemas.

Transact-SQL

Transact-SQL is the database language supported by SQL Server 2000. Transact-SQL complies with the entry-level SQL-92 standard but also supports several features from the intermediate and full levels. Transact-SQL also supports some powerful extensions to the SQL-92 standard.

The ODBC specification defines extensions to the SQL defined in the SQL-92 standard. The ODBC SQL extensions are also supported by OLE DB. Transact-SQL supports the ODBC extensions from applications using the ADO, OLE DB, or ODBC APIs, or the APIs that layer over ODBC. The ODBC SQL extensions are not supported from applications that use the DB-Library or Embedded SQL APIs.

XPath

SQL Server 2000 supports a subset of the XPath language defined by the World Wide Web Consortium (W3C). XPath is a graph navigation language used to select nodes from XML documents. First, you use a mapping schema to define an XML-based view of the data in one or more SQL Server tables and views, then you can use XPath queries to retrieve data from that mapping schema.

You usually use XPath queries in either URLs or the ADO API. The OLE DB API also supports XPath queries.

Lesson Summary

The SQL Server 2000 architecture consists of many components. One type of component in SQL Server is the database, which is where data is actually stored. A database is made up of logical components and physical components. Another component of SQL Server is the relational database engine. The relational database engine processes queries and manages memory, thread, task, and I/O activity. This engine also processes full-text queries and transactions. SQL Server 2000 supports database administration through DDL and DML, stored procedures, SQL-DMF, graphical tools, automated administration, backup and restore processes, import and export processes, data validation, and replication. In addition, SQL Server 2000 provides components that can be used to build data warehouses or data marts. SQL Server supports OLAP systems and OLTP systems. Applications use two components to access a SQL Server database: an API or a URL and a database language.

Review

The following questions are intended to reinforce key information presented in this chapter. If you are unable to answer a question, review the appropriate lesson and then try the question again. Answers to the questions can be found in the Appendix, "Questions and Answers."

1. What is SQL Server 2000?
2. What language is commonly used to work with data in a database?
3. What is XML?
4. Which edition of SQL Server 2000 includes the complete SQL Server offering?
5. What is the purpose of the SQL Server 2000 relational database engine?
6. What SQL Server 2000 technology helps you build data warehouses and data marts in SQL Server by importing and transferring data from multiple heterogeneous sources?
7. What are at least four administrative tasks that you can use the SQL Server Enterprise Manager to perform?
8. Which tool is commonly used to create queries and execute them against SQL Server databases?
9. What are at least five objects that can be included in a logical database?
10. What are the major components involved in processing a SQL statement received from a SQL Server client?
11. What two roles does Microsoft Search play in supporting SQL Server?
12. What phases does a transaction go through?

C H A P T E R   2

Using Transact-SQL on a SQL Server Database

About This Chapter

Transact-SQL is a language containing the commands that are used to administer instances of SQL Server; to create and manage all objects in an instance of SQL Server; and to insert, retrieve, modify, and delete data in SQL Server tables. Transact-SQL is an extension of the language defined in the SQL standards published by the International Organization for Standardization (ISO) and the American National Standards Institute (ANSI). This chapter introduces you to Transact-SQL and provides details about how to create and execute Transact-SQL statements in order to manage a SQL Server database and its data. The chapter also introduces you to the SQL Server programming tools that enable you to use Transact-SQL to interface with the database.

Before You Begin

To complete the lessons in this chapter, you must have SQL Server 2000 Enterprise Edition installed on a Microsoft Windows 2000 Server computer.

Lesson 1: SQL Server Programming Tools

SQL Server 2000 provides a set of tools that enable you to use Transact-SQL to interact with SQL databases and their data. This set of tools includes SQL Query Analyzer and the isqlw, isql, and osql command-prompt utilities. In this lesson, you will be introduced to each of these tools and provided with an overview of how and when these tools are used. In the lessons that follow, you will learn how to work with Transact-SQL in order to manage SQL Server databases and their data.

Note   In our discussion of Transact-SQL, you will be exposed to various database objects and to the process of querying a database and modifying objects and data within the database. For example, you will be introduced to Transact-SQL statements that enable you to create tables, execute queries, and update data. The purpose of this chapter, however, is to introduce you to using Transact-SQL in a SQL Server database. More detailed information about the various components of a database and advanced querying techniques will be provided in subsequent chapters.

After this lesson, you will be able to:
- Describe SQL Query Analyzer and the isqlw, isql, and osql command-prompt utilities.
- Navigate SQL Query Analyzer, including the query window, the Transact-SQL Debugger window, and the Open Table window.
- Run a simple query and view the result set of that query, as well as view the execution plan, trace information, statistical information, and messages that are specific to the executed query.

Estimated lesson time: 30 minutes

SQL Query Analyzer

SQL Query Analyzer is a graphical user interface (GUI) that enables you to design, test, and execute Transact-SQL statements, stored procedures, batches, and scripts interactively. You can run SQL Query Analyzer from inside SQL Enterprise Manager or run it directly from the Start menu. You can also launch SQL Query Analyzer from the command prompt by executing the isqlw utility. (The isqlw utility is discussed in more detail later in this lesson.)

Note   SQL Query Analyzer is the primary tool that you will use to run Transact-SQL statements in the exercises in this training kit, and it is one of the main tools available in SQL Server to manage database objects and the data within those objects. In addition to performing the exercise in this lesson, you should spend enough time navigating the SQL Query Analyzer interface and reviewing SQL Server Books Online to feel completely comfortable with using this tool.

The functionality within SQL Query Analyzer can be described in terms of the interface layout. SQL Query Analyzer includes a number of windows, dialog boxes, and wizards that help you to perform the tasks necessary to manage SQL Server databases and the data stored within those databases. This section discusses many of these interface objects and the functions that can be performed when you access them. For more details about any of the objects that are discussed here or any objects within the interface, refer to SQL Server Books Online.

When you launch SQL Query Analyzer, the Connect To SQL Server dialog box appears. You must specify which instance of SQL Server that you want to access and which type of authentication to use when connecting to the database. Once you have entered the appropriate information in the Connect To SQL Server dialog box and then clicked OK, SQL Query Analyzer appears and displays the Query window and the Object Browser window, as shown in Figure 2.1.

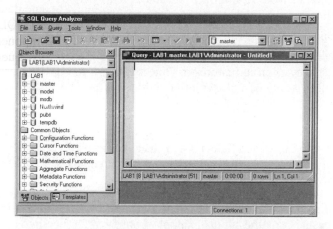

Figure 2.1.   SQL Query Analyzer displaying the Query window on the right and the Object Browser window on the left.

Note   The Object Browser window is displayed by default the first time that you use SQL Query Analyzer. If the Object Browser window was not left open when SQL Query Analyzer was last shut down, the Object Browser window will not appear when you open SQL Query Analyzer.

Query Window

The Query window is divided into two panes: The Editor pane and the Results pane. When you first open SQL Query Analyzer, only the Editor pane appears, as shown in Figure 2.1. The Results pane appears automatically when you run a Transact-SQL query. You can also open and close the Results pane manually by clicking the Show Results Pane button on the toolbar.

You can customize the window and control the behavior of the Editor pane and the Results pane. The Options dialog box, which you can access from the Tools menu, enables you to control the look and behavior of the Query window. In addition, you can specify which fonts are used for text in the window and you can change the relative size of the Editor pane and the Results pane by dragging the split bar up and down. You can also scroll through the panes (up and down or left and right) as necessary.

Editor Pane

The Editor pane is a text-editing window used to enter and execute Transact-SQL statements. You can use one of the following methods to enter code in the Editor pane:

- Type SQL statements directly in the Editor pane.
- Open a saved SQL script. The contents are displayed in the Editor pane, where they can be edited.
- Open a template file. The contents are displayed in the Editor pane, where they can be edited.
- Use the scripting features of Object Browser to copy SQL statements for the selected database object into the Editor pane.

The Editor pane in SQL Query Analyzer provides various tools to help you create and edit Transact-SQL statements, including the standard editing commands Undo, Cut, Copy, Paste, and Select All. You can also find and replace text, move the input cursor to a particular line, insert and remove indentation, force case, and insert and remove comment marks.

In addition, you can view Transact-SQL reference topics at SQL Server Books Online and copy the syntax example from the reference into the Editor pane, in order to help create a Transact-SQL statement. You can also save query definitions and other SQL scripts for reuse, and you can create templates (which are boilerplate scripts for creating objects in a database).

Color Coding in Query Analyzer

The code entered in the Editor pane is colored by category. The following table lists the default colors and what they indicate:

Color	Category
Red	Character string
Dark red	Stored procedure
Green	System table
Dark green	Comment
Magenta	System function

Color	Category
Blue	Keyword
Gray	Operator

Note   You can change these default color settings by selecting the Fonts tab on the Options dialog box.

You should use the color coding as a guide to help eliminate errors in your Transact-SQL statements. For example, if you type a keyword and it is not displayed in blue (assuming that you retained the default settings), the keyword might be misspelled or incorrect. Or, if too much of your code is displayed in red, you might have omitted the closing quotation mark for a character string.

Executing Transact-SQL Statements

You can either execute a complete script or only selected SQL statements in SQL Query Analyzer:

- Execute a complete script by creating or opening the script in the Editor pane and then pressing F5.
- Execute only selected SQL statements by highlighting the lines of code in the Editor pane and then pressing F5.

When executing a stored procedure in the Editor pane, enter the statement to execute the stored procedure and then press F5. If the statement that executes the procedure is the first in the batch, you can omit the *EXECUTE* (or *EXEC*) statement; otherwise, *EXECUTE* is required.

Results Pane

When you execute a Transact-SQL statement, the query output (result set) is displayed in the Results pane. The Results pane can include a variety of tabs. The options that you select in the interface determine which tabs are displayed. By default, only the Grids tab, which is the active tab, and the Messages tab are displayed.

Grids Tab

The Grids tab displays the result set in a grid format, as shown in Figure 2.2. The grid format is displayed much like a table and enables you to select individual cells, columns, or rows from the result set.

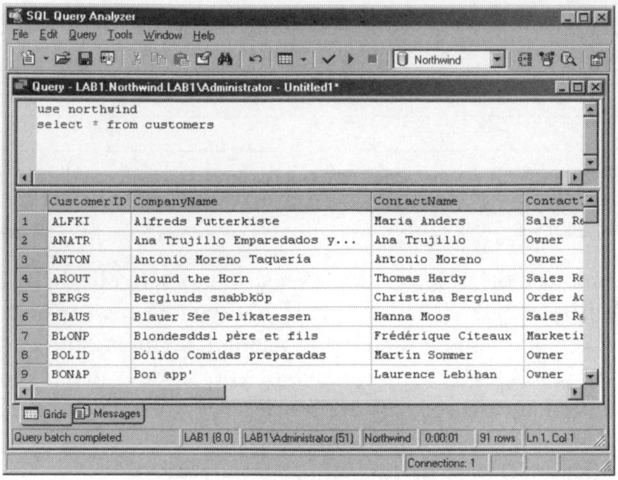

Figure 2.2. Grids tab displaying the result set generated by the executing Transact-SQL statement.

The Grids tab is always accompanied by the Messages tab, which displays messages relative to the specific query.

Results Tab

The Results tab, like the Grids tab, displays the result set generated by executing a Transact-SQL statement. In the Results tab, however, the result set is displayed as text (refer to Figure 2.3), rather than in a grid format.

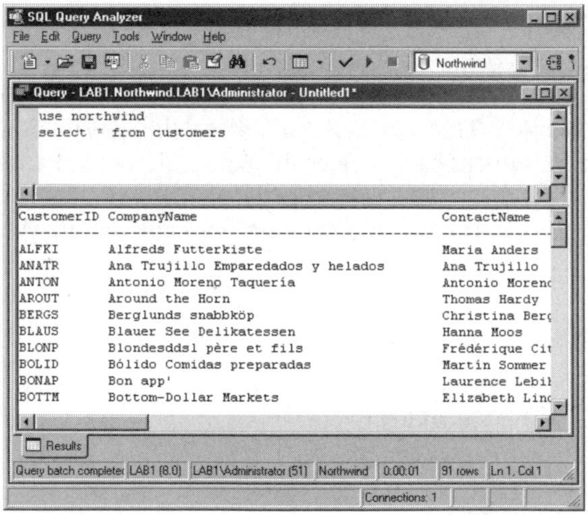

Figure 2.3. Results tab displaying the result set generated by executing a Transact-SQL statement.

The Messages tab is not displayed when the Results tab is used. Any messages pertinent to the query that has been executed are displayed in the Results tab after the result set (unless the query generated an error, in which case the Results tab contains only the error message).

You can display either the Results tab or the Grids tab, but not both. Because the Grids tab is displayed by default, you must configure SQL Query Analyzer to display the Results tab. The Results tab is then used to return queries until the end of the session or until you reconfigure SQL Query Analyzer to display the result set in the Grids tab. After you close SQL Query Analyzer and then restart it, the Grids tab will again appear in the Results pane.

To set up SQL Query Analyzer to display the Results tab, select the Execute Mode button on the toolbar, then select Results In Text. The result set from the next query that you run will be displayed in the Results tab until you select the Results In Grid option or you restart SQL Query Analyzer.

Note   You can also have the result set sent to a file, rather than to the Grids tab or to the Results tab. To send a result set to a file, select the Execute Mode button on the toolbar and then select Results To File. You will be prompted for a filename and a folder in which to store the file.

Execution Plan Tab

An important feature of SQL Query Analyzer is its set of tools that help you analyze your queries in order to ensure optimal performance. One of these tools is the Execution Plan tab of the Results pane. The Execution Plan tab displays a graphical representation of the execution plan that is used to execute the current query.

The display uses icons to represent the execution of specific statements and queries, rather than the tabular representation produced by the *SET SHOWPLAN_ALL* or *SET SHOWPLAN_TXT* statements. Figure 2.4 shows what this graphical representation looks like when you execute a simple *SELECT* statement.

By default, the Execution Plan tab is not displayed in the Results pane. To display the Execution Plan tab, select the Execute Mode button on the toolbar, then select Show Execution Plan. The next time you execute a query, the Execution Plan tab will be available—and it will show the graphical representation of the execution plan for that query. The tab will be available until you deselect the Show Execution Plan option or until you close SQL Query Analyzer.

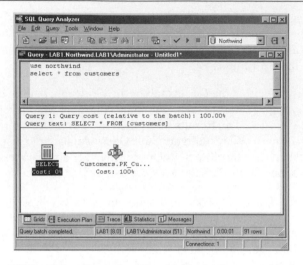

Figure 2.4. Execution Plan tab displaying a graphical representation of the executed Transact-SQL statement.

Trace Tab

The Trace tab, like the Execution Plan tab, can assist you with analyzing your queries. The Trace tab displays server trace information about the event class, subclass, integer data, text data, database ID, duration, start time, reads and writes, and Central Processing Unit (CPU) usage, as shown in Figure 2.5. The Trace tab provides information that you can use to determine the server-side impact of a query.

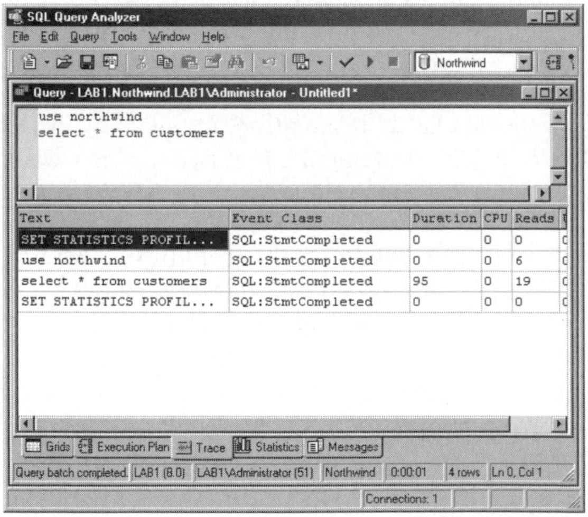

Figure 2.5. Trace tab displaying server trace information about the executed Transact-SQL statement.

By default, the Trace tab is not displayed in the Results pane. To display the Trace tab, select the Execute Mode button on the toolbar, then select Show Server Trace. The next time you execute a query, the Trace tab will be available, and it will show the server trace information. The tab will be available until you deselect the Show Server Trace option or until you close SQL Query Analyzer.

Statistics Tab

The Statistics tab provides detailed information about client-side statistics for execution of the query. The output result set displays the name of the counter, the value of the counter, and a running average from the beginning of the connection or since the last manual reset. Figure 2.6 shows the statistics that are generated after running a simple *SELECT* statement.

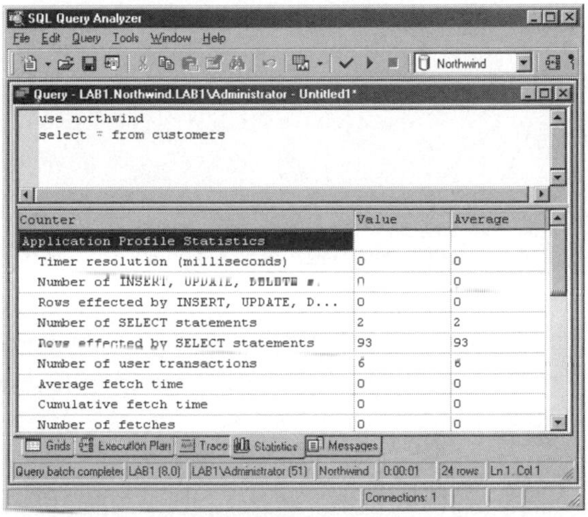

Figure 2.6.   Statistics tab displaying statistics information about the executed Transact-SQL statement.

The statistics include three groups of counters: Application Profile, Network, and Time. The statistics are displayed only when a query result is generated.

By default, the Statistics tab is not displayed in the Results pane. To display the Statistics tab, select the Execute Mode button on the toolbar, then select Show Client Statistics. The next time you execute a query, the Statistics tab will be available, and it will show the client statistics information. The tab will be available until you deselect the Show Client Statistics option or until you close SQL Query Analyzer.

Messages Tab

The Messages tab displays messages about the Transact-SQL statement that you executed (or that you tried to execute). If the query ran successfully, the message will include the number of rows returned, as shown in Figure 2.7, or it will state that the command has completed successfully. If the query did not run successfully, the Messages tab will contain an error message identifying why the query attempt was unsuccessful.

Figure 2.7.   The Messages tab displaying a message about the executed Transact-SQL statement.

The Messages tab is available in the Results pane only if the Grids tab is displayed. If the Results tab is displayed, messages appear in that tab.

Estimated Execution Plan Tab

The Estimated Execution Plan tab displays information about the execution plan that would be used for a particular query if that query were executed. Like the Execution Plan tab, the display uses icons to represent the execution of specific statements and queries. Figure 2.8 shows the estimated execution plan for a simple SELECT query. If you were to scroll down the Results pane, you would see a graphical representation similar to what you would see on the Execution Plan tab if this query were executed.

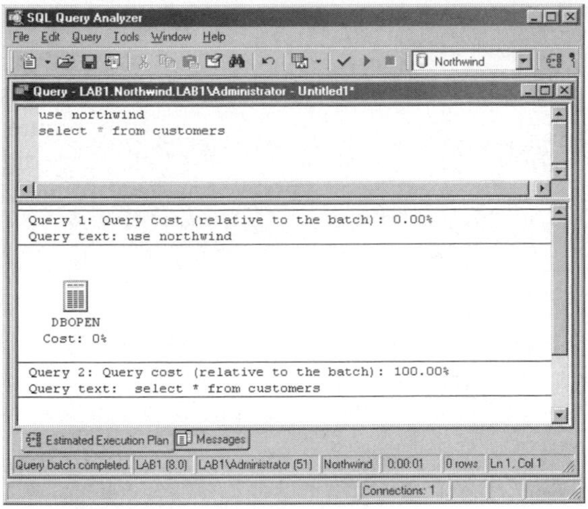

Figure 2.8.   Estimated Execution Plan Tab displaying information about the execution plan for a Transact-SQL statement.

Object Browser Window

Object Browser is a tree-based tool used to navigate among the objects in a database. In addition to navigation, Object Browser offers object scripting, stored procedure execution, and access to table and view objects.

The Object Browser window contains two tabs:

- **Objects tab.**   Lists objects within a database and lists common objects, such as built-in functions and base data types.
- **Templates tab.**   Provides access to the Templates folder.

Transact-SQL Debugger Window

SQL Query Analyzer comes equipped with a Transact-SQL debugger that enables you to control and monitor the execution of stored procedures. The debugger supports traditional functions, such as setting breakpoints, defining watch expressions, and single-stepping through procedures.

The Transact-SQL debugger in SQL Query Analyzer supports debugging against SQL Server 2000, SQL Server 7.0, and SQL Server 6.5 Service Pack 2.

Note   It is not advisable to use the Transact-SQL debugger on a production server. While in step-execution mode, the debugger can lock certain system resources that are needed by other processes.

You can run Transact-SQL Debugger only from within SQL Query Analyzer. Once started, the debugging interface occupies a window within that application, as shown in Figure 2.9.

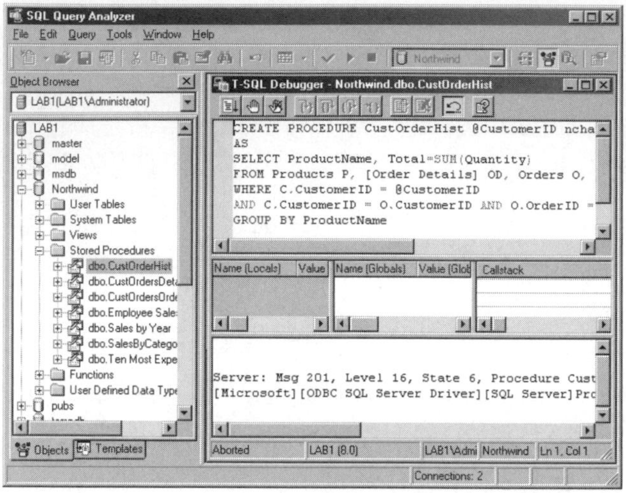

Figure 2.9. Transact-SQL Debugger window showing the result of debugging the *CustOrderHist* stored procedure in the Northwind database.

When the Transact-SQL Debugger starts, a dialog box appears prompting you to set the values of input parameter variables. It is not mandatory for these values to be set at this time. You will have the opportunity to make modifications once the Transact-SQL Debugger window appears. In the dialog box, click Execute to continue with your session.

Note   SQL Query Analyzer does not support multiple instances of the debugger. If you attempt to debug a second stored procedure, SQL Query Analyzer will prompt you to cancel the currently active debugging session.

Due to connection constraints, it is not possible to create a new query while the debugger window is in the foreground. To create a new query, either bring an existing query window to the foreground or open a new connection to the database.

The Transact-SQL Debugger window consists of a toolbar, a status bar, and a series of window panes. Many of these components have dual purposes, serving as both control and monitoring mechanisms.

Only limited functionality might be available from some of these components after a procedure has been completed or aborted. For example, you cannot set breakpoints or scroll between entries in either of the variable windows when the procedure is not running.

Open Table Window

The Open Table window displays the columns and rows from a table in a grid. You can modify the data in the grid, and you can also insert and delete rows.
Figure 2.10 shows the contents of the Customers table in the Northwind database.

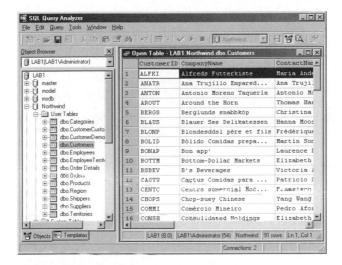

Figure 2.10.   Open Table window displaying the contents of the Customers table in the Northwind database.

Object Search Window

The Object Search window helps you to find objects in the current database server. Object Search is accessible through a button on the toolbar and through the Object Search command on the Tools menu. Figure 2.11 shows the result of searching for all user table objects in the Northwind database.

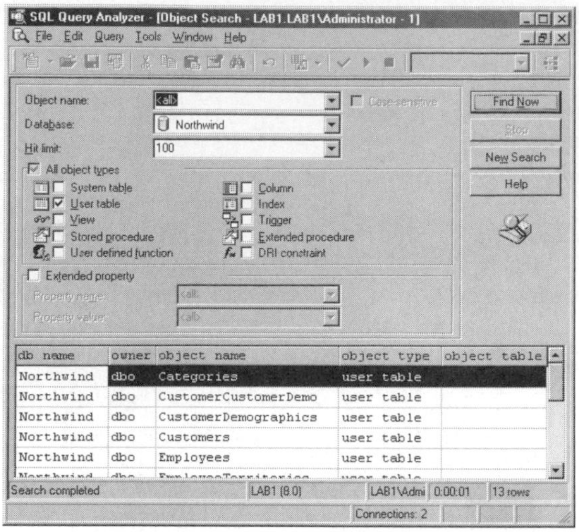

Figure 2.11.   Object Search window displaying the result of an object search of the North-wind database.

isqlw Command-Prompt Utility

The isqlw utility (SQL Query Analyzer) enables you to enter Transact-SQL state-ments, system stored procedures, and script files. You can set up a shortcut or cre-ate a batch file to launch a pre-configured SQL Query Analyzer.

You can use the isqlw utility with or without a user interface. To run isqlw without a user interface, specify valid login information (an instance of SQL Server 2000 with a trusted connection or a valid login ID and password) and input and output files. The isqlw utility executes the contents of the input file and saves the result in the output file.

If input and output files are not specified, isqlw runs interactively (starting the SQL Query Analyzer). If valid login information is specified, isqlw connects directly to an instance of SQL Server 2000. If the information specified is insufficient for a connection, the Connect To SQL Server dialog box appears.

The isqlw utility and SQL Query Analyzer use the Open Database Connectivity (ODBC) application programming interface (API), which uses the SQL Server ODBC driver default settings for SQL-92.

isql Command Prompt Utility

The isql utility enables you to enter Transact-SQL statements, system procedures, and script files. The utility uses DB-Library to communicate with SQL Server 2000.

Like most DB-Library applications, the isql utility does not set any connection options by default. You must issue *SET* statements interactively or in scripts if you want to use specific connection option settings.

The isql utility is started directly from the operating system, along with case-sensitive switches. After starting, isql accepts Transact-SQL statements and sends them to SQL Server 2000 interactively. The results are formatted and printed on the standard output device (the screen). Use *QUIT* or *EXIT* to exit from isql.

If you do not specify a username when you start isql, SQL Server 2000 checks for the environment variables and uses those. For example, *isqluser=[user]* or *isqlserver=[server]* would apply. If no environment variables are set, the workstation username is used. If you do not specify a server, the name of the workstation is used.

If neither the -U nor -P options is used, SQL Server 2000 attempts to connect by using Windows Authentication mode. Authentication is based on the Windows account of the user who is running isql. The results are printed once at the end of execution. With isql, there is a limit of 1,000 characters per line. Large statements should be spread across multiple lines.

osql Command-Prompt Utility

The osql utility enables you to enter Transact-SQL statements, system procedures, and script files. This utility uses ODBC to communicate with the server.

The osql utility is started directly from the operating system with the case-sensitive options listed previously. After osql starts, it accepts SQL statements and sends them to SQL Server interactively. The results are formatted and displayed on the screen. Use *QUIT* or *EXIT* to exit from osql.

Like the isql command-prompt utility, if you do not specify a username when you start osql, SQL Server 2000 checks for the environment variables and uses those. The osql utility uses the ODBC API, as well as the SQL Server ODBC driver default settings for the SQL Server 2000 SQL-92 connection options.

Exercise 1: Navigating SQL Query Analyzer and Running a Query

In this exercise, you will navigate through SQL Query Analyzer, execute a Transact-SQL statement, and then view the result of that query. To perform this exercise, you should be logged into your Windows 2000 Server computer as Administrator.

Note When you installed SQL Server 2000, the Northwind sample database was also installed. The Northwind database contains the sales data for a fictitious company called Northwind Traders, which imports and exports specialty foods from around the world. You will use this database for many of the exercises in this training kit.

▶ **To open SQL Query Analyzer**

1. On the Start menu, point to Programs, then Microsoft SQL Server, and then click Query Analyzer.

   As SQL Query Analyzer starts to open, the Connect To SQL Server dialog box appears.

2. In the SQL Server drop-down list, select Local. If Local is not listed, click the ellipsis button to browse for the local computer (the computer on which you are working).

3. Verify that the Windows Authentication radio button is selected.

4. Click OK.

   The SQL Query Analyzer interface appears and displays two windows: the Object Browser window and the Query Window.

Note The Object Browser window is displayed by default the first time that you use SQL Query Analyzer. If you have opened SQL Query Analyzer previously and the Object Browser window was not left open when SQL Query Analyzer was last shut down, the Object Browser window will not appear when you open SQL Query Analyzer.

---

5. If the Object Browser window did not appear, click the Object Browser button on the toolbar.

   The Object Browser window appears.

▶ **To size SQL Query Analyzer Windows**

1. Size SQL Query Analyzer as well as the Object Browser window and the Query window so that you can easily view the features within the interface.

2. Click the Show Results Pane button on the toolbar.

   The Query window is now divided into two panes: the Editor pane and the Results pane.

3. Position your mouse over the split bar between the two panes and resize them.

▶ **To configure the SQL Query Analyzer Results Pane**

1. Click the Show Results Pane button on the toolbar.

   The Results pane disappears, and the Editor pane fills the Query window.

2. On the toolbar, click the Execute Mode button and then click Show Execution Plan.

3. On the toolbar, click the Execute Mode button and then view the listed options.

   Notice that the Results In Grid option and the Show Execution Plan option are both checked. The Results In Grid option is checked by default. The options listed beneath the Execute Mode button affect how a query result is displayed and affect what information is displayed.

4. Click the Show Server Trace option.

5. On the toolbar, click the Execute Mode button and then click Show Client Statistics.

▶ **To search for an object in the database**

1. On the toolbar, click the Object Search button.

   The Object Search window appears.

2. From the Database drop-down list box, select Northwind.

3. In the All Object Types section, verify that the User Table check box is selected, then select the System Table check box.

4. Click Find Now.

   The search result appears at the bottom of the Object Search window. Notice that all entries in the db name column are listed as Northwind and that all entries in the object type column are listed as either user table or system table.

5. Close the Object Search window.

▶ **To view a table's contents**

1. In the Object Browser window, expand Northwind and then expand User Tables.

2. Right-click dbo.Employees and then select Open.

   The Open Table window appears, listing the contents of the Employees table in the Northwind database.

3. Scroll through the Open Table window to view the contents.

4. Close the Open Table window.

▶ **To debug a stored procedure**

1. In the Object Browser window, expand Northwind, and then expand Stored Procedures.

2. Right-click dbo.CustOrderHist, then click Debug.

    The Debug Procedure dialog box appears.

3. Click Execute.

    The Transact-SQL Debugger window appears as the debugging operation is executed against the *CustOrderHist* stored procedure in the Northwind database. An error message is displayed in the bottom pane indicating that the @CustomerID parameter needs to be supplied for this stored procedure to run.

4. View the result of the debugging operation.

5. Close the Transact-SQL Debugger window.

6. Close the Object Browser window.

    The Editor pane of the Query window should now be the only window displayed.

▶ **To execute a SELECT statement**

1. In the Editor pane of the Query window, enter the following Transact-SQL statement:

```
USE northwind
SELECT * FROM customers
```

    Notice that the *USE*, *SELECT*, and *FROM* all appear in blue on the screen to show that they are Transact-SQL keywords. The USE keyword changes the database context to the specified database.

2. Click the Execute Query button on the toolbar to start the query.

    The Results pane appears and displays the query result set on the Grids tab. Notice that there are four other tabs: Execution Plan, Trace, Statistics, and Messages. The Messages tab is available by default when the Grids tab is displayed. The other tabs are optional and appear now because you configured the Execute Mode options previously in this exercise.

▶ **To view query results**

1. Review the result set on the Grids tab. Select different columns and rows. Select individual cells. Scroll through the Results pane to view all of the contents on the Grids tab.

2. Click the Execution Plan tab.

    A graphical representation of the execution plan is displayed.

3. Point to each of the icons on the Execution Plan tab.

    For each icon, a pop-up menu appears, showing the result of a clustered index scan.

4. Click the Trace tab.

    Server trace information about the executed Transact-SQL statement is displayed.

5. Review the information on the Trace tab.

6. Click the Statistics tab.

    Client-side statistics for the executed query are displayed.

7. Review the statistical information.

8. Click the Messages tab.

    A message about the executed query appears.

9. Review the message.

▶ **To correct a Transact-SQL statement**

1. In the Editor pane, change customer to custom.

2. Click the Execute Query button on the toolbar.

    Notice that the Messages tab in the Results pane is active. An error message is displayed, saying that custom is an invalid object name.

3. Correct the Transact-SQL statement, then re-execute the query.

    The result set is displayed in the Grids tab.

▶ **To display the Estimated Execution Plan**

1. On the toolbar, click the Display Estimated Execution Plan button.

    The Estimated Execution Plan tab and the Messages tab appear in the Results pane. The Estimated Execution Plan tab displays the estimated execution plan for the query in the Editor window.

2. Review the information on the Estimated Execution Plan tab.

▶ **To modify how the result set is displayed**

1. On the toolbar, click the Execute Mode button and then select Results In Text.

2. Execute the query.

    The result set is displayed in text form on the Results tab of the Results pane. Notice that the Messages tab is no longer present.

3. Scroll to the bottom of the result set on the Results tab.

    The message related to the execution of this query appears beneath the result set. If the query attempt had generated an error, the error would have appeared on the Results tab.

4. On the toolbar, click the Execute Mode button and then click Show Execution Plan.

5. Repeat the previous step for the Show Server Tracer option and the Show Client Statistics option.

6. On the toolbar, click the Execute Mode button and then view the listed options. Notice that the only option now checked is Results In Text.
7. Click the Results In Grid option.
8. Re-execute the query.

   The result set is displayed in the Grids tab.
9. Close SQL Query Analyzer. When prompted to save changes, click No.

Tip   As an added exercise, try running the isql and osql command-prompt utilities. Once each utility is running, execute a *SELECT* statement against the Customers table in the Northwind database. Be sure to exit the utility after you run your query. Carefully review the information about isql and osql in SQL Server Books Online before running either of the utilities.

Lesson Summary

SQL Server 2000 provides a set of tools that enable you to use Transact-SQL to interact with SQL databases and their data. These tools include SQL Query Analyzer and the isqlw, isql, and osql command-prompt utilities. SQL Query Analyzer is a GUI that enables you to design, test, and execute Transact-SQL statements, stored procedures, batches, and scripts interactively. The functionality within SQL Query Analyzer can be described in terms of the interface layout. SQL Query Analyzer includes a number of windows, dialog boxes, and wizards that help you to perform the tasks necessary to manage SQL Server databases and the data stored within those databases. The main window that you use to execute Transact-SQL statements and to view a query result is the Query window. The Query window is divided into two panes: the Editor pane and the Results pane. SQL Query Analyzer also includes the Object Browser window, which enables you to navigate the objects in the database, and the Transact-SQL Debugger window, which enables you to control and monitor the execution of stored procedures. In addition to SQL Query Analyzer, SQL Server includes the isqlw, isql, and osql command-prompt utilities. Each of these utilities enables you to enter Transact-SQL statements, system procedures, and script files at a command prompt. You can also use the isqlw utility to launch SQL Query Analyzer.

Lesson 2: Introduction to Transact-SQL

Transact-SQL allows you to administer instances of SQL Server; create and manage all objects in an instance of SQL Server; and insert, retrieve, modify, and delete all data in SQL Server tables. Transact-SQL is an extension of the language defined in the SQL standards published by the International Organization for Standardization (ISO) and the American National Standards Institute (ANSI). This lesson introduces you to Transact-SQL and to the various types of Transact-SQL statements that are used in SQL Server, including data definition language (DDL) statements, data control language (DCL) statements, and data manipulation language (DML) statements.

After this lesson, you will be able to:
- Provide an overview of Transact-SQL and how it is used in SQL Server.
- Describe the three types of Transact-SQL statements: DDL, DCL, and DML.
- Write and execute basic DDL, DCL, and DML statements, including CREATE, GRANT, SELECT, INSERT, UPDATE, and DELETE statements.

Estimated lesson time: 35 minutes

Overview of Transact-SQL

Transact-SQL is central to the use of SQL Server. Each application that communicates with SQL Server does so by sending Transact-SQL statements to the server, regardless of the application's user interface.

SQL Server Books Online includes a complete reference for Transact-SQL statements. This reference describes each Transact-SQL element and provides examples that illustrate how to apply that element in a Transact-SQL statement. You can copy the syntax example from the reference to the Editor pane of SQL Query Analyzer to help create a Transact-SQL statement. While in the Editor pane, you can select a Transact-SQL statement, function, stored procedure, or other Transact-SQL element and then press SHIFT+F1 to view information about the selected text.

Transact-SQL Statements

A Transact-SQL statement is a set of code that performs some action on database objects or on data in a database. SQL Server supports three types of Transact-SQL statements: DDL, DCL, and DML.

Data Definition Language

Data definition language, which is usually part of a database management system, is used to define and manage all attributes and properties of a database, including row layouts, column definitions, key columns, file locations, and storage strategy.

A DDL statement supports the definition or declaration of database objects such as databases, tables, and views. The Transact-SQL DDL used to manage objects is based on SQL-92 DDL statements (with extensions). For each object class, there are usually *CREATE*, *ALTER*, and *DROP* statements (for example, *CREATE TABLE*, *ALTER TABLE*, and *DROP TABLE*).

Most DDL statements take the following form:

- *CREATE object_name*
- *ALTER object_name*
- *DROP object_name*

The following three examples illustrate how to use the Transact-SQL CREATE keyword to create, alter, and drop tables. CREATE is not limited only to table objects, however.

CREATE TABLE

The *CREATE TABLE* statement creates a table in an existing database. The following statement will create a table named Importers in the Northwind database. The table will include three columns: CompanyID, CompanyName, and Contact.

```
USE Northwind
CREATE TABLE Importers
(
CompanyID int NOT NULL,
CompanyName varchar(40) NOT NULL,
Contact varchar(40) NOT NULL
)
```

ALTER TABLE

The *ALTER TABLE* statement enables you to modify a table definition by altering, adding, or dropping columns and constraints or by disabling or enabling constraints and triggers. The following statement will alter the Importers table in the Northwind database by adding a column named ContactTitle to the table.

```
USE Northwind
ALTER TABLE Importers
ADD ContactTitle varchar(20) NULL
```

DROP TABLE

The *DROP TABLE* statement removes a table definition and all data, indexes, triggers, constraints, and permission specifications for that table. Any view or stored procedure that references the dropped table must be explicitly dropped by using the *DROP VIEW* or *DROP PROCEDURE* statement. The following statement drops the Importers table from the Northwind database.

```
USE Northwind
DROP TABLE Importers
```

Data Control Language

Data control language is used to control permissions on database objects. Permissions are controlled by using the SQL-92 *GRANT* and *REVOKE* statements and the Transact-SQL *DENY* statement.

GRANT

The *GRANT* statement creates an entry in the security system that enables a user in the current database to work with data in that database or to execute specific Transact-SQL statements. The following statement grants the Public role SELECT permission on the Customers table in the Northwind database:

```
USE Northwind
GRANT SELECT
ON Customers
TO PUBLIC
```

REVOKE

The *REVOKE* statement removes a previously granted or denied permission from a user in the current database. The following statement revokes the SELECT permission from the Public role for the Customers table in the Northwind database:

```
USE Northwind
REVOKE SELECT
ON Customers
TO PUBLIC
```

DENY

The *DENY* statement creates an entry in the security system that denies a permission from a security account in the current database and prevents the security account from inheriting the permission through its group or role memberships.

```
USE Northwind
DENY SELECT
ON Customers
TO PUBLIC
```

Data Manipulation Language

Data manipulation language is used to select, insert, update, and delete data in the objects defined with DDL.

SELECT

The *SELECT* statement retrieves rows from the database and enables the selection of one or many rows or columns from one or many tables. The following statement retrieves the CustomerID, CompanyName, and ContactName data for companies who have a CustomerID value equal to alfki or anatr. The result set is ordered according to the ContactName value:

```
USE Northwind
SELECT CustomerID, CompanyName, ContactName
FROM Customers
WHERE (CustomerID = 'alfki' OR CustomerID = 'anatr')
ORDER BY ContactName
```

INSERT

An *INSERT* statement adds a new row to a table or a view. The following statement adds a row to the Territories table in the Northwind database. The TerritoryID value for the new row is 98101; the TerritoryDescription value is Seattle; and the RegionID value is 2.

```
USE Northwind
INSERT INTO Territories
VALUES (98101, 'Seattle', 2)
```

Note The INTO keyword is an optional keyword that can be used between INSERT and the target table. Use the INTO keyword for code clarity.

UPDATE

The *UPDATE* statement changes data in a table. The following statement updates the row in the Territories table (in the Northwind database) whose TerritoryID value is 98101. The TerritoryDescription value will be changed to Downtown Seattle.

```
USE Northwind
UPDATE Territories
SET TerritoryDescription = 'Downtown Seattle'
WHERE TerritoryID = 98101
```

DELETE

The *DELETE* statement removes rows from a table. The following statement removes the row from the Territories table (from the Northwind database) whose TerritoryID value is 98101.

```
USE Northwind
DELETE FROM Territories
WHERE TerritoryID = 98101
```

Note   The FROM keyword is an optional keyword that can be used between the DELETE keyword and the target table, view, or rowset function. Use the FROM keyword for code clarity.

Exercise 2: Creating and Executing DDL, DCL, and DML Statements

In this exercise, you will create and execute DDL, DCL, and DML statements. For all procedures, you will be working with the Northwind database. To perform this exercise, you should be logged into your Windows 2000 Server computer as Administrator.

Note   The Northwind database is a sample database provided with SQL Server. If you make changes to the database and later discover that you want to restore it to its original state, you can reinstall it by running a script from the Install folder of the SQL Server 2000 installation CD-ROM.

▶   **To open SQL Query Analyzer**

1. On the Start menu, point to Programs and then to Microsoft SQL Server, then click Query Analyzer.

   As SQL Query Analyzer starts to open, the Connect To SQL Server dialog box appears.

2. In the SQL Server drop-down list, select Local. If Local is not listed, click the ellipsis button to browse for the local computer (the computer on which you are working).

3. Verify that the Windows Authentication radio button is selected.

4. Click OK.

   The SQL Query Analyzer interface appears and displays two windows: the Object Browser window and the Query Window.

5. If the Object Browser window did not appear, click the Object Browser button on the toolbar.

   The Object Browser window appears. The Object Browser window and the Editor pane (in the Query window) should now be the only windows open in SQL Query Analyzer.

6. Size SQL Query Analyzer as well as the Object Browser window and the Query window so you can comfortably view the features within the interface.

▶ **To create a table in the Northwind database**

1. In the Editor pane, enter the following *CREATE TABLE* statement:

```
USE Northwind
CREATE TABLE Investors
(
InvestorID INT NOT NULL,
FirstName varchar(30) NOT NULL,
LastName varchar(30) NOT NULL
)
```

Notice that the keywords *USE*, *CREATE TABLE*, *int*, and *varchar* all appear in blue type on the screen. If one of these words is not blue, verify that you have entered it correctly. The keywords *int* and *varchar* are data types and are discussed in later lessons.

Also notice that in the Database drop-down list on the toolbar, the Master database is displayed. This database will change to Northwind after you execute the *USE Northwind* statement.

2. Click the Execute Query button on the toolbar.

The Results pane appears with the Messages tab active, saying that the command has been completed successfully.

3. In the Object Browser window, expand Northwind and then expand User Tables.

The Investors table is listed as one of the tables. The *dbo* that appears before the table name indicates who owns the table object.

4. Right-click dbo.Investors, then click Open.

The Open Table window appears and displays the names of the three attributes that you created. No information appears in the grids below the attribute names because no data has been added to the table.

5. Close the Open Table window.

▶ **To modify a table**

1. In the Editor pane, position your cursor several lines beneath the statement that you just executed.

You will be entering a new Transact-SQL statement several lines after the preceding one so that you can copy and paste code as necessary, referring back to other statements that you executed. You can also save the code as a script file in case you want to reference it later. This process enables you to reuse code and troubleshoot problems if any should arise. For the remainder of this exercise, you should enter each Transact-SQL statement two or three lines beneath the preceding statement.

2. Enter the following *ALTER TABLE* statement:

```
ALTER TABLE Investors
ADD InvestmentCode INT NULL
```

The USE Northwind command does not need to be used here because Northwind is now the active database. The active database is displayed in the Database drop-down list box on the toolbar.

3. Highlight the *ALTER TABLE* statement, then click the Execute Query button.

Note   You can also press F5 to execute a query.

The Messages tab displays a message saying that the command has been completed successfully.

4. In the Object Browser window, right-click dbo.Investors, then click Open.

The Open Table window appears, displaying the attributes of the Investors table. The table now includes the InvestmentCode attribute.

5. Close the Open Table window.

▶ **To display information about a table**

1. In the Editor pane, enter the following code several lines beneath the *ALTER TABLE* statement:

```
EXEC sp_help Investors
```

The *sp_help* entry is a system-stored procedure that displays information about database objects. Stored procedures are discussed in Chapter 8, "Implementing Stored Procedures."

2. Highlight the *EXEC* statement, then execute it.

The Grids tab of the Results pane displays information about the Investors table. Notice that this information is similar to what you found in the Open Table window that you accessed through the Object Browser window.

3. Review the information on the Grids tab.

Note the data type for each attribute and whether that attribute is nullable. Also note the owner of the table and the type of object.

4. Close the Object Window but leave the Query window open for the next procedure.

▶ **To grant permissions on a database object**

1. In the Editor pane, enter the following *GRANT* statement beneath the last statement that you executed:

```
GRANT SELECT
ON Investors
TO PUBLIC
```

2. Highlight the *GRANT* statement, then execute it.

The Messages tab of the Results pane displays a message indicating that the command has been completed successfully.

3. Enter the following *EXEC* statement:

```
EXEC sp_helprotect Investors
```

4. Execute the *EXEC* statement.

   The Grids tab of the Results pane displays information about user permissions for the Investors table. The Public role has been granted SELECT permission for the table.

▶ **To revoke permissions on a database object**

1. Enter the following *REVOKE* statement:

```
REVOKE SELECT
ON Investors
TO PUBLIC
```

Tip   You can copy the previous *GRANT* statement that you executed and paste it at the bottom of the Editor pane. Then, simply modify the statement so that it revokes permissions rather than grants them.

The Messages tab of the Results pane displays a message indicating that the command has been completed successfully.

2. Enter the following *EXEC* statement:

```
EXEC sp_helprotect Investors
```

3. Execute the *EXEC* statement.

   The Messages tab of the Results pane displays a message indicating that there are no matching rows on which to report. Because you revoked SELECT permissions for the Public role, there are no granted or denied permissions on which to report.

Tip   You do not have to re-enter the *EXEC sp_helprotect* statement, nor do you have to copy and paste it. Simply highlight the original statement and then execute it.

▶ **To retrieve data**

1. In the Editor pane, enter the following *INSERT* statements beneath the last statement displayed:

```
INSERT Investors VALUES (01, 'Amie', 'Baldwin', 103)
INSERT Investors VALUES (02, 'Jo', 'Brown', 102)
INSERT Investors VALUES (03, 'Scott', 'Culp', 103)
INSERT Investors VALUES (04, 'Jon', 'Grande', 103)
INSERT Investors VALUES (05, 'Lani', 'Ota', 102)
```

2. Highlight the *INSERT* statements, then execute them.

The Messages tab on the Results pane displays a set of five messages, each indicating that one row has been affected.

3. Enter the following *SELECT* statement and then execute that statement:

```
SELECT * FROM Investors
```

The Grids pane displays the five rows that you entered into the Investors table.

4. Enter the following *SELECT* statement, then execute that statement:

```
SELECT FirstName, LastName FROM Investors
WHERE (InvestorID = 03 OR InvestorID = 05)
ORDER BY FirstName
```

The Grids pane displays the Lani Ota and Scott Culp rows. The only information displayed is the first and last names, and the names are displayed in alphabetical order according to first name.

▶ **To modify data**

1. Enter the following *UPDATE* statement and then execute that statement:

```
UPDATE Investors
SET InvestmentCode = 101
WHERE InvestorID = 04
```

The Messages tab displays a message indicating that one row has been affected.

2. Execute the following *SELECT* statement:

```
SELECT * FROM Investors
```

The Grids pane displays the five rows in the Investors table. Notice that Jon Grande's InvestmentCode value is now 101.

3. Enter the following *DELETE* statement, then execute that statement:

```
DELETE FROM Investors
WHERE InvestorID = 04
```

The Messages tab displays a message indicating that one row has been affected.

4. Execute the following *SELECT* statement:

```
SELECT * FROM Investors
```

The Grids pane now displays only four rows for the Investors table. Notice that Jon Grande is no longer listed.

5. Enter the following *DROP* statement, then execute that statement:

```
DROP TABLE Investors
```

The Messages tab displays a message indicating that the command was completed successfully.

6. Open the Object Browser window, expand Northwind, and expand User Tables.

The Investors table is no longer listed.

7. Close SQL Query Analyzer.

Note   When you close SQL Query Analyzer, you will be prompted to save the Transact-SQL statements in the Editor pane to a file. As an extra exercise, you can save the file and then open it again. You might try using the existing code to re-create the Investors table—adding data, manipulating data, and then dropping the table. If you do not want to save the statements, click No in the SQL Query Analyzer message box.

Lesson Summary

Transact-SQL helps you to administer instances of SQL Server; create and manage all objects in an instance of SQL Server; and insert, retrieve, modify, and delete all data in SQL Server tables. Transact-SQL is central to the use of SQL Server. The SQL Server 2000 Transact-SQL version complies with the Entry level of the SQL-92 standard and supports many additional features from the Intermediate and Full levels of the standard. SQL Server Books Online includes a complete reference on Transact-SQL statements. A Transact-SQL statement is a set of code that performs some action on database objects or on data in a database. SQL Server supports three types of Transact-SQL statements: DDL, DCL, and DML. DDL is used to define and manage database objects such as databases, tables, and views. For each object class, there are usually *CREATE*, *ALTER*, and *DROP* statements. DCL is used to control permissions on database objects. Permissions are controlled by using the SQL-92 *GRANT* and *REVOKE* statements and the Transact-SQL *DENY* statement. DML is used to select, insert, update, and delete data in the objects that are defined with DDL.

Lesson 3: Transact-SQL Syntax Elements

Transact-SQL includes many syntax elements that are used by or that influence most statements. These elements include identifiers, variables, functions, data types, expressions, control-of-flow language, and comments. This lesson discusses these elements and provides examples that illustrate how they are applied in Transact-SQL statements.

After this lesson, you will be able to:

■ Describe and use many of the syntax elements used in Transact-SQL statements, including identifiers, variables, functions, data types, expressions, control-of-flow language, and comments.

■ Create and execute Transact-SQL statements that include many of the syntax elements discussed in this lesson.

Estimated lesson time: 35 minutes

Identifiers

The database object name is known as its identifier. Everything in SQL Server can have an identifier, including servers, databases, and database objects such as tables, views, columns, indexes, triggers, procedures, constraints, and rules. Identifiers are required for most objects but are optional for some objects (such as constraints).

An object identifier is created when the object is defined. The identifier is then used to reference the object. For example, the following statement creates a table with the identifier TableX and two columns with the identifiers KeyCol and Description:

```
CREATE TABLE TableX
(KeyCol INT PRIMARY KEY, Description NVARCHAR(80))
```

This table also has an unnamed constraint, PRIMARY KEY, which has no identifier.

Classes of Identifiers

There are two classes of identifiers: regular and delimited.

Regular Identifiers

Regular identifiers conform to the rules for the format of identifiers. They are not delimited when used in Transact-SQL statements. The following *SELECT* statement includes two identifiers: TableX and KeyCol (neither of which is delimited):

```
SELECT * FROM TableX
WHERE KeyCol = 124
```

For information about how identifiers should be formatted, refer to SQL Server Books Online.

Delimited Identifiers

Delimited identifiers are enclosed in double quotation marks (" ") or in brackets ([ ]). Identifiers that comply with the rules for the format of identifiers may or may not be delimited. In the following *SELECT* statement, the delimiters are optional:

```
SELECT * FROM [TableX]
WHERE [KeyCol] = 124
```

Identifiers that do not comply with all of the rules for identifiers must be delimited in a Transact-SQL statement. In the following *SELECT* statement, you must use a delimiter for My Table because the identifier contains a space, and you must use a delimiter for Order because the identifier is also a reserved keyword.

```
SELECT * FROM [My Table]
WHERE [Order] = 10
```

For information about when and how identifiers should be delimited, refer to SQL Server Books Online.

Variables

A Transact-SQL variable is an object in Transact-SQL batches and scripts that can hold a data value. After the variable has been declared or defined, one Transact-SQL statement in a batch can set the variable to a value—and a later statement in the batch can get the value from the variable. The following Transact-SQL statements declare a variable named *EmpIDVar*, set the value for that variable to 3, and then use the variable in a *SELECT* statement:

```
USE Northwind
DECLARE @EmpIDVar INT
SET @EmpIDVar = 3
SELECT * FROM Employees
WHERE EmployeeID = @EmpIDVar + 1
```

Variables in batches and scripts are typically used for the following functions:

- As a counter, either to count the number of times a loop is performed or to control how many times the loop is performed
- To hold a data value to be tested by a control-of-flow statement
- To save a data value to be returned by a stored procedure return code

Variables are often used in a batch or procedure as counters for *WHILE* and *LOOP* statements or for *IF...ELSE* blocks. Variables can be used only in expressions, however, and not in place of object names or keywords.

Functions

A function encapsulates frequently performed logic in a subroutine made up of one or more Transact-SQL statements. Any code that must perform the logic incorporated in a function can call the function rather than having to repeat all of the function logic.

SQL Server2000 supports two types of functions:

- **Built-in functions.** These functions operate as defined in Transact-SQL and cannot be modified. The functions can be referenced only in Transact-SQL statements.
- **User-defined functions.** These functions enable you to define your own Transact-SQL functions by using the *CREATE FUNCTION* statement.

Built-In Functions

The Transact-SQL programming language contains three types of built-in functions: rowset, aggregate, and scalar.

Rowset Functions

Rowset functions can be used like table references in a Transact-SQL statement. These functions return an object that can be used in place of a table reference in a Transact-SQL statement. For example, the *OPENQUERY* function is a rowset function that executes the specified pass-through query on the given linked server, which is an OLE DB data source. The *OPENQUERY* function can be referenced in the FROM clause of a query as though it were a table name.

All rowset functions are non-deterministic; that is, they do not return the same result every time they are called with a specific set of input values. Function determinism is discussed in more detail later in this section.

Aggregate Functions

Aggregate functions operate on a collection of values but return a single, summarizing value. For example, the AVG function is an aggregate function that returns the average of the values in a group.

Aggregate functions are allowed as expressions only in the following statements:

- The select list of a *SELECT* statement (either a subquery or an outer query)
- A COMPUTE or COMPUTE BY clause
- A HAVING clause

With the exception of *COUNT*, aggregate functions ignore null values. Aggregate functions are often used with the GROUP BY clause of the *SELECT* statement.

All aggregate functions are deterministic; they return the same value any time they are called with a given set of input values.

Scalar Functions

Scalar functions operate on a single value and then return a single value. Scalar functions can be used wherever an expression is valid. Scalar functions are divided into categories, as described in the following table:

Scalar Category	Description
Configuration functions	Return information about the current configuration
Cursor functions	Return information about cursors
Date and time functions	Perform an operation on a date and a time input value and return either a string, numeric, or date and time value
Mathematical functions	Perform a calculation based on input values provided as parameters to the function and return a numeric value
Metadata functions	Return information about the database and database objects
Security functions	Return information about users and roles
String functions	Perform an operation on a string (*char* or *varchar*) input value and return a string or numeric value
System functions	Perform operations and return information about values, objects, and settings in SQL Server
System statistical functions	Return statistical information about the system
Text and image functions	Perform an operation on a text or image input value or column and return information about the value

Each category of scalar functions includes its own set of functions. For example, the *MONTH* function, which is included in the date and time category, is a scalar function that returns an integer representing the month part of a specified date.

User-Defined Functions

User-defined functions are created by using the *CREATE FUNCTION* statement, are modified by using the *ALTER FUNCTION* statement, and are removed by using the *DROP FUNCTION* statement. Each fully qualified user-defined function name (*database_name.owner_name.function_name*) must be unique.

A user-defined function takes zero or more input parameters and returns either a scalar value or a table. A function can have a maximum of 1024 input parameters. When a parameter of the function has a default value, the keyword DEFAULT must be specified when calling the function to get the default value. This behavior is different from parameters that have default values in stored procedures in which omitting the parameter also implies the default value. User-defined functions do not support output parameters.

Types of User-Defined Functions

The Transact-SQL programming language supports two types of user-defined functions: scalar and table.

Scalar Functions.

Scalar functions return a single data value of the type defined in a RETURNS clause. You can use all scalar data types, including bigint and sql_variant. The timestamp data type, user-defined data type, and non-scalar types (such as table or cursor) are not supported. The body of the function, defined in a *BEGIN...END* block, contains the series of Transact-SQL statements that return the value. The return type can be any data type except *text*, *ntext*, *image*, *cursor*, and *timestamp*.

Table Functions.

Table functions return a table. There are two types of table functions: inline and multi-statement. For an inline table function, there is no function body; instead, the table is the result set of a single *SELECT* statement. For a multi-statement table function, the function body, defined in a *BEGIN...END* block, contains the Transact-SQL statements that build and insert rows into the table that will be returned.

The statements in a *BEGIN...END* block cannot have any side effects. Function side effects are any permanent changes to the state of a resource that has a scope outside the function, such as a modification to a database table. The only changes that can be made by the statements in the function are changes to objects local to the function, such as local cursors or variables. Modifications to database tables, operations on cursors that are not local to the function, sending e-mail, attempting a catalog modification, and generating a result set that is returned to the user are examples of actions that cannot be performed in a function.

Function Determinism

SQL Server functions are either deterministic or non-deterministic. Functions are *deterministic* when they always return the same result any time they are called with a specific set of input values. Functions are *non-deterministic* when they could return a different result each time they are called, even with the same specific set of input values.

The determinism of functions dictates whether they can be used in indexed computed columns and indexed views. Index scans must always produce a consistent result. Thus, only deterministic functions can be used to define computed columns and views that are to be indexed.

Configuration, cursor, metadata, security, and system statistical functions (as well as other built-in functions) are non-deterministic.

Data Types

A *data type* is an attribute defining the type of data that an object can contain. Columns, parameters, variables, functions that return data values, and stored procedures that have a return code all have data types. Transact-SQL includes a number of base data types, such as *varchar*, *text*, and *int*. All data that is stored in SQL Server must be compatible with one of these base data types. You can create user-defined data types, but these data types are always defined in terms of a base data type.

Data types are discussed in detail in Chapter 4, "Implementing SQL Server Databases and Tables."

Expressions

An expression is a combination of identifiers, values, and operators that SQL Server can evaluate in order to obtain a result. Expressions can be used in several different places when accessing or changing data. Expressions can be used, for example, as part of the data to retrieve (in a query) or as a search condition, to look for data that meets a set of criteria.

Using Operators in Expressions

Operators enable you to perform arithmetic, comparison, concatenation, or assignment of values. For example, you can test data to verify that the country column for your customer data is populated (or not NULL).

In queries, anyone who can see the data in the table requiring an operator can perform operations. You need the appropriate permissions before you can successfully change the data.

SQL Server has seven categories of operators. The following table describes each of those categories:

Operator Category	Description
Comparison	Compares a value against another value or an expression
Logical	Tests for the truth of a condition, such as AND, OR, NOT, LIKE, ANY, ALL, or IN
Arithmetic	Performs addition, subtraction, multiplication, division, and modulo
Unary	Performs an operation on only one expression of any of the data types of the numeric data type category
Bitwise	Temporarily turns a regular numeric value (such as 150) into an integer and performs bitwise (0 and 1) arithmetic
String concatenation	Either permanently or temporarily combines two strings (character or binary data) into one string
Assignment	Assigns a value to a variable or associates a result set column with an alias

The following *SELECT* statement uses arithmetic operators to subtract the part of the year-to-date sales that the author receives (sales <;$MI> author's royalty percentage / 100) from the total sales. The result is the amount of money that the publisher receives. The product of ytd_sales and royalty is calculated first because the operator is multiplication. Next, the total is divided by 100. The result is subtracted from ytd_sales.

```
USE pubs
SELECT title_id, ytd_sales - ytd_sales * royalty / 100
FROM titles
```

Control-of-Flow Language Elements

Control-of-flow language consists of special words that control the flow of execution in Transact-SQL statements, statement blocks, and stored procedures. These words can be used in Transact-SQL statements, batches, and stored procedures.

Without control-of-flow language, separate Transact-SQL statements are performed sequentially, as they occur. Control-of-flow language permits statements to be connected, related to each other, and made interdependent by using programming-like constructs. Control-of-flow statements cannot span multiple batches or stored procedures, however.

Control-of-flow keywords are useful when you need to direct Transact-SQL to take some kind of action. For example, use a *BEGIN...END* pair of statements when including more than one Transact-SQL statement in a logical block. Use an *IF...ELSE* pair of statements when a certain statement or block of statements needs to be executed if some condition is met, and another statement or block of statements should be executed if that condition is not met (the *ELSE* condition).

The following table describes the control-of-flow keywords that are included in Transact-SQL:

Keyword	Description
BEGIN...END	Encloses a series of Transact-SQL statements so that a group of Transact-SQL statements can be executed
BREAK	Exits the innermost WHILE loop
CONTINUE	Restarts a WHILE loop
GOTO	Causes the execution of a Transact-SQL batch to jump to a label without executing the statements between the GOTO statement and the label
IF...ELSE	Imposes conditions on the execution of a Transact-SQL statement, and if ELSE is used, it introduces an alternate statement that is executed when the IF condition is not satisfied
RETURN	Unconditionally terminates a query, stored procedure, or batch
WAITFOR	Suspends the execution of a connection until either a specified time interval has passed or until a specified time of day is reached
WHILE	Repeats a statement or block of statements as long as a specified condition remains true; commonly used with *BREAK* or *CONTINUE* statements

Comments

Comments are non-executing text strings in program code (also known as remarks). Comments can be used to document code or to temporarily disable parts of Transact-SQL statements and batches that are being diagnosed. Using comments to document code makes future program-code maintenance easier. Comments are often used to record the program name, the author name, and the dates of major code changes. Comments can be used to describe complicated calculations or to explain a programming method.

SQL Server supports two types of comment characters:

- **Double hyphens (--).**   These comment characters can be used on the same line as code to be executed or on a line by themselves. Everything from the double hyphens to the end of the line is part of the comment. For a multiple-line comment, the double hyphens must appear at the beginning of each comment line, as shown in the following example:

```
USE Northwind
GO
-- First line of a multiple-line comment.
-- Second line of a multiple-line comment.
SELECT * FROM Employees
GO
```

- **Forward slash-asterisk pairs (/*...*/).**   These comment characters can be used on the same line as code to be executed, on lines by themselves, or even within executable code. Everything from the open-comment pair (/*) to the close-comment pair (*/) is considered part of the comment. For a multiple-line comment, the open-comment character pair (/*) must begin the comment, and the close-comment character pair (*/) must end the comment. No other comment characters should appear on any lines of the comment, as shown in the following example:

```
USE Northwind
GO
/* First line of a multiple-line comment.
Second line of a multiple-line comment. */
SELECT * FROM Products
GO
```

Multiple-line /* */ comments cannot span a batch. The complete comment must be contained within a batch. For example, in SQL Query Analyzer and the osql utility, the GO command signals the end of a batch. When the utilities read the characters GO in the first two bytes of a line, they send all of the code since the last GO command to the server as one batch. If a GO occurs at the start of a line between the /* and */ delimiters, then an unmatched comment delimiter will be sent with each batch (triggering syntax errors). All alphanumeric characters or symbols can be used within the comment. SQL Server ignores all characters within a comment (except the GO command). In addition, there is no maximum length for a comment within a batch. A comment can consist of one or more lines.

Exercise 3: Using Transact-SQL Syntax Elements to Create a Script

In this exercise, you will use SQL Query Analyzer to create scripts incorporating the various syntax elements of Transact-SQL that are discussed in this lesson. To perform this exercise, you should be logged into your Windows 2000 Server computer as Administrator.

▶ **To create a table in the Northwind database**

1. Open SQL Query Analyzer and connect to your local server.

2. In the Editor pane of the Query window, enter the following Transact-SQL code:

```
-- Select database.
USE Northwind
GO
-- Create the table.
CREATE TABLE [New Table] (ColumnA INT, ColumnB CHAR(3))
GO
SET NOCOUNT ON
GO
```

In this statement, you are identifying the database to be used and are creating a table whose identifier is New Table. Notice that this identifier is a delimited identifier and is enclosed in brackets. The object name contains a space as well as a Transact-SQL keyword (TABLE). The column names (ColumnA and ColumnB) are regular identifiers and do not require brackets or quotation marks. In addition, the columns are also defined with the *int* and *char* data types.

The code also includes comments that indicate that the code directly beneath the comment is used to select the database or to create a table. Comments will be used throughout this script to identify what each portion of the script is supposed to achieve.

Note   The *SET NOCOUNT ON* statement is used to stop the message indicating the number of rows affected by a Transact-SQL statement from being returned as part of the result. Use the *SET NOCOUNT OFF* statement at the end of the script to enable the message to appear in subsequent queries.

The GO keyword signals the end of a batch of Transact-SQL statements to the SQL Server utilities. GO is not a Transact-SQL statement; rather, it is a command recognized by the osql and isql utilities and by SQL Query Analyzer. SQL Server utilities interpret GO as a signal that they should send the current batch of Transact-SQL statements to SQL Server. The current batch of statements is composed of all statements entered since the last GO or since the start of the ad hoc session or script (if this GO is the first GO).

▶   **To declare and initialize a variable and use control-of-flow language**

1. Directly below the Transact-SQL statements that you just created, add the following code:

```
-- Declare the variable to be used.
DECLARE @MyCounter INT
-- Initialize the variable.
SET @MyCounter = 0
```

This statement declares the *@MyCounter* variable, defines that variable with the *int* data type, and assigns the variable a value of 0.

2. Adding to the script that you already created, enter the following code:

```
/* Use the variable to define when the loop should be completed.*/
WHILE (@MyCounter < 26)
BEGIN
   -- Insert a row into the table.
   INSERT INTO [New Table] VALUES
      -- Use the variable to provide the integer value
      -- for ColumnA. Also use it to generate a unique letter
      -- for each row. Use the ASCII function to get the
```

```
    -- integer value of 'a.' Add @MyCounter. Use the CHAR
    -- function to convert the sum back to the character
    -- @MyCounter characters after 'a.'
    (
     @MyCounter + 1,
     CHAR( ( @MyCounter + ASCII('a') ) )
    )
 /*Increment the variable to count this iteration
     of the loop.*/
  SET @MyCounter = @MyCounter + 1
END
GO
SET NOCOUNT OFF
GO
```

This statement completes the script. Notice that two control-of-flow language elements are being used here: WHILE and BEGIN...END. In addition, this statement uses expressions and operators *(@MyCounter + 1* and *@MyCounter + ASCII ('a'))* and functions *(CHAR* and *ASCII)* to determine the values to enter into the rows. At the end of the script, *SET NOCOUNT OFF* is used to enable row-count messages to be generated once more.

▶   **To execute the Transact-SQL script and then drop the table from the database**

1. Execute the script in its entirety.

   After you execute the script, the Messages tab is displayed—indicating that the command has been completed successfully. If the *SET NOCOUNT ON* statement had not been used when this script was executed, the Messages tab would have displayed a row-count message for each row that was added to the table (a total of 26).

2. Execute the following *SELECT* statement:

   ```
   SELECT * FROM [New Table]
   ```

   The result set is displayed in the Grids tab. Notice that there are 26 rows and that the values in the two columns are incremental.

3. Execute the following *SELECT* statement:

   ```
   DROP TABLE "New Table"
   ```

   The Messages tab displays a message indicating that the command has been completed successfully.

4. Close SQL Query Analyzer.

   You can save the Transact-SQL script for later use if you like; otherwise, close SQL Query Analyzer without saving the script.

Lesson Summary

Transact-SQL includes many syntax elements that are used by or that influence most statements. These elements include identifiers, variables, functions, data types, expressions, control-of-flow language, and comments. An identifier is a database object name. Every object in SQL Server can have an identifier. A variable is an object in Transact-SQL batches and scripts that can hold a data value. A function encapsulates frequently performed logic in a subroutine made up of one or more Transact-SQL statements. Transact-SQL also contains data types, which are attributes defining the type of data that an object can contain. An expression is a combination of identifiers, values, and operators that SQL Server can evaluate in order to obtain a result. Control-of-flow language consists of special words that control the flow of execution in Transact-SQL statements, statement blocks, and stored procedures. Comments are non-executing text strings in program code (also known as remarks).

Lesson 4: Executing Transact-SQL Statements

SQL Server 2000 provides several methods for executing Transact-SQL statements. You can execute single statements, or you can execute the statements as a batch (which is a group of one or more Transact-SQL statements). You can also execute Transact-SQL statements through stored procedures and triggers. This lesson introduces you to the various methods that you can use to execute statements. This lesson also provides you with an overview of how these statements are executed, depending on the method of execution. Finally, this lesson discusses how you can use scripts to execute Transact-SQL statements.

After this lesson, you will be able to:

- Identify methods used to execute Transact-SQL statements.
- Describe how Transact-SQL statements, batches, stored procedures, and triggers are processed.
- Describe Transact-SQL scripts and how they are used.

Estimated lesson time: 25 minutes

Single Transact-SQL Statements

Processing a single SQL statement is the most basic way that SQL Server 2000 executes SQL statements. How a statement is processed can best be illustrated by looking at how a *SELECT* statement is processed.

A *SELECT* statement is nonprocedural; it does not state the exact steps that the database server should use to retrieve the requested data. In other words, the database server must analyze the statement to determine the most efficient way to extract the requested data. This process is called optimizing the *SELECT* statement, and the component that performs this procedure is called the query optimizer.

The process of choosing one execution plan from several possible plans is called optimization. The query optimizer is one of the most important components of a SQL database system. While the query optimizer uses some overhead to analyze the query and choose a plan, this overhead is compensated several-fold when the query optimizer picks an efficient execution plan. For example, two construction companies can be given identical blueprints for a house. If one company spends a few days at the start to plan how it will build the house and the other company starts building without planning, the company that takes the time to plan its project will most likely finish first.

The query optimizer is important because it enables the database server to adjust dynamically to changing conditions in the database without requiring input from a programmer or from a database administrator. This process enables programmers to focus on describing the final result of the query. They can trust that the query optimizer will always build an efficient execution plan for the state of the database each time the statement is run.

Processing a *SELECT* Statement

The steps used to process a single *SELECT* statement referencing only local base tables (no views or remote tables) illustrate the basic process of executing most Transact-SQL statements. SQL Server uses the following steps to process a single *SELECT* statement:

1. The parser scans the *SELECT* statement and breaks it into logical units, such as keywords, expressions, operators, and identifiers.
2. A query tree, sometimes called a sequence tree, is built by describing the logical steps needed to transform the source data into the format needed by the result set.
3. The query optimizer analyzes all of the ways in which the source tables can be accessed and selects the series of steps that will return the result fastest while consuming the fewest resources. The query tree is updated to record this exact series of steps, and the final, optimized version of the query tree is called the execution plan.
4. The relational engine begins executing the execution plan. As steps that need data from the base tables are processed, the relational engine uses OLE DB to request the storage engine to pass up data from the row sets that are requested from the relational engine.
5. The relational engine processes the data returned from the storage engine into the format defined for the result set and returns the result set to the client.

Processing Other Statements

The basic steps described for processing a *SELECT* statement apply to other SQL statements as well, such as *INSERT*, *UPDATE*, and *DELETE*. *UPDATE* and *DELETE* statements both target the set of rows to be modified or deleted. The process of identifying these rows is the same process used to identify the source rows that contribute to the result set of a *SELECT* statement. The *UPDATE* and *INSERT* statements can both contain embedded *SELECT* statements that provide the data values to be updated or inserted.

Even DDL statements such as *CREATE PROCEDURE* or *ALTER TABLE* are ultimately resolved to a series of relational operations on the system catalog tables and sometimes (such as *ALTER TABLE* and *ADD COLUMN*) against the data tables.

Batches

A batch is a group of one or more Transact-SQL statements sent all at once from an application to SQL Server for execution. SQL Server compiles the statements of a batch into a single executable unit (called an execution plan). The statements in the execution plan are then executed one at a time.

A compile error, such as a syntax error, prevents the compilation of the execution plan so that none of the statements in the batch are executed. A run-time error, such as an arithmetic overflow or a constraint violation, has one of two effects:

- Most run-time errors stop the current statement and the statements that follow it in the batch.

- A few run-time errors, such as constraint violations, stop only the current statement. All of the remaining statements in the batch are executed.

  The statements executed before the one that encountered the run-time error are not affected. The only exception is if the batch is in a transaction and the error causes the transaction to be rolled back. In this case, any uncommitted data modifications made before the run-time error are rolled back.

For example, assume that there are 10 statements in a batch. If the fifth statement has a syntax error, none of the statements in the batch are executed. If the batch is compiled and the second statement fails while executing, the result of the first statement is not affected (because it has already been executed).

The following rules apply to batches:

- *CREATE DEFAULT*, *CREATE PROCEDURE*, *CREATE RULE*, *CREATE TRIGGER*, and *CREATE VIEW* statements cannot be combined with other statements in a batch. The *CREATE* statement must begin the batch. All other statements that follow in that batch will be interpreted as part of the definition of the first *CREATE* statement.

- A table cannot be altered and then the new columns referenced in the same batch.

- If an *EXECUTE* statement is the first statement in a batch, the *EXECUTE* keyword is not required. The EXECUTE keyword is required if the *EXECUTE* statement is not the first statement in the batch.

The GO Command

SQL Query Analyzer, the osql utility, and the isql utility use the GO command to signal the end of a batch. GO is not a Transact-SQL statement; rather, it simply signals to the utilities how many SQL statements should be included in a batch. In SQL Query Analyzer and osql, all of the Transact-SQL statements from one GO command to the next are put in the string sent to SQLExecDirect. In isql, all of the Transact-SQL statements between GO commands are placed into the command buffer before being executed.

Because a batch is compiled into a single execution plan, a batch must be logically complete. The execution plan created for one batch has no capacity to reference any variables declared in another batch. Comments must both start and end in the same batch.

The following example creates a view. Because *CREATE VIEW* must be the only statement in a batch, the GO commands are required to isolate the *CREATE VIEW* statement from the *USE* and *SELECT* statements around it.

```
USE pubs
GO
CREATE VIEW auth_titles
AS
SELECT *
FROM authors
GO
SELECT * FROM auth_titles
GO
```

Batch Processing

A batch is a collection of one or more SQL statements sent in one unit by the client. Each batch is compiled into a single execution plan. If the batch contains multiple SQL statements, all of the optimized steps needed to perform all of the statements are built into a single execution plan.

There are several ways to specify a batch:

- All of the SQL statements sent in a single execution unit from an application make up a single batch and generate a single execution plan.
- All of the statements in a stored procedure or trigger make up a single batch. Each stored procedure or trigger is compiled into a single execution plan.
- The string executed by an *EXECUTE* statement is a batch compiled into a single execution plan.
- The string executed by an *sp_executesql* system stored procedure is a batch compiled into a single execution plan.

If a batch sent from an application contains an *EXECUTE* statement, the execution plan for the executed string or stored procedure is performed separately from the execution plan containing the *EXECUTE* statement. The execution plan generated for the string executed by an *sp_executesql* stored procedure also remains separate from the execution plan for the batch containing the *sp_executesql* call.

If a statement in a batch invokes a trigger, the trigger execution plan executes separately from the original batch.

For example, a batch that contains the following four statements uses five execution plans:

- An *EXECUTE* statement executing a stored procedure
- An *sp_executesql* call executing a string
- An *EXECUTE* statement executing a string
- An *UPDATE* statement referencing a table that has an update trigger

Figure 2.12 illustrates how these four statements are processed.

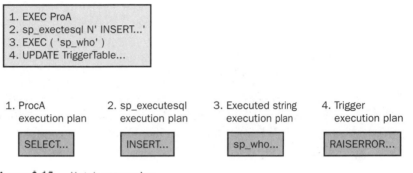

Figure 2.12.   Batch processing.

Stored Procedures and Triggers

A stored procedure is a group of Transact-SQL statements that is compiled one time and that can then be executed many times. This functionality increases performance when the stored procedure is executed because the Transact-SQL statements do not have to be recompiled.

A trigger is a special type of stored procedure that a user does not call directly. When the trigger is created, it is defined to execute when a specific type of data modification is made against a specific table or column.

A *CREATE PROCEDURE* or *CREATE TRIGGER* statement cannot span batches. In other words, a stored procedure or trigger is always created in a single batch and is compiled into an execution plan.

Stored Procedure and Trigger Execution

SQL Server 2000 stores only the source for stored procedures and triggers. When a stored procedure or trigger is first executed, the source is compiled into an execution plan. If the stored procedure or trigger is again executed before the execution plan is aged from memory, the relational engine detects the existing plan and reuses it. If the plan has aged out of memory, a new plan is built. This process is similar to the process that SQL Server 2000 follows for all SQL statements. The main performance advantage that stored procedures and triggers have in SQL Server 2000 is that their SQL statements are always the same; therefore, the relational engine matches them with any existing execution plans.

Stored procedures had a more pronounced performance advantage over other SQL statements in previous versions of SQL Server. Earlier versions of SQL Server did not attempt to reuse execution plans for batches that were not stored procedures or triggers. The only way to reuse execution plans was to encode the SQL statements in stored procedures.

The execution plan for stored procedures and triggers is executed separately from the execution plan for the batch that is calling the stored procedure or firing the trigger. This feature facilitates more frequent reuse of the stored procedure and trigger execution plans.

Stored procedures are discussed in more detail in Chapter 8, "Implementing Stored Procedures." Triggers are discussed in more detail in Chapter 9, "Implementing Triggers."

Transact-SQL Scripts

A script is a series of Transact-SQL statements stored in a file. The file can be used as input to SQL Query Analyzer or to the osql and isql utilities. The utilities then execute the SQL statements stored in the file.

Transact-SQL scripts have one or more batches. The GO command signals the end of a batch. If a Transact-SQL script does not have any GO commands, it is executed as a single batch.

You can use Transact-SQL scripts to perform the following tasks:

- Keeping a permanent copy of the steps used to create and populate the databases on your server (a backup mechanism)
- Transferring the statements from one computer to another (when necessary)
- Quickly educating new employees by enabling them to find problems in the code, to understand the code, or to change the code

Lesson Summary

SQL Server 2000 provides several methods for executing Transact-SQL statements. Processing a single SQL statement is the most basic way that SQL Server 2000 executes SQL statements. When a statement is processed, the database server analyzes the statement to determine the most efficient way to extract the requested data. The process of choosing one execution plan from several possible plans is called optimization. When processing a statement, SQL Server follows specific steps. SQL Server can process statements as a batch. A batch is a group of one or more Transact-SQL statements sent all at once from an application to SQL Server for execution. SQL Query Analyzer, the osql utility, and the isql utility use the GO command to signal the end of a batch. Each batch is compiled into a single execution plan. If the batch contains multiple SQL statements, all of the optimized steps needed to perform all of the statements are built into a single execution plan. A stored procedure is a group of Transact-SQL statements that are compiled one time and that can be executed many times. A trigger is a special type of stored procedure that a user does not call directly. SQL Server 2000 stores only the source for stored procedures and triggers. A script is a series of Transact-SQL statements stored in a file. The file can be used as input to SQL Query Analyzer or to the osql and isql utilities. The utilities then execute the SQL statements stored in the file.

Review

The following questions are intended to reinforce key information presented in this chapter. If you are unable to answer a question, review the appropriate lesson and then try the question again. You can find answers to these questions in the Appendix, "Questions and Answers."

1. In which window in SQL Query Analyzer can you enter and execute Transact-SQL statements?

2. How do you execute Transact-SQL statements and scripts in SQL Query Analyzer?

3. What type of information is displayed on the Execution Plan tab, the Trace tab, and the Statistics tab?

4. Which tool in SQL Query Analyzer enables you to control and monitor the execution of stored procedures?

5. What is Transact-SQL?

6. What are the three types of Transact-SQL statements that SQL Server supports?

7. What type of Transact-SQL statement is the *CREATE TABLE* statement?

8. What Transact-SQL element is an object in batches and scripts that can hold a data value?

9. Which Transact-SQL statements do you use to create, modify, and delete a user-defined function?

10. What are control-of-flow language elements?

11. What are some of the methods that SQL Server 2000 supports for executing Transact-SQL statements?

12. What are the differences among batches, stored procedures, and triggers?

C H A P T E R   3

Designing a SQL Server Database

About This Chapter

A SQL Server database consists of a collection of tables that contain data and other objects—including views, indexes, stored procedures, and triggers—that are defined so as to support activities performed with the data. The data stored in a database is usually related to a particular subject or process, such as a retailer's customer information or a manufacturer's sales information. This chapter introduces you to the process of creating a SQL Server database and describes the basic concepts of database design. This chapter also provides information about planning a database, identifying system requirements, and developing a logical data model.

Before You Begin

To complete the lessons in this chapter, you must have

- SQL Server 2000 Enterprise Edition installed on a Microsoft Windows 2000 Server computer.
- The ability to log on to the Windows 2000 Server computer and to SQL Server as the Windows 2000 administrator.
- Paper and a pen or pencil to complete part of the exercises.

Lesson 1: Introduction to Database Design

Before you can develop a logical data model—and subsequently create a database and the objects it contains—you should understand the fundamental concepts of database design. In addition, you should be familiar with the basic components of a database and how those components work together to provide efficient data storage and to provide access to those who require specific types of data, in specific formats, from the database. This lesson introduces you to the basic components of a database and the terminology that describes those components. The lesson then discusses normalization and entity relationships—two concepts that are integral to understanding relational database design.

After this lesson, you will be able to:

- Describe the main components of a relational database.
- Describe the process of normalization and normalize tables in a database design.
- Identify the relationships that exist between entities.

Estimated lesson time: 30 minutes

Components of a SQL Server Database

A SQL Server database consists of a collection of tables that store specific sets of structured data. A table (entity) contains a collection of rows (tuples) and columns (attributes). Each column in the table is designed to store a certain type of information (for example, dates, names, dollar amounts, or numbers). Tables have several types of controls (constraints, rules, triggers, defaults, and customized user data types) that ensure the validity of the data. Tables can have indexes (similar to those in books) that enable rows to be found quickly. You can add declarative referential integrity constraints to the tables to ensure consistency between interrelated data in different tables. A database can also store procedures that use Transact-SQL programming code to perform operations with the data in the database, such as storing views that provide customized access to table data.

For example, suppose that you create a database named MyCoDB to manage the data in your company. In the MyCoDB database, you create a table named Employees to store information about each employee, and the table contains columns named EmpID, LastName, FirstName, Dept, and Title. To ensure that no two employees share the same EmpID and that the Dept column contains only valid numbers for the departments in your company, you must add constraints to the table. Because you want to quickly find the data for an employee based on the employee's ID or last name, you define indexes. For each employee, you will have to add a row of data to the Employees table, so you create a stored procedure named AddEmployee that is customized to accept the data values for a new employee and that performs the operation of adding the row to the Employees table. You might need a departmental summary of employees, in which case you define a view named DeptEmps that combines data from the Departments and Employees tables and produces the output. Figure 3.1 shows the parts of the MyCoDB database.

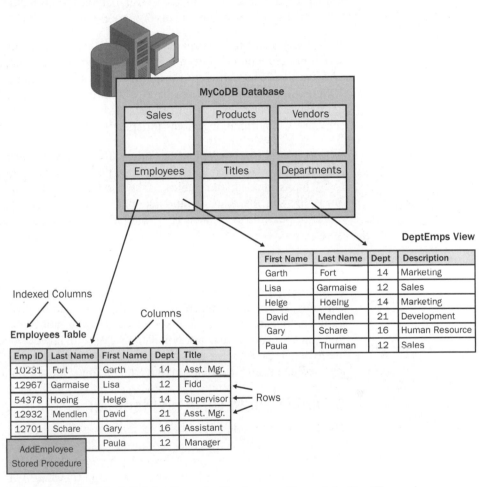

Figure 3.1. The MyCoDB database, the Employees table, and the DeptEmps view.

Normalizing a Database Design

Optimizing a database design includes the process of normalization. Normalizing a logical database design involves using formal methods to separate the data into multiple, related tables. Having a greater number of narrow tables (with fewer columns) is characteristic of a normalized database; having a few wide tables (with more columns) is characteristic of a denormalized database.

Reasonable normalization often improves performance. When useful indexes are available, the SQL Server 2000 query optimizer is efficient at selecting rapid, efficient joins between tables.

As normalization increases, so do the number and complexity of joins required to retrieve data. Too many complex relational joins between too many tables can hinder performance. Reasonable normalization should include few regularly executed queries that use joins involving more than four tables.

A database that is used primarily for decision support (as opposed to update-intensive transaction processing) might not have redundant updates and might be more understandable and efficient for queries if the design is not fully normalized. Nevertheless, data that is not normalized is a more common design problem in database applications than over-normalized data. Starting with a normalized design and then selectively denormalizing tables for specific reasons is a good strategy.

Sometimes the logical database design is already fixed, however, and total redesign is not feasible. But even then, it might be possible to normalize a large table selectively into several smaller tables. If the database is accessed through stored procedures, this schema change could take place without affecting applications. If not, it might be possible to create a view that hides the schema change from the applications.

Achieving a Well-Designed Database

In relational database design theory, normalization rules identify certain attributes that must be present or absent in a well-designed database. These rules can become quite complicated and go well beyond the scope of this book. There are a few rules that can help you achieve a sound database design, however. A table should have an identifier, it should store data for only a single type of entity, it should avoid nullable columns, and it should not have repeating values or columns.

A Table Should Have an Identifier

The fundamental rule of database design theory is that each table should have a unique row identifier, which is a column or a set of columns used to distinguish any single record from every other record in the table. Each table should have an ID column, and no two records can share the same ID value. The column (or columns) that serves as the unique row identifier for a table is the primary key of the table.

In Figure 3.2, the Employees table does not include a column that uniquely identifies each row within the table. Notice that the name David Mendlen appears twice. Because there is no unique identifier in this table, there is no way to easily distinguish one row from another. This situation could be worse if both employees worked in the same department and had the same job title.

Employees Table

Last Name	First Name	Dept ID	Title ID
Fort	Garth	17	43
Garmaise	Lisa	13	16
Hoeing	Helge	12	43
Mendlen	David	14	13
Schare	Gary	12	17
Thurman	Paula	13	16
Mendlen	David	17	12

Figure 3.2.   A table that has no unique identifier.

You can normalize the table by adding a column that uniquely identifies each row, as shown in Figure 3.3. Notice that each instance of David Mendlen has a unique EmpID value.

Employees Table

Emp ID	Last Name	First Name	Dept ID	Title ID
1067	Fort	Garth	17	43
2093	Garmaise	Lisa	13	16
2478	Hoeing	Helge	12	43
1224	Mendlen	David	14	13
1938	Schare	Gary	12	17
2066	Schare	Paula	13	16
2045	Mendlen	David	17	12

Figure 3.3.   A normalized table that has a unique identifier.

A Table Should Store Data for Only a Single Type of Entity

Attempting to store too much information in a table can prevent the efficient and reliable management of the data in the table. For example, in Figure 3.4, the Books table includes information about each book's publisher.

Books Table

BookID	Title	Publisher	PubCity	PubState	PubCountry
PC9999	Net Etiquette	Algodata Infosystems	Berkeley	CA	USA
PS2091	Is Anger the Enemy?	New Moon Books	Boston	MA	USA
BU1111	Cooking with Computers: Surreptitious Balance Sheets	Algodata Infosystems	Berkeley	CA	USA

Figure 3.4.   A table that includes title and publisher information.

Although it is possible to have columns that contain information for both the book and the publisher in the same table, this design leads to several problems. The publisher information must be added and stored redundantly for each book published by a given publisher. This information uses extra storage space in the database. If the address for the publisher changes, the change must be made for each book. Furthermore, if the last book for a publisher is removed from the Books table, the information for that publisher is lost.

In a normalized database, the information about books and publishers would be stored in at least two tables: one for book titles and one for publishers (as shown in Figure 3.5).

Books Table

BookID	Title	PubID
PC9999	Net Etiquette	1389
PS2091	Is Anger the Enemy?	736
BU1111	Cooking with Computers: Surreptitious Balance Sheets	1389

Publishers Table

BookID	Publisher	City	State	Country
PC9999	Algodata Infosystems	Berkeley	CA	USA
PS2091	New Moon Books	Boston	MA	USA
BU1111	Algodata Infosystems	Berkeley	CA	1389

Figure 3.5. A normalized database design that includes a table for book titles and a table for publisher information.

The information about the publisher now has to be entered only once and then linked to each book. If the publisher information changes, it must be changed in only one place, and the publisher information will be there even if the publisher has no books in the database.

A Table Should Avoid Nullable Columns

Tables can have columns defined to allow null values. A null value indicates that the record has no value for that attribute. Although it can be useful to allow null values in isolated cases, it is best to use them sparingly because they require special handling that increases the complexity of data operations. If you have a table that has several nullable columns and several of the rows have null values in the columns, you should consider placing these columns in another table linked to the primary table. Storing the data in two separate tables enables the primary table to be simple in design but capable of accommodating the occasional need for storing this information.

A Table Should Not Have Repeating Values or Columns

A table should not contain a list of values for a specific piece of information. For example, suppose that you want to track book titles and their authors. Although most books might have only one author, many of them might have two or more. If there is only one column in the Books table for the name of the author, this situation presents a problem. One solution is to store the name of both authors in the column, but showing a list of individual authors would then be difficult. Another solution is to change the structure of the table to add another column for the name of the second author, but this solution accommodates only two authors. Yet another column must be added if a book has three authors.

Figure 3.6 shows two methods of handling multiple authors per title.

Books Table

BookID	Title	Authors
PC9999	Net Etiquette	Charlene Locksley
PS2091	Is Anger the Enemy?	Ann Ringer, Albert Ringer
BU1111	Cooking with Computers: Surreptitious Balance Sheets	Michael O'Leary, Stearns MacFeather

Multiple Authors can be added to a single column for a particular row

BookID	Title	Author 1	Author 2	Author 3
PC9999	Net Etiquette	Charlene Locksley	NULL	NULL
PS2091	Is Anger the Enemy?	Ann Ringer	Albert Ringer	NULL
BU1111	Cooking with Computers: Surreptitious Balance Sheets	Michael O'Leary	Stearns MacFeather	NULL

One column is provided for each author - up to three authors per book

Figure 3.6. Two methods for structuring the Books table.

If you find that you need to store a list of values in a single column or if you have multiple columns for a single piece of data (Author1, Author2, and so on), you should consider placing the duplicated data in another table with a link to the primary table. In the case of the Books table, you could create an additional primary table for authors and then create a third table that matches books to authors and accommodates repeating values, as shown in Figure 3.7. This design enables any number of authors for a book without modifying the definition of the table and allocates no unused storage space for books that have a single author.

Books Table

BookID	Title	PubID
PC9999	Net Etiquette	1389
PS2091	Is Anger the Enemy?	736
BU1111	Cooking with Computers: Surreptitious Balance Sheets	1389

Authors Table

AuthID	LastName	FirstName
1786	Locksley	Charlene
2035	Ringer	Ann
3567	Ringer	Albert
2394	O'Leary	Michael
9391	MacFeather	Stearns

Authors Table

BookID	AuthID
PC9999	1786
PS2091	2035
BU1111	3567
PS2091	2394
BU1111	9391

Figure 3.7.   Three tables that store information about books and their authors.

Entity Relationships

In a relational database, relationships help to prevent redundant data. A relationship works by matching data in key columns—usually columns that have the same name in both tables. In most cases, the relationship matches the primary key from one table, which provides a unique identifier for each row with an entry in the foreign key in the other table. Primary keys and foreign keys are discussed in more detail in Chapter 5, "Implementing Data Integrity."

There are three types of relationships between tables: one-to-one, one-to-many, and many-to-many. The type of relationship depends on how the related columns are defined.

One-to-One Relationships

In a one-to-one relationship, a row in table A can have no more than one matching row in table B (and vice versa). A one-to-one relationship is created if both of the related columns are primary keys or have unique constraints. This type of relationship is not common, however, because information related in this way would usually be in one table.

One-to-Many Relationships

A one-to-many relationship is the most common type of relationship. In this type of relationship, a row in table A can have many matching rows in table B, but a row in table B can have only one matching row in table A. For example, the Publishers and Titles tables mentioned previously have a one-to-many relationship. Each publisher produces many titles, but each title comes from only one publisher. A one-to-many relationship is created if only one of the related columns is a primary key or has a unique constraint.

Many-to-Many Relationships

In a many-to-many relationship, a row in table A can have many matching rows in table B (and vice versa). You create such a relationship by defining a third table, called a junction table, whose primary key consists of the foreign keys from both table A and table B. In Figures 3-6 and 3-7, you saw how the author information could be separated into another table. The Books table and the Authors table have a many-to-many relationship. Each of these tables has a one-to-many relationship with the BookAuthor table, which serves as the junction table between the two primary tables.

Exercise 1: Exploring the Basic Concepts of Database Design

In this exercise, you will view the primary objects that are contained in a SQL Server database. You will then apply the principles of normalization to a database design and identify the relationships that exist between entities within a database. To perform this exercise, you should be logged into your Windows 2000 Server computer as Administrator. You will use SQL Query Analyzer and SQL Server Enterprise Manager for part of the exercise, and you will need paper and a pencil to complete the rest of the exercise.

▶ **To identify the main components of a SQL Server database**

1. Open SQL Query Analyzer and use Windows authentication to log on to SQL Server.

2. Open the Object Browser window if it is not already displayed.

   The Object Browser window displays a hierarchical tree of database objects contained in the instance of SQL Server that you are logged on to.

3. Review the list of database objects that appear in the tree.

   Notice that the Northwind and Pubs databases appear as objects in the tree. The tree also includes a list of common objects, such as aggregate functions and system data types.

4. Expand the Northwind node.

A list of object types appears. The list includes users tables, system tables, stored procedures, functions, and user-defined data types. Each category contains objects specific to the Northwind database.

5. Expand the Users Tables node.

A list of users tables in the Northwind database appears. Notice that each table object is preceded by the object owner (which, in this case, is dbo).

▶ **To view the contents of a table**

1. Right-click dbo.Categories, then click Open.

The Open Table window appears and displays the contents of the Categories table.

2. Review the columns and rows within the table.

What are the column names (attributes) in the Categories table, and how many rows of data are displayed?

3. Close the Open Table window.

4. Review each users' table object to determine the columns in each one. Be sure to close the Open Table window after you review that table. You can also review the system tables to view their attributes.

▶ **To use the sp_help system stored procedure to view table information**

1. In the Query window, execute the following Transact-SQL statement:

```
Use Northwind
GO
sp_help
```

2. A list of all objects in the Northwind database appears on the Grids tab of the Results pane.

Note After the result appears on the Grids tab, click within the Results pane. A second scroll bar will appear, and you can scroll through all of the objects in the database.

---

3. Close SQL Query Analyzer.

▶ **To normalize a database design**

1. Review the following table:

FirstName	LastName	City
Elizabeth	Boyle	Cleveland
Rob	Caron	Chicago

FirstName	LastName	City
Neil	Smith	Denver
Denise	Smith	Boston

2. Keeping in mind the table's design, apply the four basic rules that you should follow when designing a database. The rules are listed here for your convenience:
   - A table should have an identifier.
   - A table should store data for only a single type of entity.
   - A table should avoid nullable columns.
   - A table should not have repeating values or columns.

   Which rule is being violated in the Customers table?

3. Modify the table's design so that it adheres to the basic rules of normalization. Use your paper and pencil to draw the table and its data.

   How should you modify the data?

4. Review the following table:

CustID	FirstName	LastName	City	PurchaseType
101	Elizabeth	Boyle	Cleveland	Books, CDs
102	Rob	Caron	Chicago	Books, videos
103	Neil	Smith	Denver	CDs, videos, DVDs
104	Denise	Smith	Boston	Books

The PurchaseType column contains a list of the types of products that the customer has purchased.

5. Determine which rule or rules of normalization are being violated in the Customers table.

6. Modify the database design so that it adheres to the rules of normalization.

   How should you modify the current design?

7. Review the following table:

CustID	FirstName	LastName	City	Purchase	Manufacturer	ManContact
101	Elizabeth	Boyle	Cleveland	Spring candles	Pavlova, Ltd.	Ian Devling
102	Rob	Caron	Chicago	Sandalwood incense	Mayumi's	Mayumi Ohno
103	Neil	Smith	Denver	Sage	Pavlova, Ltd	Ian Devling
104	Denise	Smith	Boston	Hanging crystal	Leka Trading	Chandra Leka

8. Determine which rule or rules of normalization are being violated.

9. Modify the database design so that it adheres to the rules of normalization.

How should you modify the current design?

▶ **To generate a database diagram in SQL Server**

1. On the Start menu, point to Programs and then point to Microsoft SQL Server. Then, click Enterprise Manager.

SQL Server Enterprise Manager appears.

2. In the Tree tab, expand the Microsoft SQL Servers node, expand SQL Server Group, expand the node for your local computer, expand Databases, and then expand the Pubs database.

A list of object types in the Pubs database should now be displayed.

3. Right-click Diagrams, then click New Database Diagram.

The Create Database Diagram wizard appears.

4. Click Next.

The Select Tables To Be Added screen appears. The list of tables in the Pubs database appears in the left window.

5. Select the Add Selected Tables Automatically checkbox.

The How Many Levels Of Related Tables option becomes active.

6. Change the level in the How Many Levels Of Related Tables list box to 2.

7. Select the Authors table from the Available Tables list, then click Add.

The Authors table, TitleAuthor table, and Titles table are added to the Tables To Add To Diagram list.

8. Click Next.

The Completing The Create Database Diagram wizard screen appears.

9. Click Finish.

The diagram is generated and appears in a new window. The diagram includes the Authors table, the TitleAuthor table, and the Titles table.

▶ **To view entity relationships in a database diagram**

1. If the tables overlap, click the Arrange Tables button on the toolbar.

The tables should now be arranged so that you can see the relationships between them.

2. If necessary, click the Zoom button on the toolbar and select a size that would make the relationships easier to identify. Maximize the window if necessary.

3. View the connector that links the Authors table to the TitleAuthor table and the connector that links that Titles table to the TitleAuthor table.

The connector indicates that a relationship exists between the tables. Notice that there is no connector between the Author table and the Titles table because no direct relationship exists between the tables.

At one end of the connecter is a key, which indicates *one*. The other side of the connector is an infinity sign, which indicates *many*. These symbols tell you that a one-to-many relationship exists between the Authors table and the TitleAuthor table and that a one-to-many relationship exists between the Titles table and the TitleAuthor table.

What is the implied relationship between the Titles table and the Authors table?

What type of table is the TitleAuthor table (in terms of the implied relationship between Titles and Authors)?

4. Close the diagram window without saving the changes that you made, then close SQL Server Enterprise Manager.

Note   As an extra exercise, try creating diagrams for other users' tables within the Pubs database and for tables in the Northwind database. You can also try selecting levels greater than two in the How Many Levels Of Related Tables list box. Experiment with the different levels and tables.

Lesson Summary

A SQL Server database consists of a collection of tables that store a specific set of structured data. A table contains a collection of rows and columns. Each column in the table is designed to store a certain type of information (for example, dates, names, dollar amounts, or numbers). The logical design of the database, including the tables and the relationships between them, is the core of an optimized, relational database. Optimizing a database design includes the process of normalization. Normalizing a logical database design involves using formal methods to separate the data into multiple, related tables. As normalization increases, so do the number and complexity of joins that are required to retrieve data. Normalization rules identify certain attributes that must be present or absent in a well-designed database. Tables in a normalized database should have an identifier, should only store data for a single type of entity, should avoid nullable columns, and should not have repeating values or columns. You can create relationships between your tables in a database diagram to show how the columns in one table are linked to columns in another table. In a relational database, relationships help to prevent redundant data. A relationship works by matching data in key columns—usually columns that have the same name in both tables. There are three types of relationships between tables: one-to-one, one-to-many, and many-to-many. The type of relationship depends on how you define the related columns.

Lesson 2: Planning a SQL Server Database

When planning a SQL Server database, the design must take into consideration a number of factors, including database files and filegroups, transaction logs, the SQL Server installation and its operating environment, and security. This lesson discusses each of these considerations.

After this lesson, you will be able to:

- Describe many of the factors that you should take into consideration when planning a SQL Server database.

Estimated lesson time: 25 minutes

Files and Filegroups

To map a database, SQL Server 2000 uses a set of operating system files. All data and objects in the database, such as tables, stored procedures, triggers, and views, are stored within the following types of operating system files:

- **Primary.**   This file contains the startup information for the database and is used to store data. Every database has one primary data file.
- **Secondary.**   These files hold all of the data that does not fit into the primary data file. If the primary file can hold all of the data in the database, databases do not need to have secondary data files. Some databases might be large enough to need multiple secondary data files or to use secondary files on separate disk drives to spread data across multiple disks or to improve database performance.
- **Transaction Log.**   These files hold the log information used to recover the database. There must be at least one log file for each database.

A simple database can be created with one primary file that contains all data and objects and a log file that contains the transaction log information. Alternatively, a more complex database can be created with one primary file and five secondary files. The data and objects within the database spread across all six files, and four additional log files contain the transaction log information.

Filegroups group files together for administrative and data allocation/placement purposes. For example, three files (Data1.ndf, Data2.ndf, and Data3.ndf) can be created on three disk drives and assigned to the filegroup fgroup1. A table can then be created specifically on the filegroup fgroup1. Queries for data from the table will be spread across the three disks, thereby improving performance. The same performance improvement can be accomplished with a single file created on a redundant array of independent disks (RAID) stripe set. Files and filegroups, however, help to easily add new files to new disks. Additionally, if your database exceeds the maximum size for a single Windows NT file, you can use secondary data files to grow your database further.

Rules for Designing Files and Filegroups

When designing files and filegroups, you should adhere to the following rules:

- A file or filegroup cannot be used by more than one database. For example, the files sales.mdf and sales.ndf, which contain data and objects from the sales database, cannot be used by any other database.
- A file can be a member of only one filegroup.
- Data and transaction log information cannot be part of the same file or filegroup.
- Transaction log files are never part of a filegroup.

Default Filegroups

A database comprises a primary filegroup and any user-defined filegroups. The filegroup that contains the primary file is the primary filegroup. When a database is created, the primary filegroup contains the primary data file and any other files that are not put into another filegroup. All system tables are allocated in the primary filegroup. If the primary filegroup runs out of space, no new catalog information can be added to the system tables. The primary filegroup is filled only if autogrow is turned off or if all of the disks that are holding the files in the primary filegroup run out of space. If this situation happens, either turn autogrow back on or move other files off the disks to free more space.

User-defined filegroups are any filegroups that are specifically created by the user when he or she is first creating or later altering the database. If a user-defined filegroup fills up, only the users' tables specifically allocated to that filegroup would be affected.

At any time, exactly one filegroup is designated as the default filegroup. When objects are created in the database without specifying to which filegroup they belong, they are assigned to the default filegroup. The default filegroup must be large enough to hold any objects not allocated to a user-defined filegroup. Initially, the primary filegroup is the default filegroup.

The default filegroup can be changed by using the *ALTER DATABASE* statement. When you change the default filegroup, any objects that do not have a filegroup specified when they are created are allocated to the data files in the new default filegroup. Allocation for the system objects and tables, however, remains within the primary filegroup, not in the new default filegroup.

Changing the default filegroup prevents user objects that are not specifically created on a user-defined filegroup from competing with the system objects and tables for data space.

Recommendations

When implementing a database, you should try to adhere to the following guide-lines for using files and filegroups:

- Most databases will work well with a single data file and a single transaction log file.
- If you use multiple files, create a second filegroup for the additional files and make that filegroup the default filegroup. This way, the primary file will contain only system tables and objects.
- To maximize performance, you can create files or filegroups on as many different available local physical disks as possible and place objects that compete heavily for space in different filegroups.
- Use filegroups to enable the placement of objects on specific physical disks.
- Place different tables used in the same join queries in different filegroups. This procedure will improve performance due to parallel disk input/output (I/O) searching for joined data.
- Place heavily accessed tables and the non-clustered indexes belonging to those tables on different filegroups. This procedure will improve performance due to parallel I/O if the files are located on different physical disks.
- Do not place the transaction log file(s) on the same physical disk with the other files and filegroups.

Transaction Logs

A database in SQL Server 2000 has at least one data file and one transaction log file. Data and transaction log information is never mixed on the same file, and individual files are used by only one database.

SQL Server uses the transaction log of each database to recover transactions. The transaction log is a serial record of all modifications that have occurred in the database as well as the transactions that performed the modifications. The transaction log records the start of each transaction and records the changes to the data. This log has enough information to undo the modifications (if necessary later) made during each transaction. For some large operations, such as *CREATE INDEX*, the transaction log instead records the fact that the operation took place. The log grows continuously as logged operations occur in the database.

The transaction log records the allocation and deallocation of pages and the commit or rollback of each transaction. This feature enables SQL Server to either apply (roll forward) or back out (roll back) each transaction in the following ways:

- A transaction is rolled forward when you apply a transaction log. SQL Server copies the after image of every modification to the database or reruns statements such as *CREATE INDEX*. These actions are applied in the same sequence in which they originally occurred. At the end of this process, the database is in the same state that it was in at the time the transaction log was backed up.

■ A transaction is rolled back when you back out an incomplete transaction. SQL Server copies the before images of all modifications to the database since the *BEGIN TRANSACTION*. If it encounters transaction log records indicating that a *CREATE INDEX* was performed, it performs operations that logically reverse the statement. These before images and *CREATE INDEX* reversals are applied in the reverse of their original sequence.

At a checkpoint, SQL Server ensures that all transaction log records and database pages that were modified are written to disk. During each database's recovery process, which occurs when SQL Server is restarted, a transaction needs to be rolled forward only if it is not known whether all the transaction's data modifications were actually written from the SQL Server buffer cache to disk. Because a checkpoint forces all modified pages to disk, it represents the point at which the startup recovery must start rolling forward transactions. Because all pages modified before the checkpoint are guaranteed to be on disk, there is no need to roll forward anything done before the checkpoint.

Transaction log backups enable you to recover the database to a specific point in time (for example, prior to entering unwanted data) or to the point of failure. Transaction log backups should be a consideration in your media-recovery strategy.

Environment

Generally, the larger the database, the greater the hardware requirements. Database design should always take into consideration processor speeds, memory, and hard disk space and configuration. There are other determining factors, however: the number of concurrent users/sessions, transaction throughput, and the types of operations within the database. For example, a database containing infrequently updated school library data would generally have lower hardware requirements than a one-terabyte (TB) data warehouse containing frequently analyzed sales, product, and customer information for a large corporation. Aside from the disk storage requirements, more memory and faster processors would be needed for the data warehouse to cache more of the data in memory and to quickly process queries referencing large amounts of data.

Estimating the Size of a Database

When designing a database, you might need to estimate how big the database will be when it is filled with data. Estimating the size of the database can help you determine the hardware configuration that you will need to meet the following requirements:

■ Achieving the performance required by your applications

■ Ensuring the appropriate physical amount of disk space to store the data and indexes

Estimating the size of a database can also lead you to determine whether the database design needs refining. For example, you might determine that the estimated size of the database is too large to implement in your organization and that more normalization is required. Conversely, the estimated size might be smaller than expected, requiring you to denormalize the database to improve query performance.

To estimate the size of a database, estimate the size of each table individually and then add the values that you obtain. The size of a table depends on whether the table has indexes and, if so, what type of indexes. For more information about estimating the sizes of various types of tables, refer to SQL Server Books Online.

Physical Database Design

The I/O subsystem (storage engine) is a key component of any relational database. A successful database implementation usually requires careful planning in the early stages of your project. The storage engine of a relational database requires much of this planning, which includes the following:

- What type of disk hardware to use
- How to place your data onto the disks
- Which index design to use to improve query performance when accessing data
- How to set all configuration parameters appropriately for the database to perform well

SQL Server Installation

Although the installation of SQL Server is beyond the scope of this training kit, you should always take into consideration the following issues before performing an installation:

- Be sure that the computer meets the system requirements for SQL Server 2000.
- Back up your current installation of Microsoft SQL Server if you are installing SQL Server 2000 on the same computer.
- If you are installing a failover cluster, disable NetBIOS on all private network cards before running SQL Server Setup.
- Review all SQL Server installation options and be prepared to make the appropriate selections when running Setup.
- If you are using an operating system that has regional settings other than English (United States), or if you are customizing character sets or sort order settings, review topics on collation settings.

Before running SQL Server 2000 Setup, create one or more domain user accounts if you are installing SQL Server 2000 on a computer running Windows NT or Windows 2000 and want SQL Server 2000 to communicate with other clients and servers.

You should log on to the operating system under a user account that has local administrative permissions; otherwise, you should assign the appropriate permissions to the domain user account. Be sure to shut down all services dependent on SQL Server (including any service that uses ODBC, such as Internet Information Services, or IIS). In addition, shut down Windows NT Event Viewer and registry viewers (Regedit.exe or Regedt32.exe).

Security

A database must have a solid security system to control the activities that can be performed and to determine which information can be viewed and modified. A solid security system ensures the protection of data, regardless of how users gain access to the database.

Planning Security

A security plan identifies which users can see which data and perform which activities in the database. You should take the following steps to develop a security plan:

- List all of the items and activities in the database that must be controlled through security.
- Identify the individuals and groups in the company.
- Cross-reference the two lists to identify which users can see which sets of data and perform which activities in the database.

Security Levels

A user passes through two stages of security when working in SQL Server: authentication and authorization (permissions validation). The authentication stage identifies the user who is using a login account and verifies only the capability to connect to an instance of SQL Server. If authentication is successful, the user connects to an instance of SQL Server. The user then needs permissions to access databases on the server, which is done by granting access to an account in each database (mapped to the user login). The permissions validation stage controls the activities that the user is allowed to perform in the SQL Server database.

Authentication Modes

SQL Server can operate in one of two security (authentication) modes: Windows Authentication and Mixed mode. Windows Authentication mode enables a user to connect through a Windows NT 4.0 or Windows 2000 user account. Mixed mode (Windows Authentication and SQL Server Authentication) enables users to connect to an instance of SQL Server by using either Windows Authentication or SQL Server Authentication. Users who connect through a Windows NT 4.0 or Windows 2000 user account can make use of trusted connections in either Windows Authentication mode or Mixed mode.

Lesson Summary

When planning a SQL Server database, you must take into consideration database files and filegroups, transaction logs, the SQL Server installation and its operating environment, and security. All data and objects in the database are stored within primary, secondary, and transaction log files. Filegroups group files together for administrative and data allocation/placement purposes. The filegroup that contains the primary file is the primary filegroup. A database in SQL Server 2000 has at least one data file and one transaction log file. Data and transaction log information is never mixed on the same file, and individual files are used by only one database. SQL Server uses the transaction log of each database to recover transactions. Database design should always take into consideration processor speeds, memory, and hard disk space and configuration. There are other determining factors, however: the number of concurrent users/sessions, transaction throughput, and the types of operations within the database. When designing a database, you might need to estimate how big the database will be when it is filled with data. When installing SQL Server, you should take into consideration several issues. A database must have a solid security system to control the activities that can be performed and to determine which information can be viewed and modified. A security plan identifies which users can see which data and perform which activities in the database.

Lesson 3: Identifying System Requirements

Before creating a database, you must have a thorough understanding of the job that the database is expected to do. You can gain this understanding only by identifying specific types of information that are essential to developing an efficient database design. This lesson discusses the types of information that you must gather before you can begin creating a logical data model. To develop this model, you must identify the goals of your database project. You must also understand the type and amount of data with which you will be working, how you will use the data, and any business rules that apply to the new system that you are implementing.

After this lesson, you will be able to:

- Identify the goals and scope of a database development project.
- Identify the types of data that a database will manage, the current amount of data, the expected growth, and how it is currently managed.
- Identify how you will use the data in a new database.
- Identify any business rules that will be placed on the system.

Estimated lesson time: 35 minutes

The Process of Identifying System Requirements

The process of identifying system requirements includes a variety of steps. The number of steps included in this process, how these steps are defined, and the detail in which they are defined can vary greatly from resource to resource (with no one method necessarily being the most accurate). For the purpose of this training kit, however, this process has been divided into four primary tasks:

- Identifying system goals
- Identifying the amount and types of data
- Identifying how the data will be used
- Identifying business rules

You do not necessarily have to perform these tasks one at a time. For example, while identifying the amount and types of data, you might also find it useful to determine how the data will be used and what constraints should be placed on the data. Figure 3.8 illustrates the process of identifying system requirements.

Note   For additional information about designing relational database systems, refer to *Designing Relational Databases* (Microsoft Press, 1999) by Rebecca M. Riordan. This book provides a thorough discussion of database design and can be a valuable resource in building on the information in this training kit.

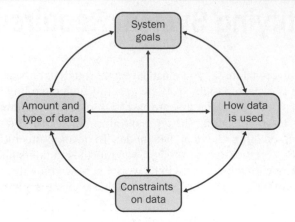

Figure 3.8. Identifying system requirements.

Identifying System Goals

Designing a database requires an understanding of the business functions that you want to model. As much as possible, your database design should accurately model the business. It is time-consuming to change the design of a database significantly once it has been implemented. A well-designed database also performs better. When designing a database, you must consider the purpose of the database and how it affects the design. In other words, you must determine the goals of the new system. Why are you creating this database?

The system goals are the reasons why you are implementing the new database. To create an effective database design, you must have thorough knowledge of the job that the database is expected to perform. Without this understanding, you cannot make informed decisions about how the database should be designed. The system goals are the reasons why the database is being developed.

Determining the system goals is not always a straightforward process. Most database development projects have many goals (both tangible and intangible), and trying to discover them can often take a fair amount of detective work. For ex ample, a manufacturing company might decide to automate its process for managing inventory. One of the company's stated goals for the project is "to make it easier to manage inventory." Your job is to take this intangible goal and try to determine the underlying tangible goal(s). Does the company want to speed up the process of managing inventory? Does it want to more accurately track inventory? Does it want to reduce costs? The intangible goal of "making it easier" might include all of these more tangible goals and more.

Although these goals are more tangible, they are still vague. Vague goals tend to be stated in general terms, such as "increase productivity" or "improve performance." As you go through the process of identifying goals, you must determine the degree to which these goals should be achieved. If the goal is to increase productivity, you should try to find out *from what to what*. Whenever possible, your goals should be directly measurable.

You should be aware, however, of the dangers of going overboard when measuring certain goals. Often, in order to determine a measurable goal, you must be able to establish an initial measurement. For example, if a goal of an inventory database is to improve accuracy, it might take a great deal of resources to study how much inaccuracy exists in the current process. A study of this sort could span years of inventory history and perhaps cost more to conduct than it would to design and implement the database. In cases such as these, it might be better to talk to managers and bookkeepers first to get a general sense of where the problems lie and what can be done to solve them. When determining the extent to which a base measurement should be studied, you should keep in mind the scale of the project and its practical application while always maintaining a sense of proportion.

Sometimes, intangible goals can be difficult to translate into more tangible goals. This situation is particularly true for goals that adopt popular marketing jargon, such as *product position*, *getting on the same page*, or *thinking out of the box*. For example, the stated goal might be something that seems to have no meaning or relevance: "We want the new system to show our clients that we're thinking out of the box and getting on the same page as them—in order to improve product positioning." In these cases, you must work closely with the organization to clearly define what its stated goal means.

After you have defined the initial goals for the new database, you can begin looking at the type and amount of data that the system will support. As you move forward with the database design process, however, be prepared to re-evaluate these goals. As projects move forward, management changes, business requirements change, and company expectations are revised. As a result, goals evolve—which means that the database design might need to be modified. You might also discover, as you dig deeper into the project, that some goals are unattainable or inappropriate. As new understandings and additional information continue to unfold, you must be prepared to act accordingly.

Identifying the Amount and Types of Data

The amount and types of data that your database will store can affect database performance and should be taken into consideration when creating your database. The amount of data will, of course, affect the size of your database, and the types of data are a factor in determining the kinds of constraints that are incorporated into the database design.

In many cases, determining the amount and types of data is a straightforward process because a system is already implemented and you are simply upgrading or replacing that system. In these situations, you can examine the body of data that already exists.

In those cases in which you are implementing a new system—or radically altering the existing one—your job might be a little more difficult because you might have to spend a fair amount of time determining what types of data will be stored and how much data there will be. You might need to interview key participants and collect copies of relevant documents and forms, such as customer statements, inventory lists, management reports, and any other documents that are currently being used.

Whatever the current system, you must determine the volume of data that the system will manage. When examining data volume, you should identify the actual amount of data and its growth pattern. For example, a warehouse might currently carry only a few thousand items, but it might be planning to add several hundred a day over the next few years to substantially increase how many items are kept on hand. Another warehouse might carry millions of items but it might plan to add only a few new items a day, never letting the inventory go much beyond its current capacity. The growth patterns for these two systems are very different, and as a result, the design approach will vary.

When looking at the types of data, you are basically trying to get a general sense of the categories of information that you will be storing and what details about the categories are necessary to store. This process will prepare you for mapping out the entities and attributes that you will incorporate into your database design. For example, if you are developing a database for a clothing retailer, the types of data might include information about customers who purchase products from the store. Customer information could include names, addresses, phone numbers, and even style preferences.

At this point in the design process, you do not have to get too specific about how data should be categorized or grouped. You are merely attempting to gain a general sense of the types of data involved and creating a centralized list for those types of data. When you actually begin to identify database objects, you will take the information you gather here and use it to develop a data model.

Identifying How the Data Will Be Used

As you gather system requirements, you must determine how information in your database will be used. The purpose of this step is to identify who will be using the data, the number of users who will be accessing the data, and the tasks they will be performing when they access that data.

When determining who will be using the data, you should think in terms of categories of users. For example, one category of users might be the general public (who accesses data through the Internet). You might also have another category of users who access data through the company's intranet. Some organizations might have only one type of user, while other organizations might have many types. In addition, there is no set minimum or maximum number of users that each category must contain. The only limitations are those dictated by hardware configurations and database design. One category might contain only one user, while another category might contain 100,000 users.

As you determine who will be using the data, you must also identify how many users in each category will be accessing the data. This estimate should include not only current numbers but projected figures, as well. In addition, you will have to define user concurrency. You should know how many people will be connected to the database at one time and how many might be trying to update the database at one time.

Once you have defined who your users are and how many there are, you must identify the tasks they will be performing when they access the database. For example, suppose a manufacturing company includes a category of users who take orders from customers. This order-taking group must be able to access and update customer information. In addition, it must be able to view inventory data in order to place these orders. The company might also include a category of users from human resources. The human resources group must be able to view and update employee information. By identifying these tasks, you can determine how the database will be accessed and how data will be viewed and manipulated. When you combine this information with the number and type of users, you will be able to implement a database design that serves the needs of everyone in the organization.

Identifying Business Rules of the System

By identifying the business rules, you are determining the constraints that govern how data and the system should be handled and protected. These constraints refer to more than the individual integrity applied to entity attributes. Business rules are much broader and incorporate all of the constraints on the system, including data integrity as well as system security. In other words, you are defining what each category of users can or cannot do.

Returning to the example of the manufacturing company, the order-taking group can access and update customer records and view inventory data. You might determine that these users should not be able to update inventory data and should not be able to view employee data, however. You might also determine that no customer records can be created without a full mailing address and phone number. Another constraint might be that any item added to a customer order should be removed from inventory. Business rules can include a wide spectrum of constraints, some pertaining to the system as a whole and others pertaining to specific types of data.

Exercise 2: Identifying the System Requirements for Your Database Design

In this exercise, you will review the following scenario. From the information in the scenario, you will identify the system requirements for a database design. You will be using this scenario and the result of this exercise in subsequent exercises. The end product will be a database that you have designed and implemented on your SQL Server computer. To complete this exercise, you need paper and a pencil. Because you need to save the result of this exercise, however, you might want to copy it into a Word processing file or text file.

Note   When designing a relational database system, your design specifications often include the applications that are necessary to access the data. For the purposes of this training kit, however, the exercises will focus on designing and implementing only the database component of the entire system.

Book Shop Scenario

The manager of a small book shop has asked you to design and implement a database that centralizes information so that it is easier and more efficient to manage inventory and track orders and sales. The shop handles rare and out-of-print books and tends to carry only a few thousand titles at any one time. Currently, the manager tracks all of the sales and inventory on paper. For each book, the manager records the title, author, publisher, publication date, edition, cost, suggested retail price, and a rating that indicates the condition of the book. Each book is assigned one of the following ratings: superb, excellent, good, fair, poor, or damaged. The manager would like to be able to add a description to each rating (just a couple of sentences), but the description should not be required. The information about each book must include the title, author, cost, suggested retail price, and rating. The publisher, publication date, and edition are not always available. If the year a book was published is available, the year will never be before 1600. And for purposes of the new database system, the publication date will never fall after the year 2099.

Because these books are rare, each title must be tracked individually—even if they are the same book (identical title, author, publisher, publication date, and edition). Currently, the manager assigns a unique ID to each book so that identical titles can be differentiated. This ID must be included with the book information. The book ID assigned by the manager is an eight-character ID made up of numbers and letters.

The manager also maintains limited information about each author whose books the store has carried or is carrying. The store might carry more than one book by an author, and sometimes more than one author will have written a book. The manager currently maintains information about approximately 2500 authors. The information includes the author's first name, last name, year of birth, and year of death (if applicable). The information must include—at the very least—the author's last name. The manager would like to include a brief description of each author, if available, when the author is added to the list. The description will usually be no longer than one or two sentences.

The bookstore has 12 employees (including the manager and assistant manager). The manager expects to hire an additional employee every year for the next few years. Both the manager and the assistant manager must be able to access and modify information about each employee as necessary. Employee information must include each employee's first name, last name, address, phone number, date of birth, hire date, and position in the store. Positions include Manager, Assistant Manager, Full Time Sales Clerk, and Part Time Sales Clerk. The manager might at some point want to add new job titles to the list or change existing ones and would eventually like to add a brief description of job duties to each title (at least, to some of the titles). An employee can hold only one position at any one time. No employee—other than the two managers—should have access to the employee information. The manager also likes to track how many books and which books each employee is selling.

The bookstore currently maintains information about customers. For each customer, the information includes the customer's first name, last name, telephone number, mailing address, books that the customer has purchased, and when the purchase was made. Because some customers do not like to give out personal information, only a first name or a last name is required. The manager currently has a list of about 2000 customers. Not all customers who are included in the list have bought books, although most have.

The manager maintains a record of sales by tracking each order from when a sales clerk takes the order to when the sale is complete. In some cases, such as for walk-in customers, these two events occur concurrently. Each order must include information about the book sold, the customer who bought the book, the salesperson who sold the book, the amount of the sale, and the date of the order. The order must also include the delivery or pickup date, which is added after the merchandise is actually picked up or delivered. An order is completed when a book has been paid for and picked up at the store or paid for and shipped to the customer. A book cannot be taken out of the store or shipped unless it is paid for. Each order includes the payment method and the status of the order. Payment methods include cash, check, and credit cards. The status of an order must be one of the following: (1) to be shipped, (2) customer will pick up, (3) shipped, or (4) picked up. An order can contain only one customer, salesperson, order date, delivery date, payment method, and order status; however, an order can contain one or more books.

Currently, orders are generated, tracked, and modified on paper order forms. The forms are used to make sure that the orders get shipped (if applicable) and to maintain a record of sales. Whenever a book is added to an order, it is removed from the inventory list. This process has been very tedious and not always very efficient. This situation can also lead to confusion and mistakes. Ideally, the manager would like sold books to remain in the list of books but be marked somehow to show that the book has been sold.

The store sells about 20 books a day. The store is open five days a week for about 10 hours a day. There are one to two salespeople working at the same time, and there are two sales counters where people pick up and pay for books and where salespeople process orders. At least one manager is in the store at one time.

The manager expects sales to increase by about 10 percent each year. As a result, the number of books on hand, authors, and customers should all increase at about the same rate.

In order to serve customers effectively, each employee must be able to access a centralized source of information about authors, books in stock, customers, and orders. Currently, employees access this information from index cards and lists. Often, these lists are not up to date, and errors are made. In addition, each employee should be able to create, track, and modify orders online, rather than having to maintain paper order forms. Only the managers should be able to modify information about authors, books, and customers, however.

Note   You can find a copy of this scenario in the BookstoreProject.doc file in the Chapter03\Exercise2 subfolder of the Training Kit Supplemental CD-ROM. You can use this copy to mark up and make notes as necessary to complete the steps in this exercise. This document will also come in handy for subsequent exercises.

▶ **To identify system goals**

1. Review the scenario. Do not try to memorize all the details; instead, try to get a general sense of what the project is trying to accomplish.
2. Write down the system goals that you can identify in the scenario.

   What are those goals?
3. Review each goal to determine whether it is measurable.

   Which goals are measurable?

▶ **To identify the amount and type of data**

1. Write down the categories of data that you can identify in this scenario.

   What categories of data can you identify?
2. For each category of data that you identified in Step 1, write down the type of information that you should track for each category.

   What types of information can you identify?
3. For each category of data that you identified in Step 1, write down the current amount of data for each category.

   What is the volume of data for each category?

4. For each category of data that you identified in Step 1, write down the expected growth pattern.

   What is the growth pattern for each category?

▶ **To identify how the data will be used**

1. Write down the categories of users that you can identify in this scenario.

   What are those categories of users?

2. For each category of user that you identified in Step 1, write down the number of users.

   What are the current number of users and the projected number of users in each category?

3. For each category of user that you identified in Step 1, write down the tasks that they will be performing.

   What tasks will each type of user be performing?

▶ **To identify business rules**

■ Write down the business rules that you can identify in this scenario.

   What are the business rules?

Lesson Summary

Before you can develop a data model, you must identify the goals of your database project, the type and amount of data that you will be working with, how the data will be used, and any business constraints that should exist on the data. You must consider the purpose of the database and how it affects the design. You should have a clear understanding of why you are creating this database. Another area of concern when identifying system requirements is the amount and types of data that your database will store. Whatever the current system, you must determine the volume of data that the system will manage. When examining data volume, you should determine the actual amount of data and its growth pattern. When looking at the types of data, you are basically trying to get a general sense of the categories of information you will be storing and what details about the categories are necessary to store. As you gather system requirements, you must identify who will be using the data, the number of users who will be accessing the data, and the tasks they will be performing when they access that data. By identifying the constraints on the data, you are determining the business rules that govern how data should be handled and protected. Business rules include data integrity as well as system security. They enable you to define what each category of users can and cannot do.

Lesson 4: Developing a Logical Data Model

Once you have identified the system requirements, you are ready to develop a logical data model. The data model is essentially an extension of the system requirements. When creating the data model, you are organizing the requirements into a logical representation of the database. The data model includes definitions of entities, their attributes, and entity constraints. The model also includes definitions of the relationships between entities and the constraints on those relationships. This lesson describes how to develop a data model by identifying the entities, their attributes and constraints, and their relationships.

After this lesson, you will be able to:
- Identify entities and their attributes.
- Identify relationships between entities.
- Define constraints on data.

Estimated lesson time: 35 minutes

Identifying Entities and Their Attributes

When you gather system requirements for a database design, one of the steps that you take is to define the types of data that the database will contain. These types of data can be separated into categories that represent a logical division of information. In most instances, each category translates to a table object within the database. Normally, there is a set of primary objects, and after they are identified, the related objects become more apparent.

For example, in the Pubs database, one of the primary objects is the Titles table. One of the objects related to the Titles table is the RoySched table, which provides information about the royalty schedules associated with each book. Another object is the TitleAuthor table, which matches authors to books.

By using the categories of data defined in the system requirements, you can start to create a map of the table objects within your new database. For example, suppose you are designing a database for a hotel's reservation system. During the process of gathering system requirements, you identify several categories of data, including rooms, guests, and reservations. As a result, you add tables to your database design that match each of these categories, as shown in Figure 3.9.

When identifying the business rules for this system, you determined that the hotel has eight types of rooms and that regular guests prefer a certain type of room. As a result, the Rooms table and the Guests table will each include a room type attribute. You decide to create a table for room types, as shown in Figure 3.10.

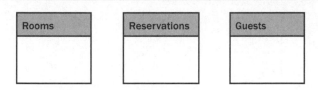

Figure 3.9.   The primary objects in a database design: the Rooms table, the Reservations table, and the Guests table.

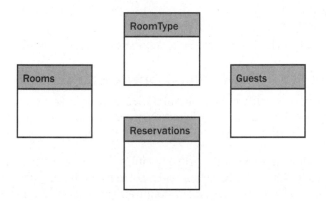

Figure 3.10.   The hotel's reservation database, which includes the RoomType table.

Now, the Rooms table and the Guests table can reference the RoomType table without having to repeat a room description for each room and each guest. In addition, as room types change, you can update the information in one location rather than having to update multiple tables and records.

Before you can complete the process of defining table objects within the database, you must define the relationships between the tables. Whenever you identify a many-to-many relationship, you will have to add a junction table. Relationships are discussed in more detail later in this lesson.

After you have defined all of the tables that you can define at this point, you can define the columns (attributes) for those tables. Again, you will be taking this information directly from the system requirements in which you identified which types of data should be included with each category of information.

Using the earlier hotel database example, suppose that you determined during the process of gathering system requirements that the Guests category of data should include information about the guests' first names, last names, addresses, telephone numbers, and room preferences. As a result, you plan to add columns to the Guests table for each of these types of information. You also plan to add a unique identifier for each guest, as is the case with any normalized entity. Figure 3.11 shows the Guests table with all of the columns that the table will contain.

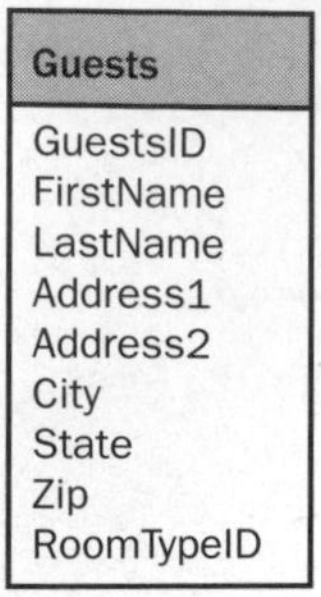

Figure 3.11.   The Guests table and its attributes.

Identifying Relationships Between Entities

After you have defined the tables and their columns, you should define the relationships between the tables. Through this process, you might discover that you need to modify the design that you have created to this point.

Start by choosing one of the primary tables and selecting the entities that have relationships to that table. Referring once more to the hotel database used in earlier examples, assume that the system requirements state that all reservations must include room and guest information. Rooms, guests, and reservations are the categories of data. As a result, you can deduce that a relationship exists between rooms and reservations and between guests and reservations. Figure 3.12 shows the relationships between these objects. A line connecting the two tables signifies a relationship. Notice that a relationship also exists between the Rooms table and the RoomType table and between the Guests table and the RoomType table.

Once you establish that a relationship exists between tables, you must define the type of relationship. In Figure 3.12, each relationship (line) is marked at each end (where it connects to the table) with the number 1 or with an infinity symbol (∞). The 1 refers to the *one* side of a relationship, and the infinity symbol refers to the *many* side of a relationship.

Note   Different sources use different types of notation to signify the types of relationships that exist between tables. For example, Database Designer in SQL Server uses a key symbol to mark the one side of a relationship and uses an infinity symbol to mark the many side of the relationship.

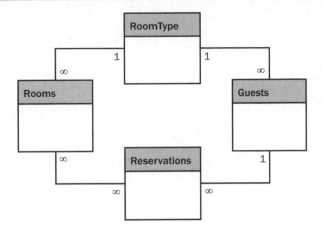

Figure 3.12.   The relationships that exist between tables in the hotel's reservation database.

To determine the types of relationships that exist between tables, you should look at the types of data that each table contains and the types of interchange between them. For example, a relationship exists between the Guests table and the Reservations table. The relationship exists because guests must be included in reservation information. According to the business rules, a guest can make one or more reservations, but each reservation record can include the name of only one guest, usually the person who is making the reservation. As a result, a one-to-many relationship exists between the two tables: one guest to many reservations.

A relationship also exists between the Reservations table and the Rooms table. According to the business rules, a reservation can be made for one or more rooms, and a room can be included in one or more reservations (on different dates). In this case, a many-to-many relationship exists: many reservations to many rooms. In a normalized database design, however, many-to-many relationships must be modified by adding a junction table and creating one-to-many relationships between each original table and the junction table, as shown in Figure 3.13.

Identifying Constraints on Data

At this point in the database design process, you should have the entities, their attributes, and the relationships between entities mapped. Now you must identify the constraints on the data that will be stored in your tables. Most of your work was already completed when you identified the business rules as you gathered system requirements. As stated previously, business rules include all constraints on a system, including data integrity and security. For this stage of the design process, your focus will be on the constraints specific to the data. You will take the data-related business rules and refine and organize them. You should try to organize the constraints based on the objects that you created in the database, and you should word them in a way that reflects those objects.

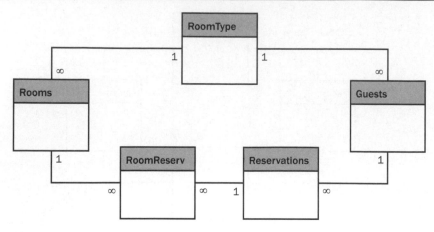

Figure 3.13.   The RoomReserv table as a junction table between the Rooms table and the Reservations table.

Returning again to the database design in Figure 3.13, suppose that one of the business rules is stated as follows: "A guest record can, but is not required to, include one of the predefined room type preferences but cannot include any other room type preference." When defining the data constraints, you should reference the relevant tables and columns and separate them so that they each focus on a single instruction:

- The RoomTypeID column in the Guests table does not require a value.
- A value other than NULL entered in the RoomTypeID column in the Guests table must be a value included in the RoomTypeID column in the RoomType table.
- A row in the Guests table can include only one value in the RoomTypeID column.

When possible, you should organize data constraints according to tables and their columns. In some cases, a constraint applies to the table as a whole, to more than one table, to a relationship between tables, or to data security. In these cases, try to organize the constraints in a way that is the most logical and the most relevant to the project you are working on. The goal of identifying the data constraints is to have a clear road map when creating database objects and their relationships and enforcing data integrity.

Exercise 3: Developing a Logical Data Model

In this exercise, you will take the steps necessary to create a logical data model. Much of this exercise involves drawing the tables, entities, and relationships that make up the database. Although you can use a drawing program such as Visio to create these objects, paper and a pencil are all that you really need. If you like, you can later transfer your model to a drawing program. In addition, you will need paper and a pencil to write the data constraints. You can also write these directly to a word processing document or a text document. Whatever method you choose, you should save the result for subsequent exercises. To perform this exercise, you will use the book shop scenario from Exercise 2 in Lesson 3.

▶ **To identify which tables to add to a database**

1. Refer to the system requirements that you developed for the book shop scenario and write down the categories of data.

   Each category represents one of the primary table objects in your database design.

2. Draw a table for each category of data. The tables should be large enough so that you can add column names. Place the tables in a way that enables you to draw relationships between the tables. You will be adding column names and defining relationships later in this exercise.

   Your drawing should include five tables.

3. Label each table with the name of one of the categories. For consistency, use the following labels for the table names: Books, Authors, Employees, Customers, and Orders.

   Your next step will be to identify any related tables. At this point, designing a database becomes a little more complicated. A good source to use for determining related tables is the list of business rules that you identified when you gathered the system requirements. Essentially, you are looking for subcategories of information or business rules that lead you to believe that additional tables are necessary. Remember, you can modify the database design as you identify relationships between tables and constraints on data.

4. Refer to the business rules in the system requirements. Notice that there are four subcategories of information: the condition of a book, the employee positions, the form of payment, and the order status.

5. Draw the four related tables to support the primary tables.

   For consistency, use the following names for your new tables: OrderStatus, FormOfPayment, Positions, and BookCondition.

6. Refer to the business rules in the system requirements. Notice that an order can contain more than one book.

7. Add one more table (BookOrders) that tracks the books ordered and the actual orders taken from customers.

   You should now have 10 tables.

▶ **To identify which columns to add to the tables**

1. Refer to the system requirements that you developed for the book shop scenario.

   For each category of data, you defined which information should be included with each category. This information makes up your columns.

2. Add column names to each table. Also remember that each row in a table must be uniquely identifiable, so the table might need an identifier. In addition, where column names are referring to information in a related table, you usually just need the identifier column from the related table. For example, the Orders table would include a StatusID column that references the OrderStatus table.

   For consistency, use the following labels for column names:

Table	Columns
Books	TitleID, AuthorID, Publisher, PubDate, Edition, Cost, SRP, ConditionID, Sold
BookCondition	ConditionID, ConditionName, Description
Authors	AuthorID, FirstName, LastName, YearBorn, YearDied, Description
Employees	EmployeeID, FirstName, LastName, Address1, Address2, City, State, Zip, Phone, DOB, HireDate, PositionID
Positions	PositionID, Title, JobDescrip
Customers	CustomerID, FirstName, LastName, Phone, Address1, Address2, City, State, Zip
Orders	OrderID, CustomerID, EmployeeID, Amount, OrderDate, DeliveryDate, PaymentID, StatusID
OrderStatus	StatusID, StatusDescrip
FormOfPayment	PaymentID, PaymentDescrip
BookOrders	OrderID, BookID

   Notice that the Employees table does not include a column for books purchased and dates of purchases. Because each customer can purchase more than one book, you would not include the information here. You could create a table to store this information, but it would be unnecessary because it would duplicate information that already exists in a database (information that can be derived through views or ad hoc queries).

► **To identify relationships between entities**

1. Determine what relationships exist between the Books table and other tables in the database. If necessary, refer to the book shop scenario and to the system requirements to help determine what relationships exist between objects.

   You are looking for direct relationships. For example, the Books table has a direct relationship with the BookCondition table. BookCondition data applies directly to Books data. In addition, Authors data is directly related to Book data (authors write books). There is also a direct relationship between Books data and BookOrders data (orders include the books being sold).

   Notice that there is no direct relationship between the Books table and the Orders table. The relationship between the two tables is indirect and is expressed through the BookOrders table.

2. For each table, draw a line from that table to any other table with which a relationship exists. You might find that you need to reposition some of your tables in order to more clearly show those relationships.

   Your database design should look similar to the schema in Figure 3.14.

3. Determine whether each relationship is one-to-one, one-to-many, or many-to-many. Write the number 1 at the *one* end of the relationship, and write the infinity (∞) symbol at the *many* end of the relationship.

   To determine the type of relationship, think in terms of the data associated with each object. For example, a relationship exists between employees and the orders that they generate. An employee can create many orders, but only one employee can create an order. Therefore, a one-to-many relationship exists between the Orders table and the Employees table (*one* employee can create *many* orders). The Employees table is on the one side of the relationship, and the Orders table is on the many side.

   Your database should now look similar to the schema in Figure 3.15.

4. Identify any many-to-many relationships in the database design.

   Which relationship is many-to-many?

5. Create a junction table named BookAuthors. The table should include the AuthorID column and the TitleID column.

6. Delete the relationship between the Books table and the Authors table, then delete the AuthorID column in the Books table.

   You are deleting the relationship between the two tables because a direct relationship no longer exists. Instead, an indirect relationship is created through the BookAuthors table. In addition, the AuthorID column is no longer necessary in the Books table because the book/author relationship is expressed in the BookAuthors table.

7. Draw the relationship between the Authors and BookAuthors tables and the relationship between the Books and BookAuthors tables.

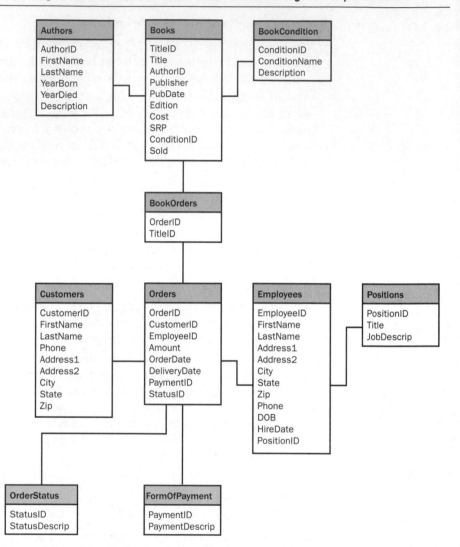

Figure 3.14.   Identifying the relationships between tables in the logical data model.

8. Determine the types of relationships that exist with the BookAuthors table. Your database design should now look similar to the schema in Figure 3.16.

▶ **To identify constraints on data**

1. On a piece of paper, write down the names of each table in your database design. Leave plenty of space between each table name to write the data constraints.

2. Review the business rule stating that book information must include the title, author, cost, suggested retail price, rating, and unique ID.

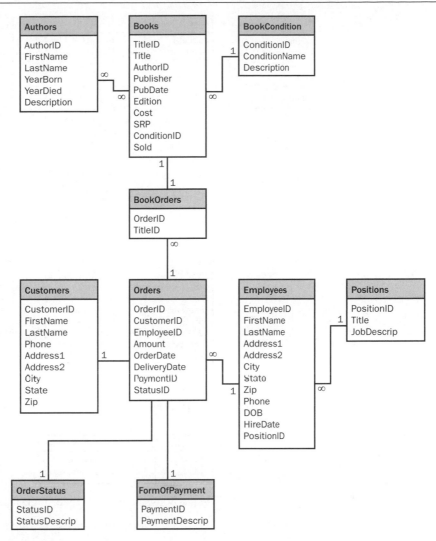

Figure 3.15. Identifying the types of relationships between tables in the logical data model.

3. Identify the object, if any, to which this business rule applies.

   To which object(s) does this business rule apply?

4. Under the Books table name and the BookAuthors table name, write the data constraints that you can derive from the business rule.

   What are the data constraints?

5. For each business rule, define the data constraints. Where applicable, write the constraints beneath the table name. If a constraint does not apply specifically to one table, write it in another space on your paper.

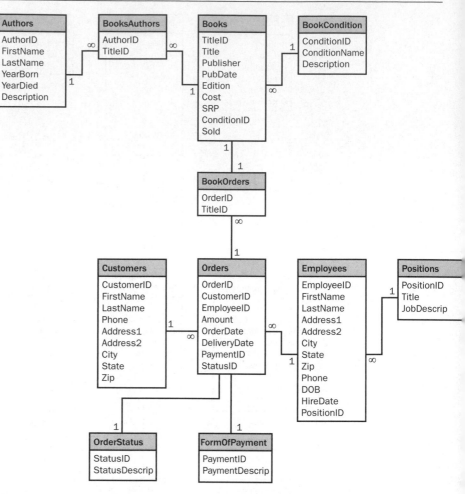

Figure 3.16.   Adding the BookAuthors table to the logical data model.

What are the data constraints for your database design?

6. Review the data constraints that you just created to ensure that every table and every column within those tables has some sort of rule associated with it.

Lesson Summary

The data model includes definitions of entities, their attributes, and entity constraints. The model also includes definitions of the relationships between entities and the constraints on those relationships. One of the first steps that you must take toward creating a data model is to identify the types of data that the database will contain. These types of data can be separated into categories that represent a logical division of information. In most instances, each category translates to a table object within the database. Once you have defined the tables and their columns, you should define the relationship between the tables. To determine the type of relationship that exists between tables, you should look at the types of data that each table contains and the types of interchanges between them. Once you determine the relationships between tables, you must identify the constraints on the data that will be stored in your tables. You should organize data constraints according to tables and their columns (when possible).

Review

The following questions are intended to reinforce key information presented in this chapter. If you are unable to answer a question, review the appropriate lesson and then try the question again. You can find answers to the questions in the Appendix, "Questions and Answers."

1. What does a SQL Server database consist of?
2. What is normalization?
3. What are the four basic rules that you should follow when normalizing a database design?
4. What are the three basic types of relationships that can exist between tables in the SQL Server database, and what are the basic differences between these types?
5. What are the three types of operating system files that SQL Server uses?
6. What two stages of security does a user pass through when working in SQL Server, and how do these stages differ?
7. What are the four primary tasks that you should perform when identifying the system requirements for a database design?
8. When determining the volume of data that the system will manage, you should identify what two types of information?
9. When determining how data will be used in a new system, you should identify what three types of information?
10. When you are gathering system requirements for a database design, one of the steps that you should take is to define the specific categories of data. What type of object within a database maps to these categories of information?
11. What task do you perform after determining that a relationship exists between two tables, and how do you perform that task?
12. What information within the system requirements should you base data constraints upon?

C H A P T E R   4

Implementing SQL Server Databases and Tables

About This Chapter

In Chapter 3, "Designing a SQL Server Database," you learned about the process of developing a logical database design. From this design, you can implement the physical database by creating the database object and the user table objects within the database. You can then view information about the database and tables, modify the objects as necessary, or delete them. This chapter explains how to create and manage a SQL Server database, then discusses data types and how to identify which ones to use when creating a table. Finally, the chapter describes how to create these tables by using the data type information and how to modify the tables after you have created them.

Before You Begin

To complete the lessons in this chapter, you must have:

- SQL Server 2000 Enterprise Edition installed on a Microsoft Windows 2000 Server computer.
- The ability to log on to the Windows 2000 Server computer and to SQL Server as the Windows 2000 Administrator.
- Paper and a pen or pencil to complete part of the exercises.
- Completed the exercises in Chapter 3, "Designing a SQL Server Database."

Lesson 1: Creating and Managing a SQL Server Database

The first step in implementing the physical database is to create the database object. By using the information that you obtained when you gathered the system requirements and the details that you identified in the logical database design, you can create the database object and define the database characteristics. You can also modify these characteristics after you have created the database object. This lesson discusses the process of creating the database object, the methods used to create the database, how to view information about the database and modify database characteristics, and how to delete a database.

After this lesson, you will be able to:

- Create a database object in SQL Server and define its characteristics.
- View information about the database and modify database characteristics.
- Delete a database object from SQL Server.

Estimated lesson time: 35 minutes

Creating a SQL Server Database

When creating a database, you must first determine the name of the database, its size, and the files and filegroups used to store it. You should consider several factors before creating your database:

- Permission to create a database defaults to members of the Sysadmin and Dbcreator fixed server roles, although permissions can be granted to other users.
- The user who creates the database becomes the owner of the database.
- A maximum of 32,767 databases can be created on a server.
- The name of the database must follow the rules for identifiers.

As stated earlier in this training kit, three types of files are used to store a database: primary files, which contain the startup information for the database; secondary files, which hold all of the data that does not fit into the primary data file; and the transaction log, which holds the log information used to recover the database. Every database has at least two files: a primary file and a transaction log file.

When you create a database, the files that make up the database fill with zeros to overwrite any existing data that previously deleted files left on the disk. Although it means that the files take longer to create, this action prevents the operating system from having to fill the files with zeros when data is written to the files for the first time during normal database operations. This feature improves the performance of day-to-day operations.

When you create the database, you should specify the maximum size that a file is permitted to grow. This specification prevents the file from growing, as data is added, until the disk space is exhausted.

SQL Server implements a new database in two steps:

1. SQL Server uses a copy of the Model database to initialize the new database and its metadata.
2. SQL Server then fills the rest of the database with empty pages (except for pages that have internal data recording how the space is used in the database).

Any user-defined objects in the Model database are copied to all newly created databases. You can add any objects to the Model database, such as tables, views, stored procedures, data types, and so on, to be included in all new databases. Each new database inherits the database option settings from the Model database.

Methods for Creating a SQL Server Database

SQL Server provides several methods that you can use to create a database: the Transact-SQL *CREATE DATABASE* statement, the console tree in SQL Server Enterprise Manager, and the Create Database Wizard, which you can access through SQL Server Enterprise Manager.

CREATE DATABASE Statement

You can use the *CREATE DATABASE* statement to create a database and the files that store the database. The *CREATE DATABASE* statement enables you to specify a number of parameters that define the characteristics of the database. For example, you can specify the maximum size to which a file can grow or the growth increment for that file. When a simple *CREATE DATABASE database_name* statement is specified with no additional parameters, the database is made the same size as the Model database. For specific information about the *CREATE DATABASE* statement and the parameters that you can define, refer to the Transact-SQL reference in SQL Server Books Online.

You can execute a *CREATE DATABASE* statement in SQL Query Analyzer. The following example creates a database called Products and specifies a single file. The file specified becomes the primary file, and a one-megabyte (MB) transaction log file is automatically created. Because neither megabytes nor kilobytes (KB) are specified in the SIZE parameter for the primary file, the primary file is allocated in megabytes. Because there is no file specification for the transaction log file, the transaction log file has no MAXSIZE and can grow to fill all available disk space:

```
USE master
GO
CREATE DATABASE Products
ON
(
   NAME = prods_dat,
   FILENAME = 'c:\program files\microsoft SQL server\mssql\data\prods.md
f',
   SIZE = 4,
   MAXSIZE = 10,
   FILEGROWTH = 1
)
GO
```

Enterprise Manager

You can create a database directly in SQL Server Enterprise Manager. To create a database in Enterprise Manager, expand the console tree for your server, right-click the Databases node, and click New Database. When the Database Properties dialog box appears, modify the default parameters as necessary in order to create the new database. Figure 4.1 shows the Database Properties dialog box when it first opens.

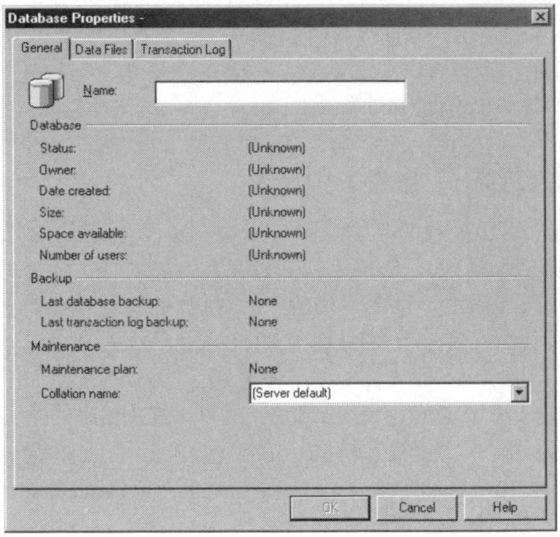

Figure 4.1.   The General tab of the Database Properties dialog box for a new database.

Create Database Wizard

The Create Database Wizard walks you through the steps necessary to create a new database. You can access the wizard by selecting Wizards from the Tools menu and then selecting Create Database Wizard. From there, complete the steps in the wizard. Figure 4.2 shows several options on the Name The Database And Specify Its Location screen that you can modify when you run the Create Database Wizard.

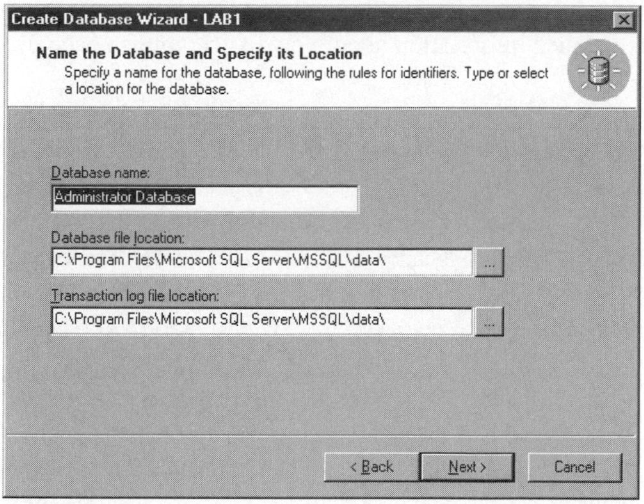

Figure 4.2.   The Name The Database And Specify Its Location screen of the Create Database Wizard.

Managing a SQL Server Database

Once you have created the new database in SQL Server, you can view information about the database, modify the characteristics of the database, or delete the database.

Viewing Information about a Database

You can view the definition of a database and its configuration settings when you are troubleshooting or considering making changes to a database. SQL Server provides several methods that you can use to view information about a database: the *sp_helpdb* system stored procedure, the *DATABASEPROPERTYEX* statement, and SQL Server Enterprise Manager.

The *sp_helpdb* system stored procedure reports information about a specified database or all databases. The *DATABASEPROPERTYEX* statement returns the current setting of the specified database option or property for the specified database. The statement returns only one property setting at a time. You can also use SQL Server Enterprise Manager to view database settings. In the console tree, open the Properties dialog box for the specific database. The Properties dialog box contains a number of tabs that include information about how the database is configured.

Modifying a Database

After you have created a database, you can modify the original definition. Before changes are made, however, it is sometimes necessary to take the database out of normal operating mode. The following table provides a list of many of the types of modifications that you can make to database properties. The table also lists the methods that you can use to complete these tasks. SQL Server Books Online provides detailed information about how to accomplish each of these tasks.

Type of Modification	Modification Methods
Increasing the size of a database	*ALTER DATABASE* statement
	The database properties in SQL Server Enterprise Manager
Changing the physical location of a database	*ALTER DATABASE* statement
Shrinking a database	*DBCC SHRINKDATABASE* statement
	The Shrink Database option in SQL Server Enterprise Manager, accessed through the node for the specific database
Setting a database to shrink automatically	The *sp_dboption* system stored procedure
	The database properties in SQL Server Enterprise Manager
Shrinking a database file	*DBCC SHRINKFILE* statement
Adding data or transaction log files	*ALTER DATABASE* statement
	The database properties in SQL Server Enterprise Manager
Deleting data or log files	*ALTER DATABASE* statement
	The database properties in SQL Server Enterprise Manager
Adding a filegroup to a database	*ALTER DATABASE* statement
	The database properties in SQL Server Enterprise Manager
Changing the default filegroup	*ALTER DATABASE* statement
Changing database options	*ALTER DATABASE* statement
	sp_dboption system stored procedure
	The database properties in SQL Server Enterprise Manager
Renaming a database	*sp_renamedb* system stored procedure
Changing the database owner	*sp_changedbowner* system stored procedure

Setting Database Options

You can set a number of database-level options that determine the characteristics of the database. Only the system administrator, database owner, and members of the Sysadmin and Dbcreator fixed server roles and db_owner fixed database roles can modify these options. These options are unique to each database and do not affect other databases. You can set the database options by using the SET clause of the

ALTER DATABASE statement, the *sp_dboption* system stored procedure, or in some cases, SQL Server Enterprise Manager.

Note   Server-wide settings are set by using the *sp_configure* system stored procedure or SQL Server Enterprise Manager. Specify connection-level settings by using *SET* statements.

After you set a database option, a checkpoint is automatically issued that causes the modification to take effect immediately.

SQL Server includes five categories of database options, which are described in the following table:

Option Type	Description
Auto options	Control certain automatic behaviors
Cursor options	Control cursor behavior and scope
Recovery options	Control the recovery model for the database
SQL options	Control American National Standards Institute (ANSI) compliance options
State options	Control whether the database is online or offline, who can connect to the database, and whether the database is in read-only mode (a termination clause can be used to control how connections are terminated when the database is transitioned from one state to another)

Deleting a SQL Server Database

You can delete a non-system database when it is no longer needed or if it is moved to another database or server. When a database is deleted, the files and their data are deleted from the disk on the server. When a database is deleted, it is permanently deleted and cannot be retrieved without using a previous backup. System databases (Msdb, Master, Model, and Tempdb) cannot be deleted.

The Master database should be backed up after a database is deleted, because deleting a database updates the system tables in the Master database. If the Master needs to be restored, any database that has been deleted since the last backup of the Master will still have references in the system tables and might generate error messages.

You can delete a database by using the *DROP DATABASE* statement or by deleting it from the console tree in SQL Server Enterprise Manager.

Exercise 1: Creating and Managing a Database

In this exercise, you will use the *CREATE DATABASE* statement to create a database that is based on the database design that you developed in Chapter 3, "Designing a SQL Server Database." You will then delete this database and use SQL Server Enterprise manager to re-create it. From there, you will view the database, expand the primary file, and add and delete a second data file. To perform this exercise, you should be logged into your Windows 2000 Server computer as Administrator. You will use SQL Query Analyzer and SQL Sèrver Enterprise Manager for the exercise.

▶ **To use the *CREATE DATABASE* statement to create a database**

1. Open SQL Query Analyzer and connect to your local server.

2. If the Object Browser window is open, close it.

   You should close the Object Browser window because later in the exercise, you will be deleting the database that you create. If the Object Browser window is open and the new database appears in the console tree, you cannot delete the database unless you close the window.

3. In the Editor pane of the Query window, enter the following Transact-SQL code:

```
USE master
GO
CREATE DATABASE BookShopDB
```

   This code creates a database with the name BookShopDB.

4. Directly beneath the code that you just entered in the Editor pane, enter the following code:

```
ON PRIMARY
(
    NAME = Bookshop_dat,
    FILENAME = 'C:\Program Files\Microsoft SQL Server\MSSQL\Data\Books
hop.mdf',
    SIZE = 4,
    MAXSIZE = 10,
    FILEGROWTH = 1
)
```

   This code defines the primary file. The logical name of the file, which is used in any Transact-SQL statements executed after the database is created, is Bookshop_dat. The path and filename used by the operating system is C:\Program Files\Microsoft SQL Server\MSSQL\Data\Bookshop.mdf. The initial size of the file is 4 MB, and the maximum size that the file can grow to is 10 MB. The growth increment of the file is 1 MB.

5. Directly beneath the code that you just entered in the Editor pane, enter the following code:

```
LOG ON
(
    NAME = bookshop_log,
    FILENAME = ' C:\Program Files\Microsoft SQL Server\MSSQL\Data\Book
shop.ldf',
    SIZE = 2,
    MAXSIZE = 5,
    FILEGROWTH = 1
)
GO
```

This code defines the log file. The logical name of the file, which is used in any Transact-SQL statements executed after the database is created, is Bookshop_log. The path and filename used by the operating system is C:\Program Files\Microsoft SQL Server\MSSQL\Data\Bookshop.ldf. The initial size of the file is 2 MB, and the maximum size that the file can grow to is 5 MB. The growth increment of the file is 1 MB.

6. Execute all of the code as one statement.

   The Messages tab of the Results pane displays two messages. One says that 4 MB of disk space has been allocated to the primary file, and the other says that 2 MB of disk space has been allocated to the transaction log file.

7. Leave SQL Query Analyzer open.

▶ **To view the BookShopDB database**

1. Open SQL Server Enterprise Manager.

2. Expand the console tree until the list of databases on your computer is displayed.

   The BookShopDB should be listed under the Databases node.

3. Right-click BookShopDB, then click Properties.

   The BookShopDB Properties window appears.

4. Click the Data Files tab.

   Notice that the bookshop_dat file is displayed in the Database Files list. The space allocated to the file is 4 MB. Also notice that the file growth is set to 1 MB and that the maximum file size is 10 MB.

5. Click the Transaction Log tab.

   Notice that the bookshop_log file is displayed in the Transaction Log Files list. The space allocated to the file is 2 MB. Also notice that the file growth is set to 1 MB and that the maximum file size is 5 MB.

6. Click the Transaction Log tab.

7. Review the remaining tabs in the BookShopDB Properties dialog box, then close the dialog box.

8. Close SQL Server Enterprise Manager.

▶ **To use the *DROP DATABASE* statement to drop a database**

1. Make SQL Query Analyzer active.

2. In the Editor pane, enter and execute the following code:

   ```
   DROP DATABASE bookshopdb
   ```

   The Messages tab of the Results pane displays two messages saying that the database files have been deleted.

3. Close SQL Query Analyzer.

▶ **To use SQL Server Enterprise Manager to create a database**

1. Open SQL Server Enterprise Manager.
2. Expand the console tree until the Databases node is displayed.
3. Right-click the Databases node, then click New Database.

   The Database Properties dialog box appears.
4. In the Name text box on the General tab, type **BookShopDB**.
5. Click the Data Files tab and review the settings on that tab.

   Notice that the initial size is 1 MB and that the file growth is unrestricted. For the purpose of this exercise, you do not need to change the default settings.
6. Click the Transaction Log tab and review the settings on that tab.

   You will notice that, like the primary data file, the initial size is 1 MB and the file growth is unrestricted. Again, you do not need to change the default settings for this exercise.
7. Click OK.
8. Expand the Database node.

   The BookShopDB has been added to the list of databases.

▶ **To view the BookShopDB database**

1. Right-click the BookShopDB node and select Properties.

   The BookShopDB Properties dialog box appears.
2. Review the Data Files tab and the Transaction Log tab.

   Notice that the database files have been configured with the default settings.
3. Review the other tabs.
4. Close the BookShopDB Properties dialog box.
5. In the console tree, expand the BookShopDB node.

   A list of object categories appears.
6. Review each category to determine which objects are created by default when you create a database.

▶ **To increase the size of a database**

1. Right-click the BookShopDB node and select Properties.

   The BookShopDB Properties dialog box appears.
2. Click the Data Files tab.
3. In the Space Allocated (MB) column of the BookShopDB_Data row (in the Database Files list), change that value from 1 MB to 2 MB.
4. Press Tab or click somewhere outside the cell where you just changed the value.

▶ **To add a data file to a database**

1. In the File Name column of the second row (in the Database Files list), type **Bookdata2**.
2. Press Tab or click somewhere outside the cell where you just entered the value.
   Default values are added to each column for the new row.
3. In the Space Allocated (MB) column of the Bookdata2 row (in the Database Files list), change that value from 1 MB to 2 MB.
4. Press Tab or click somewhere outside the cell where you just changed the value.

▶ **To delete a data file from a database**

1. Select the Bookdata2 row from the Database Files list.
2. Click the Delete button.
   The Bookdata2 file is deleted from the database.
3. Click OK.
4. Close SQL Server Enterprise Manager.

Lesson Summary

When creating a database, you must first determine the name of the database, its size, and the files and filegroups used to store it. When you create the database, you should specify the maximum size to which the file is permitted to grow. SQL Server provides several methods that you can use to create a database: the Transact-SQL *CREATE DATABASE* statement, the console tree in SQL Server Enterprise Manager, and the Create Database Wizard (which you can access through SQL Server Enterprise Manager). Once you have created the new database in SQL Server, you can view information about the database. SQL Server provides several methods that you can use to view information about a database: the *sp_helpdb* system stored procedure, the *DATABASEPROPERTYEX* statement, and SQL Server Enterprise Manager. After you have created a database, you can modify the original definition. Before changes are made, however, it is sometimes necessary to take the database out of normal operating mode. You can set a number of database-level options that determine the characteristics of the database. These options are unique to each database and do not affect other databases. You can delete a non-system database when it is no longer needed (or if it is moved to another database or server). When a database is deleted, the files and their data are deleted from the disk on the server. You can delete a database by using the *DROP DATABASE* statement or by deleting it from the console tree in SQL Server Enterprise Manager.

Lesson 2: Identifying Data Types

Once you have created a database, you can create the tables that store data within that database. In order to create those tables, however, you must first identify the data type that will be defined for each column. A *data type* is an attribute that specifies what type of data can be stored in a column, parameter, or variable. SQL Server provides a set of system-supplied data types. In addition, you can create user-defined data types that are based on the system-supplied data types. This lesson describes system-supplied data types and user-defined data types, and it explains how to identify which data type you should use when defining a column.

After this lesson, you will be able to:

- Describe system-defined data types.
- Explain how to create user-defined data types.
- Identify which data types to use when defining columns in tables.

Estimated lesson time: 25 minutes

System-Supplied Data Types

In SQL Server, each column has a related data type, which is an attribute that specifies the type of data (integer, character, monetary, and so on) that the object can hold. Certain objects other than columns also have an associated data type. The following objects have data types:

- Columns in tables and views
- Parameters in stored procedures
- Variables
- Transact-SQL functions that return one or more data values of a specific data type
- Stored procedures that have a return code (which always has an integer data type)

Assigning a data type to each column is one of the first steps to take toward designing a table. SQL Server supplies a set of system data types that define all of the types of data that you can use with SQL Server. You can use data types to enforce data integrity, because the data that is entered or changed must conform to the type specified in the original *CREATE TABLE* statement. For example, you cannot store someone's last name in a column defined with the *datetime* data type because a datetime column accepts only valid dates.

Assigning a data type to an object defines four attributes of the object:

- **The kind of data contained by the object.**   For example, the data might be character, integer, or binary.
- **The length of the stored value or its size.**   The lengths of *image*, *binary*, and *varbinary* data types are defined in bytes. The length of any of the numeric data types is the number of bytes required to hold the number of digits allowed for that data type. The lengths of character string and Unicode data types are defined in characters.
- **The precision of the number (numeric data types only).**   The precision is the number of digits that the number can contain. For example, a *smallint* object can hold a maximum of five digits; therefore, it has a precision of five.
- **The scale of the number (numeric data types only).**   The scale is the number of digits that can be stored to the right of the decimal point. For example, an *int* object cannot accept a decimal point and has a scale of zero. A money object can have a maximum of four digits to the right of the decimal point and has a scale of four.

The following table provides descriptions of the categories of data types that SQL Server supports and descriptions of the base data types that each category contains:

Category	Description	Base Data Type	Description
Binary	Binary data stores strings of bits. The data consists of hexadecimal numbers. For example, the decimal number 245 is hexadecimal F5.	*binary*	Data must have the same fixed length (up to 8 KB).
		varbinary	Data can vary in the number of hexadecimal digits (up to 8 KB).
		image	Data can be variable length and exceed 8 KB.
Character	Character data consists of any combination of letters, symbols, and numeric characters. For example, valid character data includes the "John928" and "(0*&(%B99nh jkJ" combinations.	*char*	Data must have same fixed length (up to 8 KB).
		varchar	Data can vary in the number of characters, but the length cannot exceed 8 KB.
		text	Data can be ASCII characters that exceed 8 KB.
Date and time	Date and time data consists of valid date or time combinations. There are no separate time and date data types for storing only times or only dates.	*datetime*	Date data should range from January 1, 1753 through December 31, 9999 (requires 8 bytes per value).

Category	Description	Base Data Type	Description
		smalldatetime	Date data should range from January 1, 1900 through June 6, 2079 (requires 4 bytes per value).
Decimal	Decimal data consists of data that is stored to the least-significant digit.	*decimal*	Data can be a maximum of 38 digits, all of which can be to the right of the decimal point. The data type stores an exact representation of the number; there is no approximation of the stored value.
		numeric	In SQL Server, the numeric data type is equivalent to the decimal data type.
Floating point	Approximate numeric (floating-point) data consists of data preserved as accurately as the binary numbering system can offer.	*float*	Data is a floating-point number from $-1.79E + 308$ through $1.79E + 308$.
		real	Data is a floating-point number from $-3.40E + 38$ through $3.40E + 38$.
Integer	Integer data consists of negative and positive whole numbers, such as -15, 0, 5, and 2,509.	*bigint*	Data is a number in the range from -2^{63} (-9223372036854775808) through $2^{63}-1$ (9223372036854775807). Storage size is 8 bytes.
		Int	Data is a number in the range from $-2,147,483,648$ through $2,147,483,647$ only (requires 4 bytes of storage per value).
		smallint	Data is a number in the range from $-32,768$ through $32,767$ only (requires 2 bytes of storage per value).
		tinyint	Data is a number in the range from zero through 255 only (requires 1 byte of storage per value).
Monetary	Monetary data represents positive or negative amounts of money.	*money*	Data is a monetary value in the range from $-922,337,203,685,477.5808$ through $+922,337,203,685,477.5807$ (requires 8 bytes to store value).
		smallmoney	Data is a monetary value in the range of $-214,748.3648$ through $214,748.3647$ (requires 4 bytes to store a value).

Category	Description	Base Data Type	Description
Special	Special data consists of data that does not fit in any of the other categories of data.	*Bit*	Data consists of either a 1 or a 0. Use the bit data type when representing TRUE or FALSE or YES or NO.
		cursor	This data type is used for variables or stored procedure OUTPUT parameters that contain a reference to a cursor. Any variables created with the cursor data type are nullable.
		timestamp	This data type is used to indicate the sequence of SQL Server activity on a row and is represented as an increasing number in a binary format.
		uniqueidentifier	Data consists of a 16-byte hexadecimal number indicating a globally unique identifier (GUID). The GUID is useful when a row must be unique among many other rows.
		SQL_variant	This data type stores values of various SQL Server–supported data types except *text, ntext, timestamp, image,* and *sql_variant.*
		Table	This data type is used to store a result set for later processing. The table data type can be used only to define local variables of type table or the return value of a user-defined function.
Unicode	Using Unicode data types, a column can store any character defined by the Unicode Standard, which includes all of the characters defined in the various character sets. Unicode data types take twice as much storage space as non-Unicode data types.	*nchar*	Data must have the same fixed length (up to 4000 Unicode characters).
		nvarchar	Data can vary in the number of Unicode characters (up to 4000).
		ntext	Data can exceed 4000 Unicode characters.

All data stored in SQL Server must be compatible with one of these base data types. The cursor data type is the only base data type that cannot be assigned to a table column. You can use this type only for variables and stored procedure parameters.

Several base data types have synonyms (for example, *rowversion* is a synonym for *timestamp*, and *national character varying* is a synonym for *nvarchar*).

User-Defined Data Types

User-defined data types are based on the system data types in SQL Server 2000. User-defined data types can be used when several tables must store the same type of data in a column and you must ensure that these columns have exactly the same data type, length, and nullability. For example, a user-defined data type called *postal_code* could be created based on the *char* data type.

When you create a user-defined data type, you must supply the following parameters:

- Name
- System data type upon which the new data type is based
- Nullability (whether the data type allows null values)

When nullability is not explicitly defined, it will be assigned based on the ANSI null default setting for the database or connection.

Note   If a user-defined data type is created in the Model database, it exists in all new user-defined databases. If the data type is created in a user-defined database, however, the data type exists only in that user-defined database.

You can create a user-defined data type by using the *sp_addtype* system stored procedure or by using SQL Server Enterprise Manager.

Exercise 2: Identifying Column Data Types

In this exercise, you will identify the data types that you should use in your column definitions when you create the tables for the database that you created in Exercise 1. The tables and columns will be based on the objects and data constraints that you identified when you developed your database design. You will use system-supplied base data types for your database, rather than user-defined data types. Each column must have a data type. To perform this exercise, you will need paper and a pencil to write down the data type for each column.

▶ **To review existing tables and columns and their data types**

1. Open SQL Server Enterprise Manager.
2. Expand the console tree until you can view the list of objects in the Northwind database.
3. Click the Tables node listed beneath the Northwind node.

   A list of tables in the Northwind database appears in the right pane.
4. Right-click the Employees table, then click Properties.

   The Table Properties - Employees dialog box appears.

5. Review the list of columns and their data types. Notice that the size of each column is listed to the right of the data type.

6. Close the Table Properties - Employees dialog box.

7. Right-click the Orders table, then click Properties.

   The Table Properties - Orders dialog box appears.

8. Review the list of columns and their data types.

   Close the Table Properties - Orders dialog box.

9. Open the properties for several other tables, and review the columns and data types.

▶ **To identify the data types for the Authors table**

1. Make a list of each column in the Authors table.

2. Refer to the data constraints that you identified for the Authors table when you developed your database design.

   Which data constraints apply to the AuthorID column of the Authors table?

   At this point, you are concerned only with identifying the data type for the AuthorID column and determining what type of data that column will contain. In this case, you want SQL Server to generate this ID automatically, which means that when you define this column, you will need to include the IDENTITY property in the definition. The IDENTITY property can be used only with an integer or decimal data type. You will learn more about defining this type of column in the next lesson.

   You decide to use an integer data type rather than decimal, because decimal is unnecessary as an ID. You also decide that the *smallint* data type is adequate to use to identify authors. The *smallint* data type supports an ID of up to 32,767— many more authors than you anticipate the database ever needing to store.

3. Write down **smallint** next to the AuthorID column.

4. Review the database design and the data constraints for the FirstName and LastName columns.

   What type of data will you store in this column?

   Because a name can vary in length but will not likely exceed 30 characters, you decide to use the *varchar(30)* data type for each column.

5. Review the database design and the data constraints for the YearBorn and YearDied columns.

   You can assume that each column will contain only four characters. Because date and time data types do not include a year-only data type, you decide to use a character data type.

   Which data type should you use for the YearBorn and YearDied columns?

6. Review the database design and the data constraints for the Description column.

   What type of data will you store in this column?

Because the description can vary in length but will not likely exceed 200 characters, you decide to use the *varchar(200)* data type for each column.

7. Be sure to write down the name of the correct data type next to the name of each column in the Authors table.

▶ **To identify the column data types for tables in the BookShopDB database**

1. Write down the name of each table in your database design.

2. Review the database design and the data constraints for each column in the tables.

3. Identify the data type for each column.

   What is the data type for each column in the BookShopDB tables?

   Tip   It is sometimes difficult to predict exactly what length you should use for data types such as *char* and *varchar*. You can get a feel for lengths, however, by reviewing column properties in existing databases, such as the Pubs database or the Northwind database.

   Note   Notice that the State column in the Customers table uses the *varchar(7)* data type rather than *char(2)*, as in the Employees table. Because a value is not required for this column in the Customers table, a default value of "unknown" will be defined (rather than permitting a null value). Nullability and default values are discussed in more detail in Lesson 3.

   ---

4. Be certain to write down the data type next to the name of each column (or at least record this information in some way). You will need this information for later exercises.

Lesson Summary

SQL Server provides a set of system-supplied data types, which are attributes that specify what type of data can be stored in a column, parameter, or variable. Assigning a data type to each column is one of the first steps to take toward designing a table. There are nine categories of data types: binary, character, date and time, decimal, floating point, integer, monetary, special, and Unicode. Each category contains a set of base data types. All data stored in SQL Server must be compatible with one of these base data types. You can also create user-defined data types that are based on the system-supplied data types. When a user-defined data type is created, you must supply a name for the data type, the system data type upon which the new data type is based, and nullability (whether the data type allows null values). You can create a user-defined data type by using the *sp_addtype* system stored procedure or by using SQL Server Enterprise Manager.

Lesson 3: Creating and Managing Tables

After you have created the database and identified the data types, you are ready to create the table objects that store the data within the database. When you are creating a table, the table definition should include, at the very least, the table name, the column names, the data types (and lengths, if required), and whether a column accepts NULL values. You can configure other properties at a later time, although the more properties that you configure when you create the table, the more efficient the overall process becomes. In this lesson, you will learn how to create tables, including how to specify nullability, generate column values, and define default column values. You will also learn how to view information about the table object, modify table characteristics, and delete table objects from the database.

- After this lesson, you will be able to:
- Create table objects in a SQL Server database and define their attributes.
- View information about table objects and modify table characteristics.
- Delete table objects from a SQL Server database.
- Estimated lesson time: 35 minutes

Creating Tables in a SQL Server Database

A table is a collection of data about a specific entity, such as customers, orders, or inventory. A table contains a set of columns. Each column represents an attribute of the table's data. For example, the order date might be an attribute of the orders entity. Each instance of data in a table is represented as a single record or row (sometimes referred to as a tuple).

At this point in the database development process, you should have all of the information you need to create the table in your database. Ideally, you would define everything you need in your table at one time, including PRIMARY KEY constraints as well as other constraints. For the purposes of this training kit, however, you will first learn how to create only the basic table (table name, columns, data types, nullability, and column values, where appropriate).

Determining Column Nullability

The nullability of a column determines whether the rows in the table can contain a null value for that column. A null value is not the same as zero, blank, or a zero-length character string (such as " "). Null means that no entry has been made. The presence of a null value usually implies that the value is either unknown or undefined. For example, a null value in the Price column of the Titles table of the Pubs database does not mean that the book has no price; instead, null means that the price is unknown or has not been set.

In general, avoid permitting null values because they incur more complexity in queries and updates and because they cannot be used with some column options, such as PRIMARY KEY constraints. Comparisons between two null values, or between a null value and any other value, return an unknown value because the value of each NULL is unknown. Null values cannot be used for information required to distinguish one row from another row in a table. In addition, eliminating null values when performing calculations can be important because certain calculations (such as average) can be inaccurate if NULL columns are included. If you need to create a column in which values are unknown, you can often define a default value for that column. For example, the Phone column in the Authors table of the Pubs database does not permit null values. The column does include a default value of UNKNOWN, however. If the phone number for the author is not added to the row for that author, the value in the Phone column will be UNKNOWN. Defining default values will be discussed in more detail later in this lesson.

If a row is inserted but no value is included for a column that allows null values, SQL Server supplies the null value (unless a default definition or object exists). A column defined with the keyword NULL also accepts an explicit entry of null from the user, no matter what data type it is or whether it has a default associated with it. The null value should not be placed within quotation marks, because it will be interpreted as a character string rather than the null value.

Specifying a column as not permitting null values can help maintain data integrity by ensuring that the column contains data in every row. If null values are not allowed, the user who is entering data in the table must enter a value in the column or the table row cannot be accepted into the database.

Note   Columns defined with a PRIMARY KEY constraint or IDENTITY property cannot allow null values.

You define the nullability of a column when you define the column, either when you create a table or modify a table. Whether you define columns that allow or do not allow null values, you should always use the NULL or NOT NULL keywords in every column definition because of the complexities of how null is handled in SQL Server. The NULL keyword is used if null values are allowed in the column, and the NOT NULL keywords are used if null values are not allowed.

The following example uses the *CREATE TABLE* statement to create the Employee table. The Emp_ID column and the LastName column do not allow null values, but the FirstName column does allow null values:

```
CREATE TABLE Employees
(
Emp_ID char(4) NOT NULL,
FirstName varchar(30) NULL,
LastName varchar(30) NOT NULL
)
```

Defining Default Values

Each column in a record must contain a value (even if that value is null). There are situations in which you need to load a row of data into a table but you do not know the value for a column (or the value does not yet exist). If the column allows null values, you can load the row with a null value. Because nullable columns might not be desirable, a better solution can be to define (where appropriate) a DEFAULT definition for the column. For example, it is common to specify zero as the default for numeric columns or N/A as the default for string columns when no value is specified.

Note   A DEFAULT definition in a *CREATE TABLE* statement is considered a type of constraint although it does not really enforce anything. Although constraints are discussed in detail in Chapter 5, "Implementing Data Integrity," DEFAULT definitions are discussed here to provide an alternative to defining columns that allow null values.

When you load a row into a table with a default definition for a column, you implicitly instruct SQL Server to load a default value in the column when you do not specify a value for the column.

If a column does not allow null values and does not have a default definition, you must specify a value for the column explicitly or SQL Server will return an error indicating that the column does not allow null values.

You can create a default definition in one of two ways:

- By creating the default definition when you create the table (as part of the table definition)
- By adding the default to an existing table (each column in a table can contain a single default definition)

The following example uses the *CREATE TABLE* statement to create the Employees table. None of the three columns allow null values; however, the FirstName column does provide for the possibility of an unknown first name by adding a default definition to the column definition. The *CREATE TABLE* statement uses the DEFAULT keyword to define the default value.

```
CREATE TABLE Employees
(
Emp_ID char(4) NOT NULL,
FirstName varchar(30) NOT NULL DEFAULT 'unknown',
LastName varchar(30) NOT NULL
)
```

You can modify or delete an existing default definition. For example, you can modify the value inserted in a column when no value is entered.

Note   When using Transact-SQL to modify a default definition, you must first delete the existing DEFAULT definition and then re-create it with the new definition.

DEFAULT definitions cannot be created on columns defined with any of the following:

- A *timestamp* data type
- An IDENTITY or ROWGUIDCOL property
- An existing default definition or default object

Note   The default value must be compatible with the data type of the column to which the DEFAULT definition applies. For example, the default value for an *int* column must be an integer number, not a character string.

When a DEFAULT definition is added to an existing column in a table, SQL Server (by default) applies the new default only to new rows of data added to the table. Existing data inserted by using the previous default definition is unaffected. When adding a new column to an existing table, however, you can specify for SQL Server to insert the default value (specified by the default definition) rather than a null value into the new column for the existing rows in the table.

Autonumbering and Identifier Columns

For each table, you can create a single identifier column containing system-generated sequential values that uniquely identify each row within the table. For example, an identifier column can generate unique customer receipt numbers for an application automatically as rows are inserted into the table. Identifier columns usually contain values unique within the table in which they are defined. In other words, other tables containing identifier columns can contain the same identity values used by another table. This situation is usually not a problem, however, because the identifier values are typically used only within the context of a single table, and the identifier columns do not relate to other identifier columns in other tables.

A single, globally unique identifier column can also be created for each table containing values that are unique across all networked computers in the world. A column guaranteed to contain globally unique values is often useful when similar data from multiple database systems must be merged (for example, in a customer billing system with data located in various company subsidiaries around the world). When the data is merged into the central site for consolidation and reporting, using globally unique values prevents customers in different countries from having the same billing number or customer ID. SQL Server uses globally unique identifier columns for merge replication to ensure that rows are uniquely identified across multiple copies of the table.

Creating Identifier Columns

Only one identifier column and one globally unique identifier column can be created for each table.

IDENTITY Property

Identifier columns can be implemented by using the IDENTITY property, which enables the application developer to specify both an identity number for the first row inserted into the table (Identity Seed property) and an increment (Identity Increment property) to be added to the seed in order to determine successive identity numbers. When inserting values into a table with an identifier column, SQL Server automatically generates the next identity value by adding the increment to the seed.

When you use the IDENTITY property to define an identifier column, consider the following:

- A table can have only one column defined with the IDENTITY property, and that column must be defined by using the *decimal*, *int*, *numeric*, *smallint*, *bigint*, or *tinyint* data type.
- The seed and increment can be specified. The default value for both is 1.
- The identifier column must not allow null values and must not contain a DEFAULT definition or object.
- The column can be referenced in a select list by using the IDENTITYCOL keyword after the IDENTITY property has been set.
- The *OBJECTPROPERTY* function can be used to determine whether a table has an IDENTITY column, and the *COLUMNPROPERTY* function can be used to determine the name of the IDENTITY column.

The following example uses the Transact-SQL *CREATE TABLE* statement to create the Employees table. Neither column allows null values. In addition, the Emp_ID column is an identity column. The seed value is 101, and the increment value is 1:

```
CREATE TABLE Employees
(
Emp_ID SMALLINT IDENTITY(101,1) NOT NULL,
EmpName VARCHAR(50) NOT NULL
)
```

Note   If an identifier column exists for a table that has frequent deletions, gaps can occur between identity values. Deleted identity values are not reused. To avoid such gaps, do not use the IDENTITY property. Instead, you can create a trigger that determines a new identifier value (based on existing values in the identifier column) as rows are inserted.

Globally Unique Identifiers

Although the IDENTITY property automates row numbering within one table, separate tables—each of which have their own identifier columns—can generate the same values. The IDENTITY property is guaranteed to be unique only for the table in which it is used. If an application must generate an identifier column that is unique across the entire database (or across every database on every networked computer in the world), use the ROWGUIDCOL property, the *uniqueidentifier* data type, and the *NEWID* function.

When you use the ROWGUIDCOL property to define a globally unique identifier column, consider the following:

- A table can have only one ROWGUIDCOL column, and that column must be defined by using the *uniqueidentifier* data type.
- SQL Server does not automatically generate values for the column. To insert a globally unique value, create a DEFAULT definition on the column that uses the *NEWID* function to generate a globally unique value.
- The column can be referenced in a select list by using the ROWGUIDCOL keyword after the ROWGUIDCOL property is set. This function is similar to the way in which you can reference an IDENTITY column by using the IDENTITYCOL keyword.
- The *OBJECTPROPERTY* function can be used to determine whether a table has a ROWGUIDCOL column, and the *COLUMNPROPERTY* function can be used to determine the name of the ROWGUIDCOL column.
- Because the ROWGUIDCOL property does not enforce uniqueness, the UNIQUE constraint should be used to ensure that unique values are inserted into the ROWGUIDCOL column.

The following example uses the *CREATE TABLE* statement to create the Employees table. The Emp_ID column automatically generates a GUID for each new row added to the table:

```
CREATE TABLE Employees
(
Emp_ID UNIQUEIDENTIFIER DEFAULT NEWID() NOT NULL,
EmpName VARCHAR(60) NOT NULL
)
```

Methods for Creating a Table

SQL Server provides several methods that you can use to create a table: the Transact-SQL *CREATE TABLE* statement, the console tree in SQL Server Enterprise Manager, and Database Designer (which you access through SQL Server Enterprise Manager).

CREATE TABLE Statement

You can use the *CREATE TABLE* statement to create a table within a SQL Server database. When you use this statement, you must define, at a minimum, the table name, the columns, and the data types (and their values, if applicable). The following example illustrates how to create a basic table:

```
CREATE TABLE Customers
(
CustID char(4),
CustName varchar(40)
)
```

In addition to the basic table elements (table name, columns, and data types), the *CREATE TABLE* statement also enables you to define a number of other properties. For example, you can specify the filegroup on which the table is stored, or you can define constraints that apply to individual columns or to the table as a whole. For a complete description of the *CREATE TABLE* statement, refer to the Transact-SQL reference in SQL Server Books Online.

Enterprise Manager

You can create tables directly in SQL Server Enterprise Manager. To create a table in an existing database, expand the console tree until the database is displayed, expand the database, right-click the Tables node, and then click New Table. When the New Table window appears, fill in the necessary information to define the table, as shown in Figure 4.3.

Database Designer

You can use Database Designer in SQL Server Enterprise Manager to add a table to your database diagram, to edit its structure, or to relate it to other tables in your diagram. You can either add existing database tables to a diagram or insert a new table that has not yet been defined in the database. Alternatively, you can use Table Designer to create a table or modify an existing table. *Table Designer* is a visual tool that enables you to design and visualize a single table in a database to which you are connected.

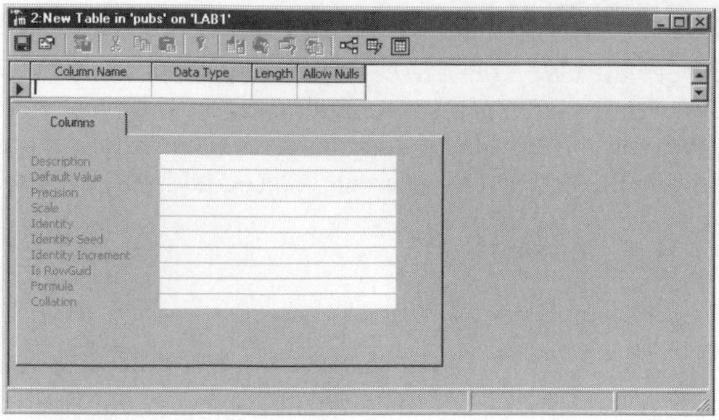

Figure 4.3.   The New Table window in SQL Server Enterprise Manager.

Managing Tables in a SQL Server Database

Once you have created a table in a SQL Server database, you can view information about the table, modify the characteristics of the table, or delete the table from the database.

Viewing Information about Tables

After you have created the tables in a database, you might need to find information about the table properties (for example, the name or data type of a column, the nature of its indexes, and so on). You can also display the dependencies of the table to determine which objects, such as views, stored procedures, and triggers, depend on the table. If you make any changes to the table, dependent objects might be affected.

SQL Server includes several methods for viewing table characteristics and dependencies:

- To view the definition of a table, use the *sp_help system* stored procedure or use SQL Server Enterprise Manager to view the table properties.
- To view the dependencies of a table, use the *sp_depends* system stored procedure or use the Display Dependencies option in SQL Server Enterprise Manager.
- To view column properties, use the *COLUMNPROPERTY* statement to return information about a column or procedure parameter.

Modifying Tables in a SQL Server Database

After a table is created, you can change many of the options that were defined for the table when it was originally created, including the following:

Columns can be added, modified, or deleted. For example, the column name, length, data type, precision, scale, and nullability can all be changed, although some restrictions exist. For more information, refer to Modifying Column Properties.

- PRIMARY KEY and FOREIGN KEY constraints can be added or deleted.
- UNIQUE and CHECK constraints and DEFAULT definitions (and objects) can be added or deleted.
- You can add or delete an identifier column by using the IDENTITY or ROWGUIDCOL property. The ROWGUIDCOL property can also be added to or removed from an existing column, although only one column in a table can have the ROWGUIDCOL property at any one time.
- A table and selected columns within the table can be registered for full-text indexing.

The name or owner of a table can also be changed. When you perform this action, you must also change the name of the table in any triggers, stored procedures, Transact-SQL scripts, or other programming code that uses the old name or owner of the table.

The following table provides a list of several types of modifications that you can make to table properties. The table also lists the methods that you can use to complete these tasks. SQL Server Books Online provides detailed information about how to accomplish each of these tasks:

Type of Modification	Modification Methods
Renaming a table	The *sp_rename* system stored procedure
	The Rename option in SQL Server Enterprise Manager
Changing the owner of a table	The *sp_changeobjectowner* system stored procedure
Modifying column properties	*ALTER DATABASE* statement
	The Design Table option in SQL Server Enterprise Manager
Renaming a column	The *sp_rename* system stored procedure
	The Design Table option in SQL Server Enterprise Manager

Deleting Tables from a SQL Server Database

At times, you need to delete a table (for example, when you want to implement a new design or free up space in the database). When you delete a table, its structural definition, data, full-text indexes, constraints, and indexes are permanently deleted from the database, and the space formerly used to store the table and its indexes is made available for other tables. You can explicitly drop a temporary table if you do not want to wait until it is dropped automatically.

If you need to delete tables that are related through FOREIGN KEY and UNIQUE or PRIMARY KEY constraints, you must delete the tables with the FOREIGN KEY constraints first. If you need to delete a table that is referenced in a FOREIGN KEY constraint but you cannot delete the entire foreign key table, you must delete the FOREIGN KEY constraint.

To delete a table from a SQL Server database, use the *DROP TABLE* statement or use Enterprise Manager to remove the table from the Tables node.

Exercise 3: Creating and Managing Tables in a SQL Server Database

In this exercise, you will use the Transact-SQL *CREATE TABLE* statement to create the tables for the database that you created in Exercise 1. You will be creating each of the tables that you identified in the database design that you developed in Chapter 3, "Designing a SQL Server Database." When you create the tables, you will define the table names, columns, data types, lengths (where applicable), and nullability. You will also define IDENTITY properties and default values for the appropriate columns within the table. You should refer to the data constraints that you identified in Chapter 3. To perform this exercise, you should be logged in to your Windows 2000 Server computer as Administrator.

▶ **To create the Authors table in the BookShopDB**

1. Open SQL Query Analyzer and connect to your local server.
2. In the Editor pane of the Query window, enter the following Transact-SQL code:

```
USE bookshopdb
CREATE TABLE Authors
      (
      AuthorID SMALLINT IDENTITY(101,1) NOT NULL,
      FirstName VARCHAR(30) NOT NULL DEFAULT 'unknown',
      LastName VARCHAR(30) NOT NULL,
      YearBorn CHAR(4) NOT NULL DEFAULT ' N/A ',
      YearDied CHAR(4) NOT NULL DEFAULT ' N/A ',
      Description VARCHAR(200) NOT NULL DEFAULT 'N/A'
      )
```

In this statement, you are creating the Authors table, which contains six columns—all of which have been defined as NOT NULL. All NOT NULL values are being used to define the nullability, because a default value is being provided for those columns that do not require a value. In addition, the AuthorID column is being defined with the IDENTITY property. The first row added to the table will be assigned an AuthorID value of 101 (the seed value). Values in this column will be generated automatically in increments of one.

3. Execute the Transact-SQL code that you just created.

   A message appears on the Messages tab saying that the command has completed successfully.

4. Open SQL Server Enterprise Manager and expand the console tree so that the objects within the BookShopDB database are displayed.

5. Click the Tables node.

Notice that the Author table appears in the list of tables in the right pane.

6. Right-click the Authors table, then click Properties.

The Table Properties—Authors dialog box appears.

7. View the properties for the Authors table.

Notice the column names, data types, size, and default values. The columns listed and their properties should reflect the table definition that you executed in SQL Query Analyzer.

▶ **To create the BookAuthors and BookCondition tables in the BookShopDB database**

1. In the Editor pane of the Query window, enter the following Transact-SQL code:

```
USE bookshopdb
CREATE TABLE BookAuthors
    (
    AuthorID SMALLINT NOT NULL,
    TitleID CHAR(8) NOT NULL
    )
CREATE TABLE BookCondition
    (
    ConditionID TINYINT NOT NULL,
    ConditionName CHAR(10) NOT NULL,
    Description VARCHAR(50) NOT NULL DEFAULT 'N/A'
    )
```

In this statement, you are creating the BookAuthors and BookCondition tables. Notice that neither table includes an IDENTITY property. The BookAuthors table is a junction table, so values are based on other tables (the Authors table and the Books table). The BookCondition table has a finite number of rows, so it is easy to generate an ID manually.

2. Return to SQL Server Enterprise Manager.

3. Click the Refresh button on the toolbar.

The BookAuthors and BookCondition tables should now be listed in the right pane.

4. Open the properties for each table, and view their settings.

Notice the column names, data types, sizes, and default values. The columns listed and their properties should reflect the table definition that you executed in SQL Query Analyzer.

5. Close the properties after you have viewed them.

▶   **To create the remaining tables in the BookShopDB database**

1. In the Editor pane of the Query window, enter and execute the Transact-SQL statements necessary to create the remaining tables in the BookShopDB database.

    When creating the Transact-SQL statements, refer to the Transact-SQL reference in SQL Server Books Online as necessary. Also refer to the database design for the BookShopDB database that you created in Chapter 3 and the data constraints that you identified in that chapter.

    What are the Transact-SQL statements that you created?

2. Save the script that you just created in case you want to use it in later exercises or to make corrections in the tables that you just created.

    Tip   You can easily re-create a table by dropping the incorrect table and then executing the Transact-SQL code that applies only to the table that you want to re-create.

    ---

3. Return to SQL Server Enterprise Manager.
4. Click the Refresh button on the toolbar.

    The tables that you just created should now be listed in the right pane.

5. Open the properties for each table, and view their settings.

    Notice the column names, data types, sizes, and default values. The columns listed and their properties should reflect the table definition that you executed in SQL Query Analyzer.

6. Close the properties after you have viewed them.
7. Close SQL Server Enterprise Manager and SQL Query Analyzer.

Lesson Summary

Once you have created the database and identified the data types, you can create the table objects that store the data within the database. A *table* is a collection of data about a specific entity, such as customers, orders, or inventory. A table contains a set of columns. Each column represents an attribute of the table's data. When defining a column, you should also define its nullability. The nullability of a column determines whether the rows in the table can contain a null value for that column. You should try to avoid permitting null values, however, because they incur more complexity in queries and updates (and because there are other column options). Each column in a record must contain a value, however (even if that value is null). Because nullable columns might not be desirable, a better solution can be to define, where appropriate, a DEFAULT definition for the column. When you load a row into a table with a default definition for a column, you implicitly instruct SQL Server to load a default value in the column when you do not specify a value for the column. For each table, a single identifier column can be created that contains system-generated sequential values that uniquely identify each row within the table. Identifier columns usually contain values unique within the table for which they are defined. In other words, a table containing identifier columns can contain the same identity values that another table is using. A single, globally unique identifier column can also be created for each table containing values that are unique across all networked computers in the world. SQL Server provides several methods that you can use to create a table: the Transact-SQL *CREATE TABLE* statement, the console tree in SQL Server Enterprise Manager, and Database Designer (which you access through SQL Server Enterprise Manager). Once you have created a table in a SQL Server database, you can view information about the table, modify the characteristics of the table, or delete the table from the database.

Review

The following questions are intended to reinforce key information presented in this chapter. If you are unable to answer a question, review the appropriate lesson and then try the question again. You can find answers to the questions in the Appendix, "Questions and Answers."

1. What is the first step toward implementing the physical database?
2. What factors should you take into consideration before creating a database?
3. What are the two steps that SQL Server uses when implementing a new database?
4. What methods can you use to create a SQL Server database object?
5. What is a data type?
6. What four attributes does a data type define for an object?
7. What are the nine categories of data types that SQL Server supports?
8. What are user-defined data types?
9. What type of information, at a minimum, should a table definition include?
10. What are you defining when you define column nullability in a table definition?
11. How do you define a default value for a column?
12. Which property can you use in the column definition of a *CREATE TABLE* statement in order to automatically generate an identity number for each new row added to a table?

C H A P T E R 5

Implementing Data Integrity

About This Chapter

Data integrity refers to the state in which all of the data values stored in the database are correct. If incorrect data values have been stored in a database, the database is said to have lost data integrity. This chapter provides an overview of the various methods that you can use to maintain data integrity and gives you a description of the types of data integrity that you will find in a SQL Server database. The chapter then provides detailed information about the various types of integrity constraints that you can use to enforce data integrity and describes how to implement them in a database.

Before You Begin

To complete the lessons in this chapter, you must have:

- SQL Server 2000 Enterprise Edition installed on a Microsoft Windows 2000 Server computer.
- The ability to log on to the Windows 2000 Server computer and to SQL Server as the Windows 2000 Administrator.
- Paper and a pen or a pencil to complete part of the exercises.
- Completed the exercises in Chapter 3, "Designing a SQL Server Database," and Chapter 4, "Implementing SQL Server Databases and Tables."

Lesson 1: Introduction to Data Integrity

Tables in a SQL Server database can include a number of different types of properties that ensure the integrity of the data. These properties include data types, NOT NULL definitions, DEFAULT definitions, IDENTITY properties, constraints, rules, triggers, and indexes. This lesson will introduce you to all of these methods for enforcing data integrity and to the types of data integrity supported by SQL Server. This lesson also discusses the various types of data integrity, including entity integrity, domain integrity, referential integrity, and user-defined integrity.

After this lesson, you will be able to:

- Identify the various table properties that can be used to ensure the integrity of data in a SQL Server database.
- Identify the various types of data integrity that SQL Server supports.

Estimated lesson time: 25 minutes

Enforcing Data Integrity

Enforcing data integrity ensures the quality of data in the database. For example, suppose that you create a Customers table in your database. The value in the Cust_ID column should uniquely identify each customer who is entered into the table. As a result, if a customer has a Cust_ID of 438, no other customer should have a Cust_ID value of 438, Next, suppose that you have a Cust_Rating column that is used to rate each customer with a rating from 1 through 8. In this case, the Cust_Rating column should not accept a value of 9 or any number other than 1 through 8. In both cases, you must use one of the methods supported by SQL Server to enforce the integrity of the data.

SQL Server supports a number of methods that you can use to enforce data integrity, including data types, NOT NULL definitions, DEFAULT definitions, IDENTITY properties, constraints, rules, triggers, and indexes. In Chapter 4, "Implementing SQL Server Databases and Tables," you already learned about several of these methods for enforcing data integrity. A brief description of these methods is included here to provide you with a cohesive overview of ways to enforce data integrity. Some of these table properties, such as NOT NULL and DEFAULT definitions, are sometimes considered a type of constraint. For the purposes of this training kit, however, they are being treated as separate from constraints.

Data Types

A data type is an attribute that specifies the type of data (character, integer, binary, and so on) that can be stored in a column, parameter, or variable. SQL Server provides a set of system-supplied data types, although you can create user-defined data types that are based on the system-supplied data types. System-supplied data types define all of the types of data that you can use with SQL Server. Data types can be used to enforce data integrity because the data entered or changed must conform to the type specified for the object. For example, you cannot store someone's last name in a column defined with the *datetime* data type, because a *datetime* column accepts only valid dates. For more information about data types, refer to Chapter 4, "Implementing SQL Server Databases and Tables."

NOT NULL Definitions

The nullability of a column determines whether the rows in the table can contain a null value for that column. A null value is not the same as zero, blank, or a zero-length character string such as " ". Null means that no entry has been made. The presence of null usually implies that the value is either unknown or undefined. You define the nullability of a column when you define the column, when you either create or modify a table. Whether you define columns that allow null values or columns that do not allow null values, you should always use the NULL or NOT NULL keywords in every column definition because of the complexities of how null is handled in SQL Server. The NULL keyword is used if null values are allowed in the column, and the NOT NULL keywords are used if null values are not allowed. For more information about data types, refer to Chapter 4, "Implementing SQL Server Databases and Tables."

DEFAULT Definitions

Defaults specify what values are used in a column if you do not specify a value for the column when inserting a row. DEFAULT definitions can be created when the table is created (as part of the table definition) or can be added to an existing table. Each column in a table can contain a single DEFAULT definition. For more information about default values, refer to Chapter 4.

IDENTITY Properties

For each table, a single identifier column can be created that contains system-generated sequential values that uniquely identify each row within the table. Identifier columns usually contain values unique within the table for which they are defined. In other words, it is possible for tables containing identifier columns to contain the same identity values used by another table. This situation is usually not a problem, however, because the identifier values are typically used only within the context of a single table—and the identifier columns do not relate to other identifier columns in other tables. For more information about the IDENTITY property, refer to Chapter 4.

Constraints

Constraints enable you to define the way that SQL Server automatically enforces the integrity of a database. Constraints define rules regarding the values allowed in columns and are the standard mechanism for enforcing integrity. Using constraints is preferred to using triggers, rules, or defaults. The query optimizer also uses constraint definitions to build high-performance query execution plans. Lesson 2 discusses constraints in more detail.

Rules

Rules are a backward-compatibility feature that performs some of the same functions as CHECK constraints. CHECK constraints are the preferred, standard way to restrict the values in a column. CHECK constraints are also more concise than rules; there can be only one rule applied to a column, but multiple CHECK constraints can be applied. CHECK constraints are specified as part of the *CREATE TABLE* statement, while rules are created as separate objects and are then bound to the column.

You should use the *CREATE RULE* statement to first create the rule, and then you should use the *sp_bindrule* system stored procedure to bind that rule to a column or to a user-defined data type. For more information about using *CREATE RULE* or *sp_bindrule*, refer to the Transact-SQL reference in SQL Server Books Online.

Triggers

Triggers are a special class of stored procedures defined to execute automatically when an *UPDATE*, *INSERT*, or *DELETE* statement is issued against a table or a view. Triggers are powerful tools that sites can use to enforce their business rules automatically when data is modified. Triggers can extend the integrity checking logic of SQL Server constraints, defaults, and rules (although constraints and defaults should be used instead whenever they provide all of the needed functionality). Triggers are discussed in more detail in Chapter 9, "Implementing Triggers."

Indexes

An index is a structure that orders the values of one or more columns in a database table. An index provides pointers to the data values stored in specified columns of the table and then orders those pointers according to the sort order you specify. The database uses the index much as you use an index in a book: it searches the index to find a particular value and then follows the pointer to the row containing that value. A unique index enforces a column's uniqueness. Indexes are discussed in more detail in Chapter 11, "Implementing Indexes."

Types of Data Integrity

SQL Server supports four types of data integrity: entity integrity, domain integrity, referential integrity, and user-defined integrity.

Note   You might find that some documentation defines more (or less) than four types of data integrity or defines types of data integrity different from the four included here. However, the four discussed here are generally considered the main types of data integrity.

Entity Integrity

Entity integrity defines a row as a unique instance of an entity for a particular table. Entity integrity enforces the integrity of the identifier column or the primary key of a table (through indexes, UNIQUE constraints, PRIMARY KEY constraints, or IDENTITY properties).

Domain Integrity

Domain integrity is the validity of entries for a given column. You can enforce domain integrity by restricting the type (through data types), the format (through CHECK constraints and rules), or the range of possible values (through FOREIGN KEY constraints, CHECK constraints, DEFAULT definitions, NOT NULL definitions, and rules).

Referential Integrity

Referential integrity preserves the defined relationships between tables when records are entered or deleted. In SQL Server, referential integrity is based on relationships between foreign keys and primary keys or between foreign keys and unique keys (through FOREIGN KEY and CHECK constraints). Referential integrity ensures that key values are consistent across tables. Such consistency requires that there be no references to non-existent values and that, if a key value changes, all references to it change consistently throughout the database.

When you enforce referential integrity, SQL Server prevents users from doing any of the following:

- Adding records to a related table if there is no associated record in the primary table
- Changing values in a primary table that result in orphaned records in a related table
- Deleting records from a primary table if there are related records in the foreign table

For example, with the Sales and Titles tables in the Pubs database, referential integrity is based on the relationship between the foreign key (title_id) in the Sales table and the primary key (title_id) in the Titles table, as shown in Figure 5.1.

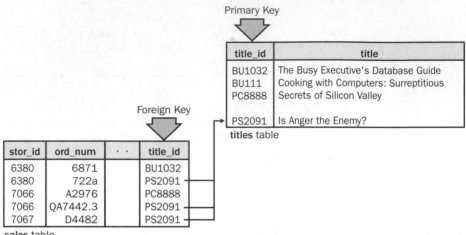

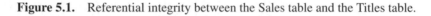

Figure 5.1.   Referential integrity between the Sales table and the Titles table.

User-Defined Integrity

User-defined integrity enables you to define specific business rules that do not fall into one of the other integrity categories. All of the integrity categories support user-defined integrity (all column-level and table-level constraints in the *CREATE TABLE* statement, stored procedures, and triggers).

Exercise 1: Identifying the Properties Used to Ensure Data Integrity

In this exercise, you will view several tables in the Pubs database and identify properties used to ensure data integrity. To perform this exercise, you should be logged into your Windows 2000 Server computer as Administrator.

▶ **To identify properties in the Employee table**

1. Open SQL Query Analyzer and connect to your local server.

2. In the Editor pane of the Query window, enter the following Transact-SQL code:

```
USE Pubs
GO
sp_help Employee
```

In this statement, you are identifying the database containing the table that you want to view and you are using the *sp_help* system stored procedure to view information about the Employee table in the Pubs database.

3. Execute the Transact-SQL statement.

Information about the Employee table appears in the Grids tab of the Results pane.

4. Scroll through the result on the Grids tab. Identify the data types, nullability, DEFAULT definitions, IDENTITY property, indexes, and constraints.

What types of constraints have been defined for the Employee table?

Which columns in the Employee table allow null values?

▶ **To identify properties in the Publishers table**

1. In the Editor pane of the Query window, enter and execute the following Transact-SQL code:

```
sp_help Publishers
```

Information about the Publishers table appears in the Grids tab of the Results pane.

2. Scroll through the result on the Grids tab. Identify the data types, nullability, DEFAULT definitions, IDENTITY property, indexes, and constraints.

What types of constraints have been defined for the Publishers table?

Which column in the Publishers table is the identity column?

Which columns in the Publishers table have been defined with the *char* data type?

▶ **To identify properties in the Titles table**

1. In the Editor pane of the Query window, enter and execute the following Transact-SQL code:

```
sp_help Titles
```

Information about the Titles table appears in the Grids tab of the Results pane.

2. Scroll through the result on the Grids tab. Identify the data types, nullability, DEFAULT definitions, IDENTITY property, indexes, and constraints.

Which column in the Publishers table has been defined with a user-defined data type?

How many columns in the Titles table allow null values?

3. Close SQL Query Analyzer.

Lesson Summary

Tables in a SQL Server database can include a number of different types of properties that ensure the integrity of the data. These properties include data types, NOT NULL definitions, DEFAULT definitions, IDENTITY properties, constraints, rules, triggers, and indexes. SQL Server supports four types of data integrity: entity integrity, domain integrity, referential integrity, and user-defined integrity. Entity integrity defines a row as a unique instance of an entity for a particular table. Domain integrity is the validity of entries for a given column. Referential integrity preserves the defined relationships between tables when records are entered or deleted. User-defined integrity enables you to define specific business rules that do not fall into one of the other integrity categories.

Lesson 2: Implementing Integrity Constraints

A constraint is a property assigned to a table or a column within a table that prevents invalid data values from being placed in the specified column(s). For example, a UNIQUE or PRIMARY KEY constraint prevents you from inserting a value that is a duplicate of an existing value; a CHECK constraint prevents you from inserting a value that does not match a search condition; and a FOREIGN KEY constraint enforces a link between data in two tables. Some documentation about constraints includes discussions about nullability and DEFAULT definitions, and in Transact-SQL, DEFAULT is indeed one type of constraint. However, because nullability and DEFAULT definitions are discussed in Chapter 4, "Implementing SQL Server Databases and Tables," this lesson focuses only on PRIMARY KEY constraints, UNIQUE constraints, FOREIGN KEY constraints, and CHECK constraints.

After this lesson, you will be able to:

- Describe the four main classes of constraints.
- Implement constraints in a SQL Server database.

Estimated lesson time: 35 minutes

Introduction to Integrity Constraints

Constraints enable you to define the way SQL Server 2000 automatically enforces the integrity of a database. Constraints define rules regarding the values allowed in columns and are the standard mechanisms for enforcing integrity. Using constraints is preferred to using triggers, rules, or defaults. The query optimizer also uses constraint definitions to build high-performance query execution plans.

Constraints can be column constraints or table constraints:

- A column constraint is specified as part of a column definition and applies only to that column.
- A table constraint is declared independently from a column definition and can apply to more than one column in a table.

Table constraints must be used when more than one column is included in a constraint. For example, if a table has two or more columns in the primary key, you must use a table constraint to include both columns in the primary key. Consider a table that records events happening in a computer in a factory. Assume that events of several types can happen at the same time, but no two events happening at the same time can be of the same type. This rule can be enforced in the table by including both the type and time columns in a two-column primary key, as shown in the following *CREATE TABLE* statement:

```
CREATE TABLE FactoryProcess
    (
    EventType INT,
    EventTime DATETIME,
    EventSite CHAR(50),
    EventDesc CHAR(1024),
    CONSTRAINT event_key PRIMARY KEY (EventType, EventTime)
    )
```

SQL Server supports four main classes of constraints: PRIMARY KEY constraints, UNIQUE constraints, FOREIGN KEY constraints, and CHECK constraints.

PRIMARY KEY Constraints

A table usually has a column (or combination of columns) whose values uniquely identify each row in the table. This column (or columns) is called the primary key of the table and enforces the entity integrity of the table. You can create a primary key by defining a PRIMARY KEY constraint when you create or alter a table.

A table can have only one PRIMARY KEY constraint, and a column that participates in the PRIMARY KEY constraint cannot accept null values. Because PRIMARY KEY constraints ensure unique data, they are often defined for identity columns. When you specify a PRIMARY KEY constraint for a table, SQL Server 2000 enforces data uniqueness by creating a unique index for the primary key columns. This index also permits fast access to data when the primary key is used in queries.

If a PRIMARY KEY constraint is defined for more than one column, values can be duplicated within one column—but each combination of values from all of the columns in the PRIMARY KEY constraint definition must be unique. Figure 5.2 illustrates how the au_id and title_id columns in the TitleAuthor table form a composite PRIMARY KEY constraint, which ensures that the combination of au_id and title_id is unique.

Creating PRIMARY KEY Constraints

You can create a PRIMARY KEY constraint by using one of the following methods:

- Creating the constraint when the table is created (as part of the table definition)
- Adding the constraint to an existing table, provided that no other PRIMARY KEY constraint already exists

You can modify or delete a PRIMARY CONSTRAINT once it has been created. For example, you might want the PRIMARY KEY constraint of the table to

Primary Key

au_id	title_id	au_ord	royaltyper
172-32-1176	PS3333	1	100
213-46-8915	BU1032	2	40
213-46-8915	BU2075	1	100
238-95-7766	PC1035	1	100
267-41-2394	BU1111	2	40

Figure 5.2.   The primary key of the TitleAuthor table in the Pubs database.

reference other columns, or you might want to change the column order, index name, clustered option, or fill factor of the PRIMARY KEY constraint. You cannot change the length of a column defined with a PRIMARY KEY constraint.

Note   To modify a PRIMARY KEY constraint by using Transact-SQL, you must first delete the existing PRIMARY KEY constraint and then re-create it with the new definition.

The following *CREATE TABLE* statement creates the Table1 table and defines the Col1 column as the primary key:

```
CREATE TABLE Table1
    (
    Col1 INT PRIMARY KEY,
    Col2 VARCHAR(30)
    )
```

You can also define the same constraint by using a table-level PRIMARY KEY constraint:

```
CREATE TABLE Table1
    (
    Col1 INT,
    Col2 VARCHAR(30),
    CONSTRAINT table_pk PRIMARY KEY (Col1)
    )
```

You can use the *ALTER TABLE* statement to add a PRIMARY KEY constraint to an existing table:

```
ALTER TABLE Table1
ADD CONSTRAINT table_pk PRIMARY KEY (Col1)
```

When a PRIMARY KEY constraint is added to an existing column (or columns) in the table, SQL Server 2000 checks the existing data in the columns to ensure that it follows the rules for primary keys:

- No null values
- No duplicate values

If a PRIMARY KEY constraint is added to a column that has duplicate or null values, SQL Server returns an error and does not add the constraint. You cannot add a PRIMARY KEY constraint that violates these rules.

SQL Server automatically creates a unique index to enforce the uniqueness requirement of the PRIMARY KEY constraint. If a clustered index does not already exist in the table (or a non-clustered index is not explicitly specified), a unique, clustered index is created to enforce the PRIMARY KEY constraint.

Important   A PRIMARY KEY constraint cannot be deleted if it is referenced by a FOREIGN KEY constraint in another table. The FOREIGN KEY constraint must be deleted first. FOREIGN KEY constraints are discussed later in this lesson.

UNIQUE Constraints

You can use UNIQUE constraints to ensure that no duplicate values are entered in specific columns that do not participate in a primary key. Although both a UNIQUE constraint and a PRIMARY KEY constraint enforce uniqueness, you should use a UNIQUE constraint instead of a PRIMARY KEY constraint in the following situations:

- **If a column (or combination of columns) is not the primary key.**   Multiple UNIQUE constraints can be defined on a table, whereas only one PRIMARY KEY constraint can be defined on a table.
- **If a column allows null values.**   UNIQUE constraints can be defined for columns that allow null values, whereas PRIMARY KEY constraints can be defined only on columns that do not allow null values.

A UNIQUE constraint can also be referenced by a FOREIGN KEY constraint.

Creating UNIQUE Constraints

You can create a UNIQUE constraint in the same way that you create a PRIMARY KEY constraint:

- By creating the constraint when the table is created (as part of the table definition)
- By adding the constraint to an existing table, provided that the column or combination of columns comprising the UNIQUE constraint contains only unique or NULL values. A table can contain multiple UNIQUE constraints.

You can use the same Transact-SQL statements to create a UNIQUE constraint that you used to create a PRIMARY KEY constraint. Simply replace the words PRIMARY KEY with the word UNIQUE. As with PRIMARY KEY constraints, a UNIQUE constraint can be modified or deleted once it has been created.

When a UNIQUE constraint is added to an existing column (or columns) in the table, SQL Server 2000 (by default) checks the existing data in the columns to ensure that all values, except null, are unique. If a UNIQUE constraint is added to a column that has duplicated values, SQL Server returns an error and does not add the constraint.

SQL Server automatically creates a UNIQUE index to enforce the uniqueness requirement of the UNIQUE constraint. Therefore, if an attempt is made to insert a duplicate row, SQL Server returns an error message saying that the UNIQUE constraint has been violated and does not add the row to the table. Unless a clustered index is explicitly specified, a unique, non-clustered index is created by default to enforce the UNIQUE constraint.

FOREIGN KEY Constraints

A foreign key is a column or combination of columns used to establish and enforce a link between the data in two tables. Create a link between two tables by adding a column (or columns) to one of the tables and defining those columns with a FOR-EIGN KEY constraint. The columns will hold the primary key values from the second table. A table can contain multiple FOREIGN KEY constraints.

For example, the Titles table in the Pubs database has a link to the Publishers table because there is a logical relationship between books and publishers. The pub_id column in the Titles table matches the primary key column in the Publishers table, as shown in Figure 5.3. The pub_id column in the Titles table is the foreign key to the Publishers table.

You can create a foreign key by defining a FOREIGN KEY constraint when you create or alter a table. In addition to a PRIMARY KEY constraint, a FOREIGN KEY constraint can reference the columns of a UNIQUE constraint in another table.

A FOREIGN KEY constraint can contain null values; however, if any column of a composite FOREIGN KEY constraint contains null values, then verification of the FOREIGN KEY constraint will be skipped.

Note   A FOREIGN KEY constraint can reference columns in tables in the same database or within the same table (self-referencing tables).

Although the primary purpose of a FOREIGN KEY constraint is to control the data that can be stored in the foreign key table, it also controls changes to data in the primary key table. For example, if the row for a publisher is deleted from the Publishers table and the publisher's ID is used for books in the Titles table, the relational integrity between the two tables is broken. The deleted publisher's books are orphaned in the titles table without a link to the data in the Publishers table. A FOREIGN KEY constraint prevents this situation. The constraint enforces referential integrity by ensuring that changes cannot be made to data in the primary key table if those changes invalidate the link to data in the foreign key table. If an attempt is made to delete the row in a primary key table or to change a primary key value, the action will fail if the deleted or changed primary key value corresponds to a value in the FOREIGN KEY constraint of another table.

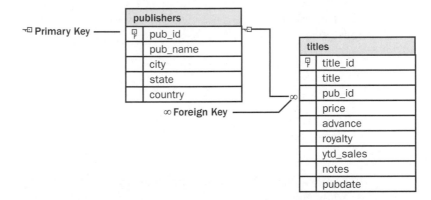

Figure 5.3.   A FOREIGN KEY constraint defined in the Titles table of the Pubs database.

To successfully change or delete a row in a FOREIGN KEY constraint, you must first either delete the foreign key data in the foreign key table or change the foreign key data in the foreign key table—thereby linking the foreign key to different primary key data.

Creating FOREIGN KEY Constraints

You can create a FOREIGN KEY constraint by using one of the following methods:

- Creating the constraint when the table is created (as part of the table definition)
- Adding the constraint to an existing table, provided that the FOREIGN KEY constraint is linked to an existing PRIMARY KEY constraint or a UNIQUE constraint in another (or the same) table

You can modify or delete a FOREIGN KEY constraint once it has been created. For example, you might want the table's FOREIGN KEY constraint to reference other columns. You cannot change the length of a column defined with a FOREIGN KEY constraint.

Note   To modify a FOREIGN KEY constraint by using Transact-SQL, you must first delete the existing FOREIGN KEY constraint and then re-create it with the new definition.

The following *CREATE TABLE* statement creates the Table1 table and defines the Col2 column with a FOREIGN KEY constraint that references the EmployeeID column, which is the primary key in the Employees table:

```
CREATE TABLE Table1
    (
    Col1 INT PRIMARY KEY,
    Col2 INT REFERENCES Employees(EmployeeID)
    )
```

You can also define the same constraint by using a table-level FOREIGN KEY constraint:

```
CREATE TABLE Table1
    (
    Col1 INT PRIMARY KEY,
    Col2 INT,
    CONSTRAINT col2_fk FOREIGN KEY (Col2)
    REFERENCES Employees (EmployeeID)
    )
```

You can use the *ALTER TABLE* statement to add a FOREIGN KEY constraint to an existing table:

```
ALTER TABLE Table1
ADD CONSTRAINT col2_fk FOREIGN KEY (Col2)
REFERENCES Employees (EmployeeID)
```

When a FOREIGN KEY constraint is added to an existing column (or columns) in the table, SQL Server 2000 (by default) checks the existing data in the columns to ensure that all values, except null values, exist in the columns of the referenced PRIMARY KEY or UNIQUE constraint. You can prevent SQL Server from checking the data in the column against the new constraint, however, and force it to add the new constraint regardless of the data in the column. This option is useful when the existing data already meets the new FOREIGN KEY constraint or when a business rule requires the constraint to be enforced only from this point forward.

You should be careful when adding a constraint without checking existing data, however, because this action bypasses the controls in SQL Server that enforce the data integrity of the table.

Disabling FOREIGN KEY Constraints

You can disable existing FOREIGN KEY constraints when performing the following actions:

- **Executing *INSERT* and *UPDATE* statements.**   Disable a FOREIGN KEY constraint during *INSERT* and *UPDATE* statements if new data will violate the constraint or if the constraint should apply only to the data already in the database. Disabling the constraint enables data in the table to be modified without being validated by the constraints.

- **Implementing replication processing.**   Disable a FOREIGN KEY constraint during replication if the constraint is specific to the source database. When a table is replicated, the table definition and data are copied from the source database to a destination database. These two databases are usually (but not necessarily) on separate servers. If the FOREIGN KEY constraints are specific to the source database but are not disabled during replication, they might unnecessarily prevent new data from being entered in the destination database.

CHECK Constraints

CHECK constraints enforce domain integrity by limiting the values that are accepted by a column. They are similar to FOREIGN KEY constraints in that they control the values that are placed in a column. The difference is in how they determine which values are valid. FOREIGN KEY constraints get the list of valid values from another table, and CHECK constraints determine the valid values from a logical expression that is not based on data in another column. For example, it is possible to limit the range of values for a salary column by creating a CHECK constraint that allows only data ranging from $15,000 through $100,000. This feature prevents the entering of salaries from outside the normal salary range.

You can create a CHECK constraint with any logical (Boolean) expression that returns TRUE or FALSE based on the logical operators. To allow only data that ranges from $15,000 through $100,000, the logical expression is as follows:

```
salary >= 15000 AND salary <= 100000
```

You can apply multiple CHECK constraints to a single column. The constraints are evaluated in the order in which they are created. In addition, you can apply a single CHECK constraint to multiple columns by creating it at the table level. For example, a multiple-column CHECK constraint can be used to confirm that any row with a country column value of USA also has a two-character value in the state column. This feature enables multiple conditions to be checked in one place.

Creating CHECK Constraints

You can create a CHECK constraint by using one of the following methods:

- Creating the constraint when the table is created (as part of the table definition)
- Adding the constraint to an existing table

You can modify or delete CHECK constraints once they have been created. For example, you can modify the expression used by the CHECK constraint on a column in the table.

Note   To modify a CHECK constraint using Transact-SQL, you must first delete the existing CHECK constraint and then re-create it with the new definition.

The following *CREATE TABLE* statement creates the Table1 table and defines the Col2 column with a CHECK constraint that limits the column-entered values to a range between 0 and 1000:

```
CREATE TABLE Table1
    (
    Col1 INT PRIMARY KEY,
    Col2 INT
    CONSTRAINT limit_amount CHECK (Col2 BETWEEN 0 AND 1000),
    Col3 VARCHAR(30)
    )
```

You can also define the same constraint by using a table-level CHECK constraint:

```
CREATE TABLE Table1
    (
    Col1 INT PRIMARY KEY,
    Col2 INT,
    Col3 VARCHAR(30),
    CONSTRAINT limit_amount CHECK (Col2 BETWEEN 0 AND 1000)
    )
```

You can use the *ALTER TABLE* statement to add a CHECK constraint to an existing table:

```
ALTER TABLE Table1
ADD CONSTRAINT limit_amount CHECK (Col2 BETWEEN 0 AND 1000)
```

When a CHECK constraint is added to an existing table, the CHECK constraint can apply either to new data only or to existing data as well. By default, the CHECK constraint applies to existing data as well as to any new data. The option of applying the constraint to new data only is useful when the existing data already meets the new CHECK constraint or when a business rule requires the constraint to be enforced only from this point forward.

For example, an old constraint might require postal codes to be limited to five digits, but a new constraint might require nine-digit postal codes. Old data with five-digit postal codes is still valid and will coexist with new data that contains nine-digit postal codes. Therefore, only new data should be checked against the new constraint.

You should be careful when adding a constraint without checking existing data, however, because this action bypasses the controls in SQL Server 2000 that enforce the integrity rules for the table.

Disabling CHECK Constraints

You can disable existing CHECK constraints when performing the following actions:

- **Executing *INSERT* and *UPDATE* statements.**   Disable a CHECK constraint during *INSERT* and *UPDATE* statements if new data will violate the constraint or if the constraint should apply only to the data already in the database. Disabling the constraint allows data in the table to be modified without being validated by the constraints.

- **Implementing replication processing.**   Disable a CHECK constraint during replication if the constraint is specific to the source database. When a table is replicated, the table definition and data are copied from the source database to a destination database. These two databases are usually (but not necessarily) on separate servers. If the CHECK constraints specific to the source database are not disabled, they might unnecessarily prevent new data from being entered into the destination database.

Exercise 2: Adding Constraints to Existing Tables

In this exercise, you will add constraints to the tables that you created in the Book-ShopDB database. You will need to refer to the data model that you developed and to the business rules that you identified in Exercise 3 of Chapter 3, "Designing a SQL Server Database." Note that every table should have a primary key. In some cases, this primary key will be made up of two columns. In addition, several tables will require foreign keys, and the Customers table will require a CHECK constraint. The business rules and data model will help you determine when to define constraints. For example, one of the business rules concerning the Books table is that the ConditionID column must contain a value that is listed in the ConditionID column of the BookCondition table. This rule tells you that you should define a FOREIGN KEY constraint for the ConditionID column of the Books table that references the ConditionID column of the BookCondition table. To perform this exercise, you should be logged into your Windows 2000 Server computer as Administrator.

▶ **To add a PRIMARY KEY constraint to the Authors table**

1. Refer to the business rules and database design and identify which column (or columns) in the Authors table should be defined with a PRIMARY KEY constraint.

   At this point in the database development process, it should be fairly obvious which column should be configured as the primary key. Remember that a PRIMARY KEY constraint is defined for a column (or columns) whose values uniquely identify each row in the table.

   Which column (or columns) in the Authors table should be defined with a PRIMARY KEY constraint?

2. Open SQL Query Analyzer and connect to your local server.

3. In the Editor pane of the Query window, enter the following Transact-SQL code:

```
USE BookShopDB
ALTER TABLE Authors
ADD CONSTRAINT authors_pk PRIMARY KEY (AuthorID)
```

In this statement, you are adding a PRIMARY KEY constraint (authors_pk) to the AuthorID column of the Authors table in the BookShopDB Database.

4. Execute the Transact-SQL statement.

A message is displayed in the Messages tab of the Results pane, stating that the command has completed successfully.

▶ **To add a PRIMARY KEY constraint to the BookAuthors table**

1. Refer to the business rules and database design and identify which column (or columns) in the BookAuthors table should be defined with a PRIMARY KEY constraint.

Which column (or columns) in the BookAuthors table should be defined with a PRIMARY KEY constraint?

2. In the Editor pane of the Query window, enter the following Transact-SQL code:

```
ALTER TABLE BookAuthors
ADD CONSTRAINT bookauthors_pk PRIMARY KEY (AuthorID, TitleID)
```

In this statement, you are adding a PRIMARY KEY constraint (bookauthors_pk) to a combination of columns: the AuthorID column and the TitleID column.

3. Execute the Transact-SQL statement.

A message is displayed in the Messages tab of the Results pane, stating that the command has completed successfully.

▶ **To add a PRIMARY KEY constraint to the remaining tables in the Book-ShopDB database**

1. Refer to the business rules and database design and identify which column (or columns) in the remaining tables should be defined with a PRIMARY KEY constraint.

2. Use SQL Query Analyzer to add a primary key to each remaining table in the BookShopDB database.

For the BookOrders table, the primary key should be created for the two columns in that table. For the other tables, use one identifier column for the primary key.

What Transact-SQL statements should you use to add the PRIMARY KEY constraints to the remaining tables?

Each table in the BookShopDB database should now be defined with a PRIMARY KEY constraint.

▶ **To add FOREIGN KEY constraints to the BookAuthors table**

1. Refer to the business rules and database design and identify which column (or columns) in the BookAuthors table should be defined with FOREIGN KEY constraints.

   Remember that a FOREIGN KEY constraint establishes and enforces a link between two tables. By looking at the business rules and the database design, you can determine what these links should be.

   Which column (or columns) in the BookAuthors table should be defined with a PRIMARY KEY constraint?

2. In the Editor pane of the Query window, enter the following Transact-SQL code:

```
ALTER TABLE BookAuthors
ADD CONSTRAINT authorid_fk FOREIGN KEY (AuthorID)
REFERENCES Authors (AuthorID)
```

   In this statement, you are adding a FOREIGN KEY constraint (authorid_fk) to the AuthorID column of the BookAuthors table. The constraint references the AuthorID column in the Authors table.

3. Execute the Transact-SQL statement.

   A message is displayed in the Messages tab of the Results pane, stating that the command has completed successfully.

4. In the Editor pane of the Query window, enter and execute the following Transact-SQL code:

```
ALTER TABLE BookAuthors
ADD CONSTRAINT titleid_fk FOREIGN KEY (TitleID)
REFERENCES Books (TitleID)
```

   A message is displayed in the Messages tab of the Results pane, stating that the command has completed successfully.

▶ **To add FOREIGN KEY constraints to the Books, BookOrders, Orders, and Employees tables**

1. Refer to the business rules and database design and identify which column (or columns) in the Books, BookOrders, Orders, and Employees tables should be defined with PRIMARY KEY constraints.

2. Use SQL Query Analyzer to add foreign keys to the Books, BookOrders, Orders, and Employees tables.

   For the BookOrders table, you should add a FOREIGN KEY constraint to each column. For the Orders table, you should add a FOREIGN KEY constraint to each of the four columns that reference other tables. For the Books table and the Employees table, you should add only one FOREIGN KEY constraint per table.

What Transact-SQL statements should you use to add the FOREIGN KEY constraints to the Books, BookOrders, Orders, and Employees tables?

The appropriate tables in the BookShopDB database should now be defined with FOREIGN KEY constraints.

▶ **To add a CHECK constraint to the Customers table**

1. Refer to the business rules and database design and identify which column (or columns) in the Customers table should be defined with a CHECK constraint.

   Remember that a CHECK constraint enforces domain integrity by limiting the values that a column will accept.

   Which column (or columns) in the Customers table should be defined with a CHECK constraint?

2. In the Editor pane of the Query window, enter the following Transact-SQL code:

```
ALTER TABLE Customer
ADD CONSTRAINT checknames_ck CHECK
(FirstName NOT LIKE 'unknown' OR LastName NOT LIKE 'unknown')
```

   In this statement, you are adding a CHECK constraint that ensures that either the FirstName column or the LastName column includes a value other than unknown, which is the DEFAULT definition for both columns. In other words, both columns in the same row cannot contain the value unknown.

3. Execute the Transact-SQL statement.

   A message is displayed in the Messages tab of the Results pane, stating that the command has completed successfully.

▶ **To add CHECK constraints to the Authors table and the Books table**

1. Refer to the business rules and database design and identify which columns in the Authors table and the Books table should be defined with CHECK constraints.

   Which columns in the Authors table and the Books table should be defined with CHECK constraints?

2. In the Editor pane of the Query window, enter the following Transact-SQL code:

```
USE BookShopDB

ALTER TABLE Authors
ADD CONSTRAINT authors1_ck
CHECK (YearBorn LIKE ('[1-2][0,6-9][0-9][0-9]')
       OR (YearBorn = 'N/A'))
ALTER TABLE Authors
ADD CONSTRAINT authors2_ck
CHECK (YearBorn NOT LIKE '[1][0][0-9][0-9]')
ALTER TABLE Authors
```

```
ADD  CONSTRAINT authors3_ck
CHECK (YearBorn NOT LIKE '[2][6-9][0-9][0-9]')

ALTER TABLE Authors
ADD CONSTRAINT authors4_ck
CHECK (YearDied LIKE ('[1-2][0,6-9][0-9][0-9]')
      OR (YearDied = 'N/A'))
ALTER TABLE Authors
ADD  CONSTRAINT authors5_ck
CHECK (YearDied NOT LIKE '[1][0][0-9][0-9]')
ALTER TABLE Authors
ADD  CONSTRAINT authors6_ck
CHECK (YearDied NOT LIKE '[2][6-9][0-9][0-9]')

ALTER TABLE Books
ADD CONSTRAINT books1_ck
CHECK (PubDate LIKE ('[1-2][0,6-9][0-9][0-9]')
      OR (PubDate = 'N/A'))
ALTER TABLE Books
ADD  CONSTRAINT books2_ck
CHECK (PubDate NOT LIKE '[1][0][0-9][0-9]')
ALTER TABLE Books
ADD  CONSTRAINT books3_ck
CHECK (PubDate NOT LIKE '[2][6-9][0-9][0-9]')
```

In this statement, you are adding CHECK constraints to the YearBorn column, the YearDied column, and the PubDate column to limit the years that can be added to these columns.

3. Execute the Transact-SQL statement.

A message is displayed in the Messages tab of the Results pane, stating that the command has completed successfully.

▶ **To verify that constraints have been added to the tables**

1. In the Editor pane of the Query window, enter and execute the following Transact-SQL code:

```
sp_helpconstraint Authors
```

The Grids tab of the Results pane displays information about the Authors table.

2. Scroll through the Grids tab until you reach the section about constraints.

The query result should include all the constraints that you have created for this table, which includes one PRIMARY KEY constraint and four DEFAULT constraints.

3. Use the *sp_helpconstraint* system stored procedure to view constraint information in the remaining tables. Verify that all appropriate constraints have been created.

4. Close SQL Query Analyzer.

Lesson Summary

Constraints define rules regarding the values allowed in columns and are the standard mechanism for enforcing integrity. Constraints can be column constraints or table constraints. Table constraints must be used when more than one column is included in a constraint. SQL Server supports four main classes of constraints: PRIMARY KEY constraints, UNIQUE constraints, FOREIGN KEY constraints, and CHECK constraints. A PRIMARY KEY constraint is defined for a column or combination of columns to ensure that the values within those columns uniquely identify each row in the table. A UNIQUE constraint is similar to a PRIMARY KEY constraint. The UNIQUE constraint ensures that no duplicate values are entered in specific columns that do not participate in a primary key. A FOREIGN KEY constraint is a column or combination of columns used to establish and enforce a link between the data in two tables. CHECK constraints enforce domain integrity by limiting the values that a column will accept.

Review

The following questions are intended to reinforce key information presented in this chapter. If you are unable to answer a question, review the appropriate lesson and then try the question again. You can find answers to the questions in the Appendix, "Questions and Answers."

1. What properties within a SQL Server database are used to enforce data integrity?
2. What is the difference between a DEFAULT definition and a NOT NULL definition?
3. What are the advantages of using CHECK constraints rather than rules?
4. What four types of data integrity does SQL Server support?
5. What are the differences between entity integrity and domain integrity?
6. Which type of integrity preserves the defined relationships between tables when records are entered or deleted?
7. What types of constraints does SQL Server support?
8. How many PRIMARY KEY constraints can be included in a table definition?
9. When should you use a UNIQUE constraint rather than a PRIMARY KEY constraint?
10. What does SQL Server check for in the existing data when a PRIMARY KEY constraint is added to an existing column (or columns)?
11. What is a FOREIGN KEY constraint, and how is it created?
12. How does a CHECK constraint determine what values are valid?

C H A P T E R   6

Accessing and Modifying Data

About This Chapter

The primary purpose of a SQL Server database is to store data and then make that data available to authorized applications and users. You can access and change data by using an application or utility to send data retrieval and modification requests to SQL Server. For the purpose of this training kit, you will use SQL Query Analyzer as your primary tool to access and modify data in a SQL Server database. SQL Query Analyzer enables you to submit Transact-SQL statements that you can use to retrieve and modify data. You can implement most of these operations by using one of four Transact-SQL statements: *SELECT*, *INSERT*, *UPDATE*, or *DELETE*. This chapter provides detailed information about each of these statements and describes how you can use each statement to retrieve and modify data. This chapter also introduces you to other methods for adding, modifying, and deleting data.

Before You Begin

To complete the lessons in this chapter, you must have:

- SQL Server 2000 Enterprise Edition installed on a Microsoft Windows 2000 Server computer.
- The ability to log on to the Windows 2000 Server computer and to SQL Server as the Windows 2000 Administrator.

Lesson 1: Accessing Data in a SQL Server Database

You can use the *SELECT* statement to retrieve data from a SQL Server database and to present the data back to the user in one or more result sets. A result set is a tabular arrangement of the data that is retrieved by executing the *SELECT* statement. Like a table, the result set comprises columns and rows. This lesson provides an overview of the main components of a *SELECT* statement and how those components—when used in a complete *SELECT* statement—can be used to retrieve specific data from a SQL Server database and present that data in a result set.

After this lesson, you will be able to:

- Describe the main components of a *SELECT* statement and how you can use those components to retrieve data.
- Define a *SELECT* statement that will retrieve specific data from a SQL Server database.

Estimated lesson time: 35 minutes

The Fundamentals of a *SELECT* Statement

A *SELECT* statement in Transact-SQL enables you to retrieve existing data from a SQL Server database. Most *SELECT* statements describe four primary properties of a result set:

- The columns to be included in the result set
- The tables from which the result set data is retrieved
- The conditions that the rows in the source table must meet in order to qualify for the result set
- The ordering sequence of the rows in the result set

For example, the following *SELECT* statement retrieves the product ID, name, and unit price of any products in the Products table whose unit price exceeds $40:

```
SELECT ProductID, ProductName, UnitPrice
FROM Products
WHERE UnitPrice > 40
ORDER BY UnitPrice ASC
```

The SELECT clause in the previous example defines which column values should be retrieved, and the FROM clause identifies the table that contains these columns. The WHERE clause limits the result set to those products whose UnitPrice value is greater than $40. The ORDER BY clause specifies that the result set is to be sorted in ascending sequence based on the value in the UnitPrice column.

The full syntax of the *SELECT* statement is complex, but the main clauses can be summarized as follows:

- SELECT *select_list*
- [INTO *new_table_name*]
- FROM *table_list*
- [WHERE *search_conditions*]
- [GROUP BY *group_by_list*]
- [HAVING *search_conditions*]
- [ORDER BY *order_list* [ASC | DESC]]

The remainder of this lesson discusses each clause in detail and provides examples of how you can define these clauses to retrieve specific data from a SQL Server database. For further details about each clause, refer to SQL Server Books Online.

The SELECT Clause

The SELECT clause includes the SELECT keyword and the select list. The select list is a series of expressions separated by commas. Each expression defines a column in the result set. The columns in the result set are in the same order as the sequence of expressions in the select list.

Using Keywords in the Select List

The select list can also contain keywords that control the final format of the result set.

The DISTINCT Keyword

The DISTINCT keyword eliminates duplicate rows from a result set. For example, the Orders table in the Northwind database contains duplicate values in the ShipCity column. To get a list of the ShipCity values with duplicates removed, enter the following code:

```
SELECT DISTINCT ShipCity, ShipRegion
FROM Orders
ORDER BY ShipCity
```

The TOP *n* Keyword

The TOP *n* keyword specifies that the first *n* rows of the result set are to be returned. If ORDER BY is specified, the rows are selected after the result set is ordered. The *n* placeholder is the number of rows to return (unless the PERCENT keyword is specified). PERCENT specifies that *n* is the percentage of rows in the result set that are returned. For example, the following *SELECT* statement returns the first 10 cities in alphabetic sequence from the Orders table:

```
SELECT DISTINCT TOP 10 ShipCity, ShipRegion
FROM Orders
ORDER BY ShipCity
```

The AS Keyword

You can improve the readability of a *SELECT* statement by giving a table an alias (also known as a correlation name or range variable). A table alias can be assigned either with or without the AS keyword:

- *table_name* AS *table_alias*
- *table_name table_alias*

In the following example, the alias p is assigned to the Publishers table:

```
USE pubs
SELECT p.pub_id, p.pub_name
FROM publishers AS p
```

Important   If an alias is assigned to a table, all explicit references to the table in the Transact-SQL statement must use the alias, not the table name.

Types of Information in the Select List

A select list can include many types of information, such as a simple expression or a scalar subquery. The following example shows many of the items that you can include in a select list:

```
SELECT FirstName + ' ' + LastName AS "Employee Name",
     IDENTITYCOL AS "Employee ID",
     HomePhone,
     Region
FROM Northwind.dbo.Employees
ORDER BY LastName, FirstName ASC
```

In this statement, the employees' first and last names are combined into one column. A space is added between the first and last names. The name of the column that will contain the employee names is Employee Name. The result set will also include the identity column, which will be named Employee ID in the result set; the HomePhone column; and the Region column. The result set is ordered first by last name and then by first name.

The INTO Clause

The INTO clause enables you to specify that the result set will be used to create a new table with the name defined in the clause. A *SELECT...INTO* statement can be used to combine data from several tables or views into one table. You can also use it to create a new table containing data selected from a linked server. The following example uses a *SELECT* statement to retrieve values from the FirstName and Last-Name columns of the Employees table:

```
SELECT FirstName, LastName
INTO EmployeeNames
FROM Employers
```

The result set that is generated by the statement creates the EmployeeNames table. The new table will contain the FirstName column and the LastName column, and those columns will contain the values from the Employees table. The result set is not displayed in the Results pane unless you specifically query the new table.

The FROM Clause

The FROM clause is required in every *SELECT* statement in which data is being retrieved from tables or views. You can use the FROM clause to list the tables and views containing the columns referenced in the select list and in the WHERE clause. You can give the table or view names aliases by using the AS clause. You can also use the FROM clause to join tables by specifying join conditions in the ON clause.

The FROM clause is a comma-separated list of table names, view names, and JOIN clauses. The following *SELECT* statement uses the FROM clause to specify the Shippers table:

```
SELECT *
FROM Shippers
```

You can also use the FROM clause to specify joins between two tables or views. Lesson 2 will discuss joins in more detail.

The WHERE, GROUP BY, and HAVING Clauses

The WHERE and HAVING clauses in a *SELECT* statement control the rows from the source tables that are used to build the result set. The WHERE and HAVING clauses are filters. They specify a series of search conditions, and only those rows that meet the terms of the search conditions are used to build the result set. Those rows that meet the search conditions are said to be qualified to participate in the result set. For example, the WHERE clause in the following *SELECT* statement returns only those rows where the region is Washington state:

```
SELECT CustomerID, CompanyName
FROM Northwind.dbo.Customers
WHERE Region = 'WA'
```

The HAVING clause is typically used in conjunction with the GROUP BY clause, although it can be specified without GROUP BY. The HAVING clause specifies more filters that are applied after the WHERE clause performs its filtering. The following SELECT statement includes a WHERE clause, a GROUP BY clause, and a HAVING clause:

```
SELECT OrdD1.OrderID AS OrderID,
    SUM(OrdD1.Quantity) AS "Units Sold",
    SUM(OrdD1.UnitPrice * OrdD1.Quantity) AS Revenue
FROM [Order Details] AS OrdD1
WHERE OrdD1.OrderID in (SELECT DISTINCT OrdD2.OrderID
    FROM [Order Details] AS OrdD2
    WHERE OrdD2.UnitPrice > $100)
GROUP BY OrdD1.OrderID
HAVING SUM(OrdD1.Quantity) > 100
```

In this *SELECT* statement, the WHERE clause returns only those orders that are selling a product with a unit price exceeding $100, and the HAVING clause further restricts the result to only those orders that include more than 100 units. The GROUP BY clause limits the rows for each distinct value in the OrderID column.

The GROUP BY Clause

The GROUP BY clause is used to produce aggregate values for each row in the result set. When used without a GROUP BY clause, aggregate functions report only one aggregate value for a *SELECT* statement.

The GROUP BY keywords are followed by a list of columns, known as the grouping columns. The GROUP BY clause restricts the rows of the result set. There is only one row for each distinct value in the grouping column or columns. Each result set row contains summary data related to the specific value of its grouping columns.

SQL Server places restrictions on the items that can be specified in the select list when a SELECT statement contains a GROUP BY clause. The select list can contain the grouping columns and expressions that return only one value for each value in the grouping columns, such as aggregate functions (vector aggregates) that have a column name as one of their parameters.

Typically, the HAVING clause is used with the GROUP BY clause, although HAVING can be specified separately. You can group by an expression as long as it does not include aggregate functions.

In a GROUP BY clause, you must specify the name of a table or view column, not the name of a result set column assigned with an AS clause. You can list more than one column in the GROUP BY clause to nest groups; that is, you can group a table by any combination of columns.

Processing the WHERE, GROUP BY, and HAVING Clauses

Understanding the correct sequence in which the WHERE, GROUP BY, and HAVING clauses are applied helps in coding efficient queries:

- The WHERE clause is used to filter the rows that result from the operations specified in the FROM clause.
- The GROUP BY clause is used to group the output of the WHERE clause.
- The HAVING clause is used to filter rows from the grouped result.

For any search conditions that could be applied either before or after the grouping operation, it is more efficient to specify them in the WHERE clause. This action reduces the number of rows that have to be grouped. The only search conditions that should be specified in the HAVING clause are those search conditions that must be applied after the grouping operation has been performed.

The ORDER BY Clause

The ORDER BY clause sorts a query result by one or more columns (up to 8060 bytes). A sort can be *ascending* (ASC) or *descending* (DESC). If neither is specified, ASC is assumed. If more than one column is named in the ORDER BY clause, sorts are nested.

The following statement sorts the rows in the Titles table, first by publisher (in descending order), then by type (in ascending order within each publisher), and finally by price (also ascending, because DESC is not specified):

```
USE Pubs
SELECT Pub_id, Type, Title_id, Price
FROM Titles
ORDER BY Pub_id DESC, Type, Price
```

Exercise 1: Using *SELECT* Statements to Access Data

In this exercise, you will use SELECT statements to retrieve data from the Pubs database. Each SELECT statement after the first one will build on the previous one as you become more specific about the data that is included in the result set. To perform this exercise, you should be logged into your Windows 2000 Server computer as Administrator.

► **To retrieve all data from the Titles table**

1. Open SQL Query Analyzer and connect to your local server.

2. In the Editor pane of the Query window, enter the following Transact-SQL code:

```
USE Pubs
SELECT * FROM Titles
```

In this statement, you are identifying the database containing the table you want to view and you are using a *SELECT* statement to retrieve all data from the Titles table in the Pubs database. The asterisk (*) in the select list indicates that data should be retrieved from all columns in the table.

3. Execute the Transact-SQL statement.

The result set appears in the Grids tab of the Results pane.

► **To retrieve data from specific columns in the Titles table**

1. In the Editor pane of the Query window, enter the following Transact-SQL code:

```
USE Pubs
SELECT Title_id, Title, Price, Ytd_sales
FROM Titles
```

In this statement, you are using a *SELECT* statement to retrieve data from the Title_id, Title, Price, and Ytd_sales columns in the Pub database.

2. Execute the Transact-SQL statement.

The result set appears in the Grids tab of the Results pane.

► **To specify the condition that the result set must meet**

1. In the Editor pane of the Query window, enter the following Transact-SQL code:

```
USE Pubs
SELECT Title_id, Title, Price, Ytd_sales
FROM Titles
WHERE Price > 10
```

The *SELECT* statement will now retrieve only those rows whose value in the Price column is greater than $10.

2. Execute the Transact-SQL statement.

The result set appears in the Grids tab of the Results pane.

► **To specify the order in which the result set appears**

1. In the Editor pane of the Query window, enter the following Transact-SQL code:

```
USE Pubs
SELECT Title_id, Title, Price, Ytd_sales
FROM Titles
WHERE Price > 10
ORDER BY Price DESC, Title
```

The result set returned by this *SELECT* statement will be ordered first by price, in descending order, and then by title, in ascending order.

2. Execute the Transact-SQL statement.

The result set appears in the Grids tab of the Results pane.

▶   **To group data in a result set**

1. In the Editor pane of the Query window, enter the following Transact-SQL code:

```
USE Pubs
SELECT Type, AVG(Price) AS AvgPrice
FROM Titles
WHERE Price > 10
GROUP BY Type
ORDER BY AvgPrice DESC
```

The result set returned by this *SELECT* statement will group together those rows with the same Type value. Rows that do not meet the conditions in the WHERE clause will be eliminated before any grouping is done. The values from the Price column will be averaged for each grouping, and that average will be inserted in the result set under the AvgPrice column. The values in the Avg-Price column will be listed in descending order.

2. Execute the Transact-SQL statement.

The result set appears in the Grids tab of the Results pane.

▶   **To create a table for the result set**

1. In the Editor pane of the Query window, enter the following Transact-SQL code:

```
USE Pubs
SELECT Type, AVG(Price) AS AvgPrice
INTO TypeAvgPrice
FROM Titles
WHERE Price > 10
GROUP BY Type
ORDER BY AvgPrice DESC
```

The *SELECT* statement will create a new table named TypeAvgPrice. The table will contain the Type column and the AvgPrice column, and those columns will contain the values from the result set.

2. Execute the Transact-SQL statement.

   A message appears in the Messages tab of the Results pane, providing the number of rows that have been affected.

3. Enter and execute the following Transact-SQL statement:

   ```
   SELECT * FROM TypeAvgPrice
   ```

   The contents of the TypeAvgPrice table are displayed in the Grids tab of the Results pane.

4. Enter and execute the following Transact-SQL statement:

   ```
   DROP TABLE TypeAvgPrice
   ```

   A message appears in the Messages tab of the Results pane, stating that the command has completed successfully.

5. Close SQL Query Analyzer.

Lesson Summary

The *SELECT* statement is used to retrieve data from a SQL Server database and to present the data back to the user in one or more result sets. The main clauses of a *SELECT* statement are the SELECT clause, the INTO clause, the FROM clause, the WHERE clause, the GROUP BY clause, the HAVING clause, and the ORDER BY clause. The SELECT clause includes the SELECT keyword and the select list. The select list defines the columns in the result set generated by a *SELECT* statement. The INTO clause enables you to specify that the result set will be used to create a new table with the name defined in the clause. The FROM clause is a comma-separated list of table names, view names, and JOIN clauses. You can use the FROM clause to list the tables and views containing the columns referenced in the select list and in the WHERE clause. You can also use the FROM clause to join types by specifying join conditions. The WHERE and HAVING clauses in a *SELECT* statement control the rows from the source tables that are used to build the result set. The GROUP BY clause is used to produce aggregate values for each row in the result set.

Lesson 2: Using Advanced Query Techniques to Access Data

Once you have grown comfortable with the fundamentals of a *SELECT* statement and are familiar with the various clauses, you are ready to learn more advanced querying techniques. One of these techniques is to combine the contents of two or more tables to produce a result set that incorporates rows and columns from each table. Another technique is to use subqueries, which are *SELECT* statements nested inside other *SELECT*, *INSERT*, *UPDATE*, or *DELETE* statements. Subqueries can also be nested inside other subqueries. You can also use Transact-SQL elements such as CUBE and ROLLUP to summarize data. This lesson reviews each of these advanced techniques and provides examples of how they are used to retrieve specific data from a SQL Server database.

After this lesson, you will be able to:

- Define joins that enable you to retrieve data from two or more tables.
- Define subqueries inside *SELECT* statements.
- Use the GROUP BY clause in a *SELECT* statement to summarize data.

Estimated lesson time: 35 minutes

Using Joins to Retrieve Data

By using joins, you can retrieve data from two or more tables based on logical relationships between the tables. Joins indicate how SQL Server should use data from one table to select the rows in another table.

Joins can be specified in either the FROM or WHERE clauses. The join conditions combine with the WHERE and HAVING search conditions to control the rows that are selected from the base tables referenced in the FROM clause. Specifying the join conditions in the FROM clause, however, helps separate them from any other search conditions that might be specified in a WHERE clause and is the recommended method for specifying joins.

When multiple tables are referenced in a single query, all column references must be unambiguous. The table name must be used to qualify any column name that is duplicated in two or more tables referenced in a single query.

The select list for a join can reference all of the columns in the joined tables or any subset of the columns. The select list is not required to contain columns from every table in the join. For example, in a three-table join, only one table can be used as a bridge from one of the other tables to the third table, and none of the columns from the middle table have to be referenced in the select list.

Although join conditions usually use the equals sign (=) comparison operator, other comparison or relational operators can be specified (as can other predicates).

When SQL Server processes joins, the query engine chooses the most efficient method (from several possibilities) of processing the join. Although the physical execution of various joins uses many different optimizations, the logical sequence is as follows:

- The join conditions in the FROM clause are applied.
- The join conditions and search conditions from the WHERE clause are applied.
- The search conditions from the HAVING clause are applied.

This sequence can sometimes influence the result of the query if conditions are moved between the FROM and WHERE clauses.

Columns used in a join condition are not required to have the same name or to be the same data type. If the data types are not identical, however, they must be compatible or be types that SQL Server can implicitly convert. If the data types cannot be implicitly converted, the join condition must explicitly convert the data type by using the CAST function.

Note   Most joins can be rewritten as subqueries (a query nested within another query), and most subqueries can be rewritten as joins. Subqueries are covered in detail later in this lesson.

Most joins can be categorized as inner joins or outer joins. Inner joins return rows only when there is at least one row from both tables that matches the join condition, eliminating the rows that do not match with a row from the other table. Outer joins, however, return all rows from at least one of the tables or views mentioned in the FROM clause as long as these rows meet any WHERE or HAVING search conditions. You can also create cross-joins and self-joins. For more information about cross-joins and self-joins, refer to SQL Server Books Online.

Inner Joins

An inner join is a join in which the values in the columns being joined are compared through the use a comparison operator. In the SQL-92 standard, inner joins can be specified in either the FROM or WHERE clause. Inner joins are the only type of join that SQL-92 supports in the WHERE clause. Inner joins specified in the WHERE clause are known as old-style inner joins.

The following *SELECT* statement uses an inner join to retrieve data from the Publishers table and the Titles table in the Pubs database:

```
SELECT t.Title, p.Pub_name
FROM Publishers AS p INNER JOIN Titles AS t
ON p.Pub_id = t.Pub_id
ORDER BY Title ASC
```

This *SELECT* statement retrieves data from the Title column in the Titles (t) table and from the Pub_name column in the Publishers (p) table. Because the statement uses an inner join, it returns only those rows for which there is an equal value in the join columns (the p.Pub_id column and the t.Pub_id column).

Outer Joins

SQL Server supports three types of outer joins: left, right, and full. All rows retrieved from the left table are referenced with a left outer join, and all rows from the right table are referenced in a right outer join. All rows from both tables are returned in a full outer join.

Using Left Outer Joins

A result set generated by a *SELECT* statement that includes a left outer join includes all rows from the table referenced to the left of LEFT OUTER JOIN. The only rows that are retrieved from the table to the right are those that meet the join condition.

In the following *SELECT* statement, a left outer join is used to retrieve the authors' first names, last names, and (when applicable) the names of any publishers that are located in the same cities as the authors:

```
USE Pubs
SELECT a.Au_fname, a.Au_lname, p.Pub_name
FROM Authors a LEFT OUTER JOIN Publishers p
     ON a.City = p.City
ORDER BY p.Pub_name ASC, a.Au_lname ASC, a.Au_fname ASC
```

The result set from this query will list the name of every author in the Authors table. The result set will include only those publishers that are located in the same cities as the authors, however. If a publisher is not located in the author's city, a null value is returned for the Pub_name column of the result set.

Using Right Outer Joins

A result set generated by a *SELECT* statement that includes a right outer join includes all rows from the table referenced to the right of RIGHT OUTER JOIN. The only rows that are retrieved from the table to the left are those that meet the join condition.

In the following *SELECT* statement, a right outer join is used to retrieve the list of publishers and the authors' first names and last names, if those authors are located in the same cities as the publishers:

```
USE Pubs
SELECT a.Au_fname, a.Au_lname, p.Pub_name
FROM Authors a RIGHT OUTER JOIN Publishers p
     ON a.City = p.City
ORDER BY p.Pub_name ASC, a.Au_lname ASC, a.Au_fname ASC
```

The result set from this query will list the name of every publisher in the Publishers table. The result set will include only those authors that are located in the same cities as the publishers, however. If an author is not located in the publisher's city, a null value is returned for the Au_fname and Au_lname columns of the result set.

Using Full Outer Joins

A result set generated by a *SELECT* statement that includes a full outer join includes all rows from both tables, regardless of whether the tables have a matching value (as defined in the join condition).

In the following *SELECT* statement, a full outer join is used to retrieve the list of publishers and authors' first and last names:

```
USE Pubs
SELECT a.Au_fname, a.Au_lname, p.Pub_name
FROM Authors a FULL OUTER JOIN Publishers p
    ON a.City = p.City
ORDER BY p.Pub_name ASC, a.Au_lname ASC, a.Au_fname ASC
```

The result set from this query lists the name of every publisher in the Publishers table and every author in the Authors table. If an author is not located in the publisher's city, a null value is returned for the Au_fname and Au_lname columns of the result set. If a publisher is not located in the author's city, a null value is returned in the Pub_name column of the result set. When the join condition is met, all columns in the result set will contain a value.

Defining Subqueries inside *SELECT* Statements

A subquery is a *SELECT* statement that returns a single value and is nested inside a *SELECT*, *INSERT*, *UPDATE*, or *DELETE* statement or inside another subquery. A subquery can be used anywhere an expression is allowed. A subquery is also called an inner query or inner select, while the statement containing a subquery is called an outer query or an outer select.

In the following example, a subquery is nested in the WHERE clause of the outer *SELECT* statement:

```
USE Northwind
SELECT ProductName
FROM Products
WHERE UnitPrice =
    (
    SELECT UnitPrice
    FROM Products
    WHERE ProductName = 'Sir Rodney''s Scones'
    )
```

The embedded *SELECT* statement first identifies the UnitPrice value for Sir Rodney's Scones, which is $10. The $10 value is then used in the outer *SELECT* statement to return the product name of all products whose unit price equals $10.

If a table appears only in a subquery and not in the outer query, then columns from that table cannot be included in the output (the select list of the outer query).

In some Transact-SQL statements, the subquery can be evaluated as if it were an independent query. Conceptually, the subquery result is substituted into the outer query (although this is not necessarily how SQL Server actually processes Transact-SQL statements that have subqueries).

Types of Subqueries

Subqueries can be specified in many places within a *SELECT* statement. Statements that include a subquery usually take one of the following formats, however:

- WHERE *<expression>* [NOT] IN (*<subquery>*)
- WHERE *<expression>* *<comparison_operator>* [ANY | ALL] (*<subquery>*)
- WHERE [NOT] EXISTS (*<subquery>*)

Subqueries that Are Used with IN or NOT IN

The result of a subquery introduced with IN (or with NOT IN) is a list of zero or more values. After the subquery returns the result, the outer query makes use of it.

In the following example, a subquery is nested inside the WHERE clause, and the IN keyword is used:

```
USE Pubs
SELECT Pub_name
FROM Publishers
WHERE Pub_id IN
    (
    SELECT Pub_id
    FROM Titles
    WHERE Type = 'business'
    )
```

You can evaluate this statement in two steps. First, the inner query returns the identification numbers of the publishers that have published business books (1389 and 0736). Second, these values are substituted into the outer query, which finds the names that match the identification numbers in the Publishers table.

Subqueries introduced with the NOT IN keywords also return a list of zero or more values. The query is exactly the same as the one in subqueries with IN, except that NOT IN is substituted for IN.

Subqueries that Are Used with Comparison Operators

Comparison operators that introduce a subquery can be modified with the keyword ALL or ANY. The SOME keyword is a SQL-92 standard equivalent for ANY. Subqueries introduced with a modified comparison operator return a list of zero or more values and can include a GROUP BY or HAVING clause. These subqueries can be restated with EXISTS.

The ALL and ANY keywords each compare a scalar value with a single-column set of values. The ALL keyword applies to every value, and the ANY keyword applies to at least one value.

In the following example, the greater than (>) comparison operator is used with the ANY keyword:

```
USE Pubs
SELECT Title
FROM Titles
WHERE Advance > ANY
    (
    SELECT Advance
    FROM Publishers INNER JOIN Titles
    ON Titles.Pub_id = Publishers.Pub_id
            AND Pub_name = 'Algodata Infosystems'
```

This statement finds the titles that received an advance larger than the minimum advance amount paid by Algodata Infosystems (which, in this case, is $5,000). The WHERE clause in the outer *SELECT* statement contains a subquery that uses a join to retrieve advance amounts for Algodata Infosystems. The minimum advance amount is then used to determine which titles to retrieve from the Titles table.

Subqueries that Are Used with EXISTS and NOT EXISTS

When a subquery is introduced with the keyword EXISTS, it functions as an existence test. The WHERE clause of the outer query tests for the existence of rows returned by the subquery. The subquery does not actually produce any data; instead, it returns a value of TRUE or FALSE.

In the following example, the WHERE clause in the outer *SELECT* statement contains the subquery and uses the EXISTS keyword:

```
USE Pubs
SELECT Pub_name
FROM Publishers
WHERE EXISTS
        (
        SELECT * FROM Titles
        WHERE Titles.Pub_id = Publishers.Pub_id
            AND Type = 'business'
        )
```

To determine the result of this query, consider each publisher's name in turn. In this case, the first publisher's name is Algodata Infosystems, which has identification number 1389. Are there any rows in the Titles table in which Pub_id is 1389 and the type is business? If so, Algodata Infosystems should be one of the values selected. The same process is repeated for each of the other publishers' names.

The NOT EXISTS keywords work like EXISTS, except the WHERE clause in which NOT EXISTS is used is satisfied if the subquery returns no rows.

Summarizing Data

Transact-SQL includes several elements that enable you to generate simple summary reports. You can use the CUBE or ROLLUP operators, which are both part of the GROUP BY clause of the *SELECT* statement. You can also use the COMPUTE or COMPUTE BY operators, which are also associated with the GROUP BY clause.

The COMPUTE and COMPUTE BY operators are supported for backward compatibility. For more details about these operators, refer to SQL Server Books Online.

Using the CUBE Operator to Summarize Data

The CUBE operator generates a result set that is a multi-dimensional cube. A multi-dimensional cube is an expansion of fact data, or data that records individual events. The expansion is based on columns that the user wants to analyze. These columns are called dimensions. The cube is a result set containing a cross-tabulation of all the possible combinations of the dimensions.

The following *SELECT* statement uses the CUBE operator in the GROUP BY clause:

```
USE Pubs
SELECT SUBSTRING(Title, 1, 65) AS Title,
    SUM(qty) AS 'Quantity'
FROM Sales INNER JOIN Titles
    ON Sales.Title_id = Titles.Title_id
GROUP BY Title
WITH CUBE
ORDER BY Title
```

This *SELECT* statement covers a one-to-many relationship between book titles and the quantity of each book sold. By using the CUBE operator, the statement returns an extra row. The extra row (which contains a null value in the Title column of the result set) represents all values in the Title column of the Titles table. The result set returns values for the quantity sold of each title and the total quantity sold of all titles. In this case, applying the CUBE operator or ROLLUP operator returns the same result.

Using the ROLLUP Operator to Summarize Data

The ROLLUP operator is useful for generating reports that contain subtotals and totals. The ROLLUP operator generates a result set that is similar to the result sets generated by the CUBE operator. The differences between CUBE and ROLLUP are as follows:

- CUBE generates a result set showing aggregates for all combinations of values in the selected columns.
- ROLLUP generates a result set showing aggregates for a hierarchy of values in the selected columns.

The following *SELECT* statement contains a ROLLUP operator in the GROUP BY clause:

```
USE Pubs
SELECT Pub_name, Au_lname, Title, SUM(qty) AS 'Sum'
FROM Authors a INNER JOIN TitleAuthor ta
    ON a.Au_id = ta.Au_id INNER JOIN Titles t
    ON t.Title_id = ta.Title_id INNER JOIN Publishers p
    ON p.Pub_id = t.Pub_id INNER JOIN Sales s
    ON s.Title_id = t.Title_id
GROUP BY Pub_name, Au_lname, Title
WITH ROLLUP
```

By using the ROLLUP operator, you can create groupings in the result set. For the grouped rows, a null value is used to represent all values for a column (except the Sum column). If you use the *SELECT* statement without the ROLLUP operator, the statement generates only a single grouping. If you use the CUBE operator, many more groupings will be returned. The ROLLUP operator returns the following data when the columns Pub_name, Au_lname, and Title are listed (in that order) in the GROUP BY clause:

- Quantity of each title that each publisher has sold for each author
- Quantity of all titles each publisher has sold for each author
- Quantity of all titles each publisher has sold
- Total quantity of all titles sold by all publishers for all authors

Exercise 2: Using Advanced Query Techniques to Retrieve Data

In this exercise, you will use SELECT statements and advanced query techniques to retrieve data from the Northwind database. The SELECT statements will include joins or subqueries, and you will use them to summarize data. To perform this exercise, you should be logged into your Windows 2000 Server computer as Administrator.

▶ **To use an inner join to retrieve data**

1. Open SQL Query Analyzer and connect to your local server.

2. In the Editor pane of the Query window, enter the following Transact-SQL code:

```
USE Northwind
SELECT o.CustomerID, o.OrderID, s.CompanyName
FROM Orders o JOIN Shippers s
ON o.ShipVia = s.ShipperID
WHERE ShipCountry = 'USA'
ORDER BY o.CustomerID, s.CompanyName
```

In this statement, you are identifying the database containing the table that you want to view, and you are using a *SELECT* statement to retrieve the customer ID, the order ID, and the name of the shipping company associated with each order. Because the name of the shipping company is in a separate table (Shippers), you must join the Orders table and the Shippers table and use the shipper ID for the join condition. The ShipVia column is a foreign key to the ShipperID column, and both columns contain the shipper IDs. Note that the Orders table is given an alias of o, and the Shippers table is given an alias of s; also note that for an inner join, you can simply use the JOIN keyword (you do not need to specify INNER JOIN)

3. Execute the Transact-SQL statement.

The result set appears in the Grids tab of the Results pane.

▶ **To use a left outer join to retrieve data**

1. In the Editor pane of the Query window, enter the following Transact-SQL code:

```
USE Northwind
SELECT o.OrderID, o.CustomerID, c.ContactName, c.City
FROM Orders o LEFT JOIN Customers c
      ON o.CustomerID = c.CustomerID
      AND o.ShipCity = c.City
ORDER BY o.OrderID
```

In this statement, you are using a *SELECT* statement to retrieve data from the OrderID and CustomerID columns in the Orders table, and the ContactName and City columns in the Customers table. The join condition uses the CustomerID columns to join the tables and further qualifies the join by specifying that values in the ShipCity column must equal the values in the City column.

2. Execute the Transact-SQL statement.

The result set appears in the Grids tab of the Results pane.

3. Click the Messages tab of the Results pane.

Notice that 830 rows are returned. Because a left outer join is used, every row in the Orders table is returned, but the only rows returned from the Customers table are those that contain the same city as where the orders are shipped.

4. Click the Grids tab of the Results pane.

5. Scroll down to row 108.

Notice that the ContactName and City columns contain null values. If you look at the data in the table, you will see that a value exists for the ContactName and City columns. Because one of the join conditions (o.ShipCity = c.City) is not met, however, null values are inserted into the columns. If you use an inner join for this query, 817 rows are returned. Only those rows that meet the join condition in both tables are returned.

▶ **To use a right outer join to retrieve data**

1. In the Editor pane of the Query window, enter the following Transact-SQL code:

```
USE Northwind
SELECT o.OrderID, o.CustomerID, c.ContactName, c.City
FROM Orders o RIGHT JOIN Customers c
    ON o.CustomerID = c.CustomerID
    AND o.ShipCity = c.City
ORDER BY o.OrderID
```

In this statement, you are using the same *SELECT* statement as in the previous procedure, only this time you are specifying a right outer join.

2. Execute the Transact-SQL statement.

The result set appears in the Grids tab of the Results pane.

3. Click the Messages tab of the Results pane.

Notice that 820 rows have been returned. Because a right outer join is used, every row in the Customers table is returned, but the only rows returned from the Orders table are those that contain the same city value as where the customers are located.

4. Click the Grids tab of the Results pane.

Notice that the first three rows of the result set contain null values for the OrderID and CustomerID columns. These rows don't meet the join condition for the Orders table.

▶ **To use a full outer join to retrieve data**

1. Use the same *SELECT* statement that you used in the two previous examples, except specify a full outer join.

2. Execute the Transact-SQL statement and view the Messages tab of the Results pane.

Notice that 833 rows have been returned. Because a full outer join is used, every row from both tables is returned.

3. Click the Grids tab of the Results pane.

   Notice that once again the first three columns contain null values in the OrderID and CustomerID columns.

4. Scroll down to row 111.

   Notice that once again the ContactName column and the City column contain null values.

▶ **To use the IN keyword in a subquery**

1. In the Editor pane of the Query window, enter the following Transact-SQL code:

```
USE Northwind
SELECT OrderID, EmployeeID AS EmpID
FROM Orders
WHERE EmployeeID IN
     (
          SELECT EmployeeID
          FROM Employees
          WHERE City = 'Seattle'
          )
ORDER BY OrderID
```

In this statement, you are using a subquery to identify the employee ID of those employees who live in Seattle. The values returned from this query are then used in the WHERE clause of the outer *SELECT* statement to limit the result set to those orders that were processed by employees in Seattle.

2. Execute the Transact-SQL statement.

   The result set appears in the Grids tab of the Results pane.

▶ **To use comparison operators and the ALL keyword in a subquery**

1. In the Editor pane of the Query window, enter the following Transact-SQL code:

```
USE Northwind
SELECT OrderID, UnitPrice
FROM [Order Details]
WHERE UnitPrice > ALL
        (
        SELECT UnitPrice
        FROM [Order Details] JOIN Orders
        ON [Order Details].OrderID = Orders.OrderID
        AND Orders.EmployeeID = 5
        )
ORDER BY UnitPrice, OrderID
```

In this statement, you are using a subquery to identify the maximum unit price of orders processed by employee 5. The WHERE clause in the outer *SELECT* statement then uses that price to limit the result set to those orders whose unit price exceeds the amount derived from the subquery.

2. Execute the Transact-SQL statement.

The result set appears in the Grids tab of the Results pane.

▶ **To use the EXISTS keyword in a subquery**

1. In the Editor pane of the Query window, enter the following Transact-SQL code:

```
USE Northwind
SELECT OrderID, CustomerID
FROM Orders
WHERE EXISTS
        (
        SELECT * FROM Customers
        WHERE Customers.CustomerID = Orders.CustomerID
                AND City = 'London'
        )
ORDER BY OrderID
```

In this statement, you are using a subquery to identify those customers who are located in London. Customers located in London evaluate to TRUE. The WHERE clause in the outer *SELECT* statement uses those rows that return TRUE to determine which orders should be returned in the result set. Any order whose customer is located in London is included.

2. Execute the Transact-SQL statement.

The result set appears in the Grids tab of the Results pane.

▶ **To use the ROLLUP operator to summarize data**

1. In the Editor pane of the Query window, enter the following Transact-SQL code:

```
USE Northwind
SELECT ProductID, UnitPrice, SUM(Quantity) AS 'Sum'
FROM [Order Details]
GROUP BY ProductID, UnitPrice
WITH ROLLUP
ORDER BY ProductID
```

In this statement, you are using a *SELECT* statement to summarize the number of products sold based on the product ID and the unit price.

2. Execute the Transact-SQL statement.

The result set appears in the Grids tab of the Results pane.

3. Review the result set in the Grids tab.

Notice that the first row of the result set contains null values in the ProductID column and in the UnitPrice column. The value in the Sum column represents the total number of all units in the result set. Also notice that the remaining rows are first grouped together by product and that each product contains sub-groups that are based on the unit price. Each product then includes a row that contains a null value in the UnitPrice column. For this row, the value in the Sum column is the total number of that type of product. For example, product 1 sold 174 units at a price of $14.40 per unit and sold 654 units at a price of $18.80 per unit. The total number of units sold with a ProductID value of 1 is 828.

4. Scroll through the result set to view the summaries of the other products.

5. Close SQL Query Analyzer.

Lesson Summary

Transact-SQL provides several advanced query techniques that you can use to retrieve data from a SQL Server database, including joins, subqueries, and the capability to summarize data. By using joins, you can retrieve data from two or more tables based on logical relationships between the tables. Most joins can be categorized as inner joins or outer joins. Inner joins return rows only if there is at least one row from both tables that matches the join condition—eliminating the rows that do not match with a row from the other table. Outer joins, however, return all rows from at least one of the tables or views mentioned in the FROM clause as long as these rows meet any WHERE or HAVING search condition. SQL Server supports three types of outer joins: left outer, right outer, and full outer. All rows are retrieved from the left table referenced with a left outer join, and all rows from the right table are referenced in a right outer join. All rows from both tables are returned in a full outer join. A subquery is a SELECT query that returns a single value and is nested inside a *SELECT*, *INSERT*, *UPDATE*, or *DELETE* statement or inside another subquery. Subqueries can be specified in many places within a *SELECT* statement. Most subqueries are specified in the WHERE clause and use the IN and NOT IN keywords, use comparison operators with the ANY or ALL keywords, or use the EXISTS and NOT EXISTS keywords. Transact-SQL also includes several elements that enable you to generate simple summary reports, including the CUBE or ROLLUP operators. The CUBE and ROLLUP operators are specified in the GROUP BY clause of a *SELECT* statement. These operators generate result sets that contain both detail rows for each item in the result set and summary rows for each group showing the aggregate totals for that group.

Lesson 3: Modifying Data in a SQL Server Database

An essential component of a database system is the capability to modify data that is stored within that system. SQL Server supports a number of methods for adding new rows of data to tables in a SQL Server database, changing the data in existing rows, and deleting rows. In this lesson, you will learn how to add, modify, and delete data in a SQL Server database.

After this lesson, you will be able to:

- Insert data into a SQL Server database.
- Modify data in a SQL Server database.
- Delete data from a SQL Server database.

Estimated lesson time: 35 minutes

Inserting Data into a SQL Server Database

SQL Server includes several methods for adding data to a database:

- The *INSERT* statement
- The *SELECT...INTO* statement
- The *WRITETEXT* statement and several database Application Programming Interface (API) options, which you can use to add ntext, text, or image data to a row
- The bulk copy component for inserting large numbers of rows

Note   An *INSERT* statement works on views as well as on tables (with some restrictions).

Using the *INSERT* Statement to Add Data

The *INSERT* statement adds one or more new rows to a table. In a simplified treatment, an *INSERT* statement takes the following form:

```
INSERT [INTO] table_or_view [(column_list)] data_values
```

The statement causes the data values (*data_values*) to be inserted as one or more rows into the named table or view. The list of column names (*column_list*), which are separated by commas, can be used to specify the columns for which data is supplied. If no columns are specified, all of the columns in the table or view receive data. If only a partial list is specified, a null value or the default value (if a DEFAULT definition exists) is inserted into any column not named in the list. All columns not specified in the column list must either allow null values or have a default assigned.

In addition, an *INSERT* statement does not specify values for the following types of columns, because SQL Server automatically generates those values:

- Columns with an IDENTITY property
- Columns with a DEFAULT definition that uses the *NEWID* function
- Computed columns

Note   The INTO keyword in an *INSERT* statement is optional and is used only to make code clearer.

The data values supplied must match the column list. The number of data values must be the same as the number of columns, and the data type, precision, and scale of each data value must match those of the corresponding column.

When defining an *INSERT* statement, you can use a VALUES clause to specify the data values for one row or you can use a SELECT subquery to specify the data values for one or more rows.

Using an *INSERT...VALUES* Statement to Add Data

A VALUES clause enables you to specify the values for one row of a table. The values are specified as a comma-separated list of scalar expressions whose data type, precision, and scale must be the same as or implicitly convertible to the corresponding column in the column list. If a column list is not specified, the values must be specified in the same sequence as the columns in the table or view.

For example, suppose you create the following table in the Pubs database:

```
USE Pubs
CREATE TABLE NewBooks
    (
    BookID INT IDENTITY(1,1) NOT NULL,
    BookTitle VARCHAR(80) NOT NULL,
    BookType CHAR(12) NOT NULL
            CONSTRAINT [booktype_df] DEFAULT ('Undecided'),
    PubCity VARCHAR(50) NULL
    )
```

Once you have created the table, you then decide to add a row of data to that table. The following *INSERT* statement uses a VALUES clause to insert a new row into the NewBooks table:

```
USE Pubs
INSERT INTO NewBooks (BookTitle, PubCity)
VALUES ('Life Without Fear', 'Chicago')
```

In this statement, values are being defined for the BookTitle column and the Pub-City column. You do not need to include the BookID column in the *INSERT* statement, however, because the BookID column is defined with the IDENTITY property. Therefore, values for that column are generated automatically. In addition, because you did not define a value for the BookType column, SQL Server automatically inserts the default value (Undecided) into the column when you run the *INSERT* statement.

Using a SELECT Subquery to Add Data

You can use a SELECT subquery in the *INSERT* statement to add values to a table from one or more other tables or views. A subquery enables you to add more than one row at a time.

Note   A SELECT subquery in an *INSERT* statement is used to add subsets of existing data to a table, whereas a VALUES clause is used in an *INSERT* statement to add new data to a table.

The following *INSERT* statement uses a SELECT subquery to insert rows into the NewBooks table:

```
USE Pubs
    INSERT INTO NewBooks (BookTitle, BookType)
        SELECT Title, Type
        FROM Titles
        WHERE Type = 'mod_cook'
```

This *INSERT* statement uses the output of the SELECT subquery to provide the data that will be inserted into the NewBooks table.

Using a *SELECT... INTO* Statement to Add Data

The *SELECT INTO* statement enables you to create a new table and populate it with the result set of the *SELECT* statement. Lesson 1 discusses the INTO clause of a *SELECT* statement in more detail.

Adding ntext, text, or image Data to Inserted Rows

SQL Server includes several methods for adding ntext, text, or image values to a row:

- You can specify relatively short amounts of data in an *INSERT* statement in the same way that you specify char, nchar, or binary data.
- You can use a *WRITETEXT* statement, which permits non-logged, interactive updating of an existing text, ntext, or image column. This statement completely overwrites any existing data in the column that it affects. A *WRITETEXT* statement cannot be used on text, ntext, and image columns in views.

- Active Data Object (ADO) applications can use the AppendChunk method to specify long amounts of ntext, text, or image data.
- OLE DB applications can use the ISequentialStream interface to write new ntext, text, or image values.
- Open Database Connectivity (ODBC) applications can use the data-at-execution form of SQLPutData to write new ntext, text, or image values.
- DB-Library applications can use the *Dbwritetext* function.

Using Bulk Copy Operations to Add Data

The bulk copy components of SQL Server enable you to insert large numbers of rows into a table or view and to retrieve large numbers of rows from a table, view, or query. Bulk copy is the fastest way to add large numbers of rows in SQL Server. Bulk copy operations are discussed in more detail in Chapter 7, "Managing and Manipulating Data."

Modifying Data in a SQL Server Database

After the tables have been created and the data has been added, changing or updating data in the tables becomes one of the day-to-day processes of maintaining a database. SQL Server provides several methods for changing data in an existing table:

- The *UPDATE* statement
- Database APIs and cursors
- The *UPDATETEXT* statement

Updates work on views as well as on tables (with some restrictions).

Using an *UPDATE* Statement to Modify Data

The *UPDATE* statement can change data values in single rows, in groups of rows, or in all of the rows in a table or view. You can also use this statement to update rows in a remote server by using either a linked server name or the *OPENROWSET*, *OPENDATASOURCE*, and *OPENQUERY* functions (as long as the OLE DB provider used to access the remote server supports updates). An *UPDATE* statement referencing a table or a view can change the data in only one base table at a time.

Note   An update is successful only if the new value is compatible with the data type of the target column and adheres to all constraints that apply to the column.

The *UPDATE* statement has these major clauses:

- SET
- WHERE
- FROM

Using a SET Clause to Modify Data

SET specifies the columns to be changed and the new values for the columns. The values in the specified columns are updated with the values given in the SET clause in all rows that match the WHERE clause search condition. If no WHERE clause is specified, all rows are updated.

For example, the following *UPDATE* statement includes a SET clause that increases the prices of the books in the NewBooks table by 10 percent:

```
USE Pubs
UPDATE NewBooks
SET Price = Price * 1.1
```

In this statement, no WHERE clause is used, so all rows in the table will be updated (unless the Price column contains a null value).

Using a WHERE Clause to Modify Data

The WHERE clause performs two functions:

- Specifies the rows to be updated
- Indicates the rows from the source tables that qualify to supply values for the update if a FROM clause is also specified

If no WHERE clause is specified, all rows in the table are updated.

In the following *UPDATE* statement, the WHERE clause is used to limit the update to only those rows that meet the condition defined in the clause:

```
USE Pubs
UPDATE NewBooks
SET BookType = 'popular'
WHERE BookType = 'popular_comp'
```

This statement changes the name popular_comp to popular. If the WHERE clause was not included, all BookType values would be changed to popular.

Using a FROM Clause to Modify Data

You can use the FROM clause to pull data from one or more tables or views into the table that you want to update. For example, in the following *UPDATE* statement, the FROM clause includes an inner join that joins the titles in the NewBooks and Titles tables:

```
USE Pubs
UPDATE NewBooks
SET Price = Titles.Price
FROM NewBooks JOIN Titles
    ON NewBooks.BookTitle = Titles.Title
```

In this statement, the Price values in the NewBooks table are being updated to the same values that are in the Price column of the Titles table.

Using APIs and Cursors to Modify Data

The ADO, OLE DB, and ODBC APIs support updating the current row on which the application is positioned in a result set. In addition, when using a Transact-SQL server cursor, you can update the current row by using an *UPDATE* statement that includes a WHERE CURRENT OF clause. Changes made with this clause affect only the row on which the cursor is positioned. Cursors are discussed in more detail in Chapter 7, "Managing and Manipulating Data."

Modifying ntext, text, or image Data

SQL Server provides a number of methods that enable you to update ntext, text, or image values in a row when replacing the entire value:

- You can specify relatively short amounts of data in an *UPDATE* statement in the same way that you update char, nchar, or binary data.
- You can use the Transact-SQL *WRITETEXT* or *UPDATETEXT* statements to update ntext, text, or image values.
- ADO applications can use the AppendChunk method to specify long amounts of ntext, text, or image data.
- OLE DB applications can use the ISequentialStream interface to write new ntext, text, or image values.
- ODBC applications can use the data-at-execution form of SQLPutData to write new ntext, text, or image values.
- DB-Library applications can use the *Dbwritetext* function.

SQL Server also supports updating only a portion of an ntext, text, or image value. In DB-Library, this procedure can be done using the *Dbupdatetext* function. All other applications and Transact-SQL scripts, batches, stored procedures, and triggers can use the *UPDATETEXT* statement to update only a portion of an ntext, text, or image column.

Deleting Data from a SQL Server Database

SQL Server supports several methods that you can use to delete data in an existing table:

- The *DELETE* statement
- APIs and cursors
- The *TRUNCATE TABLE* statement

The data-modification statements work on views as well as on tables (with some restrictions).

Using a *DELETE* Statement to Delete Data

A *DELETE* statement removes one or more rows in a table or a view. The following syntax is a simplified form of a *DELETE* statement:

```
DELETE table_or_view FROM table_source WHERE search_condition
```

The *table_or_view* placeholder names a table or a view from which the rows are to be deleted. All rows in a table or view that meet the qualifications of the WHERE search condition are deleted. If a WHERE clause is not specified, all of the rows in a table or view are deleted. The FROM clause specifies additional tables or views and join conditions that can be used by the predicates in the WHERE clause search condition to qualify the rows to be deleted from a table or view. Rows are not deleted from the tables named in the FROM clause, only from the tables named in the DELETE clause.

Any table that has had all rows removed remains in the database. The *DELETE* statement deletes only rows from the table. The table must be removed from the database by using the *DROP TABLE* statement.

Consider the following *DELETE* statement:

```
USE Pubs
DELETE NewBooks
FROM Titles
WHERE NewBooks.BookTitle = Titles.Title
      AND Titles.Royalty = 10
```

In this statement, rows are deleted from the NewBooks table if the royalty on those books is 10 percent. The royalty is based on the values in the Royalty column of the Titles table.

Using APIs and Cursors to Delete Data

The ADO, OLE DB, and ODBC APIs support deleting the current row on which an application is positioned in a result set. In addition, Transact-SQL scripts, stored procedures, and triggers can use the WHERE CURRENT OF clause on a *DELETE* statement to delete the cursor row on which they are currently positioned. Cursors are discussed in more detail in Chapter 7, "Managing and Manipulating Data."

Using the *TRUNCATE TABLE* Statement to Delete Data

The *TRUNCATE TABLE* statement is a fast, non-logged method of deleting all rows in a table. This method is almost always faster than a *DELETE* statement with no conditions, because DELETE logs each row deletion and TRUNCATE TABLE logs only the deallocation of whole data pages. The *TRUNCATE TABLE* statement immediately frees all of the space occupied by that table's data and indexes. The distribution pages for all indexes are also freed.

The following *TRUNCATE TABLE* statement deletes all rows from the NewBooks table in the Pubs database:

```
USE Pubs
TRUNCATE TABLE NewBooks
```

As with a *DELETE* statement, the table definition remains in the database after you have used the *TRUNCATE TABLE* statement (along with its indexes and other associated objects). The *DROP TABLE* statement must be used to drop the definition of the table.

Exercise 3: Modifying Data in a SQL Server Database

In this exercise, you will create a table in the BookShopDB database and add data to that table. You will modify the data that you inserted into the table and then delete that data. When you have finished modifying and deleting the data, you will remove the table from the database. To complete this exercise, you should be logged into your Windows 2000 Server computer as Administrator.

▶ **To create a test table in the BookShopDB database**

1. Open SQL Query Analyzer and connect to your local server.

2. In the Editor pane of the Query window, enter the following Transact-SQL code:

```
USE BookShopDB
CREATE TABLE Test1
    (
    RowID INT IDENTITY(1,1) NOT NULL,
    Title VARCHAR(80) NOT NULL,
    Type CHAR(12) NOT NULL DEFAULT ('Unknown'),
    City VARCHAR(50) NULL,
    Cost MONEY NULL
    )
```

In this statement, you are creating a table named Test1. The table contains five columns.

3. Execute the Transact-SQL statement.

A message appears in the Messages tab of the Results pane, stating that the command has been completed successfully.

▶ **To use an *INSERT...VALUES* statement to add data to the Test1 table**

1. In the Editor pane of the Query window, enter the following Transact-SQL code:

```
INSERT INTO Test1 (Title, Type, Cost)
VALUES ('Test Title', 'business', 27.00)
```

In this statement, you are inserting a row into the Test1 table. The row includes values for the Title, Type, and Cost columns.

2. Execute the Transact-SQL statement.

   A message appears in the Messages tab of the Results pane, stating that one row is affected.

3. Write a *SELECT* statement that enables you to view all of the data in the Test1 table.

   What statement should you use?

4. Execute the *SELECT* statement.

   The contents of the Test1 table appear in the Grids tab of the Results pane.

5. Review the contents of the Test1 table.

   Notice that the table contains only one row—the one that you added by using the *INSERT* statement. SQL Server automatically generated the value in the RowID column. The value in the City column is null because no value was defined for that column.

▶ **To use an *INSERT…SELECT* statement to add data to the Test1 table**

1. In the Editor pane of the Query window, enter the following Transact-SQL code:

```
INSERT INTO Test1 (Title, Type, Cost)
    SELECT Title, Type, Price
    FROM Pubs.dbo.Titles
```

   In this statement, you are taking data from the Titles table in the Pubs database and inserting that data into the Test1 table.

2. Execute the Transact-SQL statement.

   A message appears in the Messages tab of the Results pane, stating the number of rows that have been affected.

3. Use a *SELECT* statement to view the data in the Test1 table.

   Notice that the RowID values have been generated automatically and that each row in the City column contains a null value.

▶ **To use an *UPDATE* statement to modify data**

1. View the data in the Test1 table.

   If the Results pane still shows the query result from the last procedure, you can refer to that result. Otherwise, use a *SELECT* statement to view the table's contents.

2. Make a note of several books that have a business value in the Type column, and note the price of those books. You will need to refer to these notes as you modify data in the table.

3. In the Editor pane of the Query window, enter the following Transact-SQL code:

```
UPDATE Test1
SET Cost = Cost * 2
WHERE Type = 'business'
```

In this statement, you are increasing the value in the Cost column to twice the original amount for business books.

4. Execute the Transact-SQL statement.

A message appears in the Messages tab of the Results pane, stating the number of rows that have been affected.

5. Use a *SELECT* statement to view the data in the Test1 table.

Notice that the value in the Cost column has been doubled for each business book.

▶ **To use a *DELETE* statement to remove data from the Test1 table**

1. In the Editor pane of the Query window, enter the following Transact-SQL code:

```
DELETE Test1
WHERE Title = 'Test Title'
```

In this statement, you are deleting any rows from the table that contain a value of Test Title in the Title column.

2. Execute the Transact-SQL statement.

A message appears in the Messages tab of the Results pane, stating the number of rows that have been affected.

3. Use a *SELECT* statement to view the data in the Test1 table.

Notice that the Test Title row has been removed from the table.

4. In the Editor pane of the Query window, enter the following Transact-SQL code:

```
DELETE Test1
```

In this statement, you are deleting all rows from the Test1 table.

5. Execute the Transact-SQL statement.

A message appears in the Messages tab of the Results pane, stating the number of rows that have been affected.

6. Use a *SELECT* statement to view the data in the Test1 table.

Notice that the table now contains no data.

▶ **To use a *DROP TABLE* statement to remove the Test1 from the database**

1. In the Editor pane of the Query window, enter the following Transact-SQL code:

```
DROP TABLE Test1
```

In this statement, you are removing the Test1 table from the BookShopDB database.

2. Execute the Transact-SQL statement.

   A message appears in the Messages tab of the Results pane, stating that the command has been completed successfully.

3. Use the Object Browser window to ensure that the Test1 table has been removed from the database.

4. Close SQL Query Analyzer.

Lesson Summary

SQL Server supports a number of methods for adding new rows of data to tables in a SQL Server database, for changing the data in existing rows, and for deleting rows. Methods for inserting data include the *INSERT* statement; the *SELECT... INTO* statement; the *WRITETEXT* statement and several database API options, which can be used to add ntext, text, or image data to a row; and the bulk copy component for inserting large numbers of rows. Methods that you can use to modify data include the *UPDATE* statement, database APIs and cursors, and the *UPDATETEXT* statement. You can delete data from a database by using *DELETE* statements, by deleting the current row in a cursor or result set, or by using the *TRUNCATE TABLE* statement.

Review

The following questions are intended to reinforce key information presented in this chapter. If you are unable to answer a question, review the appropriate lesson and then try the question again. You can find answers to the questions in the Appendix, "Questions and Answers."

1. What are the four primary properties that most *SELECT* statements describe in a result set?

2. What are the main clauses of a *SELECT* statement?

3. What are several keywords that you can use in a select list?

4. What types of objects can you specify in the FROM clause of a *SELECT* statement?

5. What purpose does a join provide when used in a *SELECT* statement?

6. What are the differences between inner joins and outer joins?

7. What is a subquery?

8. What are the differences between a CUBE operator and a ROLLUP operator?

9. For what types of columns can you not specify values in an *INSERT* statement?

10. What methods can you use to modify data in a SQL Server database?

11. What are the major clauses contained in an *UPDATE* statement?

12. Which statement should you use to delete all rows in a table without having the action logged?

C H A P T E R   7

Managing and Manipulating Data

About This Chapter

In Chapter 6, "Accessing and Modifying Data," you learned how to view and modify data in a SQL Server database. In this chapter, you will learn more techniques for managing and manipulating data, including how to import and export data, how to manipulate heterogeneous data, how to use Transact-SQL cursors, and how to extract data in Extensible Markup Language (XML) format.

Before You Begin

To complete the lessons in this chapter, you must have:

- SQL Server 2000 Enterprise Edition installed on a Microsoft Windows 2000 Server computer.
- The ability to log on to the Windows 2000 Server computer and to SQL Server as the Windows 2000 Administrator.
- Completed the exercises in Chapter 3, "Designing a SQL Server Database," Chapter 4, "Implementing SQL Server Databases and Tables," and Chapter 5, "Implementing Data Integrity."

Lesson 1: Importing and Exporting Data

Importing data from an external source into an instance of SQL Server is likely to be the first step that you will perform once you set up your database. After data has been imported into your database, you can start working with that data by using Transact-SQL statements and other tools to view and modify the data. You might also find that you need to export that data out of the database. Importing data is the process of retrieving data from sources external to SQL Server (for example, an ASCII text file) and inserting it into SQL Server tables. Exporting data is the process of extracting data from an instance of SQL Server into some user-specified format (for example, copying the contents of a SQL Server table to a Microsoft Access database). In this lesson, you will learn how to use the bcp command prompt utility to copy data to and from a SQL Server database and will learn how to use the *BULK INSERT* statement to import data from a data file to a database. With Data Transformation Services (DTS), you will also be able to extract, transform, and consolidate data from disparate sources.

After this lesson, you will be able to:

- Use the bcp command prompt utility to import and export data.
- Use the *BULK INSERT* statement to import data.
- Describe how DTS is used to extract, transform, and consolidate data.

Estimated lesson time: 30 minutes

Using the bcp Utility and the *BULK INSERT* Statement

The bcp command prompt utility copies SQL Server data to or from a data file. You will use this utility most frequently to transfer large volumes of data into a SQL Server table from another program often from another database management system (DBMS). When the bcp utility is used, the data is first exported from the source program to a data file and is then imported from the data file into a SQL Server table. Alternatively, bcp can be used to transfer data from a SQL Server table to a data file for use in other programs such as Microsoft Excel.

Data can also be transferred into a SQL Server table from a data file by using the *BULK INSERT* statement. The *BULK INSERT* statement cannot bulk copy data from an instance of SQL Server to a data file, however. With the *BULK INSERT* statement, you can bulk copy data to an instance of SQL Server by using the functionality of the bcp utility in a Transact-SQL statement (rather than from the command prompt).

In order for the bcp utility and the *BULK INSERT* statement to insert data, the data file must be in row and column format. SQL Server can accept data in any ASCII or binary format as long as the terminators (characters used to separate columns and rows) can be described. The structure of the data file does not need to be identical to the structure of the SQL Server table, because bcp and *BULK INSERT* enable columns to be skipped or reordered during the bulk copy process.

Data that is bulk copied into an instance of SQL Server is appended to any existing contents in a table. Data that is bulk copied from an instance of SQL Server to a data file overwrites the previous contents of the data file.

You should keep in mind the following guidelines when you bulk copy data:

- If you are importing data, the destination table must already exist. If you are exporting to a file, bcp will create the file. The number of fields in the data file does not have to match the number of columns in the table or be in the same order.
- The data in the data file must be in character format or in a format that the bcp utility generated previously, such as native format. Each column in the table must be compatible with the field in the data file being copied. For example, it is not possible to copy an int field to a datetime column using native format bcp.
- Relevant permissions to bulk copy data are required for source and destination files and tables. To bulk copy data from a data file into a table, you must have INSERT and SELECT permissions for the table. To bulk copy a table or view to a data file, you must have SELECT permission for the table or view being bulk copied.

The following bcp command copies data from the Publishers table in the Pubs database and into the Publishers.txt file:

```
bcp pubs..publishers out publishers.txt -c -T
```

The command first identifies the database (Pubs) and the table (Publishers) from which the data will be extracted. The *out* keyword specifies that the data will be exported from the table and into the Publishers.txt file; the -c switch specifies that a character (*char*) data format should be used; and the -T switch specifies that bcp should use a trusted connection to connect to SQL Server. The contents of the Publishers.txt file will include all of the data from the Publishers table. You can use a text editor, such as Notepad, to view the data.

You can also use the bcp command prompt utility to bulk copy data from the Publishers.txt file into the Publishers2 table in the Pubs database:

```
bcp pubs..publishers2 in publishers.txt -c -T
```

Notice that this command uses the *in* keyword rather than the *out* keyword. By running this command, you insert all data from the Publishers.txt file into the Publishers2 table.

You can also use the *BULK INSERT* statement from a query tool, such as Query Analyzer, to bulk copy the data into the Publishers2 table:

```
Use Pubs
BULK INSERT Publishers2
FROM 'c:\publishers.txt'
WITH (DATAFILETYPE = 'CHAR')
```

Note   The Publishers2 table must already exist before you can bulk copy data into that table.

Using Data Formats

The bcp utility can create or read data files in the default data formats by specifying a switch at the command prompt. The following table includes a description of the four default data formats:

Data Format	Bcp Switch	BULK INSERT Clause	Description
Native	-n	DATAFILETYPE = 'native'	Uses native (database) data types. Storing information in native format is useful when information must be copied from one instance of SQL Server to another. Using native format saves time and space, preventing unnecessary conversion of data types to and from character format. A data file in native format cannot be read by any program other than bcp, however.
Character	-c	DATAFILETYPE = 'char'	Uses the character (*char*) data format for all columns, providing tabs between fields and a new-line character at the end of each row as default terminators. Storing information in character format is useful when the data is used with another program, such as a spreadsheet, or when the data needs to be copied into an instance of SQL Server from another database. Character format tends to be used when copying data from other programs that have the functionality to export and import data in plain-text format.

Data Format	Bcp Switch	BULK INSERT Clause	Description
Unicode character	-w	DATAFILETYPE = 'widechar'	The -w switch (or *widechar* value for the DATAFILETYPE clause of the *BULK INSERT* statement) uses the Unicode character data format for all columns, providing (as default terminators) tabs between fields and a newline character at the end of each row. This format allows data to be copied from a server (that is using a code page different from the code page used by the client running bcp) to another server that uses the same or different code page as the original server. This format prevents the loss of any character data, if the source and destination are Unicode data types. In addition, only a minimum number of extended characters are lost if the source and destination are not Unicode data types.
Unicode native	-N	DATAFILETYPE = 'widenative'	Uses native (database) data types for all non-character data and uses Unicode character data format for all character (*char*, *nchar*, *varchar*, *nvarchar*, *text*, and *ntext*) data.

By default, the bcp utility operates in interactive mode and queries SQL Server and the user for information required to specify the data format. When using the -n, -c, -w, or -N switches, however, bcp does not query for information about the SQL Server table on a column-by-column basis. Instead, SQL Server reads or writes the data by using the default format specified.

By default, the *BULK INSERT* statement operates in character mode (*char*). Interactive mode does not apply.

When using interactive mode to bulk copy data, the bcp utility prompts you for information regarding the storage type, prefix length, field length, and field and row terminators. The file used to store the format information for each field in the data file is called the format file. This format file provides the default information that is used either to bulk copy the data in the data file back into an instance of SQL Server or to bulk copy data from the table another time (without needing to respecify the format).

Using DTS

SQL Server DTS is a set of graphical tools and programmable objects that enable you to extract, transform, and consolidate data from disparate sources into single or multiple destinations. By using DTS tools, you can create DTS packages that enable you to create custom data-movement solutions tailored to the specialized business needs of your organization. The capability to import and export data is among the tasks that you can perform using DTS tools and packages.

DTS Tools

Data Transformation Services includes a set of tools that enable you to create, schedule, and execute DTS packages. The following table describes DTS tools:

Tool	Description
DTS Import/ Export wizard	Wizard used to copy data to and from an instance of SQL Server and to map transformations on the data. Of all the DTS tools, the DTS Import/Export wizard provides the simplest method of copying data between OLE DB data sources.
DTS Designer	Graphical tool used to build complex packages with workflows and event-driven logic. DTS Designer can also be used to edit and customize packages created with the DTS Import/ Export wizard.
DTS and Enterprise Manager	Options available for manipulating packages and accessing package information from Enterprise Manager.
DTS Package Execution Utilities	Package execution utilities include the following: The dtswiz command prompt utility enables you to start the DTS Import/Export wizard from a command prompt. The dtswiz command includes a set of command switches. The dtsrun command prompt utility enables you to execute an existing package from a command prompt. The dtsrun command includes a set of command switches. The DTS Run utility provides a set of dialog boxes that are used to execute an existing package. You can run the DTS Run utility by executing dtsrunui from a command prompt without any command switches.
DTS Query Designer	A graphical tool used to build queries in DTS.

DTS Packages

A DTS package is an organized collection of connections, DTS tasks, DTS transformations, and workflow constraints that are assembled either with a DTS tool or programmatically, and then saved to SQL Server, SQL Server 2000 Meta Data Services, a structured storage file, or a Microsoft Visual Basic file.

Each package contains one or more steps that are executed sequentially or in parallel when the package is run. When executed, the package connects to the correct data sources, copies data and database objects, transforms data, and notifies other users or processes of events. Packages can be edited, password protected, scheduled for execution, and retrieved by version.

DTS Tasks

A DTS task is a discrete set of functionalities executed as a single step in a package. Each task defines a work item to be performed as part of the data movement and data transformation process or as a job to be executed.

Data Transformation Services supplies a number of tasks that are part of the DTS object model and that can be accessed graphically through DTS Designer or accessed programmatically. These tasks, which can be configured individually, cover a wide variety of data copying, data transformation, and notification situations. For example, the following types of tasks represent some actions that you can perform by using DTS:

- **Importing and exporting data.** DTS can import data from a text file or from an OLE DB data source (for example, a Microsoft Access 2000 database) into SQL Server. Alternatively, data can be exported from SQL Server to an OLE DB data destination (for example, a Microsoft Excel 2000 spreadsheet). DTS also enables high-speed data loading from text files into SQL Server tables.

- **Transforming data.** DTS Designer includes a Transform Data task that enables you to select data from a data source connection, map the columns of data to a set of transformations, and send the transformed data to a destination connection. DTS Designer also includes a Data-Driven Query task that enables you to map data to parameterized queries.

- **Copying database objects.** With DTS, you can transfer indexes, views, logins, stored procedures, triggers, rules, defaults, constraints, and user-defined data types in addition to the data. In addition, you can generate the scripts to copy the database objects.

- **Sending and receiving messages to and from other users and packages.** DTS includes a Send Mail task that enables you to send an e-mail if a package step succeeds or fails. DTS also includes an Execute Package task that enables one package to run another as a package step and includes a Message Queue task that enables you to use Message Queuing to send and receive messages between packages.

- **Executing a set of Transact-SQL statements or ActiveX scripts against a data source.** The Execute SQL and ActiveX Script tasks enable you to write your own SQL statements and scripting code and execute them as a step in a package workflow.

Because DTS is based on an extensible Component Object Model (COM), you can create your own custom tasks. You can integrate custom tasks into the user interface of DTS Designer and save them as part of the DTS object model.

DTS Transformations

A DTS transformation is one or more functions or operations applied against a piece of data before the data arrives at the destination. The source data is not changed. For example, you can extract a substring from a column of source data and copy it to a destination table. The particular substring function is the transformation mapped onto the source column. You also can search for rows that have certain characteristics (for example, specific data values in columns) and apply functions against only the data in those rows. Transformations make it easy to implement complex data validation, data scrubbing, and conversions during the import and export process.

Data transformations enable you to perform the following operations against column data:

- **Manipulating column data.**   For example, you can change the type, size, scale, precision, or nullability of a column.
- **Applying functions written as ActiveX scripts.**   These functions can apply specialized transformations or include conditional logic. For example, you can write a function in a scripting language that examines the data in a column for values greater than 1000. Whenever such a value is found, a value of -1 is substituted in the destination table. For rows that have column values less than 1000, the value is copied to the destination table.
- **Choosing from among a number of transformations supplied with DTS.**   Examples would include a function that reformats input data by using string and date formatting; various string conversion functions; and a function that copies to a destination column the contents of a file specified by a source column.
- **Writing your own transformations.**   As COM objects and applying those transformations against column data.

DTS Connections

Data Transformation Services is based on an OLE DB architecture that enables you to copy and transform data from a variety of data sources:

- SQL Server and Oracle directly (using native OLE DB providers)
- ODBC sources (using the Microsoft OLE DB Provider for ODBC)
- Access 2000, Excel 2000, Visual FoxPro, dBase, Paradox, HTML, and additional file data sources
- Text files (by using the built-in DTS flat file OLE DB provider)
- Microsoft Exchange Server, Microsoft Active Directory, and other non-relational data sources
- Other data sources provided by third-party vendors

DTS functionality might be limited by the capabilities of specific databases, ODBC drivers, or OLE DB providers.

DTS Package Workflow

Data Transformation Services steps and precedence constraints order work items in a DTS package. You can design the DTS package workflow graphically through DTS Designer or design the workflow programmatically. You also can use an ActiveX script to customize step execution.

Steps control the order in which tasks are executed in a DTS package. Steps represent the execution units in the DTS object model, and they define which tasks execute in what sequence when the package is run.

You can define the sequence of step execution in a package with precedence constraints that link two tasks based on whether the first task executes, whether it executes successfully, or whether it executes unsuccessfully. You can use precedence constraints to build conditional branches in a workflow. Steps without constraints are executed immediately, and several steps can execute in parallel. You can also use ActiveX scripts to modify workflow.

Exercise 1: Importing and Exporting Data

In this exercise, you will import data from text files into tables in the BookShopDB database. You will first import data into lookup tables, such as BookCondition and Position, and you will then populate other tables in the database. When you have completed importing data, you will export data from the BookShopDB database into text files that are created on your hard drive. To complete this exercise, you must copy the text files in the \Chapter07\Exercise1 folder of the Training Kit Supplemental CD-ROM to the root directory of the C drive on your Windows 2000 computer. In addition, you should be logged into your Windows 2000 Server computer as Administrator.

Note   You are not limited to the C drive or to the root folder. You can select another drive or folder in which to store the files as long as you can run the bcp command from that folder. However, the root folder on the C drive is used throughout this exercise.

▶ **To use the bcp command prompt utility to import data into the Book-Condition table**

1. Click Start, then click Run.

   The Run dialog box appears.

2. In the Open text box, type **cmd**.

3. Click OK.

   A command prompt window appears.

4. If the command prompt is not located at the root directory, type **cd c:** and then press ENTER.

5. At the C: command prompt, type **bcp bookshopdb..bookcondition in bookcondition.txt -c -T**, and then press ENTER.

    The bcp command identifies the database (BookShopDB) and table (BookCondition) that will receive the imported data. The data source (BookCondition.txt) is also identified. The *in* keyword is used when importing data into a table. The -c switch specifies that a character (*char*) data type should be used, and the -T switch specifies that a trusted connection should be used.

    After you press Enter, the bcp utility copies the data from the Book-Condition.txt file into the BookCondition table. Once the data has been copied, a message appears and provides the number of rows copied, the network packet size, and the clock time.

▶ **To view the contents of the BookCondition table**

1. Open Query Analyzer and connect to your local server.

2. In the Editor pane of the Query window, enter the following Transact-SQL code:

    ```
    USE BookShopDB
    SELECT * FROM BookCondition
    ```

    In this statement, you are using a *SELECT* statement to retrieve data from the BookCondition table in the BookShopDB database.

3. Execute the Transact-SQL statement.

    The result set appears in the Grids tab of the Results pane. Notice that each row in the Description column contains a value of N/A. This value can be changed at any time to include a more detailed description of what each book condition means.

▶ **To use a *BULK INSERT* statement to import data into the Positions table**

1. In the Editor pane of the Query window, enter the following Transact-SQL code:

    ```
    USE BookShopDB
    BULK INSERT Positions
    FROM 'c:\positions.txt'
    WITH (DATAFILETYPE = 'CHAR')
    ```

    In this *BULK INSERT* statement, you are identifying the table that will receive the data (Positions) and the data source (Positions.txt). The statement uses a *CHAR* data type.

2. Execute the Transact-SQL statement.

    A message appears in the Messages tab of the Results pane, providing the number of rows affected.

3. Use a *SELECT* statement to view the data in the Positions table. Notice that a PositionID value has been provided for each type of position.

▶ **To use *BULK INSERT* statements to import data into the OrderStatus and FormOfPayment tables**

1. Use *BULK INSERT* statements to insert data from the FormOfPayment.txt file to the FormOfPayment table and from the OrderStatus.txt file to the Order-Status table.

   What statements should you use?

2. Use *SELECT* statements to view the data within the OrderStatus table and the FormOfPayment table.

   Both tables should now be populated with the appropriate data.

▶ **To use *BULK INSERT* statements to import data into the Authors table, Books table, Customers table, and Employees table**

1. Use *BULK INSERT* statements to insert data from the Authors.txt file into the Authors table, from the Books.txt file into the Books table, from the Customers.txt file into the Customers table, and from the Employees.txt file into the Employees table.

   What statements should you use?

2. Use *SELECT* statements to view the data within the four tables.

Note   The data used to populate these tables is for demonstration purposes only. The data is by no means factual, although real authors and real books have been used. In addition, the amount of data is less than would be expected for the database. You might also notice that information about customers is similar to information about employees. At this point, you should be concerned only with the functionality of the database and how relational data is being stored in the tables, not with the accuracy of the data itself (other than the fact that it adheres to constraints defined for the system).

▶ **To use the bcp command prompt utility to import data into the BookAuthors table**

1. Use the bcp utility to copy data from the BookAuthors.txt file into the Book-Authors table.

   What bcp command should you use?

2. Use a *SELECT* statement in Query Analyzer to view the contents of the Book-Authors table.

   Notice that author 102 appears in the table twice. If more than one author wrote a book, the TitleID value for that book would appear in more than one row.

3. Close Query Analyzer.

   Every table in the BookShopDB database (except for the Orders table and the BookOrders table) should now be populated with data. Data is not added to the Orders table or to the BookOrders table until new orders are generated.

▶ **To use the bcp command prompt utility to export data into a text file**

1. At the C: command prompt, type **bcp bookshopdb..books out Books2. txt -c -T**, and then press ENTER.

   The bcp command identifies the database (BookShopDB) and table (Books) from which data will be exported. A text file (Books2.txt) will be created, and the data from the Books table will be copied into that file. The *out* keyword is used when exporting data from a table.

   After you press Enter, the bcp utility copies the data from the Books table into the Books2.txt file. Once the data has been copied, a message appears providing the number of rows copied, the network packet size, and the clock time.

2. Use a text editor such as Notepad to view the contents of the Books2.txt file.

   Notice that each row in the table is on a separate line and that a tab separates each column value within a row.

3. Close the Books2.txt file and the command prompt window.

Lesson Summary

Importing data is the process of retrieving data from sources external to SQL Server and inserting the data into SQL Server tables. Exporting data is the process of extracting data from an instance of SQL Server into some user-specified format. The bcp command prompt utility copies SQL Server data to or from a data file. Data can also be transferred into a SQL Server table from a data file by using the *BULK INSERT* statement. The *BULK INSERT* statement cannot bulk copy data from an instance of SQL Server to a data file, however. Data that is bulk copied into an instance of SQL Server is appended to any existing contents in a table. Data that is bulk copied from an instance of SQL Server to a data file overwrites the previous contents of the data file. DTS is a set of graphical tools and programmable objects that enable you to extract, transform, and consolidate data from disparate sources into single or multiple destinations. By using DTS tools, you can create DTS packages with custom data-movement solutions tailored to your organization's business needs. A DTS package is an organized collection of connections, DTS tasks, DTS transformations, and workflow constraints that are assembled either with a DTS tool or programmatically and saved to SQL Server, SQL Server 2000 Meta Data Services, a structured storage file, or a Microsoft Visual Basic file.

Lesson 2: Using Distributed Queries to Access External Data

By using distributed queries, you can access data stored in multiple instances of SQL Server and heterogeneous data stored in various relational and non-relational data sources. SQL Server 2000 supports distributed queries through the use of OLE DB, the Microsoft specification of an Application Programming Interface (API) for universal data access. In this lesson, you will learn how to use distributed queries to access data in external data sources. The lesson focuses on how to use linked servers for frequent queries against OLE DB data sources and how to use ad hoc names for infrequent queries against OLE DB data sources.

After this lesson, you will be able to:

- Use linked servers, Transact-SQL statements, and the *OPENQUERY* function to access external data.
- Use ad hoc computer names and the *OPENROWSET* and *OPENDATASOURCE* functions to access external data.

Estimated lesson time: 30 minutes

Introduction to Distributed Queries

In SQL Server 2000, a distributed query is a single query that can access data from multiple data sources, including distributed data and heterogeneous data. Distributed queries can access data from external sources by using OLE DB. OLE DB providers expose data in tabular objects called *rowsets*. SQL Server 2000 enables rowsets from OLE DB providers to be referenced in Transact-SQL statements as if they were SQL Server tables.

Tables and views in external data sources can be referenced directly in *SELECT*, *INSERT*, *UPDATE*, and *DELETE* Transact-SQL statements. Because they use OLE DB as the underlying interface, distributed queries can access traditional RDBMS systems having SQL query processors as well as data that is managed by data sources of varying capabilities and sophistication. As long as the software owning the data exposes it in a tabular rowset through an OLE DB provider, the data can be used in distributed queries.

Note   Using distributed queries in SQL Server is similar to the linked table functionality through ODBC, which Microsoft Access previously supported. This functionality is now built into SQL Server with OLE DB as the interface to external data.

To access data from an OLE DB data source, you must provide SQL Server with the following information:

- The name of the OLE DB provider that exposes the data source
- Any information that the OLE DB provider needs to locate the source of the data
- Either the name of an object that the OLE DB data source can expose as a rowset, or a query that can be sent to the OLE DB provider that will cause it to expose a rowset. (The objects that can be exposed as rowsets are known as remote tables. The queries that generate rowsets are known as pass-through queries.)
- Optionally, valid login IDs for the OLE DB data source

SQL Server 2000 supports two methods for referencing heterogeneous OLE DB data sources in Transact-SQL statements: the linked server name and the ad hoc computer name.

Using Linked Server Names in Distributed Queries

You can use linked server names in Transact-SQL statements to identify external data sources. Once the linked server is defined, the linked server name can be used as the server name in a four-part name (in a table or view reference) or as an input parameter to an *OPENQUERY* function.

Linked Servers

A linked server is a virtual server that has been defined in SQL Server. The linked server definition includes all of the information needed to access an OLE DB data source. You can set up a linked server by using Enterprise Manager or by using the *sp_addlinkedserver* system-stored procedure. The linked server definition contains all of the information needed to locate the OLE DB data source.

Note Linked server names are most often referenced in distributed queries. Remote stored procedures can also access linked servers, however. Stored procedures can be executed against the linked server by using a four-part name.

A linked server definition specifies an OLE DB provider, such as Microsoft OLE DB Provider for SQL Server, and an OLE DB data source, such as an instance of SQL Server. An OLE DB provider is a dynamic link library (DLL) that manages and interacts with a specific data source. An OLE DB data source identifies the specific database that is accessible through OLE DB. Although data sources that are queried through linked server definitions are usually databases, OLE DB providers exist for a wide variety of files and file formats, including text files, spreadsheet data, and the results of full-text content searches.

Four-Part Names

After a linked server is defined, a four-part name in the form *linked_server_name.catalog.schema.object_name* can be used in Transact-SQL statements to reference data objects in that linked server. The following table describes the parts of a four-part name:

Part Name	Description
linked_server_name	Linked server referencing the OLE DB data source
Catalog	Catalog in the OLE DB data source that contains the object
Schema	Schema in the catalog that contains the object
object_name	Data object in the schema

SQL Server uses the linked server name to identify the OLE DB provider and the data source. The *catalog, schema*, and *object_name* parameters are passed to the OLE DB provider to identify a specific data object. When the linked server refers to an instance of SQL Server, *catalog* refers to a database and *schema* refers to an owner ID.

The following *SELECT* statement returns all rows from the Contacts table:

```
SELECT *
FROM StoreOwners...Contacts
```

This *SELECT* statement uses the StoreOwners linked server name to identify the OLE DB data source. Notice that the linked server name and the object name are connected by three periods (StoreOwners...Contacts) that serve as placeholders for the catalog and schema.

The *OPENQUERY* Function

The *OPENQUERY* function is used to execute the specified pass-through query on the given linked server, which is an OLE DB data source. The *OPENQUERY* function can be referenced in the FROM clause of a query as though it were a table name. The *OPENQUERY* function can also be referenced as the target table of an *INSERT*, *UPDATE*, or *DELETE* statement (subject to the capabilities of the OLE DB provider). Although the query might return multiple result sets, *OPENQUERY* returns only the first one.

The following *SELECT* statement returns the LastName values in the contacts table:

```
SELECT *
FROM OPENQUERY (StoreOwners, 'SELECT LastName FROM Contacts')
```

This *SELECT* statement uses the *OPENQUERY* function to retrieve data from an external data source. The linked server name is one of the parameters of the *OPEN-QUERY* function.

Using Ad Hoc Computer Names in Distributed Queries

You can use an ad hoc computer name for infrequent queries against OLE DB data sources that are not defined with a linked server name. In SQL Server 2000, the *OPENROWSET* and *OPENDATASOURCE* functions provide connection information for accessing data from OLE DB data sources.

You should use the *OPENROWSET* and *OPENDATASOURCE* functions only to reference OLE DB data sources that are accessed infrequently. For any data sources that will be accessed more than a few times, define a linked server. Neither *OPENDATASOURCE* nor *OPENROWSET* provide all of the functionality of linked server definitions, such as security management or catalog information queries. Each time these functions are called, all connection information, including passwords, must be provided.

Although *OPENROWSET* and *OPENDATASOURCE* appear to be functions and are referred to as such, they are technically not functions. *OPENROWSET* and *OPENDATASOURCE* are macros and do not support supplying Transact-SQL variables as arguments.

The *OPENROWSET* Function

The *OPENROWSET* function can be used with any OLE DB provider that returns a rowset and can be used anywhere a table or view reference is used in a Transact-SQL statement. *OPENROWSET* is specified with the following information:

- All of the information needed to connect to the OLE DB data source
- Either the name of an object that will generate a rowset or a query that will generate a rowset

The following *SELECT* statement uses the *OPENROWSET* function to connect to a Microsoft Access database file and access data in the Contacts table:

```
SELECT *
FROM OPENROWSET
('Microsoft.jet.oledb.4.0',
'C:\StoreOwners.mdb'; 'admin'; '', Contacts)
```

In this *SELECT* statement, the OLE DB provider is Microsoft.jet.oledb.4.0; the data source is C:\StoreOwners.mdb; the user ID is admin; and there is no password.

The *OPENDATASOURCE* Function

The *OPENDATASOURCE* function provides connection information as part of a four-part object name. This function supports only OLE DB providers that expose multiple rowsets that use the *catalog.schema.object* notation. *OPENDATA-SOURCE* can be used in the same Transact-SQL syntax locations where a linked server name can be used. *OPENDATASOURCE* is specified with the following information:

- The name registered as the PROGID of the OLE DB provider that is used to access the data source
- A connection string that specifies the various connection properties to be passed to the OLE DB provider

---

Note   The connection string syntax is a sequence of keyword-value pairs. The basic syntax is defined in the Microsoft Data Access Software Development Kit, and each provider documents the specific keyword-value pairs that it supports.

The following *SELECT* statement uses the *OPENDATASOURCE* function to connect to a Microsoft Access database file and access data in the Contacts table:

```
SELECT *
FROM OPENDATASOURCE
('Microsoft.Jet.oledb.4.0',
'Data Source = c:\StoreOwners.mdb; User ID = Admin; Password = ')
...Contacts
```

In this *SELECT* statement, the OLE DB provider is Microsoft.jet.oledb.4.0; the data source is C:\StoreOwners.mdb; the user ID is admin; and there is no password.

Exercise 2: Using Distributed Queries to Access External Data

In this exercise, you will define a linked server and then use Transact-SQL *SELECT* statements to connect an external data source. To complete this exercise, you must copy the Test1.mdb file in the \Chapter07\Exercise2 folder of the Training Kit Supplemental CD-ROM to the root directory of the C: drive of your Windows 2000 computer. In addition, you should be logged into your Windows 2000 Server computer as Administrator.

Note   You are not limited to the C drive or to the root folder. You can select another drive or folder in which to store the files as long as you can access that file through the linked server and Transact-SQL statements.

▶ **To define a linked server**

1. Open Enterprise Manager and expand the Security tab of the local database.
2. Right-click the Linked Servers node, then click New Linked Server.

   The Linked Server Properties - New Linked Server dialog box appears.
3. Select the Other Data Source radio button.

   Many of the options on the bottom half of the dialog box become active.
4. In the Linked Server text box, type **TEST_SERVER**.
5. In the Provider Name drop-down list, select Microsoft Jet 4.0 OLE DB Provider.
6. In the Data Source text box, type **C:\Test1.mdb**.
7. Click OK.

   The Test_Server linked server is added to the console tree.

▶ **To use an *OPENQUERY* function to query an external data source**

1. Open Query Analyzer and connect to your local server.
2. In the Editor pane of the Query window, enter the following Transact-SQL code:

   ```
   SELECT *
   FROM OPENQUERY
   (Test_Server, 'SELECT FirstName, LastName FROM TestTable1')
   ```

   In this statement, you are using the *OPENQUERY* function to identify the linked server (Test_Server) and to define a *SELECT* statement that returns the FirstName and LastName values from the TestTable1 table.
3. Execute the Transact-SQL statement.

   The result set appears in the Grids tab of the Results pane.

▶ **To use a Transact-SQL statement to query an external data source**

1. In the Editor pane of the Query window, enter the following Transact-SQL code:

   ```
   SELECT FirstName, LastName
   FROM Test_Server...TestTable1
   ```

   In this statement, you are identifying the linked server as part of a four-part name. Notice that three periods (...) are used as placeholders for two of the parts. This statement returns the same result as that returned by the statement in the previous procedure.

2. Execute the Transact-SQL statement.

The result set appears in the Grids tab of the Results pane.

▶ **To use the *OPENROWSET* function to query an external data source**

1. In the Editor pane of the Query window, enter the following Transact-SQL code:

```
SELECT FirstName, LastName
FROM OPENROWSET
('Microsoft.jet.oledb.4.0', 'C:\Test1.mdb';
'admin'; '', TestTable1)
```

In this statement, you are using an *OPENROWSET* function to return the First-Name and LastName values from the TestTable1 table. Note that the OLE DB provider is Microsoft.jet.oledb.4.0; the data source is C:\Test1.mdb; the user ID is admin; and there is no password.

2. Execute the Transact-SQL statement.

The result set appears in the Grids tab of the Results pane.

Lesson Summary

By using distributed queries, you can access data stored in multiple instances of SQL Server and heterogeneous data stored in various relational and non-relational data sources. Distributed queries can access data from external sources by using OLE DB. SQL Server 2000 supports the methods for referencing heterogeneous OLE DB data sources in Transact-SQL statements: the linked server name and the ad hoc computer name. You can use linked server names in Transact-SQL statements to identify external data sources. Once the linked server is defined, the linked server name can be used as the server name in a four-part name in a table or view reference or as an *OPENQUERY* input parameter. In addition, an ad hoc computer name can be used for infrequent queries against OLE DB data sources that are not defined with a linked server name. In SQL Server 2000, the *OPENROWSET* and *OPENDATASOURCE* functions provide connection information for accessing data from OLE DB data sources.

Lesson 3: Using Cursors to Retrieve Data

A *cursor* is an entity that maps over a result set and establishes a position on a single row within the result set. After the cursor is positioned on a row, operations can be performed on that row or on a block of rows starting at that position. This lesson will introduce you to SQL Server cursors and to the three types of cursor implementations. You will also learn how to fetch (retrieve) a row from a cursor and how to specify the behavior of a cursor. In addition, you will be introduced to cursor locking.

After this lesson, you will be able to:

- Describe the three types of cursor implementations: Transact-SQL server cursors, API server cursors, and client cursors.
- Use Transact-SQL to declare, open, and close a cursor.
- Use Transact-SQL to fetch rows from a cursor.

Estimated lesson time: 30 minutes

Introduction to Cursors

Operations in a relational database act on a complete set of rows. The set of rows returned by a *SELECT* statement consists of all the rows that satisfy the conditions in the WHERE clause of the statement. This complete set of rows returned by the statement is known as the *result set*. Applications—especially interactive, online applications—cannot always work effectively with the entire result set as a unit. These applications need a mechanism to work with one row or with a small block of rows at a time. Cursors are an extension to result sets that provide that mechanism.

Cursors extend result processing by supporting the following functionalities:

- Allowing positioning at specific rows of the result set
- Retrieving one row or block of rows from the current position in the result set
- Supporting data modifications to the rows at the current position in the result set
- Supporting different levels of visibility for changes made by other users to the data in the result set
- Providing access to the data in a result set for Transact-SQL statements in scripts, stored procedures, and triggers

SQL Server supports three types of cursor implementations: Transact-SQL server cursors, API server cursors, and client cursors. Because Transact-SQL server cursors and API server cursors are implemented on the server, they are referred to collectively as server cursors.

Do not mix the use of these various types of cursors. If you execute a *DECLARE CURSOR* and *OPEN* statement from an application, first set the API cursor attributes to their defaults. If you set API cursor attributes to something other than their defaults and then execute a *DECLARE CURSOR* and *OPEN* statement, you are asking SQL Server to map an API cursor over a Transact-SQL cursor. For example, do not set the ODBC attributes that call for mapping a keyset-driven cursor over a result set and then use that statement handle to execute a *DECLARE CURSOR* and *OPEN* statement that calls for an INSENSITIVE cursor.

A potential drawback of server cursors is that they currently do not support all Transact-SQL statements. Server cursors do not support Transact-SQL statements that generate multiple result sets; therefore, they cannot be used when the application executes a stored procedure or a batch that contains more than one *SELECT* statement. Server cursors also do not support SQL statements containing the keywords COMPUTE, COMPUTE BY, FOR BROWSE, or INTO.

Transact-SQL Server Cursors

Transact-SQL Server cursors are based on the *DECLARE CURSOR* statement and are used mainly in Transact-SQL scripts, stored procedures, and triggers. Transact-SQL cursors are implemented on the server and are managed by Transact-SQL statements sent from the client to the server. They are also contained in batches, stored procedures, or triggers.

When working with Transact-SQL cursors, you use a set of Transact-SQL statements to declare, populate, and retrieve data (as outlined in the following steps):

1. Use a *DECLARE CURSOR* statement to declare the cursor. When you declare the cursor, you should specify the *SELECT* statement that will produce the cursor's result set.

2. Use an *OPEN* statement to populate the cursor. This statement executes the *SELECT* statement embedded in the *DECLARE CURSOR* statement.

3. Use a *FETCH* statement to retrieve individual rows from the result set. Typically, a *FETCH* statement is executed many times (at least once for each row in the result set).

4. If appropriate, use an *UPDATE* or *DELETE* statement to modify the row. This step is optional.

5. Use a *CLOSE* statement to close the cursor. This process ends the active cursor operation and frees some resources (such as the cursor's result set and its locks on the current row). The cursor is still declared, so you can use an *OPEN* statement to reopen it.

6. Use a *DEALLOCATE* statement to remove the cursor reference from the current session. This process completely frees all resources allocated to the cursor (including the cursor name). After a cursor is deallocated, you must issue a *DECLARE* statement to rebuild the cursor.

The following set of Transact-SQL statements illustrates how to declare a cursor, populate that cursor, retrieve data from the result set, update that data, close the cursor, and deallocate the cursor:

```
/
* Declares the AuthorsCursor cursor and associates the cursor with a SE-
LECT statement. */
USE Pubs
DECLARE AuthorsCursor CURSOR FOR
        SELECT * FROM Authors
        ORDER BY Au_lname


/
* Populates the AuthorsCursor cursor with the result set from the SELECT
  statement. */
OPEN AuthorsCursor

/* Retrieves the first row from the result set. */
FETCH NEXT FROM AuthorsCursor

/* Updates the phone number within the retrieved row. */
UPDATE Authors
SET Phone = '415 658-9932'
WHERE CURRENT OF AuthorsCursor

/* Closes the AuthorsCursor cursor. */
CLOSE AuthorsCursor

/* Deallocates the AuthorsCursor cursor. */
DEALLOCATE AuthorsCursor
```

Referencing Transact-SQL Cursors

Only Transact-SQL statements can reference Transact-SQL cursor names and variables. The API functions of OLE DB, ODBC, ADO, and DB-Library cannot reference Transact-SQL cursor names and variables. Applications that need cursor processing and are using these APIs should use the cursor support built into the database API, instead of Transact-SQL cursors.

You can use Transact-SQL cursors in applications by using *FETCH* and by binding each column returned by the *FETCH* to a program variable. The Transact-SQL *FETCH* does not support batches, however, so this method is the least efficient way to return data to an application: Fetching each row requires a round trip to the server. A more efficient way to fetch rows is to use the cursor functionality built into the database APIs that support batches.

Transact-SQL cursors are extremely efficient when contained in stored procedures and triggers. Everything is compiled into one execution plan on the server, and there is no network traffic associated with fetching rows.

API Server Cursors

API server cursors are cursors that are implemented on the server and are managed by API cursor functions. API server cursors support the API cursor functions in OLE DB, ODBC, and DB-Library. Each time a client application calls an API cursor function, the SQL Server OLE DB provider, ODBC driver, or DB-Library DLL transmits the request to the server for action against the API server cursor.

Note   Although API cursors have a different syntax from Transact-SQL cursors, API cursors follow the same general process that is used for Transact-SQL cursors. You must declare the cursor, open the cursor, retrieve data from the cursor, close the cursor, and deallocate the cursor.

The OLE DB, ODBC, ADO, and DB-Library APIs support mapping cursors over the result sets of executed SQL statements. The SQL Server OLE DB provider, SQL Server ODBC driver, and DB-Library DLL implement these operations through the use of API server cursors.

When using an API server cursor in OLE DB, ODBC, and ADO, use the functions or methods of the API to perform the following tasks:

- Opening a connection
- Setting attributes defining the characteristics of the cursor that the API automatically maps over each result set
- Executing one or more Transact-SQL statements
- Using API functions or methods to fetch the rows in the result sets

In DB-Library, use the special DB-Library Cursor Library functions to work with an API server cursor.

If the API cursor attributes are set to their default settings, the SQL Server OLE DB provider and SQL Server ODBC driver use default result sets. Although the API is technically asking for a cursor, the default cursor characteristics match the behavior of a default result set. The OLE DB provider and ODBC driver, therefore, implement the default cursor options by using a default result set. This method is the most efficient way to retrieve rows from the server. When using default result sets, an application can execute any Transact-SQL statement or batch, but it can have only one outstanding statement on a connection. In other words, the application must process or cancel all of the result sets returned by one statement before it can execute another statement on the connection.

If the API cursor attributes are set to anything other than their defaults, the SQL Server OLE DB provider and the SQL Server ODBC driver use API server cursors instead of default result sets. Each call to an API function that fetches rows generates a round trip to the server to fetch the rows from the API server cursor.

DB-Library applications use the DB-Library Cursor Library functions to request cursors. If DBCLIENTCURSOR is not set, the DB-Library Cursor Library functions use API server cursors in the same way as the SQL Server OLE DB provider and SQL Server ODBC driver.

API Server Cursor Restrictions

An application cannot execute the following statements when using API server cursors:

- Transact-SQL statements that SQL Server does not support in server cursors
- Batches or stored procedures that return multiple result sets
- *SELECT* statements that contain COMPUTE, COMPUTE BY, FOR BROWSE, or INTO clauses
- An *EXECUTE* statement referencing a remote stored procedure

Client Cursors

The SQL Server ODBC driver, the DB-Library DLL, and the ADO API DLL help implement client cursors internally. Client cursors are implemented by caching all of the client's result set rows. Each time a client application calls an API cursor function, the SQL Server ODBC driver, the DB-Library DLL, or the ADO DLL performs the cursor operation on the result set rows cached on the client.

In a client cursor, a default result set is used to cache the entire result set on the client, and all cursor operations are performed against this client cache. None of the server cursor functionality of SQL Server 2000 is used. Client cursors support only forward-only and static cursors, not keyset-driven or dynamic cursors.

The DB-Library client cursors were originally implemented before SQL Server supported server cursors. ODBC implements client cursors that use the ODBC Cursor Library. This library is intended for use with ODBC drivers that support only the default settings for cursor characteristics. Because both DB-Library and the SQL Server ODBC driver offer full support for cursor operations through server cursors, you should limit the use of client cursors.

You should use client cursors only to alleviate the restriction that server cursors do not support all Transact-SQL statements or batches. If a static, scrolling cursor is needed on a Transact-SQL statement or batch that cannot be executed with a server cursor, consider using a client cursor.

Fetching and Scrolling

The operation to retrieve a row from a cursor is called a fetch. When working with Transact-SQL cursors, you can use *FETCH* statements to retrieve rows from a cursor's result set.

A *FETCH* statement supports a number of options that enable you to retrieve specific rows:

- **FETCH FIRST.**   Fetches the first row in the cursor
- **FETCH NEXT.**   Fetches the row after the last row fetched
- **FETCH PRIOR.**   Fetches the row before the last row fetched
- **FETCH LAST.**   Fetches the last row in the cursor
- **FETCH ABSOLUTE n.**   Fetches the *n*th row from the first row in the cursor if *n* is a positive integer. If *n* is a negative integer, the row that is *n* rows before the end of the cursor is fetched. If *n* is 0, no rows are fetched.
- **FETCH RELATIVE n.**   Fetches the row that is *n* rows from the last row fetched. If *n* is positive, the row that is *n* rows after the last row fetched is fetched. If *n* is negative, the row that is *n* rows before the last row fetched is fetched. If *n* is 0, the same row is fetched again.

Note   The APIs for the actual statements, functions, or methods used have different names for fetching rows.

When a cursor is opened, the current row position in the cursor is logically before the first row.

Transact-SQL cursors are limited to fetching one row at a time. API server cursors support fetching blocks of rows with each fetch. A cursor that supports fetching multiple rows at a time is called a block cursor. For more information about retrieving data from a cursor, refer to SQL Server Books Online.

Controlling Cursor Behavior

There are two models for specifying the behavior of a cursor:

- **Cursor types.**   The database APIs usually specify the behavior of cursors by dividing them into four cursor types: forward-only, static (sometimes called snapshot or insensitive), keyset-driven, and dynamic.
- **Cursor behaviors.**   The SQL-92 standard defines the DECLARE CURSOR keywords SCROLL and INSENSITIVE to specify the behavior of cursors. Some database APIs also support defining cursor behavior in terms of scrollability and sensitivity.

ADO and DB-Library support specifying only cursor types, not cursor behaviors. ODBC supports specifying cursor behavior by using either the cursor types or the cursor behaviors of scrollability and insensitivity.

Prior to SQL Server 7.0, the *DECLARE CURSOR* statement used to define Transact-SQL cursors supported only cursor behaviors of SCROLL and

INSENSITIVE. In SQL Server 7.0, *DECLARE CURSOR* was extended to support cursor-type keywords.

OLE DB's cursor behavior model differs from both cursor behaviors and cursor types.

Do not specify both cursor types and cursor behaviors for a cursor. Use one or the other. Because ODBC and Transact-SQL cursors support both cursor behaviors and cursor types, use either ODBC or Transact-SQL when you are defining the cursor. The ODBC specification states that specifying both cursor behaviors and cursor types can lead to unpredictable results.

Cursor Locking

In SQL Server, the *SELECT* statement in a cursor definition is subject to the same transaction locking rules that apply to any other *SELECT* statement. In cursors, however, an additional set of scroll locks can be acquired based on the specification of a cursor concurrency level.

The transaction locks acquired by any *SELECT* statement, including the *SELECT* statement in a cursor definition, are controlled by the following options:

- The transaction isolation level setting for the connection
- Any locking hints specified in the FROM clause

These locks are held until the end of the current transaction for both cursors and independent *SELECT* statements. When SQL Server is running in autocommit mode, each individual SQL statement is a transaction, and the locks are freed when the statement finishes. If SQL Server is running in explicit or implicit transaction mode, then the locks are held until the transaction is either committed or rolled back.

Transactions and locking are discussed in more detail in Chapter 12, "Managing SQL Server Transactions and Locks."

Exercise 3: Creating a Cursor to Retrieve Data

In this exercise, you will declare a Transact-SQL cursor, populate that cursor, retrieve rows from the cursor's result set, close the cursor, and deallocate the cursor. To complete this exercise, you should be logged into your Windows 2000 Server computer as Administrator.

▶ **To use a DECLARE CURSOR statement to declare a cursor and an OPEN statement to populate the cursor**

1. Open Query Analyzer and connect to your local server.
2. In the Editor pane of the Query window, enter the following Transact-SQL code:

```
USE BookShopDB
DECLARE CustomerCrs CURSOR FOR
    SELECT * FROM Customers
    WHERE City = 'Seattle'
    ORDER BY LastName, FirstName
```

In this statement, you are declaring a Transact-SQL cursor named Customer-Crs. The cursor is associated with a *SELECT* statement that retrieves all the customers who live in Seattle from the Customers table.

3. Execute the Transact-SQL statement.

   A message appears in the Messages tab of the Results pane, stating that the command has been successfully completed.

4. In the Editor pane of the Query window, enter the following code:

```
OPEN CustomerCrs
```

   In this statement, you are populating the cursor with the result from the *SELECT* statement that you specified when you declared the cursor.

5. Execute the *OPEN* statement.

   A message appears in the Messages tab of the Results pane, stating that the command has been successfully completed.

▶ **To use a *FETCH* statement to retrieve rows from a cursor**

1. In the Editor pane of the Query window, enter the following Transact-SQL code:

```
FETCH NEXT FROM CustomerCrs
```

   In this statement, you are retrieving the next row from the result set. Because this is the first row that you've retrieved from this cursor in this session, the row returned will be the first row in the result set.

2. Execute the Transact-SQL statement.

   The first row of the result set appears in the Grids tab of the Results pane.

3. Execute the statement a second time.

   The second row of the result set appears in the Grids tab of the Results pane.

▶ **To use a *CLOSE* statement to close a cursor and a *DEALLOCATE* statement to deallocate the cursor**

1. In the Editor pane of the Query window, enter and execute the following Transact-SQL statement:

```
CLOSE CustomerCrs
```

   A message appears in the Messages tab of the Results pane, stating that the command has been successfully completed. The cursor has now been closed.

2. Enter and execute the following Transact-SQL statement:

    ```
    DEALLOCATE CustomerCrs
    ```

    A message appears in the Messages tab of the Results pane, stating that the command has been successfully completed. The cursor has now been deallocated.

Lesson Summary

A cursor is an entity that maps over a result set and establishes a position on a single row within the result set. Cursors extend result-set processing. SQL Server supports three types of cursor implementations: Transact-SQL server cursors, API server cursors, and client cursors. Transact-SQL Server cursors are based on the *DECLARE CURSOR* statement and are used mainly in Transact-SQL scripts, stored procedures, and triggers. API server cursors support the API cursor functions in OLE DB, ODBC, and DB-Library. Like Transact-SQL cursors, API server cursors are implemented on the server. Client cursors are implemented internally by the SQL Server ODBC driver, the DB-Library DLL, and by the DLL that implements the ADO API. The operation to retrieve a row from a cursor is called a fetch. When working with Transact-SQL cursors, you can use *FETCH* statements to retrieve rows from a cursor's result set. There are two models for specifying the behavior of a cursor: cursor types and cursor behaviors. In SQL Server, the *SELECT* statement in a cursor definition is subject to the same transaction locking rules that apply to any other *SELECT* statement. In cursors, however, an additional set of scroll locks can be acquired based on the specification of a cursor concurrency level.

Lesson 4: Retrieving XML Data

Extensible Markup Language (XML) is a hypertext programming language used to describe the contents of a set of data and how the data should be outputted to a device or displayed on a Web page. You can execute Transact-SQL queries to return a result as XML rather than as a standard rowset. These queries can be executed directly or executed from within stored procedures. In addition, you can use the Transact-SQL to access data represented as an XML document. This lesson will introduce you to XML, and you will learn how to use the FOR XML clause in a *SELECT* statement to retrieve data and the *OPENXML* function to access XML data.

After this lesson, you will be able to:

- Use Transact-SQL to return result sets as XML.
- Use Transact-SQL to access XML data.

Estimated lesson time: 30 minutes

Introduction to XML

Markup languages originated as ways for publishers to indicate to printers how the content of a newspaper, magazine, or book should be organized. Markup languages for electronic data perform the same function for electronic documents that can be displayed on different types of electronic gear.

Both XML and Hypertext Markup Language (HTML) are derived from Standard Generalized Markup Language (SGML). SGML is a very large, complex language that is difficult to fully use for publishing data on the Web. HTML is a more simple, specialized markup language than SGML but has a number of limitations when working with data on the Web. XML is smaller than SGML and more robust than HTML, so it is becoming an increasingly important language in the exchange of electronic data through the Web or through intra-company networks.

In a relational database such as SQL Server, all operations on the tables in the database produce a result in the form of a table. The result set of a *SELECT* statement is in the form of a table. Traditional client/server applications that execute a *SELECT* statement process the result by fetching one row or a block of rows at a time from the tabular result set and mapping the column values into program variables. Web application programmers, on the other hand, are more familiar with hierarchical representations of data in XML or HTML format.

SQL Server2000 includes many features that support XML's functionality. The combination of these features makes SQL Server 2000 an XML-enabled database server. The following features support XML functionality:

- The ability to access SQL Server through the use of HTTP
- Support for XML-Data Reduced (XDR) schemas and the ability to specify XPath queries against these schemas
- The ability to retrieve and write XML data
  - Retrieving XML data by using the *SELECT* statement and the FOR XML clause
  - Writing XML data by using the OPENXML rowset provider
  - Retrieving XML data by using the XPath query language
- Enhancements to the SQL Server OLE DB (SQLOLEDB) provider that enable XML documents to be set as command text and to return result sets as a stream

---

Note   XML functionality is a sophisticated and extensive component of SQL Server. This lesson can cover only a small portion of that functionality. For more information about XML, refer to SQL Server Books Online. In addition, you can refer to the XML Developer Center on MSDN (*http://msdn.microsoft.com/xml /default.asp*) for the latest updates relating to SQL Server support for XML.

Using the FOR XML Clause to Retrieve Data

You can execute SQL queries against existing relational databases in order to return a result as an XML document rather than as a standard rowset. To retrieve a result directly, use the FOR XML clause of the *SELECT* statement.

For example, the following *SELECT* statement uses a FOR XML clause that specifies the AUTO mode and the ELEMENTS keyword:

```
USE Northwind
SELECT Customers.CustomerID, ContactName, CompanyName,
       Orders.CustomerID, OrderDate
FROM Customers, Orders
WHERE Customers.CustomerID = Orders.CustomerID
       AND (Customers.CustomerID = N'ALFKI'
       OR Customers.CustomerID = N'XYZAA')
ORDER BY Customers.CustomerID
FOR XML AUTO, ELEMENTS
```

The FOR XML clause uses the following syntax:

FOR XML {RAW | AUTO | EXPLICIT} [, XMLDATA] [, ELEMENTS] [, BINARY BASE64]

RAW, AUTO, EXPLICIT

The FOR XML clause must specify one of the following XML modes: RAW, AUTO, or EXPLICIT. The XML mode determines the shape of the XML result set. The XML mode is in effect only for the execution of the query for which they are set. The mode does not affect the result of any subsequent queries.

RAW Mode

RAW mode transforms each row in the query result set into an XML element with the generic identifier row. Each column value that is not NULL is mapped to an attribute of the XML element in which the attribute name is the same as the column name.

The BINARY BASE64 option must be specified in the query in order to return the binary data in base64-encoded format. In RAW mode, retrieving binary data without specifying the BINARY BASE64 option results in an error.

When an XML-Data schema is requested, the schema, declared as a namespace, appears at the beginning of the data. In the result, the schema namespace reference is repeated for every top-level element.

AUTO Mode

AUTO mode returns query results as nested XML elements. Each table in the FROM clause, from which at least one column is listed in the SELECT clause, is represented as an XML element. The columns listed in the SELECT clause are mapped to the appropriate attribute of the element. When the ELEMENTS option is specified, the table columns are mapped to subelements instead of attributes. By default, AUTO mode maps the table columns to XML attributes.

A table name (or the alias, if provided) maps to the XML element name. A column name (or the alias, if provided) maps to an attribute name or to a non-complex subelement name when the ELEMENTS option is specified in the query.

The hierarchy (nesting of the elements) in the result set is based on the order of tables identified by the columns that are specified in the SELECT clause; therefore, the order in which column names are specified in the SELECT clause is significant.

The tables are identified and nested in the order in which the column names are listed in the SELECT clause. The first, leftmost table identified forms the top element in the resulting XML document. The second leftmost table (identified by columns in the *SELECT* statement) forms a subelement within the top element (and so on).

If a column name listed in the SELECT clause is from a table that is already identified by a previously specified column in the SELECT clause, the column is added as an attribute (or as a subelement if the ELEMENTS option is specified) of the element already created, instead of opening a new hierarchy (adding a new subelement for that table).

EXPLICIT Mode

In EXPLICIT mode, the query writer controls the shape of the XML document returned by the execution of the query. The query must be written in a specific way so that the additional information about the expected nesting is explicitly specified as part of the query. You can also specify additional configurations at the column level by using the directives. When you specify EXPLICIT mode, you must assume the responsibility for ensuring that the generated XML is well-formed and valid (in the case of an XML-DATA schema).

XMLDATA

The XMLDATA keyword specifies that an XML-Data schema should be returned. The schema is added to the document as an inline schema. The primary purpose for specifying XMLDATA in a query is to receive XML data type information that can be used where data types are necessary (for example, when handling numeric expressions). Otherwise, everything in an XML document is a textual string. Generating an XML-Data schema is an overhead on the server, is likely to affect performance, and should be used only when data types are needed.

If the database column from which values are retrieved is of the type *sql_variant*, there is no data type information in the XML-Data schema. If a given query designates different XML elements with the same name, XMLDATA might produce an invalid XML-Data schema. This will happen if element-name collisions and data type names are not resolved (you might have two elements with the same name but different data types).

ELEMENTS

If the ELEMENTS option is specified, the columns are returned as subelements. Otherwise, they are mapped to XML attributes. This option is supported in AUTO mode only.

BINARY Base64

If the BINARY Base64 option is specified, any binary data returned by the query is represented in base64-encoded format. To retrieve binary data using RAW and EXPLICIT mode, you must specify this option. In AUTO mode, binary data is returned as a reference by default.

Using the *OPENXML* Function to Access XML Data

The OPENXML function is a Transact-SQL keyword that provides a rowset over in-memory XML documents. OPENXML is a rowset provider similar to a table or a view. OPENXML enables access to XML data as if it were a relational rowset by providing a rowset view of the internal representation of an XML document. The records in the rowset can be stored in database tables (similar to the rowsets provided by tables and views).

The *OPENXML* function can be used in *SELECT* and *SELECT INTO* statements wherever a rowset provider, such as a table, a view, or *OPENROWSET*, can appear as the source.

To write queries against an XML document by using *OPENXML*, you must first call the *sp_xml_preparedocument* system-stored procedure, which parses the XML document and returns a handle to the parsed document that is ready for consumption. The parsed document is a tree representation of various nodes (elements, attributes, text, comment, and so on) in the XML document. The document handle is passed to *OPENXML*, which then provides a rowset view of the document based on the parameters passed to it.

The internal representation of an XML document must be removed from memory by calling the *sp_xml_removedocument* system-stored procedure to free the memory.

In the following example, you are declaring a variable, parsing the XML data, retrieving the data in a *SELECT* statement, and removing the representation of the XML document:

```
-- Declaring a variable.
DECLARE @hDoc INT

-- Parsing the XML data.
EXEC sp_xml_preparedocument @hDoc OUTPUT,
      N'<ROOT>
      <Customers CustomerID="XYZAA" ContactName="Joe"
        CompanyName="Company1">
       <Orders CustomerID="XYZAA"
            OrderDate="2000-08-25T00:00:00"/>
          <Orders CustomerID="XYZAA"
            OrderDate="2000-10-03T00:00:00"/>
      </Customers>
      <Customers CustomerID="XYZBB" ContactName="Steve"
        CompanyName="Company2">No Orders yet!
          <Orders CustomerID="XYZBB"
             OrderDate="2000-06-21T00:00:00"/>
          <Orders CustomerID="XYZBB"
             OrderDate="2000-10-10T00:00:00"/>
      </Customers>
      </ROOT>'

-- Using OPENXML in a SELECT statement.
SELECT *
FROM OPENXML(@hDoc, N'/ROOT/Customers/Orders')
    WITH (CustomerID NCHAR(5) '../@CustomerID',
            ContactName NVARCHAR(50) '../
@ContactName', OrderDate DATETIME)

-- Removing the internal representation of the XML document.
EXEC sp_xml_removedocument @hDoc
```

The *OPENXML* function uses the following syntax:

```
OPENXML(idoc int [in],rowpattern nvarchar[in],[flags byte[in]])
[WITH (SchemaDeclaration | TableName)]
```

XML Document Handle (idoc)

The XML document handle is the document handle of the internal representation of an XML document. The internal representation of an XML document is created by calling *sp_xml_preparedocument*.

Xpath Expression (rowpattern)

The XPath expression specified as *rowpattern* identifies a set of nodes in the XML document. Each node identified by *rowpattern* corresponds to a single row in the rowset generated by OPENXML.

The nodes identified by the XPath expression can be any XML nodes (elements, attributes, processing instructions, and so on) in the XML document. If *rowpattern* identifies a set of elements in the XML document, there is one row in the rowset for each element node identified. For example, if *rowpattern* ends in an attribute, a row is created for each attribute node selected by *rowpattern*.

Mapping (flags)

In the *OPENXML* statement, you can optionally specify the type of mapping (attribute-centric or element-centric) between the rowset columns and the XML nodes identified by the *rowpattern*. This information is used in transformation between the XML nodes and the rowset columns.

There are two ways to specify the mapping (you can specify both):

- **Using the *flags* parameter.**   The mapping specified by the *flags* parameter assumes name correspondence where the XML nodes map to corresponding rowset columns with the same name.
- **Using the *ColPattern* parameter.**   *ColPattern*, an XPath expression, is specified as part of *SchemaDeclaration* in the WITH clause. The mapping specified in *ColPattern* overwrites the mapping specified by the *flags* parameter. *ColPattern* can be used to specify the special nature of the mapping (in case of attribute-centric and element-centric mapping) that overwrites or enhances the default mapping indicated by the flags. *ColPattern* is specified if the following conditions are met:
    - The column name in the rowset is different from the element/attribute name to which it is mapped. In this case, *ColPattern* is used to identify the XML element/attribute name to which the rowset column maps.
    - You want to map a metaproperty attribute to the column. In this case, *ColPattern* is used to identify the metaproperty to which the rowset column maps.

Both the *flags* and *ColPattern* parameters are optional. If no mapping is specified, attribute-centric mapping (the default value of the *flags* parameter) is assumed by default.

SchemaDeclaration

A rowset schema must be provided to *OPENXML* to generate the rowset. You can specify the rowset schema by using the optional WITH clause. The following options are available for specifying the rowset schema:

- **Specifying the complete schema in the WITH clause.**   When you specify the rowset schema, you specify the column names and their data types and their mapping to the XML document. You can specify the column pattern (by using the ColPattern parameter in SchemaDeclaration). The column pattern specified is used to map a rowset column to the XML node identified by *rowpattern* and also to determine the type of mapping. If ColPattern is not specified for a column, the rowset column maps to the XML node with the same name based on the mapping specified by the *flags* parameter. If ColPattern is specified as part of the schema specification in the WITH clause, however, it overwrites the mapping specified in the *flags* parameter.
- **Specifying the name of an existing table in the WITH clause.**   You can simply specify an existing table name whose schema can be used by *OPENXML* to generate the rowset.
- **Not specifying the WITH clause.**   In this case, *OPENXML* returns a rowset in the edge table format. This display is called an edge table because, in this table format, every edge in the parsed XML document tree maps to a row in the rowset.

TableName

A table name can be provided instead of the schema declaration if a table with the desired schema already exists and no column patterns are required.

Exercise 4: Retrieving XML Data

In this exercise, you will use the FOR XML clause to retrieve data in an XML format and use the *OPENXML* function to return XML data. To complete this exercise, you should be logged into your Windows 2000 Server computer as Administrator.

▶ **To use the FOR XML clause to retrieve data**

1. Open Query Analyzer and connect to your local server.
2. On the toolbar, click the Execute Mode button and then click Results In Text.

    By selecting this option, you can better view the result set.

3. In the Editor pane of the Query window, enter the following Transact-SQL code:

```
USE Northwind
SELECT CustomerID, ContactName, CompanyName
FROM Customers
WHERE (CustomerID = N'ALFKI'
    OR CustomerID = N'XYZAA')
ORDER BY CustomerID
FOR XML RAW
```

In this statement, you are using the FOR XML clause to return data in an XML format. The clause specifies RAW mode.

4. Execute the Transact-SQL statement.

The result set appears in the Results tab of the Results pane. Notice how the result set differs from the typical result set that you would see if you executed the *SELECT* statement without the FOR XML clause.

▶   **To use the OPENXML function to retrieve XML data**

1. In the Editor pane of the Query window, enter the following Transact-SQL code:

```
DECLARE @TestDoc INT
EXEC sp_xml_preparedocument @TestDoc OUTPUT,
        N'<ROOT>
        <Employees EmpID="1234" FirstName="Ethan"
        Dept="Marketing">
</Employees>
        <Employees EmpID="1948" FirstName="Linda"
        Dept="Research">
        </Employees>
        </ROOT>'
```

This statement declares a variable named @TestDoc and then uses the *sp_xml_preparedocument* system-stored procedure to parse the XML data.

2. Add the following Transact-SQL code to the end of the previous statement:

```
SELECT *
FROM OPENXML(@TestDoc, N'/ROOT/Employees')
WITH (EmpID NCHAR(5) './@EmpID',
    FirstName VARCHAR(50) './@FirstName',
    Dept VARCHAR(10) './@Dept')
```

This *SELECT* statement defines the result that should be returned. The *OPENXML* function is used to extract XML data. Notice that the @TestDoc variable is being used.

3. Add the following Transact-SQL code to the end of the previous statement:

```
EXEC sp_xml_removedocument @TestDoc
```

This statement removes the internal representation of the XML document.

4. Execute all four statements (*DECLARE, EXEC sp_xml_preparedocument, SELECT*, and *EXEC sp_xml_removedocument*).

    The result set appears in the Results tab of the Results pane.

5. Close Query Analyzer.

Lesson Summary

XML is a hypertext programming language used to describe the contents of a set of data and how the data should be output to a device or displayed on a Web page. SQL Server 2000 includes many features that support XML functionality. You can execute SQL queries against existing relational databases to return a result as an XML document rather than as a standard rowset. To retrieve a result directly, use the FOR XML clause of the *SELECT* statement. The FOR XML clause must specify one of the following XML modes: RAW, AUTO, or EXPLICIT. The *OPENXML* function is a Transact-SQL keyword that provides a rowset over in-memory XML documents. *OPENXML* enables access to XML data as if it were a relational rowset by providing a rowset view of the internal representation of an XML document. *OPENXML* can be used in *SELECT* and *SELECT INTO* statements wherever a rowset provider, such as a table, a view, or *OPENROWSET*, can appear as the source.

Review

The following questions are intended to reinforce key information presented in this chapter. If you are unable to answer a question, review the appropriate lesson and then try the question again. You can find answers to the questions in the Appendix, "Questions and Answers."

1. What are the differences between importing data and exporting data?
2. What tools are available to import data into or export data out of a SQL Server database?
3. What tasks can you perform by using DTS?
4. What data access technology is used by SQL Server to support distributed queries?
5. What two methods can you use in distributed queries to reference heterogeneous OLE DB data sources?
6. What is a linked server?
7. What functionality do cursors support in order to extend result processing?
8. Which three types of cursor implementations does SQL Server support?
9. How do Transact-SQL cursors differ from API server cursors?
10. What features are included in SQL Server to support XML functionalities?
11. What does the FOR XML clause in a *SELECT* statement enable you to do?
12. What does the *OPENXML* function enable you to do?

C H A P T E R   8

Implementing Stored Procedures

About This Chapter

Stored procedures improve database performance, enhance database security, and bring programming techniques to Transact-SQL not available without this database object. This chapter introduces you to the types of stored procedures available in SQL Server 2000 and how to create, execute, and alter them. The final lesson in this chapter introduces you to programming stored procedures.

Before You Begin

To complete the lessons in this chapter, you must have:

- SQL Server 2000 Enterprise Edition installed on a Microsoft Windows 2000 Server computer.
- The ability to log on to the Windows 2000 Server computer and to SQL Server as the Windows 2000 Administrator.
- Completed the exercises in Chapter 3, "Designing a SQL Server Database," Chapter 4, "Implementing SQL Server Databases and Tables," and Chapter 5, "Implementing Data Integrity."

Lesson 1: Introduction to Stored Procedures

In Chapters 3 through 7, you used Query Analyzer to create, execute, and save Transact-SQL commands and batches of commands as scripts written using Transact-SQL language. When the scripts are executed, the commands within them are processed by SQL Server to display result sets, to administer SQL Server, and to manipulate data contained in a database. When the scripts are saved, they are stored in the file system and are commonly given a SQL extension. Alternatively, Transact-SQL scripts can be named and saved in SQL Server as stored procedures. You can then invoke stored procedures in a number of ways, such as through Query Analyzer, in order to process the Transact-SQL statements within them.

In previous chapters, you used a number of stored procedures (such as *sp_help* and *sp_helpconstraint*). These procedures are stored in the Master database and contain Transact-SQL commands that make it easy for you to view various properties of objects in the database.

After this lesson, you will be able to:

- Describe the purpose and reasons for using stored procedures.
- Explain how SQL Server processes a stored procedure.
- Determine when to use stored procedures to complete SQL Server tasks.

Estimated Lesson time: 30 minutes

Purpose and Advantages of Stored Procedures

Stored procedures provide performance benefits, a programming framework, and security features unavailable to Transact-SQL commands sent to the server for processing. Performance is enhanced through local storage (local to the database), pre-compiling the code, and caching. A programming framework is provided through common programming constructs such as input and output parameters and procedure reuse. Security features include encryption and privilege limits that keep users away from the underlying database structure while still enabling them to run stored procedures that act on the database.

Performance

Every time a Transact-SQL command (or batch of commands) is sent to the server for processing, the server must determine whether the sender has appropriate permissions to execute the commands and whether the commands are valid. Once the permissions and the syntax are verified, SQL Server builds an execution plan to process the request.

Stored procedures are more efficient in part because the procedure is stored in SQL Server when it is created. Therefore, the content in the procedure runs at the server when the stored procedure is executed. A complex Transact-SQL script contained in a stored procedure is called by a single Transact-SQL statement, rather than by sending hundreds of commands over the network.

Before a stored procedure is created, the command syntax is checked for accuracy. If no errors are returned, the procedure's name is stored in the SysObjects table and the procedure's text is stored in the SysComments table. The first time the stored procedure is run, an execution plan is created and the stored procedure is compiled. Subsequent processing of the compiled stored procedure is faster because SQL Server does not recheck command syntax, re-create an execution plan, or recompile the procedure. The cache is checked first for an execution plan before a new plan is created.

Note   The relative performance boost provided by placing stored procedure execution plans in the procedure cache is reduced because execution plans for all SQL statements are now stored in the procedure cache. A Transact-SQL statement will attempt to use an existing execution plan if possible.

Programming Framework

Once a stored procedure is created, you can call it whenever it's needed. This feature provides modularity and encourages code reuse. Code reuse increases the maintainability of a database by insulating the database from changing business practices. If business rules change in an organization, a stored procedure can be modified to comply with the new business rules. All applications that call the stored procedure will then comply with the new business rules without direct modification.

Like other programming languages, stored procedures can accept input parameters, return output parameters, provide execution feedback in the form of status codes and descriptive text, and call other procedures. For example, a stored procedure can return a status code to a calling procedure so that the calling procedure performs an operation based on the code received.

Software developers can write sophisticated programs in a language such as Visual C++; then, a special type of stored procedure called an extended stored procedure can be used to invoke the program from within SQL Server.

You should write a stored procedure to complete a single task. The more generic the stored procedure, the more useful it will be to many databases. For example, the *sp_rename* stored procedure changes the name of a user-created object, such as a table, a column, or a user-defined data type in the current database. Thus, you can use *sp_rename* to rename a table in one database or a table column in another database.

Security

Another important feature of stored procedures is that they enhance security through isolation and encryption. Database users can be given permission to execute a stored procedure without being granted permissions to directly access the database objects on which the stored procedure operates. Additionally, a stored procedure can be encrypted when it is created or modified so that users are unable to read the Transact-SQL commands in the stored procedure. These security features insulate the database structure from the database user, which further ensures data integrity and database reliability.

Categories of Stored Procedures

There are five classes of stored procedures: system stored procedures, local stored procedures, temporary stored procedures, extended stored procedures, and remote stored procedures. There are other ways to categorize stored procedures, but this organization into five groups makes it easy to identify the stored procedure's location, purpose, and capability.

System Stored Procedures

System stored procedures are stored in the Master database and are typically named with an *sp_* prefix. They perform a wide variety of tasks to support SQL Server functions (such as catalog procedures) that support external application calls for data in the system tables, general system procedures for database administration, and security management functions. For example, you can view table privileges by using the *sp_table_privileges* catalog stored procedure. The following statement uses the *sp_table_privileges* system stored procedure to show privileges to the Stores table in the Pubs database:

```
USE Pubs
GO
EXECUTE sp_table_privileges Stores
```

A common database administration task is viewing information about current database users and processes. This step is an important one before a database is shut down. The following statement uses the *sp_who* system stored procedure to display all processes in use by the LAB1\Administrator user:

```
EXECUTE sp_who @loginame='LAB1\Administrator'
```

Database security is critical to most organizations that store private data in a database. The following statement uses the *sp_validatelogins* system stored procedure to show any orphaned Windows NT or Windows 2000 user and group accounts that no longer exist but still have entries in the SQL Server system tables:

```
EXECUTE sp_validatelogins
```

There are hundreds of system stored procedures included with SQL Server. For a complete list of system stored procedures, refer to "System Stored Procedures" in SQL Server Books Online. You will notice in the system stored procedures reference that some extended stored procedures are listed. Extended stored procedures are discussed later in this lesson.

Local Stored Procedures

Local stored procedures are usually stored in a user database and are typically designed to complete tasks in the database in which they reside. A local stored procedure might also be created to customize system stored procedure code. To create a custom task based on a system stored procedure, first copy the contents of a system stored procedure and save the new stored procedure as a local stored procedure. You will create local stored procedures for the BookShopDB database in Exercise 3.

Temporary Stored Procedures

A temporary stored procedure is similar to a local stored procedure, but it exists only until either the connection that created it is closed or SQL Server is shut down. The stored procedure is deleted at connection termination or at server shutdown, depending on the type of temporary stored procedure created. This volatility exists because temporary stored procedures are stored in the TempDB database. TempDB is re-created when the server is restarted; therefore, all objects within this database disappear upon shutdown. Temporary stored procedures are useful if you are accessing earlier versions of SQL Server that do not support the reuse of execution plans and if you don't want to store the task because the same task will be executed with many different parameter values.

There are three types of temporary stored procedures: local (also called private), global, and stored procedures created directly in TempDB. A local temporary stored procedure always begins with #, and a global temporary stored procedure always begins with ##. Lesson 2 explains how to create each type of temporary stored procedure. The execution scope of a local temporary procedure is limited to the connection that created it. All users who have connections to the database, however, can see the stored procedure in the Object Browser window of Query Analyzer. Because of its limited scope, there is no chance of name collision between other connections that are creating temporary stored procedures. To ensure uniqueness, SQL Server appends the name of a local temporary stored procedure with a series of underscore characters and a connection number unique to the connection. Privileges cannot be granted to other users for the local temporary stored procedure. When the connection that created the temporary stored procedure is closed, the procedure is deleted from TempDB.

Any connection to the database can execute a global temporary stored procedure. This type of procedure must have a unique name, because all connections can execute the procedure and, like all temporary stored procedures, it is created in

TempDB. Permission to execute a global temporary stored procedure is automatically granted to the public role and cannot be changed. A global temporary stored procedure is almost as volatile as a local temporary stored procedure. This procedure type is removed when the connection used to create the procedure is closed and any connections currently executing the procedure have completed.

Temporary stored procedures created directly in TempDB are different from local and global temporary stored procedures in the following ways:

- You can configure permissions for them.
- They exist even after the connection used to create them is terminated.
- They aren't removed until SQL Server is shut down.

Because this procedure type is created directly in TempDB, it is important to fully qualify the database objects referenced by Transact-SQL commands in the code. For example, you must reference the Authors table, which is owned by dbo in the Pubs database, as pubs.dbo.authors.

Extended Stored Procedures

An extended stored procedure uses an external program, compiled as a 32-bit dynamic link library (DLL), to expand the capabilities of a stored procedure. A number of system stored procedures are also classified as extended stored procedures. For example, the *xp_sendmail* program, which sends a message and a query result set attachment to the specified e-mail recipients, is both a system stored procedure and an extended stored procedure. Most extended stored procedures use the *xp_* prefix as a naming convention. However, there are some extended stored procedures that use the *sp_* prefix, and there are some system stored procedures that are not extended and use the *xp_* prefix. Therefore, you cannot depend on naming conventions to identify system stored procedures and extended stored procedures.

Use the *OBJECTPROPERTY* function to determine whether a stored procedure is extended or not. *OBJECTPROPERTY* returns a value of 1 for IsExtendedProc, indicating an extended stored procedure, or returns a value of 0, indicating a stored procedure that is not extended. The following examples demonstrate that *sp_prepare* is an extended stored procedure and that *xp_logininfo* is not an extended stored procedure:

```
USE Master
--an extended stored procedure that uses an sp_ prefix.
SELECT OBJECTPROPERTY(object_id('sp_prepare'), 'IsExtendedProc')
```

This example returns a value of 1.

```
USE Master
--a stored procedure that is not extended but uses an xp_ prefix
SELECT OBJECTPROPERTY(object_id('xp_logininfo'), 'IsExtendedProc')
```

This example returns a value of 0.

Remote Stored Procedures

As the name suggests, a remote stored procedure executes a stored procedure on a remote SQL Server installation. Remote stored procedures remain for backward compatibility but have been replaced by distributed queries. For information about distributed queries, refer to Chapter 7, "Managing and Manipulating Data."

Exercise 1: Exploring Stored Procedures

In this exercise, you will view a number of system stored procedures contained in the Master database. To perform this exercise, you should be logged in to your Windows 2000 Server computer as Administrator.

▶ **To view system stored procedures in the Master database**

1. Open Query Analyzer and connect to your local server.

2. Open the Object Browser window if it is not already displayed.

    The Object Browser window displays a hierarchical tree of database objects.

3. Expand the master node.

    A list of object types appears. Notice the Stored Procedures and Extended Procedures nodes.

4. Expand the Stored Procedures node.

    A list of stored procedures and extended stored procedures in the Master database appears.

5. Review the names of the listed procedures. Notice that dbo owns all of the procedures.

    How can you tell the difference between a system stored procedure and an extended stored procedure from the list of procedures that appear below the Stored Procedures node?

6. Expand the *dbo.sp_who* system stored procedure.

    The Parameters and Dependencies nodes appear.

7. Expand the Parameters node.

    Notice that there are two parameters defined for this procedure: @RETURN_VALUE and @loginame. @RETURN_VALUE is built-in and is used to supply return codes. All stored procedures contain the @RETURN_VALUE parameter; @loginame is an input parameter. The second example code listed under the System Stored Procedures section in this lesson sets the @loginame equal to LAB1\Administrator.

8. Expand the Dependencies node.

Notice that there is a single dependency for this stored procedure: the dbo.sysprocesses table. This is a system table stored in the Master database. The *sp_who* system stored procedure queries the SysProcesses table and displays parts of this table in its result set. You can find this table by expanding the System Tables node.

9. If you examined the dbo.sysprocesses table in the previous step, return to the *sp_who* system stored procedure in the Object Browser.

10. Scroll down in the Object Browser until you see the Extended Procedures node.

Notice that right above the Extended Procedures node, there are three stored procedures beginning with the *xp_* prefix. These are not extended stored procedures. You can verify this fact by running the *OBJECTPROPERTY* function described in the lesson against them.

11. Expand the Extended Procedures node.

As you scroll through the objects contained in this node, notice that both system stored procedures and extended stored procedures exist. The majority of procedures under this node are extended stored procedures.

12. Keep Query Analyzer open for the next exercise.

▶ **To use two methods for viewing the contents of a stored procedure**

1. Click once on the dbo.sp_who object.

2. Right-click dbo.sp_who.

The context menu for this object appears.

3. Click Scripting Options.

The Options dialog box appears.

4. Click the Include Descriptive Headers In The Script check box and click OK.

This option will display the stored procedure name and its create date near the top of the text contained in the procedure.

5. Right-click dbo.sp_who.

The context menu for this object appears.

6. Point to Script Object To New Window As and click Create.

The *dbo.sp_who stored* procedure appears in the Query window.

Notice that the CREATE PROCEDURE keywords appear near the top of the file. In the next lesson, you will learn more about creating stored procedures using Transact-SQL. Notice that batches of commands are specified in the stored procedure text. As you examine the text, you will see that the @loginame input parameter appears in a number of places. Notice also that the SysProcesses table is queried a number of times in the stored procedure using its fully qualified name, master.dbo.sysprocesses.

Don't worry about not understanding everything in this stored procedure. In Lessons 2 and 3, you will learn more about how to manage and program stored procedures.

7. Click New Query on the toolbar or press CTRL+N.

A new query window appears in the right pane.

8. In the Editor pane of the Query window, enter the following Transact-SQL code:

```
sp_helptext [master.dbo.sp_who]
```

This code uses the *sp_helptext* system stored procedure to show the contents of the *sp_who* system stored procedure contained in the Master database. It is not necessary to fully qualify the name of the stored procedure, but it is a good practice because it guarantees that you will open the object that you are interested in viewing.

9. Execute the code.

The Grids tab of the Results pane displays the contents of the *sp_who* system stored procedure.

Lesson Summary

Stored procedures contain Transact-SQL commands that are stored in a database and are typically designed to run a single task. Stored procedures provide performance gains, programming capabilities, and security features not available when using individual Transact-SQL commands or batches. Storing the procedure in a database, checking the syntax when the procedure is created, and creating a reusable execution plan the first time the stored procedure is executed will enhance performance. Stored procedures support parameters and return codes. Because stored procedures are modular, they provide a layer of insulation between changing business practices and the underlying database. The programming capabilities of stored procedures are nearly unlimited because of support for extended stored procedures. From a security perspective, users can be granted the right to execute a stored procedure without being granted the right to manipulate the database outside the stored procedure.

There are five general categories of stored procedures: system, local, temporary, extended, and remote. SQL Server includes hundreds of system stored procedures and extended stored procedures to perform tasks such as system administration. Local stored procedures are created in a user database and are typically used to complete tasks specific to the database in which they are created. Temporary stored procedures look and act like any of the other categories of stored procedures, but they are volatile and disappear upon the termination of a user connection (or when the server is shut down). Remote stored procedures are available for backward compatibility but have been replaced by distributed queries.

Lesson 2: Creating, Executing, Modifying, and Deleting Stored Procedures

In this lesson, you will learn a number of methods for managing stored procedures. Stored procedures are commonly created, executed, modified, or deleted using Query Analyzer or Enterprise Manager.

Stored procedures can be created before the objects that they reference are created. This feature is called deferred name resolution. The keywords used to create a procedure are CREATE PROCEDURE.

Before running a stored procedure, you must provide any required parameter values. Stored procedures can be executed manually or automatically when SQL Server starts. The keyword used to run a procedure is EXECUTE. This keyword is optional if the procedure to run is a single line of code or if the procedure name is the first word in a batch.

Modifying a stored procedure after it is created is common practice; perhaps you need to add a parameter or change some other part of the code in the procedure. Modifying a procedure, rather than deleting it and recreating it, is a time-saver, because many of the stored procedure properties (such as permissions) are retained when a procedure is modified. The keywords used to modify a procedure are ALTER PROCEDURE.

Procedures are dropped from a database with the DROP keyword. You can drop a stored procedure from Enterprise Manager or Query Analyzer by selecting the stored procedure and pressing the DELETE key. A procedure shouldn't be deleted until other objects that depend on the procedure are removed or modified (to break their dependency).

After this lesson, you will be able to:

- Create and modify a stored procedure in SQL Server.
- Execute a stored procedure.
- Delete a stored procedure from SQL Server.

Estimated lesson time: 45 minutes

How a Procedure Is Stored

When a procedure is created, SQL Server checks the syntax of the Transact-SQL statements within it. If the syntax is incorrect, SQL Server will generate a "syntax incorrect" error message, and the procedure will not be created. If the procedure's text passes syntax checking, the procedure is stored by writing its name and other information (such as an auto-generated identification number) to the SysObjects table. The text used to create the procedure is written to the SysComments table of the current database.

The following *SELECT* statement queries the SysObjects table in the Pubs database to show the identification number of the *ByRoyalty* stored procedure:

```
SELECT [name], [id] FROM [pubs].[dbo].[SysObjects]
WHERE [name] = 'byroyalty'
```

This query returns the following:

name	id
Byroyalty	581577110

Using the information returned from the SysObjects table, the next *SELECT* statement queries the SysComments table by using the identification number of the *ByRoyalty* stored procedure:

```
SELECT [text] FROM [pubs].[dbo].[SysComments]
WHERE [id] = 581577110
```

This query returns the create text of the *ByRoyalty* stored procedure, whose identification number is 581577110.

Note   The two previous *SELECT* statements could have been consolidated into a single *SELECT* statement by using a JOIN. They are separated here for simplicity and clarity.

Using the *sp_helptext* system stored procedure is a better option for displaying the text used to create an object (such as an unencrypted stored procedure), because the text is returned in multiple rows. You used the *sp_helptext* stored procedure in the last practice of Exercise 1.

Methods for Creating Stored Procedures

SQL Server provides several methods that you can use to create a stored procedure: the Transact-SQL *CREATE PROCEDURE* statement, SQL-DMO (using the *StoredProcedure* object), the console tree in Enterprise Manager, and the Create Stored Procedure wizard (which you can access through Enterprise Manager).

Note   Many of the commands explored here and in other chapters are accessible through the SQL-DMO API. An exploration of SQL-DMO is beyond the scope of this training kit, however. Refer to SQL Server Books Online for more information about SQL-DMO.

The *CREATE PROCEDURE* Statement

You can use the *CREATE PROCEDURE* statement or the shortened version of the statement, *CREATE PROC*, to create a stored procedure in Query Analyzer or in a command-prompt tool such as osql. When using *CREATE PROC*, you can perform the following tasks:

- Specify grouped stored procedures
- Define input and output parameters, their data types, and their default values

  When input and output parameters are defined, they are always preceded by the "at" sign (@), followed by the parameter name and then a data type designation. Output parameters must include the OUTPUT keyword to distinguish them from input parameters.
- Use return codes to display information about the success or failure of a task
- Control whether an execution plan should be cached for the procedure
- Encrypt the stored procedure's content for security
- Control execution behavior for a replication subscriber
- Specify the actions that the stored procedure should take when executed

---

Note Lesson 3 explores input and output parameters, programming actions that a stored procedure should take when executed, and success or failure result sets. For additional syntax details concerning *CREATE PROC*, refer to the Transact-SQL reference in SQL Server Books Online.

Providing a Stored Procedure with Context

With the exception of temporary stored procedures, a stored procedure is always created in the current database. Therefore, you should always specify the current database by using the USE *database_name* statement followed by the GO batch command before creating a stored procedure. You can also use the Change Database drop-down list box in Query Analyzer to select the current database.

The following script selects the Pubs database in the first batch and then creates a procedure named ListAuthorNames, which dbo owns:

```
USE Pubs
GO
CREATE PROCEDURE [dbo].[ListAuthorNames]
AS
SELECT [au_fname], [au_lname] FROM [pubs].[dbo].[authors]
```

Notice that the procedure name is fully qualified in the example. A fully qualified stored procedure name includes the procedure's owner (in this case, dbo) and the name of the procedure, ListAuthorNames. Specify dbo as the owner if you want to ensure that the task in the stored procedure will run regardless of table ownership in the database. The database name is not part of a fully qualified stored procedure name when using the *CREATE PROCEDURE* statement.

Creating Temporary Stored Procedures

To create a local temporary stored procedure, append the procedure name with # when you create it. This pound sign instructs SQL Server to create the procedure in TempDB. To create a global, temporary stored procedure, append the procedure name with ## when it is created. This double pound sign instructs SQL Server to create the procedure in TempDB. SQL Server ignores the current database when creating a temporary stored procedure. By definition, a temporary stored procedure can only exist in TempDB. To create a temporary stored procedure directly in TempDB that is not a local or global temporary stored procedure, make TempDB the current database and then create the procedure. The following examples create a local temporary stored procedure, a global temporary stored procedure, and a stored procedure directly in TempDB:

```
--create a local temporary stored procedure.
CREATE PROCEDURE #localtemp
AS
SELECT * from [pubs].[dbo].[authors]
GO
--create a global temporary stored procedure.
CREATE PROCEDURE ##globaltemp
AS
SELECT * from [pubs].[dbo].[authors]
GO
--create a temporary stored procedure that is local to tempdb.
USE TEMPDB
GO
CREATE PROCEDURE directtemp
AS
SELECT * from [pubs].[dbo].[authors]
GO
```

Fully qualified database names are specified in the *SELECT* statements. If the procedure is not executed in the context of a specific database and the Transact-SQL commands in the stored procedure are database-specific, then fully qualified database names ensure that the proper database is referenced.

In the third example, when creating a temporary stored procedure directly in TempDB, you must make TempDB the current database (USE TempDB) before executing it, or you must fully qualify its name ([TempDB].[dbo].[directtemp]). Like system stored procedures in the Master database, local and global temporary stored procedures are available for execution using their short names (regardless of the current database).

Grouping, Caching, and Encrypting Stored Procedures

Stored procedures can be logically tied together by grouping them upon creation. This technique is useful for stored procedures that should be administered as a single unit and are used in a single application. To group stored procedures, you assign each procedure in the group the same name and append the name with a semicolon and a unique number. For example, naming the following two stored procedures *GroupedProc;1* and *GroupedProc;2* on creation logically groups them together. When you view the contents of GroupedProc, you will see the code for both *GroupedProc;1* and *GroupedProc;2*.

By default, a stored procedure's execution plan is cached the first time it is executed, and it isn't cached again until the server is restarted or until an underlying table used by the stored procedure changes. For performance reasons, you might not want to cache an execution plan for a stored procedure. For example, when a stored procedure's parameters vary considerably from one execution to the next, caching an execution plan is counterproductive. To cause a stored procedure to be recompiled every time it is executed, add the WITH RECOMPILE keywords when the stored procedure is created. You can also force a recompile by using the *sp_recompile* stored procedure or by specifying WITH RECOMPILE when the procedure is executed.

Encrypting a stored procedure protects its contents from being viewed. To encrypt a stored procedure, use the WITH ENCRYPTION keywords when creating the procedure. For example, the following code creates an encrypted procedure named Protected:

```
USE Pubs
GO
CREATE PROC [dbo].[protected] WITH ENCRYPTION
AS
SELECT [au_fname], [au_lname] FROM [pubs].[dbo].[authors]
```

The WITH ENCRYPTION keywords encrypt the procedure's text column in the SysComments table. A simple way to determine whether a procedure is encrypted is by using the *OBJECTPROPERTY* function

```
--
check if stored procedure is encrypted and if so, return 1 for IsEncrypt
ed
SELECT OBJECTPROPERTY(object_id('protected'), 'IsEncrypted')
```

or by calling the procedure with *sp_helptext*:

```
--if the stored procedure is encrypted, return
"The object comments have been encrypted."
EXEC sp_helptext protected
```

Note   An encrypted stored procedure cannot be replicated. After a stored procedure is encrypted, SQL Server decrypts it for execution. However, its definition cannot be decrypted for viewing by anyone, including the owner of the stored procedure. Therefore, make sure to place an unencrypted version of the stored procedure definition in a secure location. If the procedure needs to be modified, edit the contents of the unencrypted stored procedure and save it to the secure location. Then, use the *ALTER PROCEDURE* statement with encryption to modify the existing encrypted stored procedure. You will learn about the *ALTER PROCEDURE* statement later in this lesson.

Enterprise Manager

You can create a stored procedure directly in Enterprise Manager. To accomplish this task, expand the console tree for your server and then expand the database where a stored procedure should be created. Right-click the Stored Procedure node, and then click New Stored Procedure. When the Stored Procedure Properties - New Stored Procedure dialog box appears, enter the contents of the stored procedure. Figure 8.1 shows the Stored Procedure Properties - New Stored Procedure dialog box that contains the code from a previous example.

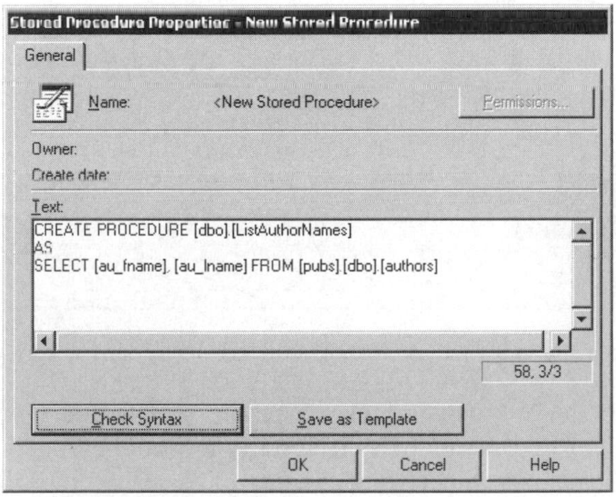

Figure 8.1.   The General tab of the Stored Procedure Properties - New Stored Procedure dialog box for a new stored procedure.

You can also check the syntax of the stored procedure before creating it and save a template that will always appear when you create a new stored procedure by using Enterprise Manager. Once the procedure is created, you can open the properties of the procedure and configure permissions. By default, the stored procedure's owner and sysadmins have full permission to the stored procedure.

Templates are useful because they provide a framework for creating consistent documentation for stored procedures. Typically, text is added to the header of the template that describes how each stored procedure should be documented.

Create Stored Procedure Wizard

The Create Stored Procedure wizard walks you through the steps necessary to create a new stored procedure. You can access the wizard by selecting Wizards from the Tools menu. In the Select Wizard window, expand the Database option, then select the Create Stored Procedure Wizard and click OK. From there, you complete the steps in the wizard. Figure 8.2 shows the options on the Welcome to the Create Stored Procedure wizard screen that you specify when you run the Create Stored Procedure wizard.

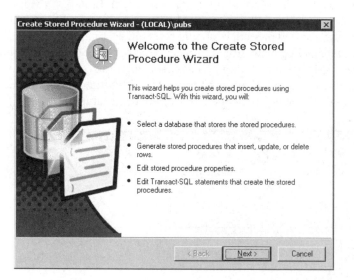

Figure 8.2.   The Welcome to the Create Stored Procedure Wizard screen.

The Create Stored Procedure wizard enables you to create procedures that insert, delete, or update data in tables. To modify the stored procedure that the wizard creates, you can edit it within the wizard or by using other tools (such as Query Analyzer).

Creating and Adding Extended Stored Procedures

After creating an extended stored procedure, you must register it with SQL Server. Only users who have the sysadmin role can register an extended stored procedure with SQL Server. To register the extended stored procedure, you can use the *sp_addextendedproc* system stored procedure in Query Analyzer or use Enterprise Manager. In Enterprise Manager, expand the Master database, right-click the Extended Stored Procedures node, and then click New Extended Stored Procedure. Extended stored procedures can be added only to the Master database.

Deferred Name Resolution

When a stored procedure is created, SQL Server does not check for the existence of any objects that are referenced in it. This feature exists because it's possible that an object, such as a table referenced in the stored procedure, does not exist when the stored procedure is created. This feature is called deferred name resolution. Object verification occurs when the stored procedure is executed.

When referring to an object (such as a table) in a stored procedure, make sure to specify the owner of the object. By default, SQL Server assumes that the creator of the stored procedure is also the owner of the objects referenced in the procedure. To avoid confusion, consider specifying dbo as the owner when creating all objects (both stored procedures and objects referenced in the stored procedures).

Executing a Stored Procedure

As you have seen in previous lessons, you can run a stored procedure in Query Analyzer simply by typing its name and any required parameter values. For example, you viewed the contents of a stored procedure by typing *sp_helptext* and the name of the stored procedure to be viewed. The name of the stored procedure to be viewed is the parameter value.

If the stored procedure isn't the first statement in a batch, in order to run it you must precede the name of the stored procedure with the EXECUTE keyword or with the shortened version of the keyword, EXEC.

Calling a Stored Procedure for Execution

When you specify the procedure name, the name can be fully qualified, such as [*database_name*].[*owner*].[*procedure_name*]. Or, if you make the database containing the stored procedure the current database (USE *database_name*), then you can execute the procedure by specifying [*owner*].[*procedure_name*]. If the 0000000procedure name is unique in the active database, you can simply specify [*procedure_name*].

Note   The identifiers ([ ]) that appear in an object name are included here for clarity and are used in the examples even when the object names do not violate the rules for identifiers. Refer to Chapter 2, "Using Transact-SQL on a SQL Server Database" (Lesson 3) for details.

Fully qualified names are not necessary when executing system stored procedures that have an *sp_* prefix, local temporary stored procedures, or global temporary stored procedures. SQL Server will search the Master database for any stored procedures that have an *sp_* prefix where dbo is the owner. To avoid confusion, do not name local stored procedures with the same names as stored procedures located in the Master database. If you do name a local stored procedure with the same name as a system stored procedure, make sure to append the procedure name with an owner other than dbo. SQL Server does not automatically search the Master database for extended stored procedures. Therefore, either fully qualify the name of an extended stored procedure or change the active database to the location of the extended stored procedure.

Specifying Parameters and Their Values

If a stored procedure requires parameter values, you must specify them when executing the procedure. When input and output parameters are defined, they are preceded by the "at" sign (@), followed by the parameter name and the data type designation. When they are called for execution, you must include a value for the parameter (and optionally, the parameter name). The next two examples run the *au_info* stored procedure in the Pubs database with two parameters: @lastname and @firstname:

```
--call the stored procedure with the parameter values.
USE Pubs
GO
EXECUTE au_info Green, Marjorie
--call the stored procedure with parameter names and values.
USE Pubs
GO
EXECUTE au_info
@lastname = 'Green', @firstname = 'Marjorie'
```

In the first example, the parameter values were specified but the parameter names were not. If the values are specified without their corresponding names, the values must be called in the same order as they were specified when the procedure was created. In the second example, the parameter names and values were specified. When both the names and the values are specified, they can be listed in any order. Parameters assigned default values when a stored procedure is created might run successfully without specifying a value upon execution.

The following list shows some of the optional syntax available when executing stored procedures:

- A return code variable of integer data type to store values returned from the stored procedure

  The RETURN keyword with an integer value (or values) must be specified in the stored procedure for this optional variable to work.

- A semicolon followed by a group number

  For grouped stored procedures, you can either execute all stored procedures in the group by simply specifying the stored procedure name, or you can include a number to select which procedure in the group you wish to execute. For example, if you create two stored procedures named *GroupedProc;1* and *GroupedProc;2*, you can run both of the stored procedures by typing **EXEC groupedproc**. Or, you can run procedure 2 by typing **EXEC groupedproc;2**.

If parameter names are defined in grouped stored procedures, each parameter name must be unique to the group. Parameter values are then specified in grouped stored procedures in the same way that they are specified when running individual stored procedures.

■ Variables to hold the parameters defined in the stored procedure

Variables are defined by using the DECLARE keyword before using EXECUTE. You will work with variables in Exercise 3.

Note   For additional syntax details about EXECUTE, refer to the Transact-SQL reference in SQL Server Books Online.

Executing Stored Procedures when SQL Server Starts

For performance, administration, or background task completion, you can mark stored procedures to run when SQL Server starts by using the *sp_procoption stored* procedure. This procedure accepts three parameters: @ProcName, @OptionName, and @OptionValue. The following statement configures a procedure named AutoStart to start automatically:

```
USE Master
GO
EXECUTE sp_procoption
@procname = autostart,
@optionname = startup,
@optionvalue = true
```

Only procedures owned by dbo and located in the Master database can be configured to start automatically. To automatically start procedures in other databases, you can call them from a procedure located in the Master database that is configured to start automatically. Calling one procedure from another is called nesting.

You can configure a stored procedure to start automatically by using Enterprise Manager. Access the Master database, then click the Stored Procedures node. Select a stored procedure that you wish to start automatically, and then right-click it. On the properties dialog box of the stored procedure, select the Execute Whenever SQL Server Starts check box.

To determine whether a procedure is set to start automatically, run the *OBJECT-PROPERTY* function and check the ExecIsStartup property. For example, the following code checks to determine whether the *AutoStart* stored procedure is configured to start automatically:

```
USE Master
--determine whether a stored procedure is set to start automatically
SELECT OBJECTPROPERTY(object_id('autostart'), 'ExecIsStartup')
```

To disable stored procedures from starting automatically, you can run the *sp_configure* stored procedure. The following statement configures SQL Server so that stored procedures flagged to start automatically will not be started the next time SQL Server is started:

```
EXECUTE sp_configure
@configname = 'scan for startup procs', @configvalue = 0
RECONFIGURE
GO
```

Modifying Stored Procedures

You can use the *ALTER PROCEDURE* statement or the shortened version of this statement, *ALTER PROC*, to modify the contents of a user-defined stored procedure by using Query Analyzer or a command-prompt tool such as osql. The *ALTER PROCEDURE* syntax is nearly identical to the *CREATE PROCEDURE* syntax.

The value of using *ALTER PROCEDURE* rather than deleting the procedure and recreating it is that *ALTER PROCEDURE* retains most of the procedure's properties, such as its object ID, the permissions set for the procedure, and its startup flag. To retain encryption or recompile settings, you must specify them (WITH ENCRYPTION and/or WITH RECOMPILE keywords) when running the *ALTER PROCEDURE* statement.

You can use Enterprise Manager and Query Analyzer to alter user-defined stored procedures. In Enterprise Manager, right-click a user-defined stored procedure and then click Properties. In the Stored Procedure Properties dialog box, modify the stored procedure statements appearing in the Text box, and then click OK. Using Query Analyzer, right-click a user-defined stored procedure and click Edit or point to Script Object to New Window As, and then click Alter. After altering the text, execute the stored procedure.

To modify the name of a user-defined stored procedure, use the *sp_rename* stored procedure. The following statement renames the *ByRoyalty* stored procedure to *RoyaltyByAuthorID*:

```
USE PUBS
GO
EXECUTE sp_rename
@objname = 'byroyalty', @newname = 'RoyaltyByAuthorID',
@objtype = 'object'
```

User-defined stored procedures can be renamed in Enterprise Manager by right-clicking the stored procedure name and clicking Rename.

You should exercise caution when renaming stored procedures and other objects (such as tables). Stored procedures can be nested. If a call is made to a renamed object, the original stored procedure will be incapable of locating the object.

Deleting Stored Procedures

You can use the *DROP PROCEDURE* statement or the shortened version of this statement, *DROP PROC*, to delete a user-defined stored procedure, several procedures at once, or a set of grouped procedures. The following statement drops two procedures in the Pubs database: *Procedure01* and *Procedure02*:

```
USE pubs
GO
DROP PROCEDURE procedure01, procedure02
```

Notice in the example that Pubs was made the current database. You cannot specify the database name when specifying a procedure to drop. The fully qualified name of the procedure is [*owner*].[*procedure_name*]. If you have created a user-defined system stored procedure (*sp_* prefix), the *DROP PROCEDURE* statement will search the current database. If it doesn't find a user-defined system stored procedure of the same name, it will search the Master database.

To drop a group of stored procedures, specify the name of the procedure. You cannot delete part of a grouped procedure by using *DROP PROCEDURE*. For example, if you have a set of grouped procedures named *GroupedProc* containing *GroupedProc;1* and *GroupedProc;2*, you cannot drop *GroupedProc;1* without also dropping *GroupedProc;2*. If you need to delete part of a grouped procedure, drop the grouped procedure and re-create it.

Before dropping a stored procedure, you should check whether other database objects depend on the stored procedure you are dropping. Use the *sp_depends* system stored procedure to check for dependent objects. You need to be concerned only with the objects that depend on the stored procedure you intend to delete.

Tip   You can create, execute, alter, and drop user-defined stored procedures in Query Analyzer by right-clicking the stored procedure and pointing to any of the *Script Object To...* options. To generate the script in Query Analyzer, click Script Object To New Window.

Exercise 2: Working with Stored Procedures

In this exercise, you will create a stored procedure in the Northwind database and verify that it was created. In the remaining practices for this lesson, you will execute, alter, and drop this procedure. In Exercise 3, you will create stored procedures for the BookShopDB database.

▶ **To create a stored procedure in the Northwind database**

1. Open Query Analyzer and connect to your local server.

2. Close the Object Browser window if it is displayed.

3. Expand the Query window so that it occupies all of the workspace in Query Analyzer.

4. In the Editor pane of the Query window, enter and execute the following code:

```
USE northwind
GO
CREATE PROCEDURE dbo.CustOrderHistRep
@CustomerID char(5)
AS
SELECT ContactName, ContactTitle
FROM Customers WHERE CustomerID = @CustomerID
SELECT ProductName, Total=SUM(Quantity)
FROM Products P, [Order Details] OD, Orders O, Customers C
WHERE
C.CustomerID = @CustomerID AND C.CustomerID = O.CustomerID
AND O.OrderID = OD.OrderID AND OD.ProductID = P.ProductID
GROUP BY ProductName
GO
```

The Northwind database is made the current database in the first batch. Then, a procedure named CustOrderHistRep is created and a single input parameter, @CustomerID, is defined. The input parameter can appear on the same line as the *CREATE PROCEDURE* line, but it appears on its own line here for clarity. A similar approach for separating the code appears below the *SELECT* statements. Notice that the data type for @CustomerID is set to char(5). If you query the [northwind].[dbo].[customers] table, you will see that all customer IDs are five characters long. The line that has a single keyword, AS, is the demarcation line between the procedure's creation in the SysObjects table and the text contained in the procedure and stored in the SysComments table.

5. Review but do not spend too much time on the *SELECT* statements that appear below the AS keyword.

When the query is executed, the first *SELECT* statement displays a person's name and title for the customer ID entered. The second *SELECT* statement displays all product names purchased by the customer and the total quantity (SUM) of each product. The result set returns the data grouped by product name. You might notice that multiple joins were accomplished by the WHERE clause, rather than by the FROM clause. When the procedure is modified, you will move the JOIN expressions to the FROM clause.

Note   You should be somewhat familiar with the code in the *SELECT* statements. If you need a review of the language in the *SELECT* statement, refer to Chapter 6, "Accessing and Modifying Data."

▶ **To view the stored procedure object in Query Analyzer**

1. Open the Object Browser in Query Analyzer and expand the Northwind database.

2. Expand the Stored Procedures node.

   All stored procedures created for the Northwind database appear.

3. Expand the *dbo.CustOrderHistRep* stored procedure.

   Notice that the stored procedure is owned by dbo and that two nodes appear below *dbo.CustOrderHistRep*: Parameters and Dependencies.

4. Expand the Parameters node.

   Notice that there are two parameters for this stored procedure: the @CustomerID parameter that you created and the built-in return code parameter, @RETURN_VALUE.

5. Expand the Dependencies node.

   Notice that this stored procedure depends on four objects: the Orders, Products, Order Details, and Customers tables in the Northwind database. No objects depend on this stored procedure.

6. Switch to the Editor pane of the Query window.

7. On a blank line at the bottom of the Editor pane, enter and execute the following line:

   ```
   sp_depends custorderhistrep
   ```

   The *sp_depends* stored procedure checks the *CustOrderHistRep* stored procedure to determine dependencies.

   Notice that the Name column contains duplicate entries, but that for any duplicate entries, the row values are different.

8. Do not close Query Analyzer, because you will use it in the next practice.

▶ **To execute the stored procedure**

1. On a blank line at the bottom of the Editor pane, enter and execute the following code:

   ```
   EXEC [northwind].[dbo].[custorderhistrep]
   @CustomerID = 'thecr'
   ```

   The shortened version of the EXECUTE keyword, EXEC, is used to run the stored procedure, *CustOrderHistRep*. Notice that the fully qualified name of the procedure was specified. This specification is not necessary, but it enables you to run the procedure without first making sure that the current database is Northwind.

   Two result sets are returned. The first result set (contact name and contact title) appears in the upper portion of the Results pane. The second result set (product name and product totals) appears in the bottom portion of the Results pane.

In the previous example, EXEC was specified to run the stored procedure. Was it necessary to use this keyword?

2. Find the *dbo.CustOrderHistRep* stored procedure in the Object Browser and right-click it.

3. From the context menu, point to Script Object to New Windows As and then click Execute.

   Query Analyzer loads a new page into the Query Window editor, and the *EXECUTE* statement for *dbo.CustOrderHistRep* appears. Notice that two variables are declared: @RC and @CustomerID. The first variable is used to hold any return codes that are part of the procedure, and the second variable holds the value of the input parameter, @CustomerID. Notice that in the *EXEC* statement, @RC is equal to the stored procedure. This relationship captures any return codes from the procedure and places them into @RC. In Lesson 3, you will learn more about declaring variables when executing a stored procedure and setting the return code parameter equal to the stored procedure.

4. In the Editor pane, click the mouse at the end of the *EXEC* statement so that a blinking cursor appears after the word @CustomerID. Append the following line to the end of the line: = 'thecr'. The *EXEC* statement should look like the following:

   ```
   EXEC @RC = [Northwind].[dbo].[CustOrderHistRep] @CustomerID = 'thecr'
   ```

5. Execute the query.

   The query returns the same result set observed previously in this practice.

6. Close the new page created in the Query window, but do not close Query Analyzer or the original page that appears in the Editor pane.

   A Query Analyzer message appears, asking you whether you want to save the changes.

7. Click No.

   The original page in the Editor pane appears.

▶ **To modify the stored procedure**

1. In the Editor pane of the Query window, locate the following code:

   ```
   USE Northwind
   GO
   CREATE PROCEDURE dbo.CustOrderHistRep
   @CustomerID char(5)
   AS
   SELECT ContactName, ContactTitle
   FROM Customers WHERE CustomerID = @CustomerID
   SELECT ProductName, Total=SUM(Quantity)
   FROM Products P, [Order Details] OD, Orders O, Customers C
   WHERE
      C.CustomerID = @CustomerID AND C.CustomerID = O.CustomerID
   ```

```
        AND O.OrderID = OD.OrderID AND OD.ProductID = P.ProductID
GROUP BY ProductName
GO
```

2. Change the CREATE keyword to ALTER.

   When the text in the procedure is changed, the ALTER keyword will enable the stored procedure to be changed without losing any properties configured for the object.

3. You want the order quantity to be listed in Descending order. Add the following statement below the *GROUP BY ProductName* statement:

```
ORDER BY Total DESC
```

4. You have also decided to move the table joins from the WHERE clause to the FROM clause. The final form of the code should be similar to the following:

```
USE Northwind
GO
ALTER PROCEDURE dbo.CustOrderHistRep
@CustomerID char(5)
AS
SELECT ContactName, ContactTitle
FROM Customers WHERE CustomerID = @CustomerID
SELECT ProductName, Total=SUM(Quantity)
FROM Products P INNER JOIN [Order Details] OD
  ON P.ProductID = OD.ProductID JOIN Orders O
  ON OD.OrderID = O.OrderID JOIN Customers C
  ON O.CustomerID = C.CustomerID
WHERE C.CustomerID = @CustomerID
GROUP BY ProductName
ORDER BY Total DESC
GO
```

5. Execute the query.

6. To verify that the changes were made, go to the bottom of the Editor pane, press ENTER, then enter and execute the following statement:

```
sp_helptext custorderhistrep
```

   The stored procedure text appears on the Grids tab in the Results pane.

7. Leave the Query Analyzer open for the next exercise.

▶ **To delete the stored procedure**

1. Go to the bottom of the Editor pane, press ENTER, then enter and execute the following statement:

```
DROP PROCEDURE dbo.custorderhistrep
```

   The stored procedure is deleted from the Northwind database.

2. Use the Object Browser in Query Analyzer or Enterprise Manager to verify that the stored procedure was removed.

3. Close the Query Analyzer.

   You are prompted to save the script.

4. If you wish to save this script, select Yes. Otherwise, press No.

Lesson Summary

The CREATE PROCEDURE keywords are used to create procedures that are stored in a database. Procedures are created using graphical tools such as Enterprise Manager or command-prompt tools such as osql. Upon creation, the name of the procedure appears in SysObjects, and the procedure's content is stored in SysComments. When a procedure is created, it can be grouped, include return codes, require input parameters, supply default values for parameters, specify output parameters, be encrypted, or specify whether an execution plan should be created and whether the procedure should execute on a replication subscriber. The fundamental reason for creating a procedure is to complete a task when the procedure is executed. The EXECUTE keyword is used to run a procedure. A procedure can be run manually or flagged so that it starts when SQL Server starts. If a procedure requires modification, it is more efficient to use the *ALTER PROCEDURE* statement instead of deleting a procedure and recreating it. *ALTER PROCEDURE* maintains most of the original stored procedure object's properties. Deleting a stored procedure is accomplished by using the *DROP PROCEDURE* statement. If a user-defined system stored procedure is not located in the current database, SQL Server will search the Master database to delete the procedure.

Lesson 3: Programming Stored Procedures

Stored procedures provide a powerful method for coding tasks in the Transact-SQL language. In the previous lesson, you learned how to create, alter, drop, and execute stored procedures. You also saw how to use an input parameter to pass a value to a stored procedure when it executes. This lesson explores the use of both input and output parameters and introduces variables. You will also learn how to handle errors in your stored procedures with return codes and the @@ERROR function. The last part of this lesson introduces you to nesting and using cursors in stored procedures.

After this lesson, you will be able to:

- Use parameters, return codes, variables, and cursors in stored procedures.
- Create nested stored procedures and error-handling code.

Estimated lesson time: 45 minutes

Parameters and Variables

Parameters and variables are a fundamental part of making a stored procedure dynamic. Input parameters enable the user who is running the procedure to pass values to the stored procedure, making the result set unique to the request. Output parameters extend the output of your stored procedures beyond the standard result sets returned from a query. The data from an output parameter is captured in memory when the procedure executes. To return a value from the output parameter, you must create a variable to hold the value. You can display the value with SELECT or PRINT commands, or you can use the value to complete other commands in the procedure.

You might be a bit more familiar with input parameters than with output parameters. You used an input parameter (@CustomerID) when you created the *CustOrderHistRep* stored procedure in Lesson 2. Before running *CustOrderHistRep*, you set the @CustomerID parameter equal to the *RC*, and then you executed the procedure.

In summary, an input parameter is defined in a stored procedure, and a value is provided to the input parameter when the procedure is executed. An output parameter is defined in a stored procedure by using the OUTPUT keyword. When the procedure executes, a value for the output parameter is stored in memory. To put the value somewhere useful, you declare a variable to hold the value. Output values are typically displayed when the procedure execution completes.

The following procedure shows the use of both input and output parameters:

```
USE Pubs
GO
CREATE PROCEDURE dbo.SalesForTitle
    @Title varchar(80),   -- This is the input parameter.
    @YtdSales int OUTPUT, -- This is the first output parameter.
    @TitleText varchar(80) OUTPUT --This is the second output parameter.
AS
-- Assign the column data to the output parameters and
-- check for a title that's like the title input parameter.
SELECT @YtdSales = ytd_sales, @TitleText=title
FROM titles WHERE title LIKE @Title
GO
```

The input parameter is @Title, and the output parameters are @YtdSales and @TitleText. Notice that all three parameters have defined data types. The output parameters include the mandatory OUTPUT keyword. After the parameters are defined, the *SELECT* statement uses all three parameters. First, the output parameters are set equal to the column names in the query. When the query is run, the output parameters will contain the values from these two columns. The WHERE clause of the *SELECT* statement contains the input parameter, @Title. When the procedure is executed, you must provide a value for this input parameter or the query will fail. Later in this lesson, you will learn how to handle errors and provide default values for parameters.

The following statement executes the stored procedure that you just examined:

```
-- Declare variables to receive output values from procedure.
DECLARE @y_YtdSales int, @t_TitleText varchar(80)
EXECUTE SalesForTitle
--set the values for output parameters to the variables.
@YtdSales = @y_YtdSales OUTPUT,
@TitleText = @t_TitleText OUTPUT,
@Title = "%Garlic%" --specify a value for input parameter.
-- Display the variables returned by executing the procedure.
Select "Title" = @t_TitleText, "Number of Sales" = @y_YtdSales
GO
```

Two variables are declared: @y_YtdSales and @t_TitleText. These two variables will receive the values stored in the output parameters. Notice that the data types declared for these two variables match the data types of their corresponding output parameters. These two variables can be named the same as the output parameters because the variables in a stored procedure are local to the batch that contains them. For clarity, the variable names are different from the output parameters. When the variable is declared, it is not matched with an output parameter. Variables are matched with output parameters after the *EXECUTE* statement. Notice that the OUTPUT keyword is specified when the output parameters are set as equal to the variables. If OUTPUT is not specified, the variables cannot display values in the *SELECT* statement at the bottom of this batch. Finally, notice that the input parameter @Title is set equal to %Garlic%. This value is sent to the WHERE clause of the stored procedure's *SELECT* statement. Because the WHERE clause uses the LIKE keyword, you can use wildcards such as % so that the query searches for titles that contain the word "Garlic."

A more succinct way to execute the procedure is shown next. Notice that it is not necessary to specifically assign the variables from the stored procedure to the value of the input parameter or the output variables declared here:

```
DECLARE @y_YtdSales int, @t_TitleText varchar(80)
EXECUTE SalesForTitle
"%Garlic%", --sets the value of the input parameter.
@y_YtdSales OUTPUT, --receives the first output parameter
@t_TitleText OUTPUT --receives the second output parameter
-- Display the variables returned by executing the procedure.
Select "Title" = @t_TitleText, "Number of Sales" = @y_YtdSales
GO
```

When the procedure is executed, it returns the following:

Title	Number of Sales
Onions, Leeks, and Garlic: Cooking Secrets of the Mediterranean	375

An interesting result of this procedure is that only a single row of data is returned. Even if the *SELECT* statement in the procedure returns multiple rows, each variable holds a single value (the last row of data returned). Several solutions to this problem are explained later in this lesson.

The *RETURN* Statement and Error Handling

Often, the majority of coding in a well-written stored procedure (or in any program, for that matter) involves error handling. SQL Server provides functions and statements to deal with errors that occur during procedure execution. The two primary categories of errors are computer errors, such as an unavailable database server, and user errors. Return codes and the @@*ERROR* function are used to handle errors that occur when a procedure is executed.

Return codes can be used for other purposes besides error handling. The *RETURN* statement is used to generate return codes and exit a batch, and it can provide any integer value to a calling program. You will see code samples in this section that use the *RETURN* statement to supply a value for both error-handling and other purposes. The *RETURN* statement is used primarily for error handling because when the *RETURN* statement runs, the stored procedure exits unconditionally.

Consider the *SalesForTitle* procedure that you created and executed in the last section. If the value specified for the input parameter (@Title) does not exist in the database, executing the procedure returns the following result set:

Title	Number of Sales
NULL	NULL

It is more instructive to explain to the user that there were no matching records. The following example shows how to modify the *SalesForTitle* stored procedure to use a RETURN code (and thus provide a more useful message):

```
ALTER PROCEDURE dbo.SalesForTitle
@Title varchar(80), @YtdSales int OUTPUT,
@TitleText varchar(80) OUTPUT
AS
--Check to see if the title is in the database. If it isn't,
--exit the procedure and set the return code to 1.
IF (SELECT COUNT(*) FROM titles WHERE title LIKE @Title) = 0
    RETURN(1)
ELSE
SELECT @YtdSales = ytd_sales, @TitleText=title
FROM titles WHERE title LIKE @Title
GO
```

The *IF* statement below the AS keyword determines whether the input parameter is provided when the procedure is executed and matches any records in the database. If the *COUNT* function returns 0, then the return code is set to 1, RETURN(1). If the *COUNT* function returns anything else, the *SELECT* statement queries the Title table for annual sales and book title information. In this case, the return code is equal to 0.

Note   The initial USE Pubs statement has been removed from the script because it isn't the focus of the sample code. If you run this code make sure that you have switched to the Pubs database first. As you move through the code examples, you might notice other space-saving code consolidations (such as removing code comments and adding others). You should make a point of commenting your code so that it is maintainable and relatively easy to understand.

Some recoding of the execution statement is necessary to use the return code. The following example sets the input parameter @Title equal to Garlic%:

```
--Add @r_Code to hold the result code.
DECLARE @y_YtdSales int, @t_TitleText varchar(80), @r_Code int
--Run the procedure and set @r_Code equal to the procedure.
EXECUTE @r_Code = SalesForTitle
@YtdSales = @y_YtdSales OUTPUT,
@TitleText = @t_TitleText OUTPUT,
```

```
@Title = "Garlic%"
--Determine the value of @r_Code and execute the code.
IF @r_Code = 0
SELECT "Title" = @t_TitleText,
"Number of Sales" = @y_YtdSales, "Return Code" = @r_Code
ELSE IF @r_Code = 1
PRINT 'No matching titles in the database. Return code=' + CONVERT(varch
ar(1),@r_Code)
GO
```

A new variable has been added to the end of the *DECLARE* statement: @r_Code. Later in the code, this variable contains the value provided by the RETURN keyword. This variable is defined as an integer data type because the return code sends an integer value. The @r_Code variable is set to the return code on the EXECUTE line. Notice that @r_Code is set equal to the stored procedure. The value for the input parameter, @Title, is now Garlic% rather than %Garlic%. In other words, the *SELECT* statement in the procedure will search for records in the Titles table starting with the word "Garlic." Conditional logic appears below the parameters and comments. The first *IF* statement is tested. If the procedure finds a record, then the return code is 0, and the *SELECT* statement runs. If the procedure doesn't find any matching records, @r_Code will equal 1 and the *PRINT* statement will run. Because there isn't a title in the database that begins with the word "Garlic," executing the procedure returns the *PRINT* statement:

```
No matching titles in the database. Return code=1
```

Changing the input parameter to %Garlic% and executing the code returns the following result set:

Title	Number of Sales	Return Code
Onions, Leeks, and Garlic: Cooking Secrets of the Mediterranean	375	0

If you don't enter a value for the @Title input parameter, the result of executing the query is the following message:

```
Server: Msg 201, Level 16, State 3, Procedure SalesForTitle, Line 0
Procedure 'SalesForTitle' expects parameter '@Title', which was not supp
lied.
```

Default Values and Setting a Parameter to NULL

To test for a NULL value for the @Title input parameters, you must set a default value for the input parameter and modify the stored procedure by adding another conditional statement. Setting a default value is a powerful error-avoidance technique. If you set @Title to a value contained in the database, the *SELECT* statement would use the default for the input parameter. In this case, it's more instructive to the user if you set a default of NULL for the input parameter and let a RETURN code instruct the user on how to properly execute the procedure. Modifying the procedure in the following way accomplishes this goal:

```
ALTER PROCEDURE dbo.SalesForTitle
@Title varchar(80) = NULL, @YtdSales int OUTPUT,
@TitleText varchar(80) OUTPUT
AS
IF @Title IS NULL
    RETURN(2)
ELSE
IF (SELECT COUNT(*) FROM titles WHERE title LIKE @Title) = 0
    RETURN(1)
ELSE
SELECT @YtdSales = ytd_sales, @TitleText=title
FROM titles WHERE title LIKE @Title
GO
```

Notice that @Title is set to a default value of NULL. A conditional *IF* statement was added right after the AS keyword. This test must occur before the *SELECT COUNT* statement, however, because the *SELECT COUNT* statement will test true with a value of NULL.

When you execute the procedure, you must include a test for a return code of 2, as shown in the following example:

```
DECLARE @y_YtdSales int, @t_TitleText varchar(80), @r_Code int
EXECUTE @r_Code = SalesForTitle
@YtdSales = @y_YtdSales OUTPUT,
@TitleText = @t_TitleText OUTPUT
--No value specified for the @Title input parameter.
IF @r_Code = 0
SELECT "Title" = @t_TitleText,
"Number of Sales" = @y_YtdSales, "Return code" = @r_Code
ELSE IF @r_Code = 1
PRINT 'No matching titles in the database. Return code=' + CONVERT(varch
ar(1),@r_Code)
ELSE IF @r_Code = 2 --test for a return code of 2.
PRINT 'You must add a value for @Title for this procedure to function pr
operly.
Return code=' + CONVERT(varchar(1),@r_Code)
GO
```

Testing for Server Errors

Another important category of error to test for is database errors. The *@@ERROR* function enables you to test for more than 3000 different database-related errors. This function captures database error numbers as a procedure executes. You can use each return number to display a message to the user explaining the reason for the error. Common user errors that lead to database errors occur in *INSERT* and *UPDATE* statements in which a user attempts to add data that violates the integrity of the data (such as adding an invalid identification number). The error numbers and their descriptions are stored in the master.dbo.sysmessages table. You can query this table with the following *SELECT* statement:

```
SELECT error, description from master.dbo.sysmessages
```

If a procedure executes successfully, *@@ERROR* is set to 0. If an error occurs, an error number other than 0 is returned to *@@ERROR*. When another Transact-SQL statement runs in a procedure, the value of *@@ERROR* changes. Therefore, *@@ERROR* should be stored in a variable or provide a return code after each Transact-SQL statement completes. The following example demonstrates how to generate a return code if there is a database error:

```
ALTER PROCEDURE dbo.SalesForTitle
@Title varchar(80) = NULL, @YtdSales int OUTPUT,
@TitleText varchar(80) OUTPUT
AS
IF @Title IS NULL
    RETURN(2)
ELSE
IF (SELECT COUNT(*) FROM dbo.titles
WHERE title LIKE @Title) = 0
    RETURN(1)
ELSE
SELECT @YtdSales = ytd_sales, @TitleText=title
FROM dbo.titles WHERE title LIKE @Title
-- Check for SQL Server database errors.
IF @@ERROR <> 0
    RETURN(3)
GO
```

Notice that the procedure checks for the value of *@@ERROR* after the *SELECT* statement that returns a result set when the procedure is executed. This function is important, because the goal of *@@ERROR* is to check for database errors after the core task of the stored procedure occurs.

The following code executes the procedure and displays a generic error message if a database error occurs:

```
DECLARE @y_YtdSales int, @t_TitleText varchar(80), @r_Code int
EXECUTE @r_Code = SalesForTitle
@YtdSales = @y_YtdSales OUTPUT,
@TitleText = @t_TitleText OUTPUT, @Title = "%Garlic%"
IF @r_Code = 0
SELECT "Title" = @t_TitleText,
"Number of Sales" = @y_YtdSales, "Return code" = @r_Code
ELSE
```

```
IF @r_Code = 1
PRINT 'No matching titles in the database. Return code=' + CONVERT(varch
ar(1),@r_Code)
ELSE
IF @r_Code = 2
PRINT 'You must add a value for @Title for this procedure to function pr
operly.
Return code=' + CONVERT(varchar(1),@r_Code)
ELSE
IF @r_Code = 3
    PRINT 'There was a database error.'
GO
```

When you create a stored procedure for a production database system, you will become familiar with the types of errors that users will make when they execute the procedure. With this experience and your understanding of result codes, you can write additional error-handling conditions into your procedures.

Note   For more information about result codes and using the *@@ERROR* function, perform a search for RESULT and @@ERROR in SQL Server Books Online.

Nesting Procedures

Nesting stored procedures simply involves calling one stored procedure from another. A single stored procedure can perform multiple tasks, but it is better to create simpler, more generic stored procedures that can call other stored procedures to complete additional tasks. For example, you might write a stored procedure called *Procedure_A* that inserts data into an existing table, and you might write another stored procedure called *Procedure_B* that displays data from the table. *Procedure_A* could call *Procedure_B* after successfully inserting data into a table. Users can still run *Procedure_B* to view table information without having to run *Procedure_A* to insert data into the table.

Procedures can be nested together up to 32 levels deep. However, there is no limit to how many procedures a single procedure can call. A procedure can also call itself recursively. A procedure is called from another procedure by using the *EXECUTE* statement. You will nest a procedure for the BookShopDB database in Exercise 3.

Cursors

You can use cursors in stored procedures; however, you should avoid them if you can find a way to do the same thing by using result sets. Procedures that use result sets are more efficient on the database and on the network, and they are typically less complex to write than cursors. Cursors are explored in Chapter 7, but are discussed here so that you can see how to use them in stored procedures. To learn more about cursors, read Lesson 3 in Chapter 7 of SQL Server Books Online and *Inside Microsoft SQL Server 2000* by Microsoft Press.

Data Retrieval Methods

The stored procedure code example used throughout this lesson is limited to returning a single row of data. For example, an input parameter value of "The%" will return a single row of data, with the last title starting with "The%" (as shown in the following result):

Title	Number of Sales	Return Code
The Psychology of Computer Cooking	NULL	0

A single row appears because the result set returned by the *SELECT* statement is passed to a variable capable of holding only a single value.

There are a number of solutions to this problem. The simplest solution is to eliminate the output parameters in the *SELECT* statement and return a record set from the stored procedure, as shown:

```
ALTER PROCEDURE dbo.SalesForTitle
@Title varchar(80)
AS
SELECT Title = title, [Number of Sales]=ytd_sales
FROM titles WHERE title LIKE @Title
GO
```

Notice that all output parameters were removed from the stored procedure. To execute this simple stored procedure, you can use the following sample code:

```
EXECUTE SalesForTitle
@Title = "The%"
```

When you execute this procedure, the result set is as follows:

Title	Number of Sales
The Busy Executive's Database Guide	4095
The Gourmet Microwave	22,246
The Psychology of Computer Cooking	NULL

For clarity, the return code syntax has been removed from the stored procedure; thus, the Return Code column does not appear. All book titles starting with "The%" appear in the result set.

The same data can be returned with cursors. The following stored procedure places each row of data into a cursor output parameter and returns the row of data before fetching the next row:

```
ALTER PROCEDURE dbo.SalesForTitle
@ResultCrsr CURSOR VARYING OUTPUT, @Title varchar(80) = NULL
AS
```

```
SET @ResultCrsr = CURSOR FOR SELECT ytd_sales, title
FROM dbo.titles WHERE title LIKE @Title
OPEN @ResultCrsr
GO
```

The second line of code creates an output parameter called @ResultCrsr of the data type *cursor*. This output parameter will hold each record returned by the cursor. After the AS keyword, @ResultCrsr is set equal to the cursor that will eventually contain each record of the *SELECT* statement. After the *SELECT* statement, the *OPEN* statement populates the result set into the cursor.

The following code can be used to execute this stored procedure:

```
DECLARE @r_ResultCrsr CURSOR
EXECUTE dbo.SalesForTitle
@ResultCrsr = @r_ResultCrsr OUTPUT, @Title = "The%"
FETCH NEXT FROM @r_ResultCrsr
WHILE (@@FETCH_STATUS <> -1)
    BEGIN
       FETCH NEXT FROM @r_ResultCrsr
    END
CLOSE @r_ResultCrsr
DEALLOCATE @r_ResultCrsr
GO
```

All three records from the database are returned. The output data is the same as the result set example shown earlier in this section, except that each record appears separately in the results pane. An additional empty row is returned because the *@@FETCH_STATUS* is not set to –1 until after an empty row is retrieved.

Exercise 3: Programming Stored Procedures to Insert and Retrieve Data

In this exercise, you will create a stored procedure to insert new customer records into the BookShopDB database. You will then create a stored procedure that checks for duplicate customer records in the database. The second procedure you create will be nested in the first procedure. The stored procedures will include parameters, variables, return codes, the *@@ERROR* function, and control of flow language.

▶ **To create an insert customer stored procedure**

1. Open Query Analyzer and connect to your local server.

2. In the Editor pane of the Query window, enter and execute the following code:

```
USE BookShopDB
GO
CREATE PROCEDURE dbo.AddCustomer
--CustomerID not included as an input parameter because
```

```
--the ID is automatically generated (Identity column)
@FirstName varchar(30), @LastName varchar(30),
@Phone varchar(24), @Address1 varchar(60),
@Address2 varchar(60) = 'unknown', @City varchar(15),
@State varchar(7), @Zip varchar(12)
AS
INSERT [BookShopDB].[dbo].[Customers]
(FirstName, LastName, Phone, Address1,
Address2, City, State, Zip)
VALUES
(@FirstName, @LastName, @Phone, @Address1,
@Address2, @City, @State, @Zip)
RETURN(SELECT @@IDENTITY AS 'Identity')
GO
```

In this statement, you create a stored procedure named AddCustomer. You specify all of the required input parameters. Notice that a default value of 'unknown' is provided for Address2. Address2 isn't always part of a customer's address. The value of 'unknown' matches the default value of the check constraint applied to this column. At the end of the code, the *RETURN* statement contains the customer ID value, which is retrieved by the *@@IDENTITY* function.

3. In the Editor pane of the Query window, enter and execute the following code:

```
DECLARE @r_Code int
EXECUTE @r_Code=dbo.AddCustomer
@FirstName = 'Jamie', @LastName = 'Marra',
@Phone = '425-555-1212', @Address1 = '20 Oak St., SE',
@City = 'Remy', @State = 'WA', @Zip = '98888'
SELECT [Customer ID] = 'The new customer ID is:' + CONVERT(CHAR(2), @
r_Code)
```

The code creates a variable of type integer named *@r_Code*. This variable is set equal to the stored procedure name upon execution. Lesson 3's code examples showed an example of using a return code for error handling. In this procedure, the return code will contain the value of the *@@IDENTITY* function when the stored procedure executes.

▶ **To add error-handling techniques to the stored procedure**

1. The *AddCustomer* stored procedure does not contain any error handling. The procedure needs to be modified to include error-handling logic. In the Editor pane of the Query window, enter and execute the following code:

```
ALTER PROCEDURE dbo.AddCustomer
@FirstName varchar(30)= 'unknown',
@LastName varchar(30)= 'unknown', @Phone varchar(24) = NULL,
@Address1 varchar(60) = NULL,
@Address2 varchar(60) = 'unknown', @City varchar(15) = NULL,
@State varchar(7) = NULL, @Zip varchar(12) = NULL
AS
IF (@FirstName = 'unknown') AND (@LastName = 'unknown')
```

```
RETURN(1)
ELSE IF @Phone IS NULL
RETURN(2)
ELSE IF
  @Address1 IS NULL OR @City IS NULL OR
  @State IS NULL OR @Zip IS NULL
RETURN(3)
ELSE
INSERT [BookShopDB].[dbo].[Customers]
(FirstName, LastName, Phone, Address1,
Address2, City, State, Zip)
VALUES
(@FirstName, @LastName, @Phone, @Address1,
@Address2, @City, @State, @Zip)
RETURN(SELECT @@IDENTITY AS 'Identity')
IF @@ERROR <> 0
RETURN(4)
GO
```

All input variables now contain default values. This method is an important error-avoidance technique. For example, if no value is specified for @First-Name, it will default to 'unknown' and the procedure will execute properly. If the user doesn't enter a first name or a last name for the customer, however, the procedure returns a value of 1. This part of the code complies with the business rule that a first name or a last name is required, and it matches with the check constraint applied to the FirstName and LastName columns of BookShopDB. If no phone number is entered, the default value of NULL is used, and a return code of 2 is sent to the executing procedure. If any address information is missing, a return code of 3 is sent to the executing procedure. Notice that the @Address2 input parameter is not part of address error checking because it is not always required. If all input parameters are specified, the *INSERT* statement is called. If the *INSERT* statement fails because of a database error, a return code of 4 is sent to the executing program.

As you work with the stored procedure, you will want to add additional error handling to the code. For example, you should check the database for duplicate customer information before creating a new customer record.

Comments were left out of the code to save space. Make sure that any code you write is fully commented inline so that others will understand the purpose of your code (and to help you remember the purpose of your code). Add comments to the beginning of your code to summarize the purpose of the procedure, the creation date, and your name or initials.

2. In the Editor pane of the Query window, enter and execute the following code:

```
DECLARE @r_Code int
EXECUTE @r_Code=dbo.AddCustomer
@FirstName= 'Jamie', @LastName = 'Marra',
@Phone = '425-555-1212', @Address1 = '20 Oak St., SE',
@City = 'Remy', @State = 'WA', @Zip = '98888'
```

```
IF @r_Code = 4
BEGIN
PRINT 'A database error has occured.
Please contact the help desk for assistance.'
END
IF @r_Code = 1
PRINT 'You must specify a value for the firstname or lastname'
ELSE IF @r_Code = 2
PRINT 'You must specify a value for the phone number'
ELSE IF @r_Code = 3
PRINT 'You must provide all address information, Street address, City
, State and Zipcode'
ELSE IF @r_Code = @@IDENTITY
SELECT [Customer ID] = 'The new customer ID is: ' + CONVERT(CHAR(2),
@r_Code)
```

A new customer record is added to the database. Error-checking code appears throughout the execution code. Examine each @r_Code value and the information returned to the user in the event of an error.

Notice that the same customer information was entered as in the previous procedure execution. In the next exercise, you will create a stored procedure to check the Customers table to avoid creating duplicate customer information.

▶ **To create a stored procedure to protect against customer record duplication**

1. Checking for duplicate record information is an important part of record entry. Without this check, it is inevitable that tables will contain duplicate entries. In the Editor pane of the Query window, enter and execute the following code:

```
CREATE PROCEDURE dbo.CheckForDuplicateCustomer
@1_FirstName varchar(30)= 'unknown',
@1_LastName varchar(30)= 'unknown',
@1_City varchar(15) = NULL, @1_State varchar(7) = NULL,
@1_Phone varchar(24) = NULL, @o_FirstName varchar(30) OUTPUT,
@o_LastName varchar(30) OUTPUT, @o_City varchar(15) OUTPUT,
@o_State varchar(7) OUTPUT, @o_Phone varchar(24) OUTPUT
AS
SELECT @o_FirstName=firstname, @o_LastName=lastname,
@o_City=city, @o_State=state, @o_Phone=phone
FROM customers
  WHERE firstname=@1_FirstName AND lastname=@1_LastName
  AND city=@1_City AND state=@1_State AND phone=@1_Phone
IF @@ROWCOUNT <> 0
RETURN(5)
```

This stored procedure checks the Customers table to determine whether there is a record with the same first name, last name, city, or phone number as the input parameters specified. The input parameters begin with 1 to distinguish them from the input parameters in the *AddCustomer* stored procedure. The output parameters are set equal to the corresponding Customers table columns in the

SELECT statement. A test for a record match is made in the WHERE clause. The column values are tested against the input parameters. If the *@@ROW-COUNT* function returns a value greater than 0, then a return code of 5 is set for the stored procedure.

2. In the Editor pane of the Query window, enter and execute the following code:

```
ALTER PROCEDURE dbo.AddCustomer
@FirstName varchar(30)= 'unknown',
@LastName varchar(30)= 'unknown', @Phone varchar(24) = NULL,
@Address1 varchar(60) = NULL,
@Address2 varchar(60) = 'unknown', @City varchar(15) = NULL,
@State varchar(7) = NULL, @Zip varchar(12) = NULL
AS
IF (@FirstName = 'unknown') AND (@LastName = 'unknown')
  RETURN(1)
ELSE IF @Phone IS NULL
  RETURN(2)
ELSE IF @Address1 IS NULL OR @City IS NULL
OR @State IS NULL OR @Zip IS NULL
  RETURN(3)
--begin nesting
DECLARE @r_Code int, @v_FirstName varchar(30),
@v_LastName varchar(30), @v_City varchar(15),
@v_State varchar(7), @v_Phone varchar(24)
EXECUTE @r_Code=dbo.CheckForDuplicateCustomer
@1_FirstName = @FirstName, @1_LastName = @LastName,
@1_City = @City, @1_State = @State, @1_Phone = @Phone,
@o_FirstName = @v_FirstName OUTPUT,
@o_LastName = @v_LastName OUTPUT, @o_City = @v_City OUTPUT,
@o_State = @v_State OUTPUT, @o_Phone = @v_Phone OUTPUT
IF @@ROWCOUNT > 0
BEGIN
  PRINT 'A duplicate record was found for ' + @v_FirstName + ' ' + @v_LastName
  PRINT 'in ' + @v_City + ' ' + @v_State + ' with a phone number '
PRINT 'of ' + @v_Phone + '.'
  RETURN(5)
END
--end nesting
INSERT [BookShopDB].[dbo].[Customers]
(FirstName, LastName, Phone,
Address1, Address2, City, State, Zip)
VALUES
(@FirstName, @LastName, @Phone,
@Address1, @Address2, @City, @State, @Zip)
RETURN(SELECT @@IDENTITY AS 'Identity')
IF @@ERROR <> 0
RETURN(4)
GO
```

The *CheckForDuplicateCustomer* stored procedure is nested into the *AddCustomer* stored procedure. The point at which nesting begins and ends has been commented in the code. Variables beginning with *v_* are created to hold the output parameter values. Each input parameter beginning with 1_ is set equal to the corresponding input parameter supplied when the *AddCustomer* stored procedure executes. The output parameters from the *CheckForDuplicateCustomer* stored procedure are then set equal to their corresponding output variables beginning with *v_*. The variable values are used in the sequence of *PRINT* statements that are called if the *@@ROWCOUNT* returns anything greater than 0.

▶ **To test the stored procedures**

1. In the Editor pane of the Query window, enter and execute the following code:

```
DECLARE @r_Code int
EXECUTE @r_Code=dbo.AddCustomer
@FirstName= 'Jamie', @LastName = 'Marra',
@Phone = '425-555-1212', @Address1 = '20 Oak St., SE',
@City = 'Remy', @State = 'WA', @Zip = '98888'
IF @r_Code = 4
BEGIN
        PRINT 'A database error has occured.
        Please contact the help desk for assistance.'
END
IF @r_Code = 1
PRINT 'You must specify a value for the firstname or lastname'
ELSE IF @r_Code = 2
PRINT 'You must specify a value for the phone number'
ELSE IF @r_Code = 3
PRINT 'You must provide all address information, Street address, City
, State and Zipcode'
ELSE IF @r_Code = @@IDENTITY
SELECT [Customer ID] = 'The new customer ID is: ' + CONVERT(CHAR(2),
@r_Code)
```

The stored procedure returns a message stating that the record already exists.

2. Change the value of @FirstName to Jeff and @LastName to Fellinge, then execute the query again.

The stored procedure returns a message with the new customer ID.

Lesson Summary

Important programming features available to stored procedures include parameters, variables, return codes, functions, default values, nesting, and cursors. Input parameters pass data to a stored procedure upon execution. Output parameters receive data from the stored procedure. Variables are used to hold values from output parameters. You specify an output parameter by using the OUTPUT keyword.

You specify a variable by using the DECLARE keyword. Return codes are primarily used for error handling. Return codes are supplied by using the RETURN keyword, followed by an integer. When the *RETURN* statement is called, the stored procedure code exits unconditionally. If an integer is supplied in the *RETURN* statement, it is sent to a variable when the procedure is executed. The variable is set as equal to the stored procedure. Then, conditional programming language is used to match the return code with a task in the program. The *@@ERROR* function is combined with return codes in the stored procedure to capture database errors. Some errors can be avoided by setting default values for parameters.

You should write stored procedures to complete a single task. You can then execute one procedure from another procedure. Executing one procedure from another is called nesting. A stored procedure that calls itself is known as recursion. Procedures can be nested up to 32 levels deep. A powerful feature of SQL Server 2000 is returning records from the database via cursors. Cursors can be created in a stored procedure and called from an executing program. You should use cursors only when absolutely necessary, because if they are misused, they can severely impact database and network performance.

Review

The following questions are intended to reinforce key information presented in this chapter. If you are unable to answer a question, review the appropriate lesson and then try the question again. You can find answers to the questions in the Appendix, "Questions and Answers."

1. You create a local temporary stored procedure and ask a colleague to execute the stored procedure. Your colleague claims that she cannot execute the stored procedure. Why can't she execute the stored procedure?

2. Why do complex stored procedures typically execute faster the second time they are run than the first time?

3. What security features are available for stored procedures?

4. What function can you use to check the properties of a stored procedure and other objects in SQL Server?

5. Why is it more efficient to modify a stored procedure by using the ALTER PROCEDURE keywords than it is to drop and re-create a stored procedure?

6. You set the current database to Northwind, and then you create a stored procedure named *#Procedure01*. You then check the Northwind database for the stored procedure, but it doesn't appear. You can run the stored procedure using Northwind as the current database. Why are you able to execute this stored procedure but it doesn't appear in the Northwind database?

7. In what three ways is the *RETURN* statement used in a stored procedure?

C H A P T E R   9

Implementing Triggers

About This Chapter

Triggers are a special class of stored procedure defined to execute automatically in place of or after data modification. The three commands that fire a trigger are UPDATE, INSERT, and DELETE. Use triggers to extend data integrity and to implement complex business logic. In this chapter, you will learn when it is appropriate to implement triggers and when basic constraints will suffice. Create triggers by using Transact-SQL language or SQL Enterprise Manager. Management tasks include altering, renaming, viewing, dropping, and disabling triggers. Triggers use two pseudo tables, Inserted and Deleted, to detect data modifications. Programming triggers requires a thorough understanding of these pseudo tables and the Transact-SQL language. In this chapter, you will learn how to program triggers and how to use a number of system commands and functions commonly used in trigger programming. Tasks commonly completed by implementing triggers include maintaining running totals and other computed values, creating an audit record of data modifications, invoking external actions, and implementing complex data integrity.

Before You Begin

To complete the lessons in this chapter, you must have:

- SQL Server 2000 Enterprise Edition installed on a Microsoft Windows 2000 Server computer.
- The ability to log on to the Windows 2000 Server computer and to SQL Server as the Windows 2000 Administrator.
- Completed the exercises in Chapter 3, "Designing a SQL Server Database," Chapter 4, "Implementing SQL Server Databases and Tables," Chapter 5, "Implementing Data Integrity," and in Chapter 7, "Managing and Manipulating Data."

Lesson 1: Introduction to Triggers

Implementing data integrity features is critical for maintaining the accuracy and consistency of the database. Complex procedural data integrity methods and business logic can be added to a database using triggers, a special type of stored procedure that is applied to tables and views. Data modification events cause triggers to fire automatically. In this lesson, you will learn when to use triggers and when to apply other less resource-intensive data integrity measures, such as cascading referential integrity. You will also learn about the various types and classes of triggers and their features and limitations.

After this lesson, you will be able to:

- Explain how to use trigger types (INSERT, UPDATE, and DELETE triggers) and trigger classes (INSTEAD OF and AFTER triggers) to extend data integrity.
- Apply cascading referential integrity in place of triggers.
- Describe trigger features and limitations.

Estimated Lesson time: 30 minutes

Extending Data Integrity with Triggers

The quality of a database is measured partly by the consistency and accuracy of the data in the database. Declarative data integrity and procedural data integrity are used to maintain data consistency and accuracy. Chapter 5, "Implementing Data Integrity," explored declarative data integrity methods. This chapter explores a common procedural data integrity method, triggers.

Triggers enable you to write a procedure that is invoked when table data is modified with an INSERT, UPDATE, or DELETE action. A trigger is applied to either a table or a view. Triggers are used to enforce business rules in the database. For example, one business rule identified for the BookShopDB database is as follows: When a book is added to an order, it is marked as sold in the inventory. A trigger applied to the BookOrders table can fire when a book order is inserted. The business logic in the trigger locates the book in the Books table and flags the book as sold. You will create this trigger in Exercise 3.

Procedural Data Integrity

Before choosing to implement a trigger, consider whether the same results can be achieved by using constraints or rules. Use entity integrity to uniquely identify rows of table data (primary key and unique key constraints). Use domain integrity to define default values (default constraints) and to restrict column data to acceptable values (check and referential constraints). Use referential integrity to enforce logical relationships between tables (foreign key and check constraints). Use default constraints to provide a value for a required field when the field is not specified in an *INSERT* statement. Use constraints before choosing to use triggers and rules. Rules remain in SQL Server 2000 for backward compatibility, and the overuse of triggers can degrade system performance. The query optimizer uses constraint definitions to build high-performance query-execution plans. Chapter 5 discusses all data integrity methods (except for triggers). Triggers are especially useful because they can contain significantly more complex processing logic than is possible with declarative integrity methods. Use triggers in the following instances:

- If using declarative data integrity methods does not meet the functional needs of the application. For example, create a trigger that changes a numeric value in a table when a record in the same table is removed.
- Changes must cascade through related tables in the database. For example, create and apply a trigger to an Orders table so that when an order is placed, stock quantity in an inventory table is changed. Create and apply another trigger to the Inventory table so that when the quantity changes, a purchase request is added to the Purchasing table.

    Use cascading referential integrity constraints instead of a custom trigger if your goal is to update or delete a foreign key constraint.
- If the database is denormalized and requires an automated way to update redundant data contained in multiple tables.
- If a value in one table must be validated against a non-identical value in another table.
- If customized messages and complex error handling are required.

Trigger Features and Limitations

Cascading referential integrity extends the accuracy and consistency of data by applying updates or deletions to foreign keys within the database. Triggers go further by extending data integrity to any table column in the database or even to objects outside the current database. You can also apply triggers to views.

A single trigger can run multiple actions, and it can be fired by more than one event. For example, you can create a single trigger that runs when any valid event, INSERT, UPDATE, or DELETE occurs. Within the Transact-SQL code, you can define business logic to handle each type of event.

Triggers cannot be created on a temporary or system table, although the Transact-SQL language within the trigger can reference temporary tables or system tables. An important limitation to be aware of is that INSTEAD OF DELETE and INSTEAD OF UPDATE triggers cannot be defined on tables that have corresponding ON DELETE or ON UPDATE cascading referential integrity defined. You will learn more about INSTEAD OF triggers later in this lesson.

Trigger Events

Three events automatically fire a trigger: INSERT, UPDATE, and DELETE events that occur on a table or on a view. Triggers cannot be fired manually. The trigger syntax always includes defining one or more of these events before the task-specific Transact-SQL language is specified. Trigger types correspond to the event. For example, you can create an update trigger so that when an update occurs to a table, the update trigger is fired. A single trigger can be assigned multiple events so that you could have a procedure that is both an update and an insert trigger. The events can be listed in any order within the trigger definition. You will learn more about trigger syntax in Lesson 2.

There are certain instances when an event that modifies or deletes data does not fire a corresponding trigger. For example, the *TRUNCATE TABLE* statement does not fire triggers defined for DELETE events. An important feature of triggers is that unsuccessful transactions are automatically rolled back. Because *TRUNCATE TABLE* is not a logged event, it cannot be rolled back so it doesn't fire the DELETE trigger. Additionally, the *WRITETEXT* statement does not cause the INSERT or UPDATE triggers to fire.

Trigger Execution

When a table insert or update fires a trigger, the trigger stores the new or modified data in a table named Inserted. When a table delete fires a trigger, the trigger stores the deleted data in a table named Deleted. The table exists in memory and is queried within the trigger by using Transact-SQL commands. This capability is critical to the function of most triggers because the task within the trigger, such as modifying a value in an associated table, compares the data contained in the Inserted or Deleted tables to the data in the modified table before the changes are committed. By using the information stored in the Inserted or Deleted table, a trigger can roll back a transaction to enforce business rules.

There are two classes of triggers in SQL Server 2000: INSTEAD OF and AFTER. INSTEAD OF triggers bypass the triggering action and run in their place. For example, an update to a table containing an INSTEAD OF trigger will run the trigger Transact-SQL code rather than the update statement. This feature enables you to specify complex processing statements within the trigger to augment the table-modification statement. AFTER triggers fire as a supplement to the triggering action and are the default trigger class. A trigger can be applied to only a single table or view.

There are a number of important differences between these trigger classes, as shown in the following table:

Characteristic	INSTEAD OF	AFTER
Applied to	Defined on a table or a view. Defining a trigger on a view extends the types of updates that a view can support.	Defined on a table. Modifications to views will fire AFTER triggers when table data is modified in response to the view modification.
Number allowed	Only one per triggering action is allowed on a table or view. You can define views of other views where each view has its own INSTEAD OF trigger.	More than one allowed on a table.
Order of execution	Only one per triggering action is allowed on a table or view, so the order is irrelevant.	Can define which trigger fires first and last. Use the *sp_settriggerorder* system stored procedure to define the first and last trigger. All other triggers applied to a table execute in random order.

You can apply both classes of triggers to a table. If you have defined both trigger classes and constraints for a table, the INSTEAD OF trigger fires. Then, constraints are processed and AFTER triggers fire. If constraints are violated, INSTEAD OF trigger actions are rolled back. AFTER triggers do not execute if constraints are violated or if some other event causes the table modification to fail.

Like stored procedures, triggers can be nested up to 32 levels deep and can be fired recursively. For more information about trigger nesting and recursion, search the Transact-SQL Reference in SQL Server Books Online for a page titled "CREATE TRIGGER."

Exercise 1: Applying Cascading Referential Integrity Constraints

In this exercise, you will add cascading referential integrity constraints to the BookShopDB database. This new SQL Server 2000 feature takes the place of a common trigger task, performing cascading deletes and updates to foreign keys.

▶ **To configure cascading referential integrity on BookShopDB for the TitleID key**

1. Open Query Analyzer and connect to your local server.

2. In the Editor pane of the Query window, enter and execute the following code:

```
USE BookShopDB
INSERT Orders (CustomerID, EmployeeID, Amount, OrderDate, DeliveryDat
e, PaymentID, StatusID)
VALUES (10, 1, 30, GetDate(), DATEADD(day, 5, GetDate()), 1, 1)
INSERT BookOrders (titleid, orderid) VALUES ('aust1234', 3)
```

The first *INSERT* statement adds an order to the Orders table. The OrderDate and DeliveryDate values are provided by functions. The first function returns today's date (as specified by your computer). The second function adds five days onto the value returned by GetDate. The second *INSERT* statement adds a record to the BookOrders table. These two insert statements are important for testing the effect of enabling cascading referential integrity for the TitleID foreign key in the BookOrders table.

3. In the Editor pane of the Query window, enter and execute the following Transact-SQL code:

```
UPDATE Books
SET TitleID = 'AUST1235'
WHERE TitleID = 'AUST1234'
```

The following error message appears in the Message tab of the Results pane:

```
Server: Msg 547, Level 16, State 1, Line 1
UPDATE statement conflicted with COLUMN REFERENCE constraint 'titleid
_fk'. The conflict occurred in database 'BookShopDB', table 'BookAuth
ors', column 'TitleID'.
The statement has been terminated.
```

This error message is caused because the foreign key constraint, titleid_fk, is violated by attempting to change the TitleID primary key value in the Books table.

4. In the Editor pane of the Query window, enter and execute the following Transact-SQL code:

```
ALTER TABLE BookAuthors DROP CONSTRAINT titleid_fk
```

This *ALTER TABLE* statement removes the titleid_fk foreign key constraint from the BookAuthors table.

5. In the Editor pane of the Query window, enter the following Transact-SQL code:

```
ALTER TABLE BookAuthors
ADD CONSTRAINT titleid_fk FOREIGN KEY (TitleID) REFERENCES Books (Tit
leID)
ON UPDATE CASCADE ON DELETE CASCADE
```

This *ALTER TABLE* statement adds cascading referential integrity to the foreign key constraint (titleid_fk) in the BookAuthors table. When an update to the TitleID primary key occurs in the Books table, the corresponding foreign key will be changed in the BookOrders table. The titleid_fk foreign key constraint makes the Books table the parent of the BookAuthors table.

6. Execute the Transact-SQL code.

7. In the Editor pane of the Query window, enter and execute the following Transact-SQL code:

```
UPDATE Books
SET TitleID = 'AUST1235'
WHERE TitleID = 'AUST1234'
```

An error message appears because the foreign key constraint, titleid2_fk, applied to the BookOrders table, was violated by attempting to change the TitleID primary key value in the Books table.

8. In the Editor pane of the Query window, enter and execute the following Transact-SQL code:

```
ALTER TABLE BookOrders DROP CONSTRAINT titleid2_fk
ALTER TABLE BookOrders
ADD CONSTRAINT titleid2_fk FOREIGN KEY (TitleID) REFERENCES Books (Ti
tleID)
ON UPDATE CASCADE ON DELETE CASCADE
```

The first *ALTER TABLE* statement drops the titleid2_fk constraint from the BookOrders table. The second *ALTER TABLE* statement adds cascading referential integrity to the titleid2_fk foreign key constraint. The titleid2_fk foreign key constraint makes the Books table the parent of the BookOrders table.

9. In the Editor pane of the Query window, enter and execute the following Transact-SQL code:

```
UPDATE Books
SET TitleID = 'AUST1235'
WHERE TitleID = 'AUST1234'
```

The TitleID is updated in the Books table, and because of cascading referential integrity, it is also updated in the BookAuthors and BookOrders tables.

10. In the Editor pane of the Query window, enter and execute the following Transact-SQL code:

```
SELECT "Books TitleID" = b.titleID, "BookAuthors TitleID"
= ba.titleID,
"BookOrders TitleID" = bo.titleID
FROM books b INNER JOIN bookauthors ba ON b.titleID=ba.titleID
INNER JOIN bookorders bo ON b.titleID=bo.titleID
WHERE b.titleid='aust1235'
```

The Grids tab of the Results pane shows that the TitleID column has been updated in all three tables.

11. In the Editor pane of the Query window, enter and execute the following Transact-SQL code:

```
DELETE FROM Books where TitleID = 'AUST1235'
```

Because of cascading referential integrity being defined for deletions, the *DELETE* statement removes the record from the Books, BookOrders, and BookAuthors tables. You can verify this fact by running the *SELECT* statement that appears in step 10.

12. In the Editor pane of the Query window, enter and execute the following Transact-SQL code:

```
ALTER TABLE BookAuthors DROP CONSTRAINT titleid_fk
ALTER TABLE BookOrders DROP CONSTRAINT titleid2_fk
ALTER TABLE BookAuthors
  ADD CONSTRAINT titleid_fk FOREIGN KEY (TitleID) REFERENCES Books (T
itleID)
ALTER TABLE BookOrders
  ADD CONSTRAINT titleid2_fk FOREIGN KEY (TitleID) REFERENCES Books (
TitleID)
INSERT Books (TitleID, Title, Publisher, PubDate, Edition, Cost, SRP,
 ConditionID, Sold)
VALUES ('AUST1234', 'Sense and Sensibility', 'N/
A', 1811, 1, 3000, 5900, 3,0)
GO
```

These statements return the database to its previous state.

Lesson Summary

Procedural data integrity is often implemented by using triggers. Triggers are invoked when table data is modified by an INSERT, UPDATE, or DELETE event. Depending on the trigger class, a trigger can be applied to a table or view. Triggers extend data integrity by enforcing complex business rules in the database. Always implement constraints and rules before using triggers, because triggers will degrade performance more quickly than constraints or rules. There are certain instances in which a trigger is the best option (for example, when custom error messages are required). Triggers can reference data inside or outside the current database. A single trigger can run multiple tasks and can be fired by more than one event. You cannot create a trigger on a temporary or system table, but these objects can be referenced in a trigger. Some events, such as a truncate table event, do not cause a DELETE trigger to fire. Triggers use Inserted and Deleted pseudo tables to store modified or deleted data. These pseudo tables are referenced in the trigger code. There are two classes of triggers: INSTEAD OF and AFTER. INSTEAD OF triggers bypass the view or table modification that fired them and the code in the trigger runs. AFTER triggers fire right after table constraints are processed. If the INSERT, UPDATE, or DELETE event does not complete properly, the trigger rolls back the transaction.

Lesson 2: Creating and Managing Triggers

In this lesson, you will learn a number of methods for creating and managing triggers. Triggers are commonly created and managed by using Query Analyzer or the Manage Triggers option in Enterprise Manager. A trigger is created by using the *CREATE TRIGGER* statement. In the trigger creation process, the trigger is applied to a table or a view. After a trigger is created, it is modified by using the *ALTER TRIGGER* statement. Triggers are renamed and viewed by using system stored procedures or Enterprise Manager. The *DROP TRIGGER* statement is used to delete a trigger, and the *ALTER TABLE* statement is used to enable or disable triggers.

After this lesson, you will be able to:

- Create triggers.
- Rename triggers and modify their contents.
- View, drop, and disable triggers.

Estimated Lesson time: 40 minutes

Creating Triggers Using Transact-SQL

You can use the *CREATE TRIGGER* statement to create a trigger by using Query Analyzer or a command-prompt tool such as osql. When using *CREATE TRIGGER*, you must specify the trigger name, the table or view upon which the trigger is applied, the class of trigger (INSTEAD OF or AFTER), the event or events that fire the trigger, and the task that you wish the trigger to perform. Optionally, you can specify whether the trigger should be replicated or encrypted. The WITH APPEND clause remains for backward compatibility but shouldn't be used to create triggers for a SQL Server 2000 database.

The main clauses in a *CREATE TRIGGER* statement can be summarized as follows:

CREATE TRIGGER *trigger_name*

ON *table_name* or *view_name*

FOR *trigger_class* and *trigger_type(s)*

AS *Transact-SQL statements*

This section discusses the CREATE TABLE, ON, and FOR/AFTER/INSTEAD OF clauses in detail and provides examples of how they are used in a trigger statement. Lesson 3 discusses the Transact-SQL statements appearing after the AS clause. For more details about trigger clauses not shown here, refer to SQL Server Books Online.

The CREATE TRIGGER Clause

Trigger creation begins with the CREATE TRIGGER clause followed by a trigger name. Triggers do not allow specifying the database name as a prefix to the object name. Therefore, select the database with the USE *database_name* clause and the GO keyword before creating a trigger. GO is specified because CREATE TRIGGER must be the first statement in a query batch.

Permission to create triggers defaults to the table owner. For consistency, consider creating tables, triggers, and other database objects so that dbo is the owner. For example, to create a trigger named Alerter in the BookShopDB database, you can use the following Transact-SQL code:

```
USE BookShopDB
GO
CREATE TRIGGER dbo.alerter
```

Trigger names must follow the rules for identifiers. For example, if you decide to create a trigger named Alerter for the Employees Table, you must enclose the name in brackets as shown:

```
CREATE TRIGGER dbo.[alerter for employees table]
```

Administering the trigger object, such as deleting it, also requires that you follow the rules for identifiers.

The ON Clause

Triggers must be assigned to a table or view. Use the ON clause to instruct the trigger on to what table or view it should be applied. When a trigger is applied, the table or view is referred to as the trigger table or the trigger view. For consistency, specify the table or view owner after the ON clause. For example, to apply a trigger to the Employees table named Alerter (where both objects—the table and the trigger—are owned by dbo), you can use the following Transact-SQL code:

```
CREATE TRIGGER dbo.alerter
ON dbo.employees
```

A trigger is applied only to a single table or view. If you need to apply the same trigger task to another table in the database, create a trigger of a different name that contains the same business logic. Then, apply the new trigger to the other table. The default trigger class, AFTER, can be applied only to a table. The new trigger class, INSTEAD OF, can be applied to either a table or a view.

The FOR, AFTER, and INSTEAD OF Clauses

A trigger event type must be specified when the trigger is created. Valid event types include INSERT, UPDATE, and DELETE. A single trigger can be fired because of one, two, or all three of the events occurring. If you want a trigger to fire on all events, follow the FOR, AFTER, or INSTEAD OF clause with INSERT, UPDATE, and DELETE. The event types can be listed in any order. For example, to make the trigger named Alerter fire on all events, you can use the following Transact-SQL code:

```
CREATE TRIGGER dbo.alerter
ON dbo.employees
FOR INSERT, UPDATE, DELETE
```

The FOR clause is synonymous with the AFTER clause. Therefore, the previous code example creates an AFTER trigger. To create Alerter as an INSTEAD OF trigger, you can use the following Transact-SQL code:

```
CREATE TRIGGER dbo.alerter
ON dbo.employees
INSTEAD OF INSERT, UPDATE, DELETE
```

Notice that the FOR clause is replaced with INSTEAD OF.

The AS Clause

The AS clause and the Transact-SQL language following it designates the task that the trigger will perform. The following example shows how to create an Alerter trigger that sends an e-mail to a user named BarryT when an INSERT, UPDATE, or DELETE occurs on the employees table:

```
USE BookShopDB
GO
CREATE TRIGGER dbo.alerter
ON dbo.employees
AFTER INSERT, UPDATE, DELETE
AS
EXEC master..xp_sendmail 'BarryT',
'A record was just inserted, updated or deleted in the Employees table.'
GO
```

This example is kept simple so that you can see clearly how a task is created in a trigger. There are a number of ways to make the task more useful. For example, you could write the task so that the e-mail message details the exact change that occurred. Lesson 3 explores more complex trigger tasks.

Creating a Trigger Using Enterprise Manager

You can create triggers by using the SQL-DMO interface or by using applications such as Enterprise Manager. To create a trigger in Enterprise Manager, you must first select the database. Next, right-click the table or view to which the trigger is applied, point to All Tasks, and then click Manage Triggers. In the text box of the

Trigger Properties dialog box, enter the trigger statement. Figure 9.1 shows the Trigger Properties dialog box containing the code from the previous example.

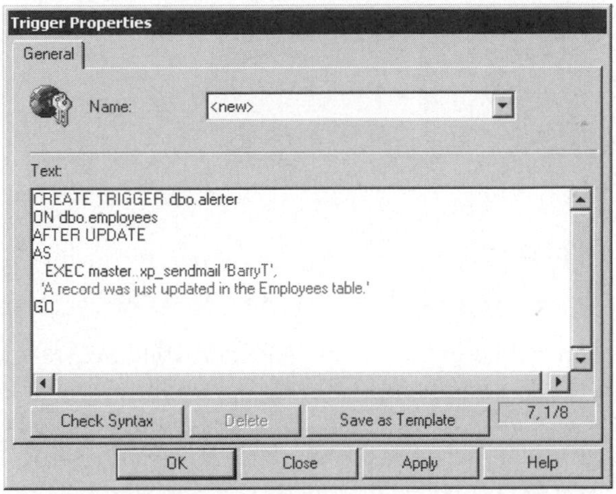

Figure 9.1.   The General tab of the Trigger Properties dialog box for a new trigger.

Trigger Management

Triggers are powerful database objects that run automatically when a table or view is modified. There are a number of database tools and commands used to manage triggers. Triggers can be:

- Modified by using the *ALTER TRIGGER* statement.
- Renamed with the *sp_rename* system stored procedure.
- Viewed by querying system tables or by using the *sp_helptrigger* and *sp_helptext* system stored procedures.
- Deleted by using the *DROP TRIGGER* statement.
- Disabled or enabled by using the DISABLE TRIGGER and ENABLE TRIGGER clauses of the *ALTER TABLE* statement.

You can also use the Manage Triggers option in Enterprise Manager to modify, view, and delete triggers. The remainder of this lesson provides details about how to perform these management tasks.

Altering and Renaming Triggers

To modify the text in a trigger, you can delete and recreate it. Alternatively, to skip the deletion step, use the *ALTER TRIGGER* statement. The *ALTER TRIGGER* statement syntax is similar to the *CREATE TRIGGER* statement syntax, but *ALTER TRIGGER* does not remove the trigger from the SysComments and SysObjects system tables. The following example shows how you can modify the Alerter trigger so that it only reports updates to the Employees table:

```
ALTER TRIGGER dbo.alerter
ON dbo.employees
AFTER UPDATE
AS
  EXEC master..xp_sendmail 'BarryT',
  'A record was just updated in the Employees table.'
GO
```

Notice that UPDATE is the only event specified following the AFTER clause, and notice that the text in the e-mail message was changed.

Triggers are modified in Enterprise Manager from the Manage Triggers option. You learned about the Manage Triggers option in the previous section of this lesson. After you display the Trigger Properties dialog box, select the trigger that you wish to modify. Then, change the word CREATE to ALTER. Figure 9.2 shows how to alter the Alerter trigger using Enterprise Manager.

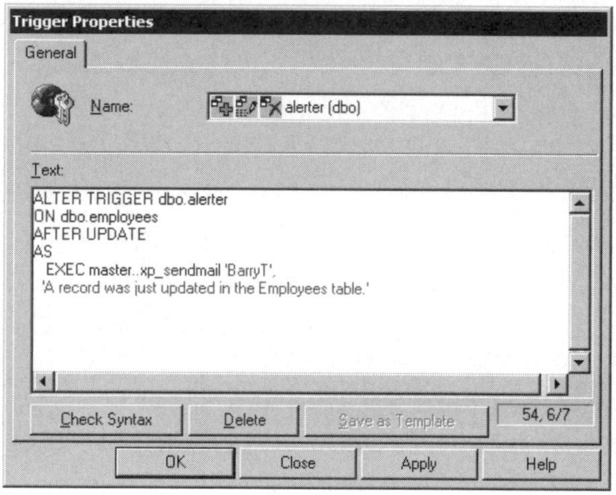

Figure 9.2.   The General tab of the Trigger Properties dialog box with the ALTER syntax shown.

Notice that the GO batch command has been removed. In the first released version of SQL Server 2000, the GO batch command causes an error in Enterprise Manager when attempting to modify a trigger.

There might be times that you need to rename a trigger to comply with new naming conventions or because you are implementing more than one trigger on a table. You can rename a trigger by using the *sp_rename* system stored procedure. The following example shows how to rename the Alerter trigger to EmpAlerter:

```
sp_rename @objname = alerter, @newname = empalerter
```

Notice that dbo was not specified in the rename syntax. Trigger ownership cannot be transferred by using the *sp_rename* system stored procedure. If you need to change the ownership of a stored procedure, you must use *CREATE TRIGGER*. If you are nesting a trigger that you rename, make sure that the calling trigger is modified to call the correct trigger name.

Viewing, Dropping, and Disabling Triggers

When a stored procedure is created, its name and other identifying information are stored in the SysObjects system table of the current database. The trigger text is stored in the SysComments system table. The following *SELECT* statement will show any triggers applied to tables in the BookShopDB database:

```
select * from bookshopdb..SysObjects where type = 'tr'
```

The type column always lists triggers with a value of tr.

Use the *sp_helptrigger* system stored procedure to show the properties of a trigger. For example, to show the properties of all triggers defined for the Employees table, type the following:

```
sp_helptrigger @tabname = employees
```

You can query the Text column of the SysComments system table to see the contents of the stored procedure. For a more organized display of information, use the *sp_helptext* system stored procedure. For example, to show the text contained in a trigger named alerter, type the following:

```
sp_helptext @objname = alerter
```

You can also use the Manage Triggers option of Enterprise Manager to view trigger text.

Deleting a trigger removes it from the SysComments and SysObjects system tables. Use the *DROP TRIGGER* statement to delete one or more triggers from a database. If you drop a trigger table or a trigger view, any triggers assigned to the table or view are also dropped. To delete the Alerter trigger in the BookShopDB database, type the following:

```
USE BookShopDB
DROP TRIGGER [dbo].[alerter]
```

As with the *CREATE TRIGGER* statement, you cannot specify the database name in the *DROP TRIGGER* statement. Unlike *CREATE TRIGGER*, *DROP TRIGGER* does not have to be the first statement in the batch. For this reason, the code example does not include a GO command between the *USE* and *DROP TRIGGER* statements.

You might have to disable a trigger (or triggers) on a table if, for example, you are troubleshooting a problem with a database, testing a database modification, or running a procedure that requires a trigger to be disabled on a table. To disable a trigger, use the *ALTER TABLE* statement. The following code disables the Alerter trigger on the Employees table:

```
ALTER TABLE employees DISABLE TRIGGER alerter
```

To disable all triggers on a table, use the ALL keyword following the DISABLE TRIGGER clause. To enable one or all triggers, change DISABLE to ENABLE in your *ALTER TABLE* statement.

Exercise 2: Creating and Managing Triggers

In this exercise, you create and test a trigger that displays a message indicating that the trigger fired. You will then manage the trigger by renaming it, modifying its contents, viewing it, disabling it, and then dropping it from the database. The Transact-SQL code appearing below the AS clause is intentionally simplistic, because Lesson 3 explores this aspect of triggers.

Note For the purpose of this exercise, it's fine to display a message when a trigger fires. However, you should design triggers for your databases that do not display result sets and that do not print messages to the screen.

▶ **To create simple triggers on the Authors table in the BookShopDB database**

1. Open Query Analyzer and connect to your local server.

2. In the Editor pane of the Query window, enter and execute the following code:

```
USE BookShopDB
GO
CREATE TRIGGER dbo.insertindicator
ON dbo.authors
AFTER INSERT
AS
PRINT 'The insert trigger fired.'
```

The *CREATE TRIGGER* statement creates a trigger named InsertIndicator and applies the trigger to the Authors table of the BookShopDB database. When an insert to the Authors table occurs, this trigger fires and prints a message on the Grids tab in the Results pane.

3. In the Editor pane of the Query window, enter and execute the following code:

```
CREATE TRIGGER dbo.updateindicator
ON dbo.authors
AFTER UPDATE
AS
PRINT 'The update trigger fired.'
GO
```

```
CREATE TRIGGER dbo.deleteindicator
ON dbo.authors
AFTER DELETE
AS
IF @@ROWCOUNT <> 0
PRINT 'The delete trigger fired.'
```

The *CREATE TRIGGER* statements create triggers named UpdateIndicator and DeleteIndicator. These triggers are applied to the Authors table in the Book-ShopDB database. When an UPDATE or DELETE occurs, these triggers print a message on the Grids tab in the Results pane. Notice that the DeleteIndicator trigger tests the @@ROWCOUNT value. If one or more rows are deleted, the message prints.

▶ **To test the triggers on the Authors table**

1. In the Editor pane of the Query window, enter and execute the following code:

```
INSERT INTO authors (firstname, lastname, yearborn, yeardied)
VALUES ('Max', 'Doe', 1962, 'N/A')
```

A record is inserted into the Authors table, and the InsertIndicator trigger fires and prints the trigger's message to the Messages tab of the Results pane.

2. In the Editor pane of the Query window, enter and execute the following code:

```
UPDATE authors
SET authors.firstname - 'Tucker'
WHERE authors.firstname = 'Max'
```

A record is updated in the Authors table, and the UpdateIndicator trigger fires and prints the trigger's message to the Messages tab of the Results pane.

3. In the Editor pane of the Query window, enter and execute the following code:

```
DELETE authors where firstname = 'Tucker'
```

A record is deleted in the Authors table, and the DeleteIndicator trigger fires and prints the trigger's message to the Messages tab of the Results pane.

▶ **To rename, modify, and view a trigger**

1. In the Editor pane of the Query window, enter the following stored procedure code:

```
sp_rename @objname=insertindicator, @newname=insupdcontrol
```

The *sp_rename* system stored procedure renames the InsertIndicator trigger to InsUpdIndicator. Later, you will modify the trigger to fire upon INSERT and UPDATE events.

2. Execute the query.

The Messages tab of the Results pane cautions you that renaming an object could cause scripts and stored procedures to fail. The message also indicates that the rename operation was successful.

3. In the Editor pane of the Query window, enter and execute the following stored procedure code:

```
sp_helptrigger @tabname = authors
```

The *sp_helptrigger* system stored procedure displays a list of triggers applied to the Authors table.

4. In the Editor pane of the Query window, enter and execute the following code:

```
ALTER TRIGGER dbo.insupdcontrol
ON dbo.authors
INSTEAD OF INSERT, UPDATE
AS
PRINT 'Inserts and updates are not allowed at this time.'
```

The trigger modification converts the renamed trigger into an INSTEAD OF trigger that prevents any inserts and updates to the Authors table. You might want to use this type of trigger to temporarily prevent changes to a table. You can disable and enable triggers by using the *ALTER TABLE* statement.

5. In the Editor pane of the Query window, enter and execute the following code:

```
SET NOCOUNT ON
INSERT INTO authors (firstname, lastname, yearborn, yeardied)
VALUES ('Max', 'Doe', 1962, 'N/A')
SET NOCOUNT OFF
```

The INSTEAD OF trigger fires and displays a message stating that updates are not allowed at this time. NOCOUNT is enabled so that a row-affected message does not appear in the Messages tab of the Results pane.

6. Run a *SELECT* statement against the Authors table to verify that no record was added.

7. In the Editor pane of the Query window, enter and execute the following stored procedure code:

```
sp_helptext @objname=insupdcontrol
```

The stored procedure displays the contents of the InsUpdControl trigger.

▶ **To disable and drop a trigger**

1. In the Editor pane of the Query window, enter and execute the following code:

```
ALTER TABLE authors DISABLE TRIGGER insupdcontrol
```

The *ALTER TABLE* statement disables the InsUpdControl trigger on the Authors table.

2. In the Editor pane of the Query window, enter and execute the following code:

```
INSERT INTO authors (firstname, lastname, yearborn, yeardied)
VALUES ('Max', 'Doe', 1962, 'N/A')
SELECT * FROM Authors where Firstname = 'Max'
```

A record is successfully inserted into the Authors table, and the record appears in the Grids tab of the Results pane.

3. In the Editor pane of the Query window, enter and execute the following code:

```
DROP TRIGGER insupdcontrol, updateindicator, deleteindicator
DELETE authors where firstname = 'Max'
```

The *DROP TRIGGER* statement deletes all three triggers applied to the Authors table. The *DELETE* statement removes the record added to the Authors table.

Lesson Summary

In this lesson, you learned how to create a trigger by using the *CREATE TRIGGER* statement. You must specify the table or view to which the trigger is applied, the event or events that fire the trigger, and any Transact-SQL code that should run when the trigger fires. You have the option of specifying the trigger class, AFTER or INSTEAD OF. AFTER is synonymous with FOR and is the more common trigger to apply to tables. INSTEAD OF can be applied to tables or views. When using *CREATE TRIGGER*, you must use it as the first statement in a batch. You can also use Enterprise Manager to create triggers.

Triggers are managed using tools and Transact-SQL statements. In Enterprise Manager, you can perform a number of trigger management tasks using the Manage Triggers option. To modify a trigger in Query Analyzer, use *ALTER TRIGGER*. To rename a trigger, use the *sp_rename* system stored procedure. To view the contents of a trigger, use the *sp_helptext* system stored procedure. To view a trigger's properties, use the *sp_helptrigger* system stored procedure or the *OBJECTPROPERTY* function. Triggers are deleted using the *DROP TRIGGER* statement and are enabled or disabled using the *ALTER TABLE* statement.

Lesson 3: Programming Triggers

After this lesson, you will be able to:

- Create triggers to apply business logic to the database.
- Determine how to use the Inserted and Deleted pseudo tables.
- Use common trigger system functions.

Estimated Lesson time: 40 minutes

The Inserted and Deleted Pseudo Tables

When an INSERT, UPDATE, or DELETE trigger fires, the event creates one or more pseudo tables (also known as logical tables). These logical tables can be thought of as the transaction logs of the event. There are two types of logical tables: the Inserted table and the Deleted table. An insert or update event creates an Inserted logical table. The Inserted logical table contains the record set that has been added or changed. The UPDATE trigger also creates a Deleted logical table. The Deleted logical table contains the original record set as it appeared before the update. The following example creates a trigger that displays the contents of the Inserted and Deleted tables following an update event to the Authors table:

```
CREATE TRIGGER dbo.updatetables
ON dbo.authors
AFTER UPDATE
AS
SELECT "Description" = 'The Inserted table:'
SELECT * FROM inserted
SELECT "Description" = 'The Deleted table:'
SELECT * FROM deleted
```

Following a simple *UPDATE* statement that changes an author's name from Dean to Denby, the trigger displays the following results:

The Inserted table:

Straight   Denby   Oakland   CA   94609

The Deleted table:

Straight   Dean   Oakland   CA   94609

The Authors table (trigger table) contains the updated record after the update trigger runs. When the trigger fires, the update to the Authors table can be rolled back by programming logic into the trigger. This transaction rollback capability also applies to INSERT and DELETE triggers.

When a delete trigger fires, the Deleted logical table contains the deleted record set. The Inserted table is not part of a DELETE event.

Note   The *SELECT* statement appears in the previous code example for illustrative purposes only. Never use statements in triggers that return a result unless you are sure that the result returned by the trigger can be handled by any applications that cause the trigger to fire.

Trigger Syntax, System Commands, and Functions

Now that you understand the purpose of triggers and the various types of triggers, the next step is to investigate the syntax for creating and altering a trigger. Functions and system commands augment triggers by allowing you to implement business logic in the trigger.

UPDATE (*column_name*) and (*COLUMNS_UPDATED()*) Clauses

Two important clauses that are part of the *CREATE TRIGGER* and *ALTER TRIGGER* statements are UPDATE (*column_name*) and (*COLUMNS_UPDATED()*). These two clauses can be part of an Insert or Update trigger and can appear anywhere in the *CREATE TRIGGER* or *ALTER TRIGGER* statement.

The IF UPDATE (*column_name*) clause determines whether an INSERT or UPDATE event occurred to the column named *column_name*. If you need to specify more than one column, separate each column name with UPDATE (*column_name*). For example, the following code segment checks to determine whether the First_Name and Last_Name columns were inserted or updated and does something as a result of an INSERT or UPDATE to either of these columns:

```
IF UPDATE (first_name) OR UPDATE (Last_Name)
BEGIN
    Do some conditional processing when either of these columns are upda
ted.
END
```

Because of deferred name resolution, the column specified by *column_name* does not need to exist when the trigger is applied to the table. However, the column must exist when the trigger fires. For more information about deferred name resolution, refer to Chapter 8, "Implementing Stored Procedures."

If the *column_name* is replaced with a value, the UPDATE clause returns TRUE. The (*COLUMNS_UPDATED()*) clause also tests for updated columns. Instead of returning true or false, (*COLUMNS_UPDATED()*) returns a varbinary bit pattern that indicates which of the tested columns were inserted or updated.

The (*COLUMNS_UPDATED()*) clause is more complex to write than the UPDATE (*column_name*) clause, but it returns exactly which tested columns were inserted or updated. You specify which columns to test by using a bit mask to represent each column (ordinal) position in the table. The following table shows the first eight columns and the bit mask assigned to each column:

Column	1	2	3	4	5	6	7	8
Bit Mask	1	2	4	8	16	32	64	128

To test whether columns 4 or 6 were updated, you can use the following code:

```
IF (COLUMNS_UPDATED() & 40) > 0
```

The value of 40 is derived from summing 8 for column 4 and 32 for column 6. The (*COLUMNS_UPDATED()*) expression tests whether the return value is greater than 0. In other words, if either or both of the columns are updated, the columns updated condition is met. If you set (COLUMNS_UPDATED() & 40) = 40, then you are testing whether both of the columns are updated. Updates to one or the other column do not meet the columns updated condition.

To test more than eight columns, you must use the *SUBSTRING* function so that the trigger knows which bit mask to test. For example, to test for an update to the ninth column, you can use the following code:

```
IF ((SUBSTRING(COLUMNS_UPDATED(),2,1)=1))
```

The *SUBSTRING* function tells the (*COLUMNS_UPDATED()*) clause to move to the second octet of columns and then test for an update to column 1 of the second octet (which is actually in ordinal position 9). The varbinary return value for this column is 1. The following table shows the *SUBSTRING* function necessary to test columns 9 through 16:

```
IF ((SUBSTRING(COLUMNS_UPDATED(),2,y)=z))
```

Column	9	10	11	12	13	14	15	16
y and z	1	2	4	8	16	32	64	128

To test modifications to multiple columns, simply add the bit values for each column. For example, to test columns 14 and 16, specify **160 (32 + 128)** for the z value.

Functions and System Commands

Numerous functions and system commands are used in triggers to implement business logic. A function commonly used in triggers is @@*ROWCOUNT*. This function returns the number of rows affected by the previous Transact-SQL statement in the trigger. If no rows are affected by an INSERT, UPDATE, or DELETE event, the trigger still fires. Therefore, use the RETURN system command to exit the trigger transparently when no table modifications are made.

In the event of an error, you might want to display a message describing the reason for the error. The RAISERROR system command is used to display error messages. You can create custom error messages with the *sp_addmessage* system stored procedure, or you can display ad hoc error messages when calling the RAISERROR system command. Refer to SQL Server Books Online for more information about the *sp_addmessage* system stored procedure.

The ROLLBACK TRANSACTION system command might also appear in the Transact-SQL code for the trigger. This command explicitly rolls back the entire batch of the trigger. A fatal error also causes an implicit rollback. You don't have to specify ROLLBACK TRANSACTION in the trigger code if your goal is to complete the transaction in all cases except if a fatal error occurs during the transaction.

Transact-SQL Language Precautions

You can use *SELECT* and *PRINT* statements or assign variables in the trigger's code, but using them to return result sets, messages, or values is dangerous. When an event causes a trigger to fire, the trigger is usually transparent to the user or application. If the application isn't designed to handle return code, such as a result set from a *SELECT* statement, then the application might fail. Using a *SELECT* statement to provide a value to a conditional statement is perfectly acceptable. For example, you might want to use a *SELECT* statement to test for the existence of a value and return that value to the *IF EXISTS* statement so that additional processing is performed. If you need to assign variables in a trigger's code, include SET NOCOUNT ON in the trigger code.

The following Transact-SQL statements are not allowed in a trigger:

- *ALTER*, *CREATE*, *DROP*, *RESTORE*, and *LOAD DATABASE*
- *LOAD* and *RESTORE LOG*
- *DISK RESIZE* and *DISK INIT*
- *RECONFIGURE*

Common Trigger Programming Tasks

Triggers are used to execute all types of business logic before (INSTEAD OF) or after (AFTER) an *INSERT*, *UPDATE*, or *DELETE* statement is run against a table or a view. Triggers are written for common tasks such as the following:

- Maintaining running totals and other computed values.

Databases constantly change as data is added, deleted, and modified in tables. In some cases, a column value in one table is computed from data modifications in another table. Triggers are ideal for maintaining computed columns. Figure 9.3 shows a trigger used to update the retail price of an item in the Inventory table when the average wholesale price changes in the Purchasing table.

inventory	
⚷ item_num	
item_desc	
qty_in_stock	
retail	inventory

purchasing
⚷ order_id
item_num
wholesale_price
qty_ordered
total cost

Figure 9.3. The Inventory and Purchasing tables.

The following trigger is applied to the Purchasing table. It calculates the average wholesale cost of inventory and increases the price by 30 percent, in addition to updating the retail_price column of the inventory table with the new value:

```
CREATE TRIGGER Retail_Price_Update
ON purchasing
AFTER INSERT, UPDATE, DELETE AS
SET NOCOUNT ON
IF EXISTS (SELECT item_num FROM inserted)
BEGIN
 UPDATE inventory
  SET retail_price =
 (SELECT (SUM(pur.total_cost)/SUM(pur.qty_ordered) * 1.30)
  FROM purchasing pur INNER JOIN inserted ins
   ON pur.item_num = ins.item_num)
 FROM inventory inv, inserted ins
 WHERE inv.item_num = ins.item_num
END
ELSE IF EXISTS (SELECT item_num from deleted)
BEGIN
 UPDATE inventory
  SET retail_price =
 (SELECT (SUM(pur.total_cost)/SUM(pur.qty_ordered) * 1.30)
  FROM purchasing pur INNER JOIN deleted del
   ON pur.item_num = del.item_num)
 FROM inventory inv, deleted del
 WHERE inv.item_num=del.item_num
END
ELSE
 BEGIN
  RAISERROR ('The retail price has not been adjusted for the product.',
16, 1)
  RETURN
END
```

The trigger uses the *SET NOCOUNT ON* statement so that when the trigger fires and updates information in the Inventory table, the *SELECT* statement result is not displayed. Conditional processing checks for the existence of the Inserted or Deleted tables. If neither the Inserted nor Deleted tables contain records, the trigger uses RAISERROR to display an ad hoc message that no prices were adjusted. You can use *sp_addmessage* to add a custom message to the SysMessages system table and then specify the message number in place of the custom message.

- **Creating audit records.**   For security reasons or to simply track activity on a table (or tables) in the database, you can create a trigger to update a table with data inserted, updated, or deleted from another table or view.
- **Invoking external actions.**   A trigger can specify an action outside of standard database processing to occur when it fires. For example, in Lesson 2 you saw an example of using the *xp_sendmail* extended stored procedure in a trigger to send a message to an e-mail account when the trigger fires.
- **Implementing complex data integrity.**   Sometimes standard data integrity measures are not enough. For example, the cascading delete action deletes records in other tables when a delete action would violate referential integrity between the tables. However, you might not want to allow a cascading delete action to occur. You could use an INSTEAD OF trigger to delete records from related tables but then log the deleted result to another table for later review. If you use an INSTEAD OF trigger to delete records, you cannot implement a delete action by using cascading referential integrity. To accomplish the same task, you must program the cascading delete action in the trigger.

Exercise 3: Creating a Trigger to Update a Column Value

In this exercise, you will create and test a trigger that updates the value to 1 in the Sold column of the Books table in BookShopDB. You will add conditional processing so that if the book is returned, the Sold column is updated with a value of 0.

▶ **To create an INSERT trigger to apply to the BookOrders table**

1. Open Query Analyzer and connect to your local server.

2. In the Editor pane of the Query window, enter and execute the following code:

```
CREATE TRIGGER dbo.update_book_status
 ON dbo.bookorders
 AFTER INSERT
AS
 UPDATE books
  SET Sold = 1
   WHERE titleid =
   (SELECT bo.titleid
     FROM bookorders bo INNER JOIN inserted i
     ON bo.orderid = i.orderid)
```

The *CREATE TRIGGER* statement creates a trigger named Update_Book_Status and applies the trigger to the BookOrders table of the BookShopDB database. When an insert to the BookOrders table occurs, this trigger fires and updates the Sold column for the matching TitleID value of the Books table.

► **To alter the trigger to accommodate BookOrders table deletions and updates**

1. In the Editor pane of the Query window, enter and execute the following code:

```
ALTER TRIGGER dbo.update_book_status
 ON dbo.bookorders
 AFTER INSERT, DELETE
AS
 SET NOCOUNT ON
 IF EXISTS (SELECT * FROM inserted)
 BEGIN
  UPDATE books
   SET Sold = 1
    WHERE titleid =
    (SELECT bo.titleid
      FROM bookorders bo INNER JOIN inserted i
      ON bo.orderid = i.orderid)
 END
 ELSE
 BEGIN
  UPDATE books
   SET Sold = 0
    WHERE titleid =
    (SELECT d.titleid
      FROM books b INNER JOIN deleted d
      ON b.titleid = d.titleid)
 END
```

The *ALTER TRIGGER* statement modifies the trigger named Update_Book_Status and applies the trigger to the BookOrders table of the BookShopDB database. The DELETE event appears after the *INSERT* statement in the third line of code. When a delete in the BookOrders table occurs, this trigger fires and updates the Sold column to 0 for the matching TitleID. This business logic is important to accommodate books that are returned. Notice that the *SELECT* statement for the delete condition (after the ELSE clause) matches the TitleID in the books table and the TitleID in the Deleted table. This modification is necessary because the BookOrders table no longer contains the deleted record.

2. The previous code does not handle updates. The only update that is relevant to the Books table is an update to the TitleID column of the BookOrders table. If the OrderID is changed in the BookOrders table, the book should still have a Sold value of 1. You must be able to handle updates to the TitleID value. In the Editor pane of the Query window, enter and execute the following code:

```
ALTER TRIGGER dbo.update_book_status
 ON dbo.bookorders
 AFTER INSERT, UPDATE, DELETE
AS
 SET NOCOUNT ON
 IF EXISTS (SELECT * FROM inserted)
```

```
BEGIN
 UPDATE books
  SET Sold = 1
   WHERE titleid =
   (SELECT bo.titleid
     FROM bookorders bo INNER JOIN inserted i
     ON bo.orderid = i.orderid)
 END
IF EXISTS (SELECT * FROM deleted)
 BEGIN
  UPDATE books
   SET Sold = 0
    WHERE titleid =
    (SELECT d.titleid
      FROM books b INNER JOIN deleted d
      ON b.titleid = d.titleid)
 END
```

The trigger is modified to include UPDATES. Notice that the ELSE clause has been removed. An UPDATE event always creates both the Inserted and Deleted tables. Therefore, the first part of the code sets the Sold status to 1 for the new TitleID value. The second part of the code detects the Deleted table and sets the Sold status for the original TitleID to 0.

▶   **To test the trigger**

1. In the Editor pane of the Query window, enter and execute the following code:

```
SET IDENTITY_INSERT orders ON
INSERT INTO orders
(orderid, customerid, employeeid, amount, orderdate, deliverydate, pa
ymentid, statusid)
VALUES (20, 10, 1, 500, GETDATE(), GETDATE() + 5, 2, 1)
SET IDENTITY_INSERT orders OFF
GO
```

An order is inserted into the Orders table.

2. In the Editor pane of the Query window, enter and execute the following code:

```
INSERT INTO bookorders
(orderid, titleid)
values (20, 'carr9675')
```

A book order for CustomerID 20 for TitleID carr9675 is inserted into the BookOrders table.

3. In the Editor pane of the Query window, enter and execute the following code:

```
SELECT * from Books where titleid = 'carr9675'
```

This command verifies that the Sold status for this book has changed to 1.

4. In the Editor pane of the Query window, enter and execute the following code:

```
UPDATE bookorders
set titleID = 'aust1234' where titleid = 'carr9675'
```

5. In the Editor pane of the Query window, enter and execute the following code:

    ```
    SELECT * from Books WHERE titleid = 'carr9675' OR titleid = 'aust1234'
    ```

    This command verifies that the Sold status for the original TitleID is 0 and that the new TitleID is 1.

6. In the Editor pane of the Query window, enter and execute the following code:

    ```
    DELETE bookorders WHERE titleid = 'aust1234'
    ```

    This command removes the book order from the BookOrders table, and the trigger changes the Sold status back to 0.

7. In the Editor pane of the Query window, enter and execute the following code:

    ```
    SELECT * from Books WHERE titleid = 'aust1234'
    ```

8. In the Editor pane of the Query window, enter and execute the following code:

    ```
    DROP TRIGGER dbo.update_book_status
    ```

    This command removes the trigger from the BookOrders table.

Lesson Summary

In this lesson, you learned how to program triggers. Triggers create two logical tables when an INSERT, UPDATE, or DELETE event occurs in a table to which a trigger is applied. These tables enable you to determine exactly what data modifications were made to a table when the trigger fired. Detecting data modifications is an essential step toward programming business logic into triggers. *CREATE* and *ALTER TRIGGER* syntaxes include two useful clauses for detecting column inserts or updates: UPDATE (*column_name*) and (*COLUMNS_UPDATED()*). The UPDATE (*column_name*) clause enables you to take an action based on modifications occurring to a specific column. The (*COLUMNS_UPDATED()*) clause enables you to detect multiple changes in columns designated by a varbinary bit mask value. The first eight columns are represented by a bit mask ranging from 1 for column 1 to 128 for column 8. Column changes beyond column eight can be detected using the *SUBSTRING* function.

Other functions exist besides *SUBSTRING* and system commands that are commonly used in triggers. The *@@ROWCOUNT* function returns the number of rows affected by a table modification. The RAISERROR system command displays either custom messages or messages contained in the SysMessages system table. Another important system command used in triggers is ROLLBACK TRANSACTION. This command enables you to control events that cause the UPDATE, INSERT, or DELETE event to be backed out. Use SET NOCOUNT ON in a trigger to prevent it from returning the rows-affected message to the calling application. Triggers are often used to maintain running totals or other computed values across tables, to create audit records to track table data modifications, to invoke external actions, and to implement complex data integrity features.

Review

The following questions are intended to reinforce key information presented in this chapter. If you are unable to answer a question, review the appropriate lesson and then try the question again. You can find answers to the questions in the Appendix, "Questions and Answers."

1. You have applied constraints, an INSTEAD OF trigger, and three AFTER triggers to a table. A colleague tells you that there is no way to control trigger order for the table. Is he correct? Why or why not?

2. You need to make sure that when a primary key is updated in one table, all foreign key references to it are also updated. How should you accomplish this task?

3. Name four instances when triggers are appropriate.

4. When a trigger fires, how does it track the changes that have been made to the modified table?

5. Name a table deletion event that does not fire a DELETE trigger.

6. Name a system stored procedure and a function used to view the properties of a trigger.

7. Using Transact-SQL language, what are two methods to stop a trigger from running?

8. Write a (COLUMNS_UPDATED()) clause that detects whether columns 10 and 11 are updated.

9. Name three common database tasks accomplished with triggers.

10. What command can you use to prevent a trigger from displaying row count information to a calling application?

11. What type of event creates both Inserted and Deleted logical tables?

12. Is it possible to instruct a trigger to display result sets and print messages?

C H A P T E R   1 0

Implementing Views

About This Chapter

A view is a virtual table whose contents are defined by a query. Like a real table, a view consists of a set of named columns and rows of data. However, a view does not exist as a stored set of data values in a database. The rows and columns of data come from tables referenced in the query that defines the view and are produced dynamically when the view is referenced. In this chapter, you will be introduced to views and the various functionalities that they support. You will also learn how to create, modify, and delete views. Finally, you will learn how to use views to insert, update, and modify data.

Before You Begin

To complete the lessons in this chapter, you must have:

- SQL Server 2000 Enterprise Edition installed on a Microsoft Windows 2000 Server computer.
- The ability to log on to the Windows 2000 Server computer and to SQL Server as the Windows 2000 Administrator.
- Completed the exercises in Chapter 3, "Designing a SQL Server Database," Chapter 4, "Implementing SQL Server Databases and Tables," Chapter 5, "Implementing Data Integrity," and Chapter 7, "Managing and Manipulating Data."

Lesson 1: Introduction to Views

Views are generally used to focus, simplify, and customize each user's perception of the database. You can use a view as a security mechanism by allowing a user to access data through the view without granting the user permission to directly access the underlying base tables of the view. You can also use views to improve performance and to partition data when you are copying data to and from SQL Server 2000. This lesson will introduce you to views and the various functionalities that they support.

After this lesson, you will be able to:

■   Define what a view is and describe the functionalities that views support.

Estimated lesson time: 20 minutes

Overview of Views

A view acts as a filter on the underlying tables referenced in the view. The query that defines the view can be from one or more tables or from other views in the current database or other databases. You can also use distributed queries to define views that use data from multiple heterogeneous sources. This functionality is useful, for example, if you want to combine similarly structured data from different servers, each of which stores data for a different region of your organization.

A view can be thought of as either a virtual table or a stored query. The data accessible through a standard view is not stored in the database as a distinct object. What is stored in the database is a *SELECT* statement. The result set of the *SELECT* statement forms the virtual table returned by the view. A user can use this virtual table by referencing the view name in Transact-SQL statements in the same way a table is referenced.

Figure 10.1 shows a view based on a *SELECT* statement that retrieves data from the Titles table and the Publishers table in the Pubs database.

There are no restrictions on querying through views and few restrictions on modifying data through them. In addition, a view can reference another view.

You can use a view to perform any or all of the following functions:

■   Restricting a user to specific rows in a table
■   Restricting a user to specific columns
■   Joining columns from multiple tables so that they look like a single table
■   Aggregating information instead of supplying details

Views can be used to partition data across multiple databases or instances of SQL Server 2000. Partitioned views enable you to distribute database processing across a group of servers.

title_id	title	type	pub_id	price	advance	royalty	ytd_sales
	The Busy Executive's Database Gui	business	1389	19.99	5,000.00	10	4095
	Cooking with Compter: Surreption	business	1389	11.95	5,000.00	10	3876
	You Can Combat Computer Stress!	business	0736	2.99	10.125.00	24	18722
	Straight Talk About Computers	business	1389	19.99	5,000.00	10	4095
	Silicon Valley Gastronomic Treats	mod_cook	0877	19.99	0.00	12	2032
	The Gourmet Microwave	mod_cook	0877	2.99	15,000.00	24	22246

titles table

title	price	
The Busy Executive's Database Gui	19.99	Algodata infosystems
Cooking with Compter: Surreption	11.95	Algodata infosystems
You Can Combat Computer Stress!	2.99	New Moon Books

View

pub_id	pub_name	city	
0736	New Moon Books	Boston	MA
0877	Binnet & Hardley	Washington	DC
1389	Algodata infosystems	Berkeley	CA
1622	Five Lakes Publishing	Chicago	IL
1756	Ramona Publishers	Dallas	TX

publishers table

Figure 10.1.   A view based on data from two tables.

SQL Server 2000 also supports indexed views, which greatly improve the performance of complex views such as those usually found in data warehouses or other decision support systems. With a standard view, the result set is not saved in the database. Rather, it is dynamically incorporated into the logic of the statement and is built dynamically at run time.

Complex queries, however, such as those in decision support systems, can reference large numbers of rows in base tables and aggregate large amounts of information into relatively concise aggregates (such as sums or averages). SQL Server 2000 supports creating a clustered index on a view that implements such a complex query. When the *CREATE INDEX* statement is executed, the result set of the view SELECT is stored permanently in the database. Future SQL statements that reference the view will have substantially better response times. Modifications to the base data are automatically reflected in the view.

Scenarios for Using Views

You can use views in a variety of ways to return data.

To Focus on Specific Data

Views enable users to focus on specific data that interests them and on the specific tasks for which they are responsible. You can leave out unnecessary data in the view. This action also increases the security of the data, because users can see only the data that is defined in the view and not the data in the underlying table.

To Simplify Data Manipulation

Views can simplify how users manipulate data. You can define frequently used joins, UNION queries, and SELECT queries as views so that users do not have to specify all of the conditions and qualifications each time an additional operation is performed on that data. For example, a complex query that is used for reporting purposes and that performs subqueries, outer joins, and aggregation to retrieve data from a group of tables can be created as a view. The view simplifies access to the data because the underlying query does not have to be written or submitted each time the report is generated. The view is queried instead.

You can also create inline user-defined functions that operate logically as parameterized views (views that have parameters in WHERE-clause search conditions).

To Customize Data

Views enable different users to see data in different ways, even when they are using the same data concurrently. This feature is particularly advantageous when users who have many different interests and skill levels share the same database. For example, a view can be created that retrieves only the data for the customers with whom an account manager deals. The view can determine which data to retrieve based on the login ID of the account manager who uses the view.

To Export and Import Data

You can use views to export data to other applications. For example, you might want to use the Stores and Sales tables in the Pubs database to analyze sales data in Microsoft Excel. To perform this task, you can create a view based on the Stores and Sales tables. You can then use the bcp utility to export the data defined by the view. Data can also be imported into certain views from data files by using the bcp utility or the *BULK INSERT* statement, providing that rows can be inserted into the view by using the *INSERT* statement.

To Combine Partitioned Data

The Transact-SQL UNION set operator can be used within a view to combine the result of two or more queries from separate tables into a single result set. This display appears to the user as a single table (called a partitioned view). For example, if one table contains sales data for Washington and another table contains sales data for California, a view could be created from the UNION of those tables. The view represents the sales data for both regions.

To use partitioned views, create several identical tables, specifying a constraint to determine the range of data that can be added to each table. The view is then created by using these base tables. When the view is queried, SQL Server automatically determines which tables are affected by the query and references only those tables. For example, if a query specifies that only sales data for the state of Washington is required, SQL Server reads only the table containing the Washington sales data, no other tables are accessed.

Partitioned views can be based on data from multiple heterogeneous sources (such as remote servers), not just from tables in the same database. For example, to combine data from different remote servers (each of which stores data for a different region of your organization), you can create distributed queries that retrieve data from each data source, and you can then create a view based on those distributed queries. Any queries read only data from the tables on the remote servers that contain the data requested by the query. The other servers referenced by the distributed queries in the view are not accessed.

When you partition data across multiple tables or multiple servers, queries accessing only a fraction of the data can run faster because there is less data to scan. If the tables are located on different servers or on a computer that has multiple processors, each table involved in the query can also be scanned in parallel, thereby improving query performance. Additionally, maintenance tasks (such as rebuilding indexes or backing up a table) can be executed more quickly.

By using a partitioned view, the data still appears as a single table and can be queried as such without having to reference the correct underlying table manually.

Partitioned views are updateable if either of these conditions is met:

- An INSTEAD OF trigger is defined on the view with logic to support *INSERT*, *UPDATE*, and *DELETE* statements.
- Both the view and the *INSERT*, *UPDATE*, and *DELETE* statements follow the rules defined for updateable, partitioned views.

Lesson Summary

Views are generally used to focus, simplify, and customize each user's perception of the database. A view acts as a filter on the underlying tables referenced in the view. A view can be thought of as either a virtual table or a stored query. There are no restrictions on querying through views, and few restrictions exist on modifying data through them. Views enable you to focus on specific data, simplify data manipulation, customize data, export and import data, and combine partitioned data.

Lesson 2: Creating, Modifying, and Deleting Views

As you learned in Lesson 1, a view is simply a SELECT query saved in the database. You can create a view as you would many other objects in a database, and once that view is created, you can modify the view or delete it. In this lesson, you will learn how to create views (including indexed views and partitioned views), modify those views, and then delete them.

After this lesson, you will be able to:
- Create basic views, indexed views, and partitioned views.
- Modify and delete views.

Estimated lesson time: 35 minutes

Creating Views

You can create views only in the current database. The tables and views referenced by the new view can exist in other databases or even in other servers, however, if the view is defined with distributed queries. View names must follow the rules for identifiers and must be unique for each user. Additionally, the name must not be the same as any tables owned by that user. You can build views on other views and on procedures that reference views. SQL Server 2000 enables views to be nested up to 32 levels.

When creating a view, you must adhere to the following restrictions:

- You cannot associate rules or DEFAULT definitions with views.
- You cannot associate AFTER triggers with views, only INSTEAD OF triggers.
- The query that defines the view cannot include the ORDER BY, COMPUTE, or COMPUTE BY clauses or the INTO keyword.
- You cannot define full-text index definitions on views.
- You cannot create temporary views, and you cannot create views on temporary tables.
- Views or tables that participate in a view created with the SCHEMABINDING clause cannot be dropped unless the view is dropped or changed so that it no longer has schema binding. In addition, *ALTER TABLE* statements on tables that participate in views with schema binding will fail if these statements affect the view definition.

- You cannot issue full-text queries against a view, although a view definition can include a full-text query if the query references a table that has been configured for full-text indexing.

- You must specify the name of every column in the view if any of the columns in the view are derived from an arithmetic expression, a built-in function, a constant, or if two or more of the columns in the view would otherwise have the same name (usually because the view definition includes a join and the columns from two or more different tables have the same name).

- In addition, you must specify the name of every column in the view if you want to give any column in the view a name that is different from the column from which it is derived. (You can also rename columns in the view.) A view column inherits the data type of the column from which it is derived, whether or not you rename it. Note that this restriction does not apply if a view is based on a query containing an outer join, because columns might change from not allowing null values to allowing them. Otherwise, you do not need to specify column names when creating the view. SQL Server gives the columns of the view the same names and data types as the columns in the query that defines the view. The select list can be a full or partial list of the column names in the base tables.

- To create a view, you must be granted permission to do so by the database owner, and you must have appropriate permissions for any tables or views referenced in the view definition.

By default, as rows are added or updated through a view, they disappear from the scope of the view when they no longer fall into the criteria of the query that defines the view. For example, a view can be defined that retrieves all rows in which the employee's salary is less than $30,000. If an employee's salary is increased to $32,000, then querying the view no longer displays that particular employee because the salary does not conform to the criteria set by the view. However, the WITH CHECK OPTION clause forces all data modification statements executed against the view to adhere to the criteria set within the *SELECT* statement that defines the view. If you use this clause, rows cannot be modified in a way that causes them to disappear from the view. Any modification that would cause this situation to happen is canceled, and an error is displayed.

Note   The WITH CHECK OPTION on a view does not affect the underlying tables when you modify those tables directly. Only the updates that are made through the view itself are affected by WITH CHECK OPTION.

The definition of a view can be encrypted to ensure that its definition cannot be obtained by anyone, including the owner of the view.

Creating Standard Views

You can use Enterprise Manager to create a view, or you can use the *CREATE VIEW* statement in Transact-SQL. In the following example, a *CREATE VIEW* statement is used to define a SELECT query that returns data from the Northwind database:

```
USE Northwind
GO
CREATE VIEW CustomerOrders
AS
SELECT o.OrderID, c.CompanyName, c.ContactName
  FROM Orders o JOIN Customers c
  ON o.CustomerID = c.CustomerID
```

In this statement, you are creating the CustomerOrders view in the Northwind database. The view uses a *SELECT* statement to select the order ID from the Orders table and the company name and contact name from the Customers table. A join connects the two tables.

Creating Indexed Views

Views are also known as virtual tables because the result set returned by the view has the same general form as a table (with columns and rows), and views can be referenced like tables in SQL statements. The result set of a standard view is not stored permanently in the database. Each time a query references the view, SQL Server 2000 dynamically merges the logic needed to build the view result set into the logic needed to build the complete query result set from the data in the base tables. The process of building the view result is called materializing the view.

For a standard view, the overhead of dynamically building the result set for each query that references the view can be substantial if the view involves complex processing of large numbers of rows (such as aggregating large amounts of data) or joining many rows. If such views are frequently referenced in queries, you can improve performance by creating a unique clustered index on the view. When a unique clustered index is created on a view, the view is executed and the result set is stored in the database in the same way that a table with a clustered index is stored.

Note   You can create indexed views only if you install Microsoft SQL Server 2000 Enterprise Edition or Microsoft SQL Server 2000 Developer Edition.

Another benefit of creating an index on a view is that the optimizer starts using the view index in queries that do not directly name the view in the FROM clause. Existing queries can benefit from the improved efficiency of retrieving data from the indexed view without having to be recoded.

Creating a clustered index on a view stores the data as it exists at the time the index is created. An indexed view also automatically reflects modifications made to the data in the base tables after the index is created, the same way as an index created on a base table. As modifications are made to the data in the base tables, they are also reflected in the data stored in the indexed view. Because the view's clustered index must be unique, SQL Server can more efficiently find the index rows affected by any data modification.

Indexed views can be more complex to maintain than indexes on base tables. You should create an index on a view only if the improved speed in retrieving the result outweighs the increased overhead of making modifications. This improvement usually occurs for views that are mapped over relatively static data, process many rows, and are referenced by many queries.

A view must meet the following requirements before you can create a clustered index on it:

- The ANSI_NULLS and QUOTED_IDENTIFIER options must have been set to ON when the *CREATE VIEW* statement was executed. The *OBJECTPROPERTY* function reports this setting for views through the ExecIsAnsiNullsOn or ExecIsQuotedIdentOn properties.

- The ANSI_NULLS option must have been set to ON for the execution of all *CREATE TABLE* statements that create tables referenced by the view.

- The view must not reference any other views, only base tables.

- All base tables referenced by the view must be in the same database as the view and must have the same owner as the view.

- The view must be created with the SCHEMABINDING option. SCHEMABINDING binds the view to the schema of the underlying base tables.

- User-defined functions referenced in the view must have been created with the SCHEMABINDING option.

- Tables and user-defined functions must be referenced by two-part names. One-part, three-part, and four-part names are not allowed.

- All functions referenced by expressions in the view must be deterministic. The IsDeterministic property of the *OBJECTPROPERTY* function reports whether a user-defined function is deterministic.

- If GROUP BY is not specified, the view select list cannot contain aggregate expressions.

- If GROUP BY is specified, the view select list must contain a COUNT_BIG(*) expression, and the view definition cannot specify HAVING, CUBE, or ROLLUP.

- A column resulting from an expression that either evaluates to a float value or uses float expressions for its evaluation cannot be a key of an index in an indexed view or table.

In addition to the previous restrictions, the *SELECT* statement in the view cannot contain the following Transact-SQL syntax elements:

- The asterisk (*) syntax to specify columns in a select list
- A table column name used as a simple expression that is specified in more than one view column
- A derived table
- Rowset functions
- A UNION operator
- Subqueries
- Outer or self joins
- The TOP clause
- The ORDER BY clause
- The DISTINCT keyword
- COUNT(*) (COUNT_BIG(*) is allowed)
- The *AVG*, *MAX*, *MIN*, *STDEV*, *STDEVP*, *VAR*, or *VARP* aggregate functions
- A *SUM* function that references a nullable expression
- The full-text predicates CONTAINS or FREETEXT
- The COMPUTE or COMPUTE BY clauses

Creating the Index

After you create a view, you can create an index on that view, assuming that the view adheres to the requirements for an indexed view. The first index created on a view must be a unique clustered index. After the unique clustered index has been created, you can create additional non-clustered indexes. The naming conventions for indexes on views are the same as for indexes on tables. The only difference is that the table name is replaced with the view name.

The *CREATE INDEX* statement must meet the following requirements in addition to the normal *CREATE INDEX* requirements:

- The user executing the *CREATE INDEX* statement must be the view's owner.
- The NUMERIC_ROUNDABORT option must be set to OFF.
- The view cannot include text, ntext, or image columns (even if they are not referenced in the *CREATE INDEX* statement).
- If the *SELECT* statement in the view definition specifies a GROUP BY clause, the key of the unique clustered index can reference only columns specified in the GROUP BY clause.

- The following SET options must be set to ON when the *CREATE INDEX* statement is executed:
  - ANSI_NULLS
  - ANSI_PADDING
  - ANSI_WARNINGS
  - ARITHABORT
  - CONCAT_NULL_YIELDS_NULL
  - QUOTED_IDENTIFIERS

Indexes are discussed in more detail in Chapter 11, "Implementing Indexes."

Creating Partitioned Views

A partitioned view joins horizontally partitioned data from a set of member tables across one or more servers, making the data appear as if it is from one table. SQL Server 2000 distinguishes between local and distributed partitioned views. In a xxxlocal partitioned view, all participating tables and the view reside on the same instance of SQL Server. In a distributed partitioned view, at least one of the participating tables resides on a different (remote) server. In addition, SQL Server 2000 differentiates between partitioned views that are updateable and views that are read only copies of the underlying tables.

Distributed partitioned views can be used to implement a federation of database servers. A federation is a group of servers that is administered independently but that cooperates to share the processing load of a system. Forming a federation of database servers by partitioning data is the mechanism that enables you to scale out a set of servers to support the processing requirements of large, multi-tiered Web sites.

Before implementing a partitioned view, you must first partition a table horizontally. The original table is replaced with several smaller member tables. Each member table has the same number of columns as the original table, and each column has the same attributes (such as data type, size, and collation) as the corresponding column in the original table. If you are creating a distributed partitioned view, each member table is on a separate member server. For the greatest location transparency, the name of the member databases should be the same on each member server, although this setup is not a requirement (for example, Server1.CustomerDB, Server2.CustomerDB, and Server3.CustomerDB).

You should design the member tables so that each table stores a horizontal slice of the original table, based on a range of key values. The ranges are based on the data values in a partitioning column. The range of values in each member table is enforced by a CHECK constraint on the partitioning column, and ranges cannot overlap. For example, you cannot have one table with a range from 1 through 200,000 and another with a range from 150,000 through 300,000, because it would not be clear which table contains the values from 150,000 through 200,000.

For example, suppose you are partitioning a Customer table into three tables. The CHECK constraint for these tables should be defined as follows:

```
-- On Server1:
CREATE TABLE Customer_33
(CustomerID INTEGER PRIMARY KEY
    CHECK (CustomerID BETWEEN 1 AND 32999),
    ... -- Additional column definitions)

-- On Server2:
CREATE TABLE Customer_66
(CustomerID INTEGER PRIMARY KEY
    CHECK (CustomerID BETWEEN 33000 AND 65999),
    ... -- Additional column definitions)

-- On Server3:
CREATE TABLE Customer_99
(CustomerID INTEGER PRIMARY KEY
    CHECK (CustomerID BETWEEN 66000 AND 99999),
    ... -- Additional column definitions)
```

After creating the member tables, define a distributed partitioned view on each member server, with each view having the same name. This setup lets queries referencing the distributed partitioned view name run on any of the member servers. The system operates as if a copy of the original table is on each member server, but each server has only a member table and a distributed partitioned view. The location of the data is transparent to the application.

You can build the distributed partitioned views by taking the following steps:

1. Add linked server definitions on each member server containing the connection information needed to execute distributed queries on the other member servers. This action gives a distributed partitioned view access to data on the other servers.
2. Set the lazy schema validation option (by using *sp_serveroption*) for each linked server definition used in distributed partitioned views. This setting optimizes performance by ensuring that the query processor does not request metadata for any of the linked tables until data is actually needed from the remote member table.
3. Create a distributed partitioned view on each member server. The views should use distributed *SELECT* statements to access data from the linked member server and merge the distributed rows with rows from the local member table.

To create distributed partitioned views for the preceding example, you should take the following steps:

1. Add a linked server definition named Server2 with the connection information for Server2 and a linked server definition named Server3 for access to Server3.

2. Create the following distributed partitioned view:

```
CREATE VIEW Customers AS
   SELECT *
   FROM CompanyDatabase.TableOwner.Customers_33
UNION ALL
   SELECT *
   FROM Server2.CompanyDatabase.TableOwner.Customers_66
UNION ALL
   SELECT *
   FROM Server3.CompanyDatabase.TableOwner.Customers_99
```

3. Perform the same steps on Server2 and Server3.

Modifying Views

After a view is defined, you can change its name or modify its definition without dropping and recreating the view, which would cause it to lose its associated permissions. When you rename a view, adhere to the following guidelines:

- The view to be renamed must be in the current database.
- The new name must follow the rules for identifiers.
- You can rename only views that you own.
- The database owner can change the name of any user's view.

Altering a view does not affect any dependent objects (such as stored procedures or triggers) unless the definition of the view changes in such a way that the dependent object is no longer valid.

To modify a view, you can use Enterprise Manager or the Transact-SQL *ALTER VIEW* statement to update the SELECT query, as shown in the following example:

```
ALTER VIEW CustomerOrders
AS
SELECT o.OrderID, o.OrderDate, c.CompanyName, c.ContactName
FROM Orders o JOIN Customers c
  ON o.CustomerID = c.CustomerID
```

In this statement, you are modifying the select list so that it includes the order date. The SELECT query in the *ALTER VIEW* statement replaces the SELECT query that was defined in the original *CREATE VIEW* statement.

In addition, you can modify a view to encrypt its definition or to ensure that all data modification statements executed against the view adhere to the criteria set within the *SELECT* statement that defines the view.

Deleting Views

After a view has been created, you can delete the view if it is not needed or if you want to clear the view definition and the permissions associated with it. When a view is deleted, the tables and the data upon which it is based are not affected. Any queries that use objects that depend on the deleted view fail when they are next executed (unless a view with the same name is created). If the new view does not reference objects expected by any objects dependent on the new view, however, queries using the dependent objects will fail when executed.

For example, suppose you create a view named MyView that retrieves all columns from the Authors table in the Pubs database, and this view is deleted and replaced by a new view named MyView that retrieves all columns from the Titles table instead. Any stored procedures that reference columns from the underlying Authors table in MyView now fail because those columns are replaced by columns from the Titles table instead.

To delete a view, you can use Enterprise Manager or the Transact-SQL *DROP VIEW* statement, as shown in the following example:

```
DROP VIEW CustomerOrders
```

Exercise 1: Creating and Modifying a View

In this exercise, you will use the CREATE VIEW statement to create a view in the BookShopDB database, the ALTER VIEW statement to modify this view, and the DROP VIEW statement to delete the view from the database. To perform this exercise, you should be logged onto your Windows 2000 Server computer as Administrator.

▶ **To create the BookAuthorView view in the BookShopDB database**

1. Open Query Analyzer and connect to your local server.

2. In the Editor pane of the Query window, enter the following Transact-SQL code:

```
USE BookShopDB
GO
CREATE VIEW BookAuthorView
AS
SELECT a.FirstName, a.LastName, b.Title
FROM Authors a JOIN BookAuthors ba
  ON a.AuthorID = ba.AuthorID
  JOIN Books b
  ON ba.TitleID = b.TitleID
```

In this statement, you are defining the BookAuthorView view in the Book-ShopDB database. The *CREATE VIEW* statement contains a SELECT query that joins the Authors table to the BookAuthors table and the BookAuthors table to the Books table. The result set from this query will include the author's first and last names and the books that this author has written.

3. Execute the Transact-SQL statement.

   A message appears in the Messages tab of the Results pane, stating that the command has been successfully completed.

4. If the Object Browser window is not displayed, open it now.

5. In the object tree of the Object Browser window, locate the new view that you created.

   Notice that the dbo.BookAuthorView node contains several nodes (including the Columns node and the Indexes node).

6. Expand the Columns node.

   Notice that the three columns that were included in the SELECT query of the CREATE VIEW definition are included in this node.

▶ **To modify the BookAuthorView view in the BookShopDB database**

1. In the Editor pane of the Query window, enter the following Transact-SQL code:

```
USE BookShopDB
Gо
ALTER VIEW BookAuthorView
AS
SELECT a.FirstName, a.LastName, b.TitleID, b.Title
FROM Authors a JOIN BookAuthors ba
  ON a.AuthorID = ba.AuthorID
  JOIN Books b
  ON ba.TitleID = b.TitleID
```

Tip You can copy and paste the code from the previous procedure and modify it to contain an *ALTER VIEW* statement and the TitleID column.

In this statement, you are adding the TitleID column to the *SELECT* statement. The result set will now include the additional column.

2. Execute the Transact-SQL statement.

   A message appears in the Messages tab of the Results pane, stating that the command has been successfully completed.

3. In the object tree of the Object Browser window, locate the BookAuthorView view and expand the Columns node.

   Notice that the TitleID column has been added to the list of columns.

4. Close Query Analyzer.

▶ **To delete the BookAuthorView view from the BookShopDB database**

1. In the Editor pane of the Query window, enter the following Transact-SQL code:

```
USE BookShopDB
GO
DROP VIEW BookAuthorView
```

In this statement, you are deleting the BookAuthorView view from the Book-ShopDB database.

2. Execute the Transact-SQL statement.

A message appears in the Messages tab of the Results pane, stating that the command has been successfully completed.

3. In the object tree of the Object Browser window, locate the Views node for the BookShopDB database.

Notice that the BookAuthorView view no longer appears.

Note   If the BookAuthorView view is still listed in the object tree, you will need to refresh the screen to update the listings.

Lesson Summary

You can create a view as you would many other objects in a database, and once that view is created, you can modify the view or delete it. When creating a view, you must adhere to specific restrictions. You can use Enterprise Manager to create a view, or you can use the *CREATE VIEW* statement in Transact-SQL. In addition to standard views, you can create indexed views. When a unique clustered index is created on a view, the view is executed and the result set is stored in the database in the same way as a table with a clustered index is stored. The first index created on a view must be a unique clustered index. After the unique clustered index has been created, you can create additional non-clustered indexes. In addition to indexed views, you can create partitioned views. A partitioned view joins horizontally parti-tioned data from a set of member tables across one or more servers, making the data appear as if it is from one table. After a view is defined, you can change its name or modify its definition without dropping and recreating the view, which would cause it to lose its associated permissions. You can also delete a view if it is not needed or if you want to clear the view definition and the permissions associ-ated with it. When a view is deleted, the tables and the data upon which it is based are not affected.

Lesson 3: Accessing Data through Views

Once a view has been created, you can use the view to access the data that is returned by the SELECT query defined within that view. Most operations that you can perform on a query can be performed on a view. In this lesson, you will learn how to use views to view the data returned by the SELECT query, and you will learn how to modify that data.

After this lesson, you will be able to:
- Use a view to view data.
- Use a view to insert, update, and delete data.

Estimated lesson time: 35 minutes

Viewing Data through Views

There are no restrictions on querying data through views. You can use a view in a *SELECT* statement to return data in much the same way as you use a table. The following *SELECT* statement enables you to view data returned by the Customer-Orders view in the Northwind database:

```
USE Northwind
SELECT *
FROM CustomerOrders
```

As with tables, you can be more specific about the type of data you return in a view. The following *SELECT* statement retrieves the OrderID column and the OrderDate column for any orders made for the QUICK-Stop company:

```
USE Northwind
SELECT OrderID, OrderDate
FROM CustomerOrders
WHERE CompanyName = 'quick-stop'
ORDER BY OrderID
```

In this statement, you are also specifying for the result set to be ordered by the OrderID values.

Modifying Data through Views

Views in all versions of SQL Server are updateable (can be the target of *UPDATE*, *DELETE*, or *INSERT* statements) as long as the modification affects only one of the base tables referenced by the view. SQL Server 2000 supports more complex types of *INSERT*, *UPDATE*, and *DELETE* statements that reference views. For example, INSTEAD OF triggers can be defined on a view to specify the individual updates that must be performed against the base tables to support the *INSERT*,

UPDATE, or *DELETE* statement. Also, partitioned views support *INSERT*, *UDPATE*, and *DELETE* statements that modify multiple member tables referenced by the view.

Modifying Data through Basic Views

There are few restrictions on modifying data through a view. However, if a view does not use an INSTEAD OF trigger or is not an updateable partitioned view, it can still be updateable, provided it meets the following conditions:

- The view contains at least one table in the FROM clause of the view definition. The view cannot be based solely on an expression.

- No aggregate functions (*AVG*, *COUNT*, *SUM*, *MIN*, *MAX*, *GROUPING*, *STDEV*, *STDEVP*, *VAR*, and *VARP*) or GROUP BY, UNION, DISTINCT, or TOP clauses are used in the select list. Aggregate functions, however, can be used within a subquery defined in the FROM clause, provided that the derived values generated by the aggregate functions are not modified.

- No derived columns are used in the select list. Derived columns are result set columns formed by anything other than a simple column reference.

Before you modify data through a view without using an INSTEAD OF trigger or an updateable partitioned view, consider the following guidelines:

- All data modification statements executed against the view must adhere to the criteria set within the *SELECT* statement defining the view if the WITH CHECK OPTION clause is used in the definition of the view. If the WITH CHECK OPTION clause is used, rows cannot be modified in a way that causes them to disappear from the view. Any modification that would cause this situation to happen is canceled, and an error is displayed.

- SQL Server must be capable of unambiguously resolving the modification operation to specific rows in one of the base tables referenced by the view. You cannot use data modification statements on more than one underlying table in a single statement. Therefore, the columns listed in the *UPDATE* or *INSERT* statement must belong to a single base table within the view definition.

- All of the columns in the underlying table that are being updated and that do not allow null values have values specified in either the *INSERT* statement or DEFAULT definitions. This feature ensures that all of the columns in the underlying table that require values have them.

- The modified data in the columns in the underlying table must adhere to the restrictions on those columns, such as nullability, constraints, DEFAULT definitions, and so on. For example, if a row is deleted, all of the underlying FOREIGN KEY constraints in related tables must still be satisfied for the delete to succeed.

- A distributed partition view (remote view) cannot be updated by using a keyset-driven cursor. This restriction can be resolved by declaring the cursor on the underlying tables and not on the view itself.

Additionally, to delete data in a view, only one table can be listed in the FROM clause of the view definition. The *READTEXT* and *WRITETEXT* statements cannot be used with text, ntext, or image columns in a view.

Adding Data through a View

Suppose you create a view in the Northwind database that returns the customer ID and the company name from the Customers table:

```
USE Northwind
GO
CREATE VIEW CustomerView
AS
SELECT CustomerID, CompanyName
FROM Customers
```

To insert data through the CustomerView view, you should use the *INSERT* statement (as shown in the following example):

```
USE Northwind
INSERT CustomerView
VALUES ('TEST1', 'Test Company')
```

This statement inserts a new row into the Customers table. Because all other columns in the table permit null values, you do not have to specify a value for those columns.

Changing Data through a View

To modify data through a view, you should use the *UPDATE* statement (as shown in the following example):

```
USE Northwind
UPDATE CustomerView
SET CustomerID = 'TEST2'
WHERE CustomerID = 'TEST1'
```

This statement changes the customer ID of Test Company to TEST2.

Deleting Data through a View

To delete data through a view, you should use the *DELETE* statement, as shown in the following example:

```
USE Northwind
DELETE CustomerView
WHERE CustomerID = 'TEST2'
```

This statement deletes the Test Company row from the Customers table.

Modifying Data through Partitioned Views

If a local or distributed partitioned view is not updateable, it can serve only as a read-only copy of the original table. An updateable partitioned view can exhibit all of the capabilities of the original table.

A view is considered an updateable partitioned view if it is defined with a set of *SELECT* statements whose individual result sets are combined into one by using the *UNION ALL* statement. Each individual *SELECT* statement references one SQL Server base table. The table can be either a local table or a linked table referenced using a four-part name, the *OPENROWSET* function, or the *OPENDATA-SOURCE* function (you cannot use an *OPENDATASOURCE* or *OPENROWSET* function that specifies a pass-through query).

In addition to the rules defined for updateable partitioned views, data modification statements referencing the view must adhere to the rules defined for *INSERT*, *UPDATE*, and *DELETE* statements.

Note You can modify data through a partitioned view only if you install Microsoft SQL Server 2000 Enterprise Edition or Microsoft SQL Server 2000 Developer Edition.

INSERT Statements

INSERT statements add data to the member tables through the partitioned view. The *INSERT* statements must adhere to the following rules:

- All columns must be included in the *INSERT* statement even if the column can be NULL in the base table or has a DEFAULT constraint defined in the base table.
- The DEFAULT keyword cannot be specified in the VALUES clause of the *INSERT* statement.
- *INSERT* statements must supply a value that satisfies the logic of the CHECK constraint defined on the partitioning column for one of the member tables.
- *INSERT* statements are not allowed if a member table contains a column that has an identity property.

- *INSERT* statements are not allowed if a member table contains a timestamp column.

- *INSERT* statements are not allowed if there is a self-join with the same view or with any of the member tables.

UPDATE Statements

UPDATE statements modify data in one or more of the member tables through the partitioned view. The *UPDATE* statements must adhere to the following rules:

- *UPDATE* statements cannot specify the DEFAULT keyword as a value in the SET clause, even if the column has a DEFAULT value defined in the corresponding member table.

- The value of a column with an identity property cannot be changed; however, the other columns can be updated.

- The value of a PRIMARY KEY cannot be changed if the column contains *text*, *image*, or *ntext* data.

- Updates are not allowed if a base table contains a timestamp column.

- Updates are not allowed if there is a self-join with the same view or any of the member tables.

- The DEFAULT keyword cannot be specified in the SET clause of the *UPDATE* statement.

DELETE Statements

DELETE statements remove data in one or more of the member tables through the partitioned view. The *DELETE* statements are not allowed if there is a self-join with the same view or any of the member tables.

Modifying Data when the INSTEAD OF Trigger Is Used

INSTEAD OF triggers override the standard actions of the triggering statement (*INSERT*, *UPDATE*, or *DELETE*). For example, an INSTEAD OF trigger can be defined to perform error or value checking on one or more columns and then to perform additional actions before inserting the record. For instance, when the value being updated in an hourly wage column in a payroll table exceeds a specified value, a trigger can be defined to either produce an error message and roll back the transaction or insert a new record into an audit log before inserting the record into the payroll table.

INSTEAD OF triggers can be defined on either tables or views; however, INSTEAD OF triggers are most useful for extending the types of updates that a view can support. INSTEAD OF triggers are discussed in more detail in Chapter 9, "Implementing Triggers."

Exercise 2: Using the AuthorsBooks View to Access Data

In this exercise, you will create a view on the Authors table that includes only the first and last names of the authors. You will then use this view to add an author to the database, modify that author, and then delete the author. To perform this exercise, you should be logged into your Windows 2000 Server computer as Administrator.

▶ **To create the AuthorNames view to view data**

1. Open Query Analyzer and connect to your local server.

2. In the Editor pane of the Query window, enter the following Transact-SQL code:

```
USE BookShopDB
GO
CREATE VIEW AuthorNames
AS
SELECT FirstName, LastName
FROM Authors
```

In this statement, you are creating a view that returns the first and last names of the authors listed in the Authors table of the BookShopDB database.

3. Execute the Transact-SQL statement.

A message appears in the Messages tab of the Results pane, stating that the command has been successfully completed.

▶ **To use the AuthorNames view to view data**

1. In the Editor pane of the Query window, enter the following Transact-SQL code:

```
USE BookShopDB
SELECT *
FROM AuthorNames
ORDER BY LastName
```

This statement uses the AuthorNames view to retrieve data. The result set is ordered by the last names of the authors.

2. Execute the Transact-SQL statement.

The result set is displayed in the Grids tab of the Results pane.

▶ **To use the AuthorNames view to insert data**

1. In the Editor pane of the Query window, enter the following Transact-SQL code:

```
USE BookShopDB
INSERT AuthorNames
VALUES ('William', 'Burroughs')
```

This statement uses the AuthorNames view to insert a new author.

2. Execute the Transact-SQL statement.

   A message appears in the Messages tab of the Results pane, stating that the command has been successfully completed.

3. In the Editor pane of the Query window, enter and execute the following Transact-SQL code:

```
SELECT *
FROM Authors
```

   The result set is displayed in the Grids tab of the Results pane.

4. Scroll to the last row of the result set.

   Notice that William Burroughs has been added to the list of authors. Also notice that the YearBorn, YearDied, and Description columns have been assigned the default value of N/A.

▶ **To use the AuthorNames view to modify data**

1. In the Editor pane of the Query window, enter the following Transact-SQL code:

```
USE BookShopDB
UPDATE AuthorNames
SET FirstName - 'John'
WHERE LastName = 'Burroughs'
```

   This statement changes the first name of the author whose last name is Burroughs.

2. Execute the Transact-SQL statement.

   A message appears in the Messages tab of the Results pane, stating that the command has been successfully completed.

3. In the Editor pane of the Query window, enter and execute the following Transact-SQL code:

```
SELECT *
FROM AuthorNames
```

   The result set is displayed in the Grids tab of the Results pane.

4. Scroll to the last row of the result set.

   Notice that William Burroughs has been changed to John Burroughs.

▶ **To use the AuthorNames view to delete data**

1. In the Editor pane of the Query window, enter the following Transact-SQL code:

```
USE BookShopDB
DELETE AuthorNames
WHERE LastName = 'Burroughs'
```

   This statement deletes John Burroughs from the Authors table.

2. Execute the Transact-SQL statement.

   A message appears in the Messages tab of the Results pane, stating that the command has been successfully completed.

3. In the Editor pane of the Query window, enter and execute the following Transact-SQL code:

```
SELECT *
FROM Authors
```

   The result set is displayed in the Grids tab of the Results pane.

4. Scroll to the last row of the result set.

   Notice that John Burroughs has been deleted from the Authors table.

► **To delete the AuthorNames view in the BookShopDB database**

1. In the Editor pane of the Query window, enter the following Transact-SQL code:

```
USE BookShopDB
GO
DROP VIEW AuthorNames
```

   In this statement, you are deleting the BookAuthorView view from the Book-ShopDB database.

2. Execute the Transact-SQL statement.

   A message appears in the Messages tab of the Results pane, stating that the command has been successfully completed.

Lesson Summary

Once a view has been created, you can use the view to access the data that is returned by the SELECT query defined within that view. You can use a view in a *SELECT* statement to return data in much the same way as you use a table. SQL Server also enables you to use views to modify data. In addition to modifying data through basic views, you can modify data through updateable partitioned views and views that use INSTEAD OF triggers. If a view does not use an INSTEAD OF trigger or is not an updateable partitioned view, it can still be updateable provided it meets specific conditions. If the conditions are met, you can insert, update, or delete data through the view. A view is considered an updateable partitioned view if the view is a set of *SELECT* statements whose individual result sets are combined into one by using the *UNION ALL* statement. In addition to the rules defined for updateable partitioned views, data modification statements referencing the view must adhere to the rules defined for *INSERT*, *UPDATE*, and *DELETE* statements. INSTEAD OF triggers override the standard actions of the triggering statement (*INSERT*, *UPDATE*, or *DELETE*). INSTEAD OF triggers can be defined for either tables or views; however, INSTEAD OF triggers are most useful for extending the types of updates that a view can support.

Review

The following questions are intended to reinforce key information presented in this chapter. If you are unable to answer a question, review the appropriate lesson and then try the question again. You can find the answers to these questions in the Appendix, "Questions and Answers."

1. What is a view?
2. What functions can a view be used to perform?
3. For what scenarios can views be used?
4. What are at least five restrictions that you must adhere to when creating views?
5. What two tools does SQL Server provide to create a view?
6. Where are the result sets stored for standard views and indexed views?
7. If a view is going to be indexed, what type of index must be the first index created on that view?
8. Which Transact-SQL statement or statements should you use to change the definition of a view or to delete that view from the database?
9. What Transact-SQL statement should you use if you want to view all of the data in the AuthorNames view of the Northwind database?
10. Which Transact-SQL statement or statements should you use to insert, modify, and delete data through a view?
11. What conditions must a view meet before you can modify data through that view?
12. When is a view considered to be an updateable partitioned view?

C H A P T E R   1 1

Implementing Indexes

About This Chapter

Indexes are database objects designed to improve query performance. This chapter introduces you to the structure and purpose of indexes and their types and characteristics. You will learn how to determine when an index is appropriate, the type of index to create, and how to create it. After you create indexes, you must maintain them to maximize query performance. A number of tools exist to assist you with index maintenance and administration. Administration tasks include rebuilding, renaming, and deleting indexes.

Before You Begin

To complete the lessons in this chapter, you must have:

- SQL Server 2000 Enterprise Edition installed on a Microsoft Windows 2000 Server computer.
- The ability to log on to the Windows 2000 Server computer and to SQL Server as the Windows 2000 Administrator.
- Completed the exercises in Chapter 3, "Designing a SQL Server Database," Chapter 4, "Implementing SQL Server Databases and Tables," Chapter 5, "Implementing Data Integrity," and Chapter 7, "Managing and Manipulating Data."

Lesson 1: Index Architecture

Indexes are structured to facilitate the rapid return of result sets. The two types of indexes that SQL Server supports are clustered and nonclustered indexes. Indexes are applied to one or more columns in tables or views. Indexed tables are supported on all editions of SQL Server 2000, and indexed views are supported on SQL Server Enterprise Edition and SQL Server Developer Edition. The characteristics of an index affect its use of system resources and its lookup performance. The Query Optimizer uses an index if it will increase query performance. In this lesson, you will learn about the structure, types, and characteristics of indexes.

After this lesson, you will be able to:

- Describe the purpose and structure of indexes.
- Explain the difference between clustered and nonclustered indexes.
- Describe important index characteristics.
- Use stored procedures, Query Analyzer, and Enterprise Manager to view index properties.

Estimated Lesson time: 40 minutes

Purpose and Structure

An index in SQL Server assists the database engine with locating records, just like an index in a book helps you locate information quickly. Without indexes, a query causes SQL Server to search all records in a table (table scan) in order to find matches. A database index contains one or more column values from a table (called the index key) and pointers to the corresponding table records. When you perform a query using the index key, the Query Optimizer will likely use an index to locate the records that match the query.

An index is structured by the SQL Server Index Manager as a Balanced tree (or B-tree). A B-tree is analogous to an upside-down tree with the root of the tree at the top, the leaf levels at the bottom, and intermediate levels in between. Each object in the tree structure is a group of sorted index keys called an index page. A B-tree facilitates fast and consistent query performance by carefully balancing the width and depth of the tree as the index grows. Sorting the index on the index key also improves query performance. All search requests begin at the root of a B-tree and then move through the tree to the appropriate leaf level. The number of table records and the size of the index key affect the width and depth of the tree. Index key size is called the key width. A table that has many records and a large index key width creates a deep and wide B-tree. The smaller the tree, the more quickly a search result is returned.

For optimal query performance, create indexes on columns in a table that are commonly used in queries. For example, users can query a Customers table based on last name or customer ID. Therefore, you should create two indexes for the table: a last-name index and a customer ID index. To efficiently locate records, the Query Optimizer uses an index that matches the query. The Query Optimizer will likely use the customer ID index when the following query is executed:

```
SELECT * FROM Customers WHERE customerid = 798
```

Do not create indexes for every column in a table, because too many indexes will negatively impact performance. The majority of databases are dynamic; that is, records are added, deleted, and changed regularly. When a table containing an index is modified, the index must be updated to reflect the modification. If index updates do not occur, the index will quickly become ineffective. Therefore, insert, update, and delete events trigger the Index Manager to update the table indexes. Like tables, indexes are data structures that occupy space in the database. The larger the table, the larger the index that is created to contain the table. Before creating an index, you must be sure that the increased query performance afforded by the index outweighs the additional computer resources necessary to maintain the index.

Index Types

There are two types of indexes: clustered and nonclustered. Both types of indexes are structured as B-trees. A clustered index contains table records in the leaf level of the B-tree. A nonclustered index contains a bookmark to the table records in the leaf level. If a clustered index exists on a table, a nonclustered index uses it to facilitate data lookup. In most cases, you will create a clustered index on a table before you create nonclustered indexes.

Clustered Indexes

There can be only one clustered index on a table or view, because the clustered index key physically sorts the table or view. This type of index is particularly efficient for queries, because data records—also known as data pages—are stored in the leaf level of the B-tree. The sort order and storage location of a clustered index is analogous to a dictionary in that the words in a dictionary are sorted alphabetically and definitions appear next to the words.

When you create a primary key constraint in a table that does not contain a clustered index, SQL Server will use the primary key column for the clustered index key. If a clustered index already exists in a table, a nonclustered index is created on the column defined with a primary key constraint. A column defined as the PRIMARY key is a useful index because the column values are guaranteed to be unique. Unique values create smaller B-trees than redundant values and thus make more efficient lookup structures.

Note   A column defined with a unique constraint creates a nonclustered index automatically.

To force the type of index to be created for a column or columns, you can specify the CLUSTERED or NONCLUSTERED clause in the *CREATE TABLE, ALTER TABLE,* or *CREATE INDEX* statements. Suppose that you create a Persons table containing the following columns: PersonID, FirstName, LastName, and Social-SecurityNumber. The PersonID column is defined as a primary key constraint, and the SocialSecurityNumber column is defined as a unique constraint. To make the SocialSecurityNumber column a clustered index and the PersonID column a non-clustered index, create the table by using the following syntax:

```
CREATE TABLE dbo.Persons
  (
  personid smallint PRIMARY KEY NONCLUSTERED,
  firstname varchar(30),
  lastname varchar(40),
  socialsecuritynumber char(11) UNIQUE CLUSTERED
  )
```

Indexes are not limited to constraints. You create indexes on any column or combination of columns in a table or view. Clustered indexes enforce uniqueness internally. Therefore, if you create a nonunique, clustered index on a column that contains redundant values, SQL Server creates a unique value on the redundant columns to serve as a secondary sort key. To avoid the additional work required to maintain unique values on redundant rows, favor clustered indexes for columns defined with primary key constraints.

Nonclustered Indexes

On a table or view, you can create 250 nonclustered indexes or 249 nonclustered indexes and one clustered index. You must first create a unique clustered index on a view before you can create nonclustered indexes. This restriction does not apply to tables, however. A nonclustered index is analogous to an index in the back of a book. You can use a book's index to locate pages that match an index entry. The database uses a nonclustered index to locate matching records in the database.

If a clustered index does not exist on a table, the table is unsorted and is called a heap. A nonclustered index created on a heap contains pointers to table rows. Each entry in an index page contains a row ID (RID). The RID is a pointer to a table row in a heap, and it consists of a page number, a file number, and a slot number. If a clustered index exists on a table, the index pages of a nonclustered index contain clustered index keys rather than RIDs. An index pointer, whether it is a RID or an index key, is called a bookmark.

Index Characteristics

A number of characteristics (aside from the index type, which is clustered or non-clustered) can be applied to an index. An index can be defined as follows:

- Unique duplicate records are not allowed
- A composite of columns—an index key made up of multiple columns
- With a fill factor to allow index pages to grow when necessary
- With a pad index to change the space allocated to intermediate levels of the B-tree
- With a sort order to specify ascending or descending index keys

---

Note   Additional characteristics, such as file groups for index storage, can be applied to an index. Refer to *CREATE INDEX* in SQL Server Books Online and to Lesson 2 for more information.

Indexes are applied to one or more columns in a table or view. With some limitations, you can specify indexes on computed columns.

Unique

When an index is defined as unique, the index keys and the corresponding column values must be unique. A unique index can be applied to any column if all column values are unique. A unique index can also be applied to a group of columns (a composite of columns). The composite column unique index must maintain distinctiveness. For example, a unique index defined on a lastname column and a social security number column must not contain NULL values in both columns. Furthermore, if there are values in both columns, the combination of lastname and social security number must be unique.

SQL Server automatically creates a unique index for a column or columns defined with a primary key or unique constraint. Therefore, use constraints to enforce data distinctiveness, rather than directly applying the unique index characteristic. SQL Server will not allow you to create an index with the uniqueness property on a column containing duplicate values.

Composite

A composite index is any index that uses more than one column in a table for its index key. Composite indexes can improve query performance by reducing input/output (I/O) operations, because a query on a combination of columns contained in the index will be located entirely in the index. When the result of a query is obtained from the index without having to rely on the underlying table, the query is considered covered—and the index is considered covering. A single column query, such as a query on a column with a primary key constraint, is covered by the index that is automatically created on that column. A covered query on multiple columns uses a composite index as the covering index. Suppose that you run the following query:

```
SELECT emp_id, lname, job_lvl
FROM employee01
WHERE hire_date < (GETDATE() - 30)
 AND job_lvl >= 100
ORDER BY job_lvl
```

If a clustered index exists on the Emp_ID column and a nonclustered index named INco exists on the LName, Job_Lvl, and Hire_Date columns, then INco is a covering index. Remember that the bookmark of a nonclustered index created on a table containing a clustered index is the clustered index key. Therefore, the INco index contains all columns specified in the query (the index is covering, and the query is covered). Figure 11.1 shows that the Query Optimizer uses INco in the query execution plan.

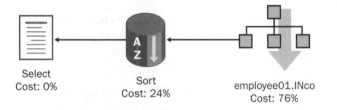

Select
Cost: 0%

Sort
Cost: 24%

employee01.INco
Cost: 76%

Figure 11.1.   The Execution Plan tab of the Results pane showing that the Query Optimizer uses the INco covering index.

Fill Factor and Pad Index

When a row is inserted into a table, SQL Server must locate some space for it. An insert operation occurs when the *INSERT* statement is used or when the *UPDATE* statement is used to update a clustered index key. If the table doesn't contain a clustered index, the record and the index page are placed in any available space within the heap. If the table contains a clustered index, SQL Server locates the appropriate index page in the B-tree and then inserts the record in sorted order. If the index page is full, it is split (half of the pages remain in the original index page, and half of the pages move to the new index page). If the inserted row is large, additional page splits might be necessary. Page splits are complex and are resource intensive. The most common page split occurs in the leaf level index pages. To reduce the occurrence of page splits, specify how full the index page should be when it is created. This value is called the fill factor. By default, the fill factor is zero, meaning that the index page is full when it is created on existing data. A fill factor of zero is synonymous with a fill factor of 100. You can specify a global default fill factor for the server by using the *sp_configure* stored procedure or for a specific index with the FILLFACTOR clause. In high-capacity transaction systems, you might also want to allocate additional space to the intermediate level index pages. The additional space assigned to the intermediate levels is called the pad index. In Lesson 2, you will learn when and how to use a fill factor.

Sort Order

When you create an index, it is sorted in ascending order. Both clustered and non-clustered indexes are sorted; the clustered index represents the sort order of the table. Consider the following *SELECT* statement:

```
SELECT emp_id, lname, job_lvl
FROM employee01
WHERE hire_date < (GETDATE() - 30)
 AND job_lvl >= 100
```

Notice that there is no sort order specified. In the previous section of this lesson, you learned that the Query Optimizer uses a composite index to return a result from this statement. The composite index is nonclustered, and the first column in the index is lname. No sort order was specified when the index was created; therefore, the result is sorted in ascending order starting with the lname column. The ORDER BY clause is not specified, thus saving computing resources. But the result appears sorted first by lname. The sort order is dependent on the index used to return the result (unless you specify the ORDER BY clause or you tell the *SELECT* statement which index to use). If the Query Optimizer uses a clustered index to return a result, the result appears in the sort order of the clustered index, which is equivalent to the data pages in the table. The following Transact-SQL statement uses the clustered index on the Emp_ID column to return a result in ascending order:

```
SELECT emp_id, lname, fname FROM employee01
```

Note   Lesson 2 describes how to determine when to use an index, how to choose the appropriate index characteristics, and how to create an index.

Index Information

You can use system stored procedures, the Object Browser in Query Analyzer, or Enterprise Manager to view indexes and index properties. Knowing the indexes applied to a table or view helps you optimize your queries. You can analyze indexes to design *SELECT* statements that return results efficiently, or you can create new indexes to accommodate your queries. Use the *sp_help* or *sp_helpindex* system stored procedures to view the indexes applied to a table or view. The following Transact-SQL command shows all indexes created for the Employee01 table:

```
sp_helpindex employee01
```

The result that is returned from *sp_helpindex* includes the index name, the index type, the database file location, and the column(s) contained in the index.

Query Analyzer's Object Browser provides similar information. In the Object Browser, expand a table node and then expand the Indexes node. Next, right-click an index and choose Edit to display the Edit Existing Index dialog box. Figure 11.2 shows the properties of an index as it appears in the Edit Existing Index dialog box.

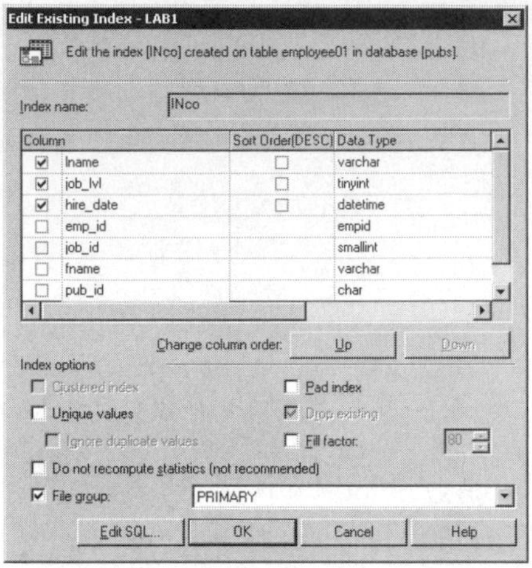

Figure 11.2.   The properties of the INco nonclustered index created on the Employee01 table in the Pubs database.

You can also view the properties of an index and access the Edit Existing Index dialog box from an Execution plan. Right-click an index that appears in the Execution Plan tab and choose Manage Indexes. Doing so displays the Manage Indexes dialog box. From there, you can click the Edit button to display the Edit Existing Index dialog box. The Manage Indexes dialog box is also available in Enterprise Manager. First, locate the Tables node of a database in the console tree. In the Details pane, right-click a table, point to All Tasks, then click Manage Indexes. You can modify, create, and delete existing indexes from the Manage Indexes dialog box. You will learn about index administration tasks such as modifying, creating, and deleting indexes in Lesson 2.

To view all indexes assigned to a database, you can query the sysindexes system table in a database. For example, to query selected index information in the Pubs database, execute the following Transact-SQL code:

```
USE PUBS
GO
SELECT name, rows, rowcnt, keycnt from sysindexes
WHERE name NOT LIKE '%sys%'
ORDER BY keycnt
```

Full-Text Indexing

Full-text indexing is not part of the indexing function described in this chapter, but you should understand how it differs from the built-in SQL Server indexing system. A full-text index enables you to perform full-text queries to search for character string data in the database. A full-text index is contained in a full-text catalog. The Microsoft Search engine, not SQL Server, maintains the full-text index and catalog. For more information about this feature, search for "Full-Text Query Architecture" in SQL Server Books Online.

Exercise 1: Viewing Index Properties and Using an Index

In this exercise, you will use the sp_helpindex system stored procedure and Query Analyzer to view the properties of an index. You will then create SELECT statements to make use of various indexes. After each SELECT statement runs, you will view the execution plan to determine which index was used by the Query Optimizer. In the last practice, you will create a composite index and run a query that uses this index.

▶ **To view index properties in the Northwind database**

1. Open Query Analyzer and connect to your local server.

2. In the Editor pane of the Query window, enter and execute the following code:

```
USE Northwind
GO
sp_helpindex customers
```

   Five indexes appear in the Grids tab of the Results pane.

   Which index represents the sort order of the Customers table?

   Does the Customers table contain a composite index?

▶ **To run queries and examine the execution plan**

1. In Query Analyzer, click Query and then click Show Execution Plan.

2. In the Editor pane of the Query window, enter and execute the following code:

```
USE Northwind
GO
SELECT * FROM customers
```

   A result set appears in the Grids tab of the Results pane. Notice that the result set is sorted by CustomerID.

3. Click the Execution Plan tab.

   The execution plan appears in the Execution Plan tab of the Results pane. Notice that the Query Optimizer used the PK_Customers clustered index. The PK_Customers index name is truncated to PK_Cu... in the Execution Plan tab.

4. In the Editor pane of the Query window, enter and execute the following code:

```
SELECT city, customerid from customers
```

A result set appears in the Grids tab of the Results pane. Notice that the result set is sorted by City.

5. Click the Execution Plan tab.

The execution plan indicates that the Query Optimizer used the City nonclustered index.

6. Why did the Query Optimizer choose the City index rather than the PK_Customers index in this case?

7. In the Editor pane of the Query window, enter and execute the following code:

```
SELECT companyname, contactname, city, country, phone FROM customers
```

A result set appears in the Grids tab of the Results pane. Notice that the result set appears to be sorted by the CompanyName column. This sort order is actually that of the CustomerID column, which contains at least the first three characters of the CompanyName column.

8. Click the Execution Plan tab.

The execution plan indicates that the Query Optimizer used the PK_Customers index. The PK_Customers index was used because no other index was covering for this query. In the next practice, you will create a covering index for this query.

9. Leave the Execution Plan tab active for the next practice.

▶   **To create a composite index and a query that uses the index**

This practice is designed to show you how to use a composite index. Therefore, do not focus on index creation here. In Lesson 2, you will learn more about creating indexes.

1. In the Execution Plan pane, right-click Customers.PK_Cu... and then click Manage Indexes.

The list of indexes created for the Customers table appears in the Manage Indexes dialog box.

2. Click New.

The Create New Index dialog box appears.

3. In the Index name text box, type **Contact**.

4. In the column appearing below the Index name text box, select the CompanyName, ContactName, City, Country, and Phone check boxes.

5. Select the City row and click the UP button until the City row is the first selected row.

6. Click OK.

The Contact index appears in the index list of the Manage Indexes dialog box.

7. Click Close.

8. In the Editor pane of the Query window, enter and execute the following code:

```
SELECT companyname, contactname, city, country, phone FROM customers
ORDER BY city
```

A result set appears in the Grids tab of the Results pane. Notice that the result set is sorted by City.

9. Click the Execution Plan tab.

The execution plan indicates that the Query Optimizer used the Contact nonclustered index. Notice that sorting the list requires no processing because the Contact composite index is sorted first on the City column.

10. In the Editor pane of the Query window, enter and execute the following code:

```
SELECT companyname, contactname, city, country, phone FROM customers
ORDER BY country
```

A result set appears in the Grids tab of the Results pane. Notice that the result set is sorted by Country.

11. Click the Execution Plan tab.

The execution plan indicates that the Query Optimizer used the Contact nonclustered index. Notice that there is processing required to sort the list because the Contact composite index is not sorted first by Country.

Lesson Summary

Indexes improve query performance by facilitating the location of records. An index contains index keys organized in index page groupings. The pages are further structured into a B-tree. The B-tree structure maintains high-performance lookup capabilities even if the index grows large. Before creating an index, consider the ways in which a table or view is queried. The Query Optimizer chooses an index if it will facilitate the return of matching records. Indexes should be created sparingly in dynamic databases, because the system must update each index as records are inserted into tables.

One clustered index is allowed per table or view. An index is created automatically when a primary key or unique constraint is defined for a table. Multiple nonclustered indexes are allowed on a table or view. The leaf level index pages of a nonclustered index contain either RIDs for an unsorted heap or clustered index keys for a sorted table. Indexes are defined as unique or nonunique. An index is made up of one or more columns. A multi-column index is called a composite index. A fill factor and pad index value are specified for an index to reduce the frequency of page splits. Indexes are automatically sorted in ascending order unless a sort order is specified. An index that returns a result without consulting the underlying table or heap is a covering index. A query whose result set is returned entirely from the covering index is called a covered query.

Lesson 2: Index Creation and Administration

In this lesson, you will learn how to create, rebuild, rename, and delete an index using Transact-SQL, Query Analyzer, and Enterprise Manager. Before creating an index for a production database, you must understand how data is accessed. You should only create indexes that serve the majority of queries that users request. The way in which the database is used dictates how liberal you can be about creating indexes. There are important performance optimization features included with SQL Server 2000 to help you determine what indexes to create or delete and to help you maintain existing indexes. This lesson concludes with a survey of these features.

After this lesson, you will be able to:

- Create, rebuild, rename, and delete indexes.
- Determine when an index is appropriate.
- Describe the key performance optimization tools for indexes in SQL Server 2000.

Estimated lesson time: 45 minutes

Index Creation

There are a number of ways to create an index in SQL Server. You can create a custom application that uses the SQL-DMO interface to create an index. As you saw in Lesson 1, you can use the Manage Indexes option from the Object Browser or access it from an execution plan in Query Analyzer. The Manage Indexes option is also available from the context menu of a table or view in Enterprise Manager. Enterprise Manager also offers a Create Index wizard to step you through index creation. You create an index for a table or view by using the *CREATE INDEX* Transact-SQL statement. You can specify index properties of a primary key or unique constraint during table creation (*CREATE TABLE*) or table modification (*ALTER TABLE*).

Using a Graphical Interface

To access the Manage Indexes option in Enterprise Manager, expand a database in the console tree and then select a table or view. In the Details pane, right-click a table, select All Tasks, and then select Manage Indexes. From the Manage Indexes dialog box, click the New button to access the Create New Index dialog box. Figure 11.3 shows the Create New Index dialog box.

From the Create New Index dialog box, you can provide an index name, the column or columns to include in the index, the type of index (clustered or nonclustered), and index properties (unique, pad index, fill factor, and the file group where the index should be created, to name a few). You can also change

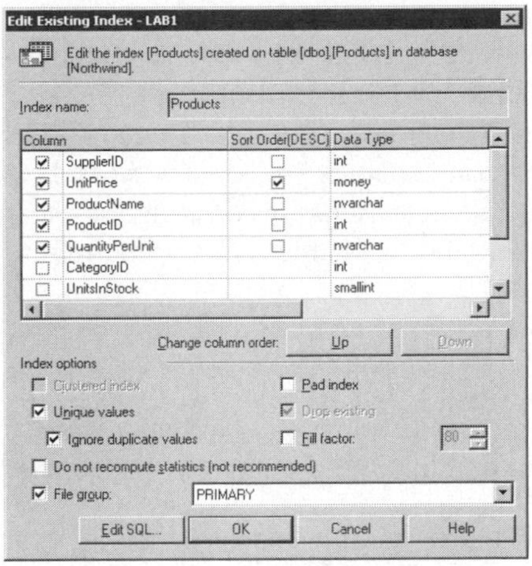

Figure 11.3. The Create New Index dialog box for the Products table of the Northwind database.

the order of the columns that are part of a composite index key by selecting the column and clicking the Up and Down buttons. The column that is first in the list of selected columns will define the primary sort order of the index key. Notice that you can also specify a descending sort order for any part of the index key. The Query Optimizer chooses the Product index that appears in Figure 11.3 when the following *SELECT* statement executes:

```
SELECT supplierid, unitprice, productname
FROM products
```

The result set shows the SupplierID in ascending order, followed by the UnitPrice in descending order. The index sorts ProductName in ascending order, but this order doesn't appear in the result set because SupplierID and UnitPrice supersede the order of the ProductName column. Here are a few records from the result set to illustrate this point:

supplierid	unitprice	productname
1	19.0000	Chang
1	18.0000	Chai
1	10.0000	Aniseed Syrup
2	22.0000	Chef Anton's Cajun Seasoning
2	21.3500	Chef Anton's Gumbo Mix
2	21.0500	Louisiana Fiery Hot Pepper Sauce
2	17.0000	Louisiana Hot Spiced Okra
3	40.0000	Northwoods Cranberry Sauce
3	30.0000	Uncle Bob's Organic Dried Pears

If you prefer more help with creating indexes, use the Create Index wizard in Enterprise Manager. The Create Index wizard is available in the wizards option under the Tools menu. Clicking wizards displays the Select Dialog box. In the Select Dialog box, expand Database, select the Create Index wizard, and click OK to start the wizard. The wizard enables you to view the indexes already created on a table or view and to create a new index by selecting the column (or columns) that should be part of the index and by setting index properties.

Using Transact-SQL Statements

The *CREATE INDEX*, *CREATE TABLE*, and *ALTER TABLE* statements participate in index creation. You can create an index with these Transact-SQL statements by using Query Analyzer or a command prompt tool such as osql.

When using *CREATE INDEX*, you must specify the index name, the table or view, and the column(s) upon which the index is applied. Optionally, you can specify whether the index should contain only unique values, the index type (clustered or nonclustered), the column sort order for each column, index properties, and the file group location for the index. The default settings are as follows:

- Create a nonclustered index.
- Sort all columns in ascending order and use the current database for sorting the index.
- Use SQL Server global settings for the pad index and fill factor.
- Create all sort results during index creation in the default file group.
- Update index statistics.
- Roll back a batch of multiple inserts if a unique index is violated by any of the records being inserted.
- Prevent an existing index from being overwritten.

The main clauses in a *CREATE INDEX* statement are summarized as follows:

- CREATE
- [UNIQUE] [CLUSTERED | NONCLUSTERED] INDEX
- *index_name*
- ON [*table_name* | *view_name*](*column_name* [,...*n*])
- [WITH [*index_ property* [,...*n*]]
- [ON *file_ group*]

So far, you have learned the meaning of these clauses, which clauses are optional, and what the default settings are for any clause not specified in the *CREATE INDEX* statement. In summary, the UNIQUE and CLUSTERED or NONCLUS-TERED clauses are optional. It is also optional to specify index properties by using the WITH clause and to specify the file group where the index is created by using the second ON clause.

The following *CREATE INDEX* statement uses default settings for all optional clauses:

```
CREATE INDEX index01 ON table01(column01)
```

An index named Index01 is created on Table01. The index key for the table is Column01. The index is not unique and is nonclustered. All index properties match the default settings for the database.

Using optional clauses customizes the following *CREATE INDEX* statement:

```
CREATE UNIQUE CLUSTERED INDEX index01
ON table01(column01, column03 DESC)
WITH FILLFACTOR = 60,
IGNORE_DUP_KEY, DROP_EXISTING,
SORT_IN_TEMPDB
```

An index named Index01 replaces the existing index of the same name created on Table01. The DROP_EXISTING keyword instructs Index01 to be replaced. The index key includes Column01 and Column03, making Index01 a composite index. The DESC keyword sets the sort order for Column03 to descending (rather than ascending). The FILLFACTOR keyword configures the index so that the leaf level index pages are 60 percent full, leaving 40 percent of the space to contain additional index key entries. The CLUSTERED and UNIQUE clauses configure the index as clustered and unique; the table is physically sorted by the index; and duplicate keys are not allowed. The IGNORE_DUP_KEY keyword enables a batch containing multiple *INSERT* statements to succeed by ignoring any *INSERT* statements that would violate the uniqueness index requirement. The SORT_IN_TEMPDB keyword instructs the index to perform intermediate sort operations in TempDB. This keyword is typically used to improve the speed at which a large index is created or rebuilt and to decrease index fragmentation. Because the second ON clause does not appear, Index01 is created in the default file group for the database.

Creating a primary key constraint or a unique constraint automatically creates an index. You define these constraints when you create or alter a table definition. The *CREATE TABLE* and *ALTER TABLE* statements include index settings so that you can customize the indexes that accompany these constraints.

The main clauses in *CREATE TABLE* statements that relate to index creation are as follows:

- CREATE TABLE *table_name*
- *(column_name data_type*

- CONSTRAINT *constraint_name*
- [PRIMARY KEY | UNIQUE]
- [CLUSTERED | NONCLUSTERED]
- [WITH FILLFACTOR = *fill_ factor*]
- [ON *file_ group*])

A primary key constraint is always set to NOT NULL. You can specify NOT NULL, but it is implicit in the definition of a primary key constraint. The following *CREATE TABLE* statement uses default index settings when creating a table with a primary key constraint:

```
CREATE TABLE table01 (column01 int
CONSTRAINT pk_column01
PRIMARY KEY)
```

A table named Table01 is created with a single column named Column01. The PRIMARY KEY clause defines Column01 with a primary key constraint named Pk_Column01. The primary key constraint, Pk_Column01, is a unique and clustered index by default.

Using optional clauses for index creation customizes the following *CREATE TABLE* statement:

```
CREATE TABLE table01 (column01 int
CONSTRAINT pk_column01
PRIMARY KEY
WITH FILLFACTOR = 50
ON SECONDARY)
```

The *ALTER TABLE* syntax for creating or modifying primary key or unique constraints is similar to the *CREATE TABLE* statement. In the *ALTER TABLE* statement, you must specify whether you are altering, adding, or dropping a constraint. For example, the following *ALTER TABLE* statement adds a column with a unique constraint to Table01:

```
ALTER TABLE table01 ADD column02 int
CONSTRAINT uk_column02
UNIQUE
```

The unique constraint is named uk_column02 and is a nonclustered index. A unique constraint creates a nonclustered index unless CLUSTERED is specified and a clustered index does not already exist for the table.

Index Administration

Maintenance tasks include rebuilding, deleting, and renaming indexes. Delete an index if it is no longer needed or if it is corrupted. Rebuild an index to maintain a custom fill factor or to reorganize the storage of the index data so that the index is contiguous in the database. Rename an index if your naming conventions change or if an existing index doesn't follow existing naming conventions.

Deleting an Index

Unused indexes for tables that are frequently updated with new information should be removed. Otherwise, SQL Server will waste processing resources to maintain unused indexes. Use the following syntax to delete an index:

DROP INDEX *table_name.index_name* | *view_name.index_name* [,...*n*]

The table name or view name must be included in the *DROP INDEX* statement. You can drop multiple indexes in a single *DROP INDEX* statement. The following example deletes a table and a view index:

```
DROP INDEX table01.index01, view01.index02
```

You can delete an index using the Object Browser in Query Analyzer or using Enterprise Manager. In the Object Browser, right-click an index name and then click Delete. In Enterprise Manager, open the Manage Indexes dialog box, select an index, and then click Delete.

Rebuilding an Index

If a clustered index exists on a table or view, any nonclustered indexes on the same table or view will use the clustered index as their index key. Dropping a clustered index by using the *DROP INDEX* statement causes all nonclustered indexes to be rebuilt so that they use a RID (rather than an index key) as a bookmark. If a clustered index is then re-created by using the *CREATE INDEX* statement, all nonclustered indexes are rebuilt so that the clustered index key replaces the RID as the index bookmark. For large tables or views that have many indexes, this rebuild process is resource intensive. Fortunately, there are other ways to rebuild an index. There are two alternatives to deleting and re-creating an index: issuing the *DBCC DBREINDEX* statement or specifying the DROP_EXISTING clause in the *CREATE INDEX* statement.

The *DBCC DBREINDEX* statement rebuilds one or more indexes on a table or view by using a single statement. This approach saves you from having to issue multiple *DROP INDEX* and *CREATE INDEX* statements to rebuild multiple indexes. To rebuild all indexes, instruct *DBCC DBREINDEX* to rebuild the clustered index, thereby causing a rebuild of all indexes on a table or view. Alternatively, you can simply leave the index name out of the *DBCC DBREINDEX* statement, and when the statement runs, all indexes are rebuilt. *DBCC DBREINDEX* is especially useful for rebuilding indexes on primary key and unique constraints, because unlike *DROP INDEX*, it isn't necessary to drop the constraint first before rebuilding the index. For example, the following statement will fail to delete an index on a primary key constraint named Pk_Column01:

```
DROP INDEX table01.pk_column01
```

However, the following *DBCC DBREINDEX* statement will rebuild the index for the primary key constraint:

```
DBCC DBREINDEX (table01, pk_column01, 60)
```

The index Pk_column01 on the primary key constraint Pk_column01 is rebuilt with a fill factor of 60 percent. *DBCC DBREINDEX* is commonly used to reestablish fill factor settings on indexes and thus decreases the frequency of page splits.

The DROP_EXISTING clause of the *CREATE INDEX* statement replaces a table or view index of the same name. As a result, the index is rebuilt. DROP_EXISTING brings efficiencies to the rebuild process (much like *DBCC DBREINDEX*). If you use *CREATE INDEX* with the DROP_EXISTING clause to replace a clustered index with an identical clustered index key, the nonclustered indexes are not rebuilt—and the table is not resorted. If the clustered index key is changed, the nonclustered indexes are rebuilt only once—and the table is resorted.

Renaming an Index

You can rename an index by deleting and recreating it. A simpler way to rebuild an index, however, is with the *sp_rename* system stored procedure. The following example demonstrates how to rename an index named index01 to index02:

```
sp_rename @objname = 'table01.index01', @newname = 'index02', @objtype =
  'INDEX'
```

The table qualifier was included with the @objname input parameter. If you don't include the table name, the system stored procedure is incapable of locating the index to rename. However, the table qualifier was intentionally excluded from the @newname input parameter. If you do include the table name with the new index name, the index will be named after the table. For example, if you specify @newname = table01.index02, then the index is named table01.index02 instead of index02. The table qualifier is unnecessary on @newname because the table is assumed from @objname. The @objtype input parameter must be set to "INDEX" or the system stored procedure will be incapable of locating the correct object type to rename.

Choosing to Index

Thus far, you have learned what an index is and how to create and administer it. Additionally, in Exercise 1 you saw examples of how to increase the frequency of index use by carefully designing your queries and indexes. This section provides additional guidelines on determining when to create an index and deciding which index properties to configure for optimal performance. Keep in mind that only one clustered index is allowed on a table or view. Therefore, a carefully designed clustered index is more important then a carefully designed nonclustered index.

You create indexes to accommodate the types of queries that users commonly run against a database. The Query Optimizer then uses one or more indexes to satisfy the query. The following query types, separately or in combination, benefit from indexes:

- **Exact match queries.**   Queries that use the WHERE clause for finding a specific value:

```
SELECT contactname, customerid
FROM customers
WHERE customerid = 'bergs'
```

A clustered index is a good choice for exact match queries if the WHERE clause returns a distinct value. For this reason, creating a clustered index is the default for primary key constraints. Online transaction processing (OLTP) applications also benefit from clustered indexes on unique keys.

Use a nonclustered index for an exact match query that does not return a unique record. For example, if users often query on a specific first name and last name, such as Bob Smith, an exact match query might return multiple records from the database.

- **Wildcard queries.**   Queries that use the LIKE clause for finding values:

```
SELECT contactname, customerid
FROM customers
WHERE customerid LIKE 'b1%'
```

Wildcard queries starting with the percentage sign (%) are not aided by indexes, because index keys start with a specific character or numeric value.

- **Range queries.**   Queries that search for a sequence of values:

```
SELECT contactname, customerid FROM customers WHERE customerid
BETWEEN 'b%' AND 'c%'
```

Clustered indexes are an excellent choice for this type of query because the index pages are physically sorted in sequential order. Therefore, once the first record is located, it is likely that the other records in the range will be adjacent or at least nearby.

- **Table joins.**   Queries that build a result set based on values in another table:

```
SELECT c.contactname, c.customerid c, o.orderid
FROM customers c INNER JOIN orders o ON c.customerid = o.customerid
```

- **Sorted output without an ORDER BY clause.**   You saw examples of this situation in Lesson 1 and Exercise 1.

If a specific column or combination of columns is often sorted in a specific way, consider a clustered index to accommodate the sort order.

- **Covered queries.**   Queries that make use of covering indexes.

  You should keep clustered index keys as small as possible, because nonclustered indexes use the clustered index key as their bookmark. As a result, a wide clustered index key creates large, nonclustered indexes. If you decide to create a clustered index as covering, use as few columns as possible to cover your queries. If you need a wide index for a covered query, create a nonclustered index as a covering index.

- **Queries that return large result sets.**

  ```
  SELECT * FROM customers
  ```

  For a large result set, don't create a covering index that includes all columns. Instead, create a clustered index on one or a few columns. The Query Optimizer will use the clustered index to look up matching values.

  Creating indexes for almost every query that you can imagine or creating very wide index keys containing many columns will negatively impact processor performance and increase disk capacity requirements to store the indexes. Processor performance is impacted by indexes because table and view modifications require indexes to be updated regularly. Use indexes sparingly on tables and views that undergo frequent modification. Do not use indexes for small tables and views that change infrequently, because an index could actually decrease the speed at which records are returned from a query. Conversely, indexing large tables will significantly improve query performance.

Index Performance

Designing and maintaining appropriate indexes for a database is difficult, especially if common database queries change or if the database structure is modified. SQL Server includes the Index Tuning wizard to assist you with choosing indexes for a table or view. The Index Tuning wizard analyzes a representative sample of database activity (a workload) to recommend an ideal set of indexes for a database. If the database workload or structure changes, rerun the Index Tuning wizard to reanalyze indexes for a database. The workload input for the wizard can be a SQL script (.SQL) file, a SQL Profiler Trace (.TRC or .LOG) file, a trace table, or a script selected in Query Analyzer.

Index Statistics

SQL Server maintains statistics concerning the distribution of values in columns that indexes use. The Query Optimizer depends on these statistics to make accurate choices on the appropriate indexes to use for a query. You can disable statistics updates by using the STATISTICS_NORECOMPUTE clause of the *CREATE INDEX* statement. This clause disables the automatic re-computation of outdated index statistics. Disabling statistics is inadvisable if a table or view changes frequently. To restore automatic statistics updating, execute the *UPDATE STATISTICS* statement on the index without including the NORECOMPUTE clause, or you can use the *sp_autostats* system stored procedure. The *sp_autostats* procedure displays or changes the automatic UPDATE STATISTICS setting.

Note   For more information about UPDATE STATISTICS and *sp_autostats*, refer to SQL Server Books Online. For more details about index performance, refer to Chapter 14, "SQL Server Monitoring and Tuning," and SQL Server Books Online.

Exercise 2: Creating a Clustered Index

In this exercise, you will create a clustered index and some nonclustered indexes for several tables in the BookShopDB database and run several *SELECT* statements to observe their use. You will then administer the indexes by changing the fill factor, renaming the index, and dropping the indexes from the database.

▶   **To create and test a nonclustered index**

1. Open Query Analyzer and connect to your local server.

2. In the Editor pane of the Query window, enter and execute the following code:

```
USE bookshopdb
sp_helpindex books
```

The Results pane in the Grids tab shows that a clustered, unique index on the TitleID index key exists for the primary key constraint Books_pk.

You observe how employees access data in the Books table, and you cannot justify changing this index in any way. Employees often query on the TitleID, Title, and Sold columns to let customers know if a book is available. The Title column value can be long, so you decide that it would be best to create a nonclustered index to cover a query on the TitleID, Title, and Sold columns.

3. In the Editor pane of the Query window, enter and execute the following code:

```
CREATE NONCLUSTERED INDEX TitleSoldStatus
ON books(title, sold)
```

There could be two titles of the same name that have the same sold status. Therefore, this index is being created as nonunique (the UNIQUE keyword is not included).

4. If the Execution Plan tab does not appear in the Results pane of the Query Analyzer, click Query and then click Show Execution Plan.

5. To test that the nonclustered index is used by the Query Optimizer, enter and execute the following code in the Editor pane of the Query window:

```
SELECT titleid, title, sold from books
```

The result set appears in the Grids tab of the Results pane.

6. Click the Execution Plan tab and move the mouse pointer over the Books.Title-Sold... index.

   A box appears, showing index scan statistics for the TitleSoldStatus index. Notice that the fully qualified index name appears at the bottom of the box.

7. Why didn't the Query Optimizer use the clustered index Books_pk?

▶ **To prepare a table for a new index configuration**

1. In the Editor pane of the Query window, enter and execute the following code:

```
sp_helpindex orders
```

   The Results pane in the Grids tab shows that Orders_pk is a clustered, unique index containing the OrderID index key. Orders_pk is a primary key constraint.

   You observe that employees usually query on both the OrderID and the CustomerID in the Orders table; therefore, you decide to create a clustered index containing the OrderID and CustomerID columns. To accomplish this task, you must change the Orders_pk clustered index to a nonclustered index.

2. In the Editor pane of the Query window, enter and execute the following code:

```
CREATE UNIQUE NONCLUSTERED INDEX orders_pk
ON orders(orderid)
WITH DROP_EXISTING
```

   The Results pane in the Grids tab displays an error message, indicating that you cannot convert a clustered index to a nonclustered index.

   To change a clustered index to a nonclustered index, you must drop and re-create the index. Because the index is part of a primary key constraint and a foreign key constraint on another table, you must use *ALTER TABLE* to drop the constraints, starting with the foreign key constraint.

3. In the Editor pane of the Query window, enter and execute the following code:

```
ALTER TABLE bookorders
DROP CONSTRAINT orderid_fk
```

   The foreign key constraint is dropped from the BookOrders table. Any foreign key constraints must be removed before primary key constraints are dropped. Later in this practice, you will re-create the foreign key constraint.

   Next, you will drop the primary key constraint.

4. In the Editor pane of the Query window, enter and execute the following code:

```
ALTER TABLE orders
DROP CONSTRAINT orders_pk
```

   The primary key constraint is dropped from the Orders table.

   In the next practice, you will re-create this constraint and the foreign key constraint after you create a clustered index for the Orders table.

▶ **To create a clustered index**

1. In the Editor pane of the Query window, enter the following code:

```
CREATE UNIQUE CLUSTERED INDEX CustomerOrder
ON orders(customerid, orderid)
WITH FILLFACTOR = 70
```

This Transact-SQL statement creates a clustered index named CustomerOrder with a composite index key. It is a composite key because it contains the CustomerID and OrderID columns.

2. Execute the code.

The CustomerOrder clustered index is created from the Orders table. For efficiency, you can create the clustered index before creating the nonclustered index. This sequence is more efficient than creating the nonclustered index first because the nonclustered index is built only once, using the clustered index key as its bookmark.

Now that you have created the clustered index, you will restore the primary key constraint and the foreign key constraint, starting with the primary key constraint.

3. In the Editor pane of the Query window, enter and execute the following code:

```
ALTER TABLE orders
ADD CONSTRAINT orders_pk
PRIMARY KEY NONCLUSTERED (orderid)
```

The primary key constraint is re-created on the Orders table. The index of this primary key constraint is nonclustered. Notice that the NONCLUSTERED keyword is specified. This keyword is unnecessary, however, because a clustered index already exists for the table. It is included as good measure to document the intent of the programmer.

Now that you have created the primary key constraint, you will re-create the foreign key constraint.

4. In the Editor pane of the Query window, enter and execute the following code:

```
ALTER TABLE bookorders
ADD CONSTRAINT orderid_fk
FOREIGN KEY (orderid)
REFERENCES orders(orderid)
```

5. In the Editor pane of the Query window, enter and execute the following code:

```
sp_helpindex orders
GO
sp_helpindex bookorders
```

From the result sets appearing in the Results pane, review the indexes configured for the Orders and BookOrders tables.

▶ **To rename and drop indexes**

1. In the Editor pane of the Query window, enter the following code:

```
sp_rename
@objname ='orders.customerorder',
@newname = 'IN_CustomerOrder',
@objtype = 'INDEX'
```

The CustomerOrder index is being renamed to IN_CustomerOrder to comply with a company nomenclature policy that all indexes not tied to a primary key constraint must be prefixed with IN_.

2. Execute the code.

The Results pane in the Grids tab displays a message indicating that the index was renamed to IN_CustomerOrder and displays a caution message that changing an object name could break scripts and stored procedures that use the object.

Next, you will delete the IN_CustomerOrder index.

3. In the Editor pane of the Query window, enter and execute the following code:

```
DROP INDEX orders.in_customerorder, books.titlesoldstatus
```

The IN_CustomerOrder index is deleted from the Orders table, and the Title-SoldStatus index is deleted from the Books table.

4. In the Editor pane of the Query window, enter and execute the following code:

```
CREATE UNIQUE CLUSTERED INDEX orders_pk
ON orders(orderid)
WITH DROP_EXISTING
```

The Orders_pk index on the Orders_pk primary key constraint is converted from a unique, nonclustered index to a unique, clustered index. Notice that you converted a nonclustered index to a clustered index here, but earlier in this exercise, a clustered index could not be directly converted to a nonclustered index.

Lesson Summary

You create indexes by using the *CREATE INDEX* statement or by using graphical tools such as the Object Browser in Query Analyzer or Enterprise Manager. In addition, Enterprise Manager contains the Create Index wizard to step you through index creation. Indexes are created automatically for primary key and unique constraints. These constraints are created by using the *CREATE TABLE* and *ALTER TABLE* statements or a graphical tool such as Enterprise Manager. When creating an index, you specify index properties, such as index type, sort order, and fill factor.

Administration tasks include rebuilding, deleting, and renaming indexes. Delete an index with the *DROP INDEX* statement or by using graphical tools such as the Object Brower in Query Analyzer. An index is most efficiently rebuilt with the *DBCC DBREINDEX* statement or the DROP_EXISTING clause of the *CREATE INDEX* statement. Use the *sp_rename* system stored procedure to change the name of an index.

Careful index design is critical to improving query performance without significantly degrading database performance. Create indexes based on the most common queries performed against the database. Indexes are especially useful for exact match queries, certain types of wildcard queries, range queries, queries involving table joins, sorted output queries, covered queries, and queries that create large result sets. Use the Index Tuning wizard to aid in the design of appropriate queries. The Index Tuning wizard analyzes the database's workload and then suggests appropriate indexes to accommodate database activity. SQL Server automatically maintains statistics regarding the distribution of column values that make up an index key. The Query Optimizer depends on these statistics to satisfy query requests appropriately.

Review

The following questions are intended to reinforce key information presented in this chapter. If you are unable to answer a question, review the appropriate lesson and then try the question again. You can find answers to the questions in the Appendix, "Questions and Answers."

1. Can a clustered index also be a unique index?

2. If you query a Customers table containing a clustered index on the primary key column, CustomerID, and a nonclustered index on the LastName column, is the nonclustered index a covering index for the following Transact-SQL statement?

   ```
   SELECT LastName, CustomerID FROM Customers WHERE LastName LIKE 'nej'
   ```

3. Is a composite index key always part of a covering index?

4. How does the global fill factor affect existing indexes and new indexes where a fill factor is not specified?

5. How do you maintain a fill factor in existing indexes?

6. What type of index can assist the following query?

   ```
   SELECT productname FROM products WHERE productname LIKE '%tool'
   ```

7. You create the following composite index:

   ```
   CREATE UNIQUE CLUSTERED INDEX index01
   ON employees(socialsecuritynumber, lastname)
   ```

   Is Index01 ideal for the following query? Explain your answer.

   ```
   SELECT socialsecuritynumber, lastname
   FROM employees
   WHERE lastname = 'kaviani'
   ```

8. Why is it unwise to create wide, clustered index keys?

9. Which index type, clustered or nonclustered, must be most carefully designed? Explain your answer.

10. If a table contains a single nonclustered index, what is its bookmark?

11. What is the default sort order for an index key?

12. You wish to create a nonclustered index on a view in SQL Server 2000 Enterprise Edition, but an error message is returned indicating that you cannot create a nonclustered index on the view. What is the most likely reason for this error message?

C H A P T E R   1 2

Managing SQL Server Transactions and Locks

About This Chapter

SQL Server uses transactions and locks to ensure the consistency and integrity of each database, despite errors that might occur in the system. A transaction is a logical unit of work that consists of a series of statements, such as *SELECT* or *UPDATE* statements. Locks prevent conflicts so that users cannot read or modify data that other users are in the process of changing. Transactions use locking to prevent users from modifying data affected by transactions that have not been completed. This chapter introduces you to the fundamentals of transactions and locks and then describes how transactions and locks are used to process data modifications.

Before You Begin

To complete the lessons in this chapter, you must have:

- SQL Server 2000 Enterprise Edition installed on a Microsoft Windows 2000 Server computer.
- The ability to log on to the Windows 2000 Server computer and to SQL Server as the Windows 2000 Administrator.
- Completed the exercises in Chapter 3, "Designing a SQL Server Database," Chapter 4, "Implementing SQL Server Databases and Tables," Chapter 5, "Implementing Data Integrity," and Chapter 7, "Managing and Manipulating Data."

Lesson 1: Transaction and Locking Architecture

SQL Server uses transactions to process a set of Transact-SQL statements as a unit. As a transaction is executed, locks are used to prevent other users from accessing the data affected by that transaction. To support transactional processing, SQL Server contains a number of architectural components, including transaction logs, concurrency control, locks, and support for distributed queries. This lesson discusses each of these components and provides an overview of how they support transactions in SQL Server.

After this lesson, you will be able to:

- Identify and describe the architectural components in SQL Server that support transactions.

Estimated lesson time: 30 minutes

Transaction Log Architecture

Every SQL Server database has a transaction log that records all transactions and the database modifications made by each transaction. This record of transactions and their modifications supports three operations:

- **Recovery of individual transactions.**   If an application issues a *ROLLBACK* statement or if SQL Server detects an error (such as the loss of communication with a client), the log records are used to roll back any modifications made during an incomplete transaction.

- **Recovery of all incomplete transactions when SQL Server is started.**   If a server running SQL Server fails, the databases might be left in a state where some modifications were never written from the buffer cache to the data files, and there might be some modifications from incomplete transactions in the data files. When a copy of SQL Server is started, it runs a recovery of each database. Every modification recorded in the log that was not written to the data files is rolled forward. Every incomplete transaction found in the transaction log is then rolled back to ensure that the integrity of the database is preserved.

- **Rolling a restored database forward to the point of failure.**   After the loss of a database, as is possible if a hard drive fails on a server that does not have a Redundant Array of Independent Disks (RAID), you can restore the database to the point of failure. You first restore the last full or differential database backup and then restore the sequence of transaction log backups to the point of failure. As you restore each log backup, SQL Server reapplies all of the modifications recorded in the log to roll forward all of the transactions. When the last log backup is restored, SQL Server then uses the log information to roll back all transactions that were not complete at that point.

The transaction log is not implemented as a table but as a separate file or set of files in the database. The log cache is managed separately from the buffer cache for data pages, resulting in simple, fast, and robust code within the database engine. The format of log records and pages is not constrained to follow the format of data pages.

You can implement the transaction log on several files. You can also define the files to autogrow as required, which reduces the potential of running out of space in the transaction log and reduces administrative overhead. The mechanism for truncating unused parts of the log is quick and has a minimal effect on transaction throughput.

Write-Ahead Transaction Log

SQL Server 2000, like many relational databases, uses a write-ahead log. A write-ahead log ensures that no data modifications are written to disk before the associated log record.

SQL Server maintains a buffer cache into which it reads data pages when data must be retrieved. Data modifications are not made directly to disk but are instead made to the copy of the page in the buffer cache. The modification is not written to disk until either the database is checkpointed or until the modifications are written to disk so that the buffer can be used to hold a new page. Writing a modified data page from the buffer cache to disk is called flushing the page. A page modified in the cache but not yet written to disk is called a dirty page.

At the time a modification is made to a page in the buffer, a log record is built into the log cache and records the modification. This log record must be written to disk before the associated dirty page is flushed from the buffer cache to disk. If the dirty page were flushed before the log record, it would create a modification on disk that could not be rolled back if the server failed before the log record was written to disk. SQL Server has logic that prevents a dirty page from being flushed before the associated log record. Because log records are always written ahead of the associated data pages, the log is called a write-ahead log.

Transaction Log Logical Architecture

The SQL Server transaction log operates logically as if it is a serial string of log records. A log sequence number (LSN) identifies each log record. Each new log record is written to the logical end of the log with an LSN higher than the LSN of the record before it.

Log records for data modifications record either the logical operation performed or record before-and-after images of the modified data. A before image is a copy of the data before the operation is performed; an after image is a copy of the data after the operation has been performed.

Many types of operations are recorded in the transaction log:

- The start and end of each transaction
- Every data modification (insert, update, or delete)
- Every extent allocation or deallocation
- The creation or dropping of a table or index

Log records are stored in a serial sequence as they are created. Each log record is stamped with the ID of the transaction to which it belongs. For each transaction, all log records associated with the transaction are singly linked in a chain using backward pointers that speed the rollback of the transaction.

Rollback statements are also logged. Each transaction reserves space on the transaction log to ensure that enough log space exists to support a rollback if an error is encountered. This reserve space is freed when the transaction is completed. The amount of space reserved depends on the operations performed in the transaction but is generally equal to the amount of space used to log each operation.

Checkpoints and the Active Portion of the Log

Checkpoints minimize the portion of the log that must be processed during the full recovery of a database. During a full recovery, you must perform two types of actions:

- The log might contain records of modifications that were not flushed to disk before the system stopped. These modifications must be rolled forward.
- All of the modifications associated with incomplete transactions (transactions for which there is no COMMIT or ROLLBACK log record) must be rolled back.

Checkpoints flush dirty data and log pages from the buffer cache of the current database, minimizing the number of modifications that have to be rolled forward during a recovery. A checkpoint writes to the log file a record marking the start of the checkpoint and stores information recorded for the checkpoint in a chain of checkpoint log records. The LSN of the start of this chain is written to the database boot page.

Checkpoints occur for the following events:

- When a *CHECKPOINT* statement is executed
- When an *ALTER DATABASE* statement is used to change a database option
- When an instance of SQL Server is stopped by executing a *SHUTDOWN* statement or by using the SQL Server Service Control Manager to stop the service from running an instance of the database engine
- When an instance of SQL Server periodically generates automatic checkpoints in each database in order to reduce the amount of time that the instance would take to recover the database

SQL Server 2000 always generates automatic checkpoints. The interval between automatic checkpoints is based on the number of records in the log, not on the amount of time. The time interval between automatic checkpoints can vary greatly. The time interval can be long if few modifications are made in the database. Automatic checkpoints occur frequently if a considerable amount of data is modified.

Truncating the Transaction Log

If log records were never deleted from the transaction log, the logical log would grow until it filled all of the available space on the disks that hold the physical log files. At some point in time, old log records no longer necessary for recovering or restoring a database must be deleted to make way for new log records. The process of deleting these log records to reduce the size of the logical log is called truncating the log.

The active portion of the transaction log can never be truncated. The active portion is needed to recover the database at any time, so you must have the log images needed to roll back all incomplete transactions. The log images must always be present in the database in case the server fails, because the images are required to recover the database when the server is restarted. The record at the start of the active portion of the log is identified by the minimum recovery log sequence number (MinLSN).

Log truncation occurs at the completion of any *BACKUP LOG* statement and occurs every time a checkpoint is processed, provided the database is using the simple recovery model.

Transaction Log Physical Architecture

The transaction log in a database maps over one or more physical files. Conceptually, the log file is a serial string of log records. Physically, the sequence of log records must be stored efficiently in the set of physical files that implement the transaction log.

SQL Server 2000 segments each physical log file internally into a number of virtual log files. Virtual log files have no fixed size, and there is no fixed number of virtual log files for a physical log file. SQL Server chooses the size of the virtual log files dynamically while creating or extending log files. SQL Server tries to maintain a small number of virtual files. The size of the virtual files after a log file name extension is based on the size of the existing log and the size of the new file increment. The size or number of virtual log files cannot be configured or set by administrators; rather, it is determined dynamically by the SQL Server code.

The only time virtual log files affect system performance is if the log files are defined with small size and growth_increment values. If these log files grow to a large size through many small increments, they will have a lot of virtual log files, which can slow down recovery. The recommendation is for log files to be defined with a size value that is close to the final size needed. Also, they should have a relatively large growth_increment value.

Shrinking the Transaction Log

The physical size of the log file is reduced when a *DBCC SHRINKDATABASE* statement is executed, when a *DBCC SHRINKFILE* statement referencing a log file is executed, or when an autoshrink operation occurs.

Shrinking a log depends first on truncating the log. Log truncation does not reduce the size of a physical log file; instead, it reduces the size of the logical log and marks as inactive the virtual logs that do not hold any part of the logical log. A log shrink operation removes enough inactive virtual logs to reduce the log file to the requested size.

The unit of size reduction is a virtual log. For example, if you have a 600 MB log file that has been divided into six 100 MB virtual logs, the size of the log file can only be reduced in 100 MB increments. The file size can be reduced to sizes such as 500 MB or 400 MB, but it cannot be reduced to sizes such as 433 MB or 525 MB.

Virtual logs that hold part of the logical log cannot be freed. If all the virtual logs in a log file hold parts of the logical log, the file cannot be shrunk until a truncation marks one or more of the virtual logs at the end of the physical log as inactive.

When any file is shrunk, the space freed must come from the end of the file. When a transaction log file is shrunk, enough virtual logs from the end of the file are freed to reduce the log to the size that the user requested. The target_size specified by the user is rounded to the next-highest virtual log boundary. For example, if a user specifies a target_size of 325 MB for our sample 600 MB file with 100 MB virtual log files, the last two virtual log files are removed. The new file size is 400 MB.

In SQL Server 2000, a *DBCC SHRINKDATABASE* or *DBCC SHRINKFILE* operation attempts to shrink the physical log file to the requested size immediately (subject to rounding) if the following conditions are met:

- If no part of the logical log is in the virtual logs beyond the target_size mark, the virtual logs after the target_size mark are freed, and the successful DBCC statement is completed with no messages.
- If part of the logical log is in the virtual logs beyond the target_size mark, SQL Server 2000 frees as much space as possible and issues an informational message. The message tells you what actions you need to perform to get the logical log out of the virtual logs at the end of the file. After you perform this action, you can then reissue the DBCC statement to free the remaining space.

In the following statement, *DBCC SHRINKFILE* is used to reduce the TestDB_Log file in the TestDB database to 1 MB:

```
USE TestDB
GO
DBCC SHRINKFILE (TestDB_Log, 1)
GO
```

Concurrency Architecture

When many people attempt to modify data in a database at the same time, a system of controls must be implemented so that modifications made by one person do not adversely affect those of another person. This process is referred to as concurrency control.

Two classifications exist for instituting concurrency control:

- **Pessimistic concurrency control.**   A system of locks prevents users from modifying data in a way that affects other users. After a user performs an action that causes a lock to be applied, other users cannot perform actions that would conflict with the lock until the owner releases it. This process is called pessimistic control because it is mainly used in environments where there is high contention for data.
- **Optimistic concurrency control.**   In optimistic concurrency control, users do not lock data when they read it. When an update is performed, the system checks to see whether another user changed the data after it was read. If another user updated the data, an error occurs. Typically, the user who receives the error rolls back the transaction and starts again. This situation is called optimistic because it is mainly used in environments where there is low contention for data.

SQL Server 2000 supports a wide range of optimistic and pessimistic concurrency control mechanisms. Users specify the type of concurrency control by specifying a transaction isolation level for a connection and concurrency options on cursors. These attributes can be defined by using either Transact-SQL statements or through the properties and attributes of database application programming interfaces (APIs) such as ADO, OLE DB, and ODBC.

Locking Architecture

A lock is an object that software uses to indicate that a user has some dependency on a resource. The software does not allow other users to perform operations on the resource that would adversely affect the dependencies of the user who owns the lock. Locks are managed internally by system software and are acquired and released based on actions that the user takes.

SQL Server 2000 uses locks to implement pessimistic concurrency control among multiple users who are performing modifications in a database at the same time. By default, SQL Server manages both transactions and locks on a per-connection basis. For example, if an application opens two SQL Server connections, locks acquired by one connection cannot be shared with the other connection. Neither connection can acquire locks that would conflict with locks held by the other connection. Only bound connections are not affected by this rule.

SQL Server locks are applied at various levels of granularity in the database. Locks can be acquired on rows, pages, keys, ranges of keys, indexes, tables, or databases. SQL Server dynamically determines the appropriate level at which to place locks for each Transact-SQL statement. The level at which locks are acquired can vary for different objects referenced by the same query. For example, one table might be very small and have a table lock applied, while another larger table might have row locks applied. The level at which locks are applied does not have to be specified by users and needs no configuration by administrators. Each instance of SQL Server ensures that locks granted at one level of granularity respect locks granted at another level.

Several lock modes exist: shared, update, exclusive, intent, and schema. The lock mode indicates the level of dependency that the connection has on the locked object. SQL Server controls how the lock modes interact. For example, an exclusive lock cannot be obtained if other connections hold shared locks on the resource.

Locks are held for the length of time needed to protect the resource at the level requested.

If a connection attempts to acquire a lock that conflicts with a lock held by another connection, the connection attempting to acquire the lock is blocked until one of the following events occurs:

- The conflicting lock is freed and the connection acquires the lock that it requested.
- The timeout interval for the connection expires. By default, there is no timeout interval, but some applications set a timeout interval to prevent an indefinite wait.

If several connections become blocked while waiting for conflicting locks on a single resource, the locks are granted on a first-come, first-served basis as the preceding connections free their locks.

SQL Server has an algorithm to detect deadlocks, a condition in which two connections have blocked each other. If an instance of SQL Server detects a deadlock, it will terminate one transaction, allowing the other to continue.

SQL Server might dynamically escalate or de-escalate the granularity or type of locks. For example, if an update acquires a large number of row locks and has locked a significant percentage of a table, the row locks are escalated to a table lock. If a table lock is acquired, the row locks are released. SQL Server 2000 rarely needs to escalate locks; Query Optimizer usually chooses the correct lock granularity at the time the execution plan is compiled.

Distributed Transaction Architecture

Distributed transactions are transactions that involve resources from two or more sources. SQL Server 2000 supports distributed transactions, allowing users to create transactions that update multiple SQL Server databases and other sources of data.

There are several ways in which applications can include SQL Server 2000 in a distributed transaction:

- If an application has a local transaction and issues a distributed query, the local transaction is escalated to a distributed transaction.
- A *BEGIN DISTRIBUTED TRANSACTION* statement can be issued.
- If an application has a local transaction and the option *REMOTE_PROC_TRANSACTIONS* is set to ON, calling a remote stored procedure escalates the local transaction to a distributed transaction.
- Applications using the Microsoft OLE DB Provider for SQL Server or the SQL Server ODBC driver can use OLE DB methods or ODBC functions to have a SQL Server connection join a distributed transaction that the application started.

Exercise 1: Accessing and Modifying the Transaction Log

In this exercise, you will view the properties of the BookShopDB database and change the size of the transaction log. You will then use a Transact-SQL statement to reduce the size of the log file. To perform this exercise, you should be logged into your Windows 2000 Server computer as Administrator.

▶ **To view the properties of the BookShopDB database and change the size of the transaction log**

1. Open Enterprise Manager.
2. Expand the console tree until the BookShopDB is displayed.
3. Right-click the BookShopDB node and click Properties.

   The BookShopDB Properties dialog box appears.
4. Click the Transaction Log tab.

   Notice that the space allocated for the transaction log is 1 MB and that the file is set to automatically grow by 10 percent.
5. In the Space Allocated (MB) box of the BookShopDB_Log row, change 1 to **3**.
6. Click OK.

   The transaction log is allocated 3 MB of space.
7. Leave Enterprise Manager open for a later procedure.

▶ **To shrink the transaction log**

1. Open Query Analyzer and connect to your local server.
2. In the Editor pane of the Query window, enter the following Transact-SQL code:

```
USE BookShopDB
GO
DBCC SHRINKFILE (BookShopDB_Log, 1)
GO
```

   In this statement, you are shrinking the size of the BookShopDB_Log file in the BookShopDB database from 3 MB to 1 MB.
3. Execute the Transact-SQL statement.

   Information about the log file is displayed in the Grids tab of the Results pane.
4. Close Query Analyzer.

▶ **To view the properties of the BookShopDB database and the transaction log**

1. In Enterprise Manager, right-click the BookShopDB node and click Properties.

   The BookShopDB Properties dialog box appears.
2. Click the Transaction Log tab.

   Notice that the space allocated for the transaction log is once again 1 MB.
3. Close Enterprise Manager.

Lesson Summary

To support transactional processing, SQL Server contains a number of architectural components, including transaction logs, concurrency control, locks, and support for distributed queries. Every SQL Server database has a transaction log that records all transactions and the database modifications made by each transaction. This record of transactions and their modifications supports three operations: recovery of individual transactions, recovery of all incomplete transactions when SQL Server is started, and rolling a restored database forward to the point of failure. SQL Server 2000, like many relational databases, uses a write-ahead log to ensure that no data modifications are written to disk before the associated log record. The SQL Server transaction log operates logically as if it is a serial string of log records. The physical size of the log file is reduced when a *DBCC SHRINK-DATABASE* statement is executed, when a *DBCC SHRINKFILE* statement referencing a log file is executed, or when an autoshrink operation occurs. In SQL Server, a system of controls is implemented so that modifications made by one person do not adversely affect those of another. SQL Server 2000 uses locks to implement pessimistic concurrency control among multiple users who are performing modifications in a database at the same time. SQL Server locks are applied at various levels of granularity in the database. Distributed transactions are transactions that involve resources from two or more sources. SQL Server 2000 supports distributed transactions, enabling users to create transactions that update multiple SQL Server databases and other sources of data.

Lesson 2: Managing SQL Server Transactions

Almost all Transact-SQL statements can run in a transaction. If the transaction does not generate any errors when it is being executed, all of the modifications in the transaction become a permanent part of the database. All transactions that include data modifications will either reach a new point of consistency and become committed or will be rolled back to the original state of consistency. Transactions are not left in an intermediate state if the database is not consistent. There are several different types of transactions. Each transaction must exhibit specific characteristics to qualify as a transaction. In this lesson, you will learn about these characteristics and about the types of transactions supported in SQL Server. You will also learn how to use Transact-SQL to start and end a transaction.

After this lesson, you will be able to:
- Identify the characteristics of a transaction.
- Define the various types of transactions.
- Use Transact-SQL to start and stop a transaction.

Estimated lesson time: 35 minutes

Overview of SQL Server Transactions

A transaction is a sequence of operations performed as a single, logical unit of work. To qualify as a transaction, a logical unit of work must exhibit four properties, called the ACID properties (atomicity, consistency, isolation, and durability):

- **Atomicity.**   A transaction must be an atomic unit of work (either all of its data modifications are performed, or none of them is performed).
- **Consistency.**   When completed, a transaction must leave all data in a consistent state. In a relational database, all rules must be applied to the transaction's modifications in order to maintain all data integrity. All internal data structures, such as B-tree indexes or doubly linked lists, must be correct at the end of the transaction.
- **Isolation.**   Modifications made by concurrent transactions must be isolated from the modifications made by any other concurrent transactions. A transaction either sees data in the state it was in before another concurrent transaction modified it or it sees the data after the second transaction has completed, but it does not see an intermediate state. This situation is referred to as serializability, because it results in the capability to reload the starting data and replay a series of transactions in order to end up with the data in the same state it was in after the original transactions were performed.

- **Durability.**   After a transaction has completed, its effects are permanently in place in the system. The modifications persist even in the event of a system failure.

SQL Server provides locking facilities that preserve transaction isolation. SQL Server also provides facilities that ensure transaction durability. Even if the server hardware, operating system, or SQL Server itself fails, SQL Server uses the transaction logs, upon restart, to automatically roll back any uncompleted transactions to the point of the system failure. In addition, SQL Server provides transaction management features that enforce transaction atomicity and consistency. After a transaction has started, it must be successfully completed or SQL Server will undo all of the data modifications made since the transaction started.

Applications control transactions mainly by specifying when a transaction starts and ends. You can specify this information by using either Transact-SQL statements or database API functions. The system must also be capable of correctly handling errors that terminate a transaction before it completes.

Transactions are managed at the connection level. When a transaction is started on a connection, all Transact-SQL statements executed on that connection are part of the transaction until the transaction ends.

Specifying Transaction Boundaries

You can identify when SQL Server transactions start and end by using Transact-SQL statements or by using API functions and methods:

- **Transact-SQL statements.**   Use the *BEGIN TRANSACTION*, *COMMIT TRANSACTION*, *COMMIT WORK*, *ROLLBACK TRANSACTION*, *ROLLBACK WORK*, and *SET IMPLICIT_TRANSACTIONS* statements to delineate transactions. These are primarily used in DB-Library applications and in Transact-SQL scripts, such as the scripts that are run using the osql command-prompt utility.
- **API functions and methods.**   Database APIs such as ODBC, OLE DB, and ADO contain functions or methods used to delineate transactions. These are the primary mechanisms used to control transactions in a SQL Server application.

Each transaction must be managed by only one of these methods. Using both methods on the same transaction can lead to undefined results. For example, you should not use the ODBC API functions to start a transaction and then use the Transact-SQL *COMMIT* statement to complete the transaction. This action would not notify the SQL Server ODBC driver that the transaction was committed. In this case, use the ODBC SQL *EndTran* function to end the transaction.

Transact-SQL Statements Allowed in Transactions

You can use all Transact-SQL statements in a transaction except the following statements:

ALTER DATABASE	*LOAD DATABASE*
BACKUP LOG	*LOAD TRANSACTION*
CREATE DATABASE	*RECONFIGURE*
DISK INIT	*RESTORE DATABASE*
DROP DATABASE	*RESTORE LOG*
DUMP TRANSACTION	*UPDATE STATISTICS*

Also, you cannot use *sp_dboption* to set database options or use any system procedures that modify the master database inside user-defined transactions.

Coding Efficient Transactions

You must keep transactions as short as possible. When a transaction is started, a DBMS must hold many resources to the end of the transaction to protect the ACID properties of the transaction. If data is modified, the modified rows must be protected with exclusive locks that prevent any other transaction from reading the rows, and exclusive locks must be held until the transaction is committed or rolled back. Depending on transaction isolation level settings, *SELECT* statements may acquire locks that must be held until the transaction is committed or rolled back. Especially in systems that have many users, transactions must be kept as short as possible to reduce locking contention for resources between concurrent connections. Long-running, inefficient transactions might not be a problem with a small number of users, but they are intolerable in a system that has thousands of users.

You should use the following guidelines to code efficient transactions:

- Do not require input from users during a transaction.
- Do not open a transaction while browsing through data (if at all possible).
- Keep the transaction as short as possible.
- Make intelligent use of lower transaction isolation levels.
- Make intelligent use of lower cursor concurrency options, such as optimistic concurrency options.
- Access the least amount of data possible while in a transaction.

Avoiding Concurrency Problems

To prevent concurrency problems, manage implicit transactions carefully. When using implicit transactions, the next Transact-SQL statement after *COMMIT* or *ROLLBACK* automatically starts a new transaction. This situation can cause a new transaction to be opened while the application browses through data, or even when it requires input from the user. After completing the last transaction required to protect data modifications, turn off implicit transactions until a transaction is once again required to protect data modifications. This process enables SQL Server to use autocommit mode while the application is browsing data and is getting input from the user.

Errors During Transaction Processing

If a severe error prevents the successful completion of a transaction, SQL Server automatically rolls back the transaction and frees all resources held by the transaction. If the client's network connection to SQL Server is broken, any outstanding transactions for the connection are rolled back when the network notifies SQL Server of the break. If the client application fails or if the client computer goes down or is restarted, the connection breaks and SQL Server rolls back any outstanding transactions when the network notifies it of the break. If the client logs off the application, any outstanding transactions are rolled back.

If a run-time statement error (such as a constraint violation) occurs in a batch, the default behavior in SQL Server is to roll back only the statement that generated the error. You can change this behavior by using the *SET XACT_ABORT* statement. After *SET XACT_ABORT ON* is executed, any run-time statement error causes an automatic rollback of the current transaction. *SET XACT_ABORT* does not affect compile errors (such as syntax errors).

The programmer has the responsibility of coding the application to specify the correct action (*COMMIT* or *ROLLBACK*) if a run-time or compile error occurs.

Types of Transactions

SQL Server supports three types of transactions: explicit, autocommit, and implicit.

Explicit Transactions

An explicit transaction is one in which you explicitly define both the start and the end of the transaction. Explicit transactions were also called user-defined or user-specified transactions in earlier versions of SQL Server.

DB-Library applications and Transact-SQL scripts use the *BEGIN TRANSACTION, COMMIT TRANSACTION, COMMIT WORK, ROLLBACK TRANSACTION*, or *ROLLBACK WORK* Transact-SQL statements to define explicit transactions:

- **BEGIN TRANSACTION.**   Marks the starting point of an explicit transaction for a connection.

- **COMMIT TRANSACTION or COMMIT WORK.**   Used to end a transaction successfully if no errors were encountered. All data modifications made in the transaction become a permanent part of the database. Resources held by the transaction are freed.

- **ROLLBACK TRANSACTION or ROLLBACK WORK.**   Used to erase a transaction in which errors are encountered. All data modified by the transaction is returned to the state it was in at the start of the transaction. Resources held by the transaction are freed.

In the following transaction, the *ROLLBACK TRANSACTION* statement rolls back any changes made by the *UPDATE* statement:

```
BEGIN TRANSACTION
GO
USE Northwind
GO
UPDATE Customers
SET ContactName = 'Hanna Moos'
WHERE CustomerID = 'BLAUS'
GO
ROLLBACK TRANSACTION
GO
```

If a *COMMIT TRANSACTION* statement had been used in this example, rather than a *ROLLBACK TRANSACTION* statement, the update would have been made to the database.

You can also use explicit transactions in the OLE DB, ADO, and ODBC APIs. For more information about using explicit transactions with these APIs, refer to SQL Server Books Online.

Explicit transaction mode lasts only for the duration of the transaction. When the transaction ends, the connection returns to the transaction mode that it was in before the explicit transaction was started (either implicit or autocommit mode).

Autocommit Transactions

Autocommit mode is the default transaction management mode of SQL Server. Every Transact-SQL statement is committed or rolled back when it is completed. If a statement completes successfully, it is committed; if it encounters any error, it is rolled back. A SQL Server connection operates in autocommit mode whenever this default mode has not been overridden by either explicit or implicit transactions. Autocommit mode is also the default mode for ADO, OLE DB, ODBC, and DB-Library.

A SQL Server connection operates in autocommit mode until a *BEGIN TRANSAC-TION* statement starts an explicit transaction or until implicit transaction mode is set to ON. When the explicit transaction is committed or rolled back or when implicit transaction mode is turned off, SQL Server returns to autocommit mode.

Compile and Run-Time Errors

In autocommit mode, it sometimes appears as if SQL Server has rolled back an entire batch instead of just one SQL statement. This situation happens only if the error encountered is a compile error, not a run-time error. A compile error prevents SQL Server from building an execution plan, so nothing in the batch is executed. Although it appears that all the statements before the one that generated the error were rolled back, the error prevented anything in the batch from being executed.

In the following example, none of the *INSERT* statements in the third batch is executed because of a compile error in the third *INSERT* statement. The first two *INSERT* statements are rolled back because of the error, and no data is added to the TestBatch table:

```
USE Pubs
GO
CREATE TABLE TestBatch (Cola INT PRIMARY KEY, Colb CHAR(3))
GO
INSERT INTO TestBatch VALUES (1, 'aaa')
INSERT INTO TestBatch VALUES (2, 'bbb')
INSERT INTO TestBatch VALUE (3, 'ccc') /* Syntax error */
GO
SELECT * FROM TestBatch /* Returns no rows */
GO
```

In the next example, the third *INSERT* statement generates a run-time, duplicate primary key error. The first two *INSERT* statements are successful and committed, so the values are added to the TestBatch table:

```
USE Pubs
GO
CREATE TABLE TestBatch (Cola INT PRIMARY KEY, Colb CHAR(3))
GO
INSERT INTO TestBatch VALUES (1, 'aaa')
INSERT INTO TestBatch VALUES (2, 'bbb')
INSERT INTO TestBatch VALUES (1, 'ccc') /* Duplicate key error */
GO
SELECT * FROM TestBatch /* Returns rows 1 and 2 */
GO
```

SQL Server uses delayed name resolution, in which object names are not resolved until execution time. In the following example, the first two *INSERT* statements are executed and committed, and those two rows remain in the TestBatch table after the third *INSERT* statement generates a run-time error (by referring to a table that does not exist):

```
USE Pubs
GO
CREATE TABLE TestBatch (Cola INT PRIMARY KEY, Colb CHAR(3))
GO
INSERT INTO TestBatch VALUES (1, 'aaa')
INSERT INTO TestBatch VALUES (2, 'bbb')
INSERT INTO TestBch VALUES (3, 'ccc') /* Table name error */
GO
SELECT * FROM TestBatch /* Returns rows 1 and 2 */
GO
```

Implicit Transactions

When a connection is operating in implicit transaction mode, SQL Server automatically starts a new transaction after the current transaction is committed or rolled back. You do nothing to delineate the start of a transaction; you only commit or roll back each transaction. Implicit transaction mode generates a continuous chain of transactions.

After implicit transaction mode has been set to ON for a connection, SQL Server automatically starts a transaction when it first executes any of the following statements:

ALTER TABLE	*INSERT*
CREATE	*OPEN*
DELETE	*REVOKE*
DROP	*SELECT*
FETCH	*TRUNCATE TABLE*
GRANT	*UPDATE*

The transaction remains in effect until you issue a *COMMIT* or *ROLLBACK* statement. After the first transaction is committed or rolled back, SQL Server automatically starts a new transaction the next time any of these statements is executed by the connection. SQL Server keeps generating a chain of implicit transactions until implicit transaction mode is turned off.

Implicit transaction mode is set either by using the Transact-SQL SET statement or by using database API functions and methods.

Transact-SQL Implicit Transactions

DB-Library applications and Transact-SQL scripts can use the Transact-SQL *SET IMPLICIT_TRANSACTIONS ON* statement to start implicit transaction mode. You should use the *SET IMPLICIT_TRANSACTIONS OFF* statement at the end of the batch to turn implicit transaction mode off. Use the *COMMIT TRANSACTION*, *COMMIT WORK*, *ROLLBACK TRANSACTION*, or *ROLLBACK WORK* statements to end each transaction.

The following statement first creates the ImplicitTran table, then starts implicit transaction mode, then runs two transactions, and then turns off implicit transaction mode:

```
USE Pubs
GO
CREATE TABLE ImplicitTran
    (
    Cola INT PRIMARY KEY,
    Colb CHAR(3) NOT NULL
    )
GO
SET IMPLICIT_TRANSACTIONS ON
GO
/* First implicit transaction started
by an INSERT statement */
INSERT INTO ImplicitTran
VALUES (1, 'aaa')
GO
INSERT INTO ImplicitTran
VALUES (2, 'bbb')
GO
/* Commit first transaction */
COMMIT TRANSACTION
GO
/* Second implicit transaction started
by an INSERT statement */
INSERT INTO ImplicitTran
VALUES (3, 'ccc')
GO
SELECT *
FROM ImplicitTran
GO
/* Commit second transaction */
COMMIT TRANSACTION
GO
SET IMPLICIT_TRANSACTIONS OFF
GO
```

API Implicit Transactions

You can use the ODBC and OLE DB APIs to set implicit transactions. Refer to SQL Server Books Online for more information. ADO does not support implicit transactions. ADO applications use either autocommit mode or explicit transactions.

Distributed Transactions

Distributed transactions span two or more servers known as resource managers. The management of the transaction must be coordinated among the resource managers by a server component called a transaction manager. SQL Server can operate as a resource manager in distributed transactions coordinated by transaction managers such as the Microsoft Distributed Transaction Coordinator (MS DTC), or by other transaction managers that support the X/Open XA specification for Distributed Transaction Processing.

A transaction within a single SQL Server that spans two or more databases is actually a distributed transaction. SQL Server, however, manages the distributed transaction internally. To the user, it operates as a local transaction.

At the application, a distributed transaction is managed in much the same way as a local transaction. At the end of the transaction, the application requests the transaction to be either committed or rolled back. A distributed commit must be managed differently by the transaction manager to minimize the risk that a network failure might result in some resource managers successfully committing while others are rolling back the transaction. You can achieve this goal by managing the commit process in two phases:

- **Prepare phase.**   When the transaction manager receives a commit request, it sends a prepare command to all of the resource managers involved in the transaction. Each resource manager then does everything required to make the transaction durable, and all buffers holding log images for the transaction are flushed to disk. As each resource manager completes the prepare phase, it returns success or failure of the prepare phase to the transaction manager.

- **Commit phase.**   If the transaction manager receives successful prepares from all of the resource managers, it sends commit commands to each resource manager. The resource managers can then complete the commit. If all of the resource managers report a successful commit, the transaction manager then sends a success notification to the application. If any resource manager reports a failure to prepare, the transaction manager sends a ROLLBACK command to each resource manager and indicates the failure of the commit to the application.

SQL Server applications can manage distributed transactions either through Transact-SQL or through the database API.

Transact-SQL Distributed Transactions

The distributed transactions started in Transact-SQL have a relatively simple structure:

1. A Transact-SQL script or application connection executes a Transact-SQL statement that starts a distributed transaction.

2. The SQL Server instance executing the statement becomes the controlling server in the transaction.

3. The script or application then executes either distributed queries against linked servers or remote stored procedures against remote servers.

4. As distributed queries and remote procedure calls are made, the controlling server automatically calls MS DTC to enlist the linked and remote servers in the distributed transaction.

5. When the script or application issues either a *COMMIT* or *ROLLBACK* statement, the controlling SQL Server calls MS DTC to manage the two-phase commit process or to notify the linked and remote servers to roll back their transactions.

Required Transact-SQL Statements

The Transact-SQL statements controlling the distributed transactions are few because SQL Server and MS DTC do most of the work internally. The only Transact-SQL statements required in the Transact-SQL script or application are those required to perform the following tasks:

- Starting a distributed transaction
- Performing distributed queries against linked servers or executing remote procedure calls against remote servers
- Calling the standard Transact-SQL *COMMIT TRANSACTION*, *COMMIT WORK*, *ROLLBACK TRANSACTION*, or *ROLLBACK WORK* statements to complete the transaction

For any Transact-SQL distributed transaction, the SQL Server processing the Transact-SQL script or connection automatically calls MS DTC to coordinate the transaction's commit or rollback.

MS DTC Distributed Transactions

Applications written by using OLE DB, ODBC, ADO, or DB-Library can use Transact-SQL distributed transactions by issuing Transact-SQL statements to start and stop Transact-SQL distributed transactions. OLE DB and ODBC, however, also contain support at the API level for managing distributed transactions. OLE DB and ODBC applications can use these API functions to manage distributed transactions that include other COM resource managers that support MS DTC transactions other than SQL Server. They can also use the API functions to gain more control over the boundaries of a distributed transaction that includes several SQL Servers. The distributed transactions started in Transact-SQL have a relatively simple structure. The Transact-SQL statements controlling the distributed transactions are few because SQL Server and MS DTC do most of the work internally.

Exercise 2: Implementing Explicit Transactions

In this exercise, you will use Transact-SQL statements to perform explicit, auto-commit, and implicit transactions. You will be performing these transactions in the BookShopDB database. To perform this exercise, you should be logged into your Windows 2000 Server computer as Administrator.

▶ **To perform an explicit transaction**

1. Open Query Analyzer and connect to your local server.

2. In the Editor pane of the Query window, enter the following Transact-SQL code:

```
BEGIN TRANSACTION
GO
USE BookShopDB
GO
UPDATE Authors
SET Description =
'English author whose novels are highly regarded
for humor, irony, and depiction of English life.'
WHERE LastName = 'Austen'
GO
COMMIT TRANSACTION
GO
```

   In this statement, you are first using the *BEGIN TRANSACTION* statement to begin the transaction. You are then updating the Authors table in the Book-ShopDB database. Finally, you are committing the transaction by using the *COMMIT TRANSACTION* statement.

3. Execute the Transact-SQL statement.

   A message appears in the Messages tab of the Results pane, stating that one row has been affected by the transaction.

4. In the Editor pane of the Query window, enter and execute the following Transact-SQL code:

```
SELECT * FROM Authors
```

   The result set is displayed in the Grids tab of the Results pane. Notice that the row for Jane Austen now contains the description specified in the transaction.

5. In the Editor pane of the Query window, enter and execute the following Transact-SQL code:

```
UPDATE Authors
SET Description = 'N/A'
WHERE LastName = 'Austen'
```

   A message appears in the Messages tab of the Results pane, stating that one row has been affected by the transaction.

► **To perform an autocommit transaction**

1. In the Editor pane of the Query window, enter the following Transact-SQL code:

```
USE BookShopDB
GO
CREATE TABLE TestTable (Col1 INT PRIMARY KEY, Col2 CHAR(3))
GO
INSERT INTO TestTable VALUES (101, 'ABC')
INSERT INTO TestTable VALUES (102, 'DEF')
INSERT INTO TestTable VALUSE (103, 'GHI')
GO
SELECT * FROM TestTable
GO
```

In this statement, you are defining four autocommit transactions. The first transaction identifies the database (BookShopDB) to be used. In the second transaction, you are creating the TestTable table. In the third transaction, you are adding values to the table, and in the fourth transaction, you are performing a SELECT query against the table.

2. Execute the Transact-SQL statement.

A message appears in the Messages tab of the Results pane, stating that incorrect syntax (VALUSE) has been used.

3. Click the Grids tab.

Notice that Col1 and Col2 are displayed but that no values have been added. When the script was executed, the table was created and the SELECT query was executed. However, because the third transaction included a syntax error, none of the values were inserted in the table.

4. In the Editor pane of the Query window, enter and execute the following Transact-SQL code:

```
DROP TABLE TestTable
```

A message appears in the Messages tab of the Results pane, stating that the command has been successfully completed.

5. In the Editor pane of the Query window, enter and execute the following Transact-SQL code:

```
USE BookShopDB
GO
CREATE TABLE TestTable (Col1 INT PRIMARY KEY, Col2 CHAR(3))
GO
INSERT INTO TestTable VALUES (101, 'ABC')
INSERT INTO TestTable VALUES (102, 'DEF')
INSERT INTO TestTable VALUES (103, 'GHI')
GO
SELECT * FROM TestTable
GO
```

The result set is now correctly displayed in the Grids tab of the Results pane.

6. In the Editor pane of the Query window, enter and execute the following Transact-SQL code:

```
DROP TABLE TestTable
```

A message appears in the Messages tab of the Results pane, stating that the command has been successfully completed.

▶ **To perform an implicit transaction**

1. In the Editor pane of the Query window, enter the following Transact-SQL code:

```
SET IMPLICIT_TRANSACTIONS ON
GO
USE BookShopDB
CREATE TABLE TestTable (Col1 INT PRIMARY KEY, Col2 CHAR(3))
GO
COMMIT TRANSACTION
GO
INSERT INTO TestTable VALUES (101, 'ABC')
INSERT INTO TestTable VALUES (102, 'DEF')
INSERT INTO TestTable VALUES (103, 'GHI')
GO
COMMIT TRANSACTION
GO
SELECT * FROM TestTable
GO
COMMIT TRANSACTION
GO
SET IMPLICIT_TRANSACTIONS OFF
GO
```

In this statement, you are first setting implicit transactions to ON. The first implicit transaction creates TestTable in the BookShopDB database. The next transaction inserts values into the table, and the final transaction performs a SELECT query against the table. Once all three implicit transactions have been executed, implicit transactions are set to OFF.

2. Execute the Transact-SQL statement.

The result set is displayed in the Grids tab of the Results pane.

3. In the Editor pane of the Query window, enter and execute the following Transact-SQL code:

```
DROP TABLE TestTable
```

A message appears in the Messages tab of the Results pane, stating that the command has been successfully completed.

Lesson Summary

A transaction is a sequence of operations performed as a single, logical unit of work. To qualify as a transaction, a logical unit of work must exhibit four properties, called the ACID properties (atomicity, consistency, isolation, and durability). You can identify when SQL Server transactions start and end with Transact-SQL statements or with API functions and methods. SQL Server supports three types of transactions: explicit, autocommit, and implicit. An explicit transaction is one in which you explicitly define both the start and the end of the transaction. An autocommit transaction is the default transaction management mode of SQL Server. Every Transact-SQL statement is committed or rolled back when it is completed. When a connection is operating in implicit transaction mode, SQL Server automatically starts a new transaction after the current transaction is committed or rolled back. Distributed transactions span two or more servers known as resource managers. The management of the transaction must be coordinated between the resource managers by a server component called a transaction manager.

Lesson 3: Managing SQL Server Locking

SQL Server 2000 uses locking to ensure transactional integrity and database consistency. Locking prevents users from reading data being changed by other users and prevents multiple users from changing the same data at the same time. If locking is not used, data within the database might become logically incorrect, and queries executed against that data might produce unexpected results. Although SQL Server enforces locking automatically, you can design applications that are more efficient by understanding and customizing locking in your applications. This lesson provides information about locking and concurrency in a SQL Server database. The lesson also discusses how to customize locking.

After this lesson, you will be able to:
- Identify the various types of concurrency problems.
- Describe optimistic and pessimistic concurrency.
- Set isolation levels and customize locking.

Estimated lesson time: 35 minutes

Types of Concurrency Problems

If locking is not available and several users access a database concurrently, problems might occur if their transactions use the same data at the same time. Concurrency problems can include any of the following situations:

- Lost or buried updates
- Uncommitted dependency (dirty read)
- Inconsistent analysis (non-repeatable read)
- Phantom reads

Lost Updates

Lost updates occur when two or more transactions select the same row and then update the row based on the value originally selected. Each transaction is unaware of other transactions. The last update overwrites updates made by the other transactions, which results in lost data.

For example, two editors make an electronic copy of the same document. Each editor changes the copy independently and then saves the changed copy, thereby overwriting the original document. The editor who saves the changed copy last overwrites the changes made by the first editor. This problem could be avoided if the second editor could not make changes until the first editor had finished.

Uncommitted Dependency (Dirty Read)

Uncommitted dependency occurs when a second transaction selects a row that is already being updated by a transaction. The second transaction is reading data that has not been committed yet and might be changed by the transaction updating the row.

For example, an editor is making changes to an electronic document. During the changes, a second editor takes a copy of the document that includes all of the changes made so far and distributes the document to the intended audience. The first editor then decides the changes made so far are wrong and removes the edits and saves the document. The distributed document contains edits that no longer exist and should be treated as if they never existed. This problem could be avoided if no one could read the changed document until the first editor determined that the changes were final.

Inconsistent Analysis (Non-repeatable Read)

Inconsistent analysis occurs when a second transaction accesses the same row several times and reads different data each time. Inconsistent analysis is similar to uncommitted dependency in that another transaction is changing the data that a second transaction is reading. In inconsistent analysis, however, the data read by the second transaction was committed by the transaction that made the change. Also, inconsistent analysis involves multiple reads (two or more) of the same row and each time the information is changed by another transaction (hence the term non-repeatable read).

For example, an editor reads the same document twice, but between each reading, the writer rewrites the document. When the editor reads the document for the second time, it has changed. The original read was not repeatable. This problem could be avoided if the editor could read the document only after the writer has finished writing it.

Phantom Reads

Phantom reads occur when an insert or delete action is performed against a row that belongs to a range of rows being read by a transaction. The transaction's first read of the range of rows shows a row that no longer exists in the second or succeeding read as a result of a deletion by a different transaction. Similarly, as the result of an insert by a different transaction, the transaction's second or succeeding read shows a row that did not exist in the original read.

For example, an editor makes changes to a document submitted by a writer, but when the changes are incorporated into the master copy of the document by the production department, they find that new, unedited material has been added to the document by the author. This problem could be avoided if no one could add new material to the document until the editor and production department finish working with the original document.

Optimistic and Pessimistic Concurrency

SQL Server 2000 offers both optimistic and pessimistic concurrency control. Optimistic concurrency control uses cursors. Pessimistic concurrency control is the default for SQL Server.

Optimistic Concurrency

Optimistic concurrency control works on the assumption that resource conflicts between multiple users are unlikely (but not impossible) and enables transactions to execute without locking any resources. Only when attempting to change data are resources checked to determine whether any conflicts have occurred. If a conflict occurs, the application must read the data and attempt the change again.

Pessimistic Concurrency

Pessimistic concurrency control locks resources as they are required, for the duration of a transaction. Unless deadlocks occur, a transaction is assured of successful completion.

Isolation Levels

When locking is used as the concurrency control mechanism, it solves concurrency problems. This feature enables all transactions to run in complete isolation from one another, although there can be more than one transaction running at any time.

Serializability is achieved by running a set of concurrent transactions equivalent to the database state that would be achieved if the set of transactions were executed serially.

SQL-92 Isolation Levels

Although serialization is important to transactions to ensure that the data in the database is correct at all times, many transactions do not always require full isolation. For example, several writers are working on different chapters of the same book. New chapters can be submitted to the project at any time; however, after a chapter has been edited, a writer cannot make any changes to the chapter without the editor's approval. This way, the editor can be assured of the accuracy of the book project at any point in time, despite the arrival of new, unedited chapters. The editor can see both previously edited chapters and recently submitted chapters.

The level at which a transaction is prepared to accept inconsistent data is termed the isolation level. The isolation level is the degree to which one transaction must be isolated from other transactions. A lower isolation level increases concurrency, but at the expense of data correctness. Conversely, a higher isolation level ensures that data is correct but can negatively affect concurrency. The isolation level required by an application determines the locking behavior that SQL Server uses.

SQL-92 defines the following isolation levels, all of which are supported by SQL Server:

- Read uncommitted (the lowest level, at which transactions are isolated only enough to ensure that physically corrupt data is not read)
- Read committed (SQL Server default level)
- Repeatable read
- Serializable (the highest level, at which transactions are completely isolated from one another)

If transactions are run at an isolation level of serializable, any concurrent, overlapping transactions are guaranteed to be serializable.

The following isolation levels enable different types of behavior:

Isolation Level	Dirty Read	Non-Repeatable Read	Phantom Read
Read uncommitted	Yes	Yes	Yes
Read committed	No	Yes	Yes
Repeatable read	No	No	Yes
Serializable	No	No	No

Transactions must be run at an isolation level of repeatable read or higher to prevent lost updates that can occur when two transactions each retrieve the same row and update the row later based on the originally retrieved values. If the two transactions update rows by using a single *UPDATE* statement and do not base the update on the previously retrieved values, lost updates cannot occur at the default isolation level of read committed.

Customizing Locking

Although SQL Server implements locking automatically, it is possible to customize this feature in applications by performing the following tasks:

- Handling deadlocks and setting the deadlock priority
- Handling timeouts and setting the lock timeout duration
- Setting the transaction isolation level
- Using table-level locking hints with the *SELECT*, *INSERT*, *UPDATE*, and *DELETE* statements
- Configuring the locking granularity for an index

Managing Deadlocks

A deadlock occurs when there is a cyclic dependency between two or more threads for a set of resources. Deadlock can occur on any system that has multiple threads, not just on a relational database management system. A thread in a multi-threaded system can acquire one or more resources (locks, for example). If the resource being acquired is currently owned by another thread, the first thread might have to wait for the owning thread to release the target resource. The waiting thread is said to have a dependency on the owning thread for that particular resource.

If the owning thread wants to acquire another resource that is currently owned by the waiting thread, the situation becomes a deadlock. Both threads cannot release the resources that they own until their transactions are committed or rolled back, and their transactions cannot be committed or rolled back because they are waiting on resources that the other owns.

Figure 12.1 provides an example of two transactions attempting to access data in two tables. Thread T1 running transaction 1 has an exclusive lock on the Supplier table. Thread T2 running transaction 2 obtains an exclusive lock on the Part table and then wants a lock on the Supplier table. Transaction 2 cannot obtain the lock because transaction 1 has it. Transaction 2 is blocked because it is waiting on transaction 1. Transaction 1 then wants a lock on the Part table but cannot obtain it because transaction 2 has it locked. The transactions cannot release the locks that they are holding until the transaction is committed or rolled back. The transactions cannot commit or roll back because, in order to continue, they require a lock held by the other transaction.

Note   Deadlocking is often confused with normal blocking. When one transaction has a lock on a resource that another transaction wants, the second transaction waits for the lock to be released. By default, SQL Server transactions do not time out (unless LOCK_TIMEOUT is set). The second transaction is blocked, not dead-locked.

In Figure 12.1, thread T1 has a dependency on thread T2 for the Part table lock resource. Similarly, thread T2 has a dependency on thread T1 for the Supplier table lock resource. Because these dependencies form a cycle, there is a deadlock between threads T1 and T2.

Minimizing Deadlocks

Although deadlocks cannot be avoided completely, the number of deadlocks can be minimized. Minimizing deadlocks can increase transaction throughput and reduce system overhead because fewer transactions are rolled back, undoing all of the work performed by the transaction. In addition, fewer transactions are resubmitted by applications because they were rolled back when they were deadlocked.

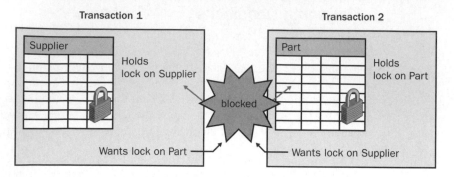

Figure 12.1.   A deadlock on two transactions accessing the Supplier table and the Part table.

You should adhere to the following guidelines to help minimize deadlocks:

- Access objects in the same order.
- Avoid user interaction during transactions.
- Keep transactions short and in one batch.
- Use a low isolation level.
- Use bound connections.

Note   Bound connections enable two or more connections to share the same transaction and locks. Bound connections can work on the same data without lock conflicts. Bound connections can be created from multiple connections within the same application or from multiple applications with separate connections. Bound connections also make coordinating actions across multiple connections easier. For more information about bound connections, refer to SQL Server Books Online.

Customizing Timeouts

When SQL Server cannot grant a lock to a transaction on a resource because another transaction already owns a conflicting lock on that resource, the first transaction becomes blocked while waiting on that resource. If this situation causes a deadlock, SQL Server terminates one of the participating transactions (with no timeout involved). If there is no deadlock, the transaction requesting the lock is blocked until the other transaction releases the lock. By default, there is no mandatory timeout period and no way to test whether a resource is locked before locking it, except to attempt to access the data (and potentially get blocked indefinitely).

Note   The *sp_who* system stored procedure can be used to determine whether a process is being blocked and who is blocking it.

The LOCK_TIMEOUT setting enables an application to set a maximum time that a statement will wait on a blocked resource. When a statement has waited longer than the LOCK_TIMEOUT setting, the blocked statement is canceled automatically, and error message 1222, "Lock request time-out period exceeded," is returned to the application.

However, any transaction containing the statement is not rolled back or canceled by SQL Server. Therefore, the application must have an error handler that can trap error message 1222. If an application does not trap the error, it can proceed unaware that an individual statement within a transaction has been canceled, and errors can occur because statements later in the transaction might depend on the statement that was never executed.

Implementing an error handler that traps error message 1222 enables an application to handle the timeout situation and take remedial action (for example, automatically resubmitting the statement that was blocked or rolling back the entire transaction).

You can use the *SET LOCK_TIMEOUT* statement to specify the number of milliseconds that a statement will wait for a lock to be released, as shown in the following example:

```
SET LOCK_TIMEOUT -1
SELECT @@LOCK_TIMEOUT
```

The *SET LOCK_TIMEOUT* statement enables an application to set the maximum time that a statement will wait for a blocked resource. When a statement has waited longer than the LOCK_TIMEOUT setting, the blocked statement is automatically canceled and an error message is returned to the application.

To determine the current lock timeout setting (in milliseconds) for the current session, you can use the *@@LOCK_TIMEOUT* function, as shown in the following example:

```
SELECT @@LOCK_TIMEOUT
```

If a LOCK_TIMEOUT value has not been set for a session, the *@@LOCK_TIMEOUT* function will return a value of 21.

Setting Transaction Isolation Levels

By default, SQL Server 2000 operates at an isolation level of READ COMMITTED. An application might have to operate at a different isolation level, however. To make use of either more or less strict isolation levels in applications, locking can be customized for an entire session by setting the isolation level of the session with the *SET TRANSACTION ISOLATION LEVEL* statement.

When the isolation level is specified, the locking behavior for all *SELECT* statements in the SQL Server session operates at that isolation level and remains in effect until the session terminates or until the isolation level is set to another level.

In the following example, the transaction isolation level is being set to SERIALIZ-ABLE, which ensures that no phantom rows can be inserted into the Authors table by concurrent transactions:

```
USE Pubs
SET TRANSACTION ISOLATION LEVEL READ COMMITTED
```

Note The isolation level can be overridden, if necessary, for individual *SELECT* statements by specifying a table-level locking hint. Specifying a table-level locking hint does not affect other statements in the session. You should use table-level locking hints to change the default locking behavior only if absolutely necessary.

To determine the transaction isolation level currently set, use the *DBCC USEROPTIONS* statement, as shown in the following example:

```
USE Pubs
SET TRANSACTION ISOLATION LEVEL READ COMMITTED
```

Implementing Table-Level Locking Hints

A range of table-level locking hints can be specified along with the *SELECT*, *INSERT*, *UPDATE*, and *DELETE* statements in order to direct SQL Server 2000 to the type of locks to be used. Use table-level locking hints for finer control of the types of locks acquired on an object. Locking hints override the current transaction isolation level for the session.

Note The SQL Server query optimizer automatically makes the correct determination. You should use table-level locking hints to change the default locking behavior only when necessary. Disallowing a locking level can affect concurrency adversely.

The following table provides a description of the available locking hints:

Locking Hint	Description
HOLDLOCK	Hold a shared lock until completion of the transaction instead of releasing the lock as soon as the required table, row, or data page is no longer required. HOLDLOCK is equivalent to SERIALIZABLE.
NOLOCK	Do not issue shared locks, and do not honor exclusive locks. When this option is in effect, it is possible to read an uncommitted transaction or a set of pages that are rolled back in the middle of a read. Dirty reads are possible. This hint only applies to the *SELECT* statement.
PAGLOCK	Use page locks where a single table lock would usually be taken.

Locking Hint	Description
READCOMMITTED	Perform a scan with the same locking semantics as a transaction running at the READ COMMITTED isolation level. By default, SQL Server 2000 operates at this isolation level.
READPAST	Skip locked rows. This option causes a transaction to skip rows locked by other transactions that would ordinarily appear in the result set, rather than block the transaction waiting for the other transactions to release their locks on these rows. The READPAST lock hint applies only to transactions operating at READ COMMITTED isolation and will read only past row-level locks. Applies only to the *SELECT* statement.
READUNCOMMITTED	Equivalent to NOLOCK.
REPEATABLEREAD	Perform a scan with the same locking semantics as a transaction that is running at the REPEATABLE READ isolation level.
ROWLOCK	Use row-level locks instead of the coarser-grained page- and table-level locks.
SERIALIZABLE	Perform a scan with the same locking semantics as a transaction that is running at the SERIALIZABLE isolation level. Equivalent to HOLDLOCK.
TABLOCK	Use a table lock instead of the finer-grained row- or page-level locks. SQL Server holds this lock until the end of the statement. If you also specify HOLDLOCK, however, the lock is held until the end of the transaction.
TABLOCKX	Use an exclusive lock on a table. This lock prevents others from reading or updating the table and is held until the end of the statement or transaction.
UPDLOCK	Use update locks instead of shared locks while reading a table, and hold locks until the end of the statement or transaction. UPDLOCK has the advantage of allowing you to read data (without blocking other readers) and update it later with the assurance that the data has not changed since you last read it.
XLOCK	Use an exclusive lock that will be held until the end of the transaction on all data processed by the statement. This lock can be specified with either PAGLOCK or TABLOCK, in which case the exclusive lock applies to the appropriate level of granularity.

In the following example, the transaction isolation level is set to SERIALIZABLE, and the table-level locking hint NOLOCK is used with the *SELECT* statement:

```
USE Pubs
GO
SET TRANSACTION ISOLATION LEVEL SERIALIZABLE
GO
```

```
BEGIN TRANSACTION
SELECT Au_lname FROM Authors WITH (NOLOCK)
GO
```

When the *SELECT* statement is executed, the key-range locks typically used to maintain serializable transactions are not taken.

Customizing Locking for an Index

The SQL Server 2000 dynamic locking strategy automatically chooses the best locking granularity for queries in most cases. In cases where access patterns are well understood and consistent, limiting the locking levels available for an index can be beneficial.

For example, a database application uses a lookup table that is refreshed weekly in a batch process. The most efficient locking strategy is to turn off page and row locking and to enable all concurrent readers to get a shared (S) lock on the table, thereby reducing overhead. During the weekly batch update, the update process can take an exclusive (X) lock and then update the entire table.

The granularity of locking used on an index can be set using the *sp_indexoption* system stored procedure. To display the current locking option for a given index, use the *INDEXPROPERTY* function. Page-level locks, row-level locks, or a combination of page-level and row-level locks can be disallowed for a given index, as described in the following table:

Disallowed Locks	Index Accessed by
Page level	Row-level and table-level locks
Row level	Page-level and table-level locks
Page level and row level	Table-level locks

For example, when a table is known to be a point of contention, it can be beneficial to disallow page-level locks, thereby allowing only row-level locks. Or, if table scans are always used to access an index or table, disallowing page-level and row-level locks can help by allowing only table-level locks.

Important   The SQL Server query optimizer automatically makes the correct determination. You should not override the choices the optimizer makes. Disallowing a locking level can affect the concurrency for a table or index adversely. For example, specifying only table-level locks on a large table accessed heavily by many users can affect performance significantly. Users must wait for the table-level lock to be released before accessing the table.

Exercise 3: Configuring Transaction Properties

In this exercise, you will use Transact-SQL statements to configure transaction timeouts, isolation levels, and locking hints. To perform this exercise, you should be logged into your Windows 2000 Server computer as Administrator.

▶ **To use Transact-SQL to configure a session timeout**

1. Open Query Analyzer and connect to your local server.

2. In the Editor pane of the Query window, enter the following Transact-SQL code:

```
SELECT @@LOCK_TIMEOUT
```

   In this statement, you are requesting the LOCK_TIMEOUT setting for the current session.

3. Execute the Transact-SQL statement.

   A value of 21 appears in the Grids tab of the Results pane. This value is returned if no LOCK_TIMEOUT setting has been implemented for this session.

4. In the Editor pane of the Query window, enter the following Transact-SQL code:

```
SET LOCK_TIMEOUT 1800
SELECT @@LOCK_TIMEOUT
```

   In this statement, you are first using the *SET LOCK_TIMEOUT* statement to set the timeout value to 1800 milliseconds. You are then using the *@@LOCK_TIMEOUT* function to view the new setting.

5. Execute the Transact-SQL statement.

   A value of 1800 appears in the Grids tab of the Results pane.

▶ **To use Transact-SQL to set the session isolation level**

1. In the Editor pane of the Query window, enter the following Transact-SQL code:

```
USE BookShopDB
SET TRANSACTION ISOLATION LEVEL SERIALIZABLE
```

   In this statement, you are setting the isolation level to SERIALIZABLE for the current session.

2. Execute the Transact-SQL statement.

   A message appears in the Messages tab of the Results grid, stating that the command has been successfully completed.

3. In the Editor pane of the Query window, enter and execute the following Transact-SQL code:

```
DBCC USEROPTIONS
```

The Grids tab of the Results pane displays the SET option values. The isolation level value is now set to SERIALIZABLE.

▶ **To use Transact-SQL to set a table-level locking hint**

1. In the Editor pane of the Query window, enter the following Transact-SQL code:

```
USE BookShopDB
SELECT TitleID, Title
FROM Books WITH (NOLOCK)
```

In this statement, you are setting a table-level locking hint (NOLOCK) for the *SELECT* statement. The NOLOCK locking hint does not issue shared locks and does not honor exclusive locks.

2. Execute the Transact-SQL statement.

The result set appears in the Grids tab of the Results pane.

3. Close Query Analyzer.

Lesson Summary

Locking prevents users from reading data being changed by other users and prevents multiple users from changing the same data at the same time. If locking is not available and several users access a database concurrently, problems might occur if their transactions use the same data at the same time. Concurrency problems can include lost or buried updates, uncommitted dependency (dirty reads), inconsistent analysis (non-repeatable reads), or phantom reads. SQL Server 2000 offers both optimistic and pessimistic concurrency control. Optimistic concurrency control works on the assumption that resource conflicts between multiple users are unlikely (but not impossible) and enables transactions to execute without locking any resources. Pessimistic concurrency control locks resources as they are required for the duration of a transaction. Unless deadlocks occur, a transaction is assured of successful completion. The level at which a transaction is prepared to accept inconsistent data is termed the isolation level. The isolation level is the degree to which one transaction must be isolated from other transactions. SQL Server supports the following isolation levels: read uncommitted, read committed, repeatable read, and serializable. Although SQL Server implements locking automatically, you can customize locking by handling deadlocks and setting the deadlock priority, handling timeouts and setting the lock time-out duration, setting the transaction isolation level, using table-level locking hints, and configuring locking granularity for an index.

Review

The following questions are intended to reinforce key information presented in this chapter. If you are unable to answer a question, review the appropriate lesson and then try the question again. You can find answers to the questions in the Appendix, "Questions and Answers."

1. What three operations do transaction logs support?
2. What events are recorded in a transaction log?
3. When are checkpoints created in a transaction log?
4. When does log truncation occur?
5. What is a transaction?
6. What three types of transactions does SQL Server support, and how do they differ?
7. What Transact-SQL statement is used to mark the starting point of an explicit transaction?
8. What two phases are used to manage the commit process in the distributed transaction?
9. What are the differences between lost updates and uncommitted dependencies?
10. What are the differences between optimistic concurrency and pessimistic concurrency?
11. What isolation levels does SQL Server support?
12. What guidelines should you follow to help minimize deadlocks?

C H A P T E R   1 3

Designing and Administering SQL Server 2000 Security

About This Chapter

Security is an integral part of any properly designed database. This chapter introduces you to SQL Server security by presenting a layered model of database security. Following an overview of security, you will learn how to design SQL Server security to accommodate user requirements and to protect the database from unauthorized access. The chapter concludes by presenting the primary tools that you will use to implement and administer database security.

Before You Begin

To complete the lessons in this chapter, you must have:

- SQL Server 2000 Enterprise Edition installed on a Microsoft Windows 2000 Server computer.
- The ability to log on to the Windows 2000 Server computer and to SQL Server as the Windows 2000 Administrator.
- Completed the exercises in Chapter 3, "Designing a SQL Server Database," Chapter 4, "Implementing SQL Server Databases and Tables," Chapter 5, "Implementing Data Integrity," and Chapter 7, "Managing and Manipulating Data."
- Paper and a pencil to complete part of the exercises.

Lesson 1: Overview of SQL Server 2000 Security

In this lesson, you will learn about SQL Server security by using a six-layer model. The lowest layer is *physical security*. Physical security includes securing access to the facilities that contain the internal network and server equipment used to support SQL Server. *Network protocol security* is the second layer. This layer includes items such as transport protocol isolation and packet encryption. The third layer is *domain security*. Domain security is implemented in a Microsoft network by using Microsoft Active Directory (AD) directory services and domains. The fourth layer is *local computer security*. This layer includes operating system auditing, file permissions, registry access, and file encryption services. The fifth layer is *SQL Server security*. SQL Server security includes authentication, authorization, encryption, and auditing services. The sixth layer is *application security*. An application can enhance SQL Server security by providing its own security features.

After this lesson, you will be able to:

- Describe SQL Server security architecture by using a six-layer paradigm.

Estimated Lesson time: 35 minutes

Physical Security

Physical security applies to all forms of computer data protection, not just to SQL Server database protection. This vital layer of security is overlooked in many networks and leaves a company vulnerable to data theft, vandalism, and environmental calamities. Physical security includes securing vital server and network hardware by placing it in limited-access spaces. For very large networks, this space could be an entire building or campus of buildings, and for medium-sized networks it could be a data center. For small networks, it could be a closet. To protect against environmental calamities, regular backups must be scheduled and stored off site.

Note For more information about security basics, refer to Microsoft's security Web site at *http://www.microsoft.com/security/*.

Network Protocol Security

Data traveling from a client to SQL Server can be encrypted so that anyone who is intercepting the packets from the network using a packet analyzer will not be able to read the contents of the packets. Packet encryption is implemented between the client and SQL Server (application layer encryption) by using the Secure Socket Layer (SSL) protocol or remote procedure call (RPC) encryption. Packet encryption is implemented between two computers running Windows 2000 by using IP

Security (IPSec). IPSec is also supported in many modern routers. Use the SQL Server 2000 Client Network Utility to configure SSL for Net-Libraries. Figure 13.1 shows how to enable encryption in the Client Network Utility.

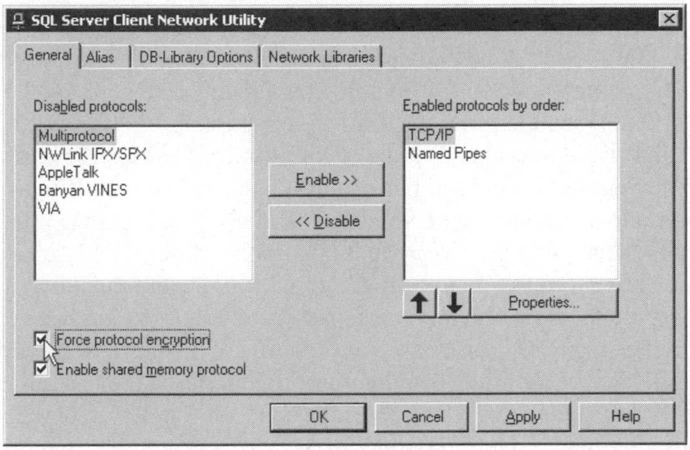

Figure 13.1.   Enabling packet encryption for all enabled protocols.

Note   SSL also requires SQL Server to be assigned a certificate. For more information, refer to the Windows 2000 Server Resource Kit.

Enabling encryption slows SQL Server network performance. Create a performance baseline before enabling encryption. After enabling encryption, determine whether the performance degradation warrants enabling this feature. Some of the Net-Library protocols contain their own security features. For example, the Multiprotocol Net-Library uses RPCs and the RPC encryption application programming interface (API), so enabling SSL packet encryption for this protocol is unnecessary.

There are other protocol-specific security features. For example, use a unique port rather than the default of 1433 for Transmission Control Protocol/Internet Protocol (TCP/IP), and use IPSec as the underlying security protocol for TCP/IP. Stop Named Pipes server announcements so that the server does not appear in graphical interfaces such as the SQL Server drop-down list box in Query Analyzer. Disable Mailslots broadcast so that the server's NetBIOS name does not appear on the network.

Another common network protocol security method is to implement a firewall solution, such as Microsoft Internet Security and Acceleration Server, or a dedicated hardware solution. A simple security measure is to create a protocol firewall by using a protocol on the internal network that differs from the external network protocol, such as IPX/SPX internally and TCP/IP externally. The internal network can then be accessed from the outside by a virtual private network (VPN) connection.

Note   Refer to the Windows 2000 Server Resource Kit for more information about network security technologies.

Domain Security

A SQL Server 2000 computer that is a member server of a Windows 2000 or Microsoft Windows NT domain can authenticate users by the security identifiers (SIDs) associated with the user. To accomplish Windows authentication, a database administrator assigns Windows NT/Windows 2000 user or group accounts with privileges to access and perform tasks in SQL Server. Windows domain user accounts provide secure validation and account lockout. Windows domain passwords are encrypted to prevent unauthorized network interception, are case-sensitive to make them difficult to determine, and include policies such as password expiration and minimum password length. A password assigned to a SQL Server login ID is also case-sensitive if a case-sensitive sort order is specified when SQL Server is installed. Windows domain passwords are always case-sensitive when logon occurs from a Windows NT or Windows 2000 client. The SQL Server facility that makes it possible for Windows domain accounts to establish a connection with SQL Server is discussed in the SQL Server Security section of this lesson.

Security account delegation is another powerful feature available to Windows 2000 networks that are running Active Directory directory services and the Kerberos mutual authentication protocol. This feature enables a user's identity to be verified when one computer connects to another computer on the network. The user logs on once and the first computer verifies the user's identity to the second computer on the user's behalf.

Note   For more information about configuring security account delegation, refer to "Security Account Delegation" in SQL Server Books Online and refer to "Impersonation" and "Service Principal Names" in the Windows 2000 Server Resource Kit.

Local Computer Security

SQL Server 2000 runs on top of Windows 98, Windows Millennium Edition (ME), Windows NT, and Windows 2000. Windows NT Server, Windows 2000 Server, and more advanced editions of these two operating system products provide the highest level of local computer security available to SQL Server 2000. For this reason, the minimum operating system requirement for SQL Server 2000 Enterprise Edition is Windows NT Server or Windows 2000 Server. Windows NT Server and Windows 2000 Server provide security auditing through the Event Log service so that you can track events such as user logons and attempts to access file objects (such as the database files). File object auditing is available for all partitions running the New Technology File System (NTFS). NTFS is a requirement for running SQL Server 2000 on Windows NT or Windows 2000. NTFS provides additional security features, including local directory and file permissions and encryption services. Finally, SQL Server Setup automatically configures restrictions on sensitive SQL-related registry settings. Whenever you change your operating system's security, carefully test SQL Server operation to verify that performance levels are maintained and that the restrictions you configure will not disable SQL Server functions.

SQL Server Security

SQL Server provides a robust set of security services to protect the databases it maintains. The four categories of SQL Server security are authentication, authorization, auditing, and encryption. Database access occurs in two stages, first by connecting to SQL Server (authentication) and second by accessing a database and its objects (authorization). Object permissions either authorize or deny a user the ability to perform actions against database objects such as tables or views. Statement permissions either authorize or deny a user the ability to create objects or back up database and log files. Activity that occurs within the database is tracked through SQL Server auditing. This auditing mechanism is specifically designed to audit database objects, unlike the Windows NT and Windows 2000 Event Log service. Optionally, database objects such as stored procedures can be encrypted within the database to protect their contents.

Authentication

SQL Server 2000 supports two modes of authentication: Windows Authentication and SQL Server Authentication. Windows Authentication enables a local user account or a user account in a Windows domain (Windows NT or Windows 2000) to establish a connection with SQL Server. SQL Server Authentication enables a user to establish a connection with SQL Server by using a SQL Server login ID. Configure the server for an authentication method during SQL Server installation or afterwards from the SQL Server Properties (Configure) dialog box in Enterprise Manager, as shown in Figure 13.2.

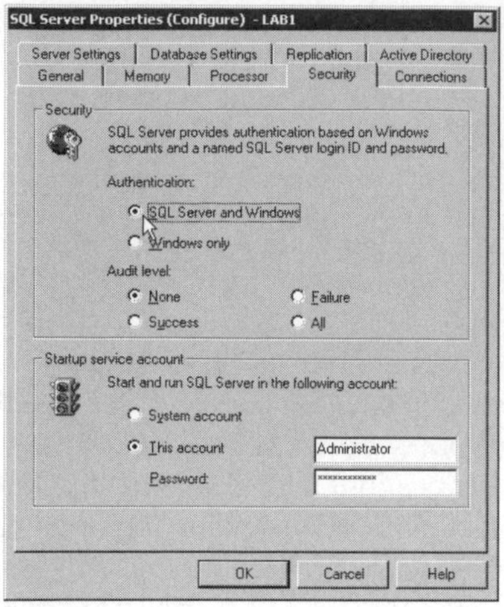

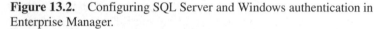

Figure 13.2.   Configuring SQL Server and Windows authentication in Enterprise Manager.

The authentication mode options are either to use both Windows Authentication and SQL Server Authentication, or to use just Windows Authentication. Configuring the server for both authentication modes is called *Mixed Mode*.

Using Windows Authentication achieves logon security integration because SQL Server depends on the local computer operating system or a domain controller to validate and maintain the user account. For example, if User01 is a local user account created on a standalone SQL Server named Server01, you can grant or deny SERVER01\User01 the connect right to SQL Server. If User02 is a domain user account created on a domain controller in Domain01, you can grant or deny DOMAIN01\User02 the connect right to SQL Server.

You can also grant or deny Windows NT and Windows 2000 groups authentication privileges. Members of the group inherit the grant or deny privilege configured for the group. A deny privilege supersedes a connect privilege assigned to a user or to any other groups of which the user might be a member. There are two types of groups in Windows NT and Windows 2000 that are granted the connect privilege: local computer groups and domain groups. *Local computer groups* are stored in the operating system on the computer running SQL Server. The two types of local computer groups are built-in local groups and user-created local groups. *Domain groups* are stored on Windows domain controllers. The three types of domain groups are domain local groups, global groups, and universal groups. Lesson 3 describes how to assign each type of group in SQL Server.

Note   Windows user and group accounts are generically referred to as Windows accounts.

Authentication succeeds if the account or group of which the user is a member is granted the connect right to SQL Server. Windows Authentication enables a user to log on to the local SQL Server computer or to the domain without having to separately log on to SQL Server. If SQL Server is configured for Mixed Mode, Windows Authentication is the default connection method.

In certain circumstances, SQL Server Authentication is the only way to establish a connection with SQL Server. The following situations require SQL Server Authentication in order to successfully establish a SQL Server connection:

- When the client and the server are not part of the same logon namespace

    If the computer running SQL Server is configured as a standalone server and the client is logged on to a domain, the client must use SQL Server authentication. If SQL Server is configured as a standalone server, the client is logged on locally, and the same user account and password combination exists on both the client and the server, then the client can use Windows authentication.

- When SQL Server is running on Windows 98 or Windows ME

    SQL Server Authentication is the only authentication mode supported by SQL Server that runs on Windows 98 and Windows ME.

- When applications are written specifically to use SQL Server Authentication

    Several SQL Server account objects are created when SQL Server is installed. The system administrator (sa) SQL Server login ID is created when SQL Server is installed. This account is assigned to the SysAdmin fixed server role and cannot be changed or deleted. A special user account object, the database owner (dbo), is mapped to sa and is created in each database. This mapping makes dbo a member of SysAdmin, as well. You will learn about server roles in the next section of this lesson. Another special account is the guest account, which enables any SQL Server authenticated user to access a database.

Authorization

Authentication alone is not enough to allow a user account to access a database. You must also assign permissions to an authenticated user account, group or role, object, or statement. Authorization is primarily assigned within the context of a database. This approach limits the scope of a user's access. For example, assigning permission to access a table within the Pubs database does not allow the user to access objects in the Master database. However, there are special administrative assignments whose scope is SQL Server.

Groups and Roles

Assigning permissions to individual users is time-consuming and difficult to maintain in databases that have a moderate to large number of users. SQL Server 2000 supports Windows groups and SQL Server roles to ease the administrative burden of assigning per-user permissions. The same groups available for authentication are also available for authorization. For example, you can assign a domain global group, GlobalGroup01 in Domain01, privileges to establish a connection with SQL Server (authentication) and to run a *SELECT* statement against a specific table or view in the database. Any domain users that are members of GlobalGroup01 will be able to run the *SELECT* statement providing that the Deny permission state isn't assigned elsewhere. You will learn about the Deny permission state later in this lesson.

Roles are similar to groups, but they are created and maintained within SQL Server. There are two types of roles: standard roles and application roles. Standard roles are assigned privileges that users inherit through role membership. Groups can contain Windows users, and depending on the group type, they can also contain other Windows groups. In contrast, a standard role can contain all security account types: Windows user and group accounts, SQL Server login IDs, and other standard roles.

Group and standard role nesting (groups containing other groups and roles containing groups or other roles) enable you to build a privilege hierarchy because privileges are cumulative. For example, if User01 is a member of Role02 and Role02 is a member of Role01, Role02 is subordinate to Role01. If you then assign a privilege to Role01 and a privilege to Role02, User01 is assigned both privileges. Figure 13.3 demonstrates this hierarchical relationship.

SQL Server includes predefined standard roles to simplify server and database administration. The two primary categories of predefined roles are fixed server and fixed database. Fixed server roles enable role members to administer the server. For example, if you make a user a member of the ServerAdmin fixed server role, the user can configure server-wide settings. SQL Server Setup adds the Windows Administrators group (BUILTIN\Administrators) as a member of the SysAdmin fixed server role. Fixed database roles enable role members to administer a specific database. For example, if you make a user a member of the db_BackupOperator fixed database role, the user can backup the database. To see the privileges assigned to each fixed database role, run the *sp_dbfixedrolepermission fixed_db_role_name* system stored procedure. To see the privileges assigned to each fixed server role, run the *sp_srvrolepermission fixed_server_role_name* system stored procedure.

Note   For a list of predefined roles, refer to "Adding a Member to a Predefined Role" in SQL Server Books Online.

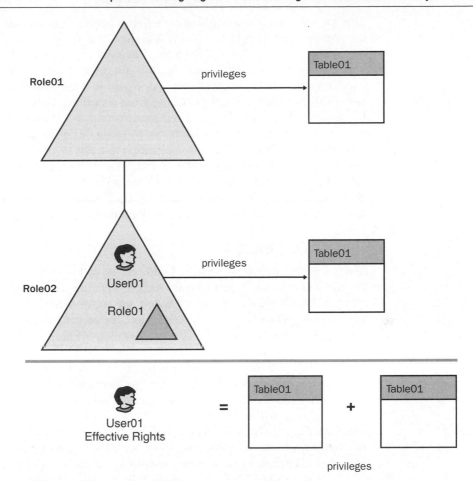

Figure 13.3.   A hierarchical relationship showing that User01 inherits the privileges assigned to Role01 and Role02.

The Public role automatically contains all database users, groups, and roles. This special role is similar to the Everyone special group in Windows NT and Windows 2000. You cannot add or remove members from this role or delete the role. The Public role is contained in every database and is assigned default permissions to each database. You can revoke permissions from the Public role to secure the database. Create standard roles in the database if Windows groups do not meet your administrative requirements.

There are times when an application requires permissions that are incongruent with user permissions. In this case, using SQL Server permissions to configure application security is impractical. SQL Server includes application roles to accommodate application-specific permissions. Application roles contain a password and do not contain members. This special role is designed to control what privileges are available to all users accessing the database from a specific application. The application role is assigned permissions in a database. After a user is authenticated to SQL Server, you activate the application role by using the *sp_setapprole* system stored procedure. The password for the application role can be encrypted by *sp_setapprole* before the password is sent to SQL Server. When an application role is active, all other user permissions are revoked until the session or application is closed. If an application must access another database when an application role is active, permission to the other database is only available through the guest user account.

Permission States

There are three permission states: Grant, Deny, and Revoke. When you *Grant* a permission, the user, group, or role (security account) is explicitly assigned the permission. When you *Revoke* a permission, the permission is removed from the security account. When you *Deny* a permission, the security account is explicitly restricted from the permission. A user's permissions are the sum of all permissions that are assigned directly to the user or to a group or role of which the user is a member. SQL Server processes Deny permission states first, which negates the permissions granted elsewhere. Therefore, if a user inherits this permission state or if it is directly assigned to the user, all other permissions are irrelevant. For example, suppose that User01 is granted the SELECT permission to Table01 and User01 is a member of Group01, which is granted the INSERT permission to Table01. As a result, the user account's effective rights are SELECT and INSERT for Table01. However, if Group01 is a member of Role01, which is assigned Deny for the SELECT and INSERT permissions on Table01, User01 cannot query or add to Table01.

Object and Statement Permissions

There are three types of permissions in SQL Server: object, statement, and implied. *Object* permissions apply to database objects and vary by object. For example, you can assign EXECUTE permission for a stored procedure and SELECT permission for a table. *Statement* permissions apply to the *CREATE* and *BACKUP* Transact-SQL statements that are run against a database. For example, the *CREATE TABLE* statement permission allows a user to create tables in a database. The following list shows object and statement permissions for various database objects:

Permission	For
CREATE (statement permission)	database, table, view, stored procedure, default, rule and function creation
BACKUP (statement permission)	database and log file backup
SELECT and UPDATE (object permission)	query and modify tables, views, and columns in tables and views
INSERT and DELETE (object permission)	add and remove tables, views, and records in tables and views
EXECUTE (object permission)	run stored procedures

Implied permissions are assigned to object owners, fixed server roles, and fixed database roles and cannot be revoked from the owners or roles. Some implied statement permissions are assigned only through fixed role membership. For example, a user must be a member of the ServerAdmin fixed server role to execute the *SHUT-DOWN* statement.

Auditing

General operating system auditing is a feature made possible in Windows NT and Windows 2000 by the Event Log service. SQL Server includes SQL Server login and security event auditing. Login authentication success and failure is a server option that you configure by using *xp_loginconfig* extended stored procedure or by using the Security tab of the SQL Server Properties (Configure) dialog box of Enterprise Manager (refer to Figure 13.2).

In order to audit events, use SQL Profiler to configure security audit events. The security events are logged to a file or to a database table. Configure the events to audit, the data columns to be traced, and the storage properties for the trace file or trace table. After tracing security events with SQL Profiler, you can open the trace file (.trc) in SQL Profiler or query on a trace table. To see an event class and data column matrix for security events, refer to "Security Audit Event Category" in SQL Server Books Online.

Object Encryption

Encrypting data keeps information confidential by storing it in a format that is difficult to decipher. Programs decipher encrypted data by using a decryption algorithm or decryption key. SQL Server 2000 contains a decryption algorithm to decipher and parse database objects that are encrypted in SQL Server. Passwords and encrypted objects in SQL Server are not viewable by any database user (including members of the SysAdmin fixed server role). SQL Server 2000 automatically encrypts passwords associated with SQL Server login IDs, and you can optionally encrypt the contents of stored procedures, user-defined functions, views, and triggers by specifying the WITH ENCRYPTION clause when creating these database objects.

Application

Applications accessing a database can call the *sp_setapprole* system stored procedure to activate an application role. In addition, applications can implement their own security that is outside of database control. Applications can use data access APIs supported by SQL Server, such as ActiveX Data Objects (ADO), OLE DB, and Open Database Connectivity (ODBC), in order to insulate the application from data access details. Applications should include security features when accessing data in SQL Server. For example, Internet Explorer includes Security Zone settings to protect against malicious scripts being run against the database.

Lesson Summary

One way to conceptualize database security is by using a six-layer model. The first layer is physical security. Vital servers, including the server running SQL Server 2000, and critical network equipment, such as backbone hardware, should be placed in a secure location. The second layer is network protocol security. Network protocol security provides encryption, mutual authentication, multiprotocol support, and firewall services in order to enhance database security. Encryption is implemented by using network security protocols such as IPSec or by using database Net-Library encryption services. Mutual authentication, multiprotocol support, and firewall services are implemented outside SQL Server network services. The third layer is domain security. SQL Server security is integrated with and benefits from Microsoft domain security. Domain user accounts and groups are assigned permissions in SQL Server to securely connect to and access the database. The fourth layer of security is local computer security. The local computer operating system provides security auditing, file and registry protection, and file encryption services. The fifth layer is SQL Server security. Authentication, authorization, auditing, and encryption services are built into SQL Server. The sixth layer is application security. Applications can use SQL Server application roles and implement their own security features to enhance database security.

Lesson 2: Designing a Database Security Plan

Once you understand database security architecture, the next step is to design a security plan that protects the database without being unnecessarily restrictive. To design a security plan, you identify security requirements contained in a list of system requirements, translate the rules into a set of user activities, and then create a User-to-Activity Map. The User-to-Activity Map serves as a security implementation guide. This lesson focuses on SQL Server security, described as layer five in Lesson 1. Network administrators, systems administrators, and engineers are responsible for implementing layers one through four of database security; database administrators and designers are responsible for implementing layer five, and application developers are responsible for implementing layer six. A security specialist typically oversees the entire security design. This lesson explores how to create a database security plan and how the security architecture explained in Lesson 1 relates to designing an efficient and effective plan.

After this lesson, you will be able to:

- Extract database security requirements from system requirements.
- Design security for a SQL Server 2000 database.
- Determine how to assign security to users, groups, and roles.
- Explain the purpose of object chaining and forming a security hierarchy through nesting.

Estimated Lesson time: 25 minutes

Requirements

In Chapter 3, "Designing a SQL Server Database," you learned that a security plan identifies database users, the data objects that they can access, and activities that they can perform in the database. Gather this information by extracting security requirements from system requirements and by determining any other security requirements that might not be part of the system requirements. For example, system requirements might not include security administrative activities such as auditing the execution of a stored procedure or running a database backup. After listing the data objects that need protection and the restricted activities that users perform in the database, create a list of unique users or classes of users and groups that access the database. Armed with this information, create a User-to-Activity Map. The map is a table that cross-references the two lists to identify which users can access protected data objects and which restricted activities they can perform in the database.

Suppose you have an employee database that is accessed by 100 users. The database contains an employee information table (Employees), a salary grade table (Salaries), and an employee location table (Locations). All employees access the

Employees table and the office location information in the Locations table. A small group of employees can access the Salaries table and the home address information in the Locations table. The same small group of employees can add, delete, and modify data in all of these tables. Another user is responsible for performing nightly backups, and another group of users can create and delete data objects in the database. The security requirements for this simple database example are as follows:

- All employees run *SELECT* statements against the Employees table.
- All employees run *SELECT* statements on the office location information in the Locations table.
- A small group of employees runs *INSERT*, *DELETE*, and *UPDATE* statements against all columns in all three tables.
- A user runs nightly database backups and performs general database administration and requires full server access.
- A group of users runs *CREATE* and *DROP* statements in the database.

The list of unique users, classes of users, and groups that access this database is as follows:

- All employees are a class of users covered by the Public database role.
- Members of the HumanResources Windows 2000 group require restricted access to the database.
- User account JDoe is a database administrator.
- Company database developers create and delete objects in SQL Server.

The following User-to-Activity Map is constructed from the information provided:

User Account, Group, or Role	Activity
Public (role)	Read-only access to the Employees table
Public (role)	Read-only access to office location columns in the Location table
DOMAIN01\HumanResources (group)	Full access to the Employees, Location, and Salaries tables
DOMAIN01\Jdoe	Full access to the database
DOMAIN01\dbDev	Create databases

For additional security examples, refer to "Planning Security" in SQL Server Books Online and to the exercise in this lesson.

Nesting and Ownership Chains

There are many ways to implement a security design in SQL Server. The goal is to implement security as efficiently as possible without compromising security requirements. For example, if 100 users all require the same level of access to the database, it is more efficient to use groups or roles than to implement security for each individual user. Both approaches will achieve the same goal, but the former design (using groups or roles) is easier to maintain and faster to implement. There are a number of security features, such as nesting, ownership chains, and pre-defined roles, that will help you design an efficient security plan.

Nesting

Nesting helps you avoid redundant permission assignments. For example, assign the Public role SELECT permission to tables that all authenticated users are allowed to access. Assign restricted object and statement permissions to a group (named Group01 for this example) that requires the same restrictions. Then, assign special permissions to a user or smaller group (named SpecialGroup01) that requires special permissions. The Public role contains all users, groups, and roles (including Group01 and SpecialGroup01). These two groups inherit the permissions assigned to the Public role. Group01 contains SpecialGroup01 so that SpecialGroup01 inherits the permissions assigned to Group01. Members of the group inherit special permissions assigned to SpecialGroup01.

Note   Windows 2000 native-mode domains also support nested groups.

Ownership Chains

Certain privileges are implied, either by predefined role membership or through object ownership. Implied permissions help you minimize the amount of manual assignment that you must undertake to meet security requirements. Consistent object ownership and forming ownership chains are other effective ways to limit and consolidate permission assignments. An *ownership chain* exists when a set of nested objects and the original calling object are owned by the same user and are located in the same database. Ownership chains allow database users to access data and to perform activities if they are only granted permissions to the calling object (either a stored procedure or a view). SQL Server checks only the calling stored procedure or view for object or statement permissions when the entire chain is owned by a single user account.

A chain is possible because views can call tables or nest other views. Additionally, stored procedures can call tables, views, or nest other stored procedures. The calling object depends on the underlying called objects. For example, a view that calls a table depends on the table in order to return a result set. As long as the same owner of the calling object owns all called objects, an ownership chain is formed. The object owner, not the user running the procedure, owns any objects created within a stored procedure. Ownership chains only apply to *SELECT*, *INSERT*, *UPDATE*, and *DELETE* statements.

Note   Recursive nesting does not provide security indirection because the calling and the called object are identical (and thus require identical permissions).

If an ownership chain is not formed, due to inconsistent object ownership, SQL Server checks permissions on each object in the chain whose next-lowest link is owned by a different user. The owner of any nested object retains access control. To optimize permission assignment, consider specifying the database owner (dbo) when creating database objects.

Security Design Recommendations

There are general guidelines for implementing SQL Server security. The network environment influences how you apply security accounts (users, groups, and roles) to your database security design. Existing permissions help you build an efficient database security design.

Users, Groups, and Roles

Determining whether to assign permissions to groups, roles, or users depends on who needs permissions. For example, assign permissions to an individual user account if a single user requires unique permissions. The type of server environment in which SQL Server runs also affects to whom you will assign permissions (groups, roles, or users). For example, assign permissions to Windows domain users if the server is part of a domain and is accessed by using Windows authentication. If possible, add a user to a predefined role rather than assigning individual permissions. Assign users to roles if there is not a Windows group that adequately represents a set of users who need database permissions, if SQL Server is not running in a Windows domain, if Windows does not authenticate access to SQL Server, or if you do not have permissions to modify group membership. For example, there is a Windows 2000 group called developers that includes all company developers, but the database developers are the only members that require full access to SQL Server. Therefore, create a role named dbDev, and add all database developers to this role. Assign database permissions to groups if there is a Windows group that contains an appropriate set of members and users who connect to the database via Windows authentication.

Permissions

Use predefined roles (public, fixed database, and fixed server roles) rather than directly assigning object and statement permissions to roles, groups, and users. Fixed roles imply wide-reaching database and server permissions that cannot be changed. Therefore, carefully assign users to fixed roles. Assign permissions to groups and roles before assigning them to users.

Design your permission structure so that permission assignments that apply to all users are at the top of the security hierarchy, and place restricted permission assignments lower in the security hierarchy. Create objects with a consistent owner so that you can create ownership chains. Create views and stored procedures that make use of ownership chains and that assign permissions to the calling stored procedure or view.

When granting object permissions to a user account, you can allow the user account to grant object permissions to others. Delegating this ability to other users means that you do not have to assign all permissions in the database. Assign the Deny permission state carefully. The effective right of any users who are directly assigned this permission state or who inherit it from a group or role membership is *deny*, regardless of permissions *granted* elsewhere.

Exercise 1: Designing Security for BookShopDB

In this exercise, you will extract security requirements from the system requirements outlined for BookShopDB in Chapter 3 and add additional security requirements to the list. You will then create a User-to-Activity Map in preparation for implementing security in Lesson 3, Exercise 2. To complete this exercise, you need paper and a pencil or a word processor.

▶ **To identify security requirements**

1. Return to Chapter 3 and review Exercise 2, "Identifying the System Requirements for Your Database Design."

2. Identify and write down the security requirements contained in the system requirements.

3. Identify and write down two security requirements that do not appear in the list extracted from the system requirements.

▶ **To determine users, groups, and roles for security and create a User-to-Activity Map**

1. Assuming that SQL Server is running in a Windows domain named BOOK-SHOP, create a list of unique users, roles, and groups to accommodate the security requirements. List only the users, roles, or groups that you believe are required to accommodate the security requirements.

2. Create a User-to-Activity Map that ties the security requirements to the unique users, roles, and groups that you defined in the previous step.

   In Lesson 3, you will implement security for BookShopDB by using the security design that you created in this exercise. In an actual database security implementation, many more additions and modifications are likely to be made to the security design.

Lesson Summary

Designing a security plan starts with understanding SQL Server security architecture and then extracting security requirements from a list of identified system requirements. However, system requirements might not include all security requirements, such as security for system administration. Therefore, the next step is to resolve additional security requirements that are not part of the system requirements. Next, identify users, groups, and roles to which privileges are assigned. Finally, tie security requirements together with identified users, groups, and roles to create a User-to-Activity Map. A security design is improved by considering the permissions to be assigned and the SQL Server network environment. For example, if two users need the same permissions, use a group or a role. Additionally, consider using existing groups in a Windows domain before creating new groups, and use predefined roles before creating new roles. Wherever possible, optimize a security design by using group and role nesting and ownership chains. Build a security hierarchy with group and role nesting. Consolidate permissions on fewer database objects by building ownership chains.

Lesson 3: Database Security Implementation and Administration

Implement a security design and administer it by using database tools such as Enterprise Manager and Query Analyzer. Verify a security design by connecting to the database with various security accounts, testing permissions, and auditing activity with SQL Profiler. In this lesson, you will see how to use database tools to configure authentication and authorization. You will also learn how to administer permissions after granting a security account with access to a database. Permission administration involves granting, revoking, and denying permissions to security accounts. In the last part of the lesson, you will learn how to administer roles. Role administration involves adding and removing roles from a database and controlling role membership in both user-defined and predefined roles.

After this lesson, you will be able to:

- Configure authentication and authorization for a SQL Server 2000 database.
- Administer permissions and roles.

Estimated Lesson time: 45 minutes

Administering Authentication

Before a user can connect to SQL Server, a security account must be added to the server and given SQL Server access. You accomplish this task by using Enterprise Manager or the Transact-SQL language.

Configuring Authentication in Enterprise Manager

In the Enterprise Manager console tree, expand the Security node and click Logins. Right-click in the details pane, and click New Login. In the SQL Server Login Properties - New Login dialog box, type the name of a Windows account. A domain Windows account, user, or group account includes the domain name. A workgroup Windows account, user account, or user-created group includes the computer name. A Windows local group that is predefined includes BUILTIN. For example, to add User01 from DOMAIN01, a local user (User01) on the SQL Server named SQLSERVER01, and the local PowerUsers predefined Windows group, the names to be added are as follows:

DOMAIN01\User01, SQLSERVER01\User01 and BUILTIN\PowerUsers

To add a SQL Server login ID from the SQL Server Login Properties - New Login dialog box, click SQL Server Authentication and then type the name of the login ID. Adding a SQL Server Login ID creates the ID in the database and grants the login ID access.

You can delete accounts from the Details pane of Enterprise Manager, and you can select the properties of an account and deny it access to authenticate with the server.

Configuring Authentication Using Transact-SQL

You use system stored procedures to manage SQL Server authentication. Use the *sp_grantlogin*, *sp_denylogin*, and *sp_revokelogin* system stored procedures to manage Windows account authentication. Use the *sp_addlogin* and *sp_droplogin* system stored procedures to manage SQL Server login ID authentication.

Windows Accounts

Use the *sp_grantlogin* system stored procedure in Query Analyzer or a command prompt tool such as osql to add and grant access to Windows accounts. The following code example shows how to use *sp_grantlogin* to add and grant access to User01 in DOMAIN01, User01 on the computer running SQL Server, SQLSERVER01, and the predefined PowerUsers group:

```
EXEC sp_grantlogin @loginame = 'DOMAIN01\user01'
EXEC sp_grantlogin @loginame = 'SQLSERVER01\user01'
EXEC sp_grantlogin @loginame = 'BUILTIN\power users'
```

Use *sp_denylogin* to deny a specific user or group access to the server without deleting the Windows account from SQL Server. You might want to perform this action to keep the database online but not allow users to connect while you are troubleshooting procedures or updating the database. The following code example shows how to use *sp_denylogin* to deny members of the predefined Power Users group from connecting to SQL Server:

```
EXEC sp_denylogin @loginame = 'BUILTIN\power users'
```

To delete a Windows account from SQL Server, use *sp_revokelogin*. The following code example shows how to use *sp_revokelogin* to remove SQLSERVER01\User01:

```
sp_revokelogin @loginame = 'SQLSERVER01\User01'
```

If a Windows account is granted privileges to one or more databases, *sp_revokelogin* will remove those privileges and delete the account from SQL Server.

SQL Server Login ID

Use the *sp_addlogin* system stored procedure to create, add, and grant access to a SQL Server login ID. The following code example shows how to use *sp_addlogin* to create, add, and grant access to User02 with a password of password02:

```
sp_addlogin
@loginame = 'user02',
@passwd = 'password02'
```

The only required parameter is @loginame. Optional input parameters other than @passwd include @defdb, @deflanguage, @sid, and @encryptopt. Use @defdb to specify a database (Master is the default). Use @deflanguage to specify a language (if no language is specified, the server's default language is used). Use @sid to define a unique security identifier (SID); otherwise, the database will auto-generate a unique SID. Use @encryptopt to skip password encryption. The default is to encrypt the password.

You cannot deny a SQL Server login ID from SQL Server authentication. Instead, you must delete the login ID. Use *sp_droplogin* to delete a SQL Server login ID. A SQL Server login ID mapped to an existing user in any database cannot be deleted until user database privileges are removed. Use the *sp_revokedbaccess* system stored procedure to remove database privileges. Refer to the next section of this lesson for details concerning *sp_revokedbaccess*.

Administering Authorization

Authentication alone is not enough to access databases in SQL Server. Security accounts (Windows accounts and SQL Server login IDs) configured for authentication are authorized to access a specific database if any one of the following three conditions is met:

- The Guest role is permitted to access the database.
- A predefined or other standard role of which the user is a member is permitted to access the database.
- A Windows group of which the user is a member is permitted to access the database.

Configuring Authorization in Enterprise Manager

In the Enterprise Manager console tree, expand the Databases node, expand a specific database, and then click Users. Right-click in the details pane and click New Database User. In the Database User Properties - New User dialog box, select the name of an authenticated security account. Only authenticated security accounts can be added. You can optionally specify a username that is different than the authenticated security account name. From this dialog box, you also specify role membership. Notice in Figure 13.4 that the Public role is automatically selected.

Any accounts added to a database are automatically added to the Public role. You cannot remove a database member from the Public role.

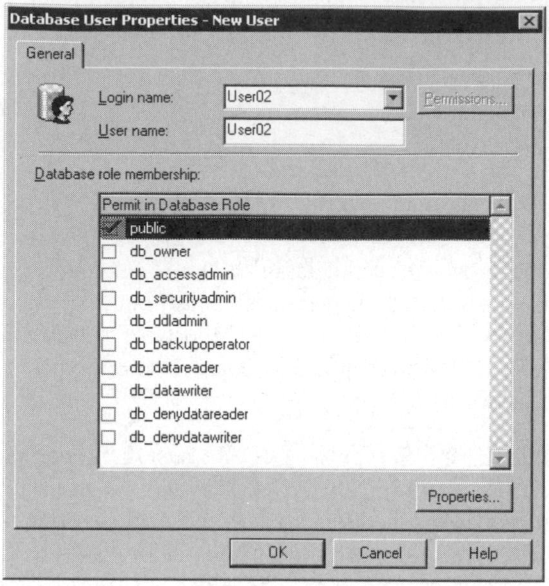

Figure 13.4.   Adding User02 to a database from the Database User Properties - New User dialog box.

Once an account is added in the Database User Properties - New User dialog box, the Permissions button appearing in Figure 13.4 becomes active. Use the Permissions button to assign permissions to the account or to view existing permissions.

Configuring Authorization Using Transact-SQL

Like authentication, system stored procedures are used to manage SQL Server authorization. Use *sp_grantdbaccess* and *sp_revokedbaccess* to grant or revoke database access to a security account. These system stored procedures work with all valid security accounts, Windows accounts, and SQL Server login IDs. Granting access is also called mapping an account to a database. The following code example shows how to use *sp_grantdbaccess* to map access for the Pubs database to the following users: User01 in DOMAIN01, User01 in the server running SQL Server (SQLSERVER01), the User01 SQL Server login ID, and the local Power Users group:

```
USE pubs
EXEC sp_grantdbaccess @loginame = 'DOMAIN01\User01'
EXEC sp_grantdbaccess @loginame = 'SQLSERVER01\User01',
@name_in_db = 'LocalUser01'
EXEC sp_grantdbaccess @loginame = 'user01',
@name_in_db = 'SQLUser01'
EXEC sp_grantdbaccess @loginame = 'BUILTIN\power users'
```

Notice that @name_in_db was specified for SQLSERVER01\User01 and for the User01 SQL Server login ID. The @name_in_db parameter allows you to alias a different name to the security account. If @name_in_db is not specified, the security account name is the username alias.

Use *sp_revokedbaccess* to remove a security account from a database. You cannot delete a SQL Server login ID until you run *sp_revokedbaccess* on any databases where privileges are granted. However, you can delete a Windows account without first removing any database mappings. The following code example shows how to use *sp_revokedbaccess* to remove User01 with an alias of SQLUser01 from the Pubs database:

```
USE pubs
EXEC sp_revokedbaccess @name_in_db = SQLUser01
```

Administering Permissions

The effective rights of a security account granted access to a database are the sum of the permissions assigned to the Public role, the permissions that the user gains as a member of other authorized roles and groups, and any permissions directly assigned to the account. The Deny permission state negates all permissions either inherited or granted directly to the security account.

Configuring Permissions in Enterprise Manager

To assign additional permissions, access the properties of a security account that appears in the Users node of a database. From there, assign the user to fixed database roles or to any custom roles defined for the database. To directly assign permissions to a user, role, or group, click the Permissions button to see the Database User Properties dialog box. From this dialog box, assign object permissions. You can also assign permissions to a specific object by accessing the properties of the object. SQL Server only allows permissions that are valid for the type of object. For example, execute (EXEC) permission is available for a stored procedure but not for a table or view. If you select a table or view in the Database User Properties dialog box, the Columns button is available. If you press the Columns button, you can assign SELECT and UPDATE object permissions on a per-column basis.

To assign the statement permissions *CREATE* and *BACKUP*, right-click on a database in the console tree and select Properties. From the *database_name* Properties dialog box that appears, click the Permissions tab. All security accounts granted access privileges appear in the Permissions tab and so do the statement permissions that can be assigned to the accounts.

For any permissions that are assigned through Enterprise Manager, a permission checkbox has three states: checked, unchecked, and marked with an X. A checked permission is granted; an unchecked permission is unassigned or revoked if previously assigned; and a check box marked with an X is a denied permission. The denied permission supercedes any assignment of the permission elsewhere.

Configuring Permissions Using Transact-SQL

Use the *GRANT*, *REVOKE*, and *DENY* statements to administer object and statement permissions from Query Analyzer, or use a command prompt tool such as osql.

The *GRANT* Statement

When using *GRANT*, you must specify the permission (or permissions) to assign and to whom they are assigned. Use the ALL keyword to assign all valid object or statement permissions. When assigning object permissions, you must also specify on what object the permissions should be applied. This specification is not required for statement permissions because they apply to a database, not to a single object in the database. Optionally, specify the WITH GRANT OPTION clause to permit a security account to grant others the same permission that has been granted to it. Use the AS keyword to specify a security account (group or role) in the current database that has the authority to execute the *GRANT* statement. If permissions are granted for an object to a group or role, you must use the AS keyword to specify the group or role with authority to assign permissions to others. SQL Server security will verify that you are a member of the specified group or role before allowing you to use the *GRANT* statement.

The main clauses in a *GRANT* statement when assigning statement permissions are summarized as follows:

GRANT ALL | *statement_ permission(s)*

TO *security_account_name(s)*

The main clauses in a *GRANT* statement when assigning object permissions are summarized as follows:

GRANT ALL | *object_ permission(s)*

(*column(s)*) ON *table_name* | *view_name*

| ON *table_name* | *view_name (column(s))*

| ON *stored_ procedure_name* | *user_defined_ function_name*

TO *security_account_name(s)*

WITH GRANT OPTION

AS *group_name* | *role_name*

The ON keyword that specifies *stored_procedure_name* includes extended stored procedures. Multiple statement and object permissions are comma-delimited, as are security account names, as shown in the following code example:

```
USE pubs
GRANT CREATE TABLE, CREATE VIEW, BACKUP DATABASE, BACKUP LOG
TO user01, [BUILTIN\power users]
```

User01 and the Power Users group are granted four statement permissions. The Power Users group is specified with brackets because of the backslash and space in the group name.

If you want to grant one or more security accounts with all valid object or statement permissions, use the ALL keyword, as shown in the following code example:

```
USE pubs
GRANT ALL
TO public
```

The Public role is granted all assignable statement permissions to the Pubs database. The result of this assignment is that all authorized users are permitted to run any statement permission against the database. Making this assignment would be atypical, but the code example demonstrates how to open the database to all authorized users. If you map the special Guest account to the Pubs database, all authenticated users who are not mapped to the Pubs database are also granted full statement permissions because the Guest account is a member of the Public role.

You can mix column and table permissions so that the last permission specified is assigned to the column. You must make sure that the last object permission is a legal column permission (SELECT or UPDATE), as shown in the following code example:

```
USE pubs
GRANT INSERT, DELETE, UPDATE, SELECT
(ord_date, ord_num, qty) ON dbo.sales
TO user01
```

User01 is granted INSERT, DELETE, and UPDATE permissions to the dbo.sales table and SELECT column permissions to the Ord_Date, Ord_Num, and Qty columns. Notice that the table name is qualified with the owner name, dbo. This specification is optional but is a good coding practice if there are other identically named tables in the database having different owners. The following code example shows how to assign UPDATE and SELECT object permissions exclusively to the columns:

```
USE pubs
GRANT UPDATE, SELECT
ON dbo.sales (ord_date, ord_num, qty)
TO test
```

The only valid object permission for a stored procedure is EXECUTE. The following code example assigns EXECUTE to Power Users for the *xp_cmdshell* extended stored procedure:

```
USE master
GRANT EXEC
ON xp_cmdshell
TO [BUILTIN\power users]
```

The *xp_cmdshell* extended stored procedure is in the Master database. Therefore, you must make Master the current database. You can only grant, revoke, or deny permissions on objects in the current database.

Note   For more information, refer to the *GRANT* statement in SQL Server Books Online.

The *Revoke* Statement

Use the *REVOKE* statement to remove previously granted permissions from a security account. The format of the *REVOKE* statement is similar to the *GRANT* statement with some exceptions. The TO keyword in the *GRANT* statement is replaced with FROM when revoking statement permissions and is either TO or FROM when revoking object permissions. The syntax for revoking object permissions includes the optional CASCADE keyword and the GRANT OPTION FOR clause. Use the GRANT OPTION FOR clause to revoke the WITH GRANT OPTION permission assigned to a security account. Use the CASCADE keyword to revoke permissions granted to the specified security account and any other security accounts that were granted permissions by the specified security account. You should include both GRANT OPTION FOR and CASCADE to revoke the Grant permission state assigned by the security account to other security accounts. The following code example revokes the EXEC permission from User01 and any other users to whom User01 assigned the EXEC permission:

```
USE master
REVOKE EXEC
ON xp_cmdshell
FROM user01
CASCADE
```

Run the following system stored procedure to view the current permissions of the extended stored procedure:

```
EXEC sp_helprotect 'xp_cmdshell'
```

The *DENY* Statement

Use the *DENY* statement to explicitly prohibit a security account from the privileges specified and to prohibit the security account from inheriting the permission through group or role membership. The format of the *DENY* statement is similar to the *GRANT* and *REVOKE* statements. Like the *GRANT* statement, the TO keyword specifies to whom the statement applies. The *DENY* statement includes the CASCADE keyword to explicitly deny permissions that were granted to the specified security account and to any other security accounts that were granted permissions by the specified security account. The following code example denies statement permissions from a SQL Server login ID and a group:

```
USE pubs
DENY CREATE TABLE, CREATE VIEW, BACKUP DATABASE, BACKUP LOG
TO user01, [BUILTIN\power users]
```

Administering Roles

You administer group membership outside SQL Server and administer role membership within SQL Server. Roles are created in Enterprise Manager or by using Transact-SQL. Predefined roles cannot be members of other roles. For example, you cannot make the SecurityAdmin fixed server role a member of the db_Owner fixed database role. All predefined roles (fixed server and fixed database) can contain groups and users as members. Fixed database roles can also contain user-defined, standard roles. User-defined, standard roles can contain other user-defined roles, groups, and users as their members. You cannot create circular role membership. For example, if Role01 is a member of Role02, Role02 cannot be a member of Role01. Application roles cannot be members of a role or contain members.

Adding and Deleting Roles

You can add and delete user-defined, standard roles in a database. You cannot delete the predefined, fixed database and fixed server roles. To add a role by using Enterprise Manager, expand the Roles node below a database in the console tree, right-click in the Details pane, and then click New Database Role. From the Database Role Properties - New Role dialog box that appears, name the role and select a role type (standard or application). If you select a standard role, you can add role members when you create the role. If you choose an application role, you can define a password for the role. To delete the role, select it in the details pane and press the DELETE key.

Use the *sp_addrole* system stored procedure to add a standard role to a database from Query Analyzer, or use a command prompt tool such as osql. The *sp_addrole* system stored procedure contains input parameters to specify the role name (and optionally, the role's owner). If you don't specify role ownership, the role owner defaults to the role creator. The following code example adds a role named Role01 to the Pubs database:

```
USE pubs
EXEC sp_addrole @rolename = 'role01'
```

Use the *sp_droprole* system stored procedure to drop a user-defined, standard role. The following code example drops a role named Role01:

```
USE pubs
EXEC sp_droprole @rolename = 'rolc01'
```

Use the *sp_addapprole* system stored procedure to add an application role to a database from Query Analyzer, or use a command prompt tool such as osql. Like *sp_addrole*, the first input parameter is @rolename. Unlike *sp_addrole*, the second input parameter for *sp_addapprole* is @password. The application role name and password are used to activate the application role, as you will see in the next section of this lesson. Use *sp_dropapprole* to delete an application role. The following code example adds an application role, AppRole01, with a password of password01 to the pubs database and then deletes the application role:

```
USE pubs
EXEC sp_addapprole @rolename = 'appRole01', @password = 'password01'
EXEC sp_dropapprole @rolename = 'appRole01'
```

Administering Role Membership

Standard roles are located in two places within Enterprise Manager. Database roles are contained in the Roles node of a database, and server roles are contained in the Server Roles node below the Security node. To add a member to a standard role in Enterprise Manager, right-click the role in the details pane and click Properties. A server role displays the Server Role Properties dialog box, and a database role displays the Database Role Properties dialog box. From the Server Role Properties dialog box, you administer role membership and view role permissions. From the Database Role Properties dialog box, you administer role membership and set permissions for user-defined roles. You cannot modify permissions on any fixed roles.

Use the *sp_addrolemember* system stored procedure to add members to a user-defined standard role or to a fixed database role. Use *sp_addsrvrolemember* to add a security account to a fixed server role. The *sp_addrolemember* system stored procedure uses @rolename and @membername as input parameters, and *sp_addsrvrolemember* uses @loginame and @rolename as input parameters. The following code example adds Role02, BUILTIN\Power Users and User01 to Role01 (a user-defined, standard role):

```
USE pubs
EXEC sp_addrolemember @rolename = 'role01',
@membername = 'role02'
EXEC sp_addrolemember @rolename = 'role01',
@membername = 'BUILTIN\power users'
EXEC sp_addrolemember @rolename = 'role01',
@membername = 'user01'
```

You must specify the mapped name for the @membername input parameter. For example, if the Power Users group alias in the database is PowerU, then the @membername value is *poweru*. Any user or group to be made a member of a role must be mapped to the database for membership addition to succeed.

Role membership restrictions control which members you can add using *sp_addrolemember*. For example, if you attempt to add a predefined role such as db_DataWriter to a user-defined role, membership will fail, as shown in the following code example:

```
USE pubs
EXEC sp_addrolemember @rolename = 'role01',
@membername = 'db_datawriter'
```

SQL Server displays the following error message:

```
Server: Msg 15405, Level 11, State 1, Procedure sp_addrolemember, Line 7
4
Cannot use the reserved user or role name 'db_datawriter'.
```

You remove role members by using the *sp_droprolemember* system stored procedure. The following code example drops User01 from Role01:

```
USE pubs
EXEC sp_droprolemember @rolename = 'role01',
@membername = 'user01'
```

Note   Enterprise Manager includes the Create Login wizard. You can use this wizard to add security accounts (authentication), to assign predefined, fixed server role membership, and to authorize database access. You cannot assign database role membership by using this wizard.

Activating an Application Role

After creating an application role, a user who authenticates with SQL Server can use an application role that is assigned to a database by activating the role. The connected user's security context is the effective rights of the application role. When the application role is activated, the user's privileges in the database are irrelevant until the session is ended. Use the *sp_setapprole* to activate an application role. The following code example uses *sp_setapprole* to activate the App1 application role with a password of secretpass. The application role is located in the Pubs database:

```
USE pubs
sp_setapprole 'app1', 'secretpass'
```

Exercise 2: Implementing Security for BookShopDB

In this exercise, you will use Query Analyzer to implement the security design you created in Exercise 1. You might want to review the security design you created in Exercise 1. In the first practice, you will create and configure Windows user accounts and a group. You will use these security accounts and a SQL Server login ID in the design implementation.

▶ **To create a Windows group and Windows users**

1. Logon to the LAB1 computer as Administrator.

2. Open a command window.

3. At the command prompt, type the following commands. Press ENTER between each line:

```
net user manager01 /add
net user manager02 /add
net user staff01 /add
net user staff02 /add
net user staff03 /add
```

A message appears, stating that each command completed successfully. The Manager01 and Manager02 Windows user accounts are added to the local computer.

4. Close the command window.

5. Using the Computer Management console, add a group named Managers and make Manager01 and Manager02 members of the Managers group.

Note The NET GROUP command line command is not used in the previous step because it functions only on domain controllers.

▶ **To configure group authentication**

1. Open Query Analyzer and connect to your local server.

2. In the Editor pane of the Query window, enter and execute the following code:

```
USE bookshopdb
EXEC sp_grantlogin @loginame = 'BUILTIN\users'
EXEC sp_grantlogin @loginame = 'LAB1\managers'
```

The Users local group and Managers local group on LAB1 are added to SQL Server so that members of these two groups can establish a connection to SQL Server.

3. In the Editor pane of the Query window, enter and execute the following code:

```
sp_addlogin @loginame = 'devuser',
@passwd = 'devpass'
```

The developer can now establish a connection with SQL Server by using the SQL Server login ID DevUser. The only optional parameter specified is @passwd, because the defaults for optional parameters not specified in the code are appropriate for this user.

4. In the Editor pane of the Query window, enter and execute the following system stored procedure:

```
sp_helplogins
```

The Results pane of the Query window shows all security accounts that can establish a connection with SQL Server. Notice that the BUILTIN\Administrator and sa accounts appear in the list as well as the three security accounts that you added in the previous steps. SQL Server Setup adds the BUILTIN\Administrator and sa security accounts. You cannot delete the sa account from the authentication list.

▶ **To authorize the security accounts in BookShopDB**

1. In the Editor pane of the Query window, enter and execute the following code:

```
EXEC sp_grantdbaccess @loginame = 'BUILTIN\users',
@name_in_db = 'All Staff'
EXEC sp_grantdbaccess @loginame = 'LAB1\managers'
EXEC sp_grantdbaccess @loginame = 'devuser'
EXEC sp_grantdbaccess @loginame = 'LAB1\manager01'
EXEC sp_grantdbaccess @loginame = 'LAB1\staff01'
EXEC sp_grantdbaccess @loginame = 'LAB1\staff02'
```

The security accounts are now mapped to BookShopDB. The Users group is given an alias of All Staff. Manager01 is added separately from the Managers group, because this user account will be assigned special privileges to the database. Two of the Staff accounts, Staff01 and Staff02, are added separately from the Users group, for the same reason.

2. In the Editor pane of the Query window, enter and execute the following code:

```
sp_helpuser
```

The Results pane of the Query window shows a list of users who are authorized to access BookShopDB. Notice that dbo appears in the list. This security account appears in each database and is the special database owner account. You cannot be authenticated or authorized to use a database using this account.

▶ **To configure permissions for the authorized accounts**

1. In the Editor pane of the Query window, enter and execute the following code:

```
sp_helprotect @name = NULL, @username = 'public'
```

The Results pane of the Query window shows a list of permissions assigned to the Public role. The Public role contains all authorized users, so permission assignment begins here to establish a security hierarchy. Notice that the list of permissions shows that Public is granted the SELECT object permission to many of the local system tables but has no object permissions for the user tables or statement permissions for the database.

2. In the Editor pane of the Query window, enter and execute the following code:

```
GRANT SELECT ON authors TO public
GRANT SELECT ON bookauthors TO public
GRANT SELECT ON bookcondition TO public
GRANT SELECT ON books TO public
GRANT SELECT ON customers TO public
GRANT SELECT ON formofpayment TO public
GRANT SELECT, INSERT, UPDATE, DELETE
ON orders TO public
GRANT SELECT, INSERT, UPDATE, DELETE
ON bookorders TO public
GRANT SELECT, INSERT, UPDATE, DELETE
ON orderstatus TO public
```

The SELECT permission is now assigned to Public for all user tables except the Employees and Positions tables. The *INSERT*, *UPDATE*, and *DELETE* object statements have also been granted to Public for the Orders, BookOrders, and OrderStatus tables.

Run *sp_helprotect* again if you wish to verify that the permissions were set or if you want to review the permissions in Enterprise Manager.

3. In the Editor pane of the Query window, enter and execute the following code:

```
GRANT INSERT, UPDATE, DELETE
ON authors TO [LAB1\managers]
GRANT INSERT, UPDATE, DELETE
ON bookauthors TO [LAB1\managers]
GRANT INSERT, UPDATE, DELETE
ON bookcondition TO [LAB1\managers]
GRANT INSERT, UPDATE, DELETE
ON books TO [LAB1\managers]
GRANT INSERT, UPDATE, DELETE
ON customers TO [LAB1\managers]
GRANT INSERT, UPDATE, DELETE
ON formofpayment TO [LAB1\managers]
GRANT ALL ON employees TO [LAB1\managers]
GRANT ALL ON positions to [LAB1\managers]
```

A security hierarchy is formed because the Managers group is a member of the Public role. The Public role has been assigned permissions that flow down to the Managers group. Permissions not assigned to the Public role are assigned to the Managers group, so the effective rights of the Managers group are all permissions to all user tables. Notice that the last two *GRANT* statements specify that all permissions should be assigned. The public role has no permissions to the Employees or Positions tables.

▶ **To assign fixed role membership**

1. In the Editor pane of the Query window, enter and execute the following code:

```
EXEC sp_addrolemember @rolename = 'db_backupoperator',
@membername = 'LAB1\staff01'
EXEC sp_addrolemember @rolename = 'db_backupoperator',
@membername = 'LAB1\staff02'
```

The two staff members are now members of the db_backupoperator fixed database role so that they can perform backups of BookShopDB.

2. In the Editor pane of the Query window, enter and execute the following code:

```
EXEC sp_addsrvrolemember @loginame = 'LAB1\managers',
@rolename = 'securityadmin'
EXEC sp_addsrvrolemember @loginame = 'LAB1\manager01',
@rolename = 'SysAdmin'
EXEC sp_addsrvrolemember @loginame = 'devuser',
@rolename = 'SysAdmin'
```

The Managers group is now a member of the SecurityAdmin fixed server role so that all managers can administer SQL Server security. Manager01 and DevUser are members of the SysAdmin fixed server role so that they have full access to SQL Server. Notice that the input parameters for *sp_addsrvrolemember* are different than the input parameters for *sp_addrolemember*.

Lesson Summary

Implement a security design by using database tools such as Enterprise Manager and Query Analyzer. The first step is to configure authentication by adding security accounts to SQL Server and permitting the accounts to establish a connection to SQL Server. Security accounts include Windows user accounts, Windows group accounts, and SQL Server login IDs. Configure security account authentication from the Logins node of Enterprise Manager or by using system stored procedures. The primary system stored procedures for configuring Windows account authentication are *sp_grantlogin*, *sp_denylogin*, and *sp_revokelogin*. The primary system stored procedures for configuring SQL Server login ID authentication are *sp_addlogin* and *sp_droplogin*.

The second step in security design implementation is authorizing security accounts to access a database. Configure security account authorization from the Users node of a database that appears in Enterprise Manager or by using system stored procedures. The primary system stored procedures for configuring security account authorization are *sp_grantdbaccess* and *sp_revokedbaccess*. Database authorization provides rudimentary permissions to the database. Administer permissions in Enterprise Manager from the properties of a security account or from the properties of an object. Administer permissions from tools such as Query Analyzer with the *GRANT*, *REVOKE*, and *DENY* statements.

The final task in security implementation is administering roles. Role administration involves adding and deleting roles and managing role membership. Add and delete roles from the Roles node in Enterprise Manager or by using system stored procedures. The system stored procedures for adding roles are *sp_addrole* and *sp_addapprole*, and the system stored procedure for deleting roles is *sp_droprole*. Manage role membership from the Roles and Server Roles nodes in Enterprise Manager. The system stored procedures for administering role membership are *sp_addrolemember*, *sp_addsrvrolemember*, and *sp_droprolemember*. Application roles do not contain members. To activate an application role, use the *sp_setapprole* system stored procedure.

Review

The following questions are intended to reinforce key information presented in this chapter. If you are unable to answer a question, review the appropriate lesson and then try the question again. You can find answers to the questions in the Appendix, "Questions and Answers."

1. Which two layers of the security architecture outlined in Lesson 1 contain SQL Server-specific security features?

2. You specifically revoke the UPDATE permission from User01 for Table01 so that the user cannot update the table. After revoking the permission, User01 still can update Table01. Name three possible reasons for this result. Four possible reasons are included in the answers.

3. You create a view and grant the Public role SELECT permission to the view. A user attempts to run the view but receives a permission conflict error message. What is the most likely reason for this result?

4. You use *sp_revokelogin*, but a Windows user is still able to authenticate to SQL Server. What is the most likely reason why the user can authenticate to SQL Server?

5. A SQL Server computer is part of a workgroup. User01 on another Windows computer that is part of the same workgroup wants to log in to SQL Server. Name two ways that the user can connect to SQL Server.

6. You use *sp_droplogin* to delete a SQL Server login ID from SQL Server, but you receive an error message stating that the security account is mapped or aliased to a database. You then use *sp_revokelogin* to delete a Windows account from SQL Server. You know that the Windows user account is mapped to several databases, but the procedure succeeds. Explain why you can delete the Windows account but you cannot delete the SQL Server login ID.

7. Why is there no place in Enterprise Manager to make a Windows user account or SQL Server login ID a member of a Windows group?

8. You map the special Guest account to a database named DB01, but you don't grant the Guest account any privileges in the database. You then run SQL Profiler and notice that a user who is not mapped to DB01 deleted a table in the database. What is the most likely reason why the user could delete a table?

9. You use the *DENY* statement to explicitly deny User01 and DOMAIN01\IT Users the CREATE VIEW permission. What Transact-SQL statement do you use to clear the explicit denial?

10. Using Enterprise Manager, you attempt to modify the permissions of a standard database role, but the Permissions button is inactive. You are connected to the database as a member of the SysAdmin role. Why is the Permissions button unavailable?

11. What are the next important steps after implementing a security design?

12. Explain the purpose of an application role and how you activate it.

C H A P T E R   1 4

SQL Server Monitoring and Tuning

About this Chapter

An important aspect of database design is continuous attention to optimizing database performance: for example, by creating stored procedures for complex tasks and by partitioning the database to improve data retrieval and updates. Tuning the database to improve performance and monitoring the server begins immediately after database implementation and continues thereafter. Lesson 1 examines how to use SQL Profiler to monitor a database system. Lesson 2 explores methods of improving database performance through partitioning and index tuning.

This chapter is not intended to provide a complete survey of database monitoring and optimization. For more information on these topics, see "Monitoring Server Performance and Activity" and "Optimizing Database Performance" in SQL Server Books Online.

Before You Begin

To complete the lessons in this chapter, you must have:

■ SQL Server 2000 Enterprise Edition installed on a Microsoft Windows 2000 Server computer.

■ The ability to log on to the Windows 2000 Server computer and to SQL Server as the Windows 2000 Administrator.

■ Completed the exercises in Chapter 3, "Designing a SQL Server Database," Chapter 4, "Implementing SQL Server Databases and Tables," Chapter 5, "Implementing Data Integrity," and Chapter 7, "Managing and Manipulating Data."

Lesson 1: Monitoring Databases with SQL Profiler

It is common for database performance to suffer as data requests and the loads placed on SQL Server change over time. A database maintains optimal performance levels through regular monitoring. Database monitoring is an important systems management task and the SQL Profiler, introduced in Chapter 13, is a key tool for completing this task. This lesson teaches you how to operate the SQL Profiler.

After this lesson, you will be able to:

- Describe tools commonly used to monitor SQL Server 2000.
- Use the SQL Profiler.
- Analyze captured SQL Profiler event data.

Estimated Lesson time: 25 minutes

SQL Server Monitoring

You will use data collected through SQL Server monitoring to determine if SQL Server is efficiently handling the workload or if the environment must be changed to handle the increased workload. Before you begin monitoring, you must determine your monitoring goals and choose an appropriate monitoring tool. Most monitoring tools capture data that you can analyze to determine which events should be monitored in the future. If the server and database environment is running efficiently, use the captured data to establish a performance baseline. Use the baseline against future captures to determine what, if anything, has changed. If the server or database is not running efficiently, use the captured data to determine how to improve performance. For example, by monitoring the response times for frequently used queries, you can determine whether changes to the query or indexes on the tables are necessary. If you are concerned about security, use the captured data to evaluate user activity; for example, you can monitor a specific database for the Transact-SQL commands users are attempting to run. If the server or database is not operating properly, use captured data to troubleshoot problems or debug application components such as stored procedures.

The primary tools for SQL Server monitoring are SQL Profiler and System Monitor (Performance Monitor in Microsoft Windows NT 4.0). The primary tool for database monitoring is SQL Profiler. In SQL Server, other tools and features available for SQL Server monitoring include the following:

- Enterprise Manager

  Monitoring features are found in the Current Activity node located below the Management node of the Enterprise Manager console tree.

- SQL Server error logs

- System stored procedures, like *sp_who* and *sp_monitor*

  SQL Profiler uses a set of stored procedures to monitor an instance of SQL Server. You can create your own monitoring application that uses these stored procedures to monitor SQL Server. For a list of SQL Profiler stored procedures, see "Creating and Managing Traces and Templates" in SQL Server Books Online.

- Built-in functions

- Trace flags or the Show Server Trace option in Query Analyzer

  Use trace flags to temporarily configure server behavior and then diagnose performance problems or debug stored procedures.

- Simple Network Management Protocol (SNMP)

  SQL Server includes Management Information Base (MIB) files that load into a Network Management System (NMS), such as HP OpenView, to monitor server and database activity.

- Windows Management Instrumentation (WMI) SQL Server Provider

This lesson explores SQL Profiler. Consult SQL Server Books Online, the *Windows 2000 Server Resource Kit, Microsoft Press 1999*, and the WMI SQL Server Administration Provider (on the SQL Server installation CD-ROM) for information on using the other tools listed.

SQL Profiler

Use the SQL Profiler graphical tool to monitor server and database activities such as auditing logins and determining the worst performing queries. SQL Profiler logs data to a SQL Server table or a file. To enhance capture analysis, you can replay logged data. SQL Profiler tracks events, such as the start of a batch or a transaction.

Monitoring with SQL Profiler

SQL Profiler monitors server and database activity and categorizes the activity as events. Logged events are called traces. A trace to a file is called a trace file and a trace to a table is called a trace table. After tracing events, you can replay traces in SQL Profiler against an instance of SQL Server to rerun the saved events. If traces are too large, you can filter the data so that only a subset of the event data is collected. Monitoring too many events adds overhead to the server and the monitoring process and can cause the trace file or trace table to grow very large, especially when monitoring over a long period of time. Define the data in a trace by using a trace template.

SQL Profiler is useful for completing the following tasks:

- Monitoring SQL Server performance
- Debugging Transact-SQL statements and stored procedures

  Use SQL Profiler to trace Transact-SQL statements and stored procedures during database development. Replay the trace to confirm that the code works properly and that it runs efficiently.

- Identifying slow-executing queries
- Troubleshooting problems in SQL Server

  To troubleshoot an event, capture it on a production system and then replay it on a test system. This approach is useful for thorough troubleshooting without interfering with user activity on the production system.

- Auditing server and database activity

  The security administrator can review any of the audited events, including the success or failure of a login attempt and the success or failure of permission requests in accessing statements and objects. Chapter 13, "Designing and Administering SQL Server 2000 Security," explores these topics.

Choosing Events, Data Columns, and Filters

SQL Profiler groups event classes into 13 categories or collections, which appear in the Events tab of the Event Properties dialog box. For example, you can expand the Performance collection and select the Show Execution Plan event class to show a plan tree for any SQL Statement being executed. Clicking the Add button (Figure 14.1) moves the event class to the Selected Event Classes box. Any event classes appearing in this box define the events that are captured when SQL Profiler is running.

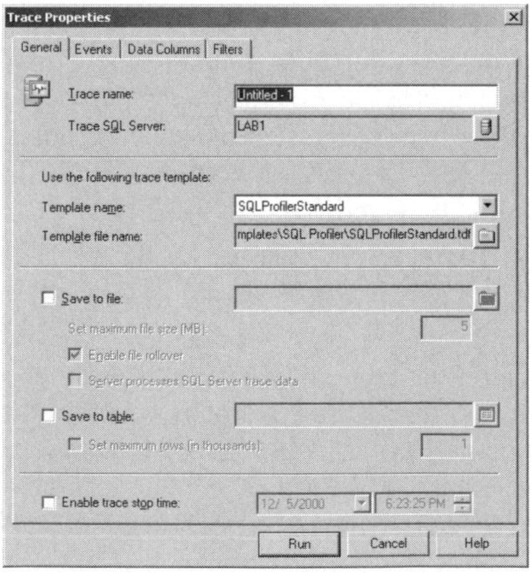

Figure 14.1. Adding the Execution Plan event class in the Performance Collection as a monitored event in SQL Profiler.

The Audit Login Event, Audit Logout Event, Existing Connection, RPC:Completed and SQL:BatchCompleted event classes appear in all SQL Profiler traces by default. You can remove any or all of these event classes or define templates that do not include these event classes. For a complete list of event collections and the event classes associated with each collection, see "Monitoring with SQL Profiler Event Categories" in SQL Server Books Online.

SQL Profiler contains a set of data columns that you select in the Data Columns tab of the Event Properties dialog box. Select columns based on the information you want returned and the way in which you want it returned when the trace is running. SQL Profiler displays the capture either in the order the events occur or sorted by group, based on one data column or a combination of data columns. If SQL Profiler can connect to the SQL Server where the trace data was captured, it will populate the Database ID, Object ID, and Index ID data columns with the names of the database, object, and index respectively. Otherwise, it will display identification numbers (IDs).

You can limit the amount of trace data captured by being selective about event classes and data columns in a trace. You can further restrict the amount of data captured by applying data filters in the Filters tab of the Event Properties dialog box. Filters serve to limit the events collected in the trace. For example, limiting the event capture to event failures will reduce the output data to only failed events Event failures are configured in the Success event criteria.

SQL Profiler categorizes filters by event criteria. Each event criteria contains a set of operators appropriate to the criteria. For example, the TargetLoginName criteria contains the Like and Not Like operators and the Duration criteria contains Equals, Not Equal To, Greater Than or Equal, and Less Than or Equal operators.

Preparing to Run a Trace in SQL Profiler

Run SQL Profiler from the Microsoft SQL Server program group by clicking the Profiler icon or from the Enterprise Manager Tools menu by clicking SQL Profiler. When SQL Profiler opens, you are presented with an empty window. From this window, you must connect to an instance of SQL Server using a security account that has authentication privileges to SQL Server and EXECUTE permission for SQL Profiler stored procedures. You can connect by clicking the New Trace icon on the toolbar or from the File menu by pointing to New and then clicking Trace. Once connected, you are presented with a Trace Properties dialog box, as shown in Figure 14.2.

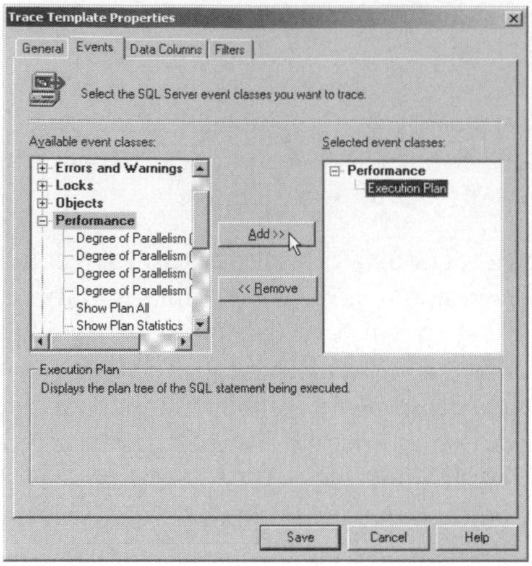

Figure 14.2.   The Trace Properties dialog box, which is used to connect to the database and define a new trace.

From the Trace Properties dialog box, you name the trace, select the server (if it is different than the server you connected to originally), specify the trace template to use, choose a trace file or trace table for logging the events, and choose whether to automatically start and stop the trace. If you do not create a trace file or trace table, the trace appears only in SQL Profiler and is lost when SQL Profiler is closed. A trace file uses a .trc extension and if you choose the trace file option, you must specify a maximum file size, whether the file rollover feature is enabled, and whether SQL Server processes trace data. The file rollover feature instructs SQL Profiler to create a new file when the original trace file reaches its maximum size. The new file name will be the original .trc file name with a number appended to it. Enabling the Server Process SQL Server Trace Data checkbox instructs SQL Server to process trace data and to not skip any events defined in the template, even under stress conditions. If this checkbox is not checked, the client application processes trace data and may skip trace data processing under heavy stress conditions. The trace table feature instructs SQL Profiler to create a table in the database. The default database for table creation is the database that the authenticated user is configured to use upon establishing a connection with the server. SQL Profiler creates the table in the database automatically. You can restrict trace table growth by specifying maximum rows in thousands.

Note   There must be at least 10 MB of free space to run SQL Profiler. If free space drops below 10 MB, SQL Profiler will stop.

Using a Trace Template

A trace template defines the criteria (events, data columns, and filters) for each trace. The trace data captured is based upon the options specified in the template. SQL Profiler contains a number of pre-defined templates and you can define your own custom templates. A template uses a .tdf extension and is stored by default in the %Program Files%\Microsoft SQL Server\80\Tools\Templates\SQL Profiler folder. Figure 14.1 shows the SQL Profiler Standard predefined template whose file name is SQLProfilerStandard.tdf.

Controlling the Trace

After choosing the template and other options shown in Figure 14.1, click Run to start the trace. A two-pane window, showing the trace name and the server name, appears in SQL Profiler. The top pane in the trace window contains records and the data columns defined in the template. The bottom pane contains descriptive text about the record selected in the top pane. After starting a trace, you can modify the name of the trace or generate a SQL script containing the SQL Profiler stored procedures and other settings that SQL Profiler uses to capture the trace. The .sql file can then be used to create a .trc file from an application other than SQL Profiler, such as Query Analyzer.

In SQL Profiler you can pause or stop a trace from the toolbar or from the File menu. Pausing a trace prevents further event data from being captured until the trace is restarted. Restarting a trace resumes trace operations without losing previously captured data. Stopping a trace stops data from being captured. After a trace is stopped, it cannot be restarted without losing any previously captured data, unless the data has been captured to a trace file or trace table. All trace properties that were previously selected are preserved when a trace is stopped. When a trace is paused, you can change the name, events, columns, and filters but you cannot change the template used or the trace's target storage location. However, when a trace is stopped, you can change any trace properties, including the template used and the trace's target location.

Replaying a Trace

Replaying a trace is useful for debugging and includes common debugging features like single-step and breakpoint setting capabilities. There are specific event classes and data columns that must be captured to replay a trace. Use the SQLProfilerTSQL_Replay.tdf trace template to ensure that you are capturing all of the appropriate event classes and data columns to replay a trace.

Exercise 1: Capturing Events Using SQL Profiler

In this exercise, you will create a SQL Profiler template and then use that template to capture data to a trace file. The trace file will be loaded into the Index Tuning wizard in Exercise 2.

▶ **To create a SQL Profiler template**

1. Click Start, point to Programs, point to Microsoft SQL Server, and then click Profiler.

   The SQL Profiler window appears.

2. Click the File menu, point to New, and then click Trace Template.

   The Trace Template Properties dialog box appears.

3. In the General tab, click Save As.

   The Save As window appears.

4. In the Filename text box, type **SQLProfiler_Exercise1** and click Save.

   The file path and filename appear in the General tab.

5. Click the Events tab.

6. In the Available Event Classes box, scroll down and select TSQL and then click Add.

   All Transact-SQL event classes are added to the Selected Event Classes box.

7. Click the Data Columns tab.

8. In the Unselected Data box, scroll down and select the TextData column and click Add.

   The TextData column appears in the Selected Data box.

9. Click the Up button so TextData appears first in the column list.

10. In the Selected Data box, click Groups.

11. In the Unselected Data box, click CPU and then click Add.

    The CPU column appears under Groups in the Selected Data box.

12. Click the Filters tab.

13. In the Trace Event Criteria box, expand ApplicationName.

    The Like and Not Like criteria appear.

14. Expand the Like criteria and in the empty text box that appears, type **Query Analyzer**.

15. Click Save.

16. Leave SQL Profiler open to complete the next practice.

▶   **To prepare SQL Profiler to run a trace**

1. On the SQL Profiler toolbar, click the New Trace icon. New Trace is the first icon on the toolbar.

    The Connect to SQL Server dialog box appears.

2. Verify that the Windows Authentication radio button is selected, and click OK.

    The Trace Properties dialog box appears and the General tab has the focus.

3. In the Trace Name text box, type **Trace01**.

4. In the Template Name drop-down list box select SQLProfiler_Exercise1.

5. Click the Save To File check box.

    The Save As window appears and Trace01 is the default filename.

6. Click Save.

    The trace file is saved to the My Documents folder and the Trace Properties dialog box reappears. Notice in the Trace Properties dialog box, that the maximum file size is set to 5 MB and that file rollover is enabled. The client processes the event data because the Server Processes SQL Server Trace Data is not checked.

7. Click and review the settings displayed in the Events, Data Columns, and Filters tabs.

    The settings in these tabs are identical to the template settings.

8. Leave SQL Profiler open but do not click Run on the Trace Properties dialog box.

▶   **To generate SQL Server activity and run a trace**

1. Open Query Analyzer, and connect to your local server.

2. In the Editor pane of the Query window, enter and execute the following code:

```
USE bookshopdb
IF EXISTS (SELECT name from dbo.sysobjects
where name = 'table01' AND type = 'U')
DROP TABLE table01
CREATE TABLE table01 (uniqueID int IDENTITY, longcol02 char(300) DEFA
ULT 'This is the default value for this column', col03 char(1))
GO
DECLARE @counter int
SET @counter = 1
WHILE @counter <= 5000
BEGIN
INSERT table01 (col03) VALUES ('a')
INSERT table01 (col03) VALUES ('b')
INSERT table01 (col03) VALUES ('c')
INSERT table01 (col03) VALUES ('d')
INSERT table01 (col03) VALUES ('e')
SET @counter = @counter + 1
END
```

The first part of the code checks for a table named Table01 in the BookShopDB database. If a table with this name is found, it is dropped. Then, the table is re-created with three columns and the table is populated with 5000 rows of data. Inserting rows into the table will take a few moments.

3. In the Editor pane of the Query window, enter but do not execute the following code:

```
SELECT col03, longcol02 FROM table01 WHERE col03 = 'a'
SELECT uniqueID, longcol02 FROM table01 WHERE uniqueID = 10000
SELECT * FROM table01 WHERE uniqueid BETWEEN 5000 AND 10000
GO
```

These Transact-SQL statements run queries against Table01. The SQL Profiler will trace the execution of this statement. Typically, you run SQL Profiler traces several times a day to gather a representative sample of database activity.

4. Switch to the SQL Profiler window that you left open in the previous practice.

5. In the Trace Properties dialog box, click Run.

The two-paned trace window appears and four data columns appear in the top pane.

6. Switch to the Query Analyzer and run the *SELECT* statements entered in step 3 of this practice.

7. Switch to the SQL Profiler and watch as the trace captures the Transact-SQL activity.

Trace data appears in the top pane of the trace window.

8. When a record containing SQL:BatchCompleted in the EventClass column appears, click the red square on the toolbar to stop the trace.

An additional row is added to the top pane of the trace window, indicating that the trace stopped. Notice that the CPU data column appears only for SQL:Stmt-Completed and SQL:BatchCompleted event classes. The CPU data column is not available or relevant to the other event classes. Also notice that the event classes with CPU values are grouped together.

▶ **To analyze the trace data**

1. The statements are grouped by CPU time. The CPU time shows the amount of CPU time, in milliseconds, used by the event.

2. Click each of the rows containing a value in the CPU column.

The text data for each Transact-SQL event appears in the bottom pane.

Which statement in the batch required the most CPU time to execute?

Which event required the most CPU time? Explain your answer.

3. Switch to Query Analyzer and insert the GO command between each *SELECT* statement. The code should now look like this:

```
SELECT col03, longcol02 FROM table01 WHERE col03 = 'a'
GO
SELECT uniqueID, longcol02 FROM table01 WHERE uniqueID = 10000
GO
SELECT * FROM table01 WHERE uniqueid BETWEEN 5000 AND 10000
GO
```

4. Switch to the SQL Profiler and restart the trace.

5. Switch to the Query Analyzer and execute the code you modified in step 5 of this practice.

6. Switch back to SQL Profiler and examine how the positioning of the GO command changed the output of the trace.

7. When the query is finished, stop the trace.

    How does the trace output differ from the trace you created in the previous practice?

8. Close SQL Profiler and Query Analyzer.

Lesson Summary

There are a number of tools designed to monitor SQL Server. SQL Profiler is the primary tool for monitoring SQL Server activity. Enterprise Manager, SQL Server error logs, system stored procedures, built-in functions, trace flags, SNMP, and WMI are other ways to monitor SQL Server activity.

SQL Profiler is a graphical tool that uses SQL Profiler stored procedures to trace SQL Server activity. The trace configuration can be defined in a trace template and the trace data is saved in a trace file or a trace table. SQL Server activity is grouped by event categories or collections. Each collection contains event classes. The event classes define the actual events that can be traced. To limit trace data, carefully select event classes and data columns for a trace. Use filters to further define the trace output you desire.

Lesson 2: Index Tuning and Database Partitioning

Database optimization begins during the design process and is further refined by tuning, using tools such as the System Monitor and implementing system configuration changes such as upgrading SQL Server computers with multiple disk controllers, redundant array of independent disks (RAID) disk controllers, and disk arrays. A thorough exploration of database optimization is a book unto itself and is thus beyond the scope of a single lesson. Therefore, this lesson explores one optimization tool, the Index Tuning wizard, and a system configuration change to improve performance, reorganizing data through partitioning. For more information on database optimization, see "Optimizing Database Performance" in SQL Server Books Online.

After this lesson, you will be able to:

- Explain how partitioning is an important part of database optimization.
- Use the Index Tuning wizard to improve query performance.

Estimated Lesson time: 25 minutes

SQL Server Tuning

Achieving excellent database performance begins with careful database and application design. For example, building a normalized or moderately denormalized database, creating effective indexes, only using cursors when absolutely necessary, and using stored procedures instead of Transact-SQL batches. Upgrading the database hardware and relocating elements of the database, such as the underlying files or tables in a database, can also improve performance. Before making system changes, establish a performance baseline by using tools such as SQL Profiler and System Monitor. Then, after any tuning procedure, rerun the performance tests and compare the results to the benchmark. These steps will help you determine the impact of your change. Sometimes an intended tuning procedure actually causes performance degradation. The baseline data helps you determine if the change was positive and if so, how large of a performance gain was achieved by the change.

Index Tuning Wizard Overview

In earlier chapters, you learned about and used the Show Execution Plan option in Query Analyzer. By enabling this option, you are able to view a graphical representation of the execution plan selected by the Query Optimizer. Another way to view a query plan selected by the Query Optimizer, without also returning a result set from executing a query, is by enabling the SET SHOWPLAN_TEXT or SET SHOWPLAN_ALL commands. Query Optimizer determines the best way to execute a query based on such things as available indexes and the database table structure, but it doesn't recommend ways to improve query performance. A sound database design is always the first way to optimize query performance. Once the database is constructed properly, you can then use the Show Execution Plan option and the SHOWPLAN commands to help you figure out ways to optimize query performance. However, the most direct way to improve query performance is by running the Index Tuning wizard.

Using the Index Tuning wizard, you select and create an optimal set of indexes and statistics for a database even if you don't have an expert understanding of database structure, workload, or SQL Server architecture. Index Tuning wizard analyzes a workload to determine the optimal set of indexes that should be in place. A workload consists of a SQL script or a SQL Profiler file trace or table trace. The SQL Profiler trace must contain either the SQL:Batch event classes in the TSQL collection or the RPC event classes in the Stored Procedures collection and the Text and Event Class data columns to provide meaningful data for analysis. In Exercise 1, you created a workload using a template containing SQL:Batch event classes and both the Text and Event Class data columns, among others.

Using the workload and the execution plans built by the Query Optimizer, the Index Tuning wizard:

- Recommends the best mix of indexes for a database and ways to tune the database for a set of problem queries.
- Analyzes the effects of the proposed changes, including index usage, distribution of queries among tables, and performance of queries in the workload.

You can customize the recommendations by specifying advanced options such as how much disk space can be used by new indexes. A recommendation consists of SQL statements that, when executed, create more effective indexes and optionally drop existing indexes that are inefficient or unnecessary. Index Tuning wizard recommendations are applied immediately, scheduled for later application, or saved to a script for manual execution. Index Tuning wizard recommendations are somewhat limited in that they do not include index creation for tables referenced by cross-database queries and system tables. Tables created with PRIMARY KEY constraints and unique keys automatically generate indexes for these keys. Therefore, the Index Tuning wizard does not recommend indexes for tables containing these attributes, but it can drop or replace a clustered index that is not unique or is not created on a PRIMARY KEY constraint. There are other limits associated with the Index Tuning wizard. For more information, see SQL Server Books Online.

Note   The Index Tuning wizard does not generate an error when saving a SQL Script to a disk with insufficient space.

Running the Index Tuning Wizard

You can start the Index Tuning wizard from Enterprise Manager, Query Analyzer, or SQL Profiler. In Enterprise Manager, the Index Tuning wizard is a listed wizard in the Select wizard window. In Query Analyzer, the Index Tuning wizard is an option in the Query menu, and in SQL Profiler it's an option in the Tools menu. When you start the Index Tuning wizard, an introductory screen appears, as shown in Figure 14.3.

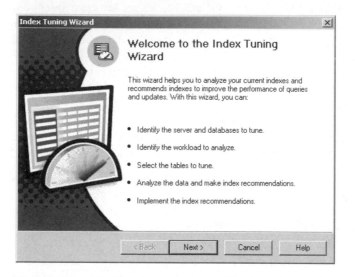

Figure 14.3.   The introductory screen of the Index Tuning wizard.

After connecting to the server, the Index Tuning wizard requires that you select a database and specify whether you want to keep the existing indexes, whether you want to create indexed views, and how thorough of an analysis should be performed. The wizard does not recommend that any indexes be dropped if the Keep All Existing Indexes checkbox is selected. Recommendations will include only new indexes. If you are running SQL Server 2000 Enterprise Edition or Developer Edition, the Index Tuning wizard can create indexes on views if the Add Indexed Views checkbox is selected. The more thorough the analysis, the more significant will be the CPU consumption while analysis is being performed. If CPU consumption is a problem, take any of the following measures:

- Lower the level of analysis by selecting the Fast or Medium tuning modes. However, a thorough analysis can result in a greater overall improvement in performance.
- Analyze a smaller workload and fewer tables.
- Run the analysis against a test version of the production server. Save the results to a script and then run the script against the production server.
- Run the wizard on a client computer, not the SQL Server.

After you select the Index Tuning wizard configuration, you must select a workload. Workload data comes from a trace file or trace table or a selection in the Query Analyzer. The Query Analyzer selection option is available only if you start the Index Tuning wizard from the Query Analyzer. Do not include index or query hints in the workload. If you do, the Query Optimizer formulates an execution plan based on the index hints, which might prevent the selection of an ideal execution plan.

After you select the workload, you can change the default index tuning parameters, select the tables for the wizard to analyze, and then run the analysis. Following the analysis, the wizard might not make index suggestions if there isn't enough data in the tables being sampled or if recommended indexes do not offer enough projected improvement in query performance over existing indexes.

Partitioning Overview

There are a number of ways to partition the components that make up a database system. For example, the database and log files can be moved to drives that provide fast disk I/O, tables can be split across member databases, additional processors can service individual SQL Server worker threads, and the processing load can be split across multiple servers. Adding hardware increases the partitioning options available to you.

File and Disk Partitioning

Spreading the database files and log files across multiple disks can improve disk I/O, leave room for additional file growth, and decrease the amount of file fragmentation that might occur on a single disk. Create files or filegroups on as many different available local physical disks as possible and place objects that compete heavily for space in different filegroups. Add multiple disk controllers, RAID disk controllers, and RAID arrays. If you create a RAID array, configure the array into a fault-tolerant stripe for critical data. You might consider placing temporary tables on a striped array that is not fault-tolerant. This type of array configuration provides the best performance, but you run the risk of data loss.

Federated and Clustered Servers

Federated servers are computers that are managed independently, but cooperate to process the database requests from applications. Clustered servers are a group of computer systems known as nodes or hosts that work together as a single system to improve availability. A database located on federated servers optimizes performance only if the application sends each SQL statement to the server that has most of the data required by the statement. This is called collocating the SQL statement with the data required by the statement.

Distributed Partitioned Views

In a federation of servers, each server runs SQL Server 2000 and is called a member server. Each federated server runs a member database that contains part of the data. The tables in the database are horizontally partitioned into member tables. There is one member table per member database, and distributed partitioned views are used to make it appear as if there is a full copy of the original table on each member server. A distributed partitioned view is composed of multiple tables that are spread across more than one server. To create a distributed partitioned view, you replace the original table with several smaller member tables that are located on member databases. Each member table has the same number of columns as the original table, and each column has the same attributes (such as data type, size, and collation) as the corresponding column in the original table.

Exercise 2: Tuning Queries Using the Index Tuning Wizard

In this exercise, you will run the Index Tuning wizard and load the SQL Profiler trace you created in Exercise 1. You will then allow the Index Tuning wizard to create the recommended indexes. In the last two practices, you will rerun the SQL Profiler trace using the trace template created in Exercise 1 and then you will open Trace01 to see if query performance improves from index creation.

▶ **To configure and run the Index Tuning wizard**

1. Open Query Analyzer, and connect to your local server.

2. In the Editor pane of the Query window, type any character or press the space bar.

    You must take this action for the Index Tuning wizard to be an available option in the Query pull-down menu.

3. Click the Query menu and then click Index Tuning wizard.

    The Welcome to the Index Tuning wizard screen appears.

4. Click Next.

    The Select Server And Database screen appears.

5. Select BookShopDB from the Database drop-down list box and click Next.

    The Specify Workload screen appears. Notice that the Query Analyzer radio button is selected. This option is available only when you start the Index Tuning wizard from Query Analyzer.

6. Click the My Workload File radio button.

    An Open window appears and Trace01.trc is listed in the folder and file pane.

7. Double-click Trace01.trc.

    The path and file name of the trace file appears in the Specify Workload screen.

8. Press the Advanced Options button to review the index tuning parameters and then click Cancel.

9. Press Next on the Specify Workload screen.

   The Select Tables to Tune screen appears.

10. Scroll down in the list and select the [dbo].[table01] checkbox.

11. Click Next.

    The analysis runs as the Index Tuning wizard determines the type of indexes to recommend. When the analysis completes, the Index Recommendations screen appears and two indexes are recommended. Below the index recommendations a bullet shows the estimated query performance improvement based on the sampled workload.

    The Index Tuning wizard recommends a clustered index named Table011 with a key on the UniqueID column and a nonclustered index named Table012 with a key on the Col03 and LongCol02 columns. Later in the Index Tuning wizard screens, you can choose to save a script to create these indexes. You can customize the script before executing it. For example, you might want to name the indexes differently.

12. Click the Analysis button and review the various reports available from the Reports drop-down list box, then click Close.

13. In the Index Recommendations screen, click Next.

    The Schedule Index Update Job screen appears.

14. Click the Apply Changes checkbox and then click Next.

    The Completing The Index Tuning wizard screen appears.

15. Click Finish.

    The database is updated with the recommended changes and then a message box appears, indicating that the Index Tuning wizard has successfully completed.

16. Click OK to close the Index Tuning wizard.

17. Leave Query Analyzer open to complete the next practice.

▶ **To test query performance**

1. Open SQL Profiler.

2. Click File, point to New, and then click Trace.

   The Connect to SQL Server dialog box appears.

3. Click OK.

   The Trace Properties dialog box appears.

4. In the Trace Name text box, type **Trace02**.

5. In the Template Name drop-down list box, select SQLProfiler_Exercise1.

6. Click the Save To File checkbox.

   The Save As window appears and Trace02 is the default file name.

7. Click Save.

   The trace file is saved to the My Documents folder and the Trace Properties dialog box reappears.

8. Leave SQL Profiler open but do not click Run on the Trace Properties dialog box.

9. Switch to Query Analyzer.

10. In the Editor pane of the Query window, enter but do not execute the following code:

```
USE bookshopdb
SELECT col03, longcol02 FROM table01 WHERE col03 = 'a'
SELECT uniqueID, longcol02 FROM table01 WHERE uniqueID = 10000
SELECT * FROM table01 WHERE uniqueid BETWEEN 5000 AND 10000
GO
```

11. Switch to the SQL Profiler window.

12. In the Trace Properties dialog box, click Run.

    The two-paned trace window appears and four data columns appear in the top pane.

13. Switch to the Query Analyzer and run the *SELECT* statements.

14. Switch to the SQL Profiler and watch as the trace captures the Transact-SQL activity.

    Trace data appears in the top pane of the trace window.

15. When a record appears containing SQL:BatchCompleted in the EventClass column, click the red square on the toolbar to stop the trace.

16. An additional row is added to the top pane of the trace window, indicating that the trace stopped.

17. Leave SQL Profiler and Query Analyzer open to complete the next exercise.

▶ **To test for improved query performance**

1. In the SQL Profiler, click File, point to Open, and then click Trace File.

   The Open window appears and the Folder And File pane lists Trace01.

2. Double-click Trace01.

   Trace01 appears in the SQL Profiler window.

3. Click Window and then click Tile Horizontally.

   Trace01 and Trace02 are rearranged in the SQL Profiler window.

4. Scroll down in both trace file displays until you see all of the CPU values.

   Notice that Trace02 shows significantly less CPU consumption for the query than Trace01. Consider adding the Duration event class to the trace template to determine how long each SQL statement takes to execute.

5. Close the SQL Profiler and the Query Analyzer.

Lesson Summary

Database optimization occurs during the design process and after implementation through tuning. At the conclusion of the design and implementation process, a performance baseline should be created using SQL Profiler and System Monitor. The baseline provides the data you need to determine to what extent performance is improved through tuning. A way to improve query performance is by running the Index Tuning wizard and implementing index recommendations provided by the wizard. The wizard requires a workload to analyze. The workload is a trace or a Transact-SQL script. After the workload is analyzed, the Index Tuning wizard makes recommendations. You implement the recommendations immediately, schedule the changes for later, or create a script so that you can manually execute the recommended changes.

Server and database performance is improved through partitioning. There are many different ways to partition a database. Implement federated servers or clusters and split the database across member servers. After creating a federation of servers, create distributed partitioned views to obtain data from horizontally partitioned member tables. Add additional processors so that SQL Server divides the worker threads among the available processors. Add disks, controllers, and RAID arrays, and then split the database and log files among the disks.

Review

The following questions are intended to reinforce key information presented in this chapter. If you are unable to answer a question, review the appropriate lesson and then try the question again. Answers to the questions can be found in the Appendix, "Questions and Answers."

1. Name a monitoring feature that sends database information to a Network Management System (NMS).

2. Name a SQL Server tool you can use to monitor current SQL Server activity.

3. Several users inform you that database performance levels seem to change right around the time that staff rotations occur. How can you use SQL Profiler to determine if the staff rotation has anything to do with changing performance levels?

4. You are concerned about database security. How can you use the SQL Profiler to alleviate your concerns?

5. How can you reduce the amount of data collected by a trace?

6. Where can trace data be stored?

7. As you move through the Index Tuning wizard screens, you see that choosing a script from the Query Analyzer is not an option. What is the most likely reason for this result?

8. How can you start a trace in Query Analyzer?

9. What application requirement must be met for the application to benefit from a federation of servers?

10. How must member tables be configured to support distributed partitioned views?

11. What are two ways that CPU consumption can be reduced when performing an analysis with the Index Tuning wizard?

12. The Index Tuning wizard can create indexed views on what SQL Server editions?

PART 2

Preparation for MCP Exam 70-229

O B J E C T I V E   D O M A I N   1

Developing a Logical Data Model

The Developing a Logical Data Model domain focuses on the skills required to build the foundation for any database system—the **logical data model**. This model is used to validate and document the business rules and functions of the database in a graphic manner.

The first step in developing the model consists of defining the pertinent business entities, determining the relationships between these entities, and identifying the **cardinality** of these relationships. Then the defining **attributes** are added to each entity, and the model is checked for **normalization**. Next the **primary keys** are determined, and through the relationships, the **foreign keys** are defined. Once the fundamental entity relationships are understood, attribute data types, **scale** and **precision**, allowed values, and **nullability** are determined. All of these steps are covered in this section of the exam.

Although any modeling tool can be used to create a logical model (especially because a logical model should be product-independent), Microsoft Visio, with its data modeling stencils, is an excellent modeling tool that can be used throughout the database design and implementation phases.

Tested Skills and Suggested Practices

The skills that you need to successfully master the Developing a Logical Data Model objective domain on the *Designing and Implementing Databases with Microsoft SQL Server 2000 Enterprise Edition* exam include:

- **Defining entities; considerations include entity composition and normalization.**

  - Practice 1: For this practice, create a list of all of the reasonable entities, with the entity name only, that would exist for a sample business function.

- Practice 2: Add the attributes that describe the entity.

- Practice 3: Validate that the model meets the three main requirements for normal form. Ensure that there are no repeating groups, that all of the attributes in an entity depend on the whole primary key, and that attributes depend only on the primary key and not on any other attributes.

- **Defining entity keys; considerations include primary keys, foreign keys, and unique constraints.**

  - Practice 1: Using the logical entity model created in the previous practice, determine the relationships between the entities, identifying the cardinality as one-to-one, one-to-many, or many-to-many. If your chosen design tool does not include the ability to model a many-to-many relationship, you can add an associative entity in between.

  - Practice 2: Evaluate your logical model for redundancies, circular relationships, and invalid assumptions. Determine whether all business objects are included. It is critical that this simple logical model be flexible, stable, and appropriate for the business function being modeled because it will provide the foundation for all remaining work on the project. Take the time to validate the relationships.

  - Practice 3: Determine all possible candidate keys for each entity and identify the primary keys. Add the primary key names to the models, as well as the corresponding foreign key names, based on the relationships already defined.

- **Defining attribute domain integrity; considerations include CHECK constraints, data types, and nullability.**

  - Practice 1: Determine the data types, including the scale and precision of each attribute, the allowable values, and the nullability of each attribute.

  - Practice 2: Validate the logical model against the business rules and functions and ensure that all possible requirements that can be met are met by the relational model. Keep in mind that businesses change over time, and it is not to your advantage to have to change the fundamentals of the model to include these types of business rules.

Further Reading

This section lists supplemental readings by objective. Study these sources thoroughly before taking exam 70-229.

Objective 1.1

Date, C. J. *An Introduction to Database Systems*. Reading, Mass.: Addison-Wesley, 1995. Review Chapter 4, "Relational Data Objects: Domains and Relations." This is the fundamental book about database systems.

Fleming, Candace C. and Barbara von Halle. *Handbook of Relational Database Design*. Reading, Mass.: Addison-Wesley, 1989. Review Chapter 5, "Build Skeletal User Views," in Part Two, "Building a Logical Data Model." This book is considered a classic for an introduction to relational design.

Elmasri, Ramez A. and Shamkant B. Navathe. *Fundamentals of Database Systems*. Reading, Mass.: Addison-Wesley, 1994. Review Chapter 3, "Data Modeling using the Entity-Relationship Approach," and Chapter 6, Section 1, "Relational Model Concepts." This book is fairly academic, but provides a concise description of the fundamentals.

Litwin, Paul. "Fundamentals of Relational Database Design." (This paper can be downloaded for free at *http://www.microsoft.com/TechNet*. You can find this paper by searching on the title.) Review the sections on relationships and normalization. This paper provides a good, short overview of relational database design.

Simsion, Graeme C. *Data Modeling Essentials: Analysis, Design, and Innovation*. Boston, Mass.: International Thompson Computer Press, 1993. Review Chapter 1, "What is Data Modeling?"; Chapter 2, "Basic Normalization"; Chapter 3, "The Entity Relationship Approach"; Chapter 6, "More About Relationships and Foreign Keys"; and Chapter 7, "Advanced Normalization." These chapters provide user-friendly descriptions of data modeling fundamentals.

Teorey, Toby J. *Database Modeling and Design*. San Francisco: Morgan Kaufmann, 1999. Review Chapter 3, "ER Modeling in Logical Database Design," and Chapter 5, "Normalization." These chapters provide user-friendly descriptions of data modeling fundamentals.

Microsoft SQL Server 2000 product documentation. To access Books Online (BOL), click the Start button, and point to Programs, then Microsoft SQL Server, and then Books Online. Click the Contents tab and double-click any of the following topics: "Database Design Considerations," "Creating a Database Plan," "Logical Database Modeling," and "Normalization." Although the BOL information about database design is limited, it is a good starting place.

Microsoft Corporation. *MCSE Training Kit: Microsoft SQL Server 2000 Database Design and Implementation*. Redmond, Washington: Microsoft Press, 2001. Read and complete the practices in Lessons 1 and 2 in Chapter 3, "Designing SQL Server Database."

Objective 1.2

Date, C. J. *An Introduction to Database Systems*. Reading, Mass.: Addison-Wesley, 1995. Review Chapter 5, "Relational Data Integrity: Candidate Keys and Related Matters."

Fleming, Candace C. and Barbara von Halle. *Handbook of Relational Database Design*. Reading, Mass.: Addison-Wesley, 1989. Review Chapter 6, "Add Keys to User Views," in Part Two, "Building a Logical Data Model."

Litwin, Paul. "Fundamentals of Relational Database Design." (This paper can be downloaded for free at *http://www.microsoft.com/TechNet*. You can find this paper by searching on the title.)

Simsion, Graeme C. *Data Modeling Essentials: Analysis, Design, and Innovation*. Boston, Mass.: International Thompson Computer Press, 1993. Review Chapter 8, "Primary Keys and Identity," and Chapter 9, "Attributes."

Microsoft SQL Server 2000 product documentation. To access Books Online, click the Start button, and point to Programs, then Microsoft SQL Server, and then Books Online. Click the Contents tab, double-click "Creating and Maintaining Databases," and review the following topics: "Primary Key Constraints," "Foreign Key Constraints," and "Unique Constraints."

Objective 1.3

Fleming, Candace C. and Barbara von Halle. *Handbook of Relational Database Design*. Reading, Mass.: Addison-Wesley, 1989. Review Chapter 9, "Determine Additional Attribute Business Rules," in Part Two, "Building a Logical Data Model."

Simsion, Graeme C. *Data Modeling Essentials: Analysis, Design, and Innovation*. Boston, Mass.: International Thompson Computer Press, 1993. Review Chapter 8, "Primary Keys and Identity," and Chapter 9, "Attributes."

Microsoft SQL Server 2000 product documentation. To access Books Online, click the Start button, and point to Programs, then Microsoft SQL Server, and then Books Online. Click the Contents tab and double-click the "Creating and Maintaining Databases" section. Review the "Data Integrity" topic.

In Part 1, read and complete the practices in Lessons 2 and 3 in Chapter 4, "Implementing SQL Server Databases and Tables," and Lessons 1 and 2 in Chapter 5, "Implementing Data Integrity."

OBJECTIVE 1.1

Define entities.

The first step to a well-designed database model to be implemented in SQL Server 2000 is to determine the valid entities for the model. Although this phase might seem simple at first glance—just a diagram of a group of boxes with titles in them—this phase is critical to the success of any dependent project. Changes to a logical model after development has begun, or worse, has been implemented, can have huge implications, much like a pebble thrown into a pond. The ripples affect every part of an organization's code, documentation, and users. It is critical to understand the business functions and their relationships at a deep and fundamental level. The logical model allows you to work your way to this understanding, by the iterative process of the modeling, discussion with the pertinent business and subject matter experts, and validation of the model.

This model must also be flexible and it should be considered as part of an enterprise data model. Although you might not be modeling the entire organization's data at this time, there is a very good chance that the model will need to be extended to a new area or incorporated with an independently designed model. It is to the organization's best advantage to ensure that the model adheres to fundamental modeling concepts and the enterprise perspective. Consider all of the code, documentation, training manuals, **stored procedures**, business objects and components, and so on that need to be changed if the basic logical model is flawed and invalid for the organization. The cost of such a change is huge, so the time spent getting it right at this point is worth the effort.

A well-designed data model must not only be valid for the business, but also it needs to be scalable, maintainable, and extensible. An elegant data model will encompass all of these attributes.

Many examples of "generic" data models have already been created, validated, and implemented that might fit your needs. Usually you will need to customize these, or slice off the particular parts that are pertinent to your project, but adhering to these common models will help to ensure extensibility.

The last critical piece to a logical data model is to ensure that the appropriate resources are available to help validate the model. This will need to include business people, who might have no understanding of databases, but who understand the business and its processes, and a database architect who can translate the business into a model.

After the entities have been determined, adding the attributes for the entities helps validate that the correct entity selections have been made. When the entities and their attributes have been designed, the model should be checked to verify that it meets at least the first three levels of normal form. These levels are

- No repeating groups or multivalue attributes.

- Every attribute in the entity must be dependent on the whole primary key.

- Every attribute in the entity must be dependent only on the primary key.

You can easily remember the last two by the following saying: "All attributes must be dependent on the key, the whole key, and nothing but the key."

Objective 1.1 Questions

70-229.01.01.001

You design the following entities for a school course system. You would like to normalize the entities. What should you do?

Examine the entities shown here.

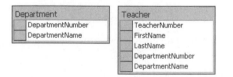

A. Remove the CourseTitle1, CourseTitle2, and CourseTitle3 attributes in the Student entity.

B. Remove the Course entity.

C. Add enough CourseTitle attributes in the Student entity to accommodate all of the courses that a student might take.

70-229.01.01.002

You have created a model with two entities for a school course system. You would like to normalize the entities. What should you do?

Examine the entities shown here.

A. Add a TeacherNumber to the Department entity.

B. Replace the FirstName and LastName attributes in the Teacher entity with TeacherName.

C. Remove the DepartmentName from the Teacher entity.

70-229.01.01.003

You design a logical model for current enrollment in a university. You want to remove any redundant attributes or derived attributes that are dependent on other attributes. What should you do?

Examine the entities shown here.

Student
StudentID
StudentName

Instructor
InstructorID
InstructorName
CoursesTaught

Course
CourseID
CourseName
CourseLevel

Schedule
CourseID
InstructorID
Quarter

A. Remove the InstructorID from the Schedule entity.

B. Remove the CoursesTaught attribute from the Instructor entity.

C. Remove the CourseName from the Course entity.

D. Remove the CourseID from the Schedule entity.

70-229.01.01.004

You are designing a logical model to track airline flights. In your system, an airplane is owned by one airline, and a flight would always be flown by one airplane. You create the following entities:

- Airplane

- Flight

- Airline

In the following sentence diagrams, the arrows indicate a one-to-many relationship. Which of the following diagrams describes the relationship between these three entities that meets the scenario requirements?

A. Flight --> Airline --> Airplane

B. Airplane --> Airline --> Flight

C. Airplane --> Flight --> Airline

D. Airline --> Airplane --> Flight

Objective 1.1 Answers

70-229.01.01.001

▶ **Correct Answers: A**

   A. **Correct:** The multiple CourseTitle attributes are an example of repeating groups, and are a violation of first normal form. This will obviously waste space and is inflexible.

   B. **Incorrect:** The Course entity will be needed. Removing it will do nothing to normalize the Student entity, and the CourseTitle attributes are still left as repeating groups.

   C. **Incorrect:** This proposed solution is a violation of first normal form, in that there are repeating groups. This causes many problems, including wasted space, and is very difficult to program against.

70-229.01.01.002

▶ **Correct Answers: C**

   A. **Incorrect:** The TeacherNumber is not part of the Department entity and does not describe the Department entity in any way, but rather describes the Teacher.

   B. **Incorrect:** Combining the names does not address any normalization problems. It does not remove repeating groups.

   C. **Correct:** The DepartmentName is dependent on the DepartmentNumber and anything that would be considered a primary key for a Teacher. Leaving this in can cause data inconsistency in that a change to a DepartmentName will require not only a change to the Department entity, but also to all of the Teacher rows that have the same name.

70-229.01.01.003

▶ **Correct Answers: B**

   A. **Incorrect:** The InstructorID is part of the primary key of the Schedule entity and it is required to describe a Schedule instance. It is not a derived attribute, and it is not redundant because it is also a foreign key reference to the Instructor entity.

   B. **Correct:** This attribute would need to be derived from a calculation based on the count for a teacher in the Schedule entity. This derived data would also be redundant and could lead to data inconsistencies if this attribute were changed without a change to the instances in the Schedule entity.

   C. **Incorrect:** The CourseName is not redundant or derived; it is a description that is required for the Course entity.

   D. **Incorrect:** The CourseID is part of the primary key for the Schedule entity. It is not derived, and it is not redundant because it is also a foreign key reference to the Course entity.

70-229.01.01.004

▶ **Correct Answers: D**

A. **Incorrect:** In this model, an airplane would have one foreign key reference to an airline, and an airline would have many airplanes. This is correct. However, the model shows an airline as having a foreign key relationship with a flight, which is not correct as described by the scenario. There would not be any way to determine what airplane was assigned to a flight.

B. **Incorrect:** In this model, there is a one-to-many relationship between an airplane and an airline. This is not correct because we know from the scenario that an airplane is owned by one airline. Also, in this model one airline would have many flights. Although this is correct, the relationship between an airline and a flight should be tracked through the airplane, not directly through the airline.

C. **Incorrect:** Here one airplane is allowed per flight, which is correct. However, one flight is allowed per airline, and that is obviously not accurate because an airline would have many flights.

D. **Correct:** Here one airline is allowed per airplane, and many airplanes per airline, which follows the scenario requirement that an airplane is owned by one airline. There is one airplane per flight, and many flights per airplane, which is again correct. We know that a flight is flown by only one plane.

OBJECTIVE 1.2

Design entity keys.

This section of the exam focuses on identifying the **primary keys**, **foreign keys**, and any **unique constraints**.

The first step to identifying entity keys is to determine all possible candidates for the primary key. These are any attributes, or combination of attributes, that can uniquely identify an instance of the entity, or a row. There might be more than one candidate for selection as the primary key, and each one of these possibilities needs to be identified. In collaboration with the business, a determination of the most appropriate candidate is selected as the primary key.

There are three major considerations for a primary key. A primary key should be:

- Applicable

- Minimal

- Stable

An applicable primary key simply means that this is the best selection for uniquely identifying each instance in this entity.

A minimal key means that it is as small as possible because it might be heavily used throughout the model, and subsequently the database. The combination of a customer name, address, and phone number is not a good example of a minimal primary key.

A stable primary key means that the possibility of the value changing is very small. In general, it is best not to change a primary key because if it is part of a relationship, the value will need to be migrated throughout the system. This can have a large impact.

Although every entity must, by definition, have a candidate for a primary key, it is quite common to use a system-generated key, called a **surrogate key**, as the primary key. An example of this is a people entity. A true unique identifier for a person is a large combination of many things, and it might not actually exist at all, so a unique key that has no meaning outside of the system is generated.

After a primary key is determined for each entity, this key is migrated to every entity that has a foreign key reference to it. The key can be renamed to be better understood in the context of the referring entity, but it must have the same data type.

Lastly, every candidate primary key that is not selected as the actual primary key, including attribute combinations, must have a unique constraint to enforce the logical candidate. For example, although you might decide to create a surrogate key called Country Code for a Country entity, and designate this as the primary key, the Country Name is a candidate key and could also have been selected as the primary key. It should, therefore, have a unique constraint to enforce this.

Objective 1.2 Questions

70-229.01.02.001

You are creating a database to track music compositions submitted for copyright to a large international copyright company. Copyrights might be acquired for every composition submitted, but a particular composer can submit only one composition of the same name at any time. You create a composer entity with a composer ID for the primary key. You also create a composition entity. Which of the following provides the best logical primary key for each row in the composition entity?

A. Composition name

B. Composition name and composition year

C. Composition name and composer ID

D. Composition name and copyright number

70-229.01.02.002

You are designing a data model to track software projects. A project might be undertaken in one department or in multiple departments. Each project is assigned a group of programmers. A programmer who is a staff member of one department might also be assigned to a project that is being undertaken by another department, and a programmer might perform multiple jobs on a particular project. You design the model with the foreign key relationships as follows. Which of the following is true? (Choose all that apply.)

Examine the following logical model.

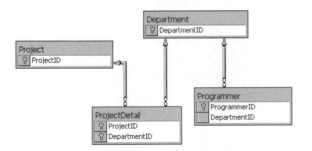

A. The programmers on each project can be determined.

B. The programmers on staff in each department can be determined.

C. The job being performed by a programmer on a project can be determined.

D. The projects being performed in a department can be determined.

70-229.01.02.003

You are creating a model to track employee reviews. Reviews are currently held at six-month intervals, and only one reviewer performs an employee's review. You create an employee entity and the following review entity. Which attributes would determine the uniqueness of a review?

Examine the Review Entity shown here.

```
EmployeeReview
   EmployeeID
   ReviewDate
   ReviewGrade
   ReviewerID
```

A. EmployeeID

B. EmployeeID, ReviewDate

C. EmployeeID, ReviewerID

D. EmployeeID, ReviewDate, ReviewGrade

70-229.01.02.004

You are creating a model of employees in a large international company. Each country provides a government-generated number given to every person authorized to work. Other information contained in the employee entity would be family name, given name, phone number, and address. Which of the following is the best choice to uniquely identify each employee?

A. Family name and given name

B. Government number

C. Family name, given name, phone number, and address

D. System-generated identity number

70-229.01.02.005

You are designing a logical model for museum art collections. You have currently designed Museum, Artist, and ArtObject entities. You want to accomplish the following results:

- Museums can be recognized as being part of a larger museum.

- The museum owning artwork created by a particular artist can be known.

- An art object that was created by more than one artist can be stored.

- A surrogate key can be used as the primary key for the museum.

- No museum can have the same name as another museum.

You perform the following actions:

- You add a one-to-many relationship between the Artist and ArtObject entities.

- You add a surrogate primary key attribute called MuseumID to the Museum entity.

- You add an attribute called ParentMuseumID and a self-referencing foreign key relationship to the Museum entity.

- You add a surrogate primary key attribute called ArtistID to the Artist table.

- You add a foreign key relationship between the ArtObject and the Museum entities.

Which of the results do these actions produce? (Choose all that apply.)

A. You ensure that museums can be recognized as being part of a larger museum.

B. You ensure that the museum holding artwork created by a particular artist can be known.

C. You ensure that an art object that was created by more than one artist can be stored.

D. You use a surrogate key for the primary key for the museum.

E. You ensure that no museum can have the same name as another museum.

70-229.01.02.006

You are creating a logical data model for tracking grants to nonprofit organizations for your company. Some organizations are part of another organization. Grants can be split between organizations. You need to be able to track how much money was given to any particular organization at any level. You design the model with the foreign key relationships as follows. Which of the following is true? (Choose all that apply.)

Examine the following logical model.

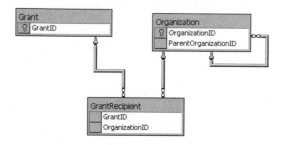

A. You are able to determine all of the organizations that are part of any particular parent organization.

B. Grants that are awarded to any organization can be determined, including any organizations for which it is considered a parent organization.

C. The organization that awards the grant can be determined.

Objective 1.2 Answers

70-229.01.02.001

▶ **Correct Answers: C**

  A. **Incorrect:** Selecting composition name for the primary key would not allow submission of more than one composition with the same name. Although this might be rare, it would not be impossible.

  B. **Incorrect:** Selecting composition name and composition year would allow for more than one composition of the same name to be submitted in the same year, but in this case, composition year is an arbitrary selection that is not indicated by any of the given business criteria. Again, more than one composition of the same name by different composers would not be allowed for submission in the same year.

  C. **Correct:** Selecting composition name and composer ID provides the best candidate key for the scenario. It allows submission of compositions with the same names, but only one per composer.

  D. **Incorrect:** This selection has two obvious problems. One is that a copyright number is not known at all times, and primary keys cannot be null. Also, if the copyright number were known, it would be assumed to be unique in itself, and a composition name would not be needed as well to uniquely identify a row in the entity.

70-229.01.02.002

▶ **Correct Answers: B and D**

  A. **Incorrect:** Although the foreign key relationships in the model describe which department a programmer is part of, they do not allow us to determine which project the programmer is working on.

  B. **Correct:** The model allows us to determine the programmers in each department because there is a foreign key in the Programmer entity that references the Department entity.

  C. **Incorrect:** There is no information about a specific job in the model.

  D. **Correct:** Because the ProjectDetail entity contains a foreign key to the Department entity, projects being performed in a department can be determined.

70-229.01.02.003

▶ **Correct Answers: B**

A. **Incorrect:** Selecting only EmployeeID as the primary key allows only one review per employee. This is not the correct primary key for this entity because the requirement is for employees to have multiple reviews.

B. **Correct:** The combination of EmployeeID and ReviewDate uniquely identifies an instance of a review for an employee. Although the scenario states that reviews are currently held at six-month intervals, the combination of the two attributes allows for this, as well as any other review interval. This makes this selection flexible. It also prohibits more than one reviewer per employee review.

C. **Incorrect:** Selecting the combination of EmployeeID and ReviewerID allows only one review per employee and reviewer combination. An employee could be reviewed more than once by the same reviewer, which this selection would prohibit.

D. **Incorrect:** There is no need to include the ReviewGrade in the primary key. This allows for multiple reviews on the same date for an employee, if there were different ReviewGrades. This is not the situation described in the scenario.

70-229.01.02.004

▶ **Correct Answers: D**

A. **Incorrect:** The selection of family name and given name for a primary key will not uniquely identify an employee because there can be many people with the same name within a large company. This selection also has one other problem, it does not meet the stability requirement for a good primary key. In many countries names change over time according to marital status. Every attempt should be made to ensure that primary keys do not change.

B. **Incorrect:** Although this might seem to be a good solution, there is no guarantee that these numbers are not recycled when a previous person has passed on (this is the case with Social Security numbers in the United States). Also, there is no guarantee that a number given out by one country will be unique in the world, or that there is a common type for these numbers (that is, numeric versus alphanumeric).

C. **Incorrect:** Although the chances are small that more than one person with the same name would have the same address and phone number, this is not impossible. (Consider George Forman and his sons, George, George, George, George, and George.) This selection does not uniquely identify an employee because the same person can be entered into the table with a different address. This selection also suffers from the instability problem and is simply too much data to use as a primary key, where the same data would need to be migrated to any tables that would refer to this entity.

D. **Correct:** Because there does not appear to be a simple, applicable, and stable candidate for a unique identifier for this entity, the best option is to create a unique number, generated by the system.

70-229.01.02.005

▶ **Correct Answers: A, B, and D**

A. **Correct:** By adding an attribute called ParentMuseumID and creating a self-referencing foreign key relationship to the Museum entity, you ensure that any museum can have another museum as a parent. This implementation allows only hierarchical relationships, and allows a museum to have only one parental museum.

B. **Correct:** Because there is a relationship between the Artist and ArtObject entities, and a relationship between the ArtObject and Museum entities, the museum that is holding artwork by a particular artist can be determined through these relationships.

C. **Incorrect:** Because there is only a one-to-many relationship between the Artist and ArtObject entities, there can only be one Artist associated with a particular ArtObject. To accomplish this result, a many-to-many relationship would need to be created and, in SQL Server 2000, this would require an associated table with a row for each Artist for an ArtObject.

D. **Correct:** Adding the MuseumID attribute to the Museum entity and then defining this attribute as the primary key produces this result.

E. **Incorrect:** There is nothing in the listed actions that ensures that only one museum has a particular name. The primary key, which will be unique by definition, has been defined on the surrogate key. A unique constraint will need to be added to the Museum name to produce this result. Whenever a surrogate key is used in an entity definition, it is important to also add any required unique constraints on candidate keys; otherwise, duplicate data can be entered.

70-229.01.02.006

▶ **Correct Answers: A and B**

A. **Correct:** The self-referencing foreign key relationship on Organization allows for all child organizations of a parent organization to be known.

B. **Correct:** Because there is a many-to-many relationship between the Organization entity and the Grant entity, all grants awarded to an institution can be determined through the GrantRecipient entity. Grants can also be summarized for parent organizations because of the self-referencing relationship on Organization.

C. **Incorrect:** This information is not contained in the model because the only relationship between an Organization and a Grant is through the GrantRecipient entity.

O B J E C T I V E   1 . 3

Design attribute domain integrity.

Determining the **domain integrity** for an attribute can include determining the data type, nullability, and other constraints on the attribute. Determining attribute domains ensures that only the allowable values can be entered into the database. This includes whether alphanumeric or numeric data is allowed, whether a value can be null, and any other type of constraint or rule on the data, such as a range of allowable values.

Generally, determining a data type is straightforward. Discussions with the business about current and future possible values usually lead to accurate data type evaluations. The same is true for range constraints and other check constraints. Consistency in data type selection is important and can prevent problems later in the development process.

However, determining whether an attribute can be null is more problematic. Excessive usage of nulls can lead to difficulties in programming because SQL queries must be written differently when a null is expected. Any expression that contains a null will evaluate as unknown.

The question of whether nulls should be used in a relational database is fairly controversial. Because the use of nulls requires a three-valued logic that not all developers are aware of, you might find that to help ensure accuracy in your systems, you need to limit null usage. The following tables show the three-valued logic truth tables.

AND	True	False	Unknown
True	True	False	Unknown
False	False	False	False
Unknown	Unknown	False	Unknown

OR	True	False	Unknown
True	True	True	True
False	True	False	Unknown
Unknown	True	Unknown	Unknown

NOT	True	False	Unknown
	False	True	Unknown

In general, it is best to use nulls very sparingly, and as little as possible for any attribute that participates in a relationship. One good practice is to allow nulls only in descriptive text attributes. Some people use codes to represent the different types of nulls. For example, some attributes need to be null because they might not be applicable in every case; or the attribute value is not known at the moment, but can be considered required later; or the attribute value truly is not known. Using a code to represent these three "null states" can help with data integrity and data cleaning.

Objective 1.3 Questions

70-229.01.03.001

Evaluate the Customer and Repair entities shown below. A customer with an order should not be deleted. How should you enforce a relationship between the Customer and Repair entities to ensure integrity?

Examine the following logical model.

A. Add a CHECK constraint to the RepairID attribute.

B. Add a CHECK constraint to the CustomerID attribute.

C. Add a DELETE trigger to the Repair entity.

D. Add the CustomerID attribute to the Repair entity with a FOREIGN KEY constraint to the Customer entity.

70-229.01.03.002

You have to enforce relationships between the entities shown below. Telephone sales agents are compensated according to the number of customer calls and the duration of the time spent on the phone talking to customers. The agents are using different extensions as they move around. How would you enforce the relationship between the Agent records and the CallDetails to calculate commissions?

Examine the following logical model.

A. Add a FOREIGN KEY constraint on the Extension attribute in CallDetails referencing the Agent entity.

B. Create a procedure to query the Agent and CallDetails entities to determine the commissions.

C. Add AgentID to the CallDetails entity and create a FOREIGN KEY constraint referencing the Agent entity.

70-229.01.03.003

You are developing a database model for a high school. Evaluate the Student and State entities below. What should you change in the model to maintain data integrity?

Examine the following logical model.

Student
- StudentID
- LastName
- FirstName
- Address
- City
- StateID
- Zipcode

State
- StateID
- StateName

A. Add a FOREIGN KEY constraint to the Student entity referencing the State entity's StateID attribute.

B. Add a CHECK constraint to the State entity on the StateID attribute.

C. Add a CHECK constraint to the Student entity on the StateID attribute.

D. Add a FOREIGN KEY constraint to the State entity referencing the Student entity's StateID attribute.

70-229.01.03.004

You are building a rent-a-car tracing program. Evaluate the Customers, Agreements, and Cars entities shown below. Each customer can rent one or more cars. Each car can be rented to only one customer at a time. A car not owned by the rent-a-car office cannot be rented. How should you enforce integrity between the Agreements and Cars entities?

Examine the following logical model.

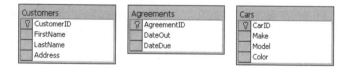

Customers
- CustomerID
- FirstName
- LastName
- Address

Agreements
- AgreementID
- DateOut
- DateDue

Cars
- CarID
- Make
- Model
- Color

A. Add a CHECK constraint to the AgreementID attribute.

B. Add the AgreementID attribute to the Cars entity with a FOREIGN KEY constraint referencing the Agreements entity.

C. Add an INSERT trigger to the rental entity.

D. Add the CarID attribute to the Agreements entity with a FOREIGN KEY constraint referencing the Cars entity.

70-229.01.03.005

You have designed an entity for tracking orders and have added all of the attributes, including one called UnitPrice that will be used to store the actual price charged per product. Which data types and nullability should be set for the UnitPrice attribute to ensure that the results of any mathematical functions on Unit-Price will always be accurate?

A. A nullable integer.

B. A nullable float.

C. A nullable money.

D. A non-nullable integer.

E. A non-nullable float.

F. A non-nullable money.

70-229.01.03.006

You are designing a logical model to collect information about the composition of fragrances for perfum-eries. This model will be used to create a database containing the recipes for different fragrances, and the percentages of each ingredient in the fragrance recipe will need to be tracked. You design an entity called PerfumeComposition and an entity called Ingredient. The percentage of each ingredient in a particular perfume will be stored in the PerfumeComposition table, one row for each ingredient. You want to ensure that the sum of the ingredient percentages for a perfume does not exceed 100. How can you accomplish this?

A. Add a CHECK constraint to the PerfumeComposition table that would disallow percentages of more than 100 per cent for a perfume.

B. Add a trigger to the PerfumeComposition table that would reject any percentage that would cause the sum of all of the percentages for a perfume to exceed 100 per cent.

C. Create a procedure to calculate any offending percentage every night and to delete the rows from the PerfumeComposition table.

D. Add a unique constraint to the percentage attribute in the PerfumeComposition table to disallow rows with the same percentages.

Objective 1.3 Answers

70-229.01.03.001

▶ **Correct Answers: D**

A. **Incorrect:** A CHECK constraint enforces strict values that can be stored in an attribute. A constraint contains a logical expression that must be evaluated before an INSERT into an attribute. Having a CHECK constraint could enforce some logical expression on the RepairID but would not prevent deletion of a customer.

B. **Incorrect:** Using a CHECK constraint on the CustomerID could enforce other rules on the CustomerID attribute but would not prevent the deletion of a customer.

C. **Incorrect:** A DELETE trigger is a stored procedure executed each time you delete a record from the Repair entity. This trigger would execute when you delete a record on the Repair entity but would not prevent a deletion of a record from the Customer entity.

D. **Correct:** You can add a CustomerID attribute to the Repair entity and configure it to have a FOREIGN KEY constraint referencing the Customer entity. You cannot delete a record from the referenced entity if you still have rows in the referencing entity. In this case, the Repair entity references the Customer entity, and rows cannot be deleted from the Customer entity until they are deleted first from the Repair entity.

70-229.01.03.002

▶ **Correct Answers: C**

A. **Incorrect:** Although the attribute referencing the agents by extension would be sufficient if they could not use more than one extension, the Extension attribute cannot be used correctly. You could associate agents with calls they did not make.

B. **Incorrect:** You cannot query the CallDetails and Agents entities to arrive at a commission because there is nothing to associate the two entities with each other. The Extension attribute cannot be used because the agents can use multiple extensions. You cannot tell who used the phone at that extension without adding an AgentID attribute to the CallDetails entity.

C. **Correct:** Adding the AgentID to the CallDetails entity and then creating the FOREIGN KEY constraint referencing the Agent entity is the correct relationship as described by the scenario.

70-229.01.03.003

▶ **Correct Answers: A**

A. **Correct:** Using a FOREIGN KEY constraint will guarantee data validity and guarantee that records cannot be deleted from the State entity while records referencing them exist in the Student entity.

B. **Incorrect:** A CHECK constraint can verify the validity of the new value. In this example you need to make sure that you cannot insert a student record without the correct StateID. A CHECK constraint placed on the State entity will validate data in the State entity but not in the Student entity. It will not guarantee data integrity between the two entities.

C. **Incorrect:** Although a CHECK constraint can determine which data can be placed in the Student entity based on the State entity, it does not stop deletion of records from the State entity.

D. **Incorrect:** A FOREIGN KEY constraint is correct, but the constraint should be placed on the Student entity referencing the State entity, not the other way around.

70-229.01.03.004

▶ **Correct Answers: D**

A. **Incorrect:** A CHECK constraint enforces domain integrity by restricting the values that can be entered into an attribute. A CHECK constraint contains a logical expression that must be true in order to accept the new value. A CHECK constraint on the AgreementID attribute would not enforce integrity between the Agreements entity and the Cars entity.

B. **Incorrect:** If a car could be rented only once, you could add the AgreementID to the Cars entity. Because a car can be rented many times, this will not work.

C. **Incorrect:** An INSERT trigger is a stored procedure that is executed automatically whenever you try to insert a record into the entity. A trigger can include most Transact-SQL (T-SQL) statements. Although a trigger could be placed on the Agreements entity to roll back the transaction if a car that is being rented is not in stock, a trigger should be used only when a constraint does not provide the necessary functionality.

D. **Correct:** You can add a CarID attribute to the Agreements entity and configure that attribute as a foreign key. This process enforces integrity between the Agreements entity and the Cars entity.

70-229.01.03.005

▶ **Correct Answers: F**

A. **Incorrect:** An integer is not the appropriate data type for UnitPrice because a price requires decimals. UnitPrice should also be non-nullable because a price is always known. It might have a UnitPrice of zero, but it would not be an unknown value.

B. **Incorrect:** A float is not the appropriate data type for UnitPrice because float data types are approximate and can have rounding errors in calculations, something that is frowned upon in money transactions. UnitPrice should also be non-nullable because a price is always known. It may have a UnitPrice of zero, but it would not be an unknown value.

C. **Incorrect:** Money is the correct data type for UnitPrice. This data type was designed specifically for monetary data, and it will not have the rounding problems that a float data type will exhibit. However, UnitPrice should be non-nullable because a price is always known. It may have a UnitPrice of zero, but it would not be an unknown value.

D. **Incorrect:** An integer would not be the appropriate data type for UnitPrice because a price will require decimals. However, UnitPrice should be non-nullable because a price is always known.

E. **Incorrect:** A float would not be the appropriate data type for UnitPrice because float data types are approximate and can have rounding errors in calculations, something that is frowned upon in money transactions. However, UnitPrice should be non-nullable because a price is always known.

F. **Correct:** Money is the correct data type for UnitPrice. This data type was designed specifically for monetary data, so it will not have the rounding problems that a float data type will exhibit. UnitPrice should also be non-nullable because a price is always known. It may have a UnitPrice of zero, but it would not be an unknown value. This combination is correct for the business function and rules required by the question.

70-229.01.03.006

▶ **Correct Answers: B**

A. **Incorrect:** It would not be possible to add a CHECK constraint to check across rows, summing the percentage.

B. **Correct:** This is the only way to implement this business rule in the database.

C. **Incorrect:** It is best not to change data after it has been entered, but rather to disallow its entry in the first place if it is incorrect. Deleting offending rows is a dangerous strategy because data would quickly become incorrect and invalid.

D. **Incorrect:** This does not address the sum of the rows in the PerfumeComposition table for a particular perfume exceeding 100 percent.

OBJECTIVE DOMAIN 2

Implementing the Physical Database

The **physical database design** maps the **logical database design** to a physical medium. To develop a physical database design, you must take the available hardware into consideration. You need to take advantage of the available hardware and keep in mind the extensibility options of the existing or new hardware. Consider how the data will be accessed throughout the hardware system. The physical design addresses how data will be accessed, whereas the logical design models your business requirements and data. Physical design tends to be very platform-specific.

A well-designed database model is key to a successful high-performance database with efficient storage and retrieval of data. The design should be carefully reviewed to assess its impact on the database. You have to take a close look at the following aspects of database operations: performance, maintainability, extensibility, scalability, availability, and security.

Performance involves not just the response time of the query but the network traffic, disk I/O, and CPU utilization.

Maintainability involves the ongoing maintenance of the database, which includes backups and restores, rebuilding and creating new indexes, updating constraints, or partitioning data.

Extensibility refers to the ability to extend new functionality built into Microsoft SQL Server 2000 and future releases. It includes the extensibility of your database design to support future releases of your software.

Scalability refers to the ability to accommodate growing databases and numbers of new users without suffering performance hits or a breakdown.

Availability involves users, application servers, or other server processes to access the data in the database. Availability is measured in system uptime and has become more and more important in current Internet commerce systems.

Security refers to the control of access in the database and determination of who can access specific data in the database.

If you intend to implement a partitioned database at some time, this is the time to determine how that implementation could be done.

You should know how a logical database design could impact database performance. You need to have a firm understanding of the key terms in the following section to successfully answer the questions.

Tested Skills and Suggested Practices

The skills that you need to successfully master the Implementing the Physical Database objective domain on the *Designing and Implementing Databases with Microsoft SQL Server 2000 Enterprise Edition* exam include:

- **Evaluating the logical database and its impact on each aspect of database operations, such as performance, maintainability, extensibility, scalability, availability, security, and partitionability.**

    - Practice 1: For this practice you must use a logical database design. Collect all tables, views, indexes, constraints, and so on. List each feature of your design. List the number of tables, views, constraints, and so on. You should know the number of projected users, the estimated database size, and the anticipated database growth. Consider the hardware and whether it is expandable to grow with your business needs. Look at each item and determine the impact on the database. For example, more triggers can dramatically impact performance. Overly complex or too many indexes can do more harm than good.

    - Practice 2: Make a list of the critical standards of database quality, such as performance, maintainability, extensibility, scalability, availability, and security. Determine how each of these items impacts your standard of database quality.

    - Practice 3: Look closely at how normalization and denormalization would affect your standard of database quality.

- **Modifying a logical database design to minimize its impact on database operations.**

    - Practice 1: Review the list you created for the first practice and take a look at what part of your database design you would change to improve maintainability. For example, you might want to limit the number of indexes or the size of the database. You might find that your database is already designed to support maximum maintainability and you do not need to make any changes.

    - Practice 2: You need to take into consideration the performance of your database and decide whether you need to make changes in your logical database design to improve performance. You might need to rework some joins, denormalize some tables, or introduce new indexes.

■ Practice 3: Based on the list you have created, look at the availability of the database design. You might consider consolidating your databases or introducing partitioning.

- **Determining the impact that database design modifications will have on database operations.**

■ Practice 1: Add a denormalized table to your database. Make sure you add the necessary indexes, triggers, views, and constraints. Look at the impact the denormalized table had on the performance and size of database operation.

■ Practice 2: Add views to your database to see how they impact the aspects of the database.

■ Practice 3: Expand the database with extra data to see how the expansion affects your database.

Further Reading

This section lists supplemental readings by objective. Study these sources thoroughly before taking exam 70-229.

Objective 2.1

Microsoft SQL Server 2000 product documentation. To access Books Online, click the Start button, point to Programs, then Microsoft SQL Server, and then click Books Online. Click the Contents tab, double-click "Creating and Maintaining Databases," and review "Databases," "Database Design Considerations," "Creating a Database," and "Optimizing Database Performance."

Delaney, Kalen. *Inside Microsoft SQL Server 2000*. Redmond, Washington: Microsoft Press, 2000. Review Chapter 5, "Databases and Database Files."

In Part 1, read and complete the practices in Lessons 1, 2, and 3 in Chapter 3, "Designing SQL Server Database," and Lesson 1 in Chapter 4, "Implementing SQL Server Databases and Tables."

Objective 2.2

Microsoft SQL Server 2000 product documentation. To access Books Online, click the Start button, point to Programs, then Microsoft SQL Server, and then click Books Online. Click the Contents tab, double-click "Creating and Maintaining Databases," and review "Tables" and "Views."

Delaney, Kalen. *Inside Microsoft SQL Server 2000*. Redmond, Washington: Microsoft Press, 2000. Review Chapter 6, "Tables."

In Part 1, read and complete the practices in Lesson 4 in Chapter 2, "Using Transact-SQL on a SQL Server Database," Lessons 1 and 3 in Chapter 4, "Implementing SQL Server Databases and Tables," Lessons 1 and 2 in Chapter 5, "Implementing Data Integrity," Lessons 1, 2, and 3 in Chapter 8, "Implementing Stored Procedures," Lessons 1, 2, and 3 in Chapter 9, "Implementing Triggers," Lessons 1, 2, and 3 in Chapter 10, "Implementing Views," and Lessons 1 and 2 in Chapter 11, "Implementing Indexes."

Objective 2.3

Microsoft SQL Server 2000 product documentation. To access Books Online, click the Start button, point to Programs, then Microsoft SQL Server, and then click Books Online. Click the Contents tab, double-click "Replication," and review "Partitioned Views."

Delaney, Kalen. *Inside Microsoft SQL Server 2000*. Redmond, Washington: Microsoft Press, 2000. Review Chapter 2, "A Tour of SQL Server: Data Replication."

In Part 1, read and complete the practices in Lesson 2, Chapter 14, "Maintaining and Optimizing SQL Server Database."

Objective 2.4

Microsoft SQL Server 2000 product documentation. To access Books Online, click the Start button, point to Programs, then Microsoft SQL Server, and then click Books Online. Click the Contents tab and review "Transact-SQL Reference" and "Trouble-shooting."

Microsoft SQL Server 2000 product documentation. To access Books Online, click the Start button, point to Programs, then Microsoft SQL Server, and then click Books Online. Click the Contents tab and double-click the "Optimizing Database Performance" topic. Then review "Physical Database Design" under "Database Design."

Microsoft SQL Server 2000 product documentation. To access Books Online, click the Start button, point to Programs, then Microsoft SQL Server, and then click Books Online. Click the Contents tab and double-click the "Creating and Maintaining Databases" topic. Then review "Creating and Modifying a Table" under "Tables."

In Part 1, read and complete the practices in Lesson 2, Chapter 14, "Maintaining and Optimizing SQL Server Database."

OBJECTIVE 2.1

Create and alter databases.

The first step to creating databases is to plan how the databases will be created and distributed across the physical media. SQL Server 2000 provides so much flexibility in database creation and placement that a plan is required to properly design the physical implementation for optimal performance and flexibility.

Start by gathering information about your system. Accurate information might not be readily available as to how usage will occur, so be prepared to change your plan later to optimize performance.

Next, consider how you will partition the databases across the physical drives (if at all). Also, you should consider how many files or filegroups will need to be created and how the database should be placed on these filegroups.

It is critical to determine the optimal placement for the transaction log as well, and to try to ensure that there is no contention between the data being written and the transaction log being written.

Part of the database creation plan must also be the database maintenance plan. What recovery model will you use, and how do you plan to back up and restore databases, as well as perform necessary database console commands (DBCCs)? All of these questions need to be taken into consideration in determining how to design databases.

Objective 2.1 Questions

70-229.02.01.001

You are managing databases for a long distance phone company. One of these databases is used to temporarily hold millions of phone call records. After the billing processes are finished, you have to delete certain records from the tables, and you need to use your system disk resources conservatively. How would you create the database and what kind of settings would you use?

A. Create a small database and use the autogrow feature.

B. Create a large database and disable the autogrow feature.

C. Create a database, allow it to automatically grow, and enable the autoclose feature.

D. Create a database, allow it to automatically grow, and enable the autoshrink feature.

70-229.02.01.002

You have just expanded your server with a second high-speed RAID controller and disk drives. You want to take advantage of this new controller and drives. You have one primary database used by an application. How can you take advantage of the new expansion while disturbing operations as little as possible?

A. Back up the database and create one large logical drive spanning the two controllers.

B. Create a second database on the logical drive of the second controller and move some tables into the new database.

C. Add files to the filegroup of the database and transaction log and place them on the new controller's logical drive.

70-229.02.01.003

You are trying to design a system and optimize it for throughput. You have to decide how to organize your drives, tables, indexes, and so on. Your system contains two RAID controllers with three channels on each controller. Each channel has 40 MB/sec throughput. You cannot create logical drives spanning controllers, but you can create logical drives spanning channels on the same controller. Which of the following solutions would provide the best performance?

A. Create a logical disk spanning all three channels and place the system files, swap file, and the SQL Server executable files on this drive. Create the second logical drive spanning the three channels of the second controller, and place the transaction log and the database files on this drive.

B. Create a logical disk spanning all three channels and place the system files, swap file, the SQL Server executable files, and the transaction log on that logical disk. Create the second logical drive spanning the three channels of the second controller, and put the database files on the second logical drive.

C. Create a logical drive on the first controller's first channel only. Place the system and the page files on this logical drive. Create a second logical drive on the first controller's second and third channels. Place the database transaction log on the second logical drive. Create a third logical drive on the second controller spanning the three channels, and place the database and index files on the third logical drive.

D. Create a logical drive on the first controller's first channel only. Place the system and the page file on this logical drive. Create a second logical drive on the first controller's second and third channels. Create a third logical drive on the second controller spanning the three channels. When you create the database in the filegroup, you specify a file on the second logical drive and a file on the third logical drive for both the database and the transaction log.

70-229.02.01.004

You have deleted 10 million rows from the CallDetails table in MyDATA. Which statement would you use to make SQL Server resize the database file to its smallest possible size?

A. ALTER DATABASE MyDATA SET RECOVERY SIMPLE

B. DBCC SHRINKDB

C. DBCC SHRINKFILE

D. DBCC SQLPERF SHRINKDB

70-229.02.01.005

You have a server with a RAID controller with three channels, and each channel has 40 MB/sec through-put. Your system drive is created on a logical drive array using the first channel only. The data drive is created with the union of the second and third channel as a second logical drive. When you look at the disk performance, you realize that the data drive is overworked but the system drive has almost no activity. How would you reconfigure this system to have better performance?

A. Reconfigure the physical disk subsystem so that both the system and the data logical drives span all three channels.

B. Reconfigure the logical disk system, creating three logical drives with each one on its own channel. Place system, page file, and data on their own logical drives.

C. Reconfigure the system creating three logical drives with each one on its own channel. Place system, data, and transaction log on their own logical drive.

70-229.02.01.006

You have decided to create two filegroups for your database, a primary and a secondary. Which of the following are advantages to this approach? (Choose all that apply.)

A. The primary filegroup can be backed up separately from the secondary filegroup.

B. The filegroups can be checked for data consistency and integrity separately.

C. By separating the filegroups, both can contain historical data and be marked as read-only.

D. The primary filegroup can be small enough to contain only the system tables and placed on the most fault-tolerant drives, to help ensure point-of-failure recovery.

70-229.02.01.007

Which of the following RAID levels is best suited to the transaction log on a system using the full recovery model?

A. RAID 0

B. RAID 1

C. RAID 5

70-229.02.01.008

You have decided that you want to use raw partitions with your SQL Server database to improve performance. Does SQL Server support raw partitions, and how many data files can you place on a raw partition?

A. SQL Server no longer supports raw partitions.

B. SQL Server supports raw partitions, and the maximum file number is unlimited.

C. SQL Server supports raw partitions, and the maximum file number is one.

Objective 2.1 Answers

70-229.02.01.001

▶ **Correct Answers: D**

A. **Incorrect:** Creating a small database and enabling the autogrow feature will conserve space. However, when the database grows after the processing is done, the database will retain its largest size. You have to enable the autoshrink feature to allow SQL Server to shrink the database.

B. **Incorrect:** Creating a large database improves performance because the database does not have to allocate data while it processes new records. In this case, after you delete the unnecessary records, the database will retain its size. You need to shrink the database as soon as possible to conserve disk space. Having a fixed-size database might interrupt your operation if the incoming data is more than the database is able to hold.

C. **Incorrect:** Although creating a database and letting it automatically grow is correct, enabling autoclose will not help to conserve disk space. Autoclose enables SQL Server to shut the database down when all resources are freed and all users are disconnected. You have to enable autoshrink to conserve disk space.

D. **Correct:** Databases are created by default with autogrow enabled. This feature allows the database to grow when it requires more space to hold the data, indexes, and other database-related information. Enabling autoshrink causes the database to resize itself when data is removed from the database. SQL Server 2000 will periodically check the database and will shrink the database files when possible. Be aware that there is a performance hit when the database is growing.

70-229.02.01.002

▶ **Correct Answers: C**

A. **Incorrect:** You could create one logical drive spanning the two controllers if the controllers allow it. It would create a relatively big interruption because you need to back up the database and then create the logical drive, format it, re-create the database, and restore the database. You should add new files to the filegroup of the database and the transaction log and place them on the new logical drive.

B. **Incorrect:** If you wouldn't break referential integrity, you can do this, but the application might have to be changed. You could horizontally partition the data, but you will have to move data from one database to the other periodically. You should add new files to the filegroup of the database and the transaction log and place them on the new logical drive.

C. **Correct:** If you expand the database this way, you will not interrupt the operation of the database at all. SQL Server will automatically start using the files on the second logical disk as soon as it requires more pages for new data.

70-229.02.01.003

▶ **Correct Answers: D**

A. **Incorrect:** In this case you will have both logical drives with the maximum of 120 MB/sec throughput. This is overkill for the system, page, and SQL Server executables. These files are accessed infrequently, whereas the database is limited to only 120 MB/sec throughput without utilizing the available system resources.

B. **Incorrect:** In this scenario you are utilizing the controllers more evenly, but you are still limiting the possible performance. Moving the transaction log to another controller improves the performance for insert, update, and delete, but it's not utilizing the resources for data retrieval.

C. **Incorrect:** In this case you are using the controller more evenly, but you still do not have the best configuration. The system files are fine on a single channel because they are accessed less frequently. The transaction log is limited to only 80 MB/sec, which can slow insert, update, and delete transactions. The database files are limited to only 120 MB/sec throughput.

D. **Correct:** This is the best configuration of the given examples. The system files are on their own logical drive and have plenty of throughput of 40 MB/sec. These files are accessed less frequently. Creating both the database and transaction log spanning two logical drives produces the maximum throughput of 200 MB/sec.

70-229.02.01.004

► **Correct Answers: C**

A. **Incorrect:** The SET RECOVERY option allows the recovery model to be set, and SIMPLE is the nonlogged option, but this will not affect any actions that were taken previously. With ALTER DATABASE you can add or remove files from the database, but before that you have to execute DBCC SHRINKFILE with the EMPTYFILE argument. You have to use DBCC SHRINKFILE to force the database to shrink the given file. You cannot make the database smaller than the model database.

B. **Incorrect:** DBCC SHRINKDB is not supported in Microsoft SQL Server 7 or SQL Server 2000. You have to shrink the data files of the database individually. You have to use DBCC SHRINKFILE to force the database to shrink one of its files. Database size will never be smaller than the model database.

C. **Correct:** DBCC SHRINKFILE is used to instruct SQL Server to try to shrink its file to a smaller size. It can be used on files in a database or in the transaction log. Database size will never be smaller than the model database.

D. **Incorrect:** DBCC SQLPERF does not have a SHRINKDB option. DBCC SQLPERF provides statistics about the use transaction log space in all databases. DBCC SHRINKFILE is used to instruct SQL Server to try to shrink its file to a smaller size. It can be used on the files in a database or in the transaction log. Database size will never be smaller than the model database.

70-229.02.01.005

► **Correct Answers: A**

A. **Correct:** In this case all logical drives will span all three channels, so the data drive will have more throughput. For example: If the channels are 40 MB/sec, you will have 120 MB/sec throughput compared with the original 80 MB/sec.

B. **Incorrect:** Configuring a RAID system this way will decrease database performance. The system did not have any problem while the system files and page file were on the same controller. So separating them and giving each its own channel will not improve the system performance. Instead, this configuration will to some degree degrade performance. In the original configuration, the data drive had 80 MB/sec throughput, but in this configuration it has only 40 MB/sec.

C. **Incorrect:** Although in some circumstances it is a good idea to separate the data and the log files onto different drives, in this case it will not improve the performance. You are still limited to the maximum 80 MB/sec throughput for the database, and this configuration will not take advantage of the remaining 40 MB/sec.

70-229.02.01.006

▶ **Correct Answers: A, B, and D**

A. **Correct:** Because there is no need to back up data that has not changed, seldom-changed data can be put on the secondary filegroup. You could then choose to back up the primary filegroup only, to ensure that the system databases are always intact. This approach allows a partial restore. Filegroups provide much more flexibility for performance and maintenance.

B. **Correct:** Filegroups can have DBCC CHECKFILEGROUP run on each separate filegroup. This approach can be advantageous when a system's maintenance window is too small for both filegroups to have DBCCs performed, or when data changes little on the secondary filegroup. Filegroups provide much more flexibility for performance and maintenance.

C. **Incorrect:** The primary filegroup can never be marked as read-only. However, by creating two or more filegroups, the secondary filegroup data can be read-only, whereas the data in the primary filegroup would be read-write.

D. **Correct:** To have point-of-failure recovery, the primary filegroup must be intact. If you make it small and protected from the rest of the data, this filegroup has a better chance of remaining intact.

70-229.02.01.007

▶ **Correct Answers: B**

A. **Incorrect:** RAID 0 is not recommended for any SQL Server files without any other availability plan because RAID 0 provides no redundancy. Because the transaction log is required for full recovery, there must be some kind of redundancy in the system.

B. **Correct:** RAID 1 is excellent for the transaction log. It provides mirroring for redundancy and is optimal for sequential writes because there is no striping involved in this level. Because the transaction log is a sequential wrap-around write, this level is both fault-tolerant and high-performing for the transaction log.

C. **Incorrect:** RAID 5 uses parity, as well as striping, to provide fault tolerance without the expense of duplicate drives used for mirroring, placing some data on all discs. This is excellent for read operations, because it uses fewer discs than RAID 1, but it is not optimal for the transaction log, which will perform mostly sequential writes.

70-229.02.01.008

▶ **Correct Answers: C**

A. **Incorrect:** SQL Server supports raw partitions and FAT and NTFS also. Although raw partitions can yield some performance improvement, they can also make SQL Server management more complex.

B. **Incorrect:** Although SQL Server supports raw partitions, the maximum file number per partition is one. A raw partition does not have a file system, so the whole partition is treated as a single file.

C. **Correct:** SQL Server supports raw partitions with a single file per partition. For each file you have to create a partition. Some of the built-in features, such as autogrow, are not available with raw partitions. You have to use just a drive letter assigned to the raw partition or a mounting point.

OBJECTIVE 2.2

Create and alter database objects.

After the databases have been created, the database objects must be created, including tables and views. Creating database objects also requires a physical implementation plan. You should already have a logical model that will guide you for the creation of the tables as far as the names, columns, data types, and constraints. However, now is the time to optimize each of these parts of the object creation for the physical implementation.

Determine how you will use **views** in your system. Some shops use views only for database access, leaving the underlying tables unavailable to developer access. This approach can be complex to work with but is quite flexible because it allows changes to be made to the underlying table objects without changing any of the code that is used against the system. In SQL Server, indexed views can now be used to help with specific performance problems that might be occurring with certain queries.

You will need a plan as to where to place the database objects within the files and filegroups. This allows you to tune your system's performance by controlling how and where data is stored physically. Separating often-used tables on separate filegroups can enhance performance by providing parallel read and write access if they are on different drives.

Again, SQL Server 2000 provides a great deal of flexibility and control over database object creation and placement for performance, as well as the ease with which objects can be modified or altered.

Objective 2.2 Questions

70-229.02.02.001

You use this syntax to create a table:

```
CREATE TABLE Customers (
CustomerID    int          IDENTITY (1,10),
LastName      varchar(25)    NOT NULL,
FirstName     varchar(25)    NOT NULL,
MiddleName    varchar(1),
Add1          varchar(20),
City          varchar(20),
State         varchar(2),
ZipCode       varchar(5)
)
```

Which results will this produce? (Choose all answers that apply.)

A. The IDENTITY value starts at 10 and gets incremented with a value of 1.

B. The IDENTITY value gets generated automatically, and this column can be updated.

C. The IDENTITY value gets generated automatically, and this column cannot be updated.

D. None of the columns can have a NULL value.

70-229.02.02.002

You use the following statement to create a table:

```
CREATE TABLE Logging (
LogID        uniqueidentifier    DEFAULT ( NEWID ()),
Title        varchar (25)        NOT NULL,
Data         text,
Status       int                 NOT NULL
)
```

Which results will this produce? (Choose all that apply.)

A. LogID, Title, and Status cannot be NULL.

B. LogID will have a default value of a new GUID and can be updated.

C. LogID and Data are nullable, whereas Title and Status must have a value other than NULL.

D. TEXT is limited to 4000 characters if no size is defined.

70-229.02.02.003

You use the following statement to create a table:

```
CREATE TABLE Orders (
OrderID        uniqueidentifier      NOT NULL DEFAULT( NEWID() )
CONSTRAINT pk_Orders PRIMARY KEY,
CustomerID    long                   NOT NULL,
Date          datetime
)
```

Which results will this produce? (Choose all that apply.)

A. The uniqueidentifier data type will generate unique integer numbers.

B. OrderID value will be a GUID, and it will be used as the PRIMARY KEY of this table.

C. Defines OrderID, CustomerID, and Date values.

70-229.02.02.004

You are planning to create an index for a large table with two columns used to identify rows. Users need to access data quickly in sorted order, and duplicates are permitted. Which indexing strategy should you choose?

A. Unique, composite, and clustered

B. Nonunique, composite, and nonclustered

C. Nonunique, composite, and clustered

D. Nonclustered

70-229.02.02.005

You need to change your Orders table by adding a new column. This column must be of integer type, cannot have a null value, and can accept the following numbers: 1, 3, 5, 7, and 9. A default value of 1 should be assigned. Which of the following is true?

A. You can achieve the requirement by executing the following Transact-SQL statement: `ALTER TABLE Orders ADD (SpecialValue int not null check (SpecialValue in (1,3,5,7,9))`

B. You can achieve the requirement by executing the following Transact-SQL statement: `ALTER TABLE Orders ADD (SpecialValue int not null default (1) check (SpecialValue in (1,3,5,7,9))`

C. Columns with a not null value cannot be added to a table.

D. You cannot add a column and a constraint in one statement.

70-229.02.02.006

You have created a view with the option of SCHEMABINDING. What effect will this have on the view?

A. Prior to execution of the view, the schema will be checked for changes to the underlying tables and views.

B. SQL Server will return information about the view instead of the underlying tables and views when browse-mode metadata is requested.

C. SCHEMABINDING binds the view to the schema, so the SELECT statement must include the two-part names of tables, views, or user-defined functions referenced.

70-229.02.02.007

You have two tables with the same schema definition. One table will store East Coast data, and the other will store the data for the West Coast. You want to create a view that returns all the rows from both tables. You write the following statement:

```
CREATE VIEW AllData as
SELECT * FROM EastCoast
UNION ALL
SELECT * FROM WestCoast
```

What is the difference between UNION and UNION ALL?

A. There is no difference between UNION and UNION ALL.

B. UNION ALL is not supported in SQL Server 2000.

C. UNION returns everything from the first table and everything that does not already exist from the second table. UNION ALL returns everything from both tables.

D. UNION returns only unique records from both tables. UNION ALL returns all records from both tables.

70-229.02.02.008

Where does SQL Server keep the scripts for views, and what happens if you use the ENCRYPTION option?

A. View scripts are kept in the syscomments system table, and using ENCRYPTION stores the script coded and the view cannot be replicated. If you use the ENCRYPTION option, you should save the script.

B. View scripts are kept in the sysviews system table, and using ENCRYPTION will garble the text output if you try to view the script. It has no effect on replication.

C. View scripts are kept in the sysviews system table, and ENCRYPTION will cause the script not to be stored in SQL Server—only the execution plan will be stored. The view cannot be replicated.

D. View scripts are kept in the sysviewdetails system table; using ENCRYPTION will store the script coded and the view can be replicated.

70-229.02.02.009

You have a stored procedure in your SQL Server database to calculate bonuses for employees. The logic for this procedure is very complex, and you do not want anyone to see the logic in your database even if they have administrative rights. What option is correct to use with your CREATE PROCEDURE statement?

A. WITH SECURITY ON

B. WITH ENCRYPTION PASSWORD 'password'

C. WITH ENCRYPTION

70-229.02.02.010

You have a stored procedure in your SQL Server database using atypical and temporary values. You do not want SQL Server to cache the execution plan for this stored procedure. What is the attribute you should use when creating the stored procedure?

A. WITH NOCACHE

B. WITH RECOMPILE

C. WITH NEW PLAN

70-229.02.02.011

After analyzing the performance of your SQL Server database, you find out that one of your tables is causing SQL Server to provide slow performance. To be precise, you find out that the indexes on a table are not effective. You come to the conclusion that your primary key should not be clustered, whereas a second index should be. Which of the following statements is correct?

A. You can re-create your primary key to use nonclustered indexes and your secondary index to use clustered indexes.

B. You cannot achieve the requirement because a primary key is always created as a clustered index.

C. You can create your primary key nonclustered as long as no other table references it with a foreign key constraint.

70-229.02.02.012

You have a table and you need to create an index on one of the columns. This column has duplicate values. You know that no more duplicate values will be entered into the table, but the existing duplicate values must be kept in the table. You do not want to allow any more duplicate keys entered into the table. Which of the following statements is true?

A. You cannot achieve the requirement. You have to remove the duplicates and then create an index with the UNIQUE option.

B. You can achieve the requirement when creating the index by using the UNIQUE and IGNORE_DUP_KEY options.

C. You can achieve the requirements using the IGNORE_DUP_KEY option.

70-229.02.02.013

You have Table1 with static data, whereas Table2 is volatile. What FILLFACTOR would you use on indexes created for both tables?

A. Low FILLFACTOR for Table1 and high FILLFACTOR for Table2

B. High FILLFACTOR for Table1 and low FILLFACTOR for Table2

C. High FILLFACTOR for both tables

Objective 2.2 Answers

70-229.02.02.001

▶ **Correct Answers: C**

A. **Incorrect:** An IDENTITY column takes the following parameters: the first is the seed value, and the second is the increment value. This example creates a Customer table; CustomerID will be generated as soon as a new record is inserted into the table. LastName and FirstName are mandatory, whereas the rest of the columns are optional.

B. **Incorrect:** Although the first part of the answer was correct, the second part is incorrect. IDENTITY columns cannot be updated.

C. **Correct:** This example creates a Customer table; CustomerID will be generated as soon as a new record is inserted into the table. An IDENTITY column is not updateable. LastName and FirstName are mandatory, whereas the rest of the columns are optional.

D. **Incorrect:** If neither NULL nor NOT NULL is defined and the data type is not an IDENTITY column, the column will be nullable. LastName and FirstName are not nullable, whereas the rest can have a NULL value.

70-229.02.02.002

▶ **Correct Answers: B and C**

A. **Incorrect:** LogID is not defined as not nullable. If you do not want to accept NULLs in this column, you should declare it as LogID uniqueidentifier NOT NULL DEFAULT(NEWID ()). This example creates a table, LogID, and Data can accept NULL, whereas Title and Status must have a value other than NULL. LogID will be populated with a new globally unique identifier (GUID), and this column can be updated.

B. **Correct:** LogID will have a new GUID as a value as soon as a new record is inserted into the table. This column can be updated or nulled. This example creates a table, LogID, and Data can accept NULL, whereas Title and Status must have a value other than NULL.

C. **Correct:** Uniqueidentifier is just another data type. It does not create a value as IDENTITY does, and IDENTITY exclusively sets the column to not updateable. This example creates a table, and LogID and Data can accept NULL, whereas Title and Status must have a value other than NULL.

D. **Incorrect:** TEXT is a data type, and its size cannot be defined as it can be with NUMERIC or VARCHAR. TEXT is capable of storing up to $2^{31} - 1$ (2,147,483,647) bytes. TEXT is used for non-Unicode strings, whereas NTEXT is used for Unicode strings.

70-229.02.02.003

▶ **Correct Answers: B and C**

  A. **Incorrect:** A uniqueidentifier column can accept only a valid GUID. In this example OrderID will have a value of a GUID, and this column will be used as the PRIMARY KEY column. CustomerID cannot have a value of NULL, whereas Date does not have to have a value.

  B. **Correct:** OrderID cannot have a value of NULL because of the NOT NULL clause; by default it will have a new GUID and be the PRIMARY KEY of this table.

  C. **Correct:** CREATE TABLE defines all the columns of a table. The column definitions of the table must include the name and type of the columns. The data type must be either a system-defined data type or a user-defined data type. In addition, you can constrain each column as a NULL or NOT NULL. You can also define default values, PRIMARY KEY constraint, and FOREIGN KEY constraints or CHECK constraints.

70-229.02.02.004

▶ **Correct Answers: C**

  A. **Incorrect:** Although composite and clustered are correct, unique is incorrect because this table must allow duplicates. A clustered index orders the data physically. You need a composite index because you have more than one column in the index. Duplicates are allowed, so a nonunique index is needed.

  B. **Incorrect:** Although nonunique and composite are correct, nonclustered is incorrect. You should create a clustered index. A clustered index is ordered physically, which is useful when data is accessed in sorted order. Data in a nonclustered index is not sorted in the order of the index.

  C. **Correct:** A clustered index orders the data physically. You need a composite index because you have more than one column in the index. Duplicates are allowed, so a nonunique index is needed.

  D. **Incorrect:** You should create a clustered index. A clustered index is ordered physically, which is useful when data is accessed in sorted order. Data in a nonclustered index is not sorted in the order of the index. You should have chosen a nonunique, composite, clustered index.

70-229.02.02.005

▶ **Correct Answers: B**

A. **Incorrect:** If you add a column to a table with a not null option, you must use a default value. Not specifying the default value will cause an error. You need to insert the default between the not null and check.

B. **Correct:** Adding a column with a not null option and defining a default value produces the result you want. The CHECK constraint will be created correctly, and the name will be generated automatically. If naming the constraint is necessary, you have to add the constraint definition after a comma in the statement.

C. **Incorrect:** Columns with a not null value can be added to an existing table; however, a default value must be defined. If you try to add a column with the not null option but without a default value, SQL Server will generate an error. You can create the constraint two different ways within the same command, either by defining the constraint as an option of the column without a defined name or by specifying it after the column definition separated with a comma.

D. **Incorrect:** You can create the column definition and the constraint with the same statement. You can create the constraint two different ways within the same command, either by defining the constraint as an option of the column without a defined name or specifying it after the column definition separated with a comma.

70-229.02.02.006

▶ **Correct Answers: C**

A. **Incorrect:** The schema will not be checked every time the view is executed. If the underlying tables or views are changed and columns are removed from the tables or views, the execution might fail based on the changes at execution time. SCHEMABINDING will force binding of the schema to the view. You must include the two-part name, like object.name, for tables, views, or user-defined functions. Objects cannot be dropped while they are referenced from a view using SCHEMABINDING. In a view created with SCHEMABINDING, all columns are updateable except a column with a type of TIMESTAMP.

B. **Incorrect:** If you have to return browse-mode metadata, you need to use the VIEW_METADATA option. SCHEMABINDING will force binding of the schema to the view. You must include the two-part name, like object.name, for tables, views, or user-defined functions. Objects cannot be dropped while they are referenced from a view using SCHEMABINDING. In a view created with SCHEMA-BINDING, all columns are updateable except a column with a type of TIMESTAMP.

C. **Correct:** SCHEMABINDING will force binding of the schema to the view. You must include the two-part name, like object.name, for tables, views, or user-defined functions. Objects cannot be dropped while they are referenced from a view using SCHEMABINDING. In a view created with SCHEMABINDING, all columns are updateable except a column with a type of TIMESTAMP.

70-229.02.02.007

▶ **Correct Answers: D**

A. **Incorrect:** UNION and UNION ALL are not the same commands. The UNION operator returns two or more SELECT statement results in a single result set. These result sets must have the same number of columns and compatible data types. By default UNION will remove duplicates from the result set; if you use UNION ALL, all records will be returned in the result set.

B. **Incorrect:** UNION ALL is a valid option statement in SQL Server 2000. The UNION operator returns two or more SELECT statement results in a single result set. These result sets must have the same number of columns and compatible data types. By default UNION will remove duplicates from the result set; if you use UNION ALL, all records will be returned in the result set.

C. **Incorrect:** This answer is incorrect because duplicate records from the first table will also be removed. The UNION operator returns two or more SELECT statement results in a single result set. These result sets must have the same number of columns and compatible data types. By default UNION will remove duplicates from the result set; if you use UNION ALL, all records will be returned in the result set.

D. **Correct:** The UNION operator returns two or more SELECT statement results in a single result set. These result sets must have the same number of columns and compatible data types. By default UNION will remove duplicates from the result set; if you use UNION ALL, all records will be returned in the result set.

70-229.02.02.008

▶ **Correct Answers: A**

A. **Correct:** View scripts are kept in the syscomments system table. Using ENCRYPTION will code the script so that it cannot be viewed and causes the view not to be replicated.

B. **Incorrect:** View scripts are kept in the syscomments system table instead of the sysviews system table. A sysviews system table does not exist in SQL Server 2000. View scripts are kept in the syscomments system table; using ENCRYPTION will store the script coded and the view cannot be replicated. If you use the ENCRYPTION option, you should save the script.

C. **Incorrect:** View scripts are kept in the syscomments system table; using ENCRYPTION will store the script coded and the view cannot be replicated. If you use the ENCRYPTION option, you should save the script.

D. **Incorrect:** View scripts are kept in the syscomments system table; using ENCRYPTION will store the script coded and the view cannot be replicated. If you use the ENCRYPTION option, you should save the script.

70-229.02.02.009

▶ **Correct Answers: C**

A. **Incorrect:** To disable the viewing of the stored procedure code, you have to use the WITH ENCRYPTION option when you create the stored procedure. After you encrypt a stored procedure, there is no way to decrypt it.

B. **Incorrect:** Although the correct attribute to encrypt a stored procedure is WITH ENCRYPTION, you cannot specify a password. After a stored procedure is encrypted, there is no way to decrypt it in SQL Server.

C. **Correct:** The WITH ENCRYPTION option on the CREATE PROCEDURE statement will force SQL Server to encrypt the Transact-SQL code within the stored procedure. After the code is encrypted, it is no longer viewable.

70-229.02.02.010

▶ **Correct Answers: B**

A. **Incorrect:** To force SQL Server to recompile and not cache the execution plan, you need to use the WITH RECOMPILE attribute when creating the stored procedure.

B. **Correct:** The WITH RECOMPILE option will force SQL Server not to cache the execution plan for the stored procedure and to recompile it each time it executes.

C. **Incorrect:** WITH NEW PLAN is not supported in SQL Server. To force SQL Server not to cache the execution plan, you need to use the WITH RECOMPILE option when creating the stored procedure.

70-229.02.02.011

▶ **Correct Answers: A**

A. **Correct:** A primary key can be created with a nonclustered index. By default SQL Server uses clustered indexes, but this can be changed when creating the table or after the table has been created.

B. **Incorrect:** A common misunderstanding is to assume that a primary key can only be a clustered index. This is the default that SQL Server provides, and most commonly it is the correct indexing for primary keys. However, it can be changed either at table creation or with the ALTER TABLE statement after the table has been created.

C. **Incorrect:** Although the first part of the answer is correct—a primary key can be created using a nonclustered index—the second part is incorrect. For foreign keys it does not matter what kind of index is used on the referenced column, if any.

70-229.02.02.012

▶ **Correct Answers: A**

A. **Correct:** When a unique index exists, UPDATE or INSERT statements that would generate duplicate key values are rolled back, and SQL Server displays an error message. This is true even if the UPDATE or INSERT statement changes many rows but causes only one duplicate. If an attempt is made to enter data for which there is a unique index and the IGNORE_DUP_KEY clause is specified, only the rows violating the UNIQUE index fail. When processing an UPDATE statement, IGNORE_DUP_KEY has no effect.

SQL Server does not allow the creation of a unique index on columns that already include duplicate values, whether or not IGNORE_DUP_KEY is set. If attempted, SQL Server displays an error message; duplicates must be eliminated before a unique index can be created on the column(s).

B. **Incorrect:** See explanation for A.

C. **Incorrect:** See explanation for A.

70-229.02.02.013

▶ **Correct Answers: B**

A. **Incorrect:** For tables with static data, you should use high FILLFACTOR so SQL Server will place more data on index pages. For volatile tables you should set a low FILLFACTOR, allowing new data to be inserted into the index pages and preventing page splits.

B. **Correct:** High FILLFACTOR allows SQL Server to place more data on index pages, whereas low FILLFACTOR leaves more room on index pages. These settings prevent SQL Server from splitting pages as frequently, which improves the performance.

C. **Incorrect:** Although high FILLFACTOR is good for static tables, it is not optimal for volatile tables. Volatile tables need space on index pages; if less space is available on the index pages, SQL Server will be forced to split the pages, which decreases performance.

OBJECTIVE 2.3

Alter database objects to support replication and partitioned views.

SQL Server 2000 allows you to replicate, copy, and modify data across SQL Server servers in your enterprise. SQL Server 2000 supports **snapshot**, **transactional**, and **merge replication**. SQL Server 2000 also includes several methods and options for replication design, monitoring, and administration that are needed for distributing data while keeping data consistent. SQL replication has many benefits, such as allowing different sites to keep a copy of the same data, allowing separate **online transaction processing (OLTP)** and **online analytical processing (OLAP)** databases, allowing users to work in disconnected environments with changes propagated when reconnected, increasing aggregate read performance, and providing support for standby databases. You should think about SQL Server replication when you have to solve one of the following problems: copy or replicate data to one or more sites, distribute data on a scheduled basis, distribute changes to other databases, allow multiple sites to change the data and then merge the changes, or use databases in an online/offline environment.

Snapshot replication distributes data as it appeared at the moment when the snapshot was taken. It does not monitor changes made between the replications; rather, it copies the whole data. Snapshot replication is best for infrequently replicated data where latency is not a problem. Snapshot replication is helpful when data is mostly static and does not change often, when it is acceptable if the data is out of date, or when replicating small amounts of data.

Transactional replication uses snapshots the first time to push the data to the subscribers, and then when changes are made at the publisher, the changes get captured and sent to the subscribers. Transactional replication is helpful when you want changes to be propagated to the subscribers as they occur, when you need transactions to support the **ACID** (**atomicity**, **consistency**, **isolation**, and **durability**) properties, and when subscribers are reliably connected to the publisher. In transactional replication, only the publisher data is changed—the subscribers should be read-only.

Merge replication works like transactional replication, but both the publisher and the subscriber can change the data. Changes will be merged together at the publisher. Merge replication allows sites to work autonomously and, at a later time, merge the updates into a single database at the publisher. After the changes are rolled up, the changes will be pushed to all subscribers. Merge replication is useful when multiple subscribers need to modify the data, when subscribers need to receive data and make changes offline and later synchronize the changes, and when you do not expect any conflicts when data is updated at multiple sites.

Objective 2.3 Questions

70-229.02.03.001

You are working for an e-commerce company. You want to ease the load on SQL Server, and you decide to add additional servers for read-only operations. The Products list is changed quite infrequently and should be rolled out as a single transaction. What kind of SQL Server replication would you use?

A. Transactional replication

B. Snapshot replication

C. Merge replication

70-229.02.03.002

You are working for a roadside service company. Data centers are located all over the country and changes are made only to the corporate database, but customer information is read on all locations. Changes to the database must be replicated as soon as possible to the subscriber servers. What kind of replication would you use?

A. Transactional replication

B. Snapshot replication

C. Merge replication

70-229.02.03.003

You are developing a database design and implementation for a sales system. The requirement is that a subset of the database will be downloaded into the salesperson's laptop and will be changed there. When the salesperson reconnects, his or her changes must be merged into the corporate database. What kind of replication would you use?

A. Transactional replication

B. Snapshot replication

C. Merge replication

70-229.02.03.004

You are scaling out your database and you add a second server. On both servers you have a table called Orders. You create a partitioned view called vOrders. RegionID is the column you have used to partition the data on, and it is part of the primary key. What do you have to do with the tables to set up partitioning correctly?

A. Create indexes on both tables on the RegionID column.

B. Create a constraint on both tables to set the acceptable values for both tables.

C. Execute `sp_EnablePartitioning` on (`Server1.MyDB.Orders, Server2.MyDB.Orders`).

D. You have to create a partitioned index on the vOrders view as follows: `CREATE NONCLUSTERED INDEX ndx_vOrders ON (RegionID) PARTITIONED ON Server1.MyDB.Orders values in (1 to 5), Server2.MyDB.Orders values in (6 to 10)`.

70-229.02.03.005

What configuration do you have to set up on a database server to enable partitioning and get it to perform correctly?

A. Create remote servers in each server pointing to the other servers in the federated server cluster and enable lazy schema validation.

B. Create linked servers in each server pointing to other servers in the federated server cluster and enable lazy schema validation.

C. Create linked servers in each server pointing to other servers in the federated server cluster and disable lazy schema validation.

D. Create remote servers in each server pointing to the other servers in the federated server cluster and disable lazy schema validation.

70-229.02.03.006

You have a partitioned view. You want to create an index on this partitioned view so that you will have an indexed view. Which statement is correct?

A. You can create an indexed view on a partitioned view.

B. You cannot create an indexed view on a partitioned view.

C. You can create an indexed view on a partitioned view as long as the index is clustered.

70-229.02.03.007

You want to create indexed views. Which of the following SQL Server editions support indexed views? (Choose all that apply.)

A. SQL Server Developer Edition

B. SQL Server Standard Edition

C. SQL Server Enterprise Edition

Objective 2.3 Answers

70-229.02.03.001

▶ **Correct Answers: B**

A. **Incorrect:** Transactional replication is used to propagate changes to the subscribers as soon as they happen. Although this type of replication will do the job, it will introduce unnecessary processing on the publisher and the subscribers as well. You do not need to have the changes sent to the subscribers because they happen on an infrequent basis.

B. **Correct:** Snapshot replication is the correct answer because you do not need to have the changes as they happen. Transactional replication would introduce unnecessary processing on the servers. Merge replication would be also an incorrect answer because changes will only happen on the publisher server.

C. **Incorrect:** Merge replication is used when data can be changed either on the publisher or on the subscriber servers. In this case changes will be made only on the publisher server, and changes will be replicated on an infrequent basis. Both merge and transactional replication would introduce unnecessary processing and work on the servers.

70-229.02.03.002

▶ **Correct Answers: A**

A. **Correct:** Transactional replication is used to propagate changes to the subscribers as soon as they happen. Key features of the requirement are that changes are made only at the corporate office and changes must be replicated as soon as possible.

B. **Incorrect:** Snapshot replication is used when the data is changed very infrequently and data can be out of date while the updates happen on different servers. Key features of the requirement are that changes are made only at the corporate office and changes must be replicated as soon as possible. Only transactional replication can fulfill these requirements.

C. **Incorrect:** Merge replication is used when data can be changed on either the publisher or the subscriber servers. In this case data can be changed only at the corporate office, and changes must be replicated as soon as possible. Although merge replication would work correctly, the merge aspect of this replication would introduce unwanted overhead on the servers, which was not part of the requirement.

70-229.02.03.003

▶ **Correct Answers: C**

A. **Incorrect:** Transactional replication only allows data to be changed at the publisher. In this case data will be changed both at the publisher and at the subscribers. Based on the requirements, merge replication should be implemented. Merge replication allows data to be changed both at the publisher and at the subscribers.

B. **Incorrect:** Snapshot replication allows data to be changed at the publisher; also, snapshot replication is an expensive operation because the entire data set must be copied each time instead of just changes. Merge replication is the correct answer because merge replication allows data to be changed both at the publisher and at the subscribers.

C. **Correct:** Merge replication is the correct answer because it allows the data to be changed both at the publisher and at the subscribers. It will fulfill all the requirements in the scenario.

70-229.02.03.004

▶ **Correct Answers: B**

A. **Incorrect:** This is incorrect because it might speed up some of your queries, but you have to create a constraint on the RegionID and set the range for each partition. These constraints will be used by the query engine to determine which tables to access to satisfy your query. This will save valuable time for the server because it will not have to go across each and every machine for data.

B. **Correct:** You have to create a constraint on the RegionID columns in both databases on the Orders tables. The query engine will use these values to evaluate which servers it has to access to retrieve data to satisfy the query.

C. **Incorrect:** Sp_EnablePartitioning is not a valid SQL Server stored procedure. You have to create a constraint on the RegionID columns in both databases in the Orders tables. The query engine will use these values to evaluate which servers it has to access to retrieve data to satisfy the query.

D. **Incorrect:** This statement is incorrect. Although you can create an index on the view, it is not required. You have to create a constraint on the RegionID columns in both databases on the Orders tables. The query engine will use these values to evaluate which servers it has to access to retrieve data to satisfy the query.

70-229.02.03.005

▶ **Correct Answers: B**

    A. **Incorrect:** Remote servers are used to enable stored procedure execution on a remote server. A client connected to one server can execute a stored procedure on a remote server without establishing a connection to the remote server. To enable partitioning, you have to set up linked servers and lazy schema validation using the sp_serveroption stored procedure. This optimizes performance by ensuring that the query processor does not request metadata for any of the linked tables until data is actually needed from the remote member table.

    B. **Correct:** You have to create linked servers and use the sp_serveroption to enable lazy schema validation. This optimizes performance by ensuring that the query processor does not request metadata for any of the linked tables until data is actually needed from the remote member table.

    C. **Incorrect:** The first part of the answer is correct, but the second is not. You need to have linked servers and enable lazy schema validation with the sp_serveroption stored procedure. Lazy schema validation optimizes performance by ensuring that the query processor does not request metadata for any of the linked tables until data is actually needed from the remote member table.

    D. **Incorrect:** This answer is wrong in both ways; neither the server connection nor the lazy schema validation was presented correctly. Remote servers are used to enable stored procedure execution on a remote server. A client connected to one server can execute a stored procedure on a remote SQL Server without establishing a connection to the remote server. To enable partitioning, you have to set up linked servers and lazy schema validation using the sp_serveroption stored procedure. This optimizes performance by ensuring that the query processor does not request metadata for any of the linked tables until data is actually needed from the remote member table.

70-229.02.03.006

▶ **Correct Answers: B**

    A. **Incorrect:** To create an indexed view, all referenced tables must be in the same database. This exclusivity prohibits a partitioned view. You can improve performance by creating indexes on each table used by the partitioned view.

    B. **Correct:** You cannot use indexed and partitioned views together. Indexed views require that the tables reside in the same database.

    C. **Incorrect:** Indexed views and partitioned views are mutually exclusive. Indexed views require the underlying tables to reside in the same database, whereas partitioned views are scattered across multiple instances of SQL Server.

70-229.02.03.007

▶ **Correct Answers: A and C**

A. **Correct:** SQL Server Developer Edition and SQL Server Enterprise Edition are the only editions that support indexed views.

B. **Incorrect:** SQL Server Standard Edition does not support indexed views.

C. **Correct:** SQL Server Developer Edition and SQL Server Enterprise Edition are the only editions that support indexed views.

OBJECTIVE 2.4

Troubleshoot failed object creation.

The first step in troubleshooting failed object creation is to check the syntax of your Transact-SQL statement. If the syntax is correct, check the relationships of the SQL Server objects involved in the operation. Usually the problem lies either in the object relationship or in not providing enough information for SQL Server to fulfill your request.

Dropping an object is most commonly interrupted because of the relationship with other objects such as foreign keys or constraints such as NOT NULL.

Modifying a column can be interrupted because the change would cause data corruption or truncation. Expanding a table with new columns could be interrupted because you did not supply enough information even though the syntax is correct. A good example of this is adding a new column to a table with the NOT NULL attribute but without including a default value.

Troubleshooting failed object creation is much more difficult than creating new objects. You have to look at existing objects and their interactions with changes and new objects.

Objective 2.4 Questions

70-229.02.04.001

You have an existing Customers table with customers' information. You need to add a column called Privileged with a data type of int. This column cannot have the value of NULL. You execute the following Transact-SQL statement and receive the following error code. How can you modify your statement to execute successfully and achieve the desired result?

```
ALTER TABLE Customers ADD Test INT NOT NULL
ERROR CODE:
Server: Msg 4901, Level 16, State 1, Line 1
ALTER TABLE only allows columns to be added that can contain nulls or have a DEFAULT
definition specified. Column 'test' cannot be added to table 'customers' because it
does not allow nulls and does not specify a DEFAULT definition.
```

A. You cannot modify the statement to achieve the required result without removing all the data from the table, making the changes, and then repopulating the table. If a default is defined, SQL Server will be able to update all existing records to this value, so it will not have to break the NOT NULL constraint.

B. You cannot modify the statement because you cannot add a NOT NULL column to a table.

C. You have to modify the statement as follows: ALTER TABLE Customers ADD Test INT NOT NULL WITH FORCE.

D. You have to define a default value.

70-229.02.04.002

You have modified your Customer table with the following Transact-SQL statement: ALTER TABLE Customers ADD Privileged INT NOT NULL DEFAULT (0). The business requirements have changed and you no longer need the Privileged column. You execute the following statement and receive the following error message. How can you resolve the problem?

```
ALTER TABLE DROP COLUMN Privileged
Server: Msg 5074, Level 16, State 1, Line 1
The object 'DF__customers__privileged__5441852A' is dependent on column 'privileged'.
Server: Msg 4922, Level 16, State 1, Line 1
```

A. You have to drop the foreign key constraint referencing the Privileged column before you can drop the column itself.

B. You have to drop the default value (DF) before you can drop the column itself.

C. You have to drop the constraint (NOT NULL) before you can drop the column itself.

70-229.02.04.003

You created a view on a table called Testing123 with the following code: `CREATE VIEW vTesting123 AS SELECT * FROM Testing123`. After a few days you receive e-mails from the users with the following error message:

```
Server: Msg 208, Level 16, State 1, Procedure vTesting123, Line 1
Invalid object name 'Testing123'.
Server: Msg 4413, Level 16, State 1, Line 1
Could not use view or function 'vTesting123' because of binding errors.
```

What could cause this error?

A. Someone has modified the Testing123 table and did not rebind it with the view. The view still has the previous compilation and could not bind to the table.

B. Testing123 has been removed or renamed from the database, and the view cannot bind to it because it no longer exists.

C. Access rights have been changed, and users have no longer have access to the Testing123 table, only to the vTesting123 view.

Objective 2.4 Answers

70-229.02.04.001

▶ **Correct Answers: D**

    A. **Incorrect:** Although this response would work, it does not achieve the requested modification. SQL Server allows you to add a column with a NOT NULL column as long as you also provide a default value.

    B. **Incorrect:** A table can be modified with a column of NOT NULL constraint if a default is also provided. If a default is defined, SQL Server will be able to update all existing records to this value so it will not have to break the NOT NULL constraint.

    C. **Incorrect:** SQL Server does not have an option to force an alteration on a table. You should define a default value. If a default is defined, SQL Server will be able to update all existing records to this value so it will not have to break the NOT NULL constraint.

    D. **Correct:** If you define a default value, SQL Server will be able to add the new column to the table. SQL Server will use this value and update all existing records. This value will also be used when new records are inserted into the table and no value has been defined for the new record.

70-229.02.04.002

▶ **Correct Answers: C**

    A. **Incorrect:** The error message does not imply a foreign key constraint referencing the Privileged column. It shows that a constraint is defined on the column. This constraint was created by the usage of the NOT NULL attribute when the column was created. The constraint must be removed before the column can be dropped.

    B. **Incorrect:** This error message shows that a constraint is on the column. Defining a column with a default value does not create a constraint on the column. In the example code, we used the NOT NULL and it will create a constraint on the column. You have to drop the constraint before you can drop the column.

    C. **Correct:** SQL Server reminded you that you still have a dependency issue before you can remove the column. The NOT NULL clause caused SQL Server to place a constraint on the column when it was created. Dropping the constraint will allow you to drop the column from the table.

70-229.02.04.003

▶ **Correct Answers: B**

   A. **Incorrect:** SQL Server does not keep binding information between objects; therefore, every time the view is compiled or accessed, dependencies will be checked.

   B. **Correct:** Someone has removed or renamed the Testing123 table. As a result, when the view is executed, SQL Server cannot find the table and the execution fails.

   C. **Incorrect:** First, the error message would reflect permission violation and not invalid object names. Second, if the users have access privileges to access vTesting123, they do not need additional access rights for the Testing123 table.

OBJECTIVE DOMAIN 3

Retrieving and Modifying Data

The Retrieving and Modifying Data objective domain deals with building and executing Transact-SQL statements and processing **result sets**. Result sets can be retrieved either in a tabular (or relational) result set or in **eXtensible Markup Language (XML)** format.

Microsoft SQL Server applications connect to a database using one of the following two methods:

- Applications can use database **application programming interfaces (APIs)** such as **ADO**, **OLE DB**, or **ODBC**. With these access methods, SQL Server returns results in a tabular result set.

  Internet applications can use ADO or **Uniform Resource Locators (URLs)** to execute **XPath** queries on the computer running SQL Server. (XPath is a language used to access an XML document.)

- Data also can be manipulated by using the **bulk copy program (BCP)** or **Data Transformation Services (DTS)**.

  The BCP utility is used to export and import data between servers and data files and provides excellent performance. The BCP utility also allows the database operator to specify file formats.

DTS provides great flexibility to export and import data from different file formats and providers. You can export and import data from an ODBC or OLE DB data source and manipulate the data. These jobs can be saved in different packages and reused repeatedly. DTS provides a rich interface for application developers to interface with SQL Server.

Heterogeneous data can be manipulated, including other ODBC data sources and XML documents.

SQL Server 2000 also introduces new XML support, including the FOR XML clause for SELECT statements, which returns result sets in a number of different XML formats.

Tested Skills and Suggested Practices

The skills that you need to successfully master the Retrieving and Modifying Data objective domain on the *Designing and Implementing Databases with Microsoft SQL Server 2000 Enterprise Edition* exam include:

- **Using DTS and BCP.**

    - Practice 1: Use BCP to export data from a database to a file in text format and load the data into another table.

    - Practice 2: Load data into a table containing data and indexes. Examine the performance when no indexes exist on the table compared to the performance when indexes already exist.

    - Practice 3: Use DTS to load data in a comma-delimited format into a SQL Server database.

    - Practice 4: Use DTS to export data using a Transact-SQL SELECT statement, performing a simple data transformation, such as concatenation of character columns.

- **Using Transact-SQL statements to query a SQL Server database.**

    - Practice 1: Use SELECT statements to perform basic data access queries. Select all the columns in a table, and then restrict the returned results. Use the Northwind database shipped with SQL Server 2000 to practice writing different queries.

    - Practice 2: Use the SELECT statement to query more than one table using joins. Predefine the columns you will use to join the tables. After you have joined two tables, try to join three tables and then four tables.

    - Practice 3: Use subqueries nested in the WHERE clause of the SELECT statement. The subquery will return a single value to compare it with the outer query.

- Practice 4: Use a cursor to walk through the records in the recordset. Declare, open, close, and fetch data from a cursor. After closing the cursor, make sure you deallocate it.

- Practice 5: Use the statistical functions of Structured Query Language (SQL), such as COUNT, SUM, MIN, MAX, and AVG.

- **Using Transact-SQL to manipulate data in a SQL Server database.**

  - Practice 1: Use the INSERT statement to insert records into tables. It is necessary to view the schema definition of the table before inserting data. Take a close look at which columns require a value. Try to insert data without specifying each column. Also try to insert data without listing the columns in which you want to place data.

  - Practice 2: Use the UPDATE statement to update a record's columns. Try to use the WHERE clause to update more than one record in the database.

  - Practice 3: Use the DELETE statement to delete all the rows from a table. Use the WHERE clause to delete a set of records based on criteria requiring two joined tables.

- **Using cursors with a SQL Server database.**

  - Practice 1: Create cursors and familiarize yourself with their operations.

  - Practice 2: Create different types of cursors and examine their usage pattern.

  - Practice 3: Use cursors to manipulate data, including updating, inserting, and deleting rows.

- **Working with XML data.**

  - Practice 1: Retrieve XML data in different formats using the correct keyword, such as AUTO, RAW, or EXPLICIT.

  - Practice 2: Use OpenXML to open a rowset over a small XML document, selecting from the XML, and returning a result set.

  - Practice 3: Use XML queries via a URL and return data directly to the browser.

Further Reading

This section lists supplemental readings by objective. Study these sources thoroughly before taking exam 70- 229.

Objective 3.1

Microsoft SQL Server 2000 product documentation. To access Books Online (BOL), click the Start button, point to Programs, then Microsoft SQL Server, and then click Books Online. Click the Contents tab and double-click the "Using the SQL Server Tools" topic. Then review "BCP Utility" under "Command Prompt Utilities."

Microsoft SQL Server 2000 product documentation. To access Books Online, click the Start button, point to Programs, then Microsoft SQL Server, and then click Books Online. Click the Contents tab, double-click "Data Transformation Services," and review "DTS Overview," "DTS Basics," and "DTS Tools."

In Part 1, read and complete the practices in Lesson 1, Chapter 7, "Managing and Manipulating Data."

Objective 3.2

Microsoft SQL Server 2000 product documentation. To access Books Online, click the Start button, point to Programs, then Microsoft SQL Server, and then click Books Online. Click the Contents tab and double-click "Accessing and Changing Relational Data."

Microsoft SQL Server 2000 product documentation. To access Books Online, click the Start button, point to Programs, then Microsoft SQL Server, and then click Books Online. Click the Contents tab and double-click the "Administering SQL Server" topic. Then review "Configuring Linked Servers" under "Managing Servers."

Microsoft SQL Server 2000 product documentation. To access Books Online, click the Start button, point to Programs, then Microsoft SQL Server, and then click Books Online. Click the Contents tab, double-click "SQL Server Architecture," and review "Distributed Query Architecture."

Delaney, Kalen. *Inside Microsoft SQL Server 2000*. Redmond, Washington: Microsoft Press, 2000. Review Chapter 7, "Querying Data."

In Part 1, read and complete the practices in Lesson 2, Chapter 7, "Managing and Manipulating Data."

Objective 3.3

Microsoft SQL Server 2000 product documentation. To access Books Online, click the Start button, point to Programs, then Microsoft SQL Server, and then click Books Online. Click the Contents tab, double-click "Accessing and Changing Relational Data," and review "Query Fundamentals," "Advanced Query Concepts," "Modifying Data," "Locking," "Cursors," and "Distributed Queries."

Delaney, Kalen. *Inside Microsoft SQL Server 2000*. Redmond, Washington: Microsoft Press, 2000. Review Chapter 7, "Querying Data.

In Part 1, read and complete the practices in Lessons 1, 2, and 3 in Chapter 6, "Accessing and Modifying Data."

Objective 3.4

Microsoft SQL Server 2000 product documentation. To access Books Online, click the Start button, point to Programs, then Microsoft SQL Server, and then click Books Online. Click the Contents tab, double-click "Accessing and Changing Relational Data," and review "Cursors."

Delaney, Kalen. *Inside Microsoft SQL Server 2000*. Redmond, Washington: Microsoft Press, 2000. Review Chapter 12, "Special Transact-SQL Operations: Working with Cursors and Large Objects."

In Part 1, read and complete the practices in Lessons 1, 2, and 3 in Chapter 6, "Accessing and Modifying Data," and Lesson 3 in Chapter 7, "Managing and Manipulating Data."

Objective 3.5

Microsoft SQL Server 2000 product documentation. To access Books Online, click the Start button, point to Programs, then Microsoft SQL Server, and then click Books Online. Click the Contents tab and double-click "XML and Internet Support."

In Part 1, read and complete the practices in Lesson 4, Chapter 7, "Managing and Manipulating Data."

O B J E C T I V E   3 . 1

Import and export data.

Three main methods are provided by SQL Server 2000 to import and export data: the **BCP** utility, the **BULK INSERT** Transact-SQL command, and DTS.

The BCP utility is a fast method to import data from a file to a SQL Server table or view, or to export data from a SQL Server table, query, or view to a file. The BCP utility is the best choice when data is being moved from or to a file, and the move needs to be fast, with no transformations or other manipulations of any kind. The BCP operations might be logged, depending on a number of factors.

The BULK INSERT command is a regular Transact-SQL statement, much like the INSERT command, but it is used to insert data from a data file into a SQL Server table or view. BULK INSERT is significantly faster than BCP or DTS for text file imports. However, when importing native data, BCP performance is comparable to BULK INSERT performance. One of the main advantages of BULK INSERT is that it can be used within Transact-SQL and can be used within a transaction, allowing for rollback if needed.

DTS provides a very flexible and powerful framework for moving and transforming data and database objects. It has a number of wizards and tasks built in for importing and exporting data from multiple ODBC and OLE DB data sources. It provides a GUI to create complex workflows that can be saved and scheduled to be executed at another time. DTS allows data transformations to be included in the data movement tasks. These transformations can be written in VBScript or Microsoft JScript.

DTS exposes a **COM** object model that can be used with programming languages such as Microsoft Visual C++ or Microsoft Visual Basic to write more complex data transformation tasks within a program. DTS supplies an OLE DB provider called the **DTS Data Pump**, which exposes the interfaces and methods to move and transform data.

It is important to choose the appropriate tool for each data transfer need, to ensure flexibility as well as performance. However, with the three tools provided, there is very little that you cannot accomplish in data transfer.

Objective 3.1 Questions

70-229.03.01.001

You are about to bulk load a BCP export file into your database. You want the data to be loaded as quickly as possible. Which of the following must be met to ensure that your BCP load is as fast as possible?

A. Enable Select into/bulk copy.

B. The table cannot have an index.

C. The table can be replicated.

D. The filegroup of the database cannot have more than one file.

70-229.03.01.002

You need to import about a thousand rows of data from another system into a table on the production system. You want to be able to do this within a transaction that can be rolled back, if needed. This data must also be fully logged, and you need to ensure that all referential integrity on the table is checked, whether in constraints or triggers.

Which of the following approaches will best meet these requirements?

A. Use the BCP command-line utility to bulk copy the data with the FIRE_TRIGGERS and CHECK_CONSTRAINTS options.

B. Use the BCP command-line utility to bulk copy the data after setting the Select into/bulk copy database option.

C. Use the BULK INSERT command within a transaction with the FIRE_TRIGGERS and CHECK_CONSTRAINTS options.

D. Use the BULK INSERT command with the TABLOCK option.

70-229.03.01.003

Which of the following functions can be performed using DTS? (Choose all that apply.)

A. Move data between a SQL Server table and a Microsoft Access table, converting numeric data to character data.

B. Use File Transfer Protocol (FTP) to copy data from one location to another.

C. Use Message Queuing to split a large DTS job into smaller pieces and send the tasks to multiple computers.

D. Transfer logins and user-defined error messages from one server to another.

70-229.03.01.004

You are about to use DTS to load data from an Oracle database using Microsoft OLE-DB Provider for Oracle. What operations are valid? (Choose all that apply.)

A. Change the column data types.

B. Specify a query to retrieve a subset of the Oracle data.

C. Use JScript to write transformation scripts.

D. The destination table must be dropped and re-created before the data can be imported.

70-229.03.01.005

You want to export data from SQL Server to a text file. Which utilities can you use? (Choose all that apply.)

A. Use ISQL.

B. Use the DTS Export Wizard.

C. Use BCP.

Objective 3.1 Answers

70-229.03.01.001

▶ **Correct Answers: A**

A. **Correct:** This option must be enabled on your database to allow fast data load; however, the load has to fulfill other requirements. If you want all of your databases to have this option enabled when they are created, enable this option on your model database.

B. **Incorrect:** This answer is half true. You can have a table with indexes defined, but the table must be empty, or you can have a table with data but without indexes. If your table already has data and indexes, you should consider dropping the indexes, loading the data, and then re-creating the indexes.

C. **Incorrect:** If your table is participating in replication, you cannot perform a fast load, but you can still use BCP to load the data. The operation will be logged in the transaction log, and that will slow your database load.

D. **Incorrect:** The number of files in the database filegroup, or the filegroup in which the table is created, has no effect on the BCP operation.

70-229.03.01.002

▶ **Correct Answers: C**

A. **Incorrect:** The BCP utility cannot be run from within a transaction. It is a command-line utility that runs outside SQL Server. The FIRE_TRIGGERS option will force the INSERT TABLE triggers to fire, which by default are not fired. The CHECK_CONSTRAINTS option forces constraints to be checked, which are also ignored by default with a BCP operation. Also, the FIRE_TRIGGERS option will force the BCP operation to be fully logged.

B. **Incorrect:** The BCP utility cannot be run from within a transaction. It is a command-line utility that runs outside SQL Server. Setting the Select into/bulk copy database option can cause the operation to not be logged; however, if there are indexes on the table, or if it is being replicated, it will be logged. Because the FIRE_TRIGGERS and CHECK_CONSTRAINTS options were not set, referential integrity will not be checked.

C. **Correct:** BULK INSERT is a Transact-SQL command that can be run within a transaction and rolled back if needed. The FIRE_TRIGGERS options will force the INSERT TABLE triggers to fire, which by default are not fired. The CHECK_CONSTRAINTS option forces constraints to be checked, which are also ignored by default. Also, the FIRE_TRIGGERS option ensures that the operation is fully logged.

D. **Incorrect:** The BULK INSERT command can be used in a Transact-SQL transaction, but the TABLOCK option will cause only the table to be locked for the duration of the operation. Because triggers are not fired and constraints not checked by default, the referential integrity will not be checked.

70-229.03.01.003

▶ **Correct Answers: A, B, C, and D**

A. **Correct:** With DTS, Data can be moved between SQL Server and Access.

B. **Correct:** The built-in DTS File Transfer Protocol Task will allow files to be copied from one location to another, as well as entire directories.

C. **Correct:** Message Queuing can be used to send and receive messages between DTS packages for asynchronous processing. Messages can be received by multiple computers to perform different tasks. However, Message Queuing cannot take part in a DTS transaction.

D. **Correct:** The built-in DTS Transfer Logins Task can be used to transfer logins from one system to another, and the built-in Transfer Error Messages Task will transfer any error messages that have been added to the system with the sp_addmessage system stored procedure.

70-229.03.01.004

▶ **Correct Answers: A, B, and C**

A. **Correct:** You can convert from almost any SQL Server data type to any other data type. If simple conversion is not available, you can always write a script to transform the data.

B. **Correct:** If the data source driver or database supports SQL, you can always specify a SELECT statement to retrieve data.

C. **Correct:** SQL Server allows you to use VBScript or JScript to write your data transformation script.

D. **Incorrect:** You can import data into an existing table, or you can ask DTS to drop it for you. If the table does not exist, DTS will create it for you.

70-229.03.01.005

▶ **Correct Answers: B and C**

A. **Incorrect:** ISQL is a command-based query utility. It is used to execute batched jobs from the command line. You can use DTS Export Wizard or BCP to accomplish this task.

B. **Correct:** SQL Server includes a service called Data Transformation Services (DTS). DTS is used to transfer data to and from SQL Server from different data sources, such as ODBC, OLE DB, or text files. DTS allows you to specify the data you want to export and the format. You can also save the job in a package and reuse it at a later time.

C. **Correct:** BCP is a command-line utility used to import and export data in a native SQL Server format or in text format. BCP is used to transfer large amounts of data. BCP uses the ODBC API Bulk Copy interface, whereas earlier versions of BCP used DB-Library's bulk copy API.

OBJECTIVE 3.2

Manipulate heterogeneous data.

SQL Server 2000 offers a number of ways to manipulate external data from data sources other than SQL Server. These can include ODBC data sources, OLE DB data sources, and XML documents. They can also include Oracle databases, Access databases, Microsoft Excel files, and flat files.

The five main methods to manipulate heterogeneous data and produce distributed queries are as follows:

- **Linked servers**—Servers can be added as remote servers and then given a name that can be used within regular Transact-SQL statements. Objects on remote linked servers are identified by fully qualifying the object names, following the standard of server.database.owner.table.

- **OPENQUERY**—Allows a named server that is already identified as a linked server with the sp_addlinkedserver system stored procedure to be queried as a table within a Transact-SQL statement. A query to be run against the remote server is supplied and returns a result set to the calling server.

- **OPENDATASOURCE**—Allows a remote table to be opened by supplying ad hoc connection information in place of a table reference in a Transact-SQL statement. This function should be used only for infrequent queries against OLE DB data sources that are not defined as a linked server.

- **OPENROWSET**—Returns the result of a supplied query, as opposed to the entire table. Over a network, this method can be more efficient, and allows some of the work to be performed on the remote query. This allows a disparate data source to be accessed as a table in a Transact-SQL statement by indicating the connection parameters, as well as passing a statement that is run against the remote server, returning the result sets to the calling server.

- **OPENXML**—Allows a small XML document to have a rowset opened over it, with the results returned as a table and included in a Transact-SQL statement.

There are limitations in what statements can be used in a distributed query, depending on the capabilities of the remote server, and the type of query being written. Stored procedures can be run only against other SQL Server data sources. In general, SQL Server tries to run the remote query on the remote server, returning only the result sets to the calling server, to limit network traffic.

Note OPENDATASOURCE and OPENROWSET are actually **macros**, and do not allow any parameters. They also do not provide metadata for the remote results.

Objective 3.2 Questions

70-229.03.02.001

You need to create a one-time ad hoc distributed query against a remote computer running SQL Server. You have the connection string and the query. Which of the following rowset functions would be the best approach for this need?

A. Parse the connection string and add a linked server using the sp_addlinkedserver system stored procedure. Then write the query using the fully qualified, four-part object name.

B. Parse the connection string and add a linked server using the sp_addlinkedserver system. You can then use the OPENQUERY rowset function, supplying the linked server name and the query.

C. Use the OPENROWSET function, supplying the connection string and the query statement.

D. Use the DTS wizard to create a table and import the data from the other data source. Then run the query against the imported table.

70-229.03.02.002

You currently have all of your customer data in four separate servers, with the data partitioned by region. You want to be able to create a partitioned view for the Customers table that contains the SELECT...UNION ALL syntax for each of the four servers. This solution provides an abstraction layer for your client applications, so that developers do not need to know which physical server contains the required results. This solution also allows flexibility in the physical partitioning of the data because the implementation is hidden from the client users. Which of the following heterogeneous access methods will best support these requirements?

A. Add linked servers for each of the three remote servers on each server. Then create the view using the four-part, fully qualified object name in the SELECT...UNION ALL syntax.

B. Add linked servers for each of the three remote servers on each server. Then create the view using the OPENQUERY clause in the SELECT...UNION ALL syntax.

C. Create the partitioned view on each server using the OPENROWSET function in the SELECT...UNION ALL syntax, supplying the connection string for each of the three remote servers.

D. Create the partitioned view on each server using the OPENDATASOURCE clause in the SELECT...UNION ALL syntax, supplying the connection string for each of the three remote servers.

70-229.03.02.003

You need to query data from a large Access table without setting up a linked server. You want to filter the data in Access with a query before it is returned to the server. Which of the following approaches will best meet these requirements?

A. Use the OPENQUERY function.

B. Use the OPENXML function.

C. Use the OPENDATASOURCE function.

D. Use the OPENROWSET function.

Objective 3.2 Answers

70-229.03.02.001

▶ **Correct Answers: C**

A. **Incorrect:** Although you could parse the connection string to get the server name, this would be more work than necessary. Creating a linked server is also too much overhead for a one-time ad hoc query against a remote SQL Server.

B. **Incorrect:** Although you could parse the connection string to get the server name, this would be more work than necessary. Creating a linked server is also too much overhead for a one-time ad hoc query against a remote computer running SQL Server. The OPENQUERY clause does use a linked server name, but again, defining a linked server is too much overhead.

C. **Correct:** The OPENROWSET function is good for a one-time ad hoc distributed query. It doesn't require the overhead of adding a linked server, and it takes connection information and a remote query as parameters. OPENROWSET does not allow variables for any parameters and it will return only the first result set if the query returns multiple result sets.

D. **Incorrect:** This would work for a long-term solution, but creating a new table and DTS task and then importing the data is too much work and overhead for a one-time distributed query. It would also be extremely resource-intensive if the data set were large.

70-229.03.02.002

▶ **Correct Answers: A**

A. **Correct:** This solution is the best. Although OPENROWSET and OPENDATASOURCE can in some situations be used to create partitioned views, they are not the best approach because they are not as functional as linked servers. The overhead of creating a linked server is justified because the Customer partitioned view will be used often.

B. **Incorrect:** Although this would work, once linked servers are added, using the four-part, fully qualified object name is more understandable and easier to use than the OPENQUERY function. OPENQUERY provides no added functionality or performance in this situation.

C. **Incorrect:** Using OPENROWSET requires a connection string and does not support all of the functionality of linked servers.

D. **Incorrect:** Using OPENDATASOURCE requires a connection string and does not support all of the functionality of linked servers. It also does not allow a query to be supplied.

70-229.03.02.003

▶ **Correct Answers: D**

A. **Incorrect:** OPENQUERY requires a linked server, so using it does not meet all the requirements. You specify a query with OPENQUERY, so the result set would be limited to only the requested rows.

B. **Incorrect:** OPENXML requires an XML document for input, and although the data could be returned programmatically from the other servers as XML, this would be extremely limited and clumsy. Because XML is not required in this scenario, there is no need for it or major benefit from using it.

C. **Incorrect:** Although the OPENDATASOURCE function does not require a linked server, and it takes a connection string, it does not allow a query to limit the results returned from the remote provider. Therefore, more data than might be required would be returned. This does not meet the requirement.

D. **Correct:** This is the best solution. Using the OPENROWSET function with a query to limit the returned results would best meet the requirements. OPENROWSET also requires a connection string, not a linked server name.

Retrieve, filter, group, summarize, and modify data by using Transact-SQL.

The **INSERT** statement is used to enter new rows into a database table. INSERT has three major parts: specifying the target table, specifying the columns where you want to place data, and specifying the values for those columns.

The **UPDATE** statement is used to update from one to many records in a database table. It also has three parts: specifying the target table, specifying the columns and their new values, and using the WHERE clause to specify the records to be modified. More complex UPDATE statements can have joins to specify the set of records to be updated.

The **DELETE** statement is used to delete one or more records from a database table. It has two parts: first, specifying the target table, and second, using the WHERE clause, specifying the records to be deleted. DELETE has the same capability as UPDATE to use joins to specify records to be deleted.

The **SELECT** statement is used to retrieve data from a database. You can indicate that you want all columns from the table returned or specify which columns you want returned. The FROM clause specifies the table or tables from which the data should be returned. The WHERE clause can contain a list of expressions to allow you to filter the results returned. Transact-SQL provides many conditional operators, such as AND, OR, BETWEEN, LIKE, IN, >, <, <>, =, >=, and <=. You can use DISTINCT to eliminate duplicate records.

The SELECT statement can be used to insert data into another table. The INSERT…SELECT statement can be used to add records to an existing table.

TOP can be used to specify the maximum number of records to be returned. By also using PERCENT you can specify a percentage of records to be returned.

Aggregation results are obtained by using the **MIN, MAX, COUNT, AVG, CUBE,** and **ROLLUP** functions to calculate the processed result set.

GROUP BY can be used to divide the table into groups. Groups can consist of columns, results, and computed columns.

ORDER BY is used to specify the sequencing of the returned result set. ORDER BY is invalid in views, inline functions, subqueries, and derived tables unless TOP is specified.

In this objective, you should have a good working knowledge of the INSERT, UPDATE, DELETE, and SELECT statements.

Objective 3.3 Questions

70-229.03.03.001

You have two computers running SQL Server named SERVER1 and SERVER2. Both of them have a SALES database with the same database schema. Which line of the following query will return an error when used as a distributed query against these servers?

```
SELECT c.CustomerID, COUNT(*) FROM
SERVER1.SALES..Customers c,
SERVER2.SALES.dbo.Orders o
WHERE c.CustomerID = o.CustomerID
GROUP BY c.CustomerID
```

A. SERVER1.SALES..Customers c

B. SERVER2.SALES.dbo.Orders o

C. WHERE c.CustomerID = o.CustomerID

D. GROUP BY c.CustomerID

70-229.03.03.002

You execute the following SQL statement:

```
SELECT CustomerID, COUNT(*) FROM Orders GROUP BY CustomerID HAVING COUNT(*) > 10
```

What result will SQL Server generate?

A. Incorrect syntax. You cannot use HAVING and COUNT together.

B. Incorrect syntax. You have to alias COUNT(*), and then you can use it in the HAVING clause.

C. Correct syntax. It will return all the records where COUNT(*) is greater than 10.

D. Incorrect syntax. The COUNT(*) must be in the GROUP BY column list.

70-229.03.03.003

You have the following statement:

```
SELECT TOP 10 ProductName,UnitPrice FROM Products ORDER BY UnitPrice DESC
```

Which of the following statements is true?

A. This statement returns the top 10 percent of the records, ordered by the UnitPrice.

B. This statement returns the first 10 rows, ordered by the UnitPrice in descending order.

C. You will receive an error message. All columns specified in the SELECT list must be in ORDER BY, just as with GROUP BY.

70-229.03.03.004

You want to decrease the price of 10 percent of the most expensive data in your inventory. Which Transact-SQL statement will do that?

A. UPDATE Products

```
SET UnitPrice = UnitPrice * 0.9
WHERE ProductID = ( SELECT TOP 10 ProductID FROM Products ORDER BY UnitPrice DESC )
```

B. UPDATE Products

```
SET UnitPrice = UnitPrice * 0.9
WHERE ProductID IN ( SELECT TOP 10 ProductID FROM Products ORDER BY UnitPrice DESC )
```

C. UPDATE Products

```
SET UnitPrice = UnitPrice * 0.9
WHERE ProductID IN ( SELECT TOP 10 PERCENT ProductID FROM Products ORDER BY UnitPrice
DESC )
```

D. UPDATE Products

```
SET UnitPrice = UnitPrice * .9
FROM Product a,Products b
WHERE a.ProductId = b.ProductId ORDER BY a.UnitPrice DESC TOP 10 PERCENT
```

70-229.03.03.005

Evaluate the following statement:

```
SELECT 4 / 4 + 2 * 5 - 5
```

Which operator will be evaluated first?

A. The addition operator will be evaluated first.

B. The multiplication operator will be evaluated first.

C. The subtraction operator will be evaluated first.

D. The division operator will be evaluated first.

70-229.03.03.006

Evaluate the following script:

```
DECLARE @rows INT, @errors INT
SELECT 5, 10, 15
IF @@ERROR > 0
    SET @errors = 1
ELSE
    SET @errors = 0
IF @@ROWCOUNT > 0
    SET @rows = @@ ROWCOUNT
ELSE
    SET @rows = -9999
SELECT @errors, @rows
```

What will be in the result set?

A. 0, -9999

B. 0, 0

C. 1, 1

D. 1, -9999

70-229.03.03.007

You have a SELECT statement that joins a table on a local server to a table on a linked server. The linked server has much more memory and processors than the local server. How can you ensure that the optimizer performs the join operation on the linked server?

A. Write the join as an OUTER join on the side that references the table on the linked server.

B. Use the fully qualified name for the linked server table.

C. Use the REMOTE table hint in the SELECT statement.

D. Use the MERGE join table hint in the SELECT statement.

70-229.03.03.008

You need to retrieve results from a table of employees that includes a NOT NULL EmployeeID column, a NULL Name column, and a NOT NULL Salary column.

- The required result is the sum of all of the employee salaries.

- The first optional result is the number of rows in the table.

- The second optional result is to return the largest salary.

You create the following Transact-SQL query:

```
SELECT SUM(Salary), COUNT(Name) from Employee
```

Which result will this query provide?

A. The required result and all optional results.

B. The required result and one optional result.

C. The required result and none of the optional results.

D. The query does not provide the required result.

70-229.03.03.009

You are designing a sales database application that will require the use of many transactions to ensure data consistency. You will deploy this application with many users, and you want to ensure that it is as scalable as possible. Which of the following will help to ensure that blocking is kept to a minimum, ensuring scalability? (Choose all that apply.)

A. Allow user input inside a transaction.

B. Keep transactions short and in small batches.

C. Use as low a level of transaction isolation as is allowable.

D. Use NOLOCK hints in SELECT statements where allowable.

70-229.03.03.010

How can using a stored procedure to insert data into the OrderDetails table reduce network traffic and increase database performance?

A. The number of requests between the server and the client is reduced.

B. The execution plan is stored in the cache after it was executed the first time.

C. Stored procedures accept parameters.

D. You can bypass permission checking on stored procedures.

Objective 3.3 Answers

70-229.03.03.001

▶ **Correct Answers: A**

   A. **Correct:** This line is incorrect. You have to specify the object owner when using distributed queries. The correct syntax is server.database.owner.table.

   B. **Incorrect:** This line is correct and well formed.

   C. **Incorrect:** This line is correct. It is a well-formed condition used to build a join between the two referenced tables.

   D. **Incorrect:** This line is correct. For the GROUP BY to be valid, you must have the column name listed in the SELECT part of the query.

70-229.03.03.002

▶ **Correct Answers: C**

   A. **Incorrect:** You can use COUNT with HAVING; the only requirement is that the COUNT must be in the column list of the SELECT statement.

   B. **Incorrect:** You can use the COUNT alias in the columns list of the SELECT statement, but you cannot use the alias in the HAVING clause.

   C. **Correct:** This statement is correctly formed. The correct column names and expressions are in the SELECT statement. GROUP BY and HAVING are well formed statements.

   D. **Incorrect:** You cannot use an aggregate in the GROUP BY clause. COUNT(*) must be listed in the columns list of the SELECT statement, but not in the columns list of the GROUP BY.

70-229.03.03.003

▶ **Correct Answers: B**

A. **Incorrect:** This statement will return the first 10 records from the Products table, ordered by the Unit-Price in a descending order. If you need to return the top 10 percent, use SELECT TOP 10 PER-CENT. DESC causes the ordering to be descending, from high to low.

B. **Correct:** TOP specifies the number of rows to return. ORDER BY and DESC cause the result set to be ordered in high-to-low UnitPrice order.

C. **Incorrect:** ORDER BY does not work the same way as GROUP BY. You can base ordering on one or more columns. Columns used in ORDER BY do not have to be in the SELECT column list. The following code would execute correctly: SELECT TOP 10 ProductName FROM Products ORDER BY UnitPrice DESC.

70-229.03.03.004

▶ **Correct Answers: C**

A. **Incorrect:** This answer is wrong because you needed to return the top 10 percent of the most expensive items. You should have used TOP 10 PERCENT instead of TOP 10. Also, the WHERE clause has a problem: if your subquery returns more than one row, you have to use IN; otherwise, the query will fail.

B. **Incorrect:** This query will execute successfully, but it won't provide the required result. You should have updated the top 10 percent of the most expensive items; instead, you updated the top 10 most expensive items.

C. **Correct:** This Transact-SQL statement will produce the required result.

D. **Incorrect:** If you update a table using UPDATE…FROM, you cannot use ORDER BY. ORDER BY can be used only with the SELECT statement. TOP 10 PERCENT is also usable only with a SELECT statement and must follow the SELECT keyword.

70-229.03.03.005

▶ **Correct Answers: D**

A. **Incorrect:** The addition operator will be evaluated third.

B. **Incorrect:** The multiplication operator will be evaluated second.

C. **Incorrect:** The subtraction operator will be evaluated fourth.

D. **Correct:** Like most languages, SQL Server 2000 has an operator precedence in which multiple operators can be used within one expression. Multiplication and division are evaluated before addition and subtraction. Operators with the same order of precedence are evaluated left to right. This statement will be evaluated as follows:

```
SELECT (((4 / 4) + (2 * 5)) - 5)
```

70-229.03.03.006

▶ **Correct Answers: B**

A. **Incorrect:** -9999 can never be returned from the @rows local variable because the @@ROWCOUNT global variable has been reset at the IF statement.

B. **Correct:** There are no errors in this statement because it is a simple SELECT statement using constants, so the @@ERROR global variable will return 0. However, because the IF statement always resets the results of the @@ROWCOUNT global variable to 0, the value of the @rows local variable can never be evaluated to -9999, but will always return 0.

C. **Incorrect:** There are no errors in the SELECT statement, so 1 will not be returned for the @errors local variable and, because of the reset of the @@ROWCOUNT global variable after the IF statement, 1 will never be returned from the @rows local variable.

D. **Incorrect:** There are no errors in the SELECT statement, so 1 will not be returned for the @errors local variable. The script never enters the ELSE clause for the @rows local variable because the @@ROWCOUNT global variable has been reset after the first IF statement, so -9999 will never be returned.

70-229.03.03.007

▶ **Correct Answers: C**

A. **Incorrect:** An OUTER join indicates a type of join, not the location of the join operation being performed. This solution has other problems because the result set from an OUTER join is different from the result set from an INNER join.

B. **Incorrect:** Using fully qualified names does not affect where the actual join operation will be performed.

C. **Correct:** Using the REMOTE hint will force the optimizer to perform the actual join operation on the remote server. This can be used only with an INNER join, and the remote table should be on the right side of the join.

D. **Incorrect:** The MERGE hint forces the optimizer to use the merge algorithm for performing the join. It does not determine where the actual operation will be performed.

70-229.03.03.008

▶ **Correct Answers: C**

A. **Incorrect:** The proposed query satisfies only the required result.

B. **Incorrect:** The proposed query satisfies only the required result.

C. **Correct:** The query returns the sum of all of the salaries in the table with the use of the SUM function. There is a COUNT function to return the number of rows in the table, but it will not return an accurate number because the Name column is used as the input for the COUNT function. Because the Name column will allow null values, the COUNT function will count only the rows that have a value for the Name column. The asterisk (*) should always be used with the COUNT function if the number of rows in the table is the desired result, regardless of null values in specific columns. Also, there is no function to return the largest salary value from the table. The MAX function could have been used, with the Salary column as input to provide this result.

D. **Incorrect:** The proposed query satisfies the required result.

70-229.03.03.009

▶ **Correct Answers: B, C, and D**

A. **Incorrect:** It is critical to not allow user input inside a transaction. You have no control over how long a user will keep that transaction open if input is required. The user might go to lunch, leaving the transaction open and the locks held against the tables used in the transaction. It is best to collect user input before the transaction begins.

B. **Correct:** Keeping the transaction and batch size small will ensure that locks are held for a minimal time and allow other users to get access to the resources. This is critical to ensure database scalability.

C. **Correct:** Setting the transaction isolation level to a lower level than the default of READ COMMIT-TED can help to keep locking at a minimum. The READ COMMITTED level, which is the SQL Server 2000 default, holds shared locks to ensure that there are no dirty reads, but data can be changed by another user in the middle of a transaction, which can cause phantoms and nonrepeatable reads. Setting the level to READ UNCOMMITTED means that no shared locks are acquired and exclusive locks are not honored. This is the lowest and least intrusive isolation level, but it must be used only in appropriate situations. This has the same effect as using the NOLOCK hint in a SELECT statement.

D. **Correct:** The NOLOCK hint in the SELECT statement is an excellent way to minimize locking in transactions where it is appropriate. It will take any locks on the tables included in the SELECT statement.

70-229.03.03.010

▶ **Correct Answers: A and B**

A. **Correct:** Stored procedures are a collection of Transact-SQL Statements. You do not have to send the statements down to the server one by one. The code is kept on the server side, just the parameters have to be sent to the server.

B. **Correct:** The first time a stored procedure is executed a plan is created. The compiled plan is then placed into the procedure cache. Subsequent execution of the stored procedure will be faster because the compiled plan is already in cache.

C. **Incorrect:** Although stored procedures accept parameters, this process does not reduce network traffic and does not increase performance.

D. **Incorrect:** In SQL Server, you cannot bypass permission and security checking for any kind of object. Stored procedures yield improved performance because the Transact-SQL code does not have to be sent down to the server, and the stored procedure execution plan can be cached on the server side after it was executed once.

Manage result sets by using cursors and Transact-SQL.

A SELECT statement with a WHERE clause will return only those records that satisfy the WHERE condition. This complete set of rows is known as a **result set**.

Transact-SQL cursors are an extension of the result set, and they provide ways to manipulate the result set one row at a time. Cursors provide the way to "walk" the result set forward and backward. The cursor acts as a pointer in the result set, pointing at a specific row. The cursor also provides ways to modify the data in the rows and support different levels of visibility of changes made by other users.

In SQL Server 2000, you can use cursors in two different ways. The first is using Transact-SQL, and the second is using the API cursor functions. All cursors require temporary resources in the cache. These resources can include memory, paging files, temporary files, or databases. Large cursors or unnecessary cursors can degrade the performance of SQL Server.

SQL Server supports three different types of cursors: static, dynamic, and keyset.

- Static cursors return a result set that is a snapshot of the data when the recordset is opened. Changes made to the membership, order, and data values in the database after the result set is returned are not visible in the static result set.

- Dynamic cursors return a result set that is the opposite of the static result set. All changes made to the membership, order, and data values of the rows in the result set are visible when you scroll through the result set.

- Keyset cursors return a result set that is controlled by a unique set of identifiers known as the keyset. As in a static result set, the membership and order are fixed at the time of the opening of the result set. The keyset is kept in the tempdb database.

SQL Server also supports forward-only cursors. Forward-only cursors are defined by the FORWARD_ONLY keyword, which can be applied to all three result set types. Forward-only cursors use resources more efficiently than scrolling cursors do. However, forward-only cursors allow only forward fetches.

For this objective you should know the differences between the different cursors. You should understand the differences in their behavior.

Objective 3.4 Questions

70-229.03.04.001

You need to create a cursor that reflects the changes made to the database table even after the result set is returned. Which cursor type would you use?

A. FORWARD_ONLY

B. Static

C. Keyset

D. Dynamic

E. FAST_FORWARD

70-229.03.04.002

You need to define a cursor. Which statement should you use?

A. DECLARE CURSOR

B. OPEN

C. FETCH

D. @@FETCH_STATUS

70-229.03.04.003

Evaluate this statement:

```
DECLARE MyCursor CURSOR
STATIC LOCAL FOR
SELECT ZipCode from ZipCodes where State='NV'
```

Which of the following is true about this statement?

A. The result set is updateable globally.

B. The result set is stored in the tempdb database and all changes made by other users are reflected in your result set.

C. The cursor can be used by other subsequent operations in different stored procedures.

D. The result set is stored in the tempdb database and available only in the current stored procedure.

Objective 3.4 Answers

70-229.03.04.001

▶ **Correct Answers: D**

A. **Incorrect:** FORWARD_ONLY is not a cursor type but rather is an option that you can use with static, keyset, or dynamic cursors. If you use FORWARD_ONLY without a cursor type specification, you will have a forward-only dynamic cursor.

B. **Incorrect:** A static cursor makes a copy of the data used by the cursor. All requests to the cursor are fulfilled from a temporary table in the tempdb database. All requests come from a copy of the original data, so changes made to the original data will not be visible in the temporary table.

C. **Incorrect:** For a keyset cursor, SQL Server builds a temporary table in the tempdb database with a set of keys that uniquely identify each record. Changes made by you or by other users will be visible to you while you are moving forward or backward in the table.

D. **Correct:** A dynamic cursor reflects all changes in the recordset, and the values, orders, and membership of each row can change with each FETCH.

E. **Incorrect:** FAST_FORWARD is not a cursor type. FAST_FORWARD defines a FORWARD_ONLY and READ_ONLY cursor with performance optimization.

70-229.03.04.002

▶ **Correct Answers: A**

A. **Correct:** DECLARE CURSOR defines the attributes of a SQL Server cursor. The statement includes the SELECT statement and variables that the cursor uses. When you need to work with cursors, your first step should be to declare a cursor. Users must have SELECT permission on the table.

B. **Incorrect:** The OPEN statement is for opening and populating the cursor. The OPEN statement cannot define a cursor.

C. **Incorrect:** The FETCH statement is used to fetch the next or previous record from an already defined and open cursor. The FETCH statement can be executed only after the OPEN statement has been executed.

D. **Incorrect:** @@FETCH_STATUS is not a statement but is instead a global status variable. When cursors are used, you should check the last status of your fetch. The @@FETCH_STATUS variable has the following three possible status values: FETCH statement was successful, FETCH failed or the cursor point was beyond the result set, or the row fetched is missing.

70-229.03.04.003

▶ **Correct Answers: D**

A. **Incorrect:** This result set is declared with the LOCAL keyword. A local cursor is available only in the stored procedure where it was created. At the end of the stored procedure, these cursors are deallocated automatically, but you should always implement the necessary code to clean up after your cursor. Cursors declared with the GLOBAL keyword are available outside the scope of the current stored procedure.

B. **Incorrect:** Although the cursors will be allocated in the tempdb database, the scope of the cursor will be local to the stored procedure. LOCAL means that the cursor will be accessible only within the scope of the stored procedure.

C. **Incorrect:** A local cursor is available only within the scope of the stored procedure. If a cursor is required to be accessible within different stored procedures, you need to declare it as global using the GLOBAL keyword.

D. **Correct:** A static local cursor is allocated in the tempdb database and is available only within the scope of the stored procedure where it was declared.

O B J E C T I V E   3 . 5

Extract data in XML format.

One of the new features in SQL Server 2000 is the ability to extract data in XML format. Results can be returned to a client in XML format by adding the FOR XML clause to the SELECT statement. You can also return result sets in XML format using templates and XPath queries. SQL Server 2000 can also be queried directly from a URL.

FOR XML returns results in a number of different ways, providing great flexibility. FOR XML is valid only for the SELECT statement, and its usage has a number of restrictions. It cannot be used within a view, with cursors, or with the COMPUTE BY or GROUP BY clauses, and it cannot be used in subqueries.

FOR XML can be used in the following ways:

- SELECT...FOR XML RAW—This returns each row in the result set as one element called "row," with columns indicated in the SELECT statement as attribute=value pairs. For example, the query `SELECT CUSTOMER.CUSTOMERNAME, ORDERS.ORDERID FROM CUSTOMER, ORDERS WHERE CUSTOMER.CUSTOMERID=ORDERS.CUSTOMERID` might return the following XML:

  `<row CUSTOMERNAME="Brown" ORDERID="101" />`

  `<row CUSTOMERNAME="Brown" ORDERID="105" />`

  `<row CUSTOMERNAME="Yates" ORDERID="225" />`

  Notice that the result is nonhierarchical and looks very much like the result sets you are used to in SQL Server. Because Brown has two orders, the name is returned twice.

- SELECT...FOR XML AUTO—This returns hierarchical data, depending on the number of tables in the join and the order of the columns. Generally, an element is created for each table, with the columns returned as attribute=value pairs. The same query as in the preceding example, SELECT CUSTOMER.CUSTOMERNAME, ORDERS.ORDERID FROM CUSTOMER, ORDERS WHERE CUSTOMER.CUSTOM-ERID=ORDERS.CUSTOMERID, would return the following XML:

```
<CUSTOMER CUSTOMERNAME="Brown" >

  <ORDERS ORDERID="101" />

  <ORDERS ORDERID="105" />

</CUSTOMER >

<CUSTOMER CUSTOMERNAME="Yates" >

  <ORDERS ORDERID="225" />

</CUSTOMER >
```

This hierarchical data return is very useful. Note that the column order in the SELECT clause is significant in determining the hierarchy.

- SELECT... FOR XML EXPLICIT—This option provides much more flexibility, but requires the query to be written in a specific way to produce the expected output. It is more functional than the RAW or AUTO clauses, but also more complicated. This option allows you to control what data is returned as elements and what is returned as attributes, which are fixed in the AUTO and RAW options.

- The XMLDATA option can be added to any of the SELECT statements described in this list to return an XML schema generated from the table structure. The schema will be returned before the actual results. XML schemas provide information about the table structure.

The entire XML functionality is implemented in Sqlxmlx.dll. When SQLOLEDB determines that the command is an XML command, the provider passes that command to Sqlxmlx.dll, which executes the command and returns the result to SQLOLEDB. There is obviously some overhead in producing XML. It is important to determine when it is necessary to extract data from SQL Server in XML format.

Objective 3.5 Questions

70-229.03.05.001

Evaluate the following XML result returned from a SELECT statement with the FOR XML option:

```
<row stor_name="Eric the Read Books" qty="5"/>
<row stor_name="Bookbeat" qty="10"/>
```

The following query was used to produce this result:

```
SELECT Stores.Stor_Name, Sales.Qty
FROM Stores JOIN Sales
ON Stores.Stor_ID = Sales.Stor_ID
WHERE Title_ID = 'BU1032'
```

Which FOR XML option was used to produce this output?

A. FOR XML RAW

B. FOR XML AUTO

C. FOR XML RAW, XMLDATA.

D. FOR XML AUTO, XMLDATA

70-229.03.05.002

You need to send an XML data stream to another business that will then use that data to create orders in its system. They do not want the data in hierarchical order, but they need to know the data types. Which of the FOR XML clauses would be best suited for these requirements?

A. FOR XML RAW

B. FOR XML AUTO

C. FOR XML RAW, XMLDATA

D. FOR XML AUTO, XMLDATA

70-229.03.05.003

Evaluate the following XML result returned from a SELECT statement with the FOR XML AUTO option:

```
<Stores Stor_Name="Eric the Read Books">
  <Sales Qty="3" Title_ID="1013">
    <Titles Title="Is Anger The Enemy?"/>
  </Sales>
</Stores>
<Stores Stor_Name="Doc-U-Mat: Quality Laundry and Books">
  <Sales Qty="20" Title_ID="1013">
    <Titles Title="Is Anger the Enemy?"/>
  </Sales>
  <Sales Qty="25" Title_ID="1043">
    <Titles Title="Life Without Fear"/>
  </Sales>
</Stores>
```

Which of the following queries was used to produce this result?

A. SELECT Titles.Title, sales.Qty, Stores.Stor_Name, Sales.Title_id FROM Stores JOIN Sales ON Stores.Stor_ID = Sales.Stor_ID JOIN Titles ON Sales.Title_ID = Titles.Title_ID WHERE State = 'WA' FOR XML AUTO

B. SELECT sales.qty, sales.title_id, stores.stor_name, titles.title FROM stores JOIN sales ON stores.stor_id = sales.stor_id JOIN titles ON sales.title_id = titles.title_id WHERE state = 'WA' FOR XML AUTO

C. SELECT stores.stor_name, sales.qty, titles.title, sales.title_id FROM stores JOIN sales ON stores.stor_id = sales.stor_id JOIN titles ON sales.title_id = titles.title_id WHERE state = 'WA' FOR XML AUTO

Objective 3.5 Answers

70-229.03.05.001

▶ **Correct Answers: A**

A. **Correct:** Because the XML RAW option displays row as the element name, we can determine that this was generated using the RAW option.

B. **Incorrect:** The AUTO option would have returned the element names as the table names.

C. **Incorrect:** Although this XML option has the generic row as the element name, this was generated by the RAW option. However, because there is no schema prefacing the results, this was not generated using the XMLDATA option.

D. **Incorrect:** The AUTO option returns the element names as the table names, and the XMLDATA would cause the schema to be generated and prepended to the results.

70-229.03.05.002

▶ **Correct Answers: C**

A. **Incorrect:** This clause produces the results in a nonhierarchical order, so RAW is the right approach, but there will not be any schema provided.

B. **Incorrect:** This clause produces the results in a hierarchical order, which does not meet the criteria. There will not be any schema provided.

C. **Correct:** This selection produces nonhierarchical data prefaced with the schema information, which meets the requirements.

D. **Incorrect:** Although this clause will produce the schema, because of the XMLDATA option, it will be returned in hierarchical order, which does not meet the requirements.

70-229.03.05.003

▶ **Correct Answers: C**

A. **Incorrect:** The hierarchy is determined by the order of the tables referenced in the columns in the SELECT statement. In the generated XML, the order of the elements is Stores, Sales, Titles—not Titles, Sales, Stores, Sales, as displayed in this query. Only the first occurrence of a table is used, and other occurrences are added as attributes to the table element.

B. **Incorrect:** The hierarchy is determined by the order of the tables referenced in the columns in the SELECT statement. In the generated XML, the order of the elements is stores, sales, titles—not sales, stores, titles as displayed in this query. Only the first occurrence of a table is used, and other occurrences are added as attributes to the table element.

C. **Correct:** In the generated XML, the order of the elements is stores, sales, titles, as displayed in this query. Only the first occurrence of a table is used, and other occurrences are added as attributes to the table element.

O B J E C T I V E   D O M A I N   4

Programming Business Logic

To access data in a Microsoft SQL Server database, you can use **Transact-SQL** statements. For complex tasks, this becomes repetitive and inefficient. You can address such tasks by creating **stored procedures**. A stored procedure is a precompiled collection of Transact-SQL statements kept as a unit under a unique name. Stored procedures are kept within the SQL Server database and can be executed with a single command. Stored procedures allow user-declared variables, groupings, conditional execution, and other programming features. Stored procedures can contain a group of statements and calls to other stored procedures. They can have input and output parameters. Stored procedures can also return status value and indicate success or failure.

A **transaction** is the basic unit for modifying data while preserving the ACID properties: atomicity, consistency, isolation, and durability. A transaction is a sequence of operations that is performed as a single unit of work.

- **Atomicity**—A transaction must be a single unit of work or modification completed or none.

- **Consistency**—When the transaction completes, the data will be in a consistent state. In a SQL Server database, this means that the data is valid, and that triggers, rules, and so on are processed without any errors. All internal structures are updated.

- **Isolation**—Transactions can be executed concurrently. Transactions must provide a total isolation from other transactions executed concurrently. If two transactions are accessing the same data, one transaction can see the data either before the other transaction begins or after, but not while the changes are being made.

- **Durability**—After the transaction is completed, all changes in the database are permanent and would survive system failure.

SQL Server supports three different kinds of transactions: **explicit transactions**, **implicit transactions**, and **distributed transactions**.

SQL Server uses different kinds of locks within the database to prevent conflicts. Locks make the serialization of transactions possible. SQL Server automatically selects the right kind of lock to the specific transaction. Locks ensure that data is being read and written cleanly.

To extend SQL Server Transact-SQL programmability, SQL Server 2000 provides user-defined functions. User-defined functions, like stored procedures, can encapsulate frequently used operations, but they can also return a scalar value or a table.

Tested Skills and Suggested Practices

The skills that you need to successfully master the Programming Business Logic objective domain on the *Designing and Implementing Databases with Microsoft SQL Server 2000 Enterprise Edition* exam include:

- **Using stored procedures to access, manipulate, and manage data in the database.**

  - Practice 1: Create stored procedures to access the database using the SELECT statement. Use parameters passed in to a stored procedure to specify the range of data you want to view.

  - Practice 2: Use stored procedures and cursors to manipulate data in tables.

  - Practice 3: Use stored procedures to insert a record into a database table. All column values should be passed into the stored procedure and inserted into a table.

  - Practice 4: Use the UPDATE statement within the stored procedure to update a table based on the passed-in values.

  - Practice 5: Write stored procedures with both input and output parameters.

- **Using triggers to enforce data integrity in a SQL Server database.**

  - Practice 1: Create an INSERT trigger on a SQL Server table. This trigger should insert another row into another table using the values available in the temporary "inserted" table.

  - Practice 2: Create an UPDATE trigger. If the values are not in the acceptable range, raise an error and roll back the transaction.

- Practice 3: Create a DELETE trigger. Based on the values, update other tables.

- Practice 4: Create INSTEAD OF triggers for INSERT, UPDATE, and DELETE operations on a table, and do the appropriate work for a table.

- **Using transactions to ensure data integrity.**

  - Practice 1: Insert, update, and delete data from different tables using transactional protection.

  - Practice 2: Use transaction and data manipulation, and then abort the transaction.

  - Practice 3: Use transaction savepoints and roll back to a savepoint.

  - Practice 4: Change the connection transaction behavior from the default, and look at the different behaviors.

- **Creating user-defined functions.**

  - Practice 1: Create a user-defined function that takes LastName, FirstName as varchars and returns a concatenation of both as varchar.

  - Practice 2: Return a table and use it in the FROM clause of a join.

Further Reading

This section lists supplemental readings by objective. Study these sources thoroughly before taking exam 70-229.

Objective 4.1

Microsoft SQL Server 2000 product documentation. To access Books Online (BOL), click the Start button, point to Programs, then Microsoft SQL Server, and click Books Online. Click the Contents tab and double-click the "SQL Server Architecture" topic. Then review "Transactions Architecture" under "Relational Database Engine Architecture."

Microsoft SQL Server 2000 product documentation. To access Books Online, click the Start button, point to Programs, then Microsoft SQL Server, and click Books Online. Click the Contents tab, double-click "Accessing and Changing Relational Data," and review "Accessing and Changing Data Fundamentals" and "Transactions."

Microsoft SQL Server 2000 product documentation. To access Books Online, click the Start button, point to Programs, then Microsoft SQL Server, and click Books Online. Click the Contents tab, double-click "Creating and Maintaining Databases," and review "Stored Procedures," "Views," "Enforcing Business Rules with Triggers," and "User-Defined Functions."

In Part 1, read and complete the practices in Lesson 3 in Chapter 2, "Using Transact-SQL on a SQL Server Database," Lessons 1, 2, and 3 in Chapter 8, "Implementing Stored Procedures," Lessons 1, 2, and 3 in Chapter 9, "Implementing Triggers," Lessons 1, 2, and 3 in Chapter 10, "Implementing Views," and Lessons 1, 2, and 3 in Chapter 12, "Managing SQL Server Transactions and Locks."

Objective 4.2

Microsoft SQL Server 2000 product documentation. To access Books Online, click the Start button, point to Programs, then Microsoft SQL Server, and then click Books Online. Click the Contents tab, double-click "Creating and Maintaining Databases," and review "Enforcing Business Rules with Triggers."

Microsoft SQL Server 2000 product documentation. To access Books Online, click the Start button, point to Programs, then Microsoft SQL Server, and click Books Online. Click the Contents tab and double-click the "Accessing and Changing Relational Data" topic. Then review "Advanced Query Concepts." Also review "Advanced Topics" under "Transactions."

In Part 1, read and complete the practices in Lesson 3 in Chapter 2, "Using Transact-SQL on a SQL Server Database," Lessons 1, 2, and 3 in Chapter 8, "Implementing Stored Procedures," Lessons 1, 2, and 3 in Chapter 9, "Implementing Triggers," Lessons 1, 2, and 3 in Chapter 10, "Implementing Views," and Lessons 1, 2, and 3 in Chapter 12, "Managing SQL Server Transactions and Locks."

Objective 4.3

Microsoft SQL Server 2000 product documentation. To access Books Online, click the Start button, point to Programs, then Microsoft SQL Server, and click Books Online. Click the Contents tab and double-click the "Accessing and Changing Relational Data" topic. Then review "Using Options in SQL Server" under "Accessing and Changing Data." Also review "Error Handling" under "Advanced Query Concepts."

Microsoft SQL Server 2000 product documentation. To access Books Online, click the Start button, point to Programs, then Microsoft SQL Server, and click Books Online. Click the Contents tab and double-click the "Using the SQL Server Tools" topic. Then double-click the "User Interface Reference" topic and review "Using Transact-SQL Debugger" under "SQL Query Analyzer Help."

In Part 1, read and complete the practices in Lesson 1, Chapter 14, "Maintaining and Optimizing SQL Server Database."

OBJECTIVE 4.1

Manage data manipulation by using stored procedures, transactions, triggers, user-defined functions, and views.

Data can be manipulated in special ways in SQL Server 2000 with stored procedures, transactions, triggers, user-defined functions, and views. Each of these methods is specialized for different uses, although their functionality might overlap in some ways.

Stored procedures are optimized for repeated usage in that the code can be created and tested, and when the code is first compiled, the execution plan will be saved for further use. One of the best ways to encapsulate known business code is to use stored procedures. By using stored procedures, you can also best ensure that the execution plan and the code will be reused. Stored procedures provide a logical abstraction layer. Using stored procedures can also help enforce some good programming habits, such as testing of SQL code, and ensuring that code is kept under source control. Client and middle-tier applications can be protected from changes to the underlying database objects when stored procedures are implemented because the procedures can be changed, with no code change to the outlying layers.

User-defined explicit transactions allow blocks of code to be handled together as one logical unit of work, with user-controlled rollback or commit.

Triggers are pieces of user-defined business logic that are fired whenever certain changes happen to a table. In SQL Server 2000, users can implement multiple AFTER triggers, which fire after a data manipulation command, as well as an INSTEAD OF trigger that will fire instead of (and hence, before) the data manipulation.

New to SQL Server 2000 are user-defined functions. These are functions that are created by the user and can be used inline in queries and to simplify coding. They provide a great deal of coding flexibility and the ability to encode some business logic in a simple-to-use function. User-defined functions can return scalar values or tables.

Views are logical abstractions over queries, commonly used to replace a complex query with a view that is easy to maintain and understand. SQL Server 2000 allows partitioned views, which provide a unioned view over multiple tables partitioned by some data constraint, as well as indexed views. Indexed views allow queries that are problematic from an optimization standpoint to be created and treated as a separate table, which the system manages, keeping it up to date when changes are made to the underlying base tables. A unique clustered index can then be created on the view, providing potentially huge performance gains. Indexed views are currently available only in the Enterprise Edition of SQL Server 2000.

Managing error handling in SQL Server code can be problematic because there is no built-in error handler. Generally, the best practice is to check the current results of the @@ERROR global variable after each statement, performing some error handling work dependent on the result. The global variable @@ROWS can also be used to determine whether any rows were affected by a statement. It is important to understand the scope of both of these variables because the next statement might immediately affect them, whether that statement returns results or not. For example, a common mistake is to run a SQL command, use the IF @@ROWCOUNT construct to check for the number of rows, and then to use the IF @@ERROR construct to check the error code and perform a function. However, the first IF statement resets the @@ERROR global variable to 0, negating the intended error-checking code.

Objective 4.1 Questions

70-229.04.01.001

In your stored procedure, you have to raise an error. What are the capabilities of RAISERROR? (Choose all that apply.)

A. It can print a message to the application.

B. It can assign an error number, state, and severity.

C. It can be logged in the error log.

D. The message string can contain substitution variables.

70-229.04.01.002

You are creating a stored procedure that will call a number of other stored procedures. If any of the inside stored procedures do not complete the required business logic, the outer stored procedure should stop execution with a message to the user. It does not need to roll back the previous work. Which of the following approaches will meet these requirements?

A. In the outer stored procedure, use a SELECT statement to check the results of @@ERROR after each inner stored procedure. If the result is zero, continue; otherwise, return an error message and stop execution.

B. Inside each inner stored procedure, store an error number as a return result from the stored procedure. In the outer stored procedure, check the result code of the inner stored procedure and continue if there is no error; otherwise, return an error message and stop execution.

C. Create a transaction inside the outer stored procedure that wraps each of the inner stored procedures. In the outer stored procedure, use a SELECT statement to check the results of @@ROWCOUNT after the execution of each inner stored procedure. If the result is zero, continue; otherwise, return an error message and stop execution.

D. In the outer stored procedure, use a SELECT statement to check the result of @@ROWCOUNT after the execution of each inner stored procedure. If the result is not zero, continue; otherwise, return an error message and stop execution.

70-229.04.01.003

Which of the following statements can cause a transaction to roll back if you have set XACT_ABORT on? (Choose all that apply.)

A. ROLLBACK TRAN

B. RAISERROR

C. In a statement, you use WHERE 1/0 and cause a divide by zero error.

D. PRINT

70-229.04.01.004

You want to create a user-defined function to parse a telephone number passed to the user-defined function. You want the return value to be a table, and if the value is invalid, you want to abort the current transaction. Which of the following statements is true?

A. You can use ROLLBACK TRAN and you can return a table.

B. You cannot use ROLLBACK TRAN and cannot return a table.

C. You can use ROLLBACK, but you cannot return a table.

D. You cannot use ROLLBACK, but you can return a table.

70-229.04.01.005

You created a partitioned view, and now you want to override the INSERT, UPDATE, and DELETE statement behavior. Which of the following statements is true?

A. You cannot use an INSTEAD OF trigger on a partitioned view.

B. You can use an AFTER trigger only on a partitioned view.

C. You can use INSTEAD OF triggers, but each type (INSERT, UPDATE, and DELETE) can have only one definition.

D. You can use INSTEAD OF triggers on tables and views in place of INSERT, UPDATE, and/or DELETE triggers.

70-229.04.01.006

You need to add business logic to an INSERT trigger to add the row to an audit table in another database for every INSERT in one table. This table has an IDENTITY column for the primary key, and the table has two triggers, one that also inserts into another table the current rows inserted. What is the best way to get the value of the identity column just inserted?

A. In the trigger, use a SELECT statement to save the value of @@IDENTITY after the INSERT statement and use this value to insert the row into the audit table.

B. In the trigger, use a SELECT statement to check the return value of the SCOPE_IDENTITY function after the INSERT statement.

C. In the trigger, use a SELECT statement to check the return value of the IDENT_CURRENT function, passing in the name of the table as the parameter after the INSERT statement, and use this value to insert the row into the audit table.

70-229.04.01.007

You need to create a stored procedure to return one calculated value converted to a string value. Which of the following methods will best produce the results you want?

A. You create the stored procedure declaring a varchar variable as output and use a SELECT statement to store the converted result into this variable.

B. Use a SELECT statement to check the value in @@ROWS after the stored procedure execution.

C. Return the result as a return code from the stored procedure.

D. Use a SELECT statement to check the result in the stored procedure.

70-229.04.01.008

You have a database that includes all of the company's employees. You currently have Employee and Job tables, which relate an employee to a manager through the Job table. The Employee table contains the rows for all employees, including managers. There is also a flag called Current in the Job table that indicates the current job for an employee. There is a constraint on the table that ensures that only one row can be indicated as the Current job for each employee. You would like to create a simple way to return an employee's current manager's ID. The approach should be flexible enough to be used in any command, including the BCP utility, if needed. Which of the following code snippets would best satisfy these requirements?

A. CREATE FUNCTION CurrentManager (@EmployeeID int) RETURNS int AS BEGIN

```
DECLARE @ManagerID int
SELECT @ ManagerID =Job.ManagerID
FROM Employee JOIN Job on Employee.EmployeeID = Job.EmployeeID
JOIN Employee as Manager ON Job.ManagerID = Manager.EmployeeID
WHERE Employee.EmployeeID = @EmployeeID
AND Job.CurrentJob = 1
RETURN @ ManagerID
END
```

B. CREATE VIEW CurrentManager AS

```
SELECT Job.ManagerID
FROM Employee JOIN Job on Employee.EmployeeID = Job.EmployeeID
JOIN Employee as Manager ON Job.ManagerID = Manager.EmployeeID
WHERE Job.CurrentJob = 1
```

C. CREATE PROCEDURE CurrentManager (@employeeid int) AS

```
BEGIN
SELECT Job.ManagerID
FROM Employee JOIN Job on Employee.EmployeeID = Job.EmployeeID
JOIN Employee as Manager ON Job.ManagerID = Manager.EmployeeID
WHERE Employee.EmployeeID = @employeeid
AND Job.CurrentJob = 1
END
```

70-229.04.01.009

You have a stored procedure that will require nested transactions to ensure that all modifications are applied. You want to ensure that there are no transactions open at the completion of the stored procedure. Which of the following global variables can be interrogated to determine if a transaction is still open?

A. @@CONNECTIONS

B. @@NESTLEVEL

C. @@.FETCH_STATUS

D. @@TRANCOUNT

Objective 4.1 Answers

70-229.04.01.001

▶ **Correct Answers: A, B, C, and D**

A. **Correct:** RAISERROR can send a message to the application just like the PRINT function, but it has more options than PRINT.

B. **Correct:** RAISERROR can assign the specific error, severity, and state numbers.

C. **Correct:** RAISERROR can request to be logged in the SQL Server Log file and/or the Microsoft Windows NT/ Microsoft Windows 2000 application log.

D. **Correct:** The message string can contain substitution variables similar to the C language printf function, as in the following example:

```
RAISERROR('The current database ID is:%d', 16, 1, @DBID)
```

70-229.04.01.002

▶ **Correct Answers: B**

A. **Incorrect:** If a stored procedure runs completely, the results of @@ERROR will not show an error, because the stored procedure ran, even though the results were not what you expected. This is much like a function in other coding languages, where the function itself runs to completion and does not return an error, but the code within the function might not complete the desired actions.

B. **Correct:** This is the best approach. Inside each inner stored procedure, check the validity of the logic, which should include @@ERROR to ensure that there were no errors. @@ROWCOUNT can also be used if the success of the stored procedure can be determined by the number of rows that were affected. A return code should then be returned to the outer stored procedure. The outer stored procedure should be executed with a variable already declared to trap the return code. The outer stored procedure can continue depending on the result of this variable.

C. **Incorrect:** There is no need to include a transaction in the outer stored procedure because the requirements indicate that no actions need to be rolled back on an error. The stored procedure should just return an error message and stop execution.

D. **Incorrect:** The results of @@ROWCOUNT might not indicate the successful completion of all of the business requirements in the inner stored procedures.

70-229.04.01.003

▶ **Correct Answers: A, B, and C**

A. **Correct:** ROLLBACK TRAN will roll back any implicit or explicit transaction to the beginning or to a named savepoint.

B. **Correct:** If you specify a high enough severity code with RAISERROR, the transaction will roll back.

C. **Correct:** Division by zero or another run-time error will cause the transaction to roll back.

D. **Incorrect:** PRINT sends a message back to the calling application but will not cause the transaction to abort.

70-229.04.01.004

▶ **Correct Answers: D**

A. **Incorrect:** You cannot use any functions that change the transaction state, such as COMMIT or ROLLBACK. You also cannot start a transaction in a function. Every scalar SQL Server type, and also tables, can be returned by a user-defined function.

B. **Incorrect:** The first part of the answer is correct. You cannot use any statement that would change the state of a transaction; however, you can return a table, not just scalar types.

C. **Incorrect:** You cannot use any functions that change the transaction state, such as COMMIT or ROLLBACK. You also cannot start a transaction in a function. Every scalar SQL Server type, and also tables, can be returned by a user-defined function.

D. **Correct:** You cannot use any functions that would change the transaction state, but you can return a table from a user-defined function.

70-229.04.01.005

▶ **Correct Answers: D**

   A. **Incorrect:** You can use an INSTEAD OF trigger on any table or view in your database. The INSTEAD OF trigger will override the default behavior of the statement you have executed (whether an INSERT, UPDATE, or DELETE) and allow you to write custom operations.

   B. **Incorrect:** You can use both INSTEAD OF and AFTER triggers on distributed views as well as tables.

   C. **Incorrect:** Although you can use an INSTEAD OF trigger with a distributed view, there is no limit on the number of same type triggers you can implement on a distributed view.

   D. **Correct:** You can use INSTEAD OF triggers on any table, view, or partitioned view without limitation on the type of the trigger.

70-229.04.01.006

▶ **Correct Answers: B**

   A. **Incorrect:** @@IDENTITY will return the last generated identity value for any table in the current session. In some situations, depending on the code run in the trigger, another table might have an identity value inserted, and this value could be returned in this trigger.

   B. **Correct:** This is the best solution because this function returns the last identity generated in the current session and the current scope, which in this case is the trigger. @@IDENTITY will return the last generated identity value for any table in the current session. In some situations, depending on the code run in the trigger, another table might have an identity value inserted, and this value could be returned in this trigger. The IDENT_CURRENT function will return the last generated identity for the table passed as a parameter. There is a possibility that another session could have inserted a row into the table in the time between the insertion of the row by the trigger and the running of the IDENT_CURRENT function.

   C. **Incorrect:** The IDENT_CURRENT function will return the last generated identity for the table passed as a parameter. There is a possibility that another session could have inserted a row into the table in the time between the insertion of the row by the trigger and the running of the IDENT_CURRENT function, depending on the amount of code and usage in the trigger. @@IDENTITY will return the last generated identity value for any table in the current session. In some situations, depending on the code run in the trigger, another table might have an identity value inserted, and this value could be returned in this trigger.

70-229.04.01.007

▶ **Correct Answers: A**

A. **Correct:** An output variable can be used to return a data value to the calling code. This is a very common method for returning scalar values from a stored procedure. The calling code must be aware of and capable of handling output parameters. Because only one value is expected, using an output parameter is more elegant than using a SELECT statement to obtain the results. Because the calling code does not need to work through multiple rows in the result set, the calling code is simpler.

B. **Incorrect:** @@ROWCOUNT does not return the result rows, but returns the number of rows that are affected by the immediately preceding command.

C. **Incorrect:** A stored procedure can return only an integer value as a result code.

D. **Incorrect:** Although simply using a SELECT statement will provide a return result, it is not the best method. Although the SELECT statement returns a scalar value, using an output parameter allows the calling code to assume one value and code for that result. Using the SELECT statement requires that calling code to handle the possibility of multiple rows, and to manage the results as if there were multiples. This requires more overhead than the output parameter method.

70-229.04.01.008

▶ **Correct Answers: A**

A. **Correct:** This is the best solution because it can be used inline almost anywhere in a command. It can be referenced in a SELECT statement and is guaranteed to return only a scalar value, so there would never be a problem with a subquery returning more than one result and then causing an error. Because a BCP command can use a query or a view as well as a table, this function can be used by the BCP utility as well.

B. **Incorrect:** There is no way to pass a parameter to a view, so in order to get the view to compile, the EmployeeID was left out, which does not meet the requirement.

C. **Incorrect:** Although you could create a stored procedure, it would not be the best option because a stored procedure cannot be invoked everywhere, such as in a query, which is necessary to meet the requirement.

70-229.04.01.009

▶ **Correct Answers: D**

A. **Incorrect:** This global variable will return the number of successful and attempted connections since the server was started.

B. **Incorrect:** @@NESTLEVEL will return the nesting level of the stored procedures, not the nesting level of transactions.

C. **Incorrect:** This returns the status of the last fetch from any cursor currently open in the connection.

D. **Correct:** This will return the number of open transactions in the connection. The BEGIN TRANS-ACTION statement will increment the @@TRANCOUNT global variable by one. COMMIT TRANSACTION will decrement this value. ROLLBACK TRANSACTION will set this variable to 0.

OBJECTIVE 4.2

Enforce procedural business logic by using stored procedures, transactions, triggers, user-defined functions, and views.

With SQL Server you can encapsulate frequently used operations in a single unit. These stored procedures can be included in other stored procedures to implement complex business logic. The included and parent stored procedures share the same transaction, and their operation is atomic.

SQL Server provides two primary mechanisms for enforcing business roles and logic: constraints and triggers. **Triggers** are special stored procedures invoked in response to an INSERT, UPDATE, or DELETE statement. Triggers can query other tables and include complex Transact-SQL statements. A trigger and the statement that fires it are handled in a single transaction. Triggers can perform more complex tasks than constraints can. Unlike constraints, triggers can reference other tables in the database. Triggers are also able to evaluate the state of the table before and after the data modification. Multiple triggers of the same type, such as INSERT, UPDATE, or DELETE, allow multiple actions to be performed in response to the same operation.

Transactions are the basic unit for modifying data in an atomic, consistent, isolated, and durable way. A transaction is a sequence of operations that is performed as a single unit of work. A transaction can be used to encapsulate a business process, including stored procedures, user-defined functions, triggers, and so on.

Objective 4.2 Questions

70-229.04.02.001

You want to create a trigger for a table so you can verify that one of the column values exists in another table and do some manipulation with the data. If the value is not found, you want to roll back the current transaction. Which statement is true?

A. You cannot access another table from a trigger, but you can abort a transaction.

B. You can access another table from a trigger, but you cannot abort a transaction, just like a user-defined function.

C. The requirements can be accomplished with a trigger. The trigger will work correctly.

D. You can neither access another table nor control the outcome of a transaction using a trigger.

70-229.04.02.002

You have the following Transact-SQL stored procedure code. Which line has an error? (Choose all that apply.)

```
CREATE PROCEDURE Test AS
BEGIN
  IF (@@ERROR > 0) THEN
    ROLLBACK TRAN
  ELSE BEGIN
    INSERT INTO Logs(Message) values('It Worked!')
  END
END
NOT FOR REPLICATION
```

A. CREATE PROCEDURE Test AS

B. IF (@@ERROR > 0) THEN

C. ROLLBACK TRAN must be in a BEGIN…END block.

D. NOT FOR REPLICATION

70-229.04.02.003

You want to write a stored procedure that will have a transaction inside. You want to ensure that the stored procedure will roll back only the actions within the procedure if it is called from code in which a transaction has already been declared, leaving the outer transaction intact. You do not know the setting for the XACT_ABORT option. Your stored procedure must run without errors when there is no outer transaction declared as well. What is the best approach to meet these requirements?

A. You do not need to do anything special to the stored procedure because if it is already in a transaction, only the stored procedure will be rolled back.

B. Use the BEGIN TRANSACTION...ROLLBACK TRANSACTION construct within the stored procedure.

C. At the beginning of the stored procedure, use the SAVE TRANSACTION construct with a transaction name and the ROLLBACK TRANSACTION construct with the same name.

D. If @@TRANCOUNT <> 0, use the SAVE TRANSACTION construct with a transaction name; otherwise, use the BEGIN TRANSACTION construct with a transaction name and the ROLLBACK TRANSACTION construct with the same name.

70-229.04.02.004

What are the internal or special (conceptual) temporary tables in a trigger, and what functions can you use to test for column states?

```
CREATE TRIGGER MyTrigger on MyTable for INSERT, UPDATE, DELETE
    AS ...
```

A. These special tables are INSERTED, UPDATED, and DELETED. Column state functions are INSERT(), UPDATE(), DELETE().

B. These special tables are INSERTED and DELETED. Column state functions are UPDATE() and COLUMNS_UPDATED().

C. These special tables are UPDATED and DELETED. Column state functions are UPDATE(), COLUMNS_UPDATED().

D. If no special tables are available within a trigger, you have to access the data tables directly.

70-229.04.02.005

You have created a table as follows:

```
CREATE TABLE Test1 (Id INT)
```

You created the following INSTEAD OF INSERT trigger on this table:

```
CREATE TRIGGER Test1_IO ON Test1
INSTEAD OF INSERT
AS
BEGIN
  INSERT INTO Test1 SELECT ID+1 FROM INSERTED
END
```

You executed the following code:

```
INSERT INTO Test1 VALUES(1)
SELECT * FROM Test1
```

What will be the result?

A. Execution will fail because inside the trigger you are inserting into the same table, and the trigger gets called over and over again until it overflows the buffer.

B. The result will be 1 because the trigger would do an infinite loop and SQL Server will not execute it.

C. The code will execute successfully, and the result will be 2.

70-229.04.02.006

You need to work procedurally through a result set of rows from a table called Employee with a primary key of EmployeeID, returning the first name concatenated to the last name. You do not want to use a cursor because of the possible locking problems. Which of the following code snippets would best satisfy this requirement?

A.
```
DECLARE @ NextID INT

SELECT @ NextID = MIN( ID ) FROM Employee
WHILE @ NextID IS NOT NULL
BEGIN
  SELECT ID, FirstName + ' ' + LastName FROM Employee
    WHERE ID = @ NextID
  SELECT @ NextID = MIN( ID ) FROM Employee WHERE ID > @ NextID
END
```

B.
```
DECLARE @NextID INT

SELECT @ NextID = MIN( ID ) FROM Employee
BEGIN
  SELECT ID, FirstName + ' ' + LastName FROM Employee
    WHERE ID = @ NextID
  SELECT @ NextID = MIN( ID ) FROM Employee WHERE ID > @ NextID
END
```

C.
```
DECLARE @ NextID INT

SELECT @ NextID = MIN( ID ) FROM Employee
IF @ NextID IS NULL GOTO Finish
BEGIN
  SELECT ID, FirstName + ' ' + LastName FROM Employee
    WHERE ID = @ NextID
  SELECT @ NextID = MIN( ID ) FROM Employee WHERE ID > @nextid
END
Finish:
```

D.
```
DECLARE @ NextID INT

SELECT @ NextID = MIN( ID ) FROM Employee
WHILE @ NextID IS NOT NULL
BEGIN
  SELECT ID, FirstName + ' ' + LastName FROM Employee
    WHERE ID = @ NextID
END
```

70-229.04.02.007

You need to create a report that will output all of the Employee rows and the Orders they have in the Northwind database. You want to see a row for every Employee, but report only the order amounts if the Employee is in the WA region and the order date is greater than 07/12/1996. You need to output a row for each Employee even if the Employee does not have an order later than that date or is not in the WA region. Which of the following queries would produce the correct result?

A. SELECT E.LastName, O.OrderID, O.OrderDate

    FROM Employees E LEFT OUTER JOIN Orders O
    ON E.EmployeeID = O.EmployeeID
    AND O.OrderDate > '1996 07-12'
    WHERE E.Region = 'WA'
    ORDER BY E.LastName

B. SELECT E.LastName, O.OrderID, O.OrderDate

    FROM Employees E LEFT OUTER JOIN Orders O
    ON E.EmployeeID = O.EmployeeID
    WHERE E.Region = 'WA'
    AND O.OrderDate > '1996-07-12'
    ORDER BY E.LastName

C. SELECT E.LastName, O.OrderID, O.OrderDate

    FROM Employees E LEFT OUTER JOIN Orders O
    ON E.EmployeeID = O.EmployeeID
    AND E.Region = 'WA'
    AND O.OrderDate > '1996-07-12'
    ORDER BY E.LastName

D. SELECT E.Lastname, O.OrderID, O.OrderDate

    FROM Employees E LEFT OUTER JOIN Orders O
    ON E.EmployeeID = O.EmployeeID
    AND E.Region = 'WA' WHERE O.OrderDate > '1996-07-12'
    ORDER BY E.LastName

Objective 4.2 Answers

70-229.04.02.001

▶ **Correct Answers: C**

A. **Incorrect:** You can both access another table from a trigger and control the outcome of the transaction.

B. **Incorrect:** You can access another table from a trigger. Although user-defined functions cannot control the outcome of a transaction, triggers can.

C. **Correct:** You can access tables from the trigger and control the outcome of the transaction.

D. **Incorrect:** Triggers, just like stored procedures, can do all kinds of access and transaction controls. Triggers are invoked by SQL Server, whereas stored procedures are called on behalf of the user.

70-229.04.02.002

▶ **Correct Answers: B and D**

A. **Incorrect:** This syntax is correct. You can also optionally define input parameters and return values when you define the stored procedure. You can define default values so that not all parameters must be passed each time when the stored procedure is being called.

B. **Correct:** The IF statement does not use THEN. THEN is used in many programming languages such as Microsoft Visual Basic or VBScript. The correct syntax is IF (condition).

C. **Incorrect:** If the IF condition precedes a single statement, you do not have to use BEGIN...END. On the other hand, if the IF condition precedes more than one statement, you have to use the BEGIN...END to enclose the statement block.

D. **Correct:** Stored procedures are created with NOT FOR REPLICATION as default behavior. If you want the stored procedure to be replicated, you must use FOR REPLICATION. NOT FOR REPLICATION will generate an error.

70-229.04.02.003

▶ **Correct Answers: D**

A. **Incorrect:** If the stored procedure is executed within a transaction and an error occurs within the stored procedure, all of the actions might not be rolled back without explicitly indicating which logic should be rolled back.

B. **Incorrect:** If there is a ROLLBACK called inside the stored procedure, all of the work will be rolled back up to that point, including the work from the outside calling code that would already have been executed before the stored procedure. This is not the behavior needed to meet the requirements.

C. **Incorrect:** Using the SAVE TRANSACTION construct with a name and then using that name with the ROLLBACK construct at the beginning of the stored procedure will cause only the work within the procedure itself to be rolled back if there is an error. This meets one of the requirements. However, the stored procedure will not run by itself outside a transaction because there is no transaction to save.

D. **Correct:** This is the best approach. Using the SAVE TRANSACTION construct with a name and then using that name with the ROLLBACK construct at the beginning of the stored procedure will cause only the work within the procedure itself to be rolled back if there is an error. This meets one of the requirements. However, the stored procedure will not run by itself outside a transaction because there is no transaction to save. It is best to check the value of @@TRANCOUNT to determine whether you are currently in a transaction, and then either create a savepoint with SAVE TRANSACTION if there is a transaction already started, or create a new one with BEGIN TRANSACTION. The same transaction name can be used for either option, so the ROLLBACK TRANSACTION would use this name and would be valid whether the SAVE TRANSACTION or BEGIN TRANSACTION construct was used.

70-229.04.02.004

▶ **Correct Answers: B**

A. **Incorrect:** SQL Server does not have INSERT(), UPDATE(), or DELETE() functions.

B. **Correct:** The INSERTED table contains all newly inserted records and all updates on existing records, and DELETED holds all deleted records. You can check whether a column is being changed with the UPDATE() function. Also, you can use the COLUMNS _UPDATED_() function to get a bit pattern representation of the changed columns.

C. **Incorrect:** There is no UPDATED table. The special tables created are the INSERTED and DELETED tables, and the UPDATE() function can be used to test whether a particular column has been updated.

D. **Incorrect:** To see the changes made by or requested with the INSERT, UPDATE, or DELETE statements, SQL Server has to provide you with the changes. SQL Server creates two special tables within the scope of a trigger. INSERTED has all the new inserts and updates, and DELETED holds all the deleted records.

70-229.04.02.005

▶ **Correct Answers: C**

A. **Incorrect:** If, in your trigger, you execute a statement against the same table that the trigger is activated on, the trigger will not be called again. SQL Server protects itself from this type of infinite loop.

B. **Incorrect:** The trigger will execute successfully, and the result will be 2. SQL Server will not call a trigger if the event comes from within a trigger.

C. **Correct:** The code example is correct. SQL Server will not execute a trigger if the code would fire the trigger on the same table.

70-229.04.02.006

▶ **Correct Answers: A**

A. **Correct:** This is one way to emulate a cursor with control-of-flow language if there is a primary key that can be used to move through the result set. The WHILE construct allows the code inside to loop until the condition is met.

B. **Incorrect:** Because there is no control-of-flow language other than a BEGIN and END, there is no loop to move through the results one row at a time. This code will execute only once. A better way would be to store either the minimum or the maximum primary key, and then move through the result set one row at a time with a WHILE clause, filtering for the current key as you go, and then getting the next key before moving on.

C. **Incorrect:** There is no loop here, only a check for a null; therefore, this code will execute only once. A better way would be to store either the minimum or the maximum primary key, and then move through the result set one row at a time with a WHILE clause, filtering for the current key as you go, and then getting the next key before moving on.

D. **Incorrect:** This code will loop an infinite number of times (or until the server crashes). There is a loop being called with the WHILE construct, but there is no change to the value being checked, so the loop will run forever. A better way would be to store either the minimum or the maximum primary key, and then move through the result set one row at a time with a WHILE clause, filtering for the current key as you go, and then getting the next key before moving on.

70-229.04.02.007

▶ **Correct Answers: C**

A. **Incorrect:** Although this query uses a left outer join, it will not return a row for employees who are not in the WA region. The result set is restricted after the join by the WHERE clause, which would restrict the rows for any employee not in the WA region.

B. **Incorrect:** Although this query uses a left outer join, it will not return a row for employees who are not in the WA region or who have orders with dates later than the orderdate. The result set is restricted after the join by the WHERE clause, which would restrict the rows for any employee not in the WA region and having orders that do not meet the criteria.

C. **Correct:** This query will return the correct results because the restrictions are placed on the JOIN clause. The OUTER JOIN then allows all rows in the employee table to be output, even if they are not in the WA region or they have no orders after the criteria date.

D. **Incorrect:** Although this query uses a LEFT OUTER JOIN, it will not return a row for employees not having orders later than the criteria date. The result set is restricted after the join by the WHERE clause.

OBJECTIVE 4.3

Troubleshoot and optimize programming objects.

A number of tools and methods are available to troubleshoot and optimize programming objects, such as stored procedures, triggers, user-defined functions, and views. These include coding statements, such as the PRINT statement and RAISERROR, to track and monitor the values of variables, as well as query and table hints to optimize the data access in a Transact-SQL statement.

One of the most valuable tools for troubleshooting stored procedures is the Transact-SQL Debugger. This tool is available in the SQL Query Analyzer and includes the most common debugging options, such as using watch expressions, stepping through code, and setting breakpoints in code.

Objective 4.3 Questions

70-229.04.03.001

You have a Web-based Online Transaction Processing (OLTP) orders application that has a few problematic SELECT queries that join six different tables and request the retrieved results in different orders. These queries are taking too long to return the results to the user. Which of the following would be the easiest and most effective way to get better performance from these few queries? (Choose all that apply.)

A. Use the OPTION (FAST n) query hint.

B. Use the ROBUST PLAN query hint.

C. Create indexed views for the queries.

D. Rewrite the statement as a view.

70-229.04.03.002

You need to troubleshoot a stored procedure, determining what the results of a particular local variable are during the execution of the store procedure. Which of the following can help to troubleshoot this procedure? (Choose all that apply.)

A. Use the SET statement to set the local variable to another value.

B. Use the PRINT statement inside the procedure to print out the local variable contents.

C. Use the RAISERROR statement.

D. Use the SQL Query Analyzer Transact-SQL Debugger.

70-229.04.03.003

You have a database application that uses dynamic SQL. The only changes to the query are the values that are used in the WHERE clause. You would like to ensure that the execution plan generated by the optimizer at compile time will be reused on subsequent executions. Which of the following approaches can help ensure cached execution plan reuse? (Choose all that apply.)

A. Rewrite the statement using the sp_executesql system stored procedure and fully qualified names.

B. Rewrite the statement as a stored procedure, using input parameters for the WHERE clause substitution.

C. Rewrite the statement using fully qualified object names.

D. Rewrite the statement as a view.

70-229.04.03.004

You have designed a database application that will be used by a large number of users, and you want to ensure that SELECT queries against the Products table do not block transactions that might be inserting data into other tables in the database. The Products table does not change except during a nightly batch job that will adjust the Products table. Which of the following SELECT statement locking hints can be used to minimize locking in this scenario?

A. HOLDLOCK

B. NOLOCK

C. PAGLOCK

D. TABLOCK

70-229.04.03.005

You are evaluating the performance of your database. Your organization allows access to the database only through stored procedures, but you notice that some of the stored procedures are recompiling. Which of the following situations can cause a stored procedure to recompile? (Choose all that apply.)

A. Changes to a large percentage of the data in the underlying objects

B. Interleaving of data manipulation language with data definition language in the stored procedure

C. Cursors created in the stored procedure that reference a temporary table in a SELECT statement

D. Statements that reference temporary tables that were created outside the stored procedure

Objective 4.3 Answers

70-229.04.03.001

▶ **Correct Answers: A and C**

  A. **Correct:** Selecting this option will cause the query to be optimized for the first number of rows that is supplied in the hint. This returns the first group of information to users as fast as possible, allowing the time that the user looks at the first group to be used to retrieve the rest of the results. This is especially helpful if you supply the approximate number of rows to the query hint that fills the first page on the user interface.

  B. **Incorrect:** This will force the optimizer to use a query execution plan that will be best for the maximum row size. This plan will be executed at the expense of performance, so this would not be a good option for this scenario.

  C. **Correct:** Creating an indexed view by creating a view for the problematic queries and then adding a clustered unique index on these views will cause the creation of a table that is maintained by the server. There is a modification cost for the extra maintenance that needs to be performed by the server for these tables, but the performance gains can be great. A number of requirements must be met for an indexed view to be used. Only the Enterprise Edition of SQL Server supports indexed views, and there are a number of other prerequisites.

  D. **Incorrect:** Writing statements as a view will not cause a query to perform faster or retrieve results faster.

70-229.04.03.002

▶ **Correct Answers: B, C, and D**

  A. **Incorrect:** Using the SET statement will not provide debugging or troubleshooting information by itself. It is simply an assignment statement.

  B. **Correct:** The PRINT statement can be used to output the value of a local variable. Using the PRINT statement at critical points in the procedure can help to troubleshoot the procedure. The PRINT statement can accept only character or Unicode values, so variables with other data types will need to be converted before they can be used with the PRINT statement.

C. **Correct:** Although RAISERROR is generally used to output error messages to clients, it can also be used to troubleshoot Transact-SQL by using the statement at critical points in the code, outputting the value of the local variable at those points in the execution of the code.

D. **Correct:** This is an excellent tool to debug a stored procedure. It can be used only within the SQL Query Analyzer, so it cannot be used during actual procedure execution from a client. However, it is very powerful and can show the value of local variables (through the watch functionality) throughout the execution of the code. It also supports stepping through code and setting breakpoints. The Transact-SQL Debugger should not be used on a production server.

70-229.04.03.003

▶ **Correct Answers: A and B**

A. **Correct:** Using the sp_executesql system stored procedure and passing the changed parameter values can help to ensure that a cached execution plan can be reused. The optimizer will give an internal name to the query and treat it as a pseudo-stored procedure, reusing the plan when possible if only the parameter values change. All object names must be fully qualified for the optimizer to reuse the plan.

B. **Correct:** Using a stored procedure will provide the best chance of an execution plan being reused. Fully qualified names are not required because the procedure name by itself will cause the optimizer to recognize the plan. However, using a stored procedure does not ensure that a cached execution plan is reused every time because there are conditions that will cause a stored procedure to recompile, such as the use of temp tables and cursors.

C. **Incorrect:** Although the optimizer might be able to reuse an execution plan if the Transact-SQL statement is very simple and fully qualified object names are used, this is very rare, and the use of fully qualified names will not in itself ensure that a cached execution plan will be reused.

D. **Incorrect:** Writing statements as a view does not ensure cached execution plan reuse, and not all dynamic statements can be rewritten as views.

70-229.04.03.004

▶ **Correct Answers: B**

A. **Incorrect:** The HOLDLOCK hint will force a lock to be held during the duration of the transaction and sets the isolation level to SERIALIZABLE. This would cause more locking on the table, and hence more blocking than no table hint at all.

B. **Correct:** Using the NOLOCK hint in this scenario would be the best approach. This hint will hold the minimal locks on the Products table, and because this table does not change during the transaction period of the day, it would not be a problem as far as uncommitted data being read by users. This will provide the best concurrency and ensure that minimal locking is held during the transaction.

C. **Incorrect:** This would force the optimizer to take a page lock instead of a table lock, but it would not provide the minimal locking in this scenario.

D. **Incorrect:** This will force the optimizer to lock the entire table, producing much more locking, hence blocking, than might have been caused without the hint.

70-229.04.03.005

▶ **Correct Answers: A, B, C, and D**

A. **Correct:** If a sufficient number of data modifications have been made to the underlying objects (such as large insertions or deletions), the stored procedure might be recompiled. This could be considered a good thing because the optimizer might select a different execution plan based on the data changes.

B. **Correct:** Using statements that create or drop objects interleaved with SELECT statements or other data manipulation statements can cause recompilation. This occurs because the objects might not exist during the first compile, so the optimizer is not able to create an execution plan. If objects, such as temporary tables and indexes, need to be created in a stored procedure, it is best to try to create them at the beginning, before they are referenced.

C. **Correct:** Creating a cursor with the DECLARE CURSOR statement that uses a temporary table in the SELECT clause of the cursor can cause a stored procedure to recompile.

D. **Correct:** A reference to a temporary table that was created outside the stored procedure can cause a recompile. It is best to create the required temporary table in the stored procedure, ensuring that the data definition statements, such as the CREATE TABLE statements, do not interleave with any data manipulation statements, such as SELECT statements.

OBJECTIVE DOMAIN 5

Tuning and Optimizing Data Access

The Tuning and Optimizing Data Access domain focuses on how to use the three main tools provided by Microsoft SQL Server 2000 to evaluate data access performance. The tools are:

- SQL Query Analyzer

- SQL Profiler

- Index Tuning Wizard

The SQL Query Analyzer is a tool that will run queries, return results, and display the **execution plan** in a graphical manner. It is the first tool used to determine whether a query is optimized for the current **data distribution** and indexes.

The Index Tuning Wizard can be run from the SQL Query Analyzer to suggest and create recommended indexes based on the queries and data in the database.

The SQL Profiler provides a great deal of information about the events on one or more servers. The SQL Profiler can help determine slow-running queries, poor execution plans, locking, **deadlocking**, and many other events that can affect performance.

Three main areas are critical to SQL Server data access performance:

- Optimal execution plans

- Cached execution plans

- Minimal locking

The SQL Query Analyzer can be used to ensure that the query has an optimal plan. This involves evaluating the graphical plan output by the Analyzer to ensure that data access is fast, that only data needed is acquired, and that indexes are being used. A short-running query will also ensure that any locks that might be required are short.

The Index Tuning Wizard can be used to determine whether the best indexes have been created for the data distribution, and it can be run against a query to ensure that the optimal plan has been selected.

You can use stored procedures or the **sp_executesql** system-stored procedure for ad hoc queries to ensure that an execution plan is cached. The SQL Profiler can also be used to monitor recompiles. Because there is substantial overhead for continuously recompiling a query or stored procedure, you should make an effort to cache as many queries as possible. The SQL Profiler can also be used to determine queries that are long-running, and hence might be holding locks for too long and blocking other connections.

All of these tools can also be used to monitor and troubleshoot performance.

Tested Skills and Suggested Practices

The skills that you need to successfully master the Tuning and Optimizing Data Access domain on the *Designing and Implementing Databases with Microsoft SQL Server 2000 Enterprise Edition* exam include:

- **Analyzing a query execution plan.**

    - Practice 1: Back up the Northwind database. Drop all of the indexes on the tables, and create a query for all of the order details for every order for a certain state.

    - Practice 2: Evaluate the execution plan and determine where the major cost of the query lies. Look especially for table scans and large numbers of rows being passed to the next step in the tree.

    - Practice 3: Rewrite the query in another manner. For instance, if you used joins, use a subselect. Run both queries at the same time in the same SQL Query Analyzer window, and determine which query method performs the best, as indicated by the batch cost. Save the results in a file for later comparison.

- **Analyzing indexes with the Index Tuning Wizard.**

    - Practice 1: Highlight the queries that you created in the previous Practice 1 in the SQL Query Analyzer, and then run the Index Tuning Wizard for all of the tables in the Northwind database. Create any indexes the wizard suggests.

    - Practice 2: Rerun both the queries and evaluate the execution plan. Evaluate the differences between the execution plans generated before the index creation and the plans after the indexes have been created.

■ **Capturing, analyzing, and replaying SQL Profiler traces.**

■ Practice 1: Create and run a SQL Profiler trace using the SQLProfilerTSQL_Duration template. Run a number of different queries in the SQL Query Analyzer, and then evaluate them in SQL Profiler, determining which queries run the longest.

■ Practice 2: Create and run a new SQL Profiler trace using the SQLProfilerTSQL template. Add the Execution Plan event class to this trace, and evaluate the same queries that were run in Practice 1 for execution plans. Try to determine from the execution plan why one query produces a longer duration than another query.

■ Practice 3: Create and run a new SQL Profiler trace with the SQLProfilerTSQL_Replay template. Open a new SQL Query Analyzer instance and run a number of queries. Save the trace to a trace file. Using the SQL Profiler, replay the trace, stepping through the statements one at a time.

Further Reading

This section lists supplemental readings by objective. Study these sources thoroughly before taking exam 70-229.

Objective 5.1

In Part 1, read and complete the practices in Lesson 1, Chapter 14, "Maintaining and Optimizing SQL Server Database."

Microsoft SQL Server 2000 product documentation. To access Books Online (BOL), click the Start button, point to Programs, then Microsoft SQL Server, and then click Books Online. Click the Contents tab, double-click "Optimizing Database Performance," and review "Query Tuning." Also, click the Contents tab and double-click the "Using the SQL Server" topic. Then review "SQL Query Analyzer Help" under "User Interface Reference."

Objective 5.2

In Part 1, read and complete the practices in Lesson 1, Chapter 14, "Maintaining and Optimizing SQL Server Database."

Microsoft SQL Server 2000 product documentation. To access Books Online, click the Start button, point to Programs, then Microsoft SQL Server, and then click Books Online. Click the Contents tab, and double-click the "Administering SQL Server" topic. Then review "Evaluating Performance" under "Monitoring Server Performance and Activity."

Objective 5.3

In Part 1, read and complete the practices in Lessons 1 and 2, Chapter 11, "Implementing Indexes."

Microsoft SQL Server 2000 product documentation. To access Books Online, click the Start button, point to Programs, then Microsoft SQL Server, and then click Books Online. Click the Contents tab, and double-click the "Creating and Maintaining Databases" topic. Then review "Designing an Index" under "Indexes."

Objective 5.4

In Part 1, read and complete the practices in Lessons 1 and 2, Chapter 11, "Implementing Indexes."

Microsoft SQL Server 2000 product documentation. To access Books Online, click the Start button, point to Programs, then Microsoft SQL Server, and then click Books Online. Click the Contents tab, and double-click the "Creating and Maintaining Databases" topic. Select "Index Tuning Wizard" and review "Indexes" under the "Designing an Index" topic.

Objective 5.5

In Part 1, read and complete the practices in Lesson 1, Chapter 14, "Maintaining and Optimizing SQL Server Database."

Microsoft SQL Server 2000 product documentation. To access Books Online, click the Start button, point to Programs, then Microsoft SQL Server, and then click Books Online. Click the Contents tab, and review the "Administering SQL Server" topic. Then review "Evaluating Performance" under "Monitoring SQL Server Performance and Activity."

OBJECTIVE 5.1

Analyze the query execution plan.

The **SQL Query Analyzer** produces a graphical representation of the execution plan of a specific query or group of queries. Understanding and analyzing this plan is your best method to ensure that your application is fast, accurate, and scalable. This analysis should be done more than just once. You should do it when you create the query, against a test database of a size that will reflect your production database, and then at larger sizes to understand what will happen as more data is acquired.

There are many things to look for in the analysis of the plan. Even though an index has been used by the optimizer, creating another, more selective, index might provide better performance. Evaluate your query for unnecessary table scans, for sorts that can be eliminated with the creation of another index, and for bookmarks that indicate that the optimizer needs to go back to the clustered index or heap table to cover the query.

You can also use the analyzer to evaluate the difference between alternate approaches; the SQL Query Analyzer will indicate what percentage of the entire batch optimization cost is allocated to each part of the batch.

The SQL Query Analyzer can also produce a server trace, a client trace, and other statistics, and it can be used to execute queries directly against a database. There are also tools for browsing the database objects, and for debugging code directly in the analyzer.

Objective 5.1 Questions

70-229.05.01.001

You run a query in the SQL Query Analyzer with the Show Execution Plan option enabled, and the following execution plan is displayed. The Orders table has a unique clustered index on the OrderID primary key, and a nonclustered index on the CustomerID column. The Customers table has only a unique clustered index on the CustomerID primary key. Why has the optimizer selected to do a sort on the Orders?

Examine the execution plan below.

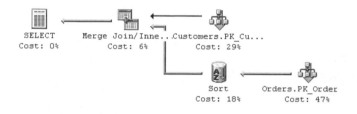

A. The optimizer has determined that a merge join would be the optimal method to retrieve this data. Because merge joins require both inputs to be in sorted order, it has added a sort operation to put the Orders table in CustomerID order, and it is using the CustomerID index on the Customers table, which will return the rows in CustomerID order as well.

B. Only merge joins can be used with clustered indexes.

C. Using an outer join will always force a merge join to be used.

D. Merge joins are the default join algorithms used by the SQL Server optimizer, unless you specify another type with a join hint in the query.

70-229.05.01.002

You run the following two queries in the same SQL Query Analyzer window with the Show Execution Plan option enabled. The following execution plan indicates that the first query's cost is 29.89 percent, relative to the batch cost of both queries. The Orders table has a unique clustered index on the OrderID primary key and a nonclustered index on the CustomerID column. The Customers table has only a unique clustered index on the CustomerID primary key. Why has the optimizer selected two different query plans when the joins are the same and there is no WHERE clause?

```
SELECT Customers.CompanyName, Orders.OrderID
FROM Customers LEFT OUTER JOIN Orders
ON Customers.CustomerID = Orders.CustomerID
SELECT *
FROM Customers LEFT OUTER JOIN Orders
ON Customers.CustomerID = Orders.CustomerID
```

Examine the execution plans below.

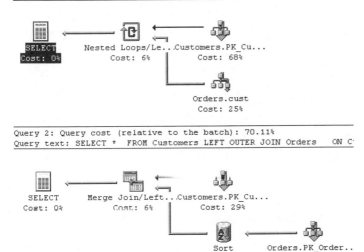

Query 1: Query cost (relative to the batch): 29.89%
Query text: SELECT Customers.CompanyName, Orders.OrderID   FROM Cus

Query 2: Query cost (relative to the batch): 70.11%
Query text: SELECT *   FROM Customers LEFT OUTER JOIN Orders   ON C

A. The optimizer has determined that a merge join would be the optimal method to retrieve this data. Because merge joins require both inputs to be in sorted order, it has added a sort operation to put the Orders table in CustomerID order, and it is using the CustomersID index on the Customers table, which will return the rows in CustomerID order as well.

B. Only merge joins can be used with clustered indexes.

C. Using an outer join will always force a merge join to be used.

D. Merge joins are the default join algorithms used by the SQL Server optimizer, unless you specify another type with a join hint in the query.

70-229.05.01.003

You run the following query in the Northwind database. On the Orders table there is a clustered index on the OrderID and a nonclustered index on the OrderDate columns. On the Customers table there is only a clustered index on the CustomerID. When the query is run, the following execution plan is displayed. (Please note that this assumes there is no index in the Northwind database on the OrderDate column.)

```
SELECT EmployeeID FROM Orders JOIN Customers
ON Orders.CustomerID = Customers.CustomerID
WHERE OrderDate > '01/15/1997'
```

Why is a bookmark being used in this plan?

Examine the execution plans below.

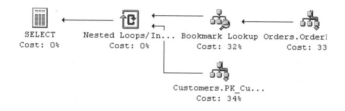

A. Because the EmployeeID is not included in the nonclustered index used to limit the results, the optimizer must use a bookmark to look up this value from the clustered index.

B. The nested loops join requires a sorted input, so the bookmark is used to look up the value of the EmployeeID from the clustered index.

C. The bookmark marks the place of each iteration through the nested loop.

70-229.05.01.004

You have noticed that some of the queries on a system are running longer than they used to. You know that statistics are important for ensuring that the optimizer can select the optimal index. How can you determine when the statistics were last updated for a particular index? (Choose all that apply.)

A. Use the SET STATISTICS IO command.

B. Run the DBCC SHOW_STATISTICS command for the index, and evaluate the UPDATE column for the last time the statistics were updated on the index.

C. Use the STATS_DATE system function to return the date an index was last updated.

D. Use the system-stored procedure sp_statistics against the table.

Objective 5.1 Answers

70-229.05.01.001

▶ **Correct Answers: A**

A. **Correct:** The optimizer has selected a merge join, which requires the input from both sides to be in sorted order. It has selected to use the clustered index of each table because we have requested all the columns to be returned. Because there are no indexes other than the clustered index that contain all the column data, the optimizer considers it to be faster to retrieve all of the data from the clustered index on the Orders table, and then sort it in CustomerID order as an input to the merge join.

B. **Incorrect:** All of the three different join algorithms can be used with clustered indexes.

C. **Incorrect:** Although the optimizer in the join algorithm selection considers the join type, it does not require a merge join.

D. **Incorrect:** There is no default join algorithm for the optimizer that will always be used unless indicated otherwise.

70-229.05.01.002

▶ **Correct Answers: A**

A. **Correct:** The optimizer has selected a merge join, which requires the input from both sides to be in sorted order. It has selected to use the clustered index of each table because we have requested all of the columns to be returned. Because there are no indexes other than the clustered index that contain all of the column data, the optimizer considers it to be faster to retrieve all of the data from the clustered index on the Orders table, and then sort it in CustomerID order as an input to the merge join.

B. **Incorrect:** All of the three different join algorithms can be used with clustered indexes.

C. **Incorrect:** Although the optimizer in the join algorithm selection considers the join type, it does not require a merge join.

D. **Incorrect:** There is no default join algorithm for the optimizer that will always be used unless indicated otherwise.

70-229.05.01.003

▶ **Correct Answers: A**

A. **Correct:** The nonclustered index on OrderDate is being used to limit the rows to those that meet the criteria. Because the EmployeeID column is not included in the nonclustered index, the EmployeeID must be pulled from the clustered index. The optimizer uses a bookmark to look up this value in the clustered index.

B. **Incorrect:** A nested loops join does not require a sorted input, and the bookmark is not needed to support the nested loops join.

C. **Incorrect:** A nested loops join does iterate through one input to the join, but the bookmark is not used to mark the place in this iteration. It indicates that data has to be retrieved from the clustered index, because it is not available in the selected index used for the criteria limitation.

70-229.05.01.004

▶ **Correct Answers: B and C**

A. **Incorrect:** The SET STATISTICS IO command will show the physical and logical reads for a SQL statement. It will not show any information about index statistics.

B. **Correct:** The DBCC SHOW_STATISTICS command will display a great deal of information about the distribution statistics for a particular index, including the last date the statistics were updated.

C. **Correct:** The STATS_DATE system function will show the date an index was last updated.

D. **Incorrect:** The system-stored procedure sp_statistics will display a list of all of the indexes and statistics for a table or indexed view, but will not display the date the statistics were last updated.

Capture, analyze, and replay SQL Profiler traces.

The SQL Profiler captures a number of events and data about these events in a file that can be used to analyze or replay these events. This tool provides the best information on what is actually happening on the server. Trace information can be captured to files as well as to SQL tables, which allows queries to be run against the data for further analysis.

There are other methods of capturing data from the server as well. Trace flags can be set to capture information, such as deadlocks, and these can be output to an error log or a trace file. Customized traces can also be created to meet custom requirements. All of the data columns and events that are available in the SQL Profiler tool can be programmatically captured in a trace created in the SQL Query Analyzer. The trace option TRACE_PRODUCE_BLACKBOX is one of the trace options that can be set when creating a custom trace. This is the equivalent of the Flight Recorder that was available in SQL Server 7.0, and it will record the last 5 MB of trace information.

SQL Profiler traces can degrade server performance, so care should be taken to use the SQL Profiler appropriately.

Objective 5.2 Questions

70-229.05.02.001

SQL Profiler can perform many functions for monitoring SQL Server activity and performance. Which of the following functions can SQL Profiler perform? (Choose all that apply.)

A. Show a textual execution plan for queries that are run against a server.

B. Show a graphical execution plan for queries that are run against a server.

C. Capture when information is written to the transaction log.

D. Capture when the database and log files autogrow.

70-229.05.02.002

You need to determine whether a stored procedure is taking more than a second when it is run under load in your test environment. You want to be sure that a minimal amount of data is being captured in the SQL Profiler trace to ensure that performance is not being degraded. Which of the following SQL Profiler trace event classes and filters will provide you with the minimal information needed to determine whether this procedure ever runs longer than 1 second?

A. You run a trace with the SP:Completed and SQL:BatchCompleted event classes and keep the remaining default settings.

B. You run a trace with the SP:Starting event class, add a filter to capture only events with TextData such as the name of the stored procedure, and keep the remaining default settings.

C. You run a trace with the SP:Completed event class, add a filter to capture only events with TextData such as the name of the stored procedure, and remove all data columns allowed except the Duration data column.

D. You run a trace with the SP:Completed event class, add a filter to capture only events with TextData such as the name of the stored procedure, remove all data columns allowed except the Duration data column, and add a filter to capture only events with a duration greater than 1 second.

70-229.05.02.003

You would like to have a trace captured on a machine and then replay that trace on a test machine. Which of the following event classes will you need to capture to be able to replay the trace if no cursors are being used? (Choose all that apply.)

A. Audit Login

B. Audit Logout

C. Existing Connection

D. RPC:Starting

E. SQL:BatchStarting

70-229.05.02.004

You have been sent a trace that was created with enough information to replay in the SQL Profiler, and you need to analyze the trace for long-running events. Which of the following methods can best be used to see only the events with duration greater than 5 seconds, grouped by the SPID?

A. Open the trace and, on the Data Columns tab of the Trace Properties dialog box, add the duration data column to the Selected Data list, and add a filter for any duration greater than 5 seconds.

B. Open the trace and, on the Data Columns tab of the Trace Properties dialog box, add the SPID data column to the Selected Data list, and add a filter for any duration greater than 5 seconds.

C. Open the trace and, on the Data Columns tab of the Trace Properties dialog box, add the SPID and Duration data columns to the Selected Data list.

70-229.05.02.005

You have a reporting server that supports ad hoc queries against the database, and you need to determine the usage of one of the major tables. You would like to be able to find the number of times that the table is accessed within a day and keep this data in such a way that it can be analyzed later in Microsoft Excel or Microsoft Access. How might you best accomplish this?

A. Create a trace with the SQL:StmtStarting event class and the TextData data column included, and set a filter to capture only events in which the TextData data column contains the table name. Set the trace stop time for 24 hours later. When the trace is completed, save it to a trace table.

B. Create a trace with the SQL:BatchStarting and SP:Starting events and the TextData data column included. Set the trace stop time for 24 hours later.

C. Create a trace with the SQL:BatchStarting and SP:Starting class events and the TextData data column included and set a filter to capture only events in which the ObjectName contains the table name. Set the trace stop time for 24 hours later.

Objective 5.2 Answers

70-229.05.02.001

▶ **Correct Answers: A, C, and D**

A. **Correct:** By adding the Execution Plan event class from the Performance event category, a textual execution plan can be captured in the SQL Profiler trace.

B. **Incorrect:** The SQL Profiler cannot show a graphical execution plan, as in the SQL Query Analyzer.

C. **Correct:** Adding the TransactionLog event class from the Transactions event category will capture when data is written to the transaction log.

D. **Correct:** Adding the Data File Auto Grow and the Log File Auto Grow event classes from the Database event category will capture data about when these events occur.

70-229.05.02.002

▶ **Correct Answers: D**

A. **Incorrect:** The SP:Completed event class is needed for the stored procedure event capture, but the SQL:BatchCompleted class will capture T-SQL commands as well. Because no filter has been applied, all instances of the stored procedure would be captured, not just those with a duration greater than 1 second.

B. **Incorrect:** Although the SP:Starting event class will capture the stored procedure event, and the filter will allow only the stored procedure event you want, duration data is captured. The duration data can be captured only on completion of an event, not the start. You would also need to add a filter to capture only instances of the stored procedure execution that exceed 1 second.

C. **Incorrect:** This proposed solution will produce a very small trace, capturing only the duration, system process ID (SPID), and event class for the stored procedure. However, because there is no filter on duration, it will not limit the instances with execution times greater than 1 second.

D. **Correct:** This proposed solution will produce the smallest amount of data for this scenario, and it will capture only the events of the stored procedure that have a duration greater than 1 second. Because the trace is so small, you can be fairly sure that the profiling itself is not interfering with the server performance.

70-229.05.02.003

▶ **Correct Answers: A, B, C, D, and E**

A. **Correct:** The Audit Login event class will capture all of the connection data needed to connect the trace when it is replayed. This event is required.

B. **Correct:** The Audit Logout event class will capture all of the disconnection data needed to disconnect the trace when it is replayed, and it should be included to complete a trace completely.

C. **Correct:** The ExistingConnection event is needed to ensure that events are captured for events occurring on connections already open on the server once the trace capture is started.

D. **Correct:** The RPC:Starting event class is needed to capture stored procedures that are executed from a client using an RPC mechanism.

E. **Correct:** The SQL:BatchStarting event class will capture any Transact-SQL batch data needed to replay these events.

70-229.05.02.004

▶ **Correct Answers: B**

A. **Incorrect:** This will cause the data to be grouped by the duration column, not the SPID column, but it will filter out any event with duration greater than 5 seconds.

B. **Correct:** This proposed solution will group the data by SPID and filter out any events except those with a duration greater than 5 seconds. This will also make the trace file smaller and easier to manage and analyze.

C. **Incorrect:** This proposed solution will group the data by both SPID and Duration, not just by SPID, and all events, regardless of duration, will be included.

70-229.05.02.005

▶ **Correct Answers: A**

A. **Correct:** The SQL:StmtStarting event will be captured for all SQL statements, not just the start of a batch. By filtering the TextData data column for occurrences that contain the table name, only the actual statements that include the table name will be captured. Saving the trace file to a SQL Server table allows it to be analyzed more easily because queries can be run against the table, and it can be accessed with Excel or Access.

B. **Incorrect:** The SQL:BatchStarting event with the TextData data column will give you every Transact SQL statement and stored procedure sent to the server and will not capture usage only of the main table. SQL:BatchStarting does not capture every SQL statement, only the start of a batch. It does not provide a good mechanism for analyzing in Excel or Access.

C. **Incorrect:** The ObjectName data column is not populated by the SQL:BatchStarting and SP:Starting events, so the filter will not be used, and all events will be captured. SQL:BatchStarting does not capture every SQL statement, only the start of a batch. This approach does not provide a good mechanism for analyzing in Excel or Access.

O B J E C T I V E   5 . 3

Create and implement indexing strategies.

Optimal index design is critical for query performance in SQL Server. There are many things to consider when designing indexes, and care should be taken to re-evaluate indexes on a database as data and queries change.

Every table in a database can have one **clustered index** and as many **nonclustered indexes** as needed. Determining which columns should be indexed with a clustered index can be considered an art. In the Enterprise Edition of SQL Server, indexes can also be created on views, providing excellent performance for often-used, complex queries.

Considerations for creating and implementing indexes include:

- Clustered indexes

- Nonclustered indexes

- Covering indexes

- Indexed views

- Statistics

Objective 5.3 Questions

70-229.05.03.001

You are designing an indexing strategy for your database and are evaluating clustered index placement. Which of the following situations can be considered good candidates for a clustered index? (Choose all that apply.)

A. Columns that contain a small number of distinct values, such as Gender

B. Columns that are frequently changed

C. Primary keys

D. Queries that will return a large range of values, such as from a BETWEEN clause

70-229.05.03.002

You are designing an indexing strategy for your database and are evaluating nonclustered index placement. Which of the following situations can be considered good candidates for a nonclustered index? (Choose all that apply.)

A. Foreign keys

B. All of the columns that are commonly accessed by a query

C. A column with a few unique values

D. Queries that return a small number of results

70-229.05.03.003

You have a database system that has been running for quite some time, with a large amount of inserts. There are a number of nonclustered indexes and a clustered index on all of the main large tables. Over time, you see that inserts are slowing down. What could you do to enhance insert performance on the large tables?

A. Using SQL Enterprise Manager, set the fill factor option to a smaller number for all of the existing indexes.

B. Drop the existing indexes and rebuild them with a smaller fill factor.

C. Run DBCC INDEXDEFRAG.

Objective 5.3 Answers

70-229.05.03.001

► **Correct Answers: C and D**

A. **Incorrect:** Generally a clustered index is wasted on a column with a very small number of unique values because the optimizer might find it less expensive to do a table scan than use an index. A better choice is a column with a large number of distinct values.

B. **Incorrect:** Columns that are frequently changed are especially bad candidates for a clustered index because all nonclustered indexes use a clustered index key as their identifier, so changing the value of a clustering key requires any nonclustered indexes to be rebuilt. Also, the data must be kept in physical order in a clustered index, so changing data in a clustered column might require the entire row to be physically moved. There are obviously large performance penalties for this.

C. **Correct:** Because primary keys are often used in joins and often require fast single-row lookups in online transaction processing (OLTP) systems, a clustered index on a primary key can be advantageous, especially if the primary key is a small surrogate key. If there is no compelling reason to put a clustered index on another column, a good default strategy is to put the index on the primary key.

D. **Correct:** Queries that return a large range of values will be in physical order if there is a clustered index on that column, so this is a good candidate for a clustered index.

70-229.05.03.002

► **Correct Answers: A, B, and D**

A. **Correct:** A foreign key column is often used in a join, so this makes a good candidate for a nonclustered index. Because merge joins require sorted input, including a nonclustered index on foreign keys can help ensure that the optimizer can consider a merge join as a possible inexpensive option.

B. **Correct:** This is called a "covering index," and it will allow a query to access only the nonclustered index without having to read data from the clustered index, eliminating accessing both the index and the main data.

C. **Incorrect:** Columns with a few unique values are not good candidates for any index because it is generally cheaper for the optimizer to do a table scan than to use an index in this situation.

D. **Correct:** Queries that do not return a large number of results are good candidates for nonclustered indexes. Because there is a good possibility that the data page will need to be accessed as well in combination with the index when a nonclustered index is used, retrieving small result sets will not cause performance problems.

70-229.05.03.003

▶ **Correct Answers: B**

A. **Incorrect:** Although setting the fill factor to a smaller value would probably be a good strategy for a table with many inserts, only when an index is created is the new fill factor followed. Changing the fill factor on all of the existing indexes will not produce smaller numbers of page splits.

B. **Correct:** Changing a fill factor is useful only when an index is created, so dropping and re-creating indexes with a smaller fill factor will leave more space open on each page. A system with a large number of inserts will therefore cause fewer page splits with a smaller fill factor.

C. **Incorrect:** The DBCC INDEXDEFRAG command will defragment and compact data and index pages, taking into account the original fill factor of the indexes when they were created. However, it cannot be used to change the fill factor so that more space is available on data and index pages as inserts are performed.

OBJECTIVE 5.4

Improve index use by using the Index Tuning Wizard.

The Index Tuning Wizard can be used to suggest and create optimal indexes for a database. The wizard can be run against a workload or against a query inside the SQL Query Analyzer. It can be used to script suggested indexes for later implementation, or it can create the indexes immediately. The Index Tuning Wizard is quite flexible in the configuration settings offered, can be run for a fast, intermediate, or thorough analysis, and can include indexed views. It also can consume CPU time and cause performance degradation, so it should be used during non-peak-usage times. Also, any index changes to a system should be thoroughly tested before implemented.

The Index Tuning Wizard can perform the following functions:

- Identify the servers and database to tune

- Identify a workload to analyze

- Select tables to tune

- Analyze the data and make index recommendations

- Implement the index recommendations

- Recommend indexes to be dropped if they are not used

Objective 5.4 Questions

70-229.05.04.001

You have a database application that has been running for about six months, and there have been no changes to the indexes since their creation. What should you do to help ensure that the optimal indexes have been created, and that indexes that are not being used are dropped?

A. Create a trace in SQL Profiler to capture an appropriately sized workload and run the Index Tuning Wizard against this workload.

B. Drop all existing indexes and run the Index Tuning Wizard against each of the common queries in the SQL Query Analyzer.

C. Create a small test database with a small number of rows for each table. Run the Index Tuning Wizard against this test database, and then implement the recommendations on the production server.

D. Run the Index Tuning Wizard against an appropriate workload created in the SQL Profiler with the Keep All Existing Indexes check box selected.

70-229.05.04.002

Which of the following will the Index Tuning Wizard not make recommendation on? (Choose all that apply.)

A. Primary key constraints

B. System tables

C. Queries that refer to tables in another database

D. Unique indexes

70-229.05.04.003

The Index Tuning Wizard can help optimize index usage. Which of the following are features of the Index Tuning Wizard? (Choose all that apply.)

A. Analyze a trace that was previously created in SQL Profiler.

B. The UI offers an option to limit the number of queries that are optimized.

C. The UI offers an option to limit the amount of memory used by the wizard.

D. Generate a script to create the recommended indexes for future use.

70-229.05.04.004

Which of the following will not be included for analysis by the Index Tuning Wizard? (Choose all that apply.)

A. Query, table, and index hints

B. Queries with quoted identifiers

C. Queries on a SQL Server 6.5 system

Objective 5.4 Answers

70-229.05.04.001

▶ **Correct Answers: A**

    A. **Correct:** The Index Tuning Wizard will recommend indexes to be created and indicate those that are not being used from a workload created in SQL Profiler. The larger the workload, the better chance that the analysis will be optimal.

    B. **Incorrect:** Dropping all indexes is a drastic approach, and indexes should not be dropped without understanding the consequences for query performance. It would take a long time to run the Index Tuning Wizard against every individual query, and this does not provide the most accurate information because a single query run by itself does not provide an accurate picture of what else might be happening on the server at the same time.

    C. **Incorrect:** The Index Tuning Wizard might not recommend an index if a table has too few rows, just as the optimizer might not use an index if there are too few rows. This is not a good strategy because the test database will not provide an accurate picture of the database for the Index Tuning Wizard.

    D. **Incorrect:** Although the workload will give the Index Tuning Wizard a good reference for recommending indexes to be created, it will not recommend any to be dropped if the Keep Existing Indexes check box is selected. Therefore, unnecessary work might be performed to keep unneeded indexes up to date.

70-229.05.04.002

▶ **Correct Answers: A, B, C, and D**

    A. **Correct:** The Index Tuning Wizard will not make a recommendation on a primary key constraint. Generally, you should always have some kind of index on a primary key constraint because this is a column that will be used often for joins and will always benefit from some kind of index, whether clustered or nonclustered.

    B. **Correct:** Indexes should not usually be generated against system tables by users, so the Index Tuning Wizard will not consider these in its analyses.

    C. **Correct:** The Index Tuning Wizard recommendation scope is only within the current database, so recommendations will not be made for an index on a table in another database, even if it is used within a query being analyzed.

    D. **Correct:** The Index Tuning Wizard will not include unique indexes in its analysis.

70-229.05.04.003

▶ **Correct Answers: A, B, and D**

   A. **Correct:** A workload that was created by monitoring a server with SQL Profiler can be saved to a trace file and then put into the Index Tuning Wizard. Capturing a full workload that exercises all the queries in a system can provide excellent information for tuning a system's queries and indexes.

   B. **Correct:** One of the advanced options in the Index Tuning Wizard is an option to limit the number of queries that the wizard will analyze.

   C. **Incorrect:** There is no option to limit the amount of memory used by the Index Tuning Wizard.

   D. **Correct:** One of the features of the Index Tuning Wizard is the option to either execute the recommendations immediately or save them to a script to be further analyzed. It is recommended to never automatically execute the Index Tuning Wizard on a production server.

70-229.05.04.004

▶ **Correct Answers: B and C**

   A. **Incorrect:** Query, table, and index hints are evaluated, but they will always be included in the Index Tuning Wizard and can actually cause the wizard to choose suboptimal indexes. It is best to remove hints before running the wizard.

   B. **Correct:** The Index Tuning Wizard will not evaluate queries with quoted identifiers set on.

   C. **Correct:** The Index Tuning Wizard cannot evaluate SQL Server 6.5 queries.

Monitor and troubleshoot database activity by using SQL Profiler.

The SQL Profiler is an excellent tool for auditing a SQL Server database. Security events, scheduled jobs, login failures, transaction log writes, and database and log file growth are some of the many events that can be monitored for both performance and security reasons. Auditing can be customized as needed and can be extensive enough to conform to the C2 auditing standards.

Operations that can cause performance problems can also be monitored, such as memory changes, large sorts, deadlocks, logical reads, physical writes, and DBCCs run during peak performance hours.

User activity can also be monitored, including determining the host name, application name, and Microsoft Windows NT domain name of logged-on users. The time that activities occur as well as the duration can also be monitored. SQL Profiler can also monitor errors, including severity.

Objective 5.5 Questions

70-229.05.05.001

Your corporation has policies in place that do not allow any administrative work to take place during the daytime hours. You think that someone might be granting permissions on objects during the day. You would like to determine whether object permissions are being granted during the day, and if so, as much information about the user as possible. Which is the best method to accomplish this?

A. You create a SQL Profiler trace that includes the SQL:BatchStarting event class, and includes the NTUserName and LoginName data columns.

B. You create a SQL Profiler trace that includes all of the Security Audit event classes, and only the TextData, SPID, and EventClass data columns.

C. You create a SQL Profiler trace that includes the Audit Object GDR Event event class and includes the NTUserName, LoginName, and StartTime data columns.

70-229.05.05.002

You receive a report that an application starts performing poorly when a large number of users are connected. You suspect that there might be transactions that have been left open for too long, because either queries are taking too long to complete, or user interaction is being requested in the middle of a transaction. What methods can you use to determine whether blocking is occurring in the database or transactions are being held open too long? (Choose all that apply.)

A. Run the system-stored procedure sp_who on the server every few seconds, and look in the BLK column of the result set for any incidence of a blocking SPID.

B. Run the DBCC OPENTRAN command every few seconds.

C. Run the SQL Profiler and capture the Lock:Deadlock event, grouping by SPID.

D. Run the SQL Profiler and capture the event classes in the Transaction event category and the command being run, and then group the events by the Duration data column.

70-229.05.05.003

You have a large database application that uses many stored procedures. Whenever the server is rebooted, the system will run a bit more slowly, because each of the stored procedures is compiled before the execution plan. The application then tends to run faster. However, a certain number of stored procedures never seem to run faster. What is the best approach to determine whether these stored procedures are reusing a cached execution plan?

A. Run a SQL Profiler trace to capture the SP:Completed event grouped by the Duration data column.

B. Run a SQL Profiler trace capturing the SP:CacheHit, SP:CacheMiss, and SP:ExecContextHit events.

C. Run the system-stored procedure sp_recompile against all of the stored procedures.

70-229.05.05.004

You have an application that is occasionally returning error message 1205, indicating that a deadlock has occurred and that the process has been chosen as the deadlock victim. Which of the following troubleshooting methods can you use to determine what query might be producing the deadlock? (Choose all that apply.)

A. Add the 1204 trace flag to the startup options of the server to capture deadlock information and output it to the error log. Restart the server.

B. Run the DBCC TRACEON (1204) command to capture deadlock information (trace flag 1204).

C. Capture the Lock:Deadlock and Lock:Deadlock Chain events in SQL Profiler.

D. Run the sp_lock system-stored procedure.

Objective 5.5 Answers

70-229.05.05.001

▶ **Correct Answers: C**

   A. **Incorrect:** The SQL:BatchStarting event class will capture the start of all SQL batches, which is too much information. The NTUserName and LoginName data columns will indicate the user information, but will not provide the time of the permissions statements.

   B. **Incorrect:** Capturing all of the Security Audit events will capture too much information, and there are no data columns for the user or the time of the event.

   C. **Correct:** The Audit Object GDR Event event class will capture events that occur when a GRANT, DENY, or REVOKE permission is made against an object. The NTUserName and LoginName data columns will indicate who is performing the operation, and the StartTime data column will show the time of the start of the permission event.

70-229.05.05.002

▶ **Correct Answers: A, B, and D**

   A. **Correct:** Although this is a very simple method, it is a quick way to determine whether a connection is blocking another connection for a long period of time. The SPID identified in the BLK column will indicate the offending connection, which can then be further examined.

   B. **Correct:** The DBCC OPENTRAN command will return information about the oldest open transaction in the database. If DBCC OPENTRAN continuously returns the same transaction as being open, there is a good possibility that something is holding the transaction open too long and should be investigated.

   C. **Incorrect:** Capturing a deadlock can be helpful for troubleshooting, but it won't provide enough information to find a long-running transaction or blocking, because it will capture events that are caused by a deadlock, a special kind of locking situation that might never occur in the database.

   D. **Correct:** The Transaction events grouped by Duration will provide information on the longest-running transaction, and include the SPID. This can then be used to further investigate the offending queries.

70-229.05.05.003

▶ **Correct Answers: B**

A. **Incorrect:** The SP:Completed event grouped by the Duration data column will show the longest-running stored procedure, which would not be helpful for determining execution plan reuse.

B. **Correct:** Capturing the cache hit, cache miss, and execution context hit events can help determine whether a stored procedure is being found in the cache and whether the execution plan is therefore reused.

C. **Incorrect:** The sp_recompile system-stored procedure will cause a stored procedure to be recompiled the next time it is executed. It will not provide any information about execution plan reuse or producer recompilation.

70-229.05.05.004

▶ **Correct Answers: A, B, and C**

A. **Correct:** The 1204 trace flag will capture deadlock information and output it to the SQL Server error log. Once the server is restarted, any deadlocks will be captured, and information determining the SPIDs involved, and other diagnostic information, will be output as well. You can then use this information to evaluate the troublesome code.

B. **Correct:** The 1204 trace flag will capture deadlock information. With this DBCC command, the server does not need to be restarted. The SQL error log can then be examined for deadlock output and the offending queries investigated and corrected.

C. **Correct:** The SQL Profiler can capture deadlock information when it occurs, and these traces can then be evaluated to determine which processes are involved, and what the query running at the time was doing.

D. **Incorrect:** The sp_lock system-stored procedure provides a great deal of valuable information on locking that is occurring on the database, including the lock type and the resources locked. However, it will not provide troubleshooting information about deadlocks.

OBJECTIVE DOMAIN 6

Designing a Database Security Plan

Microsoft SQL Server 2000 supports one of two security modes: Windows Authentication Mode (Windows Authentication) or Mixed Mode (Windows Authentication and SQL Server Authentication).

Windows Authentication Mode allows users to connect using Microsoft Windows NT 4 or Windows 2000 user accounts.

Mixed Mode Authentication allows users to connect using Microsoft Windows NT 4 or Windows 2000 user accounts or using SQL Server built-in authentication. SQL Server Authentication is provided only for backward compatibility.

When a blank login name is used for a SQL Server connection, SQL Server uses Windows Authentication. Windows Authentication has certain benefits over SQL Authentication primarily because of its integration with the Windows NT 4 and Windows 2000 operating system.

A SQL Server security system has two parts: access validation and permissions. Access validation includes the two security modes of SQL Server: Windows Authentication Mode or Mixed Mode. Permissions include object access permissions, such as INSERT, UPDATE, and DELETE, and object manipulation permissions, such as CREATE, ALTER, and DROP. SQL Server 2000 also introduced application security and application roles. Application security can be used to restrict users to access data only through a specific application, for example, Microsoft Excel. **Application roles** allow the application to take over the responsibility of user authentication.

Tested Skills and Suggested Practices

The skills that you need to successfully master the Designing a Database Security Plan objective on the *Designing and Implementing Databases with Microsoft SQL Server 2000 Enterprise Edition* exam include:

- **Controlling object access with GRANT and REVOKE.**

  - Practice 1: Create different user IDs.

  - Practice 2: Manage and modify user IDs.

  - Practice 3: Grant permissions to view and review the effects.

- **Controlling data access by using stored procedures, triggers, and user-defined functions.**

  - Practice 1: Create a stored procedure, grant user rights on it, and look at the behavior when you try to access it with different user IDs.

  - Practice 2: Create triggers and control user access with the triggers.

- **Creating and managing application roles.**

  - Practice 1: Create an application role.

  - Practice 2: Modify the application role.

Further Reading

This section lists supplemental readings by objective. Study these sources thoroughly before taking exam 70- 229.

Objective 6.1

Microsoft SQL Server 2000 product documentation. To access Books Online, click the Start button, point to Programs, then Microsoft SQL Server, and then click Books Online. Click the Contents tab and double-click the "Administering SQL Server" topic. Then review "Managing Permissions" under "Managing Security."

In Part 1, read and complete the practices in Lesson 3 in Chapter 2, "Using Transact-SQL on a SQL Server Database," Lessons 1, 2, and 3 in Chapter 8, "Implementing Stored Procedures," Lessons 1, 2, and 3 in Chapter 9, "Implementing Triggers," Lessons 1, 2, and 3 in Chapter 10, "Implementing Views," and Lessons 1, 2, and 3 in Chapter 13, "Managing SQL Server Security."

Objective 6.2

Microsoft SQL Server 2000 product documentation. To access Books Online, click the Start button, point to Programs, then Microsoft SQL Server, and then click Books Online. Click the Contents tab and double-click the "Administering SQL Server" topic. Then review "Managing Permissions" under "Managing Security."

In Part 1, read and complete the practices in Lessons 1, 2, and 3 in Chapter 13, "Managing SQL Server Security."

Objective 6.3

Microsoft SQL Server 2000 product documentation. To access Books Online, click the Start button, point to Programs, then Microsoft SQL Server, and then click Books Online. Click the Contents tab and double-click the "Administering SQL Server" topic. Then review "Advanced Security Topics" under "Managing Security."

In Part 1, read and complete the practices in Lessons 1, 2, and 3 in Chapter 13, "Managing SQL Server Security."

Control data access by using stored procedures, triggers, user-defined functions, and views.

In SQL Server 2000, the user must have sufficient rights to access and manipulate any object within the database.

Working with data or executing stored procedures requires permission. Object permissions are SELECT, INSERT, UPDATE, DELETE, and EXECUTE.

Statement permissions are activities involved in creating a database or an item in a database. Statement permissions are BACKUP DATABASE, BACKUP LOG, CREATE DATABASE, CREATE DEFAULT, CREATE FUNCTION, CREATE PROCEDURE, CREATE RULE, CREATE TABLE, and CREATE VIEW.

Permissions are managed by granting, denying, and revoking them.

GRANT allows a user to perform activities or work with data in the current database. Users can perform only the activities for which they have GRANT permission.

DENY prevents a user from performing activities or working with data in the current database and prevents the user account from inheriting permissions from other group or role memberships.

REVOKE removes the granted or denied permission only at the level revoked (user, group, or role).

Objective 6.1 Questions

70-229.06.01.001

You have a table called TABLE1 in your database. You do not want the user to access the table directly, but the user needs to insert data into the table. What can you do to fulfill this requirement? (Choose all that apply.)

A. Create a view and grant the user INSERT permission on the view.

B. Create a stored procedure and grant the user EXECUTE permission.

C. Create a stored procedure and grant the user EXECUTE and INSERT permissions.

D. You cannot fulfill this requirement.

70-229.06.01.002

In your database, you have a table with pregenerated account numbers. You do not want your users to access this table directly, but they need to be able to retrieve and remove one or more available account numbers from the table when they need them. You do not want them to execute any INSERT and UPDATE statement directly. This business logic sometimes needs to be executed as a part of a JOIN operation. How would you accomplish this?

A. Create a stored procedure and return the new account numbers.

B. Create a user-defined function and return the new account numbers.

C. You cannot fulfill this requirement.

70-229.06.01.003

You have a table called TABLE1 in your database and you are not connected to the database as the system administrator through the sa account. Why can't you set permission on a trigger for TABLE1?

A. Only the sa account can set permission on a trigger.

B. Only the creator or owner can set permission on a trigger.

C. You cannot set permission on a trigger.

70-229.06.01.004

You have OrderDetails and Products tables. You need to present the two tables as a single table using a join. You want ACCOUNTANTS to have read-only permissions, but you do not want them to access the tables directly and execute any other SELECT statements.

A. Create a view and make it perform the join. Grant SELECT permissions to ACCOUNTANTS.

B. Create two views and let ACCOUNTANTS execute a SELECT statement.

C. You cannot fulfill this requirement.

Objective 6.1 Answers

70-229.06.01.001

▶ **Correct Answers: A and B**

   A. **Correct:** If a user has been granted INSERT permission to a view, it gives the user the ability to access all underlying tables even if he or she does not have rights on that table.

   B. **Correct:** A user with EXECUTE permission on a stored procedure can accomplish work on underlying objects even if that user does not have any permission on the objects.

   C. **Incorrect:** Although creating a stored procedure and granting the user EXECUTE permission would fulfill the requirements, you cannot grant INSERT permission on a stored procedure.

   D. **Incorrect:** This requirement is easily fulfilled either by creating a view and granting INSERT permission to the user or by creating a stored procedure with EXECUTE permission for the user.

70-229.06.01.002

▶ **Correct Answers: B**

   A. **Incorrect:** Although you can implement the required business login in a stored procedure and return a result set of new account numbers, the result set cannot be used as part of a JOIN operation. To be part of a JOIN operation, you must create a user-defined function and return a table as a return value.

   B. **Correct:** Only a user-defined function can fulfill the requirements. Although a stored procedure can do the business logic, it cannot return a result set in a form that can be used in a JOIN operation.

   C. **Incorrect:** This requirement is easy to fulfill by creating a user-defined function. A user-defined function can implement the required business logic and return a table as a return value.

70-229.06.01.003

▶ **Correct Answers: C**

   A. **Incorrect:** You cannot assign permission on a trigger. You must have the appropriate permissions on the table to do the required work. If you have the appropriate permissions, the trigger will work accordingly.

   B. **Incorrect:** Triggers are part of a table and, because of that, you cannot set permission on a trigger. If you need to control access, you have to set permission on the table itself.

   C. **Correct:** You cannot set permission on a trigger. If you need to set permission, you have to set it on the table or view.

70-229.06.01.004

▶ **Correct Answers: A**

   A. **Correct:** The view can provide the join. ACCOUNTANTS do not need any permission on the tables, but they do need to have SELECT permission on the view. It will provide them with the required data, and it also prevents them from executing any query against these two tables.

   B. **Incorrect:** Although ACCOUNTANTS would be able to execute the join, they would be also able to execute other queries against these two tables. You need to provide them only with the join of these tables and not allow them to execute anything else.

   C. **Incorrect:** A view can provide the join. ACCOUNTANTS do not have to have any permission on the tables, but they do need to have SELECT permission on the view. It will provide them with the required data, and it also prevents them from executing any query against these two tables.

O B J E C T I V E   6 . 2

Define object-level security including column-level permissions by using GRANT, REVOKE, and DENY.

In SQL Server, every user must have permission to access and manipulate data in the database. These permissions are granted, revoked, and denied by using the appropriate SQL Server Transact-SQL command: GRANT, REVOKE, and DENY.

The GRANT command allows a user to perform activities or work with data in the current database. Users can perform only the activities for which they have GRANT permission. These object-level security permissions are INSERT, UPDATE, DELETE, and EXECUTE.

DENY prevents a user from performing activities or working with data in the current database and prevents the user account from inheriting permissions from other group or role memberships.

REVOKE removes the granted or denied permission only at the level revoked (user, group, or role).

In SQL Server 2000, permissions can be granted on smaller entities such as objects. You can set permissions not only on objects, but also on the columns.

Objective 6.2 Questions

70-229.06.02.001

You need to grant the SYSOPER user permission to SELECT and INSERT on Table1. You also want SYSOPER to be able to grant SELECT permission to other users with SELECT permission only. Which code block is correct?

A. ```
GRANT SYSOPER on Table1 to SELECT,INSERT

GRANT SYSOPER on Table1 to GRANT SELECT
```

B. ```
GRANT SYSOPER on Table1 to SELECT, INSERT, GRANT SELECT
```

C. ```
GRANT SELECT, INSERT on Table1 to SYSOPER WITH GRANT SELECT
```

D. ```
GRANT SELECT on Table1 to SYSOPER WITH GRANT OPTION

GRANT INSERT on Table1 to SYSOPER
```

70-229.06.02.002

You granted SELECT permissions to the PUBLIC role. You granted the MANAGERS role the permission to INSERT, UPDATE, and DELETE. You created an ACCOUNTANTS role with INSERT and UPDATE permissions. If a user is part of both ACCOUNTANTS and MANAGERS, which database operations is the user allowed?

A. The user will be able to SELECT, INSERT, and UPDATE but not to DELETE.

B. The user will be able to perform only the first granted role's permitted operations.

C. The user will be able to perform all four actions: SELECT, INSERT, UPDATE, and DELETE.

D. If a user belongs to at least one permission role other than PUBLIC, the user will not inherit the permissions of PUBLIC. Users will be able to INSERT, DELETE, and UPDATE, but not to SELECT.

70-229.06.02.003

You created table Test4 as follows:

```
CREATE TABLE Test4 (ID1 INT, ID2 INT)
GRANT SELECT (ID1) ON Test4 TO TEST
GRANT INSERT, UPDATE, DELETE ON Test4 TO Test
```

What would be the outcome if user Test executes the following code?

```
INSERT INTO Test4 (1,1)
SELECT * FROM Test4
```

A. Both INSERT and SELECT will execute successfully.

B. The INSERT statement would succeed, and the SELECT statement would fail.

C. The INSERT statement would fail, and the SELECT statement would succeed.

70-229.06.02.004

You want to prevent a user from executing an INSERT, UPDATE, or DELETE statement on a table. You want to be certain that if the user's role assignments change to a role that allows these operations, the user will still not be able to accomplish them. Which Transact-SQL command—DENY, REVOKE, or both—could accomplish this?

A. Neither command can be used to fulfill the requirements.

B. Both DENY and REVOKE could fulfill the requirements.

C. Only REVOKE can fulfill the requirements.

D. Only DENY can fulfill the requirements.

70-229.06.02.005

You do not want the ACCOUNTANTS role to have SELECT, UPDATE, and DELETE permission on the Trace table. You want to be certain if a user belongs to another role that has the right to access the Trace table, the user will still be able to do so. Which statement would accomplish this?

A. `DENY ACCOUNTANTS ON Trace TO SELECT, UPDATE, DELETE`

B. `REVOKE SELECT, UPDATE, DELETE on Trace FROM ACCOUNTANTS`

C. `REVOKE ACCOUNTANTS ON Trace TO SELECT, UPDATE, DELETE`

D. `DENY SELECT, UPDATE, DELETE ON Trace TO ACCOUNTANTS`

Objective 6.2 Answers

70-229.06.02.001

▶ **Correct Answers: D**

A. **Incorrect:** The syntax in this example is incorrect. The parameters for GRANT are first, the kind of access you want to assign, and second, the SQL Server object and to whom you are granting the rights.

B. **Incorrect:** If you want to grant a user certain rights and also enable the user to assign rights to other users, you have to do it in two separate statements.

C. **Incorrect:** Using the WITH GRANT option, you cannot specify what kind of permission the user can grant to other users. To fulfill the requirements, you have to execute two separate statements.

D. **Correct:** You must use two statements to both give a user permission to use specific commands and then to limit the user's ability to grant permission to other users to only a subset of those commands.

70-229.06.02.002

▶ **Correct Answers: C**

A. **Incorrect:** This user will inherit all permissions from all roles. If you do not want a user to have a given permission, you should revoke or deny it.

B. **Incorrect:** In SQL Server, we do not have a role that supersedes all other roles. This user will inherit all permissions from all roles.

C. **Correct:** The user will inherit the permissions from all roles. These roles cover all the required functionality.

D. **Incorrect:** The user will belong to all roles. PUBLIC is just another database role in SQL Server, such as MANAGERS and ACCOUNTANTS.

70-229.06.02.003

▶ **Correct Answers: B**

A. **Incorrect:** Test has permission to INSERT, UPDATE, and DELETE from Test4 but has only the right to SELECT from column ID1. SELECT ID1 FROM Test4 would execute successfully.

B. **Correct:** The INSERT statement would complete successfully because you granted Test INSERT, UPDATE, and DELETE permission on the whole table; however, you granted Test permission to SELECT only from ID1.

C. **Incorrect:** The INSERT statement would complete successfully because you granted Test INSERT, UPDATE, and DELETE permission on the whole table; however, you granted Test permission to SELECT only from ID1. SELECT ID1 FROM Test4 would execute successfully.

70-229.06.02.004

▶ **Correct Answers: D**

A. **Incorrect:** You can fulfill the requirement with the Transact-SQL command DENY.

B. **Incorrect:** DENY could prevent the user from inheriting permission through a group or role. REVOKE could remove only the previously granted or denied permission but would not affect inherited permissions.

C. **Incorrect:** REVOKE removes the previously granted or denied permission from the current user; it does not prevent the user from inheriting permission through a group or role.

D. **Correct:** DENY creates a record in the security system in the current database and prevents the user from inheriting permission through a group or role.

70-229.06.02.005

▶ **Correct Answers: B**

A. **Incorrect:** DENY could prevent the ACCOUNTANTS from having SELECT, UPDATE, and DELETE permissions on Trace, but it would also disable them from accessing Trace even if other roles would allow them to do so. The syntax of the statement is also incorrect.

B. **Correct:** This statement would prevent access on the object level, but it would not change the behavior of the inherited permissions.

C. **Incorrect:** Although REVOKE is the right command to achieve the desired permissions, the syntax of the statement is incorrect.

D. **Incorrect:** Although the statement syntax is correct, the statement would pose a more strict access control than was required. DENY would prevent the ACCOUNTANTS from having SELECT, UPDATE, and DELETE permissions on Trace, but it would also disable them from accessing Trace even if other roles would allow them.

OBJECTIVE 6.3

Create and manage application roles.

An application role is a new functionality in SQL Server 2000. It provides a way to restrict access to a database through a specific application. When an application role is activated for a connection by the application, the connection loses all permissions applied for the connection, including login, user account, roles, and so on. The connection gains the permissions associated with the application role. Application roles are applicable only to the database in which they exist. If an application using an application role needs to access another database, it must do so through the guest account. If a user by default would not have permission to access a table but the application needs to access the table to execute properly, the user permission will be overridden by the application permissions and the user will be able to access the table.

Application roles allow the application, rather than SQL Server, to manage user authentication. However, SQL Server still needs to authenticate the application when it accesses the database, so the application must provide a password to authenticate itself.

If ad hoc access to the database is not required, Windows NT 4 users and Windows 2000 users and groups do not need to be granted any permissions because all permissions can be assigned by the applications they use to access the database.

There are several options for managing application role passwords without hard-coding them into applications. An encrypted key stored in the registry or somewhere else, for which only the application has the decryption code, can be used. The application reads the key, decrypts it, and uses the value to set the application role.

Objective 6.3 Questions

70-229.06.03.001

You want to switch the current connection to use an application role. How would you accomplish this?

A. In the connection string, you would use the `Application Role=True` flag. Set the user name equal to the application name and the password equal to the application password.

B. Execute the sp_setapprole stored procedure to activate the permissions for an application role.

C. Execute `Setapplicationmode True, "Application Name","Password"`.

D. This option is available only if the client connects using OLE DB and uses the `Application Role=True` flag.

70-229.06.03.002

Which connection type supports application role permissions and password encryption?

A. Only OLE DB

B. Only ODBC

C. Only DBLib

D. OLE DB and ODBC

70-229.06.03.003

If a connection is switched to application role permissions, what happens to the user's permissions and application role's permissions?

A. They are fused, and the connection will have both the user's and application role's permissions.

B. The user's permissions will be discarded, and only the application role's permissions will be used.

C. If the user has higher permissions, the user's permissions will be used; otherwise, the application role's permissions will be used.

D. Only those permissions will be available that exist in both the user's permissions and the application's permissions.

70-229.06.03.004

You found out that the application role's password has been compromised. You want to change the application role's password. How would you do it?

A. You cannot do it by just changing the password. You have to drop the current application role and re-create it.

B. You have to execute sp_approlechangepassword to change the application role's password.

C. You have to execute sp_approlepassword to change the application role's password.

D. You have to create a new application role with the new password and copy the permissions over with sp_copyapprolepermissions.

70-229.06.03.005

Can a connection use more than one application role, and is the application role valid in another database in the same SQL Server instance?

A. Connections can use more than one application role but are valid only in the current database.

B. Connections can use only one application role and are valid only in the current database.

C. Connections can use more than one application role and are valid in all databases in the same instance of SQL Server 2000.

D. Connections can use more than one application role and are valid in all databases.

Objective 6.3 Answers

70-229.06.03.001

▶ **Correct Answers: B**

A. **Incorrect:** You cannot connect as an application role to the database. You have to connect to the database and then switch your connection to use an application role using the sp_setapprole stored procedure.

B. **Correct:** You can switch an existing connection to application role permissions using the sp_setapprole stored procedure.

C. **Incorrect:** Setapplicationmode is not a valid Transact-SQL stored procedure. You have to use sp_setapprole to switch to application role permissions.

D. **Incorrect:** OLE DB, ODBC, and DBLib support application mode, but DBLib does not support encrypted passwords. Switching to application role permissions is achieved using sp_setapprole instead of a flag in the connection string.

70-229.06.03.002

▶ **Correct Answers: D**

A. **Incorrect:** OLE DB supports password encryption, and ODBC does also.

B. **Incorrect:** ODBC supports password encryption, and OLE DB does also.

C. **Incorrect:** Although DBLib supports application role permissions, it does not support password encryption. Password encryption is supported only by OLE DB and ODBC.

D. **Correct:** Both OLE DB and ODBC support password encryption, whereas DBLib does not.

70-229.06.03.003

▶ **Correct Answers: B**

A. **Incorrect:** When switching to application role permission, all information associated with the user, including login, username, and permissions, will be discarded, and only the application role's permissions will be used.

B. **Correct:** The application role's permission will be used, and the user-related information will be ignored and discarded from the connection.

C. **Incorrect:** SQL Server does not differentiate between higher-level permissions. When application role permission is used, all information associated with the user, including login, username, and permissions, will be discarded and only the application role's permissions will be available.

D. **Incorrect:** SQL Server will not fuse the users and the application role's permissions. When application role permission is used, all information associated with the user, including login, username, and permissions, will be discarded, and only the application role's permissions will be available.

70-229.06.03.004

▶ **Correct Answers: C**

A. **Incorrect:** You do not have to drop the application role and re-create a new one. You need to use the sp_approlepassword Transact-SQL stored procedure to change the application role's password.

B. **Incorrect:** You can change the application role's password, but sp_approlechangepassword is not a valid Transact- SQL stored procedure. The correct stored procedure is sp_approlepassword.

C. **Correct:** The application role's password can be changed without dropping the application role and re-creating it.

D. **Incorrect:** Although you can create a new application role, you cannot copy an application role's permissions to another application role. sp_copyapprolepermissions is not a valid Transact-SQL stored procedure. You have to use the sp_approlepassword Transact-SQL stored procedure to change the password.

70-229.06.03.005

▶ **Correct Answers: B**

A. **Incorrect:** A single connection can use only one application role at a time, and it is valid only in the database it was created in. If you need to access other databases through the same connection, you have to use the guest account.

B. **Correct:** SQL Server allows only one application role per connection, and it is valid only in the current database the application role was created in.

C. **Incorrect:** The application role is valid only in the database it was created in, and the connection can use only one application role at a given time.

D. **Incorrect:** A single connection can use only one application role at a time, and the role is valid only in the database it was created in.

A P P E N D I X   A

Questions and Answers

The following questions and answers are for Part 1 of this book.

Chapter 1: Introduction to Microsoft SQL Server 2000
Review

page 44

1. What is SQL Server 2000?

    SQL Server 2000 is an RDBMS that uses Transact-SQL to send requests between a client computer and a SQL Server 2000 computer. An RDBMS includes databases, the database engine, and the applications necessary to manage the data and the components of the RDBMS. The RDBMS organizes data into related rows and columns within the database.

2. What language is commonly used to work with data in a database?

    SQL

3. What is XML?

    XML is a standard format for data on the Internet. XML consists of tags within a text document that define the structure of the document. XML documents can be easily processed through HTML. Although most SQL statements return their results in a relational (tabular) result set, the SQL Server 2000 database component supports a FOR XML clause that causes the results to be returned as an XML document. SQL Server 2000 also supports XPath queries from Internet and intranet applications.

4. Which edition of SQL Server 2000 includes the complete SQL Server offering?

    SQL Server 2000 Enterprise Edition

5. What is the purpose of the SQL Server 2000 relational database engine?

    The SQL Server 2000 relational database engine is a modern, highly scalable engine for storing data. The database engine stores data in tables. Applications submit SQL statements to the database engine, which returns the results to the application in the form of a tabular result set. Internet

applications submit either SQL statements or XPath queries to the database engine, which returns the results in the form of an XML document. The relational database engine provides support for common Microsoft data access interfaces, such as ADOs, OLE DB, and ODBC.

6. What SQL Server 2000 technology helps you build data warehouses and data marts in SQL Server by importing and transferring data from multiple heterogeneous sources?

   DTS

7. What are at least four administrative tasks that you can use the Enterprise Manager to perform?

   Any four of the following tasks:

   - **Defining groups of servers running SQL Server**
   - **Registering individual servers in a group**
   - **Configuring all SQL Server options for each registered server**
   - **Creating and administering all SQL Server databases, objects, logins, users, and permissions in each registered server**
   - **Defining and executing all SQL Server administrative tasks on each registered server**
   - **Designing and testing SQL statements, batches, and scripts interactively by invoking Query Analyzer**
   - **Invoking the various wizards defined for SQL Server**

8. Which tool is commonly used to create queries and execute them against SQL Server databases?

   Query Analyzer

9. What are at least five objects that can be included in a logical database?

   Any five of the following:

   - **Table**
   - **Data type**
   - **View**
   - **Stored procedure**
   - **Function**
   - **Index**
   - **Constraint**
   - **Rule**
   - **Default**
   - **Trigger**

10. What are the major components involved in processing a SQL statement received from a SQL Server client?

    The client, the tabular data stream, the server Net-Library, and SQL Server (the relational database engine)

11. What two roles does Microsoft Search play in supporting SQL Server?

    Indexing support and querying support

12. What phases does a transaction go through?

    A transaction goes through several phases:

    12.1. **Before the transaction starts, the database is in a consistent state.**

    12.2. **The application signals the start of a transaction. This process can be initiated explicitly with the *BEGIN TRANSACTION* statement. Alternatively, the application can set options to run in implicit transaction mode; the first Transact-SQL statement executed after the completion of a prior transaction starts a new transaction automatically. No record is written to the log when the transaction starts; the first record is written to the log when the application generates the first log record for a data modification.**

    12.3. **The application starts modifying data. These modifications are made one table at a time. As a series of modifications are made, they might leave the database in a temporarily inconsistent intermediate state.**

    12.4. **When the application reaches a point where all the modifications have completed successfully and the database is once again consistent, application commits the transaction. This step makes all of the modifications a permanent part of the database.**

    12.5. **If the application encounters some error that prevents it from completing the transaction, it undoes, or rolls back, all the data modifications. This process returns the database to the point of consistency it was at before the transaction started.**

Chapter 2: Using Transact-SQL on a SQL Server Database Review

page 94

1. In which window in Query Analyzer can you enter and execute Transact-SQL statements?

    The Editor pane of the Query window

2. How do you execute Transact-SQL statements and scripts in Query Analyzer?

    You can execute a complete script or an individual Transact-SQL statement by creating or opening the script in the Editor pane and then pressing F5. To perform this task, no other statements can be entered into the Editor pane. If there are other statements, you must highlight the script or statements that you want to execute, then press F5.

3. What type of information is displayed on the Execution Plan tab, the Trace tab, and the Statistics tab?

The Execution Plan tab displays a graphical representation of the execution plan that is used to execute the current query. The Trace tab, like the Execution Plan tab, can assist you with analyzing your queries. The Trace tab displays server trace information about the event class, subclass, integer data, text data, database ID, duration, start time, reads and writes, and CPU usage. The Statistics tab provides detailed information about client-side statistics for execution of the query.

4. Which tool in Query Analyzer enables you to control and monitor the execution of stored procedures?

Transact-SQL debugger

5. What is Transact-SQL?

Transact-SQL is a language that contains the commands used to administer instances of SQL Server; to create and manage all objects in an instance of SQL Server; and to insert, retrieve, modify, and delete data in SQL Server tables. Transact-SQL is an extension of the language defined in the SQL standards published by ISO and ANSI.

6. What are the three types of Transact-SQL statements that SQL Server supports?

DDL, DCL, and DML

7. What type of Transact-SQL statement is the *CREATE TABLE* statement?

DDL

8. What Transact-SQL element is an object in batches and scripts that can hold a data value?

Variable

9. Which Transact-SQL statements do you use to create, modify, and delete a user-defined function?

CREATE FUNCTION, *ALTER FUNCTION*, **and** *DROP FUNCTION*

10. What are control-of-flow language elements?

Control-of-flow language elements control the flow of execution of Transact-SQL statements, statement blocks, and stored procedures. These words can be used in Transact-SQL statements, batches, and stored procedures. Without control-of-flow language, separate Transact-SQL statements are performed sequentially, as they occur. Control-of-flow language elements permit statements to be connected, related to each other, and made interdependent by using programming-like constructs.

Control-of-flow keywords are useful when you need to direct Transact-SQL to take some kind of action. For example, use a *BEGIN...END* pair of

statements when including more than one Transact-SQL statement in a logical block. Use an *IF...ELSE* pair of statements when a certain statement or block of statements needs to be executed IF some condition is met, and another statement or block of statements should be executed if that condition is not met (the ELSE condition).

11. What are some of the methods that SQL Server 2000 supports for executing Transact-SQL statements?

You can execute single statements, or you can execute the statements as a batch (a group of one or more Transact-SQL statements). You can also execute Transact-SQL statements through stored procedures and triggers. In addition, you can use scripts to execute Transact-SQL statements.

12. What are the differences among batches, stored procedures, and triggers?

A batch is a group of one or more Transact-SQL statements sent at one time from an application to SQL Server for execution. SQL Server compiles the statements of a batch into a single executable unit, called an execution plan. The statements in the execution plan are then executed one at a time. A stored procedure is a group of Transact-SQL statements that is compiled one time and can then be executed many times. A trigger is a special type of stored procedure that a user does not call directly. When the trigger is created, it is defined to execute when a specific type of data modification is made against a specific table or column.

Chapter 3: Designing a SQL Server Database
Lesson 1: Introduction to Database Design
Exercise 1: Exploring the Basic Concepts of Database Design

page 104   ▶   **To view the contents of a table**

2. Review the columns and rows within the table.

What are the column names (attributes) in the Categories table, and how many rows of data are displayed?

CategoryID, CategoryName, Description, and Picture (eight rows of data are displayed, not counting the header)

page 104   ▶   **To normalize a database design**

2. Keeping in mind the table's design, apply the four basic rules that you should follow when designing a database. The rules are listed here for your convenience:

■ A table should have an identifier.

■ A table should store data for only a single type of entity.

■ A table should avoid nullable columns.

■ A table should not have repeating values or columns.

Which rule is being violated in the Customers table?

The table does not have an identifier.

3. Modify the table's design so that it adheres to the basic rules of normalization. Use your paper and pencil to draw the table and its data.

How should you modify the data?

Add a column that serves as an identifier. For example, you can add a column named CustID. For each row, add a unique value to the column so that each customer has a unique customer ID.

6. Modify the database design so that it adheres to the rules of normalization.

How should you modify the current design?

Ensure that a table exists in the database that lists the various products that the company sells. This table should include an identifier for each product. Create another table that matches customer IDs to product IDs to track which products each customer purchased.

9. Modify the database design so that it adheres to the rules of normalization.

How should you modify the current design?

Create a separate table for the products so that all product and manufacturing information is in a table separate from the Customers table. The products table should include an identifier for each product. Create another table that matches customer IDs to product IDs to track which products each customer purchased.

page 106   ▶   **To view entity relationships in a database diagram**

3. View the connector that links the Authors table to the TitleAuthor table and the connector that links the Titles table to the TitleAuthor table.

The connector indicates that a relationship exists between the tables. Notice that there is no connector between the Author table and the Titles table because no direct relationship exists between the tables.

At one end of the connector is a key, which indicates one. The other side of the connector is an infinity sign, which indicates many. These symbols tell you that a one-to-many relationship exists between the Authors table and the TitleAuthor table and that a one-to-many relationship exists between the Titles table and the TitleAuthor table.

What is the implied relationship between the Titles table and the Authors table?

Many-to-many

What type of table is the TitleAuthor table (in terms of the implied relationship between Titles and Authors)?

A junction table

Chapter 3: Designing a SQL Server Database
Lesson 3: Identifying System Requirements
Exercise 2: Identifying the System Requirements for Your Database Design

page 122 ▶ **To identify system goals**

2. Write down the system goals that you can identify in the scenario.

What are those goals?

Centralize information so that it is easier and more efficient to manage inventory and track orders and sales; maintain a central repository of information about authors, customers, and employees; and provide employees with the ability to generate, track, and modify orders online.

3. Review each goal to determine whether it is measurable.

Which goals are measurable?

The goal of centralizing information so that it is easier and more efficient to manage inventory and track orders and sales is measurable in part. Once the database is implemented, information will be centralized, so this part of the goal is measurable. The goal of making it "easier and more efficient" is not measurable, however. To make it measurable, you must establish an initial measurement. You need to ask, "How much easier and how much more efficient?" Because you are implementing a relatively small database, it would not be practical and cost-effective to conduct an in-depth study of the current system. In this case, it is enough to know that the manager says that the current system is creating a problem—a problem that can be resolved, at least in part, by implementing the database.

The goal of maintaining a centralized repository of information about authors, customers, and employees is measurable because there is currently no centralized repository (and there will be once the database is implemented). The same is true of the goal of providing employees with the ability to generate, track, and modify orders online. Once the database is implemented, they will have this ability.

page 122 ▶ **To identify the amount and type of data**

1. Write down the categories of data that you can identify in this scenario.

What categories of data can you identify?

Books, authors, employees, customers, and orders

2. For each category of data that you identified in Step 1, write down the type of information that you should track for each category.

What types of information can you identify?

Category	Types of Information
Books	Title, authors, publisher, publication date, edition, cost, suggested retail price, condition of book, unique ID
Authors	First name, last name, year of birth, year of death, description of author
Employees	First name, last name, address, phone number, date of birth, hire date, position
Customers	First name, last name, phone number, mailing address, books purchased, purchase date
Orders	Books sold, customer, salesperson, amount of the sale, order date, delivery date, form of payment, order status

3. For each category of data that you identified in Step 1, write down the current amount of data for each category.

What is the volume of data for each category?

Books   **3000**

Authors   **2500**

Employees   **12**

Customers   **2000**

Orders   **1000**

4. For each category of data that you identified in Step 1, write down the expected growth pattern.

What is the growth pattern for each category?

Books   **10 percent annually**

Authors   **10 percent annually**

Employees   **One employee annually**

Customers   **10 percent annually**

Orders   **10 percent annually**

page 123   ▶   **To identify how the data will be used**

1. Write down the categories of users that you can identify in this scenario.

What are those categories of users?

Managers, sales staff

2. For each category of user that you identified in Step 1, write down the number of users.

What are the current number of users and the projected number of users in each category?

User Type	Current Amount	Projected Growth Pattern
Managers	2	No expected growth
Sales staff	10	One annually

Only two to four employees (including managers) are in the store at the same time and are potentially accessing and updating the database concurrently.

3. For each category of user that you identified in Step 1, write down the tasks that they will be performing.

What tasks will each type of user be performing?

User Type	Tasks
Managers	Maintaining inventory (book information); maintaining information about authors; maintaining employee information; tracking how many books and which books each employee has sold; maintaining customer information; tracking orders; maintaining a record of sales (based on orders); and generating and modifying orders
Sales staff	Accessing information about authors, books, customers, and orders; creating, tracking, and modifying orders

page 123 ▶ **To identify business rules**

1. Write down the business rules that you can identify in this scenario.

What are the business rules?

- **The database system should adhere to the following business rules:**
- **Book information must include the title, author, cost, suggested retail price, rating, and the unique ID assigned to each book.**
- **The publisher, publication date, and edition are not required.**
- **The book publication date can be a year within the range of 1600 to 2099.**
- **A book must be rated as superb, excellent, good, fair, poor, or damaged.**
- **Each rating should have the capacity to include a two-sentence description, but the description is not required.**
- **Authors can write more than one book.**
- **More than one author can write one book.**
- **Author information must include the author's last name.**
- **Author information can include the author's year of birth and year of death, if applicable.**

- An author's description is no longer than two sentences.
- The author's description is not required.
- Managers must be able to access and modify employee information.
- Employee information must include the first name, last name, address, telephone number, date of birth, hire date, and position.
- An employee's position must be Manager, Assistant Manager, Full-Time Sales Clerk, or Part-Time Sales Clerk.
- Each position should have the capacity to include a two-sentence description, but the description is not required.
- An employee can hold only one position at a time.
- Only managers can access or modify employee information.
- Customer information must include a first name or a last name.
- Customer information does not require a telephone number or mailing address. Which books customers purchased and on which dates are not required because not all customers have bought books.
- Order information must include information about books sold, which customer bought the books, which employee sold the books, the amount of the sale, the date the order is placed, the form of payment, and the status of the order.
- The order information must include the date of delivery or pickup once the order is completed.
- The form of payment must be cash, check, or credit card.
- The order status must be one of the following: (1) to be shipped, (2) customer will pick up, (3) shipped, or (4) picked up.
- Orders can contain only one customer, salesperson, order data, delivery date, form of payment, and order status.
- Orders can contain one or more books.
- When a book is added to an order, it is marked as sold in the inventory.
- All employees can access information about authors, books in stock, customers, and orders.
- All employees can create, view, and modify orders online.
- Only managers can modify information about authors, books, and customers.

Chapter 3: Designing a SQL Server Database
Lesson 4: Developing a Logical Data Model
Exercise 3: Developing a Logical Data Model

page 131   ▶   **To identify relationships between entities**

    4. Identify any many-to-many relationships in the database design.

Which relationship is many-to-many?

The relationship between the Authors table and the Books table is a many-to-many relationship. Many authors can co-author one book; one author can write many books; and many authors can co-author many books.

page 132   ▶   **To identify constraints on data**

3. Identify the object, if any, to which this business rule applies.

   To which object or objects does this business rule apply?

   To the Books and BookAuthors tables

4. Under the Books table name and the BookAuthors table name, write the data constraints that you can derive from the business rule.

   What are the data constraints?

   The following constraints apply to the Books table:

   - **The TitleID column must contain a value.**
   - **The Title column must contain a value.**
   - **The Cost column must contain a value.**
   - **The SRP column must contain a value.**
   - **The ConditionID column must contain a value.**
   - **The value in the TitleID column must be unique.**

   The following constraints apply to the BookAuthors table:

   - **The AuthorID column must contain a value.**
   - **The TitleID column must contain a value.**

5. For each business rule, define the data constraints. Where applicable, write the constraints beneath the table name. If a constraint does not apply specifically to one table, write it in another space on your paper.

   What are the data constraints for your database design?

   The following constraints apply to the database design:

   Books table

   - **The TitleID column must contain a value.**
   - **The value in the TitleID column must be unique.**
   - **The Title column must contain a value.**
   - **The Title column must be able to contain a value for a long title (about one sentence).**
   - **The Publisher column does not require a value.**
   - **The PubDate column does not require a value.**

- The Edition column does not require a value.
- The Cost column must contain a value.
- The SRP column must contain a value.
- The ConditionID column must contain a value.
- The ConditionID column must contain a value that is listed in the ConditionID column of the BookCondition table.
- The Sold column must indicate whether a book is sold.
- The PubDate column does not require a value. If a value is added, it must fall within the range of 1600 to 2099.

BookAuthors table

- The AuthorID column must contain a value.
- The AuthorID column must contain a value that is listed in the AuthorID column of the Authors table.
- The TitleID column must contain a value.
- The TitleID column must contain a value that is listed in the TitleID column of the Books table.
- The combination of values in the AuthorID column and the TitleID column must be unique.

BookCondition table

- The ConditionID column must contain a value.
- The value in the ConditionID column must be unique.
- The ConditionName column must contain a value.
- The value in the ConditionName column must be unique.
- The initial values to be used in the ConditionName column are Superb, Excellent, Good, Fair, Poor, and Damaged.
- The Description column does not require a value.
- The Description column must be able to contain a two-sentence value.

Authors table

- The AuthorID column must contain a value.
- The value in the AuthorID column must be unique.
- The FirstName column does not require a value.
- The LastName column must contain a value.
- The YearBorn column does not require a value.
- The YearDied column does not require a value.
- The Description column does not require a value.
- The Description column must be able to contain a two-sentence value.

Orders table

- The OrderID column must contain a value.
- The value in the OrderID column must be unique.
- The CustomerID column must contain a value.
- The CustomerID column must contain a value that is listed in the CustomerID column of the Customers table.
- The EmployeeID column must contain a value.
- The EmployeeID column must contain a value that is listed in the EmployeeID column of the Employees table.
- The Amount column must contain a value.
- The value in the Amount column must be in United States currency.
- The OrderDate column must contain a value.
- The DeliveryDate column must contain a value when the StatusID column contains a value that is equivalent to a shipped value or to a picked up value in the StatusID column of the Orders table.
- The PaymentID column must contain a value.
- The PaymentID column must contain a value that is listed in the PaymentID column of the FormOfPayment table.
- The StatusID column must contain a value.
- The StatusID column must contain a value that is listed in the StatusID column of the OrderStatus table.
- The StatusID column must contain a value that is equivalent to a shipped value or to a picked up value in the StatusID column of the Orders table if a value is added to the DeliveryDate column.

BookOrders table

- The OrderID column must contain a value.
- The OrderID column must contain a value that is listed in the OrderID column of the Orders table.
- The TitleID column must contain a value.
- The TitleID column must contain a value that is listed in the TitleID column of the Books table.
- The combination of values in the OrderID column and the TitleID column must be unique.

OrderStatus table

- The StatusID column must contain a value.
- The value in the StatusID column must be unique.
- The StatusDescrip column must contain a value.

- **The value in the StatusDescrip column must be unique.**
- **The initial values to be used in the StatusDescrip column are To be shipped, Customer will pick up, Shipped, and Picked up.**

FormOfPayment table

- **The PaymentID column must contain a value.**
- **The value in the PaymentID column must be unique.**
- **The PaymentDescrip column must contain a value.**
- **The value in the PaymentDescrip column must be unique.**
- **The initial values to be used in the PaymentDescrip column are Cash, Check, and Credit card.**

Employees table

- **The EmployeeID column must contain a value.**
- **The value in the EmployeeID column must be unique.**
- **The FirstName column must contain a value.**
- **The LastName column must contain a value.**
- **The Address1 column must contain a value.**
- **The Address2 column does not require a value.**
- **The City column must contain a value.**
- **The State column must contain a value.**
- **The Zip column must contain a value.**
- **The Phone column must contain a value.**
- **The DOB column must contain a value.**
- **The HireDate column must contain a value.**
- **The PositionID column must contain a value.**
- **The PositionID column must contain a value that is listed in the PositionID column of the Positions table.**

Customers table

- **The CustomerID column must contain a value.**
- **The value in the CustomerID column must be unique.**
- **The FirstName column or the LastName column or both columns must contain values.**
- **The Phone column does not require a value.**
- **The Address1 column does not require a value.**
- **The Address2 column does not require a value.**
- **The City column does not require a value.**

- The State column does not require a value.
- The Zip column does not require a value.

Positions table

- The PositionID column must contain a value.
- The value in the PositionID column must be unique.
- The Title column must contain a value.
- The value in the Title column must be unique.
- The initial values to be used in the Title column are Manager, Assistant Manager, Fulltime Sales Clerk, and Part Time Sales Clerk
- The JobDescrip column does not require a value.
- The JobDescrip column must be able to contain a two-sentence value.

Multiple tables

- When a row is added to the BookOrders table, the value for the Sold column in the Books table is updated to reflect that the book in the order has been sold.
- Security Managers can view and modify data in all tables.
- All employees can view and modify data in the BookOrders and Orders tables.
- All employees can access data in the Authors table, Book Authors table, Books table, BookCondition table, BookOrders table, Customer table, Orders table, OrderStatus table, and FormOfPayment table.

Chapter 3: Designing a SQL Server Database
Review

page 136

1. What does a SQL Server database consist of?

   A SQL Server database consists of a collection of tables that store specific sets of structured data. A table (entity) contains a collection of rows (tuples) and columns (attributes). Each column in the table is designed to store a certain type of information (for example, dates, names, dollar amounts, or numbers).

2. What is normalization?

   The process of using formal methods to separate the data into multiple related tables

3. What are the four basic rules that you should follow when normalizing a database design?

   A table should have an identifier, store data for only a single type of entity, avoid nullable columns, and not have repeating values or columns.

4. What are the three basic types of relationships that can exist between tables in the SQL Server database, and what are the basic differences between these types?

The three types of relationships are one-to-one, one-to-many, and many-to-many. In a one-to-one relationship, a row in table A can have no more than one matching row in table B (and vice versa). In a one-to-many relationship, table A can have many matching rows in table B, but a row in table B can have only one matching row in table A. In a many-to-many relationship, a row in table A can have many matching rows in table B (and vice versa).

5. What are the three types of operating system files that SQL Server uses?

Primary, secondary, and transaction log

6. What two stages of security does a user pass through when working in SQL Server, and how do these stages differ?

A user passes through authentication and authorization (permissions validation). The authentication stage identifies the user who is using a login account and verifies only the capability to connect to an instance of SQL Server. If authentication is successful, the user connects to an instance of SQL Server. The user then needs permissions to access databases on the server. This process is done by granting access to an account in each database (mapped to the user login). The permissions validation stage controls the activities that the user is allowed to perform in the SQL Server database.

7. What are the four primary tasks that you should perform when identifying the system requirements for a database design?

Identifying system goals, identifying the amount and types of data, identifying how the data will be used, and identifying business rules

8. When determining the volume of data that the system will manage, you should identify what two types of information?

The actual amount of data and its growth pattern

9. When determining how data will be used in a new system, you should identify what three types of information?

Who will be using the data, the number of users who will be accessing the data, and the tasks that they will be performing when they access that data

10. When you are gathering system requirements for a database design, one of the steps that you should take is to define the specific categories of data. What type of object within a database maps to these categories of information?

A table object

11. What task do you perform after determining that a relationship exists between two tables, and how do you perform that task?

   Determine the types of relationships that exist between tables. To determine the types of relationships, you should look at the types of data that each table contains and the types of interchanges between them.

12. What information within the system requirements should you base data constraints upon?

   Business rules

Chapter 4: Implementing SQL Server Databases and Tables
Lesson 2: Identifying Data Types
Exercise 2: Identifying Column Data Types

page 153   ▶   **To identify the data types for the Authors table**

2. Refer to the data constraints that you identified for the Authors table when you developed your database design.

   Which data constraints apply to the AuthorID column of the Authors table?

   The column must contain a value, and the value must be unique.

4. Review the database design and the data constraints for the FirstName and LastName columns.

   What type of data will you store in this column?

   Character data

5. Review the database design and the data constraints for the YearBorn and YearDied columns.

   You can assume that each column will contain only four characters. Because date and time data types do not include a year-only data type, you decide to use a character data type.

   Which data type should you use for the YearBorn and YearDied columns?

   char(4), **although which data type to use is not always a clear-cut decision**

6. Review the database design and the data constraints for the Description column.

   What type of data will you store in this column?

   Character data

page 154   ▶   **To identify the column data types for tables in the BookShopDB database**

3. Identify the data type for each column.

What is the data type for each column in the BookShopDB tables?

Note   It is sometimes difficult to predict exactly what length you should use for data types such as *char* and *varchar*. You can get a feel for lengths, however, by reviewing column properties in existing databases, such as the Pubs database or the Northwind database.

The following table lists the suggested data types for each column in the tables:

Table	Column	Data Type
Books	TitleID	*char(8)*
	Title	*varchar(70)*
	Publisher	*varchar(50)*
	PubDate	*char(4)*
	Edition	*char(4)*
	Cost	*money*
	SRP	*money*
	ConditionID	*tinyint*
	Sold	*bit*
BookCondition	ConditionID	*tinyint*
	ConditionName	*char(10)*
	Description	*varchar(50)*
Authors	AuthorID	*smallint*
	FirstName	*varchar(30)*
	LastName	*varchar(30)*
	YearBorn	*char(4)*
	YearDied	*char(4)*
	Description	*varchar(200)*
BookAuthors	AuthorID	*smallint*
	TitleID	*char(8)*
Employees	EmployeeID	*smallint*
	FirstName	*varchar(30)*
	LastName	*varchar(30)*
	Address1	*varchar(60)*
	Address2	*varchar(60)*

Table	Column	Data Type
(Employees, continued)	City	*varchar(15)*
	State	*char(2)*
	Zip	*varchar(12)*
	Phone	*varchar(24)*
	DOB	*datetime*
	HireDate	*datetime*
	PositionID	*tinyint*
Positions	PositionID	*tinyint*
	Title	*varchar(30)*
	JobDescrip	*varchar(80)*
Customers	CustomerID	*smallint*
	FirstName	*varchar(30)*
	LastName	*varchar(30)*
	Phone	*varchar(24)*
	Address1	*varchar(60)*
	Address2	*varchar(60)*
	City	*varchar(15)*
	State	*varchar(7)*
	Zip	*varchar(12)*
Orders	OrderID	*smallint*
	CustomerID	*smallint*
	EmployeeID	*smallint*
	Amount	*money*
	OrderDate	*datetime*
	DeliveryDate	*datetime*
	PaymentID	*tinyint*
	StatusID	*tinyint*
OrderStatus	StatusID	*tinyint*
	StatusDescrip	*varchar(25)*
FormOfPayment	PaymentID	*tinyint*
	PaymentDescrip	*varchar(12)*
BookOrders	OrderID	*smallint*
	BookID	*char(8)*

> **Note** Notice that the State column in the Customers table uses the *varchar(7)* data type rather than *char(2)*, as in the Employees table. Because a value is not required for this column in the Customers table, a default value of "unknown" will be defined (rather than permitting a null value). Nullability and default values are discussed in more detail in Lesson 3.

```
USE bookshopdb
CREATE TABLE Books
      (
      TitleID CHAR(8) NOT NULL,
      Title VARCHAR(70) NOT NULL,
      Publisher VARCHAR(50) NOT NULL DEFAULT 'N/A',
      PubDate CHAR(4) NOT NULL DEFAULT 'N/A',
      Edition CHAR(4) NOT NULL DEFAULT 'N/A',
      Cost MONEY NOT NULL,
      SRP MONEY NOT NULL,
      ConditionID TINYINT NOT NULL,
      Sold BIT NOT NULL DEFAULT '0',
      )
CREATE TABLE BookOrders
      (
      OrderID SMALLINT NOT NULL,
      TitleID CHAR(8) NOT NULL
      )
CREATE TABLE Positions
      (
      PositionID TINYINT NOT NULL,
      Title VARCHAR(30) NOT NULL,
      JobDescrip VARCHAR(80) NOT NULL DEFAULT 'N/A'
      )
CREATE TABLE Employees
      (
      EmployeeID SMALLINT IDENTITY NOT NULL,
      FirstName VARCHAR(30) NOT NULL,
      LastName VARCHAR(30) NOT NULL,
      Addrees1 VARCHAR(60) NOT NULL,
      Address2 VARCHAR(60) NOT NULL DEFAULT 'N/A',
      City VARCHAR(15) NOT NULL,
      State CHAR(2) NOT NULL,
      Zip VARCHAR(12) NOT NULL,
      Phone VARCHAR(24) NOT NULL,
      DOB DATETIME NOT NULL,
      HireDate DATETIME NOT NULL,
      PositionID TINYINT NOT NULL
      )
CREATE TABLE Customers
      (
      CustomerID SMALLINT IDENTITY(10,1) NOT NULL,
      FirstName VARCHAR(30) NOT NULL DEFAULT 'unknown',
```

```
            LastName VARCHAR(30) NOT NULL DEFAULT 'unknown',
            Phone VARCHAR(24) NOT NULL DEFAULT 'unknown',
            Address1 VARCHAR(60) NOT NULL DEFAULT 'unknown',
            Address2 VARCHAR(60) NOT NULL DEFAULT 'unknown',
            City VARCHAR(15) NOT NULL DEFAULT 'unknown',
            State VARCHAR(7) NOT NULL DEFAULT 'unknown',
            Zip VARCHAR(12) NOT NULL DEFAULT 'unknown'
            )
CREATE TABLE Orders
            (
            OrderID SMALLINT IDENTITY NOT NULL,
            CustomerID SMALLINT NOT NULL,
            EmployeeID SMALLINT NOT NULL,
            Amount MONEY NOT NULL DEFAULT 0,
            OrderDate DATETIME NOT NULL,
            DeliveryDate DATETIME NULL,
            PaymentID TINYINT NOT NULL,
            StatusID TINYINT NOT NULL
            )
CREATE TABLE OrderStatus
            (
            StatusID TINYINT NOT NULL,
            StatusDescrip VARCHAR(25) NOT NULL
            )
CREATE TABLE FormOfPayment
            (
            PaymentID TINYINT NOT NULL,
            PaymentDescrip VARCHAR(12) NOT NULL
            )
```

Chapter 4: Implementing SQL Server Databases and Tables Review

page 168

1. What is the first step toward implementing the physical database?

   Creating a database object

2. What factors should you take into consideration before creating a database?

   You should take into consideration the following factors:

   Permission to create a database defaults to members of the sysadmin and dbcreator fixed server roles, although permissions can be granted to other users.

   The user who creates the database becomes the owner of the database.

   A maximum of 32,767 databases can be created on a server.

   The name of the database must follow the rules for identifiers.

3. What are the two steps that SQL Server uses when implementing a new database?

SQL Server implements a new database through the following two steps:

SQL Server uses a copy of the Model database to initialize the new database and its metadata.

SQL Server then fills the rest of the database with empty pages, except for pages that have internal data recording how the space is used in the database.

4. What methods can you use to create a SQL Server database object?

SQL Server provides several methods that you can use to create a database: the Transact-SQL *CREATE DATABASE* statement, the console tree in Enterprise Manager, and the Create Database wizard (which you can access through Enterprise Manager).

5. What is a data type?

A data type is an attribute that specifies the type of data (integer, character, monetary, and so on) that the object can hold. Each column in a SQL Server table has a related data type. Certain objects other than columns also have an associated data type.

6. What four attributes does a data type define for an object?

A data type defines the following four attributes:

***The kind of data contained by the object*   For example, the data might be character, integer, or binary.**

***The length of the stored value, or its size*   The lengths of image, binary, and varbinary data types are defined in bytes. The length of any of the numeric data types is the number of bytes required to hold the number of digits allowed for that data type. The length of the character string and Unicode data types is defined in characters.**

***The precision of the number (numeric data types only)*   The precision is the number of digits that the number can contain. For example, a *smallint* object can hold a maximum of five digits; therefore, it has a precision of five.**

***The scale of the number (numeric data types only)*   The scale is the number of digits that can be stored to the right of the decimal point. For example, an *int* object cannot accept a decimal point and has a scale of zero. A money object can have a maximum of four digits to the right of the decimal point and has a scale of four.**

7. What are the nine categories of data types that SQL Server supports?

Binary, character, date and time, decimal, floating point, integer, monetary, special, and Unicode

8. What are user-defined data types?

User-defined data types are data types that are based on the system data types in SQL Server 2000. User-defined data types can be used if several tables must store the same type of data in a column and if you must ensure that these columns have exactly the same data type, length, and nullability. For example, a user-defined data type named postal_code could be created based on the *char* data type.

9. What type of information, at a minimum, should a table definition include?

The table name, column names, data types (and lengths, if required), and whether a column accepts NULL values

10. What are you defining when you define column nullability in a table definition?

The nullability of a column determines whether the rows in the table can contain a null value for that column. A null value is not the same as zero, blank, or a zero-length character string such as " ". Null means that no entry has been made. The presence of null usually implies that the value is either unknown or undefined.

11. How do you define a default value for a column?

By defining a DEFAULT definition with the column definition of a *CREATE TABLE* statement; you can also add a default value to a column by modifying the column definition

12. Which property can you use in the column definition of a *CREATE TABLE* statement in order to automatically generate an identity number for each new row added to a table?

The IDENTITY property, which enables you to define the number for the first row inserted into the table (the seed value) and to define an increment to be added to the seed to determine successive identity numbers

Chapter 5: Implementing Data Integrity
Lesson 1: Introduction to Data Integrity
Exercise 1: Identifying the Properties Used to Ensure Data Integrity

page 174

▶   **To identify properties in the Employee table**

4. Scroll through the result on the Grids tab. Identify the data types, nullability, DEFAULT definitions, IDENTITY property, indexes, and constraints.

What types of constraints have been defined for the Employees table?

CHECK, DEFAULT, FOREIGN KEY, and PRIMARY KEY

Which columns in the Employees table allow null values?

The minit column and the job_lvl column

page 175   ▶   **To identify properties in the Publishers table**

2. Scroll through the result on the Grids tab. Identify the data types, nullability, DEFAULT definitions, IDENTITY property, indexes, and constraints.

What types of constraints have been defined for the Publishers table?

CHECK, DEFAULT, and PRIMARY KEY

Which column in the Publishers table is the identity column?

No identity column has been defined for this table.

Which columns in the Publishers table have been defined with the char data type?

The pub_id column and the state column

page 175   ▶   **To identify properties in the Titles table**

2. Scroll through the result on the Grids tab. Identify the data types, nullability, DEFAULT definitions, IDENTITY property, indexes, and constraints.

Which column in the Publishers table has been defined with a user-defined data type?

The title_id column has been defined with the *tid* user-defined data type.

How many columns in the Titles table allow null values?

Six

Chapter 5: Implementing Data Integrity
Lesson 2: Implementing Integrity Constraints
Exercise 2: Adding Constraints to Existing Tables

page 185   ▶   **To add a PRIMARY KEY constraint to the Authors table**

1. Refer to the business rules and database design and identify which column (or columns) in the Authors table should be defined with a PRIMARY KEY constraint.

At this point in the database development process, it should be fairly obvious which column should be configured as the primary key. Remember that a PRIMARY KEY constraint is defined for a column (or columns) whose values uniquely identify each row in the table.

Which column (or columns) in the Authors table should be defined with a PRIMARY KEY constraint?

The AuthorID column

page 186   ▶   **To add a PRIMARY KEY constraint to the BookAuthors table**

1. Refer to the business rules and database design and identify which column (or columns) in the BookAuthors table should be defined with a PRIMARY KEY constraint.

   Which column (or columns) in the BookAuthors table should be defined with a PRIMARY KEY constraint?

   The AuthorID and TitleID columns

page 186   ▶   **To add a PRIMARY KEY constraint to the remaining tables in the Book-ShopDB database**

2. Use Query Analyzer to add a primary key to each remaining table in the Book-ShopDB database.

   For the BookOrders table, the primary key should be created for the two columns in that table. For the other tables, use one identifier column for the primary key.

   What Transact-SQL statements should you use to add the PRIMARY KEY constraints to the remaining tables?

   Use the following Transact-SQL statements to add the PRIMARY KEY constraints:

```
ALTER TABLE Books
ADD CONSTRAINT books_pk PRIMARY KEY (TitleID)
ALTER TABLE BookCondition
ADD CONSTRAINT bookcondition_pk PRIMARY KEY (ConditionID)
ALTER TABLE BookOrders
ADD CONSTRAINT bookorders_pk PRIMARY KEY (OrderID, TitleID)
ALTER TABLE Customers
ADD CONSTRAINT customers_pk PRIMARY KEY (CustomerID)
ALTER TABLE Orders
ADD CONSTRAINT orders_pk PRIMARY KEY (OrderID)
ALTER TABLE Employees
ADD CONSTRAINT employees_pk PRIMARY KEY (EmployeeID)
ALTER TABLE Positions
ADD CONSTRAINT positions_pk PRIMARY KEY (PositionID)
ALTER TABLE OrderStatus
ADD CONSTRAINT orderstatus_pk PRIMARY KEY (StatusID)
ALTER TABLE FormOfPayment
ADD CONSTRAINT formofpayment_pk PRIMARY KEY (PaymentID)
```

   Each table in the BookShopDB database should now be defined with a PRIMARY KEY constraint.

page 187   ▶   **To add FOREIGN KEY constraints to the BookAuthors table**

1. Refer to the business rules and database design and identify which column (or columns) in the BookAuthors table should be defined with FOREIGN KEY constraints.

   Remember that a FOREIGN KEY constraint establishes and enforces a link between two tables. By looking at the business rules and the database design, you can determine what these links should be.

   Which column (or columns) in the BookAuthors table should be defined with a PRIMARY KEY constraint?

   The AuthorID column should be defined with a FOREIGN KEY constraint that references the AuthorID column in the Authors table, and the TitleID column should be defined with a FOREIGN KEY constraint that references the TitleID column in the Books table.

page 187   ▶   **To add FOREIGN KEY constraints to the Books, BookOrders, Orders, and Employees tables**

2. Use Query Analyzer to add foreign keys to the Books, BookOrders, Orders, and Employees tables.

   For the BookOrders table, you should add a FOREIGN KEY constraint to each column. For the Orders table, you should add a FOREIGN KEY constraint to each of the four columns that reference other tables. For the Books table and the Employees table, you should add only one FOREIGN KEY constraint per table.

   What Transact-SQL statements should you use to add the FOREIGN KEY constraints to the Books, BookOrders, Orders, and Employees tables?

   Use the following Transact-SQL statements to add the FOREIGN KEY constraints:

```
ALTER TABLE Books
ADD CONSTRAINT conditionid_fk FOREIGN KEY (ConditionID)
REFERENCES BookCondition (ConditionID)
ALTER TABLE BookOrders
ADD CONSTRAINT orderid_fk FOREIGN KEY (OrderID)
REFERENCES Orders (OrderID)
ALTER TABLE BookOrders
ADD CONSTRAINT titleid2_fk FOREIGN KEY (TitleID)
REFERENCES Books (TitleID)
ALTER TABLE Orders
ADD CONSTRAINT customerid_fk FOREIGN KEY (CustomerID)
REFERENCES Customers (CustomerID)
ALTER TABLE Orders
ADD CONSTRAINT employeeid_fk FOREIGN KEY (EmployeeID)
REFERENCES Employees (EmployeeID)
ALTER TABLE Orders
```

```
ADD CONSTRAINT paymentid_fk FOREIGN KEY (PaymentID)
REFERENCES FormOfPayment (PaymentID)
ALTER TABLE Orders
ADD CONSTRAINT statusid_fk FOREIGN KEY (StatusID)
REFERENCES OrderStatus (StatusID)
ALTER TABLE Employees
ADD CONSTRAINT positionid_fk FOREIGN KEY (PositionID)
REFERENCES Positions (PositionID)
```

The appropriate tables in the BookShopDB database should now be defined with FOREIGN KEY constraints.

page 188 ▶ **To add a CHECK constraint to the Customers table**

1. Refer to the business rules and database design and identify which column (or columns) in the Customers table should be defined with a CHECK constraint.

   Remember that a CHECK constraint enforces domain integrity by limiting the values that a column will accept.

   Which column (or columns) in the Customers table should be defined with a CHECK constraint?

   A CHECK constraint should be defined for the FirstName and LastName columns.

page 188 ▶ **To add CHECK constraints to the Authors table and the Books table**

1. Refer to the business rules and database design and identify which columns in the Authors table and the Books table should be defined with CHECK constraints.

   Which columns in the Authors table and the Books table should be defined with CHECK constraints?

   CHECK constraints should be defined for the YearBorn and YearDied columns in the Authors table and for the PubDate column in the Books table.

Chapter 5: Implementing Data Integrity
Review

page 191 1. What properties within a SQL Server database are used to enforce data integrity?

   Data types, NOT NULL definitions, DEFAULT definitions, IDENTITY properties, constraints, rules, triggers, and indexes

2. What is the difference between a DEFAULT definition and a NOT NULL definition?

   A DEFAULT definition specifies what values are used in a column if you do not specify a value for the column when inserting a row. A NOT NULL definition specifies that null values cannot be used in a column.

3. What are the advantages of using CHECK constraints rather than rules?

   Rules are a backward-compatibility feature that performs some of the same functions as CHECK constraints. CHECK constraints are the preferred, standard way to restrict the values in a column. CHECK constraints are also more concise than rules; there can only be one rule applied to a column, but multiple CHECK constraints can be applied. CHECK constraints are specified as part of the *CREATE TABLE* statement, while rules are created as separate objects and are then bound to the column.

4. What four types of data integrity does SQL Server support?

   Entity integrity, domain integrity, referential integrity, and user-defined integrity

5. What are the differences between entity integrity and domain integrity?

   Entity integrity defines a row as a unique instance of an entity for a particular table. Entity integrity enforces the integrity of the identifier column or the primary key of a table (through indexes, UNIQUE constraints, PRIMARY KEY constraints, or IDENTITY properties). Domain integrity is the validity of entries for a given column. You can enforce domain integrity by restricting the type (through data types), the format (through CHECK constraints and rules), or the range of possible values (through FOREIGN KEY constraints, CHECK constraints, DEFAULT definitions, NOT NULL definitions, and rules).

6. Which type of integrity preserves the defined relationships between tables when records are entered or deleted?

   Referential integrity

7. What types of constraints does SQL Server support?

   SQL Server supports four main classes of constraints: PRIMARY KEY constraints, UNIQUE constraints, FOREIGN KEY constraints, and CHECK constraints. DEFAULT definitions and NOT NULL definitions are sometimes considered types of constraints. Transact-SQL treats DEFAULT definitions as a type of constraint.

8. How many PRIMARY KEY constraints can be included in a table definition?

   One

9. When should you use a UNIQUE constraint rather than a PRIMARY KEY constraint?

   When a column (or combination of columns) is not the primary key or when a column allows null values

10. What does SQL Server check for in the existing data when a PRIMARY KEY constraint is added to an existing column (or columns)?

Whether any null values or duplicate values exist in the data

11. What is a FOREIGN KEY constraint, and how is it created?

A FOREIGN KEY constraint is a column or a combination of columns used to establish and enforce a link between the data in two tables. A link is created between two tables by adding a column or columns to one of the tables and defining those columns with a FOREIGN KEY constraint. The columns will hold the primary key values from the second table. A table can contain multiple FOREIGN KEY constraints.

12. How does a CHECK constraint determine what values are valid?

CHECK constraints determine the valid values from a logical expression. You can create a CHECK constraint with any logical (Boolean) expression that returns TRUE or FALSE based on the logical operators.

Chapter 6: Accessing and Modifying Data
Lesson 3: Modifying Data in a SQL Server Database
Exercise 3: Modifying Data in a SQL Server Database

page 223   ▶   **To use an *INSERT...VALUES* statement to add data to the Test1 table**

3. Write a *SELECT* statement that enables you to view all of the data in the Test1 table.

What statement should you use?

You should use the following *SELECT* statement:

```
SELECT * FROM Test1
```

Chapter 6: Accessing and Modifying Data
Review

page 227   1. What are the four primary properties that most *SELECT* statements describe in a result set?

Most *SELECT* statements describe the following four primary properties of a result set:

- **The columns to be included in the result set**
- **The tables from which the result set data is retrieved**
- **The conditions that the rows in the source table must meet to qualify for the result set**
- **The ordering sequence of the rows in the result set**

2. What are the main clauses of a *SELECT* statement?

    The main clauses of a *SELECT* statement can be summarized as follows:

    SELECT *select_list*

    [INTO *new_table_name*]

    FROM *table_list*

    [WHERE *search_conditions*]

    [GROUP BY *group_by_list*]

    [HAVING *search_conditions*]

    [ORDER BY *order_list* [ASC I DESC]]**

3. What are several keywords that you can use in a select list?

    DISTINCT, TOP *n*, **and AS**

4. What type of objects can you specify in the FROM clause of a *SELECT* statement?

    Tables, views, joins, and derived tables

5. What purpose does a join provide when used in a *SELECT* statement?

    By using joins, you can retrieve data from two or more tables based on logical relationships between the tables. Joins indicate how SQL Server should use data from one table to select the rows in another table.

6. What are the differences between inner joins and outer joins?

    Inner joins return rows only when there is at least one row from both tables that matches the join condition, eliminating the rows that do not match with a row from the other table. Outer joins, however, return all rows from at least one of the tables or views mentioned in the FROM clause (as long as these rows meet any WHERE or HAVING search conditions).

7. What is a subquery?

    A subquery is a *SELECT* statement that returns a single value and is nested inside a *SELECT*, *INSERT*, *UPDATE*, or *DELETE* statement or inside another subquery. A subquery can be used anywhere an expression is allowed. A subquery is also called an inner query or inner select, while the statement containing a subquery is called an outer query or outer select.

8. What are the differences between a CUBE operator and a ROLLUP operator?

    The ROLLUP operator generates a result set that is similar to the result sets generated by the CUBE operator. The differences between CUBE and ROLLUP are as follows:

- CUBE generates a result set showing aggregates for all combinations of values in the selected columns.

- ROLLUP generates a result set showing aggregates for a hierarchy of values in the selected columns.

9. For what types of columns can you not specify values in an *INSERT* statement?

    Columns with an IDENTITY property, columns with a DEFAULT definition that uses the *NEWID* function, and computed columns

10. What methods can you use to modify data in a SQL Server database?

    The *UPDATE* statement, database APIs and cursors, and the *UPDATE-TEXT* statement

11. What are the major clauses contained in an *UPDATE* statement?

    SET, WHERE, and FROM

12. Which statement should you use to delete all rows in a table without having the action logged?

    The *TRUNCATE TABLE* statement

Chapter 7: Managing and Manipulating Data
Lesson 1: Importing and Exporting Data
Exercise 1: Importing and Exporting Data

page 239

▶ **To use *BULK INSERT* statements to import data into the OrderStatus and-FormOfPayment tables**

1. Use *BULK INSERT* statements to insert data from the FormOfPayment.txt file to the FormOfPayment table and from the OrderStatus.txt file to the Order-Status table.

    What statements should you use?

    Use the following *BULK INSERT* statements:

    ```
    USE BookShopDB
    BULK INSERT FormOFPayment
    FROM 'c:\formofpayment.txt'
    WITH (DATAFILETYPE = 'CHAR')
    BULK INSERT OrderStatus
    FROM 'c:\orderstatus.txt'
    WITH (DATAFILETYPE = 'CHAR')
    ```

page 239

▶ **To use *BULK INSERT* statements to import data into the Authors table, Books table, Customers table, and Employees table**

1. Use *BULK INSERT* statements to insert data from the Authors.txt file into the Authors table, from the Books.txt file into the Books table, from the Customers.txt file into the Customers table, and from the Employees.txt file into the Employees table.

   What statements should you use?

   Use the following *BULK INSERT* statements:

   ```
   USE BookShopDB
   BULK INSERT Authors
   FROM 'c:\authors.txt'
   WITH (DATAFILETYPE = 'CHAR')
   BULK INSERT Books
   FROM 'c:\books.txt'
   WITH (DATAFILETYPE = 'CHAR')
   BULK INSERT Customers
   FROM 'c:\customers.txt'
   WITH (DATAFILETYPE = 'CHAR')
   BULK INSERT Employees
   FROM 'c:\employees.txt'
   WITH (DATAFILETYPE = 'CHAR')
   ```

page 239

▶ **To use the bcp command prompt utility to import data into the BookAuthors table**

1. Use the bcp utility to copy data from the BookAuthors.txt file into the Book-Authors table.

   What bcp command should you use?

   bcp bookshopdb..bookauthors in bookauthors.txt -c –T

Chapter 7: Managing and Manipulating Data
Review

page 266

1. What are the differences between importing data and exporting data?

   Importing data is the process of retrieving data from sources external to SQL Server (for example, an ASCII text file) and inserting it into SQL Server tables. Exporting data is the process of extracting data from an instance of SQL Server into some user-specified format (for example, copying the contents of a SQL Server table to a Microsoft Access database).

2. What tools are available to import data into or export data out of a SQL Server database?

   The bcp command prompt utility, the *BULK INSERT* statement, and Data Transformation Services (DTS)

3. What tasks can you perform by using DTS?

You can extract, transform, and consolidate data from disparate sources into single or multiple destinations.

4. What data access technology is used by SQL Server to support distributed queries?

OLE DB, the Microsoft specification of an API for universal data access

5. What two methods can you use in distributed queries to reference heterogeneous OLE DB data sources?

Using linked server names or ad hoc computer names

6. What is a linked server?

A linked server is a virtual server that has been defined in SQL Server. The linked server definition includes all of the information needed to access an OLE DB data source. You can set up a linked server by using Enterprise Manager or by using the *sp_addlinkedserver* system stored procedure. The linked server definition contains all of the information needed to locate the OLE DB data source.

7. What functionality do cursors support in order to extend result processing?

Cursors extend result processing by supporting the following functionality:

- **Allowing positioning at specific rows of the result set**
- **Retrieving one row or block of rows from the current position in the result set**
- **Supporting data modifications to the rows at the current position in the result set**
- **Supporting different levels of visibility to changes made by other users to the data presented in the result set**
- **Providing Transact-SQL statements in scripts, stored procedures, and triggers access to the data in a result set**

8. Which three types of cursor implementations does SQL Server support?

Transact-SQL server cursors, API server cursors, and client cursors

9. How do Transact-SQL cursors differ from API server cursors?

Transact-SQL Server cursors are based on the *DECLARE CURSOR* statement and are used mainly in Transact-SQL scripts, stored procedures, and triggers. Transact-SQL cursors are implemented on the server and are managed by Transact-SQL statements sent from the client to the server. They are also contained in batches, stored procedures, or triggers. API server cursors support the API cursor functions in OLE DB, ODBC, and DB-Library. API server cursors are implemented on the server. Each time

a client application calls an API cursor function, the SQL Server OLE DB provider, ODBC driver, or DB-Library DLL transmits the request to the server for action against the API server cursor.

10. What features are included in SQL Server to support XML functionalities?

The following features support XML functionalities:

- **The capability to access SQL Server through HTTP**
- **Support for XDR schemas and the capability to specify XPath queries against these schemas**
- **The capacity to retrieve and write XML data:**
  - **Retrieving XML data by using the *SELECT* statement and the FOR XML clause**
  - **Writing XML data by using the OPENXML rowset provider**
- **Retrieving XML data by using the XPath query language**
- **Enhancements to the SQLOLEDB that enable XML documents to be set as command text and to return result sets as a stream**

11. What does the FOR XML clause in a *SELECT* statement enable you to do?

The FOR XML clause enables you to execute SQL queries and to return the result in XML format.

12. What does the *OPENXML* function enable you to do?

The *OPENXML* function is a Transact-SQL keyword that provides a rowset over in-memory XML documents. *OPENXML* is a rowset provider similar to a table or a view. *OPENXML* enables access to XML data as if it were a relational rowset by providing a rowset view of the internal representation of an XML document. The records in the rowset can be stored in database tables (similar to the rowsets provided by tables and views).

Chapter 8: Implementing Stored Prodedures
Lesson 1: Introduction to Stored Procedures
Exercise 1: Exploring Stored Procedures

page 273   ▶   **To view system stored procedures in the Master database**

6. How can you tell the difference between a system stored procedure and an extended stored procedure from the list of procedures that appears below the Stored Procedures node?

System stored procedures usually contain an *sp_* prefix, while extended stored procedures usually contain the *xp_* prefix. There are exceptions to this rule, however. You can verify the type of stored procedure by using the *OBJECTPROPERTY* function.

Lesson 2: Creating, Executing, Modifying, and Deleting Stored Procedures
Exercise 2: Working With Stored Procedures

page 289   ▶   **To execute the stored procedure**

2. In the previous example, *EXEC* was specified to run the stored procedure. Was it necessary to use this keyword?

   No, it isn't necessary to specify *EXEC* or *EXECUTE* in this case, because the stored procedure to run is the first line in the Transact-SQL statement.

Chapter 8: Implementing Stored Prodedures
Review

page 309   1. You create a local temporary stored procedure and ask a colleague to execute the stored procedure. Your colleague claims that she cannot execute the stored procedure. Why can't she execute the stored procedure?

   Local temporary stored procedures may only be executed by the creator of the stored procedure from the connection used to create the procedure. When the connection terminates, the local temporary stored procedure is removed.

2. Why do complex stored procedures typically execute faster the second time they are run than the first time?

   The first time the stored procedure is run, an execution plan is created and the stored procedure is compiled. Subsequent processing of the compiled stored procedure is faster because SQL Server does not recheck command syntax, re-create an execution plan, or recompile the procedure. SQL Server stores the execution plan for the procedure in its procedure cache. The cache is checked first before a new execution plan is created for the procedure.

3. What security features are available for stored procedures?

   Database users can be given permission to execute a stored procedure without being granted permissions to access the database objects on which the stored procedure operates. A stored procedure can be encrypted when it is created or altered so that users cannot read the Transact-SQL commands in the stored procedure.

4. What function can you use to check the properties of a stored procedure and other objects in SQL Server?

   The *OBJECTPROPERTY* function enables you to view various attributes of database objects (including stored procedures). The following example shows how to use *OBJECTPROPERTY* to check whether a procedure is extended:

   ```
   SELECT OBJECTPROPERTY(object_id('storedprocedurename'), 'IsExtendedProc')
   ```

5. Why is it more efficient to modify a stored procedure by using the ALTER PROCEDURE keywords than it is to drop and re-create a stored procedure?

    Modifying a procedure (rather than dropping and recreating it) is a time saver, because most of the stored procedure properties (such as permissions) are retained when a procedure is modified.

6. You set the current database to Northwind, and then you create a stored procedure named *#Procedure01*. You then check the Northwind database for the stored procedure, but it doesn't appear. You can run the stored procedure using Northwind as the current database. Why are you able to execute this stored procedure but it doesn't appear in the Northwind database?

    Appending a stored procedure name with a # sign upon creation creates a local temporary stored procedure. This action instructs SQL Server to create the procedure in TempDB. Therefore, the stored procedure does not appear in the Northwind database. The procedure is available from any database without fully qualifying its name, provided that it executes from the connection that created it.

7. In what three ways is the *RETURN* statement used in a stored procedure?

    First, it is commonly used to provide a return code for error handling. Second, if no integer is specified with the *RETURN* statement, it simply exits unconditionally from a stored procedure. Third, it can be used for purposes other than error handling. For example, in Exercise 3 you used the *RETURN* statement to provide the integer value provided by the *@@IDENTITY* function.

Chapter 9: Implementing Triggers
Review

page 339

1. You have applied constraints, an INSTEAD OF trigger, and three AFTER triggers to a table. A colleague tells you that there is no way to control trigger order for the table. Is he correct? Why or why not?

    He is incorrect. INSTEAD OF triggers always fire before constraints are processed. Following constraint processing, the AFTER triggers fire. Because there are three AFTER triggers, you can be sure about their execution order by using *sp_settriggerorder* to define the first and last trigger to execute.

2. You need to make sure that when a primary key is updated in one table, all foreign key references to it are also updated. How should you accomplish this task?

    Configure cascading referential integrity to the foreign key constraints so that updates to the primary key are propagated to the other tables.

3. Name four instances when triggers are appropriate.

   Triggers are appropriate in the following instances:

   - **If using declarative data integrity methods does not meet the functional needs of the application**
   - **If changes must cascade through related tables in the database**
   - **If the database is denormalized and requires an automated way to update redundant data contained in multiple tables**
   - **If a value in one table must be validated against a non-identical value in another table**
   - **If customized messages and complex error handling are required**

4. When a trigger fires, how does it track the changes that have been made to the modified table?

   An INSERT or UPDATE trigger creates the Inserted (pseudo) table in memory. The Inserted table contains any inserted or updated data. The UPDATE trigger also creates the Deleted (pseudo) table, which contains the original data. A DELETE trigger also creates a Deleted (pseudo) table in memory. The Deleted table contains any deleted data. The transaction isn't committed until the trigger completes. Thus, the trigger can roll back the transaction.

5. Name a table deletion event that does not fire a DELETE trigger.

   TRUNCATE TABLE does not fire a DELETE trigger because the transaction isn't logged. Logging the transaction is critical for trigger functions, because without it, there is no way for the trigger to track changes and roll back the transaction if necessary.

6. Name a system stored procedure and a function used to view the properties of a trigger.

   The *sp_helptrigger* system stored procedure shows the properties of one or all triggers applied to a table or view. The *OBJECTPROPERTY* function is used to determine the properties of database objects (such as triggers). For example, the following code returns 1 if a trigger named Trigger01 is an INSTEAD OF trigger:

```
SELECT OBJECTPROPERTY (OBJECT_ID('trigger01'),
'ExecIsInsteadOfTrigger')
```

7. Using Transact-SQL language, what are two methods to stop a trigger from running?

You can use the *ALTER TABLE* statement to disable a trigger. For example, to disable a trigger named Trigger01 that is applied to a table named Table01, type the following:

```
ALTER TABLE table01 DISABLE TRIGGER trigger01.
```

A second option is to delete the trigger from the table by using the *DROP TRIGGER* statement.

8. Write a (COLUMNS_UPDATED()) clause that detects whether columns 10 and 11 are updated.

```
IF ((SUBSTRING(COLUMNS_UPDATED(),2,1)=6))
PRINT 'Both columns 10 and 11 were updated.'
```

9. Name three common database tasks accomplished with triggers.

Maintaining running totals and other computed values; creating audit records; invoking external actions; and implementing complex data integrity

10. What command can you use to prevent a trigger from displaying row count information to a calling application?

In the trigger, type the following:

```
SET NOCOUNT ON
```

There is no need to include SET NOCOUNT OFF before exiting the trigger, because system settings configured in a trigger are only in effect while the trigger is running.

11. What type of event creates both an Inserted and Deleted logical table?

An UPDATE event is the only type of event that creates both pseudo tables. The Inserted table contains the new value specified in the update, and the Deleted table contains the original value before the UPDATE runs.

12. Is it possible to instruct a trigger to display result sets and print messages?

Yes, it is possible to display result sets by using the *SELECT* statement and print messages to the screen by using the PRINT command. You shouldn't use *SELECT* and PRINT to return a result, however, unless you know that all applications that will modify tables in the database can handle the returned data.

Chapter 10: Implementing Views
Review

page 365

1. What is a view?

A view is a virtual table whose contents are defined by a query. Like a real table, a view consists of a set of named columns and rows of data. A view does not exist as a stored set of data values in a database, however. The rows

and columns of data come from tables referenced in the query defining the view and are produced dynamically when the view is referenced. Views are generally used to focus, simplify, and customize each user's perception of the database. A view acts as a filter on the underlying tables referenced in the view. The query that defines the view can be from one or more tables or from other views in the current or other databases. Distributed queries can also be used to define views that use data from multiple heterogeneous sources.

2. What functions can a view be used to perform?

A view can be used to perform any or all of the following functions:

■ **Restricting a user to specific rows in a table**

■ **Restricting a user to specific columns**

■ **Joining columns from multiple tables so that they look like a single table**

■ **Aggregating information instead of supplying details**

3. For what scenarios can views be used?

Views can be used in a variety of ways to return data:

■ **To focus on specific data**

■ **To simplify data manipulation**

■ **To customize data**

■ **To export and import data**

■ **To combine partitioned data**

4. What are at least five restrictions that you must adhere to when creating views?

You must adhere to the following restrictions:

■ **You can create views only in the current database. The tables and views referenced by the new view, however, can exist in other databases or even in other servers if the view is defined with distributed queries.**

■ **View names must follow the rules for identifiers and must be unique for each user. Additionally, a view name must not be the same as any table owned by that user.**

■ **You can build views on other views and on procedures that reference views. SQL Server 2000 enables views to be nested up to 32 levels.**

■ **You cannot associate rules or DEFAULT definitions with views.**

■ **You cannot associate AFTER triggers with views (only INSTEAD OF triggers).**

■ **The query that defines the view cannot include the ORDER BY, COM-PUTE, or COMPUTE BY clauses or the INTO keyword.**

■ **You cannot define full-text index definitions for views.**

■ **You cannot create temporary views, and you cannot create views on temporary tables.**

- **Views or tables that participate in a view created with the SCHEMAB-INDING clause cannot be dropped unless the view is dropped or changed so that it no longer has schema binding. In addition, *ALTER TABLE* statements on tables that participate in views having schema binding will fail if these statements affect the view definition.**
- **You cannot issue full-text queries against a view, although a view definition can include a full-text query if the query references a table that has been configured for full-text indexing.**

5. What two tools does SQL Server provide to create a view?

   Enterprise Manager and the *CREATE VIEW* statement in Transact-SQL

6. Where are the result sets stored for standard views and indexed views?

   For standard views, the result set is dynamically built when the view is called. For indexed views, the result set is stored in the database.

7. If a view is going to be indexed, what type of index must be the first index created on that view?

   A unique clustered index

8. Which Transact-SQL statement (or statements) should you use to change the definition of a view or to delete that view from the database?

   Use the *ALTER VIEW* statement to modify the view definition, and use the *DROP VIEW* statement to delete the view from the database.

9. What Transact-SQL statement should you use if you want to view all of the data in the AuthorNames view of the Northwind database?

   Use the following Transact-SQL statement:

   ```
   USE Northwind
   SELECT *
   FROM AuthorNames
   ```

10. Which Transact-SQL statement (or statements) should you use to insert, modify, and delete data through a view?

    Use the *INSERT* statement to add data, the *UPDATE* statement to modify data, and the *DELETE* statement to delete data.

11. What conditions must a view meet before you can modify data through that view?

    A view must meet the following conditions:

    - **The view contains at least one table in the FROM clause of the view definition; the view cannot be based solely on an expression.**

- No aggregate functions (*AVG, COUNT, SUM, MIN, MAX, GROUPING, STDEV, STDEVP, VAR*, or *VARP*) or GROUP BY, UNION, DISTINCT, or TOP clauses are used in the select list. Aggregate functions can be used within a subquery defined in the FROM clause, however, provided that the derived values generated by the aggregate functions are not modified.

- No derived columns are used in the select list. Derived columns are result set columns that are formed by anything other than a simple column reference.

12. When is a view considered to be an updateable partitioned view?

A view is considered an updateable partitioned view if the view is defined with a set of *SELECT* statements whose individual result sets are combined into one by using the *UNION ALL* statement. Each individual *SELECT* statement references one SQL Server base table. The table can be either a local table or a linked table referenced using a four-part name, the *OPEN-ROWSET* function, or the *OPENDATASOURCE* function (you cannot use an *OPENDATASOURCE* or *OPENROWSET* function that specifies a pass-through query).

Chapter 11: Implementing Indexes
Lesson 1: Index Architecture
Exercise 1: Viewing Index Properties and Using an Index

page 375   ▶ **To view index properties in the Northwind database**

3. Which index represents the sort order of the Customers table?

The PK_Customers index is a clustered index. If a table contains a clustered index, the table's sort order is the sort order of the clustered index.

4. Does the Customers table contain a composite index?

No, the Customers table does not contain any composite indexes, because each index key on the Customers table is composed of a single column.

page 375   ▶ **To run queries and examine the execution plan**

6. Why did the Query Optimizer choose the City index rather than the PK_Customers index in this case?

The City nonclustered index is a covering index for this query. The index key of the City index is the City column. The leaf level of the B-tree for the nonclustered index is the index key of the clustered index, CustomerID.

Chapter 11: Implementing Indexes
Lesson 2: Index Creation and Administration
Exercise 2: Creating a Clustered Index

page 387

▶ **To create and test a nonclustered index**

7. Why didn't the Query Optimizer use the clustered index Books_pk?

The TitleSoldStatus index is a covering index for the query. The index key contains the Title and Sold columns. The bookmark in the nonclustered index is TitleID because the Books_pk clustered index uses TitleID as its index key.

Chapter 11: Implementing Indexes
Review

page 392

1. Can a clustered index also be a unique index?

Yes, a unique index can be defined for both a clustered or nonclustered index. If you create a primary key constraint on a table that does not contain a clustered index, SQL Server automatically creates a clustered, unique index for the primary key constraint.

2. If you query a Customers table containing a clustered index on the primary key column, CustomerID, and a nonclustered index on the LastName column, is the nonclustered index a covering index for the following Transact-SQL statement?

```
SELECT LastName, CustomerID FROM Customers WHERE LastName LIKE 'nej'
```

Yes, the nonclustered index contains the LastName column as its index key, and the index pages at the leaf level of the B-tree use the clustered index key CustomerID. Therefore, the nonclustered index covers everything contained in the query.

3. Is a composite index key always part of a covering index?

No, a covering index could contain a single column. An index is considered covering when the result set of a query is provided entirely by the index. Therefore, a query of a single column is covered by an index that uses that column as its index key.

4. How does the global fill factor affect existing indexes and new indexes where a fill factor is not specified?

A global fill factor affects an index when it is created without the FILLFACTOR clause. If you change the global default fill factor from zero to another value, existing indexes are unaffected—but any new index that is created without the FILLFACTOR clause inherits the global fill factor setting.

5. How do you maintain a fill factor in existing indexes?

    A fill factor is set when the index is created and the index fills from that point. For example, if you create an index with a fill factor of 70 percent, 30 percent of the index is empty to accommodate new index entries. As new records are inserted, the index pages grow to accommodate the new entries, and the index pages become less than 30 percent empty. Eventually, the index pages will split to accommodate additional entries. To avoid or reduce the frequency of page splits, re-create the index with the original fill factor by using CREATE INDEX and specifying the DROP_EXISTING and FILLFACTOR clauses. You can also use DBCC DBREINDEX to rebuild the index.

6. What type of index can assist the following query?

    ```
    SELECT productname FROM products WHERE productname LIKE '%tool'
    ```

    The Query Optimizer might choose an index containing the ProductName index key, but parsing the index will not significantly affect the speed at which records are returned for this type of query. A full-text index applied to the ProductName column will assist with this query. The Products table containing the ProductName key should have at least one unique index. The simplest way to ensure the presence of a unique index is by applying a primary key constraint to a column (or columns) in the table.

7. You create the following composite index:

    ```
    CREATE UNIQUE CLUSTERED INDEX index01
    ON employees(socialsecuritynumber, lastname)
    ```

    Is Index01 ideal for the following query? Explain your answer.

    ```
    SELECT socialsecuritynumber, lastname FROM employees WHERE lastname =
     'kaviani'
    ```

    No, it isn't. The index key starts with the Social Security number and then the last name, but the query searches on the lastname column to find a match. The query is covered by the index, but a covering index optimized for this query contains the LastName column as the first part of the index key.

8. Why is it unwise to create wide, clustered index keys?

    A clustered index requires additional disk capacity because the index contains the table and the index key. Therefore, the wider the index key, the greater the disk capacity required to contain the index. In addition, nonclustered indexes on the same table or view use the clustered index key as their bookmarks. Therefore, wide clustered index keys create large nonclustered indexes.

9. Which index type, clustered or nonclustered, must be most carefully designed? Explain your answer.

   A clustered index must be most carefully designed because the table is physically sorted by the clustered index key, and you can create only a single clustered index on a table or view. The clustered index is typically designed to accommodate the most common queries and is most effective for range queries. The sort order of the clustered index should represent the most common sort of characteristics specified by users. When the ORDER BY clause specified in a *SELECT* statement matches the sort order of the clustered index, the Query Optimizer does not need to perform a sort operation.

10. If a table contains a single, nonclustered index, what is its bookmark?

    The bookmark of a nonclustered index is a RID when a clustered index does not exist on the table. The RID is a pointer to a table row in a heap, and it consists of a page number, file number, and slot number. A table without a clustered index is called a heap.

11. What is the default sort order for an index key?

    An index key is sorted in ascending order unless you specify descending order (the DESC keyword).

12. You wish to create a nonclustered index on a view in SQL Server 2000 Enterprise Edition, but an error message is returned indicating that you cannot create a nonclustered index on the view. What is the most likely reason for this error message?

    A unique, clustered index must exist on a view before you can create a nonclustered index on the view. The clustered index on a view is the result set returned by the view. Without the result set provided by the clustered index, there is nothing on which to create a nonclustered index.

Chapter 12: Managing SQL Server Transactions and Locks Review

page 429

1. What three operations do transaction logs support?

   Transaction logs support the following three operations:

   - **Recovery of individual transactions**
   - **Recovery of all incomplete transactions when SQL Server is started**
   - **Rolling a restored database forward to the point of failure**

2. What events are recorded in a transaction log?

The following events are recorded in a transaction log:

- **The start and end of each transaction**
- **Every data modification (insert, update, or delete)**
- **Every extent allocation or deallocation**
- **The creation or dropping of a table or index**

3. When are checkpoints created in a transaction log?

Checkpoints are created when the following events occur:

- **When a *CHECKPOINT* statement is executed**
- **When an *ALTER DATABASE* statement is used to change a database option**
- **When an instance of SQL Server is stopped by executing a *SHUT-DOWN* statement or by using the SQL Server Service Control Manager to stop the service running an instance of the database engine**
- **When an instance of SQL Server periodically generates automatic checkpoints in each database to reduce the amount of time the instance would take to recover the database**

4. When does log truncation occur?

Log truncation occurs at the completion of any *BACKUP LOG* statement and occurs every time a checkpoint is processed (provided the database is using the simple recovery model).

5. What is a transaction?

A transaction is a sequence of operations performed as a single logical unit of work. To qualify as a transaction, a logical unit of work must exhibit four properties called the ACID properties (atomicity, consistency, isolation, and durability).

6. What three types of transactions does SQL Server support, and how do they differ?

The three types of transactions are explicit, autocommit, and implicit. An explicit transaction is one in which you explicitly define both the start and the end of the transaction. An autocommit transaction is the default transaction management mode of SQL Server. Every Transact-SQL statement is committed or rolled back when it is completed. When a connection is operating in implicit transaction mode, SQL Server automatically starts a new transaction after the current transaction is committed or rolled back. You do nothing to delineate the start of a transaction; instead, you only commit or roll back each transaction. Implicit transaction mode generates a continuous chain of transactions.

7. What Transact-SQL statement is used to mark the starting point of an explicit transaction?

BEGIN TRANSACTION

8. What two phases are used to manage the commit process in the distributed transaction?

The prepare phase and the commit phase

9. What are the differences between lost updates and uncommitted dependencies?

Lost updates occur when two or more transactions select the same row and then update the row based on the value originally selected. Each transaction is unaware of other transactions. The last update overwrites updates made by the other transactions, which results in lost data. Uncommitted dependency occurs when a second transaction selects a row that is being updated by another transaction. The second transaction is reading data that has not been committed yet and might be changed by the transaction updating the row.

10. What are the differences between optimistic concurrency and pessimistic concurrency?

Optimistic concurrency control works on the assumption that resource conflicts between multiple users are unlikely (but not impossible) and enables transactions to execute without locking any resources. Only when attempting to change data are resources checked to determine whether any conflicts have occurred. If a conflict occurs, the application must read the data and attempt the change again. Pessimistic concurrency control locks resources as they are required for the duration of a transaction. Unless deadlocks occur, a transaction is assured of successful completion.

11. What isolation levels does SQL Server support?

The following isolation levels are supported:

- **Read uncommitted (the lowest level, at which transactions are isolated only enough to ensure that physically corrupt data is not read)**
- **Read committed (SQL Server default level)**
- **Repeatable read**
- **Serializable (the highest level, at which transactions are completely isolated from one another)**

12. What guidelines should you follow to help minimize deadlocks?

You should adhere to the following guidelines:

- **Access objects in the same order.**
- **Avoid user interaction in transactions.**
- **Keep transactions short and in one batch.**

- Use a low isolation level.
- Use bound connections.

Chapter 13: Designing and Administering SQL Server 2000 Security
Lesson 2: Designing a Database Security Plan
Exercise 1: Designing Security for BookShopDB

page 447

▶ **To identify security requirements**

2. Identify and write down the security requirements contained in the system requirements.

- **Managers must be able to access and modify employee information.**
- **Only managers can access or modify employee information.**
- **All employees can access information about authors, books in stock, customers, and orders.**
- **All employees can create, track, and modify orders online.**
- **Only managers can modify information about authors, books, and customers.**

3. Identify and write down two security requirements that do not appear in the list extracted from the system requirements.

There are many right answers. The following list shows three possible items to include:

- **Two employees must be able to run a backup of the database.**
- **Managers must be able to administer SQL Server security for all employees.**
- **A trusted developer who is not part of the company and one manager must have full access to the database.**

page 447

▶ **To determine users, groups, and roles for security and create a User-to-Activity Map**

1. Assuming that SQL Server is running in a Microsoft Windows domain named BOOKSHOP, create a list of unique users, roles, and groups to accommodate the security requirements. List only the users, roles, or groups that you believe are required to accommodate the security requirements.

- **BOOKSHOP\Managers (All managers are members.)**
- **BOOKSHOP\Users (All employees, including managers, are members.)**
- **Public role (All authenticated users are members.)**
- **BOOKSHOP\Staff01 and BOOKSHOP\Staff02 (The two users to be granted backup privileges for SQL Server use these Windows accounts.)**

- **db_BackupOperator fixed database role (BOOKSHOP\Staff01 and BOOKSHOP\Staff02 are members.)**
- **SecurityAdmin fixed server role (BOOKSHOP\Managers are members.)**
- **DevUser (The outside developer uses this SQL Server login ID.)**
- **BOOKSHOP\Manager01 (The manager to be granted special privileges for SQL Server uses this Windows account.)**
- **SysAdmin fixed server role (BOOKSHOP\Manager01 and DevUser are members.)**

2. Create a User-to-Activity Map that ties the security requirements to the unique users, roles, and groups that you defined in the previous step.

User Account, Group, or Role	Activity
Public (role)	Read-only access to all tables except for the Employees and Positions tables
Public (role)	Add, delete, and modify data in Orders, BookOrders, and OrderStatus tables
BOOKSHOP\Managers	Fully access all user tables
SecurityAdmin	Administer SQL Server security
db_BackupOperator	Run the database backup
SysAdmin (fixed role)	Administer SQL Server

Chapter 13: Designing and Administering SQL Server 2000 Security Review

page 465

1. Which two layers of the security architecture outlined in Lesson 1 contain SQL Server-specific security features?

   The network protocol and SQL Server security layers. The network protocol layer includes the SQL Server 2000 Client Network Utility. With this utility, you configure encryption for Net-Library protocols used between the client and the SQL Server. The SQL Server layer includes the following SQL Server-specific security features:

   - **Pass-through authentication (Windows authentication)**
   - **SQL Server Authentication**
   - **Object and statement permissions**
   - **Special security accounts, such as sa and roles (like fixed roles, the public role, and application roles)**
   - **Database object encryption**
   - **Internal auditing**

2. You specifically revoke the UPDATE permission from User01 for Table01 so that the user cannot update the table. After revoking the permission, User01 still can update Table01. Name three possible reasons for this result. Four possible reasons are included in the answers.

- **Revoking a permission does not necessarily deny a user's access to the permission. If User01 is a member of a group or a role that is granted the UPDATE permission, the user's effective right is the UPDATE permission.**

- **You have removed the permission from Table01 in the wrong database. The majority of permission setting occurs within the context of a database and only applies to objects within the current database.**

- **The Public role is assigned permissions to update Table01.**

- **User01 has been removed from the database and the Guest account is permitted to update Table01.**

3. You create a view and grant the Public role SELECT permission to the view. A user attempts to run the view but receives a permission conflict error message. What is the most likely reason for this result?

The ownership chain is broken. You own the view; another user owns the underlying table; and the user who is attempting to run the view does not have permissions to the underlying table. When an ownership chain is broken, SQL Server evaluates permissions on every object in the chain.

4. You use *sp_revokelogin*, but a Windows user is still able to authenticate to SQL Server. What is the most likely reason why the user can authenticate to SQL Server?

The user is a member of a group that has been granted the right to connect to SQL Server. The *sp_revokelogin* system stored procedure does not deny a user access to log in to SQL Server; rather, it simply removes the account specified in the @loginame input parameter.

5. A SQL Server computer is part of a workgroup. User01 on another Windows computer that is part of the same workgroup wants to log in to SQL Server. Name two ways that the user can connect to SQL Server.

There are a number of ways to connect:

- **The user can log in with a SQL Server login ID.**

- **Create a Windows user account named User01 on the SQL Server computer. Make the password for User01 on the SQL Server the same as the User01 account on the client computer.**

- **Add the local User01 account to a Windows group that has been permitted to establish a connection with SQL Server.**

6. You use *sp_droplogin* to delete a SQL Server login ID from SQL Server, but you receive an error message stating that the security account is mapped or aliased to a database. You then use *sp_revokelogin* to delete a Windows account from SQL Server. You know that the Windows user account is mapped to several databases, but the procedure succeeds. Explain why you can delete the Windows account but you cannot delete the SQL Server login ID.

   You must run *sp_revokedbaccess* against all databases where a SQL Server login ID has been granted access. Then, the security account can be deleted from SQL Server by using *sp_droplogin*. When you delete a Windows account from SQL Server by using *sp_revokelogin*, SQL Server automatically removes the account from any databases where privileges have been assigned. In Enterprise Manager, you can delete any security account without first revoking database privileges.

7. Why is there no place in Enterprise Manager to make a Windows user account or SQL Server login ID a member of a Windows group?

   Windows Group membership is assigned outside SQL Server by using Windows operating system tools such as User Manager, and only Windows accounts (users and groups) can be members of a Windows group. Therefore, you cannot assign a SQL Server login ID as a member of a Windows group.

8. You map the special Guest account to a database named DB01, but you don't grant the Guest account any privileges in the database. You then run SQL Profiler and notice that a user who is not mapped to DB01 deleted a table in the database. What is the most likely reason why the user could delete a table?

   A user who is not mapped to a database can connect to the database as the Guest account if Guest is mapped to the database. The *CREATE TABLE* statement might have been assigned to the Public role, and because Guest is mapped to the database, Guest is a member of the Public role.

page 466

9. You use the *DENY* statement to explicitly deny User01 and DOMAIN01\IT Users the CREATE VIEW permission. What Transact-SQL statement do you use to clear the explicit denial?

   Use the *REVOKE* statement to clear an explicit denial. The following *REVOKE* statement clears the denial described in the question:

   ```
   USE pubs
   REVOKE CREATE VIEW
   TO user01, [DOMAIN01\it users]
   ```

10. Using Enterprise Manager, you attempt to modify the permissions of a standard database role, but the Permissions button is inactive. You are connected to the database as a member of the SysAdmin role. Why is the Permissions button unavailable?

You are attempting to modify permissions on a fixed database role. You cannot modify permissions assigned to either predefined role type (fixed server or fixed database).

11. What are the next important steps after implementing a security design?

Verifying the security design by connecting to the database with various security accounts and testing permissions and audit activity with SQL Profiler

12. Explain the purpose of an application role and how you activate it.

Application roles provide a method of controlling access to a database from within an application. When an application role is active, the user's privileges in the database are irrelevant until the session is ended. Use the *sp_setapprole* system stored procedure to activate an application role.

Chapter 14: SQL Server Monitoring and Tuning
Lesson 1: Monitoring Databases with SQL Profiler
Exercise 1: Capturing Events Using SQL Profiler

page 476   ▶   **To analyze the trace data**

3. Which statement in the batch required the most CPU time to execute?

```
SELECT * FROM table01
WHERE uniqueid BETWEEN 5000 AND 10000
```

This statement requires the most CPU time to execute. The amount of CPU time will vary depending on the speed of the processor(s) used for this exercise.

4. Which event required the most CPU time? Explain your answer.

The SQL:BatchCompleted event appears to take the most time to execute. However, if you sum the three Transact-SQL statements, you will see that the CPU time is equivalent to the SQL:BatchCompleted CPU time. Therefore, the event that required the most CPU time is the following statement:

```
SELECT * FROM table01 WHERE uniqueid BETWEEN 5000 AND 10000
```

If you regularly execute batches of SQL Statements, the SQL:BatchCompleted event is useful in determining the most expensive batch.

10. How does the trace output differ from the trace you created in the previous practice?

The SQL:BatchCompleted event appears after each Transact-SQL statement. If you sum the CPU time for the three Transact-SQL statements, you will see that placing a *GO* statement between each SQL statement is slightly less processor intensive. However, the processor isn't the only resource to consider. Placing a *GO* statement between each statement slightly increases network traffic.

Chapter 14: SQL Server Monitoring and Tuning
Review

page 486

1. Name a monitoring feature that sends database information to a Network Management System (NMS).

   SQL Server 2000 contains MIB files that can be loaded into an NMS so that the NMS can monitor various aspects of SQL Server activity.

2. Name a SQL Server tool you can use to monitor current SQL Server activity.

   The Current Activity node of Enterprise Manager and SQL Profiler are two SQL Server tools that monitor current activity.

3. Several users inform you that database performance levels seem to change right around the time that staff rotations occur. How can you use SQL Profiler to determine if the staff rotation has anything to do with changing performance levels?

   Run a trace several times a day as staff is rotated in and out. Create or use an existing template that groups activity by users. Analyze the activity to determine if there is a user running inappropriate or intensive queries.

4. You are concerned about database security. How can you use SQL Profiler to alleviate your concerns?

   Create a trace that includes some or all of the event classes in the Security Audit collection. Run the trace continuously or intermittently depending on your security needs.

5. How can you reduce the amount of data collected by a trace?

   Be selective about which event classes and data columns should be part of a trace. Further restrict the amount of data captured by applying data filters in the Filters tab of the Event Properties dialog box.

6. Where can trace data be stored?

   When you create a trace you can instruct SQL Profiler to create a trace file or a trace table. If you don't select a trace table or trace file location, the trace will be lost when SQL Profiler is closed.

7. As you move through the Index Tuning wizard screens, you see that choosing a script from the Query Analyzer is not an option. What is the most likely reason for this result?

   You did not open the Index Tuning wizard from Query Analyzer. The script option is available in the Index Tuning wizard only when the wizard is started from Query Analyzer.

8. How can you start a trace in Query Analyzer?

Use SQL Profiler to define the properties of a trace. Then, create a script from the Script Trace option below the File menu. You can create a script for either SQL Server 7.0 or SQL Server 2000. The script trace contains SQL Profiler stored procedures and input parameters necessary to create a trace. Load the script into the Query Analyzer, make some minor modifications as explained in the script file, and run the trace by executing the script.

9. What application requirement must be met for the application to benefit from a federation of servers?

The application must send requests for data or updates to the member server with the most data required to complete the statement.

10. How must member tables be configured to support distributed partitioned views?

Each member table has the same number of columns as the original table, and each column has the same attributes (such as data type, size, and collation) as the corresponding column in the original table.

11. What are two ways that CPU consumption can be reduced when performing an analysis with the Index Tuning wizard?

Any two of the following are acceptable for reducing CPU consumption: lower the level of analysis by selecting the Fast or Medium tuning modes; analyze a smaller workload and fewer tables; run the analysis against a test version of the production server; and run the wizard on a client computer instead of the SQL Server.

12. The Index Tuning wizard can create indexed views on what SQL Server editions?

SQL Server Enterprise Edition and SQL Server Developer's Edition support indexed views. Therefore, the Index Tuning wizard can create indexed views on these platforms. If you run the Index Tuning wizard on another edition of SQL Server, such as SQL Server Personal Edition, the Add Indexed Views checkbox is not available.

Glossary

Symbols

@@ERROR A global variable that holds the error number for the last Transact-SQL statement executed. A value of 0 indicates no error. @@ERROR is reset after each statement is executed, so its value needs to be checked immediately after each Transact-SQL statement. The value must be saved to a local variable if it is to be used later in the code.

@@ROWCOUNT A global variable that holds the number of rows returned by the last Transact-SQL statement. @@ROWCOUNT is reset after each statement is executed, so its value should be saved to a local variable if it is needed later in the code.

A

ACID For a unit of work to qualify as a transaction, it must exhibit four characteristics: atomicity, consistency, isolation, and durability.

action A user-initiated operation upon a selected cube or portion of a cube. The operation can launch an application with the selected item as a parameter or retrieve information about the selected item.

active statement A SQL statement that has been executed but whose result set has not yet been canceled or fully processed.

ActiveX Data Objects (ADO) An easy-to-use application programming interface (API) that wraps OLE DB for use in languages such as Visual Basic, Visual Basic for Applications, Active Server Pages, and Microsoft Internet Explorer Visual Basic Scripting.

ad hoc connector name The OPENROWSET function in the FROM clause of a query that allows all connection information for an external server and data source to be issued every time the data must be accessed.

add-in A custom extension (written in any language that supports the Component Object Model, or COM usually Visual Basic) that interacts with Analysis Manager and provides specific functionality. Add-ins are registered with the Analysis Add-In Manager. They are called by the Analysis Add-In Manager in response to user actions in the user interface.

ADO *See* ActiveX Data Objects (ADO).

aggregate function A function that performs a calculation on a column in a set of rows and returns a single value.

aggregate query A query (SQL statement) that summarizes information from multiple rows by including an aggregate function such as SUM or AVG.

aggregation A table or structure that contains pre-calculated data for a cube. An aggregation is also a collection of objects that makes a whole. An aggregation can be a concrete or conceptual set of whole-part relationships among objects.

aggregation prefix A string that is combined with a system-defined ID to create a unique name for a partition's aggregation table.

aggregation wrapper A wrapper that encapsulates a COM object within another COM object.

alert A user-defined response to a SQL Server event. Alerts can either execute a defined task or send an e-mail or pager message to a specified operator.

alias An alternative name for a table or column in expressions that is often used to shorten the name for subsequent reference in code to prevent possible ambiguous references or to provide a more descriptive name in the query output. An alias can also be an alternative name for a server.

aliasing To allow the name of an object, property, or relationship to be reused in a new context while keeping all other attributes constant.

American National Standards Institute (ANSI) An organization of American industry and business groups that develops trade and communication standards for the United States. Through membership in the International Organization for Standardization (ISO) and the International Electrotechnical Commission (IEC), ANSI coordinates American standards with corresponding international standards.

Analysis server The server component of Analysis Services that is specifically designed to create and maintain multidimensional data structures and provide multidimensional data in response to client queries.

annotational property A property that is maintained by Meta Data Services as string data that can be attached to any repository object that exposes the IAnnotationalProps interface.

anonymous subscription An anonymous subscription is a type of pull subscription for which detailed information about the subscription and the Subscriber is not stored.

ANSI *See* American National Standards Institute (ANSI).

API *See* application programming interface (API).

API server cursor A server cursor built to support the cursor functions of an application programming interface (API) such as ODBC, OLE DB, ADO, and DB-Library. An application does not usually request a server cursor directly; rather, it calls the cursor functions of the API. The SQL Server interface for that API implements a server cursor if that is the best way to support the requested cursor functionality. *See also* server cursor.

application programming interface (API) A set of routines available in an application, such as ADO, for use by software programmers when designing an application interface.

application role A SQL Server role created to support the security needs of an application.

archive file The .CAB file created by archiving an Analysis Services database.

article An object specified for replication. An article is a component in a publication and can be a table, specified columns (using a column filter), specified rows (using a row filter), a stored procedure or view definition, the execution of a stored procedure, a view, an indexed view, or a user-defined function.

atomic A condition in which either all or none of the transaction data modifications are performed.

atomicity A state where all data modifications are performed, or none are performed; an atomic unit of work. Atomicity is one of the required characteristics for a transaction.

attribute In data mining, a single characteristic of a case. Attributes are used to provide information about a case. For example, weight can be an attribute of a case that involves shipping containers. *See also* case.

authentication The process of validating that the user who is attempting to connect to SQL Server is authorized to do so. *See also* SQL Server Authentication.

authorization The operation that verifies the permissions and access rights granted to a user.

automatic recovery Recovery that occurs every time SQL Server is restarted. Automatic recovery protects your database if there is a system failure.

autonomy The independence that one site has from other sites when performing modifications to data.

availability A measure of how often a system is running and available to users.

AVG A SQL function to calculate the average of an expression.

axis A set of tuples. Each tuple is a vector of members. A set of axes defines the coordinates of a multidimensional data set. *See also* slice, tuple.

B

backup A copy of a database, transaction log, file, or filegroup used to recover data after a system failure.

backup device A tape or disk used in a backup or restore operation.

backup file A file that stores a full or partial database, transaction log, file, or filegroup backup.

backup media The tape, disk, or named pipe used to store a backup set.

backup set The output of a single backup operation.

balanced hierarchy A dimension hierarchy in which all leaf nodes are the same distance from the root node.

base data type Any system-supplied data type, such as char, varchar, binary, and varbinary. User-defined data types are derived from base data types. *See also* data type, user-defined data type.

base table A table stored permanently in a database. Base tables are referenced by views, cursors, SQL statements, and stored procedures. *See also* underlying table.

batch A set of SQL statements submitted together and executed as a group. A script is often a series of batches submitted one after the other.

bcp files Files that store bulk copy data created by the bulk copy utility or synchronization.

bcp utility A command prompt bulk copy utility that copies SQL Server data to or from an operating system file in a user-specified format.

bigint data type An integer data type with a value from -2^{63} (-9223372036854775808) through $2^{63} -1$ (9223372036854775807).

binary data type A fixed-length binary data type with a maximum length of 8000 bytes.

binary large object (BLOB) A piece of binary data that has an exceptionally large size (such as pictures or audio tracks stored as digital data) or any variable or table column large enough to hold such values. In Transact-SQL, a BLOB is stored in an image column. Sometimes the term BLOB is also applied to large character data values, such as those stored in text or ntext columns.

binding In SQL application programming interfaces (APIs), refers to associating a result set column or a parameter with a program variable so that data is moved automatically into or out of a program variable when a row is fetched or updated.

bit data type A data type that holds a value of either 1 or 0.

bitwise operation An operation that manipulates a single bit or tests whether a bit is on or off.

BLOB *See* binary large object (BLOB).

blocks A series of Transact-SQL statements enclosed by BEGIN and END. You can nest BEGIN...END blocks within other BEGIN...END blocks.

Boolean An operation or expression that can be evaluated only as either true or false.

browse mode A function that enables you to scan database rows and update their values one row at a time. Several browse mode functions return information that an application can use to examine the structure of a complicated ad hoc query.

built-in functions A group of predefined functions provided as part of the Transact-SQL and multidimensional expressions (MDX) languages.

bulk copy program (BCP) A command-prompt bulk copy utility that copies SQL Server data to or from an operating system file in a user-specified format.

BULK INSERT A SQL statement to bulk copy data to a SQL Server instance within a SQL statement. The BULK INSERT command can be used from within a Transact-SQL statement.

business logic *See* business rules.

business rules The logical rules that are used to run a business. Business rules can be enforced in the .COM objects that make up the middle tier of a Windows DNA system. They can also be enforced in a SQL Server database by using triggers, stored procedures, and constraints.

C

cache aging The mechanism of caching that determines when a cache row is outdated and when it must be refreshed.

cached execution plan A query execution plan that has been inserted into the execution plan, cached, and is available for reuse on the next execution of the query. Cached execution plans are one of the major performance features of SQL Server and allow the optimization step of query execution, which can be time-consuming, to be avoided on subsequent query executions. Execution plans are aged out of cache when they have not been accessed for a certain amount of time and each time the server is rebooted.

calculated column A column in a table that displays the result of an expression rather than stored data (for example, CalculatedCostColumn = Price * Quantity).

calculated field A field defined in a query that displays the result of an expression, rather than stored data.

calculated member A member of a dimension whose value is calculated at run time by using an expression. Calculated member values can be derived from other members' values. A calculated member is any member that is not an input member. For example, a calculated member Profit can be determined by subtracting the value of the member Costs from the value of the member Sales. *See also* input member.

calculation condition A multidimensional expressions (MDX) logical expression used to determine whether a calculation formula will be applied against a cell in a calculation subcube. *See also* solve order.

calculation formula A multidimensional expression (MDX) used to supply a value for cells in a calculation subcube (subject to the application of a calculation condition). *See also* solve order.

calculation pass A stage of calculation in a multidimensional cube in which applicable calculations are evaluated. Multiple passes might be required to complete all calculations. *See also* solve order.

calculation subcube The set of multidimensional cube cells used to create a calculated cells definition. The set of cells is defined by a combination of multidimensional expressions (MDX) set expressions. *See also* solve order.

call-level interface (CLI) The interface supported by ODBC for use by an application.

candidate key A column (or set of columns) that has a unique value for each row in a table. Each candidate key value uniquely identifies a single row in the table. Tables can have multiple candidate keys. One candidate key in a table is specified by the database designer to be the primary key for the table, and any other candidate key is called an alternate key.

cardinality A ratio that describes the number of relationship instances (for example, one-to-many).

cascading delete An operation that deletes a row containing a primary key value that is referenced by foreign key columns in existing rows in other tables. On a cascade delete, all of the rows whose foreign key values reference the deleted primary key value are also deleted.

cascading update An operation that updates a primary key value that is referenced by foreign key columns in existing rows in other tables. On a cascade update, all of the foreign key values are updated to match the new primary key value.

case In data mining, an abstract view of data characterized by attributes and relations to other cases. A case is a distinct member of a case set and can be a member of multiple case sets. *See also* attribute, case key, case set.

case key In data mining, the element of a case by which the case is referenced within a case set. *See also* case.

case set In data mining, a set of cases. *See also* case.

cell In a cube, the set of properties, including a value, specified by the intersection when one member is selected from each dimension.

certificate A collection of data used for authentication and the secure exchange of information on non-secure networks, such as the Internet. A certificate securely binds a public encryption key to the entity that holds the corresponding private encryption key. Certificates are digitally signed by the issuing certification authority and can be managed for a user, computer, or service.

change script A text file that contains SQL statements for all changes made to a database, in the order in which they were made, during an editing session. Each change script is saved in a separate text file with a .SQL extension. Change scripts can be applied back to the database later by using a tool such as osql.

changing dimension A dimension that has a flexible member structure. A changing dimension is designed to support frequent changes to structure and data.

char data type A character data type that holds a maximum of 8000 characters.

character format Data stored in a bulk-copy data file by using text characters. *See also* native format.

character set A character set determines the types of characters that SQL Server recognizes in the char, varchar, and text data types. Each character set is a set of 256 letters, digits, and symbols specific to a country or language. The printable characters of the first 128 values are the same for all character sets. The last 128 characters, sometimes referred to as extended characters, are unique to each character set. A character set is related to, but separate from, Unicode characters.

CHECK constraint Defines which data values are acceptable in a column. You can apply CHECK constraints to multiple columns, and you can apply multiple CHECK constraints to a single column. When a table is dropped, CHECK constraints are also dropped.

checkpoint An event in which the database engine writes dirty buffer pages to disk. Dirty pages are pages that have been modified, but the modifications have not yet been written to disk. Each checkpoint writes to disk all pages that were dirty at the last checkpoint and that still have not been written to disk. Checkpoints occur periodically based on the number of log records generated by data modifications or when requested by a user or a system shutdown.

child A member in the next lower level in a hierarchy that is directly related to the current member. For example, in a Time dimension containing the levels Quarter, Month, and Day, January is a child of Qtr1.

classification *See* prediction.

clause In English Query, a sequence of related words within a sentence that have both a subject and a predicate and that function as either an independent or a dependent unit. In Transact-SQL, a clause is a subunit of a SQL statement. A clause begins with a keyword.

CLI *See* call-level interface (CLI).

client application An application that retrieves data from an Analysis server and that performs local analysis and presentation of data from relational or multidimensional databases. Client applications connect to the Analysis server through the PivotTable Service component.

client cursor A cursor implemented on the client. The entire result set is first transferred to the client, and the client application programming interface (API) software implements the cursor functionality from this cached result set.

clustered index An index in which the logical order of the key values determines the physical order of the corresponding rows in a table.

clustering A data mining technique that analyzes data in order to group records together according to their location within the multidimensional attribute space. Clustering is an unsupervised learning technique. *See also* segmentation.

code page For character and Unicode data, a definition of the bit patterns that represent specific letters, numbers, or symbols (such as 0x20 representing a blank space and 0x74 representing the character "t"). Some data types use one byte per character, and each byte can have one out of 256 different bit patterns.

collation A set of rules that determines how data is compared, ordered, and presented. Character data is sorted by using collation information, including locale, sort order, and case-sensitivity. *See also* locale, SQL collation.

column In a SQL table, the area in each row that stores the data value for some attribute of the object modeled by the table. For example, the Employees table in the Northwind sample database models the employees of the Northwind Traders company. The LastName column in each row of the Employees table stores the last name of the employee represented by that row in the same way that a Last Name field in a window or form would contain a last name. *See also* row.

column filter Column filters restrict the columns to be included as part of a snapshot or transactional or merge publication.

column-level collation The capability of SQL Server 2000 to support multiple collations in a single instance. Databases can have default collations different from the default collation of the instance. Individual columns and variables can be assigned collations different from the default collation for the instance or database. Each column in a table can have a different collation.

column-level constraint A constraint definition that is specified within a column definition when a table is created or altered. The constraint applies only to the associated column. *See also* constraint.

COM *See* Component Object Model (COM).

COM-structured storage file A Component Object Model (COM) compound file used by Data Transformation Services (DTS) to store the version history of a saved DTS package.

command relationship Provides instructions to hardware based on natural-language questions or commands (for example, "Play the album with song XXX on it").

commit An operation that saves all changes to databases, cubes, or dimensions made since the start of a transaction. A commit guarantees that all of the transaction's modifications are made a permanent part of the database, cube, or dimension. A commit also frees resources, such as locks, that are used by the transaction. *See also* rollback.

Component Object Model (COM) A Microsoft specification for developing component software. Several SQL Server and database application programming interfaces (APIs) such as SQL-DMO, OLE DB, and ADO are based on COM. Some SQL Server components, such as Analysis Services and English Query, store objects as COM objects. *See also* method.

composite index An index that uses more than one column in a table to index data.

composite key A key composed of two or more columns.

computed column A virtual column in a table whose value is computed at run time. The values in the column are not stored in the table but are computed based on the expression that defines the column.

concatenation To combine two or more character strings or expressions into a single character string or expression or to combine two or more binary strings or expressions into a single binary string or expression.

concurrency A process that allows multiple users to access and change shared data at the same time. SQL Server uses locking to allow multiple users to access and change shared data at the same time without a conflict.

connection An interprocess communication (IPC) linkage established between a SQL Server 2000 application and an instance of SQL Server 2000. The connection is a network link if the application is on a computer different from the SQL Server 2000 instance. If the application and the SQL Server 2000 instance are on the same computer, the linkage is formed through a local IPC mechanism, such as shared memory. The application uses the IPC linkage to send Transact-SQL statements to SQL Server and to receive result sets, errors, and messages from SQL Server.

consistency At the end of a transaction, all of the data must be consistent, with data integrity intact. Consistency is one of the four characteristics required for a unit of work to be considered a transaction.

constant A group of symbols that represent a specific data value. The format of a constant depends on the data type of the value that it represents. For example, "abc" is a character string constant, "123" is an integer constant, "December_16,_1999" is a datetime constant, and "0x02FA" is a binary constant.

constraint A property assigned to a table column that prevents certain types of invalid data values from being placed in the column. For example, a UNIQUE or PRIMARY_KEY constraint prevents you from inserting a value that is a duplicate of an existing value; a CHECK constraint prevents you from inserting a value that does not match a search condition; and NOT_NULL prevents you from inserting a NULL value. *See also* column-level constraint.

continuation media The backup media used when the initial medium becomes full, allowing continuation of the backup operation.

control-break report A report that summarizes data in user-defined groups or breaks. A new group is triggered when different data is encountered.

control-of-flow language Transact-SQL keywords that control the flow of execution of SQL statements and statement blocks in triggers, stored procedures, and batches.

correlated subquery A subquery that references a column in the outer statement. The inner query is executed for each candidate row in the outer statement.

CPU busy A SQL Server statistic that reports the time (in milliseconds) that the central processing unit (CPU) spent on SQL Server work.

crosstab query Displays data for summarized values from a field or a table and then groups them by two sets of facts: one down the left side and the other across the top of the data sheet.

COUNT An aggregate function to return the number of items in a group.

cube A set of data that is organized and summarized into a multidimensional structure defined by a set of dimensions and measures. *See also* multidimensional structure.

cube file *See* local cube.

cube role A collection of users and groups that have the same access to a cube. A cube role is created when you assign a database role to a cube, and it applies only to that cube. *See also* custom rule, database role.

cursor An entity that maps over a result set and establishes a position on a single row within the result set. After the cursor is positioned on a row, operations can be performed on that row or on a block of rows starting at that position. The most common operation is to fetch (retrieve) the current row (or block of rows).

cursor data type A special data type used to reference a cursor.

cursor library A part of the ODBC and DB-Library application programming interfaces (APIs) that implements client cursors. A cursor library is not commonly used in current systems; rather, server cursors are used instead.

custom rollup An aggregation calculation that is customized for a dimension level or member and that overrides the aggregate functions of a cube's measures.

custom rule In a role, a specification that limits the dimension members or cube cells that users in the role are permitted to access. *See also* cube role, database role.

D

data block In text, ntext, and image data, a data block is the unit of data transferred all at once between an application and an instance of SQL Server 2000. The term is also applied to the units of storage for these data types. In tape backup files, the data block is the unit of physical input/output (I/O).

data connection A collection of information required to access a specific database. The collection includes a data source name and logon information. Data connections are stored in a project and are activated when the user performs an action that requires access to the database. For example, a data connection for a SQL Server database consists of the name of the database, the location of the server on which it resides, network information used to access that server, and a user ID and password.

data control language (DCL) The subset of SQL statements used to control permissions on database objects (permissions are controlled by using the GRANT and REVOKE statements).

data definition The specification of the attributes, properties, and objects in a database.

data definition language (DDL) A language, usually part of a database management system, that is used to define all attributes and properties of a database, especially row layouts, column definitions, key columns (and sometimes keying methodology), file locations, and storage strategy.

data dictionary A set of system tables that are stored in a catalog and that include definitions of database structures and related information, such as permissions.

data explosion The exponential growth in size of a multidimensional structure, such as a cube, due to the storage of aggregated data. *See also* density, sparsity.

data file In bulk copy operations, the file that transfers data from the bulk copy OUT operation to the bulk copy IN operation. In SQL Server 2000 databases, data files hold the data stored in the database. Every SQL Server 2000 database has at least one primary data file and can optionally have multiple secondary data files to hold data that does not fit on the primary data file. *See also* log file.

data integrity A state in which all the data values stored in the database are correct. If incorrect data values have been stored in a database, the database is said to have lost data integrity.

data lineage Information used by Data Transformation Services (DTS), in conjunction with Meta Data Services, that records the history of package execution and data transformations for each piece of data.

data manipulation language (DML) The subset of SQL statements used to retrieve and manipulate data.

data mart A subset of the contents of a data warehouse. A data mart tends to contain data focused at the department level or on a specific business area. *See also* data warehouse.

data member A child member generated for a non-leaf member in a parent-child dimension. A data member contains a value directly associated with a non-leaf member that is independent of the summary value calculated from the descendants of the member. For example, a data member can contain a manager's salary so that either individual salaries or summarized salaries can be displayed.

data mining model *See* mining model.

data modification An operation that adds, deletes, or changes information in a database by using Transact-SQL statements such as INSERT, DELETE, and UPDATE.

data pump An OLE DB service provider that provides the infrastructure to import, export, and transform data between heterogeneous data stores by using Data Transformation Services (DTS).

data scrubbing Part of the process of building a data warehouse out of data coming from multiple online transaction processing (OLTP) systems. The process must address errors such as incorrect spellings, conflicting spelling conventions between two systems, and conflicting data (such as having two part numbers for the same part).

data source The source of data for an object, such as a cube or a dimension. The data source is also the specification of the information necessary to access source data. The data source sometimes refers to an object of ClassType clsDataSource.

data source name (DSN) The name assigned to an ODBC data source. Applications can use DSNs to request a connection to a system ODBC data source, which specifies the computer name and (optionally) the database to which the DSN maps.

data type An attribute that specifies what type of information can be stored in a column, parameter, or variable. System-supplied data types are provided by SQL Server, and user-defined data types can also be created. *See also* base data type.

data warehouse A database specifically structured for query and analysis. A data warehouse typically contains data representing the business history of an organization. *See also* data mart, fact table.

data-definition query A SQL query that contains data definition language (DDL) statements. These are statements that allow you to create or alter objects (such as tables, indexes, views, and so on) in the database and to migrate database objects from Microsoft Access.

database A collection of information, tables, and other objects organized and presented to serve a specific purpose, such as searching, sorting, and recombining data. Databases are stored in files.

database catalog The part of a database that contains the definition of all the objects in the database as well as the definition of the database. *See also* system catalog.

database diagram A graphical representation of the objects in a database. A database diagram can be either a whole or partial picture of the structure of a database. This diagram includes objects for tables, the columns they contain, and the relationship between them.

database file One of the physical files that make up a database.

database language The language used for accessing, querying, updating, and managing data in relational database systems. SQL is a widely used database language. The Microsoft SQL Server implementation of SQL is called Transact-SQL.

database object A database component, such as a table, index, trigger, view, key, constraint, default, rule, user-defined data type, or stored procedure. The term *database object* can also refer to a database.

database owner A member of the database administrator role of a database. There is only one database owner. The owner has full permissions in that database and determines the access and capabilities provided to other users.

database project A collection of one or more data connections (a database and the information needed to access that database). When you create a database project, you can connect to one or more databases through ODBC and view their components through a visual user interface that includes Database Designer for designing and creating databases and Query Designer for creating SQL statements for any ODBC-compliant database.

database role A collection of users and groups that have the same access to an Analysis Services database. You can assign a database role to multiple cubes in the database, thereby granting the role's users access to these cubes. *See also* cube role, custom rule.

database schema The names of tables, fields, data types, and primary and foreign keys of a database; also known as the database structure.

database script A collection of statements used to create database objects. Transact-SQL scripts are saved as files that usually end with .SQL.

dataset In OLE DB for OLAP, the set of multidimensional data that is the result of executing a multidimensional expressions (MDX) SELECT statement.

datetime data type A SQL Server system data type that stores a combined date and time value from January 1, 1753 through December 31, 9999 with an accuracy of three-hundredths of a second (or 3.33 milliseconds).

DBCS *See* double-byte character set (DBCS).

DCL *See* data control language (DCL).

DDL *See* data definition language (DDL).

deadlock A situation where two users, each having a lock on one piece of data, attempt to acquire a lock on the other's piece. Each user would wait indefinitely for the other to release the lock unless one of the user processes is terminated. SQL Server detects deadlocks and terminates one user's process. *See also* livelock.

decimal data type Fixed-precision and scale-numeric data from $-10^{38} -1$ through $10^{38} -1$.

decision support Systems designed to support the complex analysis required to discover business trends. The information retrieved from these systems allows managers to make business decisions based on a timely and accurate analysis of business trends.

decision tree A treelike model of data that is produced by certain data mining methods. Decision trees can be used for prediction. *See also* prediction.

declarative referential integrity (DRI) A type of data integrity enforced by FOREIGN KEY constraints. The constraints are defined as part of a table definition that enforces proper relationships between tables. The constraints ensure that proper actions are taken when DELETE, INSERT, and UPDATE statements remove, add, or modify primary or foreign key values. The DRI actions enforced by FOREIGN_KEY constraints can be supplemented with additional referential integrity logic defined in triggers on a table.

default A data value, option setting, collation, or name assigned automatically by the system if a user does not specify the value, setting, collation, or name. A default can also refer to an action taken automatically at certain events if a user has not specified the action to take.

DEFAULT constraint A property defined for a table column that specifies a constant to be used as the default value for the column. If any subsequent INSERT or UPDATE statement specifies a value of NULL for the column or does not specify a value for the column, the constant value defined in the DEFAULT constraint is placed in the column.

default database The database to which the user is immediately connected after logging in to SQL Server.

default instance The copy of SQL Server that uses the computer name on which it is installed as its name. *See also* named instance, multiple instances.

default language The language that SQL Server 2000 uses for errors and messages if a user does not specify a language. Each SQL Server 2000 login has a default language.

default member The dimension member used in a query when no member is specified for the dimension. The default member of a dimension is the All member if an (All) level exists (or else an arbitrary member of the highest level). You can also set default members for individual roles in custom rules for dimension security.

default result set The default mode that SQL Server uses to return a result set back to a client. Rows are sent to the client in the order that they are placed in the result set, and the application must process the rows in this order. After executing a SQL statement on a connection, the application cannot do anything on the connection other than retrieve the rows in the result set until all the rows have been retrieved. The only other action that an application can perform before the end of the result set is to cancel the remainder of the result set. This is the fastest method to get rows from SQL Server to the client. *See also* firehose cursor.

Delete query A query (SQL statement) that removes rows from one or more tables.

delimiter In Transact-SQL, characters that indicate the start and end of an object name by using either double quotation marks (" ") or brackets ([ ]).

denormalize To introduce redundancy into a table in order to incorporate data from a related table. The related table can then be eliminated. Denormalization can improve efficiency and performance by reducing complexity in a data warehouse schema. *See also* star schema.

density The percentage of cells that contain data in a multidimensional structure. Analysis Services stores only cells that contain data. A dense cube requires more storage than a sparse cube of identical structure design. *See also* data explosion, sparsity.

deny Removes a permission from a user account and prevents the account from gaining permission through membership in groups or roles within the permission.

dependencies The views and procedures that depend on the specified table or view.

destination object An object in a repository that participates in a relationship such that the object is the destination of the relationship. For example, the component is the destination object in the relationship project. *See also* origin object.

dictionary entry Defined words in the English Query dictionary. You can make additions to the dictionary through the English Query domain editor by specifying the word, its part of speech, and an optional, irregular form.

differential database backup A database backup that records only those changes made to the database since the last full database backup. A differential backup is smaller and faster to restore than a full backup and has a minimal effect on performance.

dimension A structural attribute of a cube, which is an organized hierarchy of categories (levels) that describe data in the fact table. These categories typically describe a similar set of members upon which the user wants to base an analysis. For example, a geography dimension might include levels for Country, Region, State or Province, and City. *See also* level, measure, member group, virtual dimension.

dimension hierarchy One of the hierarchies of a dimension. *See also* hierarchy.

dimension table A table in a data warehouse whose entries describe data in a fact table. Dimension tables contain the data from which dimensions are created. *See also* fact table, primary dimension table.

direct connect The state of being connected to a back-end database so that any changes that you make to a database diagram automatically update your database when you save the diagram or selected items in it.

direct response mode The default mode in which SQL Server statistics are gathered separately from the SQL Server Statistics display. Data is available immediately to SQL Server Performance Monitor; however, the statistics displayed are one period behind the statistics retrieved.

dirty pages Buffer pages that contain modifications that have not been written to disk.

dirty read Reads that contain uncommitted data. For example, transaction1 changes a row. Transaction2 reads the changed row before transaction1 commits the change. If transaction1 rolls back the change, transaction2 has read a row that never logically existed.

distribute To move transactions or snapshots of data from the Publisher to Subscribers, where they are applied to the destination tables in the subscription databases.

distributed query A single query that accesses data from multiple data sources.

distribution database A database on the Distributor that stores data for replication, including transactions, snapshot jobs, synchronization status, and replication history information.

distribution retention period The distribution retention period determines the amount of information stored for a replication agent and the length of time that subscriptions will remain active in the distribution database. When the distribution retention period is exceeded, the Distribution Clean Up Agent runs.

distributed transaction A single transaction that accesses data from multiple data sources. Distributed transactions are managed by the Microsoft Distributed Transaction Coordinator (MS DTC) process and allow the four characteristics of transactions to be adhered to across disparate data sources.

Distributor A server that hosts the distribution database and stores history data, transactions, and metadata. *See also* local Distributor, remote Distributor.

DML *See* data manipulation language (DML).

domain In Windows 2000 security, a collection of computers grouped for viewing and administrative purposes that share a common security database. In relational databases, a domain refers to the set of valid values allowed in a column.

domain integrity An integrity mechanism that enforces the validity of entries for a given column. The mechanism, such as the CHECK constraint, can restrict the possible data values by data type, format, or range of values allowed.

double-byte character set (DBCS) A character set that generally uses two bytes to represent a character, allowing more than 256 characters to be represented. DBCSs are typically used in environments that use ideographic writing systems, such as Japanese, Korean, and Chinese.

DRI *See* declarative referential integrity (DRI).

drill down/drill up A technique for navigating through levels of data ranging from the most summarized (up) to the most detailed (down). For example, when viewing the details of sales data by year, a user can drill down to display sales data by quarter (and furthermore, to display data by month).

drill through To retrieve the detailed data from which the data in a cube cell was summarized.

DSN *See* data source name (DSN).

DSN-less connection A type of data connection that is created based on information in a data source name (DSN) but that is stored as part of a project or application. DSN-less connections are especially useful for Web applications because they enable you to move the application from one server to another without recreating the DSN on the new server.

DTS package An organized collection of connections, Data Transformation Services (DTS) tasks, DTS transformations, and workflow constraints defined by the DTS object model and assembled either with a DTS tool or programmatically.

DTS package template A model Data Transformation Services (DTS) package. The template is used to help create and configure a particular type of package.

dump *See* backup.

dump file *See* backup file.

dynamic cursor A cursor that can reflect data modifications made to the underlying data while the cursor is open. Updates, deletes, and inserts made by users are reflected in the dynamic cursor.

dynamic filter Merge replication filters that restrict data based on a system function or a user-defined function, such as SUSER_SNAME().

dynamic locking The process that SQL Server uses to determine the most cost-effective locks to use at any one time.

dynamic recovery The process that detects and/or attempts to correct software failure or loss of data integrity within a relational database management system (RDBMS).

dynamic snapshot A snapshot of a merge publication with dynamic filters that is applied by using bulk copy files to improve performance.

dynamic SQL statements In Embedded SQL for C, a SQL statement built and executed at run time.

E

encrypted trigger A trigger that is created with an optional encryption parameter that encrypts the definition text and cannot be decrypted. Encryption makes the information indecipherable to protect it from unauthorized viewing or use.

encryption A method for keeping sensitive information confidential by changing data into an unreadable format.

English Query A Microsoft application development product that allows users to ask questions in English, rather than in a computer language such as SQL. For example, you might ask, "How many customers bought products last year?" rather than prepare an equivalent SQL statement.

entity In English Query, an entity is a real-world object referred to by a noun (person, place, thing, or idea). Entities are semantic objects.

entity integrity A state in which all the rows in a database have a not-null primary key value, all tables have primary keys, and no table has any duplicate primary key values. This ensures that there are no duplicate entries for anything represented in the database.

enumeration A data type of a property. An enumeration specifies that a property value should support a fixed set of constant strings or integer values.

equijoin A join in which the values in the columns being joined are compared for equality, and all columns are included in the results.

error log A text file that records system information from SQL Server.

error state number A number associated with SQL Server 2000 messages that helps Microsoft support engineers find the specific code location that issued the message. This information can be helpful in diagnosing errors that might have been generated from multiple locations in the SQL Server 2000 code.

escape character A character used to indicate that another character in an expression is meant literally and not as an operator. For example, in SQL, the character "%" is used as a wildcard character to mean "any number of characters in this position." However, if you want to search for a string such as "10%" (10 percent), you cannot specify "10%" alone as a search string. The "%" would be interpreted as "any number of characters in addition to 10." By specifying an escape character, you can flag instances where "%" specifically means percent. For example, if you specify the escape character "#," you can indicate a search string of "10#%" to mean "10 percent."

exclusive lock A lock that prevents any other transaction from acquiring a lock on a resource until the original lock on the resource is released at the end of the transaction. An exclusive lock is always applied during an update operation (INSERT, UPDATE, or DELETE).

execution plan The path and user context that the SQL Server query optimizer creates for the execution of a query. Every query must have an execution plan created by the SQL Server query optimizer, and plans can be cached for reuse, providing better performance.

explicit transaction A group of SQL statements enclosed within transaction delimiters. The first delimiter must be either BEGIN_TRANSACTION or BEGIN_DISTRIBUTED_TRANSACTION, and the end delimiter must be one of the following: COMMIT_TRANSACTION, COMMIT_WORK, ROLLBACK_TRANSACTION, ROLL-BACK_WORK, or SAVE_TRANSACTION.

expression In SQL, a combination of symbols and operators that evaluates to a single data value. Simple expressions can be a constant, a variable, a column, or a scalar function. Complex expressions are one or more simple expressions connected by operators.

extended stored procedure A function in a dynamic link library (DLL) that is coded by using the SQL Server 2000 Extended Stored Procedure API. The function can then be invoked from Transact-SQL by using the same statements that are used to execute Transact-SQL stored procedures. Extended stored procedures can be built to perform functionality not possible with Transact-SQL stored procedures.

eXtensible Markup Language (XML) Self-describing data in a hypertext format. XML provides for hierarchical data display and is becoming the standard data format for the Internet. Along with the data, the column or attribute names are displayed, and a schema can be included as well.

extent The unit of space allocated to a SQL Server object, such as a table or index, whenever the object needs more space. In SQL Server 2000, an extent is eight contiguous pages.

F

fact A row in a fact table in a data warehouse. A fact contains values that define a data event (such as a sales transaction).

fact table A central table in a data warehouse schema that contains numerical measures and keys relating facts to dimension tables. Fact tables contain data that describes specific events within a business, such as bank transactions or product sales. *See also* data warehouse, dimension table, star join, star schema.

Federal Information Processing Standard (FIPS) Standards that apply to computer systems purchased by the U.S. government. Each FIPS standard is defined by the National Institute of Standards and Technology (NIST). The current standard for SQL products is FIPS 127-2, which is based on the ANSI SQL-92 standard. ANSI SQL-92 is aligned with ISO/IEC SQL-92.

fetch An operation that retrieves a row or block of rows from a cursor. Transact-SQL batches, stored procedures, and triggers use the FETCH statement to fetch from Transact-SQL cursors. Applications use application programming interface (API) fetch functions.

field An area in a window or record that stores a single data value. Some databases, such as Microsoft Access, use the word "field" as a synonym for "column."

field length In bulk copy, the maximum number of characters needed to represent a data item in a bulk copy character format data file.

field terminator In bulk copy, one or more characters marking the end of a field or row, separating one field or row in the data file from the next.

file In SQL Server databases, a basic unit of storage for a database. One database can be stored in several files. SQL Server uses three types of files: data files (which store data), log files (which store transaction logs), and backup files (which store backups of a database).

file DSN Stores connection information for a database in a file that is saved on your computer. The file is a text file with the extension .DSN. The connection information consists of parameters and corresponding values that ODBC Driver Manager uses to establish a connection.

file storage type Defines the storage format used in the data file that transfers data from a bulk copy OUT operation to a bulk copy IN operation. In native mode files, all data is stored using the same internal structures that SQL Server 2000 uses to store the data in a database. In character mode files, all data is converted to character strings.

filegroup In SQL Server, a named collection of one or more files that forms a single unit of allocation.

fill factor An attribute of an index that defines the amount of free space on each page of the index. FILLFACTOR accommodates the future expansion of table data and reduces the potential for page splits. FILLFACTOR is a value from 1 through 100 that specifies the percentage of the index page to be left empty.

filter A set of criteria that controls the set of records returned as a result set. Filters can also define the sequence in which rows are returned.

filtering The ability to restrict data based upon criteria defined in the WHERE clause of a SQL statement. For replication, filtering occurs on table articles defined in a publication. The result is partitions of data that can be published to Subscribers. *See also* partitioning, vertical filtering.

FIPS *See* Federal Information Processing Standard (FIPS).

firehose cursor An obsolete term for the default result set. *See also* default result set.

fixed database role A predefined role that exists in each database. The scope of the role is limited to the database in which it is defined.

fixed server role A predefined role that exists at the server level. The scope of the role is limited to the SQL Server instance in which it is defined.

FK *See* foreign key (FK).

flattened interface An interface created to combine members of multiple interfaces.

flattened rowset A multidimensional data set presented as a two-dimensional rowset in which unique combinations of elements of multiple dimensions are combined on an axis.

float data type A data type that holds floating-point number data from −1.79E + 308 through 1.79E + 308. Float, double precision, and float(n) are SQL Server float data types.

foreign key (FK) The column or combination of columns whose values match the primary key (PK) or unique key in the same or another table. The FK is also called the referencing key.

foreign table A table that contains a foreign key.

forward-only cursor A cursor that cannot be scrolled; rows can be read only in sequence from the first row to the last row.

fragmentation Occurs when data modifications are made. You can reduce fragmentation and improve read-ahead performance by dropping and recreating a clustered index.

full outer join A type of outer join in which all rows in all joined tables are included (whether they are matched or not).

full-text catalog Stores all of the full-text indexes for tables within a database.

full-text enabling The process of allowing full-text querying to occur on the current database.

full-text index The portion of a full-text catalog that stores all of the full-text words and their locations for a given table.

full-text query As a SELECT statement, a query that searches for words, phrases, or multiple forms of a word or phrase in the character-based columns (of char, varchar, text, ntext, nchar, or nvarchar data types). The SELECT statement returns those rows meeting the search criteria.

full-text service The SQL Server component that performs the full-text querying.

function A piece of code that operates as a single, logical unit. A function is called by name, accepts optional input parameters, and returns a status and optional output parameters. Many programming languages support functions, including C, Visual Basic, and Transact-SQL. Transact-SQL supplies built-in functions, which cannot be modified, and supports user-defined functions, which can be created and modified.

G

global default A default that is defined for a specific database and is shared by columns of different tables.

global properties General properties of an English Query application, such as the default year setting or the start date of the fiscal year.

global rule A rule that is defined for a specific database and is shared by columns of different tables.

global subscriptions A subscription to a merge publication with an assigned priority value used for conflict detection and resolution.

global variable In SQL Server, a variable that can be referenced by multiple Data Transformation Services (DTS) tasks. In earlier versions of SQL Server, the term referred to the Transact-SQL system functions whose names start with two "at" signs (@@).

grant The process of applying permissions to a user account to allow the account to perform an activity or to work with data.

granularity The degree of specificity of information contained in a data element. A fact table that has fine granularity contains many discrete facts, such as individual sales transactions. A table that has coarse granularity stores facts that are summaries of individual elements, such as sales totals per day.

guest A special user account that is present in all SQL Server 2000 databases and cannot be removed from any database. If a connection is made by using a login that has not been assigned a user account in a database and the connection references objects in that database, it has the permissions assigned only to the guest account in that database.

GUID Globally unique identifier.

H

heterogeneous data Data stored in multiple formats (for example, data stored in a SQL Server database, a text file, and an Excel spreadsheet).

hierarchy A logical tree structure that organizes the members of a dimension such that each member has one parent member and zero or more child members. *See also* dimension hierarchy, level.

HOLAP *See* hybrid OLAP (HOLAP).

homogeneous data Data that comes from multiple data sources that are all managed by the same software (for example, data that comes from several Exchange spreadsheets or data that comes from several SQL Server 2000 instances). A SQL Server 2000 distributed query is homogeneous if all the data comes from SQL Server 2000 instances.

hop In data communications, one segment of the path between routers on a geographically dispersed network. A hop is comparable to one *leg* of a journey that includes intervening stops between the starting point and the destination. The distance between each of those stops (routers) would be a communications hop.

horizontal partitioning The process of segmenting a single table into multiple tables based on selected rows. Each of the multiple tables has the same columns but fewer rows. *See also* partitioning.

HTML *See* Hypertext Markup Language (HTML).

huge dimension In Analysis Services, a dimension that contains more than approximately 10 million members. Huge dimensions must use relational OLAP (ROLAP) storage mode. *See also* very large dimension.

hybrid OLAP (HOLAP) A storage mode that uses a combination of multidimensional data structures and relational database tables to store multidimensional data. Analysis Services stores aggregations for a HOLAP partition in a multi-dimensional structure and stores facts in a relational database. *See also* multidimensional OLAP (MOLAP), relational OLAP (ROLAP).

Hypertext Markup Language (HTML) A system of marking up, or tagging, a document so that it can be published on the World Wide Web. Documents prepared in HTML include reference graphics and formatting tags. You use a Web browser (such as Microsoft Internet Explorer) to view these documents.

I

identifier The name of an object in a database. An identifier can be from 1 through 128 characters.

identity column A column in a table that has been assigned the IDENTITY property. The IDENTITY property generates unique numbers.

IDENTITY property A property that generates values that uniquely identify each row in a table. When inserting rows into a table that has an identity column, SQL Server generates the next identity value automatically (based on the last-used identity value and the increment value specified during column creation).

idle time A SQL Server 2000 Agent condition that defines the level of central processing unit (CPU) usage by the SQL Server 2000 database engine that constitutes an idle state. SQL Server 2000 Agent jobs can then be created to run whenever the database engine CPU usage falls below the level defined in the idle time definition. This minimizes the impact that the SQL Server Agent jobs might have on other tasks accessing the database.

IEC *See* International Electrotechnical Commission (IEC).

image data type A SQL Server variable-length binary data type that has a maximum length of $2^{31} - 1$ (2,147,483,647) bytes.

immediate updating An option available with snapshot replication and transactional replication that allows data modifications to be made to replicated data at the Subscriber. The data modifications are then immediately propagated to the Publisher by using two-phase commit protocol (2PC).

immediate updating Subscribers *See* immediate updating subscriptions.

immediate updating subscriptions A subscription to a snapshot or transactional publication for which the user is able to make data modifications at the Subscriber. The data modifications are then immediately propagated to the Publisher by using two-phase commit protocol (2PC).

implicit transaction A connection option in which each SQL statement executed by the connection is considered a separate transaction.

implied permission Permission to perform an activity specific to a role. Implied permissions cannot be granted, revoked, or denied.

incremental update The set of operations that either adds new members to an existing cube or dimension, or adds new data to a partition. The incremental update is one of three processing options for a cube or partition and is one of two processing options for a dimension. *See also* process, refresh data.

index In a relational database, a database object that provides fast access to data in the rows of a table (based on key values). Indexes can also enforce uniqueness on the rows in a table. SQL Server supports clustered and nonclustered indexes. The primary key of a table is automatically indexed. In full-text search, a full-text index stores information about significant words and their locations within a given column.

index ORing An execution strategy that consists of looking up rows of a single table that uses several indexes, followed by producing the result (by combining the partial results). This lookup usually corresponds to an OR keyword in a WHERE_<*search_conditions*> clause.

index page A database page containing index rows.

indexed view A SQL view where the data is stored in the database in the indexed order; an indexed view can provide performance gains.

information model An object-oriented schema that defines metadata constructs used to specify the structure and behavior of an application, process, component, or software artifact.

initial media The first medium in each media family.

initial snapshot Files including schema and data, constraints, extended properties, indexes, triggers, and system tables necessary for replication. The initial snapshot is transferred to Subscribers when implementing replication. *See also* Synchronization.

inner join An operation that retrieves rows from multiple source tables by comparing the values from columns shared between the source tables. An inner join excludes rows from a source table that have no matching rows in the other source tables.

input member A member whose value is loaded directly from the data source instead of being calculated from other data. *See also* calculated member.

input set The set of data provided to a multidimensional expressions (MDX) value expression upon which the expression operates.

input source Any table, view, or schema diagram used as an information source for a query.

insensitive cursor A cursor that does not reflect data modifications made to the underlying data by other users while the cursor is open.

Insert query A query that copies specific columns and rows from one table to another or to the same table.

instance A copy of SQL Server running on a computer. A computer can run multiple instances of SQL Server 2000. A computer can run only one instance of SQL Server 7.0 or earlier, although in some cases it can also run multiple instances of SQL Server 2000.

int (integer) data type A SQL Server system data type that holds whole numbers from -2^{31} ($-2,147,483,648$) through $2^{31} -1$ ($2,147,483,647$).

integer In SQL Server 2000, a data type category that includes the bigint, int, smallint, and tinyint data types.

integrated security *See* Windows Authentication.

integrity constraint A property defined on a table that prevents data modifications that would create invalid data.

intent lock A lock placed on one level of a resource hierarchy to protect shared or exclusive locks on lower-level resources. For example, before a SQL Server 2000 database engine task applies shared or exclusive row locks within a table, it places an intent lock on the table. If another task tries to apply a shared or exclusive lock at the table level, it is blocked by the table-level intent lock held by the first task. The second task does not have to check for individual page or row locks before locking the table; rather, it only has to check for an intent lock on the table.

interactive structured query language (isql) An interactive command-prompt utility provided with SQL Server that allows users to execute Transact-SQL statements or batches from a server or workstation and view the results returned.

interface A defined set of properties, methods, and collections that forms a logical grouping of behaviors and data. Classes are defined by the interfaces that they implement. Many different classes can implement an interface.

interface implication If an interface implies another interface, then any class that implements the first interface must also implement the second interface. Interface implication is used in an information model to achieve some of the effects of multiple inheritance.

internal identifier A more compact form of an object identifier in a repository. An internal identifier is guaranteed to be unique only within a single repository. *See also* object identifier.

International Electrotechnical Commission (IEC) One of two international standards bodies responsible for developing international data communications standards. The IEC works closely with the International Organization for Standardization (ISO) to define standards for computing. They jointly published the ISO/IEC SQL-92 standard for SQL.

International Organization for Standardization (ISO) One of two international standards bodies responsible for developing international data communications standards. The ISO works closely with the International Electrotechnical Commission (IEC) to define standards for computing. They jointly published the ISO/IEC SQL-92 standard for SQL.

Internet-enabled A publication setting that enables replication to Internet Subscribers.

interprocess communication (IPC) A mechanism through which operating system processes and threads exchange data and messages. IPCs include local mechanisms such as Windows shared memory or network mechanisms such as Windows Sockets.

IPC *See* interprocess communication (IPC).

ISO *See* International Organization for Standardization (ISO).

isolation level The property of a transaction that controls the degree to which data is isolated for use by one process and is guarded against interference from other processes. Setting the isolation level defines the default locking behavior for all SELECT statements in your SQL Server session.

ISQL *See* interactive structured query language (isql).

J

job A specified series of operations, called steps, performed sequentially by SQL Server Agent.

join As a verb, to combine the contents of two or more tables and produce a result set that incorporates rows and columns from each table. Tables are typically joined by using data that they have in common. As a noun, *join* refers to the process or result of joining tables (as in the term *inner join*) to indicate a particular method of joining tables. *See also* join column.

join column A column referenced in a join condition. *See also* join.

join condition A comparison clause that specifies how tables are related by their join columns.

join field *See* join column.

join filter A row filter used in merge replication that defines a relationship between two tables that will be enforced during synchronization, which is similar to specifying a join between two tables.

join operator A comparison operator in a join condition that determines how the two sides of the condition are evaluated and which rows are returned.

join path A series of joins indicating how two tables are related.

join table *See* junction table.

junction table A table that establishes a relationship between other tables. The junction table contains foreign keys referencing the tables that form the relationship.

K

kernel In SQL Server 2000, a subset of the storage engine that is referenced in some error messages. In Windows 2000, the kernel is the core of the operating system that performs basic operations.

key A column (or group of columns) that uniquely identifies a row (PRIMARY_KEY), defines the relationship between two tables (FOREIGN_KEY), or can be used to build an index. *See also* key column.

key column A column referenced by a primary, foreign, or index key. *See also* key.

key range lock A lock used to lock ranges between records in a table to prevent phantom insertions or deletions into a set of records. A key range lock ensures serializable transactions.

keyset-driven cursor A cursor that shows the effects of updates made to its member rows by other users while the cursor is open but does not show the effects of inserts or deletes.

keyword A reserved word in SQL Server that performs a specific function, such as to define, manipulate, and access database objects.

L

large level A dimension level that contains a number of members that equals or exceeds the threshold for large levels. This threshold varies and is set in the Properties dialog box of Analysis Manager.

latency The amount of time that elapses when a data change is completed at one server and when that change appears at another (for example, the time between when a change is made at a Publisher and when it appears at the Subscriber).

LCID *See* locale identifier (LCID).

leaf In a tree structure, an element that has no subordinate elements. For example, in Analysis Services, a leaf is a dimension member that has no descendants. *See also* non-leaf.

leaf level The bottom level of a clustered or non-clustered index. In a clustered index, the leaf level contains the actual data pages of the table. In a nonclustered index, the leaf level either points to data pages or points to the clustered index (if one exists), rather than containing the data itself.

leaf member A dimension member that does not have descendants.

left outer join A type of outer join in which all rows from the left-most table in the JOIN clause are included. When rows in the left table are not matched by rows in the right table, all result set columns that come from the right table are assigned a value of NULL.

level The name of a set of members in a dimension hierarchy such that all members of the set are at the same distance from the root of the hierarchy. For example, a time hierarchy can contain the levels Year, Month, and Day. *See also* dimension, hierarchy.

level hierarchy *See* dimension hierarchy.

library In Analysis Services, a folder that contains shared objects (such as shared dimensions) that can be used by multiple objects within a database.

linked cube A cube that is based on a cube defined on another Analysis server. *See also* publishing server, source cube, subscribing server.

linked server A definition of an OLE DB data source used by SQL Server 2000 distributed queries. The linked server definition specifies the OLE DB provider required to access the data and includes enough addressing information for the OLE DB provider to connect to the data. Any rowsets exposed by the OLE DB data source can then be referenced as tables (called linked tables) in SQL Server 2000 distributed queries. *See also* local server.

linked table An OLE DB rowset exposed by an OLE DB data source that has been defined as a linked server for use in SQL Server 2000 distributed queries. The rowsets exposed by the linked server can be referenced as tables in distributed queries.

linking table A table that has associations with two other tables and is used indirectly as an association between those two tables.

livelock A request for an exclusive lock that is repeatedly denied because a series of overlapping shared locks keeps interfering. SQL Server detects the situation after four denials and refuses further shared locks. A livelock also occurs when read transactions monopolize a table or a page, forcing a write transaction to wait indefinitely. *See also* deadlock.

local cube A cube created and stored with the extension .CUB on a local computer by using PivotTable Service.

local Distributor A server that is configured as both a Publisher and a Distributor for SQL Server Replication. *See also* Distributor, remote Distributor.

local group A group in Windows NT 4.0 or Windows 2000 containing user accounts and global groups from the domain group in which they are created and any trusted domain. Local groups cannot contain other local groups.

local login identification The identification (ID) that a user must use to log in to a local server. A login ID can have up to 128 characters. The characters can be alphanumeric; however, the first character must be a letter (for example, CHRIS or TELLER8).

local server In SQL Server 2000 connections, an instance of SQL Server 2000 running on the same computer as the application. When resolving references to database objects in a Transact-SQL statement, the local server is the instance of SQL Server 2000 executing the statement. In SQL Server 2000 distributed queries, the local server is the instance of SQL Server 2000 executing the distributed query. The local server then accesses any linked servers referenced in the query. In SQL Server 2000 remote stored procedures, the local server is the instance of SQL Server executing an EXEC statement that references a remote stored procedure. The local server then passes the execution request to the remote server on which the remote stored procedure resides. *See also* linked server, remote server.

local subscription A subscription to a merge publication that uses the priority value of the Publisher for conflict detection and resolution.

local variable A user-defined variable that has an assigned value. A local variable is defined with a DECLARE statement, is assigned an initial value by a SELECT or SET statement, and is used within the statement batch or procedure in which it was declared.

locale The Windows operating system attribute that defines certain behaviors related to language. The locale defines the code page, or bit patterns, used to store character data and the order in which characters are sorted. The locale also defines language-specific items such as the format used for dates and time and the character used to separate decimals in numbers. A unique number called a locale identifier (LCID) identifies each locale. SQL Server 2000 collations are similar to locales in that the collations define language-specific types of behaviors for instances of SQL Server 2000. *See also* collation, locale identifier (LCID).

locale identifier (LCID) A number that identifies a Windows-based locale. *See also* locale.

lock A restriction on access to a resource in a multi-user environment. SQL Server automatically locks users out of a specific row, column, or file in order to maintain security or to prevent concurrent data modification problems.

lock escalation The process of converting many fine-grain locks into fewer coarse-grain locks, thereby reducing system overhead.

log file A file or set of files containing a record of the modifications made in a database. *See also* data file.

logical database design The design of a database based on business requirements, without regard for the physical implementation. Logical database design serves to verify the requirements, before physical implementation, which is much costlier to change, takes place.

logical data model A formal model of business data based on business requirements, without regard for the physical implementation. Generally, the logical model is the first tool designed for a database, and it serves to verify the business assumptions, before physical implementation of a database takes place.

logical name A name that SQL Server uses to identify a file. A logical name for a file must correspond to the rules for identifiers and can have as many as 30 characters (for example, ACCOUNTING or LIBRARY).

logical operators The operators AND, OR, and NOT, which are used to connect search conditions in WHERE clauses.

login (account) An identifier that gives a user permission to connect to SQL Server 2000 by using SQL Server Authentication. Users who connect to SQL Server 2000 by using Windows NT Authentication are identified by their Windows 2000 logon and do not need a separate SQL Server 2000 login.

login security mode A security mode that determines the manner in which a SQL Server 2000 instance validates a login request. There are two types of login security: Windows Authentication and SQL Server authentication.

lookup table A table, either in a database or hard-coded in the English Query application, that contains codes and the English words or phrases that they represent. For example, a gender lookup table contains the following code and English descriptions: M, Male.

M

macro A type of coding that is used like a function but actually consists of a set of instructions.

maintainability A measure of the ease of maintaining a system.

Make Table query A query (SQL statement) that creates a new table and then creates rows in it by copying rows from an existing table.

many-to-many relationship A relationship between two tables in which rows in each table have multiple matching rows in the related table. Many-to-many relationships are maintained by using a third table called a junction table and by adding the primary key columns from each of the other two tables to this table.

many-to-one relationship A relationship between two tables in which one row in one table can relate to many rows in another table.

MAPI *See* Messaging Application Programming Interface (MAPI).

Master database The database that controls the operation of each instance of SQL Server. This database installs automatically with each instance of SQL Server and keeps track of user accounts, remote user accounts, and remote servers with which each instance can interact. This database also tracks ongoing processes, configurable environment variables, system error messages, tapes and disks available on the system, and active locks.

master definition site *See* Publisher.

master file The file installed with earlier versions of SQL Server that is used to store the Master, Model, and Tempdb system databases and transaction logs and the pubs sample database and transaction log.

master site *See* Distributor.

MDX *See* multidimensional expressions (MDX).

measure In a cube, a set of values that are based on a column in the cube's fact table and are usually numeric. Measures are the central values that are aggregated and analyzed. *See also* dimension.

measurement In English Query, an option in the Adjective Phrasing dialog box. By using a measurement, you can specify some measurement that is represented in an entity.

media description The text describing the media set. *See also* media set.

media family All media in a set written by a single device (for example, an initial medium and all continuation media, if any). *See also* media set.

media header A header that provides information about the backup media.

media name The descriptive name for the entire backup media set.

media set All media involved in a backup operation. *See also* media description, media family.

member An item in a dimension representing one or more occurrences of data. A member can be either unique or nonunique. For example, 1997 and 1998 represent unique members in the year level of a time dimension, whereas January represents nonunique members in the month level because there can be more than one January in the time dimension if it contains data for more than one year. *See also* virtual dimension.

member delegation A modeling concept that describes how interface members are mapped from one interface to another.

member group A system-generated parent of a collection of consecutive dimension members. *See also* dimension.

member key column A dimension level's property that specifies the identifiers of the members of the level. The value of this property can specify a column that contains the identifiers or an expression that evaluates to the identifiers. *See also* member name column, member variable.

member name column A dimension level's property that specifies the names of the members of the level. The value of this property can specify a column that contains the names or an expression that evaluates to the names. *See also* member key column, member variable.

member property Information about the members of a dimension level in addition to that contained in the dimension (for example, the color of a product or the telephone number of a sales representative). *See also* virtual dimension.

member variable The value used internally by Analysis Services to identify a dimension member. The MemberKeyColumn property specifies

the member variables for a dimension. For example, a number from one through 12 could be the member variable that corresponds to a month of the year. *See also* member key column, member name column.

memo A type of column containing long strings of text, typically more than 255 characters. A memo is the Access equivalent of a SQL Server text data type.

merge The operation that combines two partitions into a single partition.

merge replication A type of replication that allows sites to make autonomous changes to replicated data (and, at a later time, merge changes and resolve conflicts when necessary). *See also* snapshot replication, transactional replication.

message number A number that identifies a SQL Server 2000 error message.

Messaging Application Programming Interface (MAPI) An e-mail application programming interface (API).

metadata Information about the properties of data, such as the type of data in a column (numeric, text, and so on) or the length of a column. Metadata can also be information about the structure of data or information that specifies the design of objects such as cubes or dimensions.

method A function that performs an action by using a COM object, as in SQL-DMO, OLE DB, and ActiveX Data Objects (ADO). *See also* Component Object Model (COM).

mining model An object that contains the definition of a data mining process and the results of the training activity. For example, a data mining model can specify the input, output, algorithm, and other properties of the process and hold the information gathered during the training activity, such as a decision tree.

mining model training The process that a data mining model uses to estimate model parameters by evaluating a set of known and predictable data. Also, this term refers to the act of causing a mining model to evaluate training data. *See also* training data set.

mirroring The process for protecting against the loss of data due to disk failure by maintaining a fully redundant copy of data on a separate disk. Mirroring can be implemented at several levels: in SQL Server 2000, in the operating system, and in the disk controller hardware.

Mixed Mode Combines Windows Authentication and SQL Server Authentication. Mixed Mode allows users to connect to an instance of SQL Server through either a Windows NT 4.0 or Windows 2000 user account or through a SQL Server login.

model In English Query, a model is the collection of all information that is known about the objects in the English Query application. This information includes the specified database objects (such as tables, fields, and joins); semantic objects (such as entities, the relationships between them, and additional dictionary entries); and global domain default options.

Model database A database installed with SQL Server that provides the template for new user databases. SQL Server 2000 creates a new database by copying in the contents of the model database and then expanding it to the size requested.

model dependency A relationship between two or more models in which one model is dependent on the information of another model.

module A group of objects in a project. You can move objects between modules in a project, thus organizing those objects for a dispersed development environment.

modulo An arithmetic operator that provides the integer remainder after a division involving two integers.

MOLAP *See* multidimensional OLAP (MOLAP).

money data type A SQL Server system data type that stores monetary values from -2^{63} ($-922,337,203,685,477.5808$) through $2^{63} -1$ ($+922,337,203,685,477.5807$) with accuracy to a ten-thousandth of a monetary unit.

multidimensional expressions (MDX) A syntax used for defining multidimensional objects and querying and manipulating multidimensional data.

multidimensional OLAP (MOLAP) A storage mode that uses a proprietary, multidimensional structure to store a partition's facts and aggregations or a dimension. The data of a partition is completely contained within the multidimensional structure. *See also* hybrid OLAP (HOLAP), relational OLAP (ROLAP).

multidimensional structure A database paradigm that treats data not as relational tables and columns but as information cubes that contain dimension and summary data in cells. Each cell is addressed by a set of coordinates that specify a position in the structure's dimensions. For example, the cell at coordinates {SALES, 1997, WASHINGTON, SOFTWARE} would contain the summary of software sales in Washington in 1997. *See also* cube.

multiple inheritance A modeling term that describes how an interface receives the characteristics of more than one parent interface.

multiple instances Multiple copies of SQL Server running on the same computer. There can be one default instance, which can be any version of SQL Server. There can be multiple named instances of SQL Server 2000. *See also* default instance, named instance.

multithreaded server application An application that creates multiple threads within a single process to service multiple user requests at the same time.

multi-user The capability of a computer to support many users operating at the same time while providing the computer system's full range of capabilities to each user.

N

name phrasing An English description of a relationship in which one entity is the name of another entity. For example, in the sentence "Custnames are the names of Customers," Custnames and Customers are both entities.

named instance An installation of SQL Server 2000 that is given a name in order to differentiate it from other named instances and from the default instance on the same computer. A named instance is identified by the computer name and instance name. *See also* default instance, multiple instances.

named pipe An interprocess communication (IPC) mechanism that SQL Server uses to provide communication between clients and servers. Named pipes permit access to shared network resources.

named set A set of dimension members or a set expression that is created for reuse, such as in multidimensional expressions (MDX) queries.

naming relationship A naming convention that identifies the destination objects of that relationship by name.

native format Bulk copy data files in which the data is stored by using the same internal data structures that SQL Server uses to store data in SQL Server databases. Bulk copy can quickly process native mode files because it does not have to convert data when transferring it between SQL Server and the bulk copy data file. *See also* character format.

nchar data type A fixed-length Unicode data type with a maximum of 4000 characters. Unicode characters use two bytes per character and support all international characters.

nested query A SELECT statement that contains one or more subqueries, or another term for subquery.

nested table A data mining model configuration in which a column of a table contains a table.

Net-Library A SQL Server communications component that isolates the SQL Server client software and database engine from the network application programming interfaces (APIs). The SQL Server client software and database engine send generic network requests to a Net-Library, which translates the requests to the specific network commands of the protocol that the user chooses.

nickname When used with merge replication system tables, a nickname is a name for another Subscriber that is known to already have a specified generation of updated data. A nickname is used to avoid sending an update to a Subscriber that has already received those changes.

niladic functions Functions that do not have any input parameters. Most niladic SQL Server functions return system information.

noise word Words that do not participate in a full-text query search (for example, a, and, the, and so on).

nonclustered index An index in which the logical order of the index is different from the physical, stored order of the rows on disk.

non-leaf In a tree structure, an element that has one or more subordinate elements (for example, in Analysis Services, a dimension member that has one or more descendants). In SQL Server indexes, a non-leaf is an intermediate index node that points to other intermediate nodes or leaf nodes. *See also* leaf.

non-leaf member A member that has one or more descendants.

non-repeatable read An inconsistent data read. A non-repeatable read occurs when a transaction reads the same row more than one time and when between the two (or more) reads a separate transaction modifies that row. Because the row was modified between reads within the same transaction, each read produces different values, which introduces inconsistency.

normalization rules A set of database design rules that minimizes data redundancy and results in a database in which the database engine and application software can easily enforce integrity.

ntext data type A variable-length Unicode data type that can hold a maximum of 2^30 –1 (1,073,741,823) characters. An ntext column stores a 16-byte pointer in the data row, and the data is stored separately.

NULL An entry that has no explicitly assigned value. NULL is not equivalent to zero or blank. A value of NULL is not considered to be greater than, less than, or equivalent to any other value (including another value of NULL).

nullability The attribute of a column, parameter, or variable that specifies whether it allows null data values.

numeric expression Any expression that evaluates to a number. The expression can be any combination of variables, constants, functions, and operators.

nvarchar data type A variable-length Unicode data type that has a maximum of 4000 characters. Unicode characters use two bytes per character and support all international characters. Note that sysname is a system-supplied, user-defined data type that is a synonym for nvarchar (128) and is used to reference database object names.

O

object In databases, one of the components of a database: a table, index, trigger, view, key, constraint, default, rule, user-defined data type, or stored procedure.

object identifier A unique name given to an object. In Meta Data Services, a unique identifier is constructed from a globally unique identifier (GUID) and an internal identifier. All objects must have an object identifier. *See also* internal identifier.

object owner The security account that controls the permissions for an object (usually the creator of the object). The object owner is also called the database object owner.

object permission An attribute that controls the capability to perform operations on an object. For example, table or view permissions control which users can execute SELECT, INSERT, UPDATE, and DELETE statements against the table or view.

object variable A variable that contains a reference to an object.

ODBC *See* Open Database Connectivity (ODBC).

ODBC data source The location of a set of data that can be accessed by using an ODBC driver. An ODBC data source is also a stored definition that contains all of the connection information that an ODBC application requires to connect to the data source. *See also* data source.

ODBC driver A dynamic link library (DLL) that an ODBC-enabled application, such as Microsoft Excel, can use to access an ODBC data source. Each ODBC driver is specific to a database management system (DBMS), such as SQL Server, Access, and so on.

ODS *See* Open Data Services (ODS).

OIM *See* Open Information Model (OIM).

OLAP *See* online analytical processing (OLAP).

OLE Automation controller A programming environment (for example, Visual Basic) that can drive Automation objects.

OLE Automation objects A Component Object Model (COM) object that provides Automation-compatible interfaces.

OLE Automation server An application that exposes programmable automation objects to other applications (which are called *automation clients*). Exposing programmable objects enables clients to automate certain functions by directly accessing those objects and by using the services that they make available. For example, a word processor might expose its spell-checking functionality so that other programs can use it.

OLE DB A COM-based application programming interface (API) for accessing data. OLE DB supports accessing data stored in any format (databases, spreadsheets, text files, and so on) for which an OLE DB provider is available. *See also* OLE DB for OLAP.

OLE DB consumer Any software that calls and uses the OLE DB application programming interface (API).

OLE DB for OLAP Formerly, the separate specification that addressed OLAP extensions to OLE DB. Beginning with OLE DB 2.0, OLAP extensions are incorporated into the OLE DB specification. *See also* OLE DB.

OLE DB provider A software component that exposes OLE DB interfaces. Each OLE DB provider exposes data from a particular type of data source (for example, SQL Server databases, Access databases, or Excel spreadsheets).

OLTP *See* online transaction processing (OLTP).

one-to-many relationship In relational databases, a relationship between two tables in which a single row in the first table can be related to one or more rows in the second table, but a row in the second table can be related only to one row in the first table.

one-to-one relationship In a relational database, a relationship between two tables in which a single row in the first table can be related only to one row in the second table, and a row in the second table can be related only to one row in the first table.

online analytical processing (OLAP) A technology that uses multidimensional structures to provide rapid access to data for analysis. The source data for OLAP is commonly stored in data warehouses in a relational database.

online redo log *See* transaction log.

online transaction processing (OLTP) A data processing system designed to record all of the business transactions of an organization as they occur. An OLTP system is characterized by many concurrent users actively adding and modifying data.

Open Data Services (ODS) The layer of the SQL Server database engine that transfers client requests to the appropriate functions in the database engine. ODS exposes the extended stored procedure application programming interface (API) used to write DLL functions that can be called from Transact-SQL statements.

Open Database Connectivity (ODBC) A data access application programming interface (API) that supports access to any data source for which an ODBC driver is available. ODBC is aligned with American National Standards Institute (ANSI) and International Organization for Standardization (ISO) standards for a database Call Level Interface (CLI).

Open Information Model (OIM) An information model published by the Meta Data Coalition (MDC) and widely supported by software vendors. The OIM is a formal description of metadata constructs organized by subject area.

OPENDATASOURCE A Transact-SQL function to allow ad hoc access to a remote server without using a linked server name.

OPENQUERY A Transact-SQL function to execute a passthrough query on a linked server.

OPENROWSET A Transact-SQL function to allow access to a remote server without using a linked server name, by providing all of the datasource information.

OPENXML A Transact-SQL function to open a rowset over an XML document, allowing the document to be part of a Transact-SQL query.

optimize synchronization An option in merge replication that allows you to minimize network traffic when determining whether recent changes have caused a row to move into or out of a partition that is published to a Subscriber.

optimizer *See* Query Optimizer.

ordered set A set of members that is returned in a specific order. The ORDER function in a multidimensional expressions (MDX) query returns an ordered set.

origin object An object in a repository that is the origin in a directional relationship. *See also* destination object, sequenced relationship.

outer join A join that includes all the rows from the joined tables that have met the search conditions (even rows from one table for which there is no matching row in the other join table). For result set rows returned when a row in one table is not matched by a row from the other table, a null value is supplied for all result set columns that are resolved to the table that had the missing row.

overfitting The characteristic of some data mining algorithms that assigns importance to random variations in data by viewing them as important patterns.

P

page In a virtual storage system, a fixed-length block of contiguous virtual addresses copied as a unit from memory to disk and back during paging operations. SQL Server allocates database space in pages. In SQL Server, a page is 8 kilobytes (KB) in size.

page split The process of moving half the rows or entries in a full data or index page to two new pages to make room for a new row or index entry.

parent A member in the next higher level in a hierarchy that is directly related to the current member. The parent value is usually a consolidation of the values of all of its children. For example, in a Time dimension containing the levels Quarter, Month, and Day, Qtr1 is the parent of January.

partition In Analysis Services, one of the storage containers for data and aggregations of a cube. Every cube contains one or more partitions. For a cube that has multiple partitions, each partition can be stored separately in a different physical location. Each partition can be based on a different data source. Partitions are not visible to users; instead, the cube appears to be a single object.

partitioning The process of replacing a table with multiple smaller tables. Each smaller table has the same format as the original table but has a subset of the data. Each partitioned table has rows allocated to it based on some characteristic of the data, such as specific key ranges. The rules that define into which table the rows go must be unambiguous. For example, a table is partitioned into two tables. All rows that have primary key values lower than a specified value are allocated to one table, and all keys equal to or greater than the value are allocated to the other. Partitioning can improve application processing speeds and reduce the potential for conflicts in multi-site update replication. You can improve the usability of partitioned tables by creating a view. The view, created by a union of select operations on all the partitioned tables, presents the data as if it all resides in a single table. *See also* filtering, horizontal partitioning, vertical partitioning.

pass order The order of evaluation (from highest to lowest calculation pass number) and calculation (from lowest to highest calculation pass number) for calculated members, custom members, custom rollup formulas, and calculated cells in a multidimensional cube. The pass order is used to determine formula precedence when calculating values for cells in multidimensional cubes across all calculation passes. *See also* solve order.

pass-through query A query passed uninterpreted to an external server for evaluation. The result set returned by a pass-through query can be used in the FROM clause of a query (like an ordinary base table).

pass-through statement A SELECT statement that is passed directly to the source database without modification or delay. In PivotTable Service, the PASSTHROUGH option is part of the INSERT_INTO statement.

persistence The saving of an object definition so that it will be available after the current session ends.

phantom By one task, the insertion of a new row or the deletion of an existing row in a range of rows previously read by another task that has not yet committed its transaction. The task that has the uncommitted transaction cannot repeat its original read because of the change to the number of rows in the range. If a connection sets its transaction isolation level to serializable, SQL Server uses key-range locking to prevent phantoms.

physical name The path where a file or a mirrored file is located. The default is the path of the Master.dat file followed by the first eight characters of the file's logical name. For example, if Accounting is the logical name and the Master.dat file is located in Sql\Data, the default physical name is Sql\Data\Accounti.dat. For a mirrored file, the default is the path of the Master.mir file followed by the first eight characters of the mirror file's logical name. For example, if Maccount is the name of the mirrored file and the Master.mir file is located in Sql\Data, the default physical name is Sql\Data\Maccount.mir.

physical reads A request for a database page in which SQL Server must transfer the requested page from disk to the SQL Server buffer pool. All attempts to read pages are called logical reads. If the page is already in the buffer, there is no associated physical read generated by the logical read. The number of physical reads never exceeds the number of logical reads. In a well-tuned instance of SQL Server, the number of logical reads is typically much higher than the number of physical reads.

pivot The process of rotating rows to columns and columns to rows in a cross-tabular data browser (to choose dimensions from the set of available dimensions in a multidimensional data structure for display in the rows and columns of a cross-tabular structure).

PK *See* primary key (PK).

position The current location of processing in a cursor. For example, after an application fetches the first 10 rows from a cursor, it is positioned on the 10th row of the cursor. Database application programming interfaces (APIs) also have functions such as the ODBC SQLSetPos function that allow an application to move directly to a specific position in a cursor without performing a fetch.

positioned update An update, insert, or delete operation performed on a row at the current position of the cursor. The actual change is made in the rows of the base tables used to build the current row in the cursor. Transact-SQL batches, stored procedures, and triggers use the WHERE_CURRENT_OF clause to perform positioned updates. Applications use application programming interface (API) functions such as the ODBC SQLSetPos function to perform positioned updates.

precision The maximum total number of decimal digits that can be stored (both to the left and right of the decimal point).

prediction A data mining technique that analyzes existing data and uses the results to predict values of attributes for new records or missing attributes in existing records. For example, you can use existing credit application data to predict the credit risk for a new application. *See also* decision tree.

prefix characters A set of one to four bytes that prefix each data field in a native-format bulk-copy data file. The prefix characters record the length of the data value in the field or contain –1 when the value is NULL.

prefix length The number of prefix characters preceding each non-character field in a bcp native-format data file.

prefix search Full-text query searching for those columns where the specified character-based text, word, or phrase is the prefix. When using a phrase, each word within the phrase is considered a prefix.

primary dimension table In a snowflake schema in a data warehouse, a dimension table that is directly related to and is usually joined to the fact table. Additional tables that complete the dimension definition are joined to the primary dimension table instead of to the fact table. *See also* dimension table, snowflake schema.

primary key (PK) A column (or set of columns) that uniquely identifies all the rows in a table. Primary keys do not allow null values. No two rows can have the same primary key value; therefore, a primary key value always uniquely identifies a single row. More than one key can uniquely identify rows in a table; each of these keys is called a candidate key. Only one candidate can be chosen as the primary key of a table. All other candidate keys are known as alternate keys. Although tables are not required to have primary keys, it is good practice to define them. In a normalized table, all of the data values in each row are fully dependent on the primary key. For example, in a normalized employee table that has EmployeeID as the primary key, all of the columns should contain data related to a specific employee. This table does not have the column DepartmentName because the name of the department is dependent on a department ID, not on an employee ID.

primary table The *one* side of two related tables in a one-to-many relationship. A primary table should have a primary key, and each record should be unique.

private dimension A dimension created for and used by a specific cube. Unlike shared dimensions, private dimensions are available only to the cube in which they are created. *See also* shared dimension.

procedure cache The part of the SQL Server memory pool that is used to store execution plans for Transact-SQL batches, stored procedures, and triggers. Execution plans record the steps that SQL Server must take to produce the results specified by the Transact-SQL statements contained in the batches, stored procedures, or triggers.

process In a cube, the series of operations that rebuilds the cube's structure, loads data into a multidimensional structure, calculates summaries, and saves the precalculated aggregations. As a verb, process refers to populating a cube with data and aggregations. A verb is one of three processing options for a cube.

In a dimension, a process is the operation that loads data from a dimension table in a data warehouse into the levels defined for a dimension and rebuilds the structure of the dimension. The process is one of two processing options for a dimension.

In a data mining model, a process is the operation that retrieves training data from a relational or OLAP data source into the structure defined for a data mining model. Statistically, it analyzes it with a data mining algorithm and saves the statistical data as data mining content. As a verb, process refers to populating a data mining model with data mining content. *See also* incremental update, refresh data.

project In English Query, a file that contains the structure of the relational database and definitions of semantic objects, such as entities, relationships, and dictionary entries. Its extension is .EQP, and it is used to test how English Query translates English questions into SQL statements. Later, it can be compiled into a deployable application file with an .EQD extension.

property A named attribute of a control, field, or database object that you set to define one of the object's characteristics (such as size, color, or screen location) or an aspect of its behavior (such as whether it is hidden).

property pages A tabbed dialog box where you can identify the characteristics of tables, relationships, indexes, constraints, and keys. Every object in a database diagram has a set of properties that determine the definition of a database object. Each set of tabs shows only the properties specific to the selected object. If multiple objects are selected, the property pages show the properties of the first object that you selected.

provider An OLE DB provider or an in-process dynamic link library (DLL) that provides access to a database.

proximity search Full-text query searching for those occurrences where the specified words are close to one another.

publication A publication is a collection of one or more articles from one database. This grouping of multiple articles makes it easier to specify a logically related set of data and database objects that you want to replicate at the same time.

publication database A database on the Publisher from which data and database objects are marked for replication as part of a publication that is propagated to Subscribers.

publication retention period A pre-determined length of time that regulates how long subscriptions will receive updates during synchronizations and remain activated in databases.

published data Data at the Publisher that has been replicated.

Publisher A server that makes data available for replication to other servers, detects changed data, and maintains information about all publications at the site.

publishing server An Analysis server that stores the source cube for one or more linked cubes. *See also* linked cube, subscribing server.

publishing table The table at the Publisher in which data has been marked for replication and is part of a publication.

Pubs database A sample database provided with SQL Server.

pull subscription A subscription created and administered at the Subscriber. Information about the publication and the Subscriber is stored. *See also* push subscription.

push subscription A subscription created and administered at the Publisher. Information about the publication and Subscriber is stored. *See also* pull subscription.

Q

Query Analyzer A tool provided with SQL Server that furnishes an environment in which to write and evaluate Transact-SQL statements. The Query Analyzer provides a graphical interface and tools for browsing the database objects, as well as help for functions.

Query Optimizer The SQL Server database engine component responsible for generating efficient execution plans for SQL statements.

question In English Query, an English form of a query (for example, "How many customers bought products last year?"). Questions can also be posed as statements to an English Query application (for example, "List the customers that bought products last year").

Question Builder A tool that supports users' needs to know more about the domain objects so that they can construct questions. They can find out what the domain objects contain, what kind of basic relationships are represented in the domain, and what English phrases they can use to ask about the relationships.

question file (.EQQ) An ASCII text file that contains questions (one to a line) that are ready for testing with the English Query engine. Question files are denoted with the .EQQ extension. Questions can be submitted to the question file automatically with the test tool, or a developer can create a list of questions.

question template A structure that describes a set of questions that can be asked by using a particular relationship or set of relationships.

queue A SQL Server Profiler queue that provides a temporary holding place for server events to be captured.

R

ragged hierarchy A dimension hierarchy in which one or more levels do not contain members in one or more branches of the hierarchy. For example, the state or province level in a geography hierarchy contains no members for countries that do not have states or provinces. *See also* unbalanced hierarchy.

range query A query that specifies a range of values as part of the search criteria, such as all rows from 10 through 100.

rank For full-text and SQL Server Books Online searches, a value indicating how closely rows or topics match the specified search criteria. For Meta Data Services and Analysis Services, a rank is a value indicating the relative positions of elements such as dimension members, hierarchy levels, or tuples in a set.

RDBMS *See* relational database management system (RDBMS).

real data type A SQL Server system data type that has seven-digit precision (floating precision number data from −3.40E + 38 through 3.40E + 38; storage size is four bytes).

record A group of related fields (columns) of information treated as a unit. A record is more commonly called a row in a SQL database.

recordset The ActiveX Database Objects (ADO) object used to contain a result set. The recordset also exhibits cursor behavior depending on the recordset properties set by an application. ADO recordsets are mapped to OLE DB rowsets.

recovery interval The maximum amount of time that the database engine should require to recover a database. The database engine ensures that the active portion of the database log is small enough to recover the database in the amount of time specified for the recovery interval.

recursive partitioning The iterative process used by data mining algorithm providers of dividing data into groups until no more useful groups can be found.

redo log file *See* backup file.

redundant array of independent disks (RAID) A method used with physical drives to provide fault tolerance. There are different levels of RAID that combine striping of data across the disks and mirroring of data in different configurations. Different RAID levels provide different mixes of cost, performance, and fault tolerance.

referenced key A primary key or unique key referenced by a foreign key.

referencing key *See* foreign key (FK).

referential integrity (RI) A state in which all foreign key values in a database are valid. For a foreign key to be valid, it must contain either a null value or an existing key value from the primary or unique key columns referenced by the foreign key.

reflexive relationship A relationship from a column or combination of columns in a table to other columns in that same table. A reflexive relationship is used to compare rows within the same table. In queries, this comparison is called a self-join.

refresh data The series of operations that clears data from a cube, loads the cube with new data from the data warehouse, and calculates aggregations. Refresh data is used when a cube's underlying data in the data warehouse changes but the cube's structure and aggregation definitions remain the same. The refresh data is one of three processing options for a cube. *See also* incremental update, process.

regular cube A cube that is based on tables and has its own aggregations.

regular dimension A dimension that is neither a parent-child dimension nor a virtual dimension.

relational database A collection of information organized in tables. Each table models a class of objects that are of interest to the organization (for example, Customers, Parts, and Suppliers). Each column in a table models an attribute of the object (for example, LastName, Price, and Color). Each row in a table represents one entity in the class of objects modeled by the table (for example, the customer name John Smith or the part number 1346). Queries can use data from one table to find related data in other tables.

relational database management system (RDBMS) A system that organizes data into related rows and columns. SQL Server is an RDBMS.

relational OLAP (ROLAP) A storage mode that uses tables in a relational database to store multidimensional structures. *See also* hybrid OLAP (HOLAP), multidimensional OLAP (MOLAP).

relationship A link between tables that references the primary key in one table to a foreign key in another table. The relationship line is represented in a database diagram by a solid line if referential integrity between the tables is enforced or a dashed line if referential integrity is not enforced for INSERT and UPDATE transactions. The endpoints of a relationship line show a primary key symbol to denote a primary key-to-foreign key relationship, or they show an infinity symbol (`) to denote the foreign key side of a one-to-many relationship.

In English Query, a relationship is an association between entities that describes what those entities have to do with one another. Relationships can be described concisely in English as simple statements about entities (for example, customers purchase products). More than one join might be required to represent a single relationship.

In Meta Data Services, a relationship is an association between a pair of objects where one object is an origin and the other object is a destination. The association repeats for each subsequent pair of objects so that the destination of one relationship becomes the origin in the next relationship. In this way, all objects in an information model are associated through a chain of relationships that extends from one object to the next throughout the information model.

relationship object An object representing a pair of objects that assume a role in relation to each other. *See also* sequenced relationship.

relationship type A definition of a relationship between two interfaces, as defined in an information model. A relationship type is similar to a class in that it describes characteristics to which specific instances must conform.

remote data Data stored in an OLE DB data source that is separate from the current instance of SQL Server. The data is accessed by establishing a linked server definition or by using an ad hoc connector name.

remote Distributor A server configured as a Distributor that is separate from the server configured as the Publisher. *See also* Distributor, local Distributor.

remote login identification The login identification (login ID) assigned to a user for accessing remote procedures on a remote server.

remote partition A partition whose data is stored on an Analysis server other than the one used to store the metadata of the partition.

remote server A definition of an instance of SQL Server used by remote stored procedure calls. Remote servers are still supported in SQL Server 2000, but linked servers offer greater functionality. *See also* local server.

remote stored procedure A stored procedure located on one instance of SQL Server that is executed by a statement on another instance of SQL Server. In SQL Server 2000, remote stored procedures are supported, but distributed queries offer greater functionality.

remote table A table stored in an OLE DB data source that is separate from the current instance of SQL Server. The table is accessed by either establishing a linked server definition or by using an ad hoc connector name.

replicated data Data at the Subscriber that has been received from a Publisher.

replication A process that copies and distributes data and database objects from one database to another and then synchronizes information between databases for consistency.

replication scripting The generation of .SQL scripts that can be used to configure and disable replication.

replication topology Defines the relationship between servers and the copies of data and clarifies the logic that determines how data flows between servers.

repository The storage container for the metadata used by Analysis Services. Metadata is stored in tables in a relational database and is used to define the parameters and properties of Analysis server objects.

repository engine Object-oriented software that provides management support for and customer access to a repository database.

repository object A COM object that represents a data construct stored in a repository type library.

Repository SQL schema A set of standard tables used by the repository engine to manage all repository objects, relationships, and collections. Repository SQL schema maps information model elements to SQL schema elements.

Repository Type Information Model (RTIM) A core object model that represents repository type definitions for Meta Data Services. This object model is composed of abstract classes upon which instances of information models are based.

republish When a Subscriber publishes data received from a Publisher to another Subscriber.

republisher A Subscriber that publishes data that it has received from a Publisher.

resolution strategy A set of criteria that the repository engine evaluates sequentially when selecting an object (where multiple versions exist and version information is unspecified in the calling program).

restatement In English Query, a query that is a check on the query entered by the end user. Restatements give end users a check that the English Query engine interpreted their question correctly. If the restatement is accurate, the correct SQL statements will be generated, and the returned answer will be valid.

result In English Query, an English answer to a question that has been posed to an English Query application.

result set The set of rows returned from a SELECT statement. The format of the rows in the result set is defined by the column list of the SELECT statement.

return parameters A legacy term for stored procedure output parameters used in the Open Data Services and DB-Library application programming interfaces (APIs).

reusable bookmark A bookmark that can be consumed from a rowset for a given table and used on a different rowset of the same table to position on a corresponding row.

revoke The process of removing a previously granted or denied permission from a user account, role, or group in the current database.

RI *See* referential integrity (RI).

right outer join A type of outer join in which all rows in the rightmost table in the JOIN clause are included. When rows in the right table are not matched in the left table, all result set columns that come from the left table are assigned a null value.

ROLAP *See* relational OLAP (ROLAP).

role A SQL Server security account that is a collection of other security accounts that can be treated as a single unit when managing permissions. A role can contain SQL Server logins, other roles, and Windows logins or groups.

In Analysis Services, a role uses Windows security accounts to limit the scope of access and permissions when users access databases, cubes, dimensions, and data mining models. *See also* rule.

roll forward To apply all the completed transactions from a database or log backup in order to recover a database to a point in time or to the point of failure (for example, after events such as the loss of a disk).

rollback To remove the updates performed by one or more partially completed transactions. Rollbacks are required to restore the integrity of a database after an application, database, or system failure. *See also* commit.

row In a SQL table, the collection of elements that forms a horizontal line in the table. Each row in the table represents a single occurrence of the object modeled by the table and stores the values for all of the attributes of that object. For example, in the Northwind sample database, the Employees table models the employees of the Northwind Traders Company. The first row in the table records all the information (for example, name and title) about the employee who has employee ID 1. *See also* column.

row aggregate function A function that generates summary values that appear as additional rows in the query results (unlike aggregate function results that appear as new columns). This function allows you to see detail and summary rows in one set of results. Row aggregate functions (SUM, AVG, MIN, MAX, and COUNT) are used in a SELECT statement with the COMPUTE clause.

row filter Specifies a subset of rows from a table to be published and when specific rows need to be propagated to Subscribers.

row lock A lock on a single row in a table.

rowset The OLE DB object used to contain a result set. The rowset also exhibits cursor behavior depending on the rowset properties that an application sets.

RTIM *See* Repository Type Information Model (RTIM).

rule A database object that is bound to columns or user-defined data types and specifies which data values are acceptable in a column. CHECK constraints provide the same functionality and are preferred because they are in the SQL-92 standard. In Analysis Services, a rule specifies restrictions such as Unrestricted, Fully Restricted, or Custom for security read and read/write role permissions. *See also* role.

S

sample data Artificially generated data presented instead of actual data when a cube is queried before it has been processed. Sample data enables you to view the effects of structure changes while modifying a cube.

savepoint A marker that allows an application to roll back part of a transaction if a minor error is encountered. The application must still commit or roll back the full transaction when it is complete.

scalar aggregate An aggregate function, such as MIN(), MAX(), or AVG(), that is specified in a SELECT statement column list that contains only aggregate functions. When the column list contains only aggregate functions, then the result set has only one row giving the aggregate values calculated from the source rows that match the WHERE clause predicates.

scheduled backup An automatic backup accomplished by SQL Server Agent when defined and scheduled as a job.

schema In the SQL-92 standard, a collection of database objects that are owned by a single user and form a single namespace. A namespace is a set of objects that cannot have duplicate names. For example, two tables can have the same name only if they are in separate schemas. No two tables in the same schema can have the same name. In Transact-SQL, database user IDs implement much of the functionalities associated with schemas. In database tools, *schema* also refers to the catalog information that describes the objects in a schema or database. In Analysis Services, a schema is a description of multidimensional objects (such as cubes and dimensions).

schema rowset A special OLE DB or Analysis Services rowset that reports catalog information for objects in databases or multidimensional cubes. For example, the OLE DB schema rowset DBSCHEMA_COLUMNS describes columns in tables, and the Analysis Services

MDSCHEMA_MEASURES schema rowset describes the measures in a cube.

script A collection of Transact-SQL statements used to perform an operation. Transact-SQL scripts are stored as files (usually with the .SQL extension).

scroll The capability to move around a cursor in directions other than forward-only. Users can move up and down the cursor.

security A system to authenticate a user's identity and grant or deny access to different database objects. In SQL Server 2000, there are two types of authentication modes: Windows Authentication Mode and Mixed Mode. Security on objects can be granted on most objects, including columns within a table.

Security Identifier (SID) A unique value that identifies a user who is logged on to the security system. SIDs can identify either one user or a group of users.

segmentation A data mining technique that analyzes data to discover mutually exclusive collections of records that share similar attribute sets. A segmentation algorithm can use unsupervised learning techniques such as clustering or supervised learning for a specific prediction field. *See also* clustering.

SELECT The Transact-SQL statement used to return data to an application or to another Transact-SQL statement or to populate a cursor. The SELECT statement returns a tabular result set consisting of data that is typically extracted from one or more tables. The result set contains only data from rows that match the search conditions specified in WHERE or HAVING clauses. In Analysis Services, SELECT is the multidimensional expressions (MDX) statement used to query cubes and return recordsets of multidimensional data.

select list The SELECT statement clause that defines the columns of the result set returned by the statement. The select list is a comma-separated list of expressions, such as column names, functions, or constants.

SELECT query A query that returns rows into a result set from one or more tables. A SELECT query can contain specifications for those columns to return, the rows to select, the order to put the rows in, and how to group (summarize) information.

self-join A join in which records from a table are combined with other records from the same table when there are matching values in the joined fields. A self-join can be an inner join or an outer join. In database diagrams, a self-join is called a reflexive relationship.

semantic object An object that can be represented by a database object or by another real-world object. For example, an entity and a relationship are semantic objects.

semi-additive measure A measure that can be summed along one or more (but not all) dimensions in a cube. For example, a quantity-on-hand measure of inventory can be summed along the geography dimension to produce a total quantity on hand for all warehouses, but it cannot be summed along the time dimension because the measure specifies snapshot quantities periodically in time.

sensitive cursor A cursor that can reflect data modifications made to underlying data by other users while the cursor is open. Updates, deletes, and inserts made by other users are reflected in the sensitive cursor. Sensitive cursors are typically used in Transact-SQL batches, stored procedures, and triggers by omitting the INSENSITIVE keyword on the DECLARE_CURSOR statement.

sequence *See* identity column.

sequenced collection A collection of destination objects of a sequenced relationship object. *See also* sequenced relationship.

sequenced relationship A relationship in a repository that specifies explicit positions for each destination object within the collection of destination objects. *See also* origin object, relationship object, sequenced collection.

serializable The highest transaction isolation level. Serializable transactions lock all rows that they read or modify to ensure that the transaction is completely isolated from other tasks. This procedure guarantees that a series of serializable transactions will always produce the same results if run in the same sequence.

server cursor A cursor implemented on the server. The cursor itself is built at the server, and only the rows fetched by an application are sent to the client. *See also* API server cursor.

server name A name that uniquely identifies a server computer on a network. SQL Server applications can connect to a default instance of SQL Server by specifying only the server name. SQL Server applications must specify both the server name and the instance name when connecting to a named instance on a server.

session In English Query, a sequence of operations performed by the English Query engine. A session begins when a user logs on and ends when the user logs off. All operations during a session form one transaction scope and are subject to permissions determined by the login username and password.

Setup initialization file A text file that uses the Windows .INI file format to store configuration information, enabling SQL Server to be installed without a user having to be present to respond to prompts from the Setup program.

severity level A number indicating the relative significance of an error generated by the SQL Server database engine. Values range from informational (1) to severe (25).

shared dimension A dimension created within a database that can be used by any cube in the database. *See also* private dimension.

shared lock A lock created by non-update (read) operations. Other users can read the data concurrently, but no transaction can acquire an exclusive lock on the data until all the shared locks have been released.

Showplan A report showing the execution plan for a SQL statement. SET_SHOWPLAN_TEXT and SET_SHOWPLAN_ALL produce textual showplan output. Query Analyzer and Enterprise Manager can display showplan information as a graphical tree.

SID *See* Security Identifier (SID).

single-user mode A state in which only one user can access a resource. Both SQL Server instances and individual databases can be put into single-user mode.

slice A subset of the data in a cube, specified by limiting one or more dimensions by members of the dimension. For example, facts for a particular year constitute a slice of multi-year data. *See also* axis.

smalldatetime data type Date and time data from January 1, 1900 through June 6, 2079 with an accuracy of one minute.

smallint data type SQL Server system integer data from -2^{15} ($-32,768$) through $2^{15} - 1$ ($32,767$).

smallmoney data type A SQL Server system data type that stores monetary values from $-214,748.3648$ through $+214,748.3647$, with accuracy to a ten-thousandth of a monetary unit. The storage size is four bytes. When smallmoney values are displayed, they are rounded up two places.

Snapshot Agent Prepares snapshot files containing the schema and data of published tables, stores the files in the snapshot folder, and inserts synchronization jobs in the publication database.

Snapshot Agent utility Configures and triggers the Snapshot Agent, which prepares snapshot files containing schema and data of published tables and database objects.

snapshot cursor *See* static cursor.

snapshot replication A type of replication that distributes data exactly as it appears at a specific moment in time and does not monitor for modifications made to the data. *See also* merge replication, transactional replication.

snowflake schema An extension of a star schema such that one or more dimensions are defined by multiple tables. In a snowflake schema, only primary dimension tables are joined to the fact table. Additional dimension tables are joined to primary dimension tables. *See also* primary dimension table, star schema.

solve order The order of evaluation (from the highest to the lowest solve order) and calculation (from the lowest to the highest solve order) for calculated members, custom members, custom rollup formulas, and calculated cells in a single calculation pass of a multidimensional cube. Solve order is used to determine formula precedence when calculating values for cells in multidimensional cubes, but only within a single calculation pass. *See also* calculation condition, calculation formula, calculation pass, calculation subcube, pass order.

sort order The set of rules in a collation that defines how characters are evaluated in comparison operations and the sequence in which they are sorted.

source and target A browsing technique in which a source object is used to retrieve its target object or objects through their relationship.

source cube The cube on which a linked cube is based. *See also* linked cube.

source database In data warehousing, the database from which data is extracted for use in the data warehouse. *See also* publication database.

source object The single object to which all objects in a particular collection are connected by way of relationships that are all of the same relationship type. For destination collections, the source object is the destination object. For origin collections, the source object is the origin object.

source partition An Analysis Services partition that is merged into another and is deleted automatically at the end of the merger process. *See also* target partition.

sparsity The relative percentage of a multidimensional structure's cells that do not contain data. Analysis Services stores only cells that contain data. A sparse cube requires less storage than a dense cube of identical structure design. *See also* data explosion, density.

SQL *See* Structured Query Language (SQL).

SQL collation A set of SQL Server 2000 collations whose characteristics match those of commonly used code page and sort order combinations from earlier versions of SQL Server. SQL collations are compatibility features that enable sites to choose collations that match the behavior of their earlier systems. *See also* collation.

SQL database A database based on Structured Query Language (SQL).

SQL expression Any combination of operators, constants, literal values, functions, and names of tables and fields that evaluates to a single value.

SQL Mail A component of SQL Server that allows SQL Server to send and receive mail messages through the built-in Windows NT or Windows 2000 Messaging Application Programming Interface (MAPI). A mail message can consist of short text strings, the output from a query, or an attached file.

SQL query A SQL statement, such as SELECT, INSERT, UPDATE, DELETE, or CREATE_TABLE.

SQL Server Authentication One of two mechanisms for validating attempts to connect to instances of SQL Server. Users must specify a SQL Server login ID and password when they connect. The SQL Server instance ensures that the login ID and password combination are valid before allowing the connection to succeed. Windows authentication is the preferred authentication mechanism. *See also* authentication, Windows Authentication.

SQL Server Event Forwarding Server A central instance of SQL Server that manages SQL Server Agent events forwarded to it by other instances. This server enables central management of SQL Server events.

SQL Server login An account stored in SQL Server that allows users to connect to SQL Server.

SQL Server role *See* role.

SQL Server user *See* user (account).

SQL statement A SQL or Transact-SQL command (such as SELECT or DELETE) that performs some action on data.

SQL-92 The version of the SQL standard published in 1992. The international standard is ISO/IEC 9075:1992 Database Language SQL. The American National Standards Institute (ANSI) also published a corresponding standard (Data Language SQL X3.135-1192), so SQL-92 is sometimes referred to as ANSI SQL in the United States.

sql_variant data type A data type that stores values of various SQL Server-supported data types except text, ntext, timestamp, and sql_variant.

standard security *See* SQL Server Authentication.

star join A join between a fact table (typically a large fact table) and at least two dimension tables. The fact table is joined with each dimension table on a dimension key. SQL Server considers special index manipulation strategies on these queries to minimize access to the fact table. An example of a schema that participates in a star join query could be a sales table, the fact table (containing millions of rows), a product table, (containing the description of several hundred products), and a store table (containing several dozen store names). In this example, the product and store tables are dimension tables. A query for selecting sales data for a small set of stores and a subset of products that are restricted by attributes not present in the sales database is an ideal candidate for the star query optimization. *See also* fact table.

star schema A relational database structure in which data is maintained in a single fact table at the center of the schema with additional dimension data stored in dimension tables. Each dimension table is directly related to and usually joined to the fact table by a key column. Star schemas are used in data warehouses. *See also* denormalize, fact table, snowflake schema.

statement permission An attribute that controls whether a user can execute CREATE or BACKUP statements.

static cursor A cursor that shows the result set exactly as it was at the time the cursor was opened. Static cursors do not reflect updates, deletes, or inserts that are made to underlying data while the cursor is open. They are sometimes called snapshot cursors.

static SQL statements In Embedded SQL for C, a SQL statement that is built at the time the application is compiled. The statement is created as a stored procedure when the application is compiled, and the stored procedure is executed when the application is run.

step object A Data Transformation Services (DTS) object that coordinates the flow of control and execution of tasks in a DTS package. A task that does not have an associated step object is never executed.

store-and-forward database *See* distribution database.

stored procedure A precompiled collection of Transact-SQL statements that are stored under a name and are processed as a unit. SQL Server supplies stored procedures for managing SQL Server and for displaying information about databases and users. SQL Server–supplied stored procedures are called system stored procedures.

string A set of contiguous bytes that contains a single, character-based or binary data value. In character strings, each byte (or pair of bytes) represents a single alphabetic letter, a special character, or a number. In binary strings, the entire value is considered to be a single stream of bits that does not have any inherent pattern. For example, the constant "I am 32." is an eight-byte character string, while the constant 0x0205efa3 is a four-byte binary string.

string functions Functions that perform operations on character or binary strings. Built-in string functions return values commonly needed for operations on character data.

Structured Query Language (SQL) A language used to insert, retrieve, modify, and delete data in a relational database. SQL also contains statements for defining and administering the objects in a database. SQL is the language supported by most relational databases and is the subject of standards published by the International Organization for Standardization (ISO) and the American National Standards Institute (ANSI). SQL Server 2000 uses a version of the SQL language called Transact-SQL.

structured storage file *See* COM-structured storage file.

subquery A SELECT statement nested inside another SELECT, INSERT, UPDATE, or DELETE statement or inside another subquery.

subscribe To request data from a Publisher.

Subscriber A server that receives copies of published data.

subscribing server An Analysis server that stores a linked cube. *See also* publishing server, linked cube.

subscription An order that defines what data will be published, when, and to what Subscriber.

subscription database A database at the Subscriber that receives data and database objects published by a Publisher.

subset A selection of tables and the relationship lines between them that is part of a larger database diagram. This selection can be copied to a new database diagram (called subsetting the diagram).

Synchronization In replication, the process of maintaining the same schema and data at a Publisher and at a Subscriber. *See also* initial snapshot.

system administrator (sa) The person or group of people responsible for managing an instance of SQL Server. System administrators have full permissions to perform all actions in an instance of SQL Server. System administrators are either members of the sysadmin fixed server role or log in by using the sa login ID.

system catalog A set of system tables that describe all the features of an instance of SQL Server. The system catalog records metadata such as the definitions of all users, all databases, all objects in each database, and system configuration information such as server and database option settings. *See also* database catalog.

system databases A set of four databases present in all instances of SQL Server that are used to store system information: The Master database

stores all instance-level metadata and records the location of all other databases. The Tempdb database stores transient objects that only exist for the length of a single statement or connection, such as worktables and temporary tables or stored procedures. The Model database is used as a template for creating all user databases. The Msdb database is used by the SQL Server Agent to record information about jobs, alerts, and backup histories. *See also* user database.

system functions A set of built-in functions that perform operations on and return the information about values, objects, and settings in SQL Server.

system stored procedures A set of SQL Server-supplied stored procedures that can be used for actions such as retrieving information from the system catalog or performing administrative tasks.

system tables Built-in tables that form the system catalog for SQL Server. System tables store all the metadata for an instance of SQL Server, including configuration information and definitions of all the databases and database objects in the instance. Users should not directly modify any system table.

T

table A two-dimensional object, consisting of rows and columns, used to store data in a relational database. Each table stores information about one of the types of objects modeled by the database. For example, an education database would have one table for teachers, a second for students, and a third for classes. The columns of a table represent an attribute of the modeled object (for example, first name, last name, and address). Each row represents one occurrence of the modeled object.

table data type A special data type used to store a result set for later processing.

table-level constraint Constraints that allow various forms of data integrity to be defined on one column (column-level constraint) or on several columns (table-level constraints) when the table is defined or altered. Constraints support domain integrity, entity integrity, and referential integrity as well as user-defined integrity.

table lock A lock on a table (including all data and indexes).

table scan A data retrieval operation where the database engine must read all the pages in a table to find the rows that qualify for a query.

Tabular Data Stream (TDS) The SQL Server internal client/server data transfer protocol. TDS allows client and server products to communicate regardless of operating-system platform, server release, or network transport.

tape backup A backup operation to any tape device supported by Windows NT 4.0 and Windows 2000. If you are creating a tape backup file, you must first install the tape device by using Windows NT 4.0 and Windows 2000. The tape device must be physically attached to the SQL Server that you are backing up.

target object *See* source and target.

target partition An Analysis Services partition into which another is merged and that contains the data of both partitions after the merger. *See also* source partition.

task *See* job.

task object A Data Transformation Services (DTS) object that defines pieces of work to be performed as part of the data transformation process. For example, a task can execute a SQL statement or move and transform heterogeneous data from an OLE DB source to an OLE DB destination by using the DTS Data Pump.

TDS *See* Tabular Data Stream (TDS).

tempdb database The database that provides a storage area for temporary tables, temporary stored procedures, and other temporary working storage needs.

temporary stored procedure A procedure placed in the temporary database, Tempdb, and is erased at the end of the session.

temporary table A table that is placed in the temporary database, Tempdb, and is erased at the end of the session.

text data type A SQL Server system data type that specifies variable-length non-Unicode data with a maximum length of $2^{31} - 1$ (2,147,483,647) characters. The text data type cannot be used for variables or parameters in stored procedures.

theta join A join based on a comparison of scalar values (=, >, >=, <, <=, < >, !<, and !>).

thread An operating system component that allows the logic of multi-user applications to be performed as several separate, asynchronous execution paths. The SQL Server relational database engine executes multiple threads in order to make use of multiple processors. The use of threads also helps ensure that work is being performed for some user connections even when other connections are blocked (for example, when waiting for a disk read or write operation to complete).

time dimension A dimension that breaks time down into levels such as Year, Quarter, Month, and Day. In Analysis Services, the time dimension is a special type of dimension created from a date/time column.

timestamp data type A SQL Server system data type that is a monotonically increasing counter whose values are always unique within a database.

tinyint data type A SQL Server system data type that holds whole numbers from 0 through 255. Its storage size is one byte.

tool A SQL Server application that has a graphical user interface (GUI) used to perform common tasks.

trace file A file that SQL Profiler uses to record monitored events.

training data set A set of known and predictable data used to train a data mining model. *See also* mining model training.

trait An attribute that describes an entity. For example, blood type is a trait of patients.

Transact-SQL The language that contains the commands used to administer instances of SQL Server, to create and manage all objects in an instance of SQL Server, and to insert, retrieve, modify, and delete all data in SQL Server tables. Transact-SQL is an extension of the language that is defined in the SQL standards published by the International Organization for Standardization (ISO) and the American National Standards Institute (ANSI).

Transact-SQL cursor A server cursor defined by using the Transact-SQL DECLARE_CURSOR syntax. Transact-SQL cursors are intended for use in Transact-SQL batches, stored procedures, and triggers.

transaction A group of database operations combined into a logical unit of work that is either wholly committed or rolled back. A transaction is atomic, consistent, isolated, and durable.

transaction log A database file in which all changes to the database are recorded. SQL Server uses the transaction log during automatic recovery.

transaction processing Data processing used to efficiently record business activities, called transactions, that are of interest to an organization (for example, sales, orders for supplies, or money transfers). Typically, online transaction processing (OLTP) systems perform large numbers of relatively small transactions.

transaction rollback Rollback of a user-specified transaction to the last savepoint inside a transaction or to the beginning of a transaction.

transactional replication A type of replication where an initial snapshot of data is applied at Subscribers, and then when data modifications are made at the Publisher, the individual transactions are captured and propagated to Subscribers. *See also* merge replication, snapshot replication.

transformable subscription A subscription that allows data movement, transformation mapping, and filtering capabilities of Data Transformation Services (DTS) during replication.

transformation In data warehousing, the process of changing data extracted from source data systems into arrangements and formats consistent with the schema of the data warehouse.

trigger A stored procedure that executes when data in a specified table is modified. Triggers are often created to enforce referential integrity or consistency among logically related data in different tables.

trusted connection A Windows network connection that can be opened only by users who have been authenticated by the network. The users are identified by their Windows login ID and do not have to enter a separate SQL Server login ID. *See also* Windows Authentication.

tuple An ordered collection of members from different dimensions. For example, (Boston,_[1995]) is a tuple formed by members of two dimensions: Geography and Time. A single member is a degenerated case of a tuple and can be used as an expression without the parentheses. *See also* axis.

two-phase commit A process that ensures that transactions applied to more than one server are completed on all servers or on none.

U

unbalanced hierarchy A dimension hierarchy in which leaf nodes differ in their distances from the root node. Component part and organization chart hierarchies are usually unbalanced. *See also* ragged hierarchy.

underlying table A table referenced by a view, cursor, or stored procedure. *See also* base table.

unenforced relationship A link between tables that references the primary key in one table to a foreign key in another table and that does not check the referential integrity during INSERT and UPDATE transactions. An unenforced relationship is represented in a database diagram by a dashed line.

Unicode Unicode defines a set of letters, numbers, and symbols that SQL Server recognizes in the nchar, nvarchar, and ntext data types. Unicode is related to but separate from character sets. Unicode has more than 65,000 possible values compared to a character set's 256 and takes twice as much space to store. Unicode includes characters for most languages.

Unicode collation This collation acts as a sort order for Unicode data. Unicode collation is a set of rules that determines how SQL Server compares, collates, and presents Unicode data in response to database queries.

Unicode format Data that is stored in a bulk copy data file by using Unicode characters.

Union query A query that combines two tables by performing the equivalent of appending one table onto the other.

UNIQUE constraints Constraints that enforce entity integrity on a non-primary key. UNIQUE constraints ensure that no duplicate values are entered and that an index is created to enhance performance.

unique index An index in which no two rows are permitted to have the same index value, thus prohibiting duplicate index or key values. The system checks for duplicate key values when the index is created and checks that each time data is added with an INSERT or UPDATE statement.

uniqueidentifier data type A data type containing a unique identification number stored as a 16-byte binary string used for storing a globally unique identifier (GUID).

update The act of modifying one or more data values in an existing row or rows (typically by using the UPDATE statement). Sometimes, the term *update* refers to any data modification (including insert, update, and delete operations).

update lock A lock placed on resources (such as row, page, or table) that can be updated. Updated locks are used to prevent a common form of deadlock that occurs when multiple sessions are locking resources and are potentially updating them later.

Update query A query that changes the values in columns of one or more rows in a table.

update statistics A process that recalculates information about the distribution of key values in specified indexes. Query Optimizer uses these statistics to determine the most efficient way to execute a query.

user (account) A SQL Server security account or identifier that represents a specific user in a database. Each user's Windows account or SQL Server login is mapped to a user account in a database. Then, the appropriate permissions are granted to the user account. Each user account can only access data with which it has been granted permission to work.

user database A database created by a SQL Server user and used to store application data. Most users connecting to instances of SQL Server reference user databases only, not system databases. *See also* system databases.

user-defined data type A data type, based on a SQL Server data type, created by the user for custom data storage. Rules and defaults can be bound to user-defined data types (but not to system data types). *See also* base data type.

user-defined event A type of message defined by a user that can be traced by SQL Profiler or used to fire a custom alert. Typically, the user is the system administrator.

user-defined function In Analysis Services, a function defined in a Microsoft ActiveX library that is created by using a Component Object Model (COM) automation language such as Visual Basic or Visual C++. Such libraries can be registered with Analysis Services, and their functions can be called from multidimensional expressions (MDX) queries.

In SQL Server, a Transact-SQL function defined by a user. Functions encapsulate frequently performed logic in a named entity that can be called by Transact-SQL statements instead of recoding the logic in each statement.

utility A SQL Server application run from a command prompt to perform common tasks.

V

value expression An expression in multidimensional expressions (MDX) that returns a value. Value expressions can operate on sets, tuples, members, levels, numbers, or strings. For example, set value expressions operate on member, tuple, and set elements to yield other sets.

varbinary data type A SQL Server system data type that holds up to 8000 bytes of variable-length binary data.

varchar data type A SQL Server system data type that holds variable-length non-Unicode data with a maximum of 8000 characters.

variables Defined entities that are assigned values. A local variable is defined with a DECLARE@localvariable statement and assigned an initial value within the statement batch where it is declared with either a SELECT or SET@localvariable statement.

vertical filtering Filtering columns from a table. When used as part of replication, the table article created contains only selected columns from the publishing table. *See also* filtering, vertical partitioning.

vertical partitioning To segment a single table into multiple tables based on selected columns. Each of the multiple tables has the same number of rows but fewer columns. *See also* partitioning, vertical filtering.

very large dimension In Analysis Services, a dimension that contains more than approximately five million members and fewer than approximately 10 million members. Special techniques are used to process very large dimensions. *See also* huge dimension.

view A database object that can be referenced the same way as a table in SQL statements. Views are defined by using a SELECT statement and are analogous to an object that contains the result set of this statement.

view generation A repository engine feature that is used to create relational views based on classes, interfaces, and relationships in an information model.

virtual cube A logical cube based on one or more regular cubes or linked cubes.

virtual dimension A logical dimension that is based on the values of properties of members of a physical dimension. For example, a virtual dimension that contains the colors red, green, and blue can be based on the Color member property of a product dimension. *See also* dimension, member, member property.

visual total A displayed, aggregated cell value for a dimension member that is consistent with the displayed cell values for its displayed children. The visual total of a cell can vary from the actual total if some children of the cell are hidden. For example, if the aggregate function is SUM, the displayed cell value for Spain is 1000, and the displayed cell value for Portugal is 2000, the visual total for Iberia is 3000.

W

WHERE clause The part of a SQL statement that specifies which records to retrieve.

wildcard characters Characters, including underscore (_), percent (%), and brackets ([ ]), that are used with the LIKE keyword for pattern matching.

wildcard search The use of placeholders (such as * or ?) to perform a search for data in a table or field. For example, searching the Last Name field in a database by using Smith* could result in finding all records in which the last name starts with Smith, including Smith, Smithson, Smithlin, and so forth.

Windows Authentication One of two mechanisms for validating attempts to connect to instances of SQL Server. Users are identified by their Windows user or group when they connect. Windows Authentication is the most secure mechanism for connecting to SQL Server. *See also* SQL Server Authentication, trusted connection.

Windows collation A set of rules that determine how SQL Server sorts character data. The collation is specified by name in the Windows Control Panel and in SQL Server 2000 during Setup.

write back To update a cube cell value, member, or member property value. *See also* write enable.

write enable To change a cube or dimension so that users in cube roles who have read/write access to the cube or dimension can change its data. *See also* write back.

write-ahead log A transaction logging method in which the log is always written prior to the data.

X

XML eXtensible Markup Language (XML).

XPath A language used to query XML data where a schema is also attached.

Index

Symbols

E

At Microsoft Press, we use tools to illustrate our books for software developers and IT professionals. Tools very simply and powerfully symbolize human inventiveness. They're a metaphor for people extending their capabilities, precision, and reach. From simple calipers and pliers to digital micrometers and lasers, these stylized illustrations give each book a visual identity, and a personality to the series. With tools and knowledge, there's no limit to creativity and innovation. Our tag line says it all: *the tools you need to put technology to work*.

Cover Designer:	Methodologie, Inc.
Interior Graphic Designer:	James D. Kramer
Principal Desktop Publisher:	Elizabeth Hansford
Interior Artist	Joel Panchot
Proofreader:	nSight, Inc.
Indexer:	Ginny Bess

Inside *security information* you can trust

Microsoft® Windows® Security Resource Kit
ISBN 0-7356-1868-2   Suggested Retail Price: $59.99 U.S., $86.99 Canada

Comprehensive security information and tools, straight from the Microsoft product groups. This official RESOURCE KIT delivers comprehensive operations and deployment information that information security professionals can put to work right away. The authors—members of Microsoft's security teams—describe how to plan and implement a comprehensive security strategy, assess security threats and vulnerabilities, configure system security, and more. The kit also provides must-have security tools, checklists, templates, and other on-the-job resources on CD-ROM and on the Web.

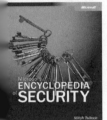

Microsoft Encyclopedia of Security
ISBN 0-7356-1877-1   Suggested Retail Price: $49.99 U.S., $72.99 Canada

The essential, one-of-a-kind security reference for computer professionals at all levels. This encyclopedia delivers 2000+ entries detailing the latest security-related issues, technologies, standards, products, and services. It covers the Microsoft Windows platform as well as open-source technologies and the platforms and products of other major vendors. You get clear, concise explanations and case scenarios that deftly take you from concept to real-world application—ideal for everyone from computer science students up to systems engineers, developers, and managers.

Microsoft Windows Server 2003 Security Administrator's Companion
ISBN 0-7356-1574-8   Suggested Retail Price: $49.99 U.S., $72.99 Canada

The in-depth, practical guide to deploying and maintaining Windows Server 2003 in a secure environment. Learn how to use all the powerful security features in the latest network operating system with this in-depth, authoritative technical reference—written by a security expert on the Microsoft Windows Server 2003 security team. Explore physical security issues, internal security policies, and public and shared key cryptography, and then drill down into the specifics of the key security features of Windows Server 2003.

Microsoft Internet Information Services Security Technical Reference
ISBN 0-7356-1572-1   Suggested Retail Price: $49.99 U.S., $72.99 Canada

The definitive guide for developers and administrators who need to understand how to securely manage networked systems based on IIS. This book presents obvious, avoidable mistakes and known security vulnerabilities in Internet Information Services (IIS)—priceless, intimate facts about the underlying causes of past security issues—while showing the best ways to fix them. The expert author, who has used IIS since the first version, also discusses real-world best practices for developing software and managing systems and networks with IIS.

To learn more about Microsoft Press® products for IT professionals, please visit:

microsoft.com/mspress/IT

In-depth, daily administration guides
for Microsoft Windows Server 2003

Microsoft® Windows® Server 2003 Administrator's Companion
ISBN 0-7356-1367-2

The in-depth, daily operations guide to planning, deployment, and maintenance. Here's the ideal one-volume guide for the IT professional who administers Windows Server 2003. This ADMINISTRATOR'S COMPANION offers up-to-date information on core system-administration topics for Windows, including Active Directory® services, security, disaster planning and recovery, interoperability with NetWare and UNIX, plus all-new sections about Microsoft Internet Security and Acceleration (ISA) Server and scripting. Featuring easy-to-use procedures and handy workarounds, this book provides ready answers for on-the-job results.

Microsoft Windows Server 2003 Security Administrator's Companion
ISBN 0-7356-1574-8

The in-depth, daily operations guide to enhancing security with the network operating system. With this authoritative ADMINISTRATOR'S COMPANION—written by an expert on the Windows Server 2003 security team—you'll learn how to use the powerful security features in the latest network server operating system. The guide describes best practices and technical details for enhancing security with Windows Server 2003, using the holistic approach that IT professionals need to grasp to help secure their systems. The authors cover concepts such as physical security issues, internal security policies, and public and shared key cryptography, and then drill down into the specifics of key security features of Windows Server 2003.

To learn more about the full line of Microsoft Press® products for IT professionals, please visit:

microsoft.com/mspress/IT

Comprehensive information and tools
for Microsoft Windows Server 2003

Microsoft® Windows® Server 2003 Resource Kit
ISBN 0-7356-1471-7

Comprehensive information and tools for maximizing the performance of Windows Server 2003. With this official Microsoft RESOURCE KIT, you can set up, manage, and optimize Windows Server 2003 with expertise from those who know the technology best. This multivolume set covers the entire server family, including Advanced Server and Datacenter Server, and features: Server Management Guide, Directory Services Guide, Distributed Services Guide, Internet Information Services (IIS) 6.0 Resource Guide, Networking Guide, and Internetworking Guide. It includes new or expanded coverage of remote administration tools, command line tasks and scenarios, policy-based administration, and registry documentation, with additional content about wireless technologies, IPv6, VPN, remote administration, operations for Active Directory® directory services, services and server roles, plus a CD-ROM packed with must-have tools and utilities.

Microsoft Windows Server 2003 Deployment Resource Kit
ISBN 0-7356-1486-5

Comprehensive information and tools for planning and deploying Windows Server 2003. This official Microsoft RESOURCE KIT provides all the information and tools you need to plan, design, and deploy Windows Server 2003 in medium to large organizations. It contains six volumes—*Deploying Network Services, Designing and Deploying Directory and Security Services, Planning Server Deployments, Automating and Customizing Installations, Designing a Managed Environment,* and *Deploying Internet Information Services (IIS) 6.0.* By focusing on deployment, this RESOURCE KIT provides exhaustive and definitive resource for a successful rollout—straight from those who know the technology best, the Microsoft Windows product team!

Microsoft Internet Information Services (IIS) 6.0 Resource Kit
ISBN 0-7356-1420-2

Comprehensive information and tools for maximizing the performance of your enterprise Web server. This official Microsoft RESOURCE KIT provides most everything you need to deploy and support Internet Information Services (IIS) 6.0—with comprehensive information and tools, straight from the source! It covers IIS architecture, migrating servers and applications, capacity planning, performance monitoring, security, top administration and troubleshooting scenarios, and IIS best practices. It's packed with over 900 pages of technical drill-down plus exclusive tools and utilities on CD, all designed to maximize performance while reducing support costs.

To learn more about the full line of Microsoft Press® products for IT professionals, please visit:

microsoft.com/mspress/IT

Get a **Free**
e-mail newsletter, updates,
special offers, links to related books,
and more when you

register on line!

Register your Microsoft Press® title on our Web site and you'll get
a FREE subscription to our e-mail newsletter, *Microsoft Press Book
Connections*. You'll find out about newly released and upcoming books
and learning tools, online events, software downloads, special offers
and coupons for Microsoft Press customers, and information about
major Microsoft® product releases. You can also read useful additional
information about all the titles we publish, such as detailed book
descriptions, tables of contents and indexes, sample chapters, links to
related books and book series, author biographies, and reviews by other
customers.

Registration is easy. Just visit this Web page and fill in your information:

http://www.microsoft.com/mspress/register

Microsoft®

- -

Proof of Purchase

Use this page as proof of purchase if participating in a promotion or rebate offer on
this title. Proof of purchase must be used in conjunction with other proof(s) of
payment such as your dated sales receipt—see offer details.

MCAD/MCSE/MCDBA Self-Paced Training Kit: Microsoft® SQL Server™ 2000 Database Design and Implementation, Exam 70-229, Second Edition

0-7356-1960-3

CUSTOMER NAME

Microsoft Press, PO Box 97017, Redmond, WA 98073-9830

MICROSOFT LICENSE AGREEMENT

Book Companion CD

IMPORTANT—READ CAREFULLY: This Microsoft End-User License Agreement ("EULA") is a legal agreement between you (either an individual or an entity) and Microsoft Corporation for the Microsoft product identified above, which includes computer software and may include associated media, printed materials, and "online" or electronic documentation ("SOFTWARE PRODUCT"). Any component included within the SOFTWARE PRODUCT that is accompanied by a separate End-User License Agreement shall be governed by such agreement and not the terms set forth below. By installing, copying, or otherwise using the SOFTWARE PRODUCT, you agree to be bound by the terms of this EULA. If you do not agree to the terms of this EULA, you are not authorized to install, copy, or otherwise use the SOFTWARE PRODUCT; you may, however, return the SOFTWARE PRODUCT, along with all printed materials and other items that form a part of the Microsoft product that includes the SOFTWARE PRODUCT, to the place you obtained them for a full refund.

SOFTWARE PRODUCT LICENSE

The SOFTWARE PRODUCT is protected by United States copyright laws and international copyright treaties, as well as other intellectual property laws and treaties. The SOFTWARE PRODUCT is licensed, not sold.

1. **GRANT OF LICENSE.** This EULA grants you the following rights:

   a. **Software Product.** You may install and use one copy of the SOFTWARE PRODUCT on a single computer. The primary user of the computer on which the SOFTWARE PRODUCT is installed may make a second copy for his or her exclusive use on a portable computer.

   b. **Storage/Network Use.** You may also store or install a copy of the SOFTWARE PRODUCT on a storage device, such as a network server, used only to install or run the SOFTWARE PRODUCT on your other computers over an internal network; however, you must acquire and dedicate a license for each separate computer on which the SOFTWARE PRODUCT is installed or run from the storage device. A license for the SOFTWARE PRODUCT may not be shared or used concurrently on different computers.

   c. **License Pak.** If you have acquired this EULA in a Microsoft License Pak, you may make the number of additional copies of the computer software portion of the SOFTWARE PRODUCT authorized on the printed copy of this EULA, and you may use each copy in the manner specified above. You are also entitled to make a corresponding number of secondary copies for portable computer use as specified above.

   d. **Sample Code.** Solely with respect to portions, if any, of the SOFTWARE PRODUCT that are identified within the SOFTWARE PRODUCT as sample code (the "SAMPLE CODE"):

      i. **Use and Modification.** Microsoft grants you the right to use and modify the source code version of the SAMPLE CODE, *provided* you comply with subsection (d)(iii) below. You may not distribute the SAMPLE CODE, or any modified version of the SAMPLE CODE, in source code form.

      ii. **Redistributable Files.** Provided you comply with subsection (d)(iii) below, Microsoft grants you a nonexclusive, royalty-free right to reproduce and distribute the object code version of the SAMPLE CODE and of any modified SAMPLE CODE, other than SAMPLE CODE, or any modified version thereof, designated as not redistributable in the Readme file that forms a part of the SOFTWARE PRODUCT (the "Non-Redistributable Sample Code"). All SAMPLE CODE other than the Non-Redistributable Sample Code is collectively referred to as the "REDISTRIBUTABLES."

      iii. **Redistribution Requirements.** If you redistribute the REDISTRIBUTABLES, you agree to: (i) distribute the REDISTRIBUTABLES in object code form only in conjunction with and as a part of your software application product; (ii) not use Microsoft's name, logo, or trademarks to market your software application product; (iii) include a valid copyright notice on your software application product; (iv) indemnify, hold harmless, and defend Microsoft from and against any claims or lawsuits, including attorney's fees, that arise or result from the use or distribution of your software application product; and (v) not permit further distribution of the REDISTRIBUTABLES by your end user. Contact Microsoft for the applicable royalties due and other licensing terms for all other uses and/or distribution of the REDISTRIBUTABLES.

2. **DESCRIPTION OF OTHER RIGHTS AND LIMITATIONS.**

   - **Limitations on Reverse Engineering, Decompilation, and Disassembly.** You may not reverse engineer, decompile, or disassemble the SOFTWARE PRODUCT, except and only to the extent that such activity is expressly permitted by applicable law notwithstanding this limitation.

   - **Separation of Components.** The SOFTWARE PRODUCT is licensed as a single product. Its component parts may not be separated for use on more than one computer.

   - **Rental.** You may not rent, lease, or lend the SOFTWARE PRODUCT.

- **Support Services.** Microsoft may, but is not obligated to, provide you with support services related to the SOFTWARE PRODUCT ("Support Services"). Use of Support Services is governed by the Microsoft policies and programs described in the user manual, in "online" documentation, and/or in other Microsoft-provided materials. Any supplemental software code provided to you as part of the Support Services shall be considered part of the SOFTWARE PRODUCT and subject to the terms and conditions of this EULA. With respect to technical information you provide to Microsoft as part of the Support Services, Microsoft may use such information for its business purposes, including for product support and development. Microsoft will not utilize such technical information in a form that personally identifies you.

- **Software Transfer.** You may permanently transfer all of your rights under this EULA, provided you retain no copies, you transfer all of the SOFTWARE PRODUCT (including all component parts, the media and printed materials, any upgrades, this EULA, and, if applicable, the Certificate of Authenticity), **and** the recipient agrees to the terms of this EULA.

- **Termination.** Without prejudice to any other rights, Microsoft may terminate this EULA if you fail to comply with the terms and conditions of this EULA. In such event, you must destroy all copies of the SOFTWARE PRODUCT and all of its component parts.

3. **COPYRIGHT.** All title and copyrights in and to the SOFTWARE PRODUCT (including but not limited to any images, photographs, animations, video, audio, music, text, SAMPLE CODE, REDISTRIBUTABLES, and "applets" incorporated into the SOFTWARE PRODUCT) and any copies of the SOFTWARE PRODUCT are owned by Microsoft or its suppliers. The SOFT-WARE PRODUCT is protected by copyright laws and international treaty provisions. Therefore, you must treat the SOFTWARE PRODUCT like any other copyrighted material **except** that you may install the SOFTWARE PRODUCT on a single computer provided you keep the original solely for backup or archival purposes. You may not copy the printed materials accompanying the SOFTWARE PRODUCT.

4. **U.S. GOVERNMENT RESTRICTED RIGHTS.** The SOFTWARE PRODUCT and documentation are provided with RESTRICTED RIGHTS. Use, duplication, or disclosure by the Government is subject to restrictions as set forth in subparagraph (c)(1)(ii) of the Rights in Technical Data and Computer Software clause at DFARS 252.227-7013 or subparagraphs (c)(1) and (2) of the Commercial Computer Software—Restricted Rights at 48 CFR 52.227-19, as applicable. Manufacturer is Microsoft Corporation/One Microsoft Way/Redmond, WA 98052-6399.

5. **EXPORT RESTRICTIONS.** You agree that you will not export or re-export the SOFTWARE PRODUCT, any part thereof, or any process or service that is the direct product of the SOFTWARE PRODUCT (the foregoing collectively referred to as the "Restricted Components"), to any country, person, entity, or end user subject to U.S. export restrictions. You specifically agree not to export or re-export any of the Restricted Components (i) to any country to which the U.S. has embargoed or restricted the export of goods or services, which currently include, but are not necessarily limited to, Cuba, Iran, Iraq, Libya, North Korea, Sudan, and Syria, or to any national of any such country, wherever located, who intends to transmit or transport the Restricted Components back to such country; (ii) to any end user who you know or have reason to know will utilize the Restricted Components in the design, development, or production of nuclear, chemical, or biological weapons; or (iii) to any end user who has been prohibited from participating in U.S. export transactions by any federal agency of the U.S. government. You warrant and represent that neither the BXA nor any other U.S. federal agency has suspended, revoked, or denied your export privileges.

DISCLAIMER OF WARRANTY

NO WARRANTIES OR CONDITIONS. MICROSOFT EXPRESSLY DISCLAIMS ANY WARRANTY OR CONDITION FOR THE SOFTWARE PRODUCT. THE SOFTWARE PRODUCT AND ANY RELATED DOCUMENTATION ARE PROVIDED "AS IS" WITHOUT WARRANTY OR CONDITION OF ANY KIND, EITHER EXPRESS OR IMPLIED, INCLUDING, WITHOUT LIMITA-TION, THE IMPLIED WARRANTIES OF MERCHANTABILITY, FITNESS FOR A PARTICULAR PURPOSE, OR NONINFRINGEMENT. THE ENTIRE RISK ARISING OUT OF USE OR PERFORMANCE OF THE SOFTWARE PRODUCT REMAINS WITH YOU.

LIMITATION OF LIABILITY. TO THE MAXIMUM EXTENT PERMITTED BY APPLICABLE LAW, IN NO EVENT SHALL MICROSOFT OR ITS SUPPLIERS BE LIABLE FOR ANY SPECIAL, INCIDENTAL, INDIRECT, OR CONSEQUENTIAL DAM-AGES WHATSOEVER (INCLUDING, WITHOUT LIMITATION, DAMAGES FOR LOSS OF BUSINESS PROFITS, BUSINESS INTERRUPTION, LOSS OF BUSINESS INFORMATION, OR ANY OTHER PECUNIARY LOSS) ARISING OUT OF THE USE OF OR INABILITY TO USE THE SOFTWARE PRODUCT OR THE PROVISION OF OR FAILURE TO PROVIDE SUPPORT SERVICES, EVEN IF MICROSOFT HAS BEEN ADVISED OF THE POSSIBILITY OF SUCH DAMAGES. IN ANY CASE, MICROSOFT'S ENTIRE LIABILITY UNDER ANY PROVISION OF THIS EULA SHALL BE LIMITED TO THE GREATER OF THE AMOUNT ACTUALLY PAID BY YOU FOR THE SOFTWARE PRODUCT OR US$5.00; PROVIDED, HOWEVER, IF YOU HAVE ENTERED INTO A MICROSOFT SUPPORT SERVICES AGREEMENT, MICROSOFT'S ENTIRE LIABILITY REGARDING SUPPORT SERVICES SHALL BE GOVERNED BY THE TERMS OF THAT AGREEMENT. BECAUSE SOME STATES AND JURISDICTIONS DO NOT ALLOW THE EXCLUSION OR LIMITATION OF LIABILITY, THE ABOVE LIMITATION MAY NOT APPLY TO YOU.

MISCELLANEOUS

This EULA is governed by the laws of the State of Washington USA, except and only to the extent that applicable law mandates governing law of a different jurisdiction.

Should you have any questions concerning this EULA, or if you desire to contact Microsoft for any reason, please contact the Microsoft subsidiary serving your country, or write: Microsoft Sales Information Center/One Microsoft Way/Redmond, WA 98052-6399.

System Requirements

To get the most out of the Training Kit, you will need a computer equipped with the following minimum configuration:

- 166-MHz or higher Pentium processor
- 128 MB RAM (minimum), 256 MB or more recommended
- SQL Server database components: 95 MB to 270 MB of free hard disk space, 250 MB typical
- CD-ROM drive
- Super VGA display with at least 256 colors
- Microsoft Mouse or compatible pointing device
- Microsoft Internet Explorer 5.0 or later

To use the electronic assessment program on the Supplemental Course Materials CD-ROM, you need a computer equipped with the following minimum configuration:

- Microsoft Windows NT 4 with Service Pack 3 or later, Microsoft Windows 98, Windows Me, Windows XP, Windows 2000 Server, or Windows Server 2003
- Multimedia PC with a 75-MHz Pentium or higher processor
- 32 MB RAM for Windows Me or Windows NT, or
- 64 MG RAM for Windows 2000 or Windows XP
- Super VGA display with at least 256 colors
- Microsoft Mouse or compatible pointing device and keyboard
- Microsoft Internet Explorer 5.01 or higher (additional 13 MB minimum hard disk space to install Internet Explorer 6 from this CD-ROM)
- 17 MB of available hard drive space for installation
- A double-speed CD-ROM drive or faster

The latest version of the HCL can be downloaded from the Hardware Compatibility List Web page at *http://www.microsoft.com/hwdq/hcl/*.